# HISTORY
# BEHIND THE
# HEADLINES

# HISTORY BEHIND THE HEADLINES

## The Origins of Conflicts Worldwide

### VOLUME 4

*Sonia G. Benson, Editor*

GALE®

Detroit • New York • San Diego • San Francisco • Cleveland • New Haven, Conn. • Waterville, Maine • London • Munich

**THOMSON**

**GALE**

History Behind the Headlines, volume 4
Sonia G. Benson

**Project Editor**
Nancy Matuszak

**Editorial**
Jason M. Everett, Rachel J. Kain

**Permissions**
Lori Hines

**Imaging and Multimedia**
Dean Dauphinais, Christine O'Bryan, Luke Rademacher

**Product Design**
Pamela A. E. Galbreath

**Composition and Electronic Capture**
Evi Seoud

**Manufacturing**
Rhonda A. Williams

ISBN 0–7876–4954–6
ISSN 1531–7307

Printed in the United States of America
10 9 8 7 6 5 4 3 2 1

# TABLE OF CONTENTS

## A

Bolstered by the powerful terrorist groups, notably al Qaeda, that it hosted within the borders of Afghanistan, the Taliban repeatedly enraged the international community with offensive acts and was forced out of power after the terrorist attacks on the United States on September 11, 2001. How did a group of religious students take power in Afghanistan?

A tragic shootdown focused the attention of the U.S. public and Congress on the "drug war," anti-drug efforts in the Andes, and the United States' expanding and controversial dealings with Latin American governments to stop the flow of illegal drugs to the United States.

The status of aborigines in Australia as compared to the rest of the population and the government's ap-

parent reluctance to embrace the indigenous reconciliation movement.

## B

From March 1, 2002, forward, 12 European countries will have one currency, the euro. Britain, or the United Kingdom, has never made the decision to abandon its own currency, the pound sterling, for the euro, repeatedly deferring the issue, and along with it, the possible advantages in trade and foreign relations.

## C

Hundreds of thousands of children throughout the world are being used as soldiers, learning the skills of warfare rather than reading and arithmetic. They are often brutalized, and worldwide efforts at rehabilitation are insufficient. The conditions that cause child soldiering, and international efforts to put an end to the practice.

China is in the process of building the largest and most powerful dam ever to be built, and there is strong disagreement about it. Proponents say it will bring clean, cheap energy into many parts of China and aid in preventing severe flood damage. Opponents say the dam will displace over one million people, destroy majestic natural beauty, cost a great deal in time, money, and effort, and may not work as planned.

Although China and the United States have been making moves toward diplomacy, unresolved friction

program to be deployed around 2005 at tremendous cost and with questionable feasibility. Critics say that deployment of the NMD could threaten the world security environment by fueling an arms race and make enemies out of current allies.

stroyed, child soldiers now facing unemployment, diamond mines still under questionable control, and ongoing fighting at Sierra Leone's borders between Liberia and Guinea, the weak new government in Freetown faces challenges ahead.

# Contents by Subject

## POLITICAL



## RELIGIOUS

# Contents by Region

## Africa



## Asia



## Australia



## Europe



## Latin America



## North America

## WORLDWIDE

# ADVISORY BOARD

**Jerry H. Bentley** is Professor of History at the University of Hawaii and editor of the *Journal of World History*. His research on the religious, moral, and political writings of Renaissance humanists led to the publication of *Humanists and Holy Writ: New Testament Scholarship in the Renaissance and Politics and Culture in Renaissance Naples*. More recently, his research has concentrated on global history and particularly on processes of cross-cultural interaction. His book *Old World Encounters: Cross-Cultural Contacts and Exchanges in Pre-Modern Times* examines processes of cultural exchange and religious conversion before the modern era, and his pamphlet "Shapes of World History in Twentieth-Century Scholarship" discusses the historiography of world history. His current interests include processes of cross-cultural interaction and cultural exchanges in modern times.

**Frank J. Coppa** is Professor of History at St. John's University, Director of their doctoral program, and Chair of the University's Vatican Symposium. He is also an Associate in the Columbia University Seminar on Modern Italy, and editor of the Lang Series on Studies on Modern Europe. He has published biographies on a series of European figures, written and edited more than twelve volumes, as well as publishing in a series of journals including the *Journal of Modern History* and the *Journal of Economic History*, among others. He is editor of the *Dictionary of Modern Italian History* and the *Encyclopedia of the Vatican and Papacy*.

**Paul Gootenberg** is a Professor of Latin American History at SUNY-Stony Brook. A graduate of the University of Chicago and of Oxford University, he specializes in the economic, social, and intellectual history of the Andes and Mexico, and more recently, the global history of drugs. He has published *Between Silver and Guano* (1989), *Imagining Development* (1993) and *Cocaine: Global Histories* (1999). Gootenberg has held many fellowships: among them, Fulbright, SSRC, ACLS, Institute for Advanced Study, Russell Sage Foundation, the Rhodes Scholarship, and a Guggenheim. He lives in Brooklyn with his wife, Laura Sainz, and son, Danyal Natan.

**Margaret Hallisey** is a practicing high school library media specialist in Burlington, MA. She has a B.A. in English from Regis College and a M.S. in Library and Information Science from Simmons College. A member of Beta Phi Mu, the International Library Science Honor Society, she has served on the executive Boards of the American Association of School Librarians (AASL), the Massachusetts School Library Media Association (MSLMA) and the New England Educational Media Association (NEEMA).

**Donna Maier** has been with the Department of History at the University of Northern Iowa since 1986. Her research interests are in nineteenth century Asante (Ghana), African Islam, and traditional African medicine. Her extensive lists of publications include "The Military Acquisition of Slaves in Asante," in *West African Economic and Social History* (1990), "Islam and the Idea of Asylum in Asante" in *The Cloths of Many-Colored Silks* (1996), and *History and Life, the World and Its Peoples*

(1977-90, with Wallbank and Shrier). She is a joint editor of the journal *African Economic History*, and a member of the African Studies Association and the Ghana Studies Council. She is currently living in Tanzania.

**Philip Yockey** is Social Sciences Bibliographer and Assistant Chief Librarian for Staff Training and Development at the Humanities and Social Sciences Library at The New York Public Library.

# ABOUT THE SERIES

In 1993 the UN Security Council created the International Criminal Tribunal for Yugoslavia and in 1995 it established another tribunal for Rwanda, in both cases as a consequence of the global community's helplessness when thousands were murdered in genocidal drives. Not since the Nuremburg and Tokyo trials after World War II has the international community felt compelled to intervene with its own justice system in crimes against peace, war crimes, and crimes against humanity. In Sierra Leone, where insurgents willfully killed, raped, and maimed innocent civilians, there will almost surely be another tribunal in the early 2000s. In the countries in which legitimate governments have failed, as we have seen in Afghanistan, political vacuums can arise that allow these areas to become centers for radical groups that export terrorism. National conflicts have in many cases become international concerns.

In the 1990s there were many kinds of conflicts in various parts of the world in which the international community was called upon to ensure that innocent groups of civilians were not intentionally destroyed by a hostile, and sometimes ruling, group. Child soldiers around the globe have received heightened attention in the last decade as the horror of their lives and the results of their training have become exposed. The Dalits, or untouchables, of India, the aboriginal peoples of Australia, the female population that is not being born due to son preference in India and China, and many others have transcended national boundaries to seek help from the rest of the world. But can standards be applied from one nation or culture to the next? How can we understand when international intervention is called for?

*History Behind the Headlines*, an ongoing series from the Gale Group, strives to answer these and many other questions in a way that television broadcasts and newspapers can not. In order to keep reports both simple and short, it is difficult for these media to give the watcher or reader enough background information to fully understand what is happening around the world today. *HBH* provides just that background, giving the general public, student, and teacher an account of each contemporary conflict, from its start to its present and even its future. This thoroughness is accomplished not just by the in-depth material covered in the main body of each essay, but also by accompanying chronologies, textual and biographical sidebars, maps, statistics, and bibliographic sources.

Not only does *HBH* provide comprehensive information on all of the conflicts it covers, it also strives to present its readers with an unbiased and inclusive perspective. Each essay, many written by an expert with a detailed knowledge of the conflict at hand, avoids taking any particular side and instead seeks to explain each vantage point. Unlike television and newspaper reports, which may only have the time, space, or even inclination to show one side of a story, *HBH* essays equally detail all sides involved.

Given the number of conflicts that beg for the fuller accounts that *History Behind the Headlines* provides, an advisory board of school and library experts helps to guide the selection process and narrow down the topics for each volume. They balance the topic lists, making sure that a proper mix of economic, political, ethnic, and geographically diverse conflicts are chosen. One to two volumes, each written in an accessible, informative way, will be released each year.

# PREFACE

## Selection and Arrangement

This volume of *History Behind the Headlines* covers 25 conflicts—including ethnic, religious, economic, political, territorial, and environmental conflicts—and provides essays exploring the background to today's events. For example, students wondering why the United States lost a seat on a UN human rights panel will find a history of the nation's relations with the organization from its establishment in 1945. Each conflict covered in HBH is contemporary—it happened within the last several years—but the roots of today's headlines are of enduring interest.

The topics were chosen following an extensive review of the conflicts covered in newspapers, magazines, and on television. A large number of potential conflicts were identified. Advisors—including academic experts, high school social study teachers, and librarians—prioritized the list, identifying those conflicts that generate the most questions. Topics were then selected to provide a regional balance and to cover various types of conflicts.

The conflicts covered are complex. Each essay discusses multiple aspects of a conflict, including economic and social aspects, the interests of other countries, international organizations and businesses, and the international implication of a conflict. The entries are arranged alphabetically by a major country, region, organization, or person in the conflict. Where this might not be clear in the table of contents, the keyword is placed in parentheses in front of the title.

## New Feature

Due to reader response, this volume launches the new feature of "Contents by Region." Now users can quickly find and locate a topic by geographic region. Users looking for all the topics in one volume covering Africa, Europe, Asia, or any other geographic region can now easily reference them through the "Contents by Region."

## Content

Each essay begins with a brief summary of the current situation, as well as some of the major factors in the conflict and a list of terms used in the essay with which the reader may be unfamiliar. Each essay contains the following sections:

- **Summary of the headline event.** An overview of the contemporary conflict that has brought the issue to public attention. For example, why the United States quit the Kyoto Protocol, the reaction of other nations, and environmental implications.

- **Historical Background.** The "Historical Background" is the heart of the essay. The author provides the historical context to the contemporary conflict, summarizing the arc of the conflict throughout history. Each essay tells the "story" of the history of the conflict, capturing important events, transfers of power, interventions, treaties, and more. The author summarizes the changes in the conflict over time, describes the role of major figures in the conflict, including individuals, political organizations, and religious organizations, and provides an overview of their positions now and in the past. Where appropriate the author may draw comparisons with similar situations in the country or region in the past. In addition, the author often attempts to put the conflict in the context of global politics and to describe the impacts the conflict has had on people around the world. Finally, the author may touch on how historians' understanding of the conflict has changed over time.

- **Recent History and the Future.** The final section brings the conflict up-to-date and may offer some projections for future resolution.

Each essay is followed by a brief bibliography that offers some suggestions of resources for further research. In addition, brief biographies may accompany the essay, profiling major figures. Sidebars may provide statistical information, a quote from a speech, a selection from a primary source document (such as a treaty), or a selection from a book or newspaper article that adds to the understanding of the conflict, or may explore an issue in greater depth (such as China's cultural preference for boys).

Images may also accompany the essay, including one or more maps showing the area of conflict. A selected bibliography providing suggestions for background information and research on the nature of conflicts and a comprehensive index appear at the back of each volume.

### *History Is To Be Read Critically*

Each of the talented writers (many academic authorities) in this volume has tried to provide an objective and comprehensive overview of the conflict and its historical context. The nature of conflict, however, involves positions strongly and passionately held; even if it were possible to write a completely objective overview of history, it would contradict with the view held by participants to the conflict. History—all history—should be read critically.

### *Acknowledgements*

Many thanks for their help to the excellent advisors who guided this project—their ongoing attention and feedback was greatly appreciated. Thanks, also, to the thoughtful and dedicated writers who lent their expertise to help others understand the complex history behind sound bites on the news.

Comments on this volume and suggestions for future volumes are welcomed. Please direct all correspondence to:

Editor, *History Behind the Headlines*
Gale Group
27500 Drake Rd.
Farmington Hills, MI 48331-3535
(800) 877-4253

# SPECIAL NOTE

*History Behind the Headlines*, volume 4, was in the middle of production when the terrorist attacks of September 11, 2001, occurred in the United States. The editors considered adjusting the content of the volume to reflect the current news emphasis on terrorism, but determined that the best way to serve you, the reader, was not to postpone volume 4 but instead devote an entire volume to terrorism topics.

Volume 5 of *History Behind the Headlines* is a special edition scheduled to publish soon after vol-

ume 4. It will contain twenty-five to thirty entries on various aspects of terrorism, from Osama bin Laden and state sponsors of terrorism to civil rights, extremism, and biological, chemical, and nuclear threats.

The editors hope that you will turn to this comprehensive special edition of *History Behind the Headlines*, authored by those knowledgeable in the field, for objective, straightforward and in-depth information on the terrorism headlines upon which global eyes are focused.

# THE AFGHAN TALIBAN STRIKES OUT

When the terrorist attacks on the World Trade Center in New York City and the Pentagon in Washington, DC, took place on September 11, 2001, the Taliban of Afghanistan—the extreme Islamic fundamentalist group that had ruled most of that nation since 1996—found themselves once again under the glare of the public eye. The prime suspects behind the attacks, exiled Saudi terrorist Osama bin Laden and his organization, al Qaeda, were based in Afghanistan, and the Taliban refused to turn them over to international authorities.

The Taliban had in fact been incurring the disfavor and often the hostility of the international community for all the years of its rule. For a tiny, impoverished country in central Asia, Afghanistan had drawn more than its share of attention as the Taliban repeatedly defied the United Nations and the Western powers as well as its moderate Muslim neighbors. Sporting its own brand of extreme Islamic rule, the Taliban inspired the devotion of many young Islamic fundamentalists, who hoped that an Islamic state in Afghanistan would pave the way for other Islamic states throughout the world. But to most moderate Muslims, humanitarian agencies, the United Nations, and Western nations, the Taliban represented a brutal and oppressive force that ran counter to the teachings of the Koran and to the interests and well-being of the people of Afghanistan.

After the terrorist attacks of September 11, 2001, President George W. Bush (2001–) delivered an ultimatum to the Taliban to hand bin Laden over or to face possible attack in retaliation for harboring a terrorist. A group of Taliban clerics, called a *ulema*, debated the issue and then announced they could not give up bin Laden with-

## THE CONFLICT

Afghanistan, having been divided and torn apart by two decades of war, was taken over in 1996 by a group of religious students professing to set up a pure Islamic state. The Taliban was harsh and oppressive, but put a stop to the violence and chaos that was rampant in Afghanistan's cities. The Taliban has repeatedly enraged the international community with a variety of offensive acts, openly defying the United Nations and its neighbors as well as the West.

### *Religious*
- The Taliban imposed a strict interpretation of Islamic law on Afghanistan in its mission to create a pure Islamic state. To most Westerners and the majority of Muslims its rule has been repressive and has denied basic human rights to a large portion of the population, but there are Muslims around the world who revere the ideals the Taliban appears to stand for.

- Although purporting to create a pure Islamic state, the Taliban has questionable credentials in this regard. Its application of Islamic law, concept of jihad, and brutality conflict sharply with most Muslims' knowledge of the Koran.

### *Political*
- Afghanistan, after being at war for more than 20 years, has a very splintered opposition group made up of ethnic minorities, with a history of corruption, betrayal, and violence. Neighboring countries have added fuel to the fire by siding with ethnic groups and supplying arms and money for war. As the Taliban exits, the danger of resuming the infighting of the civil war looms.

### *Economic*
- Afghanistan has faced the prospect of a widespread famine for several years, with millions of lives threatened by lack of food and water. Humanitarian aid workers have courageously averted total disaster at great risk to their own lives.

- When the United Nations placed sanctions on Afghanistan and isolated it from the world community, the Taliban reacted with defiance. The result has been worse suffering among an already impoverished people.

# CHRONOLOGY

**1978** Afghanistan's communist government, which is closely allied with the Soviet Union, fights a civil war against several groups of guerrillas, or mujahideen.

**1979** Soviet troops invade Afghanistan.

**1979** Osama bin Laden travels to Afghanistan to fight against the invading Soviets.

**1989** The Soviet Union withdraws its troops from Afghanistan in defeat.

**1992** Afghanistan's mujahideen fighters enter into an alliance with each other, installing a coalition government that was to rotate among the leaders of the seven mujahideen groups.

**1992** The Tajik forces of Burhanuddin Rabbani and his military commander Ahmad Shah Masud, along with the Uzbek forces of General Rashid Dostum, take the capital city of Kabul. Civil war breaks out among the different factions of mujahideen.

**1994–96** The civil war rages on. Rabbani controls Kabul; Ismail Khan governs the western province of Herat; Pashtuns govern three provinces from the city of Jalalabad; Hikmetyar holds a small region near Kabul; Dostum holds six provinces in the north; much of the south is divided among Pashtun warlords.

**November 1994** Pakistani Prime Minister Benazir Bhutto appoints the Taliban to protect a trade caravan captured by the local warlord in Kandahar, Afghanistan. Pakistan's Inter-Service Intelligence (ISI) begin training and funding the group.

**1996** The Taliban captures Kabul, the capital of Afghanistan.

**August 1998** The Taliban takes the city of Mazar-i-Sharif and massacres from one to five thousand civilians

belonging to the ethnic Shi'ite Hazara minority in a two-day rampage.

**1998** The Taliban declines to turn suspected terrorist Osama bin Laden over to the United States.

**1999** The Taliban controls more than 90 percent of Afghanistan, although it still faces considerable opposition. The United Nations imposes sanctions on the country for its refusal to extradite bin Laden.

**2000** Mullah Mohammed Omar bans the growing of poppies in Afghanistan, one of the world's largest sources of heroin.

**March 2001** The Taliban destroys two ancient statues of Buddha, giant artifacts of Afghanistan's history and culture.

**May 2001** The Taliban police arrest eight Christian humanitarian aid workers for proselytizing.

**September 11, 2001** Terrorists hijack U.S. passenger airliners and fly them into the World Trade Center and the Pentagon; another hijacked plane crashes in Pennsylvania. Thousands are killed in the attack. The United States accuses Osama bin Laden and asks the Taliban to give him up or face retribution. The Taliban refuses to give up bin Laden.

**September 25, 2001** UN Secretary-General Kofi Annan calls on the international community to help the Afghan people, who, because of a dire food shortage, face the "worst humanitarian crisis in the world."

**October 7, 2001** The United States and Great Britain start an air strike on targeted sites in Afghanistan.

**December 7, 2001** The Taliban cede Kandahar, ending their rule in Afghanistan.

out proof that he was responsible for the bombings. The Taliban leader in Afghanistan, Mullah Mohammed Omar, threatened a holy war, or *jihad*, against the United States if there was a strike against Afghanistan.

On October 7, 2001, the United States and the United Kingdom began a military strike

against the Taliban. With the aid of the air strikes, the anti-Taliban forces in Afghanistan were able to wrest Afghanistan's centers away from the Taliban within two months. On December 7 Kandahar, the spiritual center of the Taliban, was surrendered. Taliban rule was at an end, but the impact of this tough and defiant breakaway group of extremists upon the people of Afghanistan and the Muslims of the world will be tallied for many years to come. That they were able to take power and hold it against great odds is due to a number of factors, including support from al Qaeda and the government of Pakistan, a strong antipathy in many Muslim countries to the dominance of Western culture, and the deep divisions that had developed among ethnic groups and warlords in Afghanistan prior to their rule. During their reign in Afghanistan the acts of the Taliban deeply disturbed observers all over the world, and, it is becoming increasingly apparent in liberated areas of Afghanistan that their rule was highly traumatic for many Afghan citizens.

## HISTORICAL BACKGROUND

The stage was set for the Taliban takeover of Afghanistan during the Soviet-Afghanistan war (1979–89). In December 1979, after communists had taken over the Afghan government, Soviet troops invaded Afghanistan. The Soviet-Afghanistan War followed for the next ten years, a vicious fight among anti-communist Afghanistan guerrillas, the communist Afghan government, and Soviet forces. During this war, more than one million Afghans were killed. The Afghan guerrillas, known as the *mujahideen* (fighters in a holy war against infidels), considered the atheistic communist regime an affront to their religious beliefs and fought fiercely against it.

The mujahideen received help from a variety of places. Muslims came from all over the world when they learned of the Soviet invasion, particularly from Saudi Arabia, but also from Pakistan, Yemen, Libya, and Tajikistan. According to some estimates there were as many as 35,000 foreign warriors helping the Afghans against the Soviets. Among the earliest of them was Palestinian Sheik Abdallah Azzam, an early mentor to Osama bin Laden. Bin Laden was one of the first people from the Middle East to join Azzam, helping to establish the Maktab al-Khidamat (MAK, or Services Office), a center used to recruit volunteers and raise money for the Afghan struggle.

The United States secretly supported the mujahideen in their efforts to overthrow the communist government. The United States allowed the MAK to set up recruiting offices in the United States as well as in the Middle East. There are some reports that the United States funded and may well have helped train bin Laden and his colleagues. By the early 1980s the MAK had built a

network that brought thousands of Muslims from more than 50 countries to join the mujahideen in their battle against the Soviets, with training bases in Pakistan and Afghanistan.

The Soviets withdrew from Afghanistan in defeat in 1989, leaving chaos behind them. The Soviet troops had brutally raped, tortured, maimed, and massacred Afghan peasants in their path, destroying livestock and burning down towns as they passed. During the Soviet occupation one-third of Afghanistan's population fled the country; Pakistan and Iran sheltered a combined peak of more than 6 million refugees. In 1992 there were a remaining 5 million landmines in Afghanistan that the Soviets had scattered about the countryside before leaving. A decade later, in 2001, as many as 300 people are killed every month by those mines.

The president of Afghanistan at the time of the Soviet withdrawal was Muhammad Najibullah. Aligned with the Soviets, Najibullah remained in office until 1992 as the country descended into violent factional fighting. The United States rapidly withdrew its support after the Soviets left. Many Afghans accused the United States of selfishly abandoning them once the Cold War threat was past, although there was still an urgent need for help.

### The Factions Collide

Afghanistan's mujahideen fighters entered into an alliance with each other in 1992, installing a coalition government that was to rotate among the leaders of the seven mujahideen groups. But faction leaders quickly came into conflict over which group would govern Afghanistan. The victory over the Soviet empire led to a new kind of civil war based on political and ethnic disparities among the leadership.

Afghanistan's population includes several ethnic groups. The Pashtun are the majority, comprising about 38 percent of the population and living in the southeastern portion of Afghanistan as well as the northern part of Pakistan. The Tajiks make up about 25 percent of the population and live in scattered areas throughout the country. The majority of the world's Tajiks live in Tajikistan. The Hazara make up about 19 percent of the population. The Eastern Hazara are Shi'ite Muslim, a branch of Islam differing from the majority Sunni branch in its belief in the succession of Ali and the Imams with direct descent from Mohammed, as the divinely appointed leaders of Islam. The Hazara are of Mongol descent. There is also a

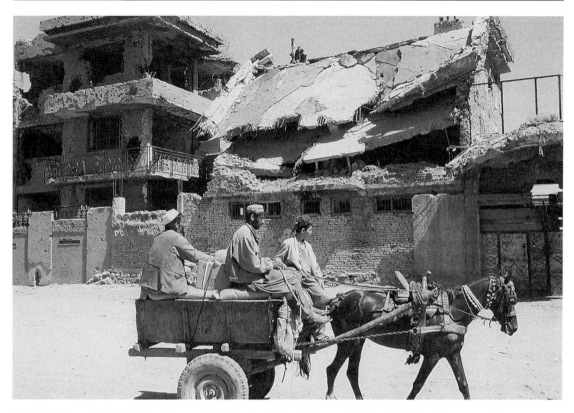

THE TALIBAN'S STRICT ENFORCEMENT OF ISLAMIC LAW HAS ALSO AFFECTED LIFE FOR THE COUNTRY'S OTHER RELIGIOUS BELIEVERS, INCLUDING HINDUS, WHO WERE REQUIRED TO WEAR IDENTITY LABELS. THIS HINDU TEMPLE WAS DESTROYED DURING FIGHTING IN MAY 2001. *(A/P Wide World. Reproduced by permission.)*

large Hazara population in Iran. Eight percent of Afghans are Uzbeks, living in the northwest part of the country. The majority of the world's Uzbek population lives in Uzbekistan. Other ethnic groups in Afghanistan include the Turkmen, Balochs, and Aimaks.

In 1992 the Tajik forces of Burhanuddin Rabbani and his military commander Ahmad Shah Masud, along with the Uzbek forces of General Rashid Dostum, took the capital city of Kabul. The city had been ruled by the Pashtuns for centuries, and Pashtun forces under General Gulbuddin Hikmetyar immediately began to fight for the city, beginning civil war. By 1994 Rabbani controlled Kabul and an area around it and claimed to be the president of Afghanistan, but he did not have power over most of the country. Anti-Soviet mujahideen Ismail Khan governed the western province of Herat; Pashtuns governed three provinces from the city of Jalalabad; Hikmetyar held a small region near Kabul; and Dostum held six provinces in the north. Much of the south was divided among Pashtun warlords who were at war with each other.

In the civil war the ex-mujahideen fought each other, often betraying one another in short-lived alliances. Half of the capital city of Kabul, which had survived the war with the Soviets, was destroyed. In the cities of Afghanistan violence and crime abounded and no one was safe. Tens of thousands of Afghan civilians were killed in the five-year period of factional fighting, and many more were displaced from their homes, raped, robbed, and otherwise traumatized.

### The Taliban

In Pakistan and in parts of Afghanistan *madrasas,* schools for training spiritual leaders, had been educating young men since the twelfth century. During the Soviet-Afghanistan War, however, the number of madrasas in Pakistan went from less than one thousand in the early 1970s to 8,000 registered and 25,000 unregistered madrasas in 1988, according to Ahmed Rashid in his acclaimed book *Taliban: Militant Islam, Oil, and Fundamentalism* (2000). These new schools had no central system to oversee their curricula. Many factions arose among the madrasas, teaching ever-changing interpretations of the Koran. By the 1980s these were the only schools in Pakistan that poor, young men could attend. Often the teachers themselves had little formal education, and many of the students came from rough backgrounds without benefit of structured family life or home.

In the past, the curriculum of a madrasa included the sciences and human values. Anis Ahmad, a religious scholar in Islamabad, Pakistan (quoted in the September 19, 2001 *Los Angeles Times*), observed that since the 1980s the madrasas "have gotten restricted to a few narrow issues," promoting a very rigid interpretation of Islamic law, or *sharia*, and particularly advocating a view of Israel and the United States as enemies of Islam.

When civil war among the warlords brought Afghanistan to desperate straits, Afghan students (or "talib," which means "student" or "seeker of truth" in Persian) in the madrasas began to seek answers to their country's woes. One of the mullahs (teachers, or givers of truth) was Mohammed Omar, who had been wounded and lost an eye fighting the Soviets before returning to his home near Kandahar to establish a madrasa. As students met in Omar's madrasa, they decided to take it upon themselves to restore peace in Afghanistan: to disarm the population and set up an Islamic society under Islamic law. They decided to call themselves the "Taliban."

The first battles the Taliban fought were small and local, freeing terrorized civilians from the violence of the military commanders stationed nearby. Then, in November 1994, Pakistani Prime Minister Benazir Bhutto appointed the Taliban to protect a trade caravan that had been captured by the local warlord in Kandahar. According to many, when Pakistan's Inter-Service Intelligence (ISI; the equivalent of the U.S. Central Intelligence Agency, or CIA) saw how successful the Taliban was in this endeavor, it began training and funding the group. Pakistan wanted to ensure that a Pashtun government would take power in Afghanistan, and it had been dissatisfied with the Pashtun leaders thus far. The Taliban was made up of Pashtuns.

At the time, the town of Kandahar had fallen into chaos, with crime and violence running out of control in its streets. After safely delivering the trade caravan they had been assigned to protect, the Taliban moved into the city and killed or drove off the criminals. They got rid of all guns in the town and then took control. Announcing that their mission was to set up the world's most pure Islamic state in Afghanistan, they applied their

## MULLAH MOHAMMED OMAR

*1958–* Leader of the Taliban, Mullah Mohammed Omar has been a mysterious figure to most of the world. He refused to meet with non-Muslims or women, and would speak only through intermediaries or over the radio. Because of the ban on photography and television, few know what he looks like.

Omar was born into the Pashtun tribe of Uruzgan, Afghanistan, in 1958 or 1959. In 1979 he arrived in Kandahar province to study at a madrasa. He then became a soldier in Afghanistan's war with the Soviet Union, suffering an injury to the head and the loss of an eye. After the defeat of the Soviets, Omar returned to the Kandahar province as a village cleric.

In 1994, Omar, like many other Afghans, was disgusted with the corrupt mujahideen, who were fighting for control of the country. Inspired by a vision of a pure Islamic Afghanistan, he began a crusade to enforce sharia, or Islamic law. He brought together and led a group of "taliban," or religious students, in vigilante actions against the warring leaders of Afghanistan, beginning the Taliban movement.

According to those who have known him, Omar strongly believed he was in direct communication with God and that his interpretations of Islamic law were absolute. Omar was not highly educated, with just a few years at the madrasa, and he only visited Afghanistan's capital Kabul twice during his career as the nation's leader. He was known to be emotional and moody. In March 2001 Omar issued an order to have the ancient statues of Buddha in the Bamiyan Province destroyed, despite a tremendous outcry from most of the nations of the world. He stood equally firm in his confrontation with the United States, refusing to turn over suspected terrorist Osama bin Laden for trial.

Until U.S. air strikes on the Taliban compound on October 7, 2001, Omar lived in relative seclusion in Kandahar with his three wives and 13 children. Interviewed after the fall of the Taliban in Afghanistan by the BBC's Pashto service on November 15, 2001, Omar listed his two priorities: "The current situation in Afghanistan is related to a bigger cause—that is the destruction of America. And on the other hand, the screening of Taleban [for those who are or are not loyal] is also in process." On ceding the Taliban's power in Kandahar on December 7, 2001, Omar promptly disappeared from sight.

# OSAMA BIN LADEN

*1957–* Osama bin Laden was the seventeenth of 52 children, born in Riyadh, Saudi Arabia. His father was a magnate in construction. His family is known in Muslim countries for financing important building projects and endowing charitable foundations. Bin Laden is said to have inherited about US$300 million.

In 1979 bin Laden traveled to Afghanistan to fight against the invading Soviets. It was there, many believe, that he became radicalized, dedicating his life to a militant Islamic creed. Supplied with American arms and intelligence, he recruited thousands of volunteer fighters, and set up training camps to aid the mujahideen in the war against the Soviet Union. In 1988 bin Laden set up al Qaeda ("the base"), a network of secret terrorist cells that operated in many countries. His goal was to stimulate extreme Islamic religious movements throughout the Muslim world and expel the corrupt Westerners, non-Muslims, and the Muslim leaders who, he believed, had strayed from the true law of Islam.

In 1991 bin Laden was enraged to learn that U.S. troops were stationed in Saudi Arabia due to the Persian Gulf War. He denounced Saudi Arabia for allowing them in the country and then announced a jihad or holy war against the Americans who, he felt, had occupied the Muslim Holy Land. That year the Saudis expelled him and revoked his citizenship, and he moved to Sudan, where he set up businesses and terrorist training camps in preparation for a war against the United States. Sudan expelled him in 1996 and he moved to Afghanistan, where he set up state-of-the-art terrorist training camps, according to some of his trainees who are now in custody.

In 1998 two U.S. embassies in Africa were bombed. The United States, convinced that bin Laden was responsible, bombed sites in Afghanistan and in Sudan where his training camps were suspected to be. The United States and then the United Nations demanded that bin Laden be extradited to a country that could try him for his terrorist acts, but the Taliban, then in power in Afghanistan, refused.

Al Qaeda is a highly secret organization. Experts believe that bin Laden and its leaders tell the operatives within the organization only what they need to know to carry out terrorist plans. Few individuals know what the group as a whole is planning. The size of the group probably varies as people are called in. It is estimated that al Qaeda draws from a group of about 50,000 Muslims worldwide, perhaps using several hundred to several thousand of them in projects. Al Qaeda is known to bankroll terrorist projects that others bring to its attention. The network is thought to be responsible for the 1993 bombing of the World Trade Center; the 1995 assassination attempt on Egyptian President Hosni Mubarak; the 1996 attack on the U.S. military headquarters in Dhahran, Saudi Arabia, killing 19 soldiers; the 1998 bombings of the U.S. embassies in Kenya and Tanzania, killing 235 and injuring more than 5,000; the bombing of the U.S.S. *Cole* in Yemen, killing 17 sailors; and the 2001 hijackings of four U.S. passenger airliners that destroyed the World Trade Center towers and a portion of the Pentagon, killing thousands of people.

fundamentalist interpretation of Islamic law to all aspects of life, banning music, photographs, and also education for girls. Women were required to cover their faces in public and could leave their homes only if accompanied by a close male relative. They were not allowed to work. Men were required to grow beards. If they shaved, they were imprisoned until the beard grew back. The right hands of thieves were amputated. Even though many citizens of Kandahar were not happy with the restrictions, there was general relief that the Taliban had stopped the violence and crime.

When news spread of the success of the Taliban, thousands of young Afghan Pashtuns arrived in Kandahar to join. Within three months, the Taliban had gained control of 12 Afghan provinces.

The leader of the Taliban, Mullah Mohammed Omar, made his base in Kandahar. Omar remained an enigmatic figure. He was in his thirties and a Pashtun. Because the Taliban prohibit taking photographs of people, few knew what Omar looked like and he tended to remain behind the scenes. Omar's opponents claimed he was ignorant of Islamic law (in fact he had just a few years in a madrasa) and was not really a Mullah or scholar of Islam. He maintained an ignorance of the world, not even traveling about in his own

AFGHAN WOMEN UNDER THE TALIBAN WERE SUBJECT TO STRICT REGULATIONS. THEY COULD NOT LEAVE THE HOUSE UNATTENDED BY A MALE FAMILY MEMBER AND HAD TO BE COVERED FROM HEAD TO TOE IN A BURQA. *(A/P Wide World. Reproduced by permission.)*

nation, in fact, only visiting Kabul twice during his reign. Many who were able to meet with him found him to be more a simple, uneducated villager than a leader of a nation. But Omar believed that he had been called by God to save Afghanistan and lead an Islamic state, and perhaps to be the political leader of all of Islam. He also believed that the edicts that he issued, which sometimes made little sense to others, were instructions from God, and he would not be dissuaded from them no matter what the consequences. Many of Omar's followers believed he was chosen by God to lead them.

The Taliban's rise to power was surprising and rapid. Its leaders did not at first speak about controlling the country—rather they professed to be setting it on a course in keeping with the Koran. According to Ahmed Rashid, this, their initial mission, appeared to be in keeping with the generally misunderstood Muslim concept of the "jihad:"

> Essentially jihad is the inner struggle of a Muslim to become a better human being, improve himself and his community... Islam also sanctions rebellion against an unjust ruler,... and jihad is the mobilizing mechanism to achieve change. Thus the life of the Prophet Mohammed has become the jihadi model of impeccable Muslim behavior and political change as the Prophet himself rebelled... The Taliban were thus acting in the spirit of the Prophet's jihad when they attacked the rapacious warlords around them.

In many cases, the Taliban did not have to fight to occupy a city; the Afghans were so tired of the civil war and of the corruption of the warlords that they welcomed the Taliban as protectors and saviors. With these successes, the Taliban attempted to take Kabul, but there resistance to them was strong.

In March 1996 Mullah Omar summoned a huge council of mullahs from all over Afghanistan to Kandahar to discuss the future of Afghanistan. It was understood that in order for the Taliban to rule Afghanistan they needed to take the city of Kabul. The mullahs from the Kandahar region, to give strength to their leader, nominated Mullah Omar as "Commander of the Faithful," the leader of the jihad and the emir of Afghanistan. On April 4, Omar unsealed a holy shrine in Kandahar containing a cloak that was believed to have once belonged to the Prophet Mohammad. The shrine had not been opened for nearly 60 years. Standing on a rooftop, he placed the prophet's cloak on his own shoulders and declared himself the commander of the faithful and the leader of all Islam. According to Tim Weiner, in an article in the December 7, 2001 *New York Times*, "No one had claimed that title since the Fourth Caliph, more than 1,000 years ago."

## International Involvement in Afghanistan's Divisions

As the Taliban fought to gain control of Kabul and the remaining cities holding out against them, their war with the warlords drew in other nations on both sides. Russia did not wish to see an extremist Islam government so close to its borders, since it had its own struggles with the Muslim state of Chechnya. Iran sympathized with the Shi'ite population of Herat, which had recently been captured by the Taliban, and supported the Hazara people against them. India was at odds with Pakistan, which supported the Taliban, and therefore supported the anti-Taliban forces. These countries sent military supplies and aid to Kabul for resistance. Pakistan and Saudi Arabia, on the other hand, supported the Taliban with supplies, arms, fuel, transport, and money. Pakistan in particular was interested in training fighters that could help them in their battles over Kashmir with India, and supported many extreme Islamic groups. Over and over again, when the Taliban needed new recruits in their battles, the madrasas in Pakistan would close down, sending thousands of students off to battle for the Taliban in Afghanistan. With support from many sources, the fighting raged on.

On August 25, 1996, the Taliban took over the city of Jalalabad and then moved on for Kabul. Taking the city by surprise on September 26, 1996, they forced Rabbani and Masud's forces to flee.

## Crossing the United Nations

The Taliban's first act in Kabul was to enter the UN compound there and drag out the former communist president Najibullah and his brother. They beat and tortured both men mercilessly before killing them and hanging their battered and mutilated bodies for the public to view. The act disgusted most of the citizens of Kabul as well as the international community. The United Nations issued a statement, quoted by Rashid: "The killing of the former President without any legitimate judicial procedure not only constitutes a grave violation of the immunity UN premises enjoy, but also further jeopardizes all the efforts which are being made to secure a peaceful settlement of the Afghan conflict." Unrelenting, the Taliban went on to impose its harshest laws on the city of Kabul, which it found to be too modern to conform to its rules without strict policing.

Resistance to the Pashtun-dominated Taliban was strongest in the city of Mazar-i Sharif, which repulsed the Taliban three times, killing an estimated 2,000 Taliban soldiers. It is reported that when the Taliban took the city in August 1998, they massacred anywhere from one to five thousand civilians belonging to the ethnic Shi'ite Hazara minority in a two-day rampage. The bloodshed and violence was so great in the city that UN humanitarian workers were forced to withdraw twice.

There were many within the Taliban who wanted to see the UN and all non-governmental organizations (NGOs) out of Afghanistan. There was a severe food shortage in the country, and millions needed the help of foreign humanitarian aid workers for daily survival. But the Taliban distrusted the influence of the foreigners despite the sufferings of the people. In 1997 the Taliban ordered some of the top UN officials to leave the country because they had defended the right of a female UN lawyer to question a leader without a curtain between them. The Taliban later arrested some Afghan UN staffers. There was ever-growing concern at the UN about the treatment of Afghanistan's women. In February 1998 the UN staff in Kandahar was beaten; the UN was forced to withdraw from the city altogether. In June of that year the Taliban ordered all female Muslim UN personnel in Afghanistan to be chaperoned by a male relative, a nearly impossible demand to fulfill. In July the Taliban closed down all NGOs' offices.

## The Taliban and Women

Shortly after capturing the capital city of Kabul, the Taliban set up a policing agency called the Ministry for the Enforcement of Virtue and Suppression of Vice, which enforced the Taliban version of Islamic law. The agency immediately began to impose strict regulations on women. Women were not allowed to work in most occupations and girls could not attend school. Women over the age of fourteen were to wear only traditional garb, including the *burqa,* an ankle-length veil that fully covered the body, making it very difficult to see and move. The windows on the lower floors of homes were blackened so that no one could look in upon the women inside.

The consequences for violating these bans were severe. Reportedly, women were shot to death for running home schools, or for attempting to leave Afghanistan without a male family member to accompany them. Women were beaten and whipped in public for such offenses as accidentally permitting an ankle to show below a veil. The whippings were extreme: the recovery period could be months, and sometimes the whippings were fatal.

Since women were not allowed to work or to go out without a male relative, widows and orphans in Afghanistan had a very rough time and were often forced to beg or turn to prostitution in order to feed themselves.

## Tough on Crime and Other Things

Not only women suffered from the harshness of the Taliban's rule. The punishment for stealing, even if it was a last resort to feed one's family, was the amputation of the right hand. If a person was caught stealing a second time, the left foot might be amputated. Homosexuals in Afghanistan were buried alive. Prostitutes were publicly hanged. Adulterers were stoned.

The Taliban banned television, all music except religious songs, movies, the Internet, card-playing, books and periodicals published outside of Afghanistan, white socks, kites, the game of chess, paper bags, and many other things, particularly things that are Western in origin. The Ministry for the Enforcement of Virtue and Suppression of Vice was well known for its brutal beatings and applications of the whip when a rule was violated. Jail terms were doled out in many cases.

## Harboring Terrorists

Throughout 1998 and 1999, the United States and the Taliban clashed over Afghanistan's harboring of Osama bin Laden, who was believed by the United States to be responsible for the August 1998 terrorist bombings of U.S. embassies in Kenya and Tanzania. From the mid-1980s bin Laden had been establishing training camps in Afghanistan and continued to attract thousands of recruits from Saudi Arabia, Algeria, Egypt, Yemen, Pakistan, and Sudan.

Although he worked with Americans during the Soviet occupation of Afghanistan, bin Laden soon became hostile to them. In Afghanistan he met Ayman al Zawahiri, a member of the Egyptian Islamic Jihad, and the two became close friends. The idea of exporting terrorism and establishing Islamic states in other Muslim countries was probably originally Zawahiri's. Using the millions he had inherited, bin Laden formed the terrorist group al Qaeda ("the base") in 1988 with these goals in mind. Al Qaeda is believed to function in as many as twenty countries.

In 1990, the Persian Gulf War brought American soldiers to Saudi Arabia. To bin Laden and his accomplices it was an outrage that Americans had set foot in the birthplace of the prophet Mohammed and the home of the two holiest Muslim shrines. He also blamed the United States for its support of Israel in the conflict with Palestine. In 1998 bin Laden announced the establishment of "The International Islamic Front for Holy War Against Jews and Crusaders." The organization, connecting Islamic extremists worldwide, announced to the world: "The ruling to kill the Americans and their allies, civilians, and the military, is an individual duty for every Muslim who can do it in any country in which it is possible to do it, in order to liberate al-Aqsa Mosque and the Holy Mosque from their grip and in order for their armies to move out of all the lands of Islam, defeated, and unable to threaten any Muslim."

In 1994, bin Laden was back in Saudi Arabia, but was soon expelled for his denouncements of the royal family. He then moved to Sudan, where he developed his business interests. In 1996 the United States convinced Sudan to expel him. He then moved to Afghanistan, where the Taliban were just taking over. By 1997 he had developed a friendship with Omar and moved his entourage to Kandahar.

According to Tim Weiner of the *New York Times*, bin Laden, looking for a place to permanently base his operations, probably flattered Omar to further his own mission. Weiner quotes a former Pakistani ambassador who had met with Omar frequently: "My very strong hunch is that bin Laden convinced this village man that he had to bring his revolution to the whole world." Rashid, in an article in *Foreign Affairs*, (November/December 1999) argues that the Taliban would not have come to political power had it not been for the support of foreigners. "Until they captured Kabul in 1996 they expressed no desire to rule the country. But ever since then—abetted by their Pakistani and Saudi backers and inspired by ideological mentors such as bin Laden—the Taliban have committed themselves to conquering the entire country and more."

From the end of the fighting against the Soviets in Afghanistan until 1998, bin Laden was suspected of organizing or being in some way linked to many terrorist acts, including an attack on a U.S. military base in Saudi Arabia in 1995 and the 1998 bombings of the U.S. embassies in Kenya and Tanzania, which killed more than two hundred people. After the bombings of the U.S. embassies, President Bill Clinton's administration (1993–2001) ordered missile strikes against suspected bin Laden training camps in Afghanistan.

The United Nations also resolved to act against the Taliban. On October 15, 1999, it

THE TALIBAN DESTROYED ANCIENT BUDDHIST STATUES IN AFGHANISTAN, PROMPTING AN INTERNATIONAL OUT-CRY AND FURTHER OSTRACISM OF THE UNPOPULAR REGIME. *(A/P Wide World. Reproduced by permission.)*

demanded that the Taliban extradite Osama bin Laden to a country that would bring him to justice. The Taliban refused, saying they had not seen evidence that bin Laden was responsible for the bombings. On November 14, 1999, the United Nations prohibited air transportation to and from Afghanistan and urged all its members to apply sanctions—freezing Taliban assets abroad and barring Afghans from investment.

## RECENT HISTORY AND THE FUTURE

Despite its control of about 90 percent of Afghanistan, the Taliban was an unrecognized political entity—only Pakistan, Saudi Arabia, and the United Arab Emirates recognized the Taliban government before the September 11 terrorist attacks in the United States. The international isolation and the sanctions deeply hurt the nation economically. Rather than capitulate to pressure, however, the Taliban further isolated itself from Western favor. Sayed Rahmatullah Hashimi, an envoy of the Taliban, commented in a PBS interview on March 29, 2001: "Well, these economic sanctions are meant to pressurize our government and this is so ridiculous for us because to try to change our ideology with economic sanctions will never work, because for us, our ideology is first."

For a time it seemed that the Taliban was deliberately pushing international buttons.

In March 2001, the Taliban destroyed a large number of statues, among them two historic treasures: giant stone Buddhas—one 165 and the other 114 feet tall (50 and 35 meters respectively), that had been carved into the sandstone mountains of Afghanistan's Bamiyan province sometime between the second and fifth centuries CE. A general worldwide protest arose when Omar announced that the Buddhas were "false idols" and would be obliterated. Hashimi said that the destruction of the Buddhas was done in anger. With a famine hitting the people of Afghanistan in the midst of worldwide sanctions, religious scholars were indignant when a group of Western historians offered to provide money for the preservation of the statues. "What do you expect from a country when you just ostracize them and isolate them and send in cruise missiles and their children are dying?" Hashimi asked. Some observers, however, noted that a council of clerics had been deliberating on the move to destroy the statues long before the Western historians expressed interest in them.

Within a couple of months of the destruction of the Buddhas, the Taliban was in the news again, this time for its unexpected help in international efforts to eliminate drug trafficking. Afghanistan had been responsible for nearly three-quarters of the poppies used to make the world's heroin. In July 2000, Omar had issued an edict banning the growing of poppies in Afghanistan, calling it a sin against the teachings of Islam. His edict went mostly unnoticed in the West until spring, when the world could clearly see that the once-abundant poppy fields in Afghanistan lay fallow. Although the Taliban said that it banned poppy crops for religious reasons, they had reason to believe that the United States and other Western nations would provide assistance to them for the tremendous loss of income the Afghans experienced. The United States did provide a US$43 million dollar grant for drought relief, but the already impoverished people of Afghanistan were suddenly without one of their major remaining sources of income.

In May 2001 the Taliban were again the focus of international protest when they proposed to force Hindus in Afghanistan to wear identification labels on their clothing. There are at least 5,000 Hindus living in Kabul and thousands elsewhere in the country. The Taliban explained that the tagging was for the Hindus' protection. Since the Ministry for the Enforcement of Virtue and Suppression of Vice patrolled Afghanistan's cities, searching out and punishing Muslims who broke the Taliban's rules, they reasoned that by wearing identification labels, the Hindus could be excluded from those punishments. Hindus, however, were not exempt from most rules. Hindu women, for example, were forced to wear the burqa. Hindus interviewed by journalists did not want to wear labels, fearing that it would make them vulnerable to more repression from the Taliban.

In August 2001 the Taliban Ministry for the Enforcement of Virtue and Suppression of Vice shut down the offices of a German-based Christian aid organization, Shelter Now, saying that the group was trying to spread Christianity among the people of Kabul. They produced evidence, including a Christian bible translated into a native language. The Taliban arrested eight of the organization's workers, two of whom were American. At the time of the terrorist attacks on the United States, the Christian aid workers were undergoing a trial in Kabul. They later escaped from the Taliban as their captors retreated from enemy forces.

### The Aftermath in Afghanistan

Because of a wide gulf in value systems, the Taliban's system of rule was very alienating to most non-fundamentalists. Their interpretations of the Koran were foreign to many Muslims. But

FOREIGN AID WORKERS WERE ARRESTED IN AFGHANISTAN FOR SEEKING TO CONVERT AFGHANS TO CHRISTIANITY, AGAIN DRAWING INTERNATIONAL ATTENTION TO THE RULING TALIBAN AS THE WORLD WAITED FOR A RESOLUTION TO THE SITUATION. *(A/P Wide World. Reproduced by permission.)*

there were some merits to their rule, and the Taliban had devotees around the world. For one thing, the Taliban did not appear to use their rule in Afghanistan to enrich themselves. They lived simply and by their own rules, for the most part. More importantly, they were highly successful in imposing order where there had been chaos and crime. A significant segment of Muslims believe in combining religion and state and look to Afghanistan as the supreme example of this. Since the Taliban's professed goal, at least originally, was to create a pure Islamic state, the question arises, was their extreme application of rules in keeping with the Koran? A lot of scholars say no. Ahmed Rashid commented that the Taliban knew little of Islamic and Afghan history, sharia, or the Koran, and thus had little historical perspective or tradition on which to base their actions.

When the Taliban was forced by U.S. air strikes and Afghan resistance to flee the city of Kabul, the change that took place there was profound. Without the dreaded Ministry for the Enforcement of Virtue and Suppression of Vice, the people in the city once again can enjoy music, film, television; young girls can go to school and women go out in public (although still, for the

# SPEECH BY TALIBAN LEADER MULLAH MOHAMMAD OMAR

Wednesday, September 19, 2001. Source: Reuters. Cited December 7, 2001. Available online at: http://www.bostonherald.com/attack/world_reaction/ausmul09192001.htm.

The Ulema have always guided the nation.

Our Islamic state is the true Islamic state in the world and for this reason the enemies of our religion and our country look on us as a thorn in their eyes and use different pretexts to try to finish it, including the one about the presence of Osama bin Laden in Afghanistan.

They put the blame for Washington and New York on him. The question is how did Osama tell the pilots? And which airports did they use? And whose planes were those? The answer is that it is America.

In this regard, Afghanistan does not have the resources and neither does Osama have the strength or resources. He is not in contact with anyone and neither have we given permission to anyone to use the Afghan land against anyone.

We have not tried to create friction with America. We have had several talks with the present and past American governments and we are ready for more talks.

We have told America that we have taken all resources from Osama and he cannot contact the outside world. And we have told America that neither the Islamic Emirate of Afghanistan or Osama are involved in the American events. But it is sad that America does not listen to our word.

America always repeats threats and makes various accusations and now it is threatening military attack.

This is being done in circumstances in which we have offered alternatives on the Osama issue.

We have said, if you have evidence against Osama, give it to the Afghan Supreme Court or the Ulema [group of mullahs or clerics] of three Islamic countries, or have OIC (Organisation of Islamic Countries) observers keep an eye on Osama.

But America rejected these, one by one. If America had considered these suggestions there would not have been a chance of such a great misunderstanding.

We appeal to the American government to exercise complete patience, and we want America to gather complete information and find the actual culprits.

We assure the whole world that neither Osama nor anyone else can use the Afghan land against anyone else.

And if even after this, America wants to use force and wants to attack Afghanistan and our innocent and oppressed people and wants to destroy the Islamic emirate, we seek your guidance and a fatwa (ruling) on the issue in the light of Islamic Sharia.

most part, dressed in burqas due to a lingering fear). Antipathy for the Taliban is widespread in Kabul, and people are particularly bitter that its brutal and oppressive regime has been associated with the peaceful Muslim religion.

Celebrations were hesitant, though, as the Taliban fled. There was much to concern the Afghan people, even supposing that the country doesn't lapse into more ethnic division and fighting amongst factions. There will be a huge recovery period after a new government is in place. There is little economic structure left to return to. The Taliban, with no respect for knowledge or professionalism, removed educated people from their posts and so administrative and technical maintenance of the nation's resources was lost. Prolonged war has torn apart energy, irrigation, and communications systems. The poppy crops that had sustained many are not a viable choice for Afghanistan's future. For five years the country has existed in enforced ignorance. For three years food and water shortages have jeopardized the lives of millions.

Afghanistan is beset with problems on all fronts. Its population is once again over-armed; some areas have already resorted to the banditry, kidnapping, and the general lawlessness that existed before Taliban rule. Beyond this, the Taliban, though scattered and no longer in power, continues to fight and mobilize. With support from many sectors within and around Afghanistan, the Taliban and its allies can still do harm to attempts to unify the country. The United States, accused of withdrawing its support from Afghanistan at a crucial time after the Soviets were defeated in 1989, is indicating that it will remain in Afghanistan this time until some stability is achieved. Yet its presence is certain to be a source of friction among the different groups in the country and a threat to some neighboring countries, such as Iran.

Only prolonged peace and stability can lead Afghanistan to recovery from decades of trauma. The new government in Afghanistan will have to ensure that the ethnic groups and religious sects are treated equitably. In the meantime, humanitarian aid agencies are fighting to maintain access to the people who face starvation without their courageous support. With such a difficult road ahead, it is to be hoped that the international community and its funding won't disappear with the Taliban.

# BIBLIOGRAPHY

Ademec, Ludwig. *Historical Dictionary of Afghanistan.* Lanham, MD: Scarecrow Press, 1997.

Auster, Bruce R. "The Recruiter for Hate," *U.S. News and World Report,* August 31,1998.

Baker, Peter. "Taliban Fortifies Capital For War: Trenches Are Dug, Men Conscripted," *Washington Post.* October 4, 2001; Page A01.

Herbert, Bob. "Fleeing the Taliban," *New York Times,* October 25, 1999, sec. A31.

Herman, Burt. "Leaders Promise Multi-Ethnic Council," American Press. Available online at http://dailynews .yahoo.com/h/ap/20011003/wl/uzbekistan_ afghanistan_1.html (cited October 3, 2001).

"Interview with Mullah Omar—Transcript," BBC News, November 15, 2001 Available online at http:// news.bbc.co.uk/hi/english/world/south_asia/newsid_ 1657000/1657368.stm (cited January 11, 2002) .

Keating, Michael. "A Women's Rights and Wrongs," *World Today* 53, no. 1 (1997): 10–12.

Maley, William, ed. *Fundamentalism Reborn? Afghanistan and the Taliban.* New York: New York University Press, 1998.

Manz, B. F. *Central Asia in Historical Perspective.* Boulder, CO: Westview Press, 1995.

Maroofi, Musa M. "The Afghan Taliban: Like It or Not, It Occupies Two-Thirds of Afghanistan and Shows No Sign of Weakening," *Washington Report,* April 1998, 47ff.

Marshall, Tyler, and John Daniszewski, "Pakistan's Muslim Schools Offer a Dark View of U.S.," *Los Angeles Times,* September 19, 2001, A-1, 4.

Miller, T. Christian, "Bin Laden Deputy: Brilliant Ideologue," *Los Angeles Times,* October 2, 2001, p. A-1, 16.

OCHA Situation Report No. 5: Afghanistan Crisis, United Nations. Available online at http://www .pcpafg.org/news/Situation_rep/Afghanistan_Crisis_ OCHA_Situation_Report_No_5_25_Sep_2001 .shtml (cited October 3, 2001).

Olesen, Asta. *Islam and Politics in Afghanistan.* London: Curzon Press, 1995.

Online Newshour: Inside Afghanistan (PBS), September 28, 2001. Available online at http://www.pbs.org/ newshour/bb/terrorism/july-dec01/afghan_9-28.html (cited October 2, 2001).

Online Newshour: Afghanistan's Agony (PBS), March 29, 2001. Available online at http://www.pbs.org/ newshour/bb/asia/jan-june01/afghanistan_3-29.html (cited October 2, 2001) .

Profile: The Lion of Panjshir, BBC News. Available online at http://news.bbc.co.uk/hi/english/world/south_asia/ newsid_1535000/1535249.stm (cited October 4, 2001).

Rashid, Ahmed. "Sister Courage," *Far Eastern Economic Review* 160, no. 48, 1997, p. 30.

———. "The Taliban: Exporting Extremism." *Foreign Affairs,* November/December 1999.

———. *Taliban: Militant Islam, Oil, and Fundamentalism in Central Asia.* New Haven, CT: Yale University Press, 2000.

Rubin, Barnett R. "Afghanistan Under the Taliban," *Current History,* February 1999, pp. 79–91.

"The Taliban Virus" *World Press Review* 45, no. 12, 1998, pp. 6–7.

Vollmann, William T. "Across the Divide," *New Yorker,* May 15, 2000.

Weiner, Tim. "Seizing the Prophet's Mantle: Muhammad Omar," *New York Times,* December 7, 2001.

*Sonia Benson*

# THE EXPANDED U.S. DRUG WAR IN LATIN AMERICA: A DOWNED MISSIONARY PLANE PLACES THE SPOTLIGHT ON THE ANDEAN INITIATIVE

## THE CONFLICT

The impact of drug abuse and drug-related violence in U.S. communities is devastating. Government estimates put the total cost at more than US$110 billion a year. Drug production and trafficking are also a serious threat to Latin American countries, eroding governments and institutions through corruption, fueling political violence and common crime, and distorting local economies.

### Political

- Colombia has been engaged in a civil conflict for over 40 years and the Colombian people are faced with severe political violence and the corrosive effects of drug trafficking. The United States has significant national interests in Colombia, including economic interests, and desires to ensure the political and economic stability of the Andean region. Many academics, policymakers, and human rights advocates differ in their views about the best way for the United States to help the Colombian government address the drug problem, particularly whether or not the United States should be involved in assisting the Colombian government to fight guerrilla groups.

- Since Richard Nixon declared a "War on Drugs" in the 1970s there has been a serious debate as to which method of drug control is most effective. Some argue that drug consumption is primarily a law enforcement challenge while others suggest that our government should view drug use as a public health problem and increase funds for treatment of addicts. There is also a debate as to whether the United States should focus funds on reducing the demand for drugs here at home, or increase spending on international programs aimed at stopping the flow of drugs to the United States.

### Economic

- In many of the Andean countries, growing coca has provided a steady income to peasants for many generations. In order to eradicate the crop, the governments must seek alternative sources of income for the farmers.

On April 20, 2001, Veronica Bowers, a U.S. Baptist missionary, and her seven-month-old daughter were flying in a small plane low over the jungle in northern Peru. When agents from the U.S. government's Central Intelligence Agency (CIA) identified the aircraft as a potential drug trafficker, the Peruvian Air Force shot the plane down, killing Bowers and her infant daughter and seriously injuring the pilot, Kevin Donaldson.

The Peruvian Air Force and the Americans were acting according to a "shootdown" policy that was adopted through a joint agreement between the U.S. and Peruvian governments in 1993 in order to block drug trafficking routes between coca growers in Peru and drug traffickers in Colombia. The United States provides financial support for the Peruvian Air Force to carry out this mission and also shares intelligence about potential drug trafficking flights.

The program is considered to be a critical part of the United States-funded "War on Drugs" in the Andes region, in which the United States works with national governments throughout Latin America to stop the flow of illegal drugs to the United States. The tragic shootdown focused the attention of the U.S. public and Congress on anti-drug efforts in the Andes and fueled an already heated debate in Washington regarding the United States' expanding role there.

The United States is providing hundreds of millions of dollars annually in counter-drug assistance to countries throughout Latin America. The bulk of the spending is currently directed to security forces in the Andean nations of Peru, Ecuador, Colombia, Bolivia, and Venezuela. To date such programs have had limited impact on the availability of drugs in the United States because drug production and trafficking constantly shift to new locations in response to new anti-drug efforts. This lack of effectiveness has left many to question whether a further investment from the United States in such programs is worthwhile. Policymakers disagree on whether the U.S. drug problem should be treated as a public health issue here at home, or approached as a law enforcement challenge in which the United States combats drug trafficking on our streets and in other countries. Critics argue that U.S. anti-drug assistance in Latin America has done more harm than good as the United States has allied itself with military forces implicated in human rights violations and political violence.

### Drug Problems in the Hemisphere

There is little question that it is in the United States' interest to work in collaboration with Latin American governments to address the hemisphere's drug problem. The United States is the world's leading consumer of illicit drugs, and the impact of drug abuse and drug-related violence across the United States is devastating. Government estimates put the cost at more than US$110 billion per year. Drug production and trafficking are also a serious threat to Latin American countries, fueling political violence and common crime, eroding government institutions through corruption, and distorting local economies. And though U.S. funding for international anti-drug efforts continues to increase year after year, there are no easy answers to the drug problem—nor is there consensus among policymakers regarding the most effective approach. U.S. international drug control programs in Latin America are currently focused in two principle areas: interdiction—law enforcement efforts to capture drugs as they are in transit to markets; and eradication—efforts to eliminate the raw materials used to make drugs at their source.

## HISTORICAL BACKGROUND

President Richard M. Nixon's administration (1969–74) first launched America's "War on Drugs" in 1971, as part of an effort to support vigorous anti-crime and law enforcement efforts and to provide programs for those servicemen who had returned from Vietnam with drug problems. Nixon declared drug abuse "enemy number one" and focused the bulk of spending on treatment programs for drug addicts. Reports indicate that such programs were effective at reducing crime related to drug abuse.

Over the past 30 years presidents have taken different approaches to the drug war. President

## CHRONOLOGY

**1972** President Nixon declares a "War on Drugs" and drastically increases federal spending on drug programs.

**1984** Nancy Reagan launches her "Just Say No" to drugs campaign.

**1986** U.S. Congress initiates the Drug Certification Process.

**1989** The first George Bush administration launches the Andean Strategy and declares a new War on Drugs.

**1993** Peru and the United States initiate an aerial shootdown program targeting drug-trafficking planes.

**1993–1994** The Colombian government breaks up the two largest Colombian drug cartels with U.S. assistance.

**1994** U.S. Congress temporarily suspends the shootdown policy in Peru due to concerns about liability.

**1998** Colombian President Andres Pastrana opens peace talks with FARC.

**2000** President Clinton approves a $1.3 billion contribution to Plan Colombia.

**2000** Bolivian President Hugo Banzer declares that Bolivia has eliminated all illegal coca.

**2001** U.S. missionary Veronica Bowers is killed in a shootdown in Peru, renewing attention to the U.S. role in the area.

Jimmy Carter (1977–81) attempted to remove federal criminal penalties for possession of minimal amounts of marijuana. As cocaine use boomed in the 1980s the Reagan administration (1981–89) drastically increased funds for anti-drug efforts, with Nancy Reagan's "Just Say No" campaign spotlighting drug education programs. Gradually, the focus of anti-drug programs in the United States shifted to law enforcement efforts, rather than treatment. As lawmakers sought new ways to get tough on the drug problem, their focus on stopping the flow of drugs into the United States also increased.

### An Anti-Drug Report Card

In 1986 the U.S. Congress established an annual "drug certification process" in which the United States judges the performance of other countries' anti-drug efforts. The process withholds several forms of aid to countries until the president

# THE HISTORY OF COCA AND COCAINE

The existence of the coca plant in the Andes dates back to 2500 BCE, centuries before the rise of the Incan empire. Coca was considered to be a sacred plant, endowed with magical powers. The leaves are traditionally used in rituals, as offerings, to forecast coming events, and to cure ailments. Individuals chew the leaf, which has a mild stimulant effect, and helps them to resist hunger and fatigue. People in the Andes also use the coca leaves in everyday products such as herbal teas, toothpaste, and wine. Historians note that that even after the Spanish conquest of the region, the use of coca played an important role, particularly in agriculture and the mining industry, as native workers would receive a ration of coca in order to curb their hunger pangs during long work shifts.

In the late nineteenth century, European doctors first began to explore the anesthetic properties of the cocaine—an active derivative of the coca leaf. Albert Niemman of Goettingen, Germany, first processed coca into cocaine in 1859. Doctors thought it would make an ideal anesthetic, as it blocked pain impulses to the brain. In 1884 doctors began to use cocaine as an anesthetic in eye operations and cocaine became a widely used pharmaceutical as the word spread about this powerful drug. In 1888 Dr. John Pemberton of Atlanta, Georgia, combined coca leaves with African cola nut extract to create what is now the world's most popular beverage: Coca-Cola. Prominent figures such as psychologist Sigmund Freud recommended the therapeutic use of cocaine to address depression. The use of the narcotic spread in the United States and Europe.

As awareness about the harmful impacts of the drug grew, the American public began to demand that the social use of cocaine be banned. Coca-Cola eliminated the use of coca leaf extracts in its soda in 1903, and the U.S. government outlawed the use of cocaine in 1914.

Coca is not cocaine. Scientific studies have revealed that the use of the coca leaf in its natural state does not have negative health impacts, nor is the consumption of the coca leaf addictive. In order to make cocaine, the coca leaf is processed using a series of chemicals including kerosene, diluted sulfuric acid, and ammonia. Through this process cocaine becomes a powerful stimulant that causes a brief sense of alertness or "high," frequently accompanied by sleep deprivation and loss of appetite. The habitual use of cocaine causes users to hallucinate and become psychotic. When frequent users stop using the drug, they experience a state of depression and withdrawal, which can lead to dependence or addiction to the drug. The long-term use of cocaine can also result in digestive disorders, weight loss, general physical deterioration, and degradation of the nervous system. An overdose of cocaine can cause death due to breathing and heart problems.

It is still legal to grow coca in some areas of Peru and Bolivia—though many areas have been targeted for reduction or elimination of coca as part of international efforts to reduce the availability of cocaine. Coca is legally sold within those countries for traditional purposes, though it is illegal to export products made with coca leaves. Coca is still used for traditional purposes in Peru, Bolivia, part of Colombia, and Northern Argentina, particularly among the native Aymara and Quechua cultures, and it remains an important symbol of cultural identity.

can certify that they are cooperating in the war on drugs. Any major drug transit or source country that is "decertified" faces a serious cutoff in U.S. financial aid, with the exception of humanitarian and anti-drug programs. The United States automatically votes against loans to "decertified" countries from multilateral banks (such as the World Bank), and the president has the authority to impose trade sanctions on such countries as well.

Many observers have suggested that this kind of pressure was necessary to gain cooperation from foreign governments in the fight against drugs. But the process has caused significant friction in Latin America, as countries resent receiving a unilateral report card from the world's largest consumer of illicit drugs. Mexican leaders have led the charge to develop a more multilateral process, calling certification "a thorn in hemispheric relations." In addition, U.S. lawmakers became concerned that the president's certification was often an arbitrary distinction, making the sanctions meaningless. Countries with whom the United States has little or no relations—such as Myanmar (Burma) and Afghanistan—were decertified year after year, while importing trading partners such as Mexico were continuously certified even during years

A CESSNA PLANE IS PULLED FROM THE AMAZON RIVER IN PERU ON APRIL 26, 2001. THE PLANE, CARRYING AMERICAN MISSIONARIES, WAS SHOT DOWN BY A PERUVIAN AIR FORCE JET THAT HAD MISTAKEN IT FOR A PLANE CARRYING DRUGS. TWO ABOARD WERE KILLED. *(A/P Wide World. Reproduced by permission.)*

when there were serious concerns about the shortcomings of their anti-drug efforts.

Throughout the late 1980s and early 1990s U.S. spending on international drug-control programs continued to rise year after year, totaling nearly $30 billion over the last decade. The first Bush administration (1989–93) focused on the Andean countries of Bolivia, Peru, and Colombia. In 1989 President George H. Bush launched the five-year, $2 million "Andean Strategy," which aimed to stop cocaine at its source. Bush declared that "the gravest domestic threat facing our nation today is drugs." The program prioritized military hardware and training for counter-narcotics operations and was a dramatic expansion of U.S. training and assistance to military and police in the region.

While this initiative placed the spotlight on Andean countries, the bulk of U.S. military anti-drug spending at that time continued to be spent on programs to detect and monitor drug transit zones in the Caribbean and the Gulf of Mexico. In 1993, President Bill Clinton (1993–2001) shifted the emphasis of military operations to dismantling the "air bridge," drug-trafficking flight routes that connect coca growers and coca paste producers in Peru to drug traffickers in Colombia. The Huallaga valley of Peru was estimated to pro-

duce two-thirds of the world's coca and cocaine paste prior to the initiation of this program. The U.S. and Peruvian governments hoped that the policy would deny traffickers their supply of paste, and that coca farmers would abandon their crops if the traffickers stopped arriving to buy the product.

The policy enabled the Peruvian Air Force to identify and shoot down suspected drug-trafficking flights. This resulted in drug traffickers abandoning air routes in favor of land and water routes, driving up the price of transporting illegal drugs. Though the policy was deemed to be a success by many officials, many question the accuracy with which planes were identified before they were shot. The program was temporarily suspended in 1994 due to the U.S. government's concerns about their legal liability if innocent civilians were killed as a result of the program, though the Clinton administration resumed the policy under significant pressure from Congress. A 2001 State Department investigation into the death of U.S. missionary Veronica Bowers, which occurred as a result of this program, revealed that U.S. and Peruvian pilots had been ignoring the safeguards in the program, which were established to ensure that only drug trafficking flights were targeted.

Throughout the 1990s, Bolivia and Peru alternately held the dubious distinction of being

## METHODS OF DRUG CONTROL

**(1) Efforts to reduce the demand for illicit drugs.**

- **Treatment** focuses on the rehabilitation of drug users, with the assumption that this is a medical or mental health issue rather than a criminal one.

- The **law enforcement** model treats drug possession, as well as sales, as a criminal matter and punishes offenders through the judicial system.

**(2) Efforts to reduce the supply of illicit drugs.**

- **Eradication** attempts to reduce production of the illegal substances in other countries.

- **Interdiction** involves reducing the flow of illegal drugs into the United States by more vigilant patrolling of the nation's borders.

*PBS Frontline.*

the world's largest producer of coca—an honor now held by Colombia. A series of factors led to this shift in cultivation. The Clinton administration's "air bridge" shootdown strategy made it far less appealing for Colombian traffickers to ship coca paste from Peru to Colombia. In 1993–94, with U.S. assistance, the Colombian government succeeded in breaking up the Medellín and Cali cartels, the two major Colombian drug trafficking syndicates. These organizations were quickly replaced by smaller trafficking organizations that were more vertically integrated; they began working within Colombia to increase coca cultivation to satisfy their needs. Thus, in the late 1990s as coca cultivation was significantly reduced in Bolivia and Peru, cultivation in Colombia boomed—increasing 150 percent over a five-year period.

Policymakers refer to this displacement as the "balloon effect." Continued demand for drugs—and the immense profits that drug trafficking promises—ensure that when drug cultivation and production are suppressed in one area, they will emerge in another. One of the greatest challenges in sustaining eradication efforts is addressing the rural poverty that lies at the root of drug cultivation. Hundreds of thousands of peasants grow coca in the Andes because the crop can be harvested four times a year and has a secure market that provides them with a steady subsistence income.

Growing alternative legal crops is often risky, as the markets are less stable and harder to reach.

In Bolivia, the United States has viewed the coca eradication efforts that it finances as a great success in recent years because the Bolivian government has drastically reduced coca cultivation. This success has come at great cost in a country where coca is deeply rooted in the culture—the traditional use of coca for medicine, as a hunger suppressant, and in rituals dates back 2,000 years and continues today. Because the Bolivian government's alternative development programs have not yet provided other sources of income for the thousands of peasant farmers whose coca crops were forcibly eradicated, social tensions in the Chapare coca-growing region have intensified. Coca growers' unions participated in nationwide road blockades in September and October 2000, and presented the government with a list of demands related to the military presence in their land and the need for alternative development. The blockades, made up of grassroots organizations from all over the country, halted transportation in the region for nearly a month, resulting in economic losses and deaths during violent confrontations between the coca growers and security forces. The coca-growing regions of Bolivia are a stage for constant protests.

### United States Turns Attention to Colombia

For more than four decades, Colombia has suffered a brutal civil war. Parties to Colombia's conflict rarely fight one another, and instead attack their enemies' alleged sympathizers—most often unarmed civilians. The impact of this violence is staggering. The Colombian Commission of Jurists estimates that political violence in Colombia has doubled in the past three years, with 20 politically motivated killings per day. One-and-a-half million internal refugees have been forced from their homes by violence. Human rights monitors, labor unionists, peace leaders, humanitarian workers, Afro-Colombians, and indigenous peoples are increasingly threatened, displaced by violence, "disappeared," and murdered.

Most analysts agree that only negotiations will bring an end to Colombia's conflict and tragic humanitarian emergency; only peace and stability will make it possible to effectively reduce drug production and trafficking. In August 1998, Colombian President Andrés Pastrana took office with the promise of seeking a peaceful resolution to the conflict. He has met with representatives of the large and well-trained anti-government guerrilla organization, the Revolutionary Armed

# PARTIES TO COLOMBIA'S CONFLICT

**Armed forces:** The primary mission of the Colombian military has been combating guerrillas in a nearly 40-year civil war, though it has increased its counterdrug operations under U.S. pressure. The Colombian army is one of the most abusive in the hemisphere. At times members of the military have made public statements that undermine the government's peace efforts and are often linked to illegal paramilitary forces and their atrocities. The State Department's February 2001 human rights report noted: "Members of the security forces collaborated with paramilitary groups that committed abuses," in some instances allowing such groups to pass through roadblocks, sharing information, or providing them with supplies or ammunition. "Impunity for military personnel who collaborated with members of paramilitary groups remained common."

**Paramilitaries:** Paramilitaries are illegal right-wing armed forces allied with the military. United under paramilitary leader Carlos Castaño's AUC (United Self-Defense Forces of Colombia), they act as private militias or death squads, often carrying out the military's "dirty work." The U.S. Drug Enforcement Agency (DEA) has identified Castaño as a "major drug trafficker." Paramilitary violence against unarmed civilians escalated sharply in 2001 as the groups vied for territorial control, access to key drug-trafficking routes, and a seat at the negotiating table. The Colombian President's Solidarity Network reported on April 17, 2001, that paramilitaries had killed 529 of the 769 people that died during massacres in 2001, compared to the 199 people the paramilitaries killed during the same period last year. Approximately 80 percent of political deaths are attributed to the paramilitaries by the Colombian Commission of Jurists (CCJ).

The State Department human rights report found: "Throughout the country, paramilitary groups killed, tor-

tured, and threatened civilians suspected of sympathizing with guerrillas in an orchestrated campaign to terrorize them into fleeing their homes.... The AUC increasingly tried to depict itself as an autonomous organization with a political agenda, although in practice it remained a mercenary vigilante force, financed by criminal activities and sectors of society that are targeted by guerrillas."

**Guerrillas:** Approximately 20,000 combatants compose the two largest guerrilla groups, the FARC (Revolutionary Armed Forces of Colombia) and ELN (National Liberation Army). They commit widespread violations of international humanitarian law, including forced recruitment of minors, civilian massacres, and kidnappings for profit. The guerrillas are responsible for approximately 15 percent of Colombia's politically motivated killings, according to the CCJ. For decades the guerrillas have waged a war against the government based on a Marxist political agenda. Both guerrilla groups are currently engaged in slow peace negotiations with the Colombian government.

Negotiations with the FARC—held in territory ceded to them by the government for peace talks—recently yielded a prisoner exchange. The ELN maintains its strategic base in key oil-producing areas in the northeastern part of the country. The FARC exerts territorial control in key coca-growing regions in southern Colombia. The guerrillas are not drug cartels, though the FARC "taxes" coca cultivation and cocaine production to fund its war effort. FARC guerrillas killed three U.S. indigenous rights activists in 1999.

All of these groups are responsible for violations of human rights and international humanitarian law.

---

Forces of Colombia (Fuerzas Armadas Revolucionarias de Colombia, usually called FARC) and created a demilitarized zone for peace negotiations in southern Colombia. To date, FARC guerrillas have not taken advantage of this opening by moving forward on peace talks. It is clear that the peace process will be long and arduous.

In 2000, the Clinton administration approved a $1.3 billion emergency aid package, the bulk of which was to support Plan Colombia, a strategy

developed by the Colombian government in consultation with Clinton officials, which would combat drugs, and strengthen Colombian government institutions. The plan also focused on advancing peace negotiations between the Colombian government and the two main guerrilla groups in Colombia, the FARC and the ELN (the National Liberation Army). The United States provided military assistance to the Colombian government, as it does for other Andean governments for anti-

A REBEL FARC SOLDIER SITS IN FRONT OF A BILLBOARD THAT SAYS, "PLAN COLOMBIA, THE GRINGOS BRING THE WEAPONS AND COLOMBIA PROVIDES THE DEAD," REFERRING TO A U.S. MILITARY PLAN TO SPRAY AND DESTROY COCA FIELDS. *(A/P Wide World. Reproduced by permission.)*

drug purposes. The U.S. government has preferred working with military forces in the region due to the widespread corruption in the local police forces in several source and transit countries. The centerpiece of U.S. assistance for Plan Colombia was equipment and training for Colombian military battalions that are leading a "Push into Southern Colombia," providing military support for anti-drug planes to spray herbicides over coca and poppy crops, the basic materials used to produce heroine and cocaine.

Clinton argued that the assistance package was critical to U.S. security and Colombia's future, pointing out that 90 percent of cocaine and two-thirds of heroin on U.S. streets came from Colombia. U.S. officials believed that eradication efforts would limit the financial base of illegal armed groups in Colombia, who profit from coca and poppy cultivation, and thus help to advance President Pastrana's peace talks.

Yet the package stirred up controversy in Congress. Critics of Plan Colombia raised doubts that the plan would succeed in slowing the flow of drugs to the United States, noting that in the last decade anti-drug programs targeting the source of drugs had not impacted the availability or price of drugs in the United States. Several representatives also speculated that by providing assistance to the

Colombian military, the United States would become embroiled in the Colombian government's struggle against guerrilla insurgents.

### The Andean Regional Initiative

In 2001 the George W. Bush administration proposed the "Andean Regional Initiative," which expands U.S. support for Plan Colombia and provides additional support to Colombia's neighbors in order to guard against the likely "spillover" of refugees, armed groups, and drug traffickers as a result of the military push in Colombia. In addition to funding for counter-drug programs, the Andean Regional Initiative also includes funding for social and economic programs, including judicial reform, assistance for government human rights programs, and alternative development programs that aim to provide a source of income for peasant farmers whose illicit crops have been eradicated.

Again the proposal sparked a significant congressional debate. Members of Congress attempted to cut funding for the Colombian military, citing its poor human rights record and persistent links to paramilitary forces—illegal right-wing death squads whose objective is to eliminate guerrillas in Colombia. Congressman James P. McGovern (D-MA) who led the effort argued,

"This House has a chance to send a straightforward message to the Colombian military: sever all ties with the paramilitary groups and sever them now. As my colleagues know, over 70 percent of the human rights crimes committed against the civilian population in Colombia, massacres, torture and the destruction of communities and the displacements of the population, are perpetrated by the paramilitaries, and the Colombian military works in collusion with those groups" (*Congressional Record*, July 24, 2001). Critics of Plan Colombia argue that the Colombian military's ties to the paramilitaries prevents progress in stopping the flow of drugs because paramilitary forces are deeply involved in drug trafficking, according to the U.S. Drug Enforcement Agency.

### Spraying Herbicides to Eradicate Coca

In 2001 the use of chemical herbicides to eradicate coca and poppy crops emerged as another controversial aspect of U.S. anti-drug efforts in Colombia. U.S. government officials assert that, because of the violence in rural areas, spraying of a chemical called "glyphosate" from airplanes was a more practical means to eradicate crops than pulling them out manually—a technique that had been used in several other countries. A growing controversy between several Colombian government agencies and elected officials regarding the impacts of the spraying on human health and legal food crops caught the attention of U.S. policymakers who waged an effort to suspend the fumigation programs. Congresswoman Jan Schakowsky (D-IL), one of the proponents of the reform stated during a July 2001 Congressional debate, "In February, I had the opportunity to go to Colombia... and we met with impoverished farmers whose legal food crops had been destroyed by U.S. fumigation planes. We heard from Colombians whose children suffered from severe rashes after being sprayed" (*Congressional Record*, July 24, 2001).

Administration officials countered such arguments from members of the House as well as environmental groups concerned about the potential consequences for the bio-diverse Amazon region, stating that glyphosate was among the safest herbicides, and noting that it is commonly used in American gardens in its commercially packaged form, known as Roundup. Rand Beers, Director of the State Department's Bureau of International Narcotics and Law Enforcement, wrote in a July 9, 2001 *Boston Globe* editorial: "There is however, a real threat to the environment of Colombia— that posed by the cutting and burning of tropical forests to clear the way for coca cultivation and the

dumping of tons of highly toxic chemicals used to process cocaine into rivers and streams of the Amazon basin by the drug producers." The State Department is currently working in collaboration with the Center for Disease Control and the Environmental Protection Agency to conduct an assessment of the environmental and health impacts of the spraying.

### Colombians Protest

"Imagine if the United States Government decided to fly planes over Florida to spray chemicals in order to eradicate marijuana, but didn't consult the governor of Florida before beginning the program." Colombian Senator Rafael Orduz posed this scenario during a recent visit to Washington to demonstrate the political tension in Colombia that occurred as a result of the fact that President Pastrana launched Plan Colombia with U.S. support, without consulting the governors in the states most dramatically impacted by the policy nor with the Colombian Congress.

Unable to reach agreement with the Pastrana government regarding the aerial eradication programs and development assistance for their departments, six governors from southern Colombia traveled to Washington and Europe to oppose the U.S.-backed Plan Colombia and seek development assistance from other international donors.

In addition to opposition from the governors, the fumigation programs have come under fire from the Colombian government's Human Rights Ombudsman and the Ministry of Environment. Several Colombian legislators proposed that chemical spraying of crops be prohibited by Colombian law. In response, the U.S. Embassy countered that the aerial eradication programs were critical to the success of U.S. and Colombian anti-drug efforts, and suspension of the programs would put further U.S. assistance to Colombia at risk. Faced with a significant political dilemma President Pastrana opted to continue the programs as additional U.S. military hardware arrived to support the spraying.

## RECENT HISTORY AND THE FUTURE

The death of Veronica Bowers in Peru serves as a reminder to the public that the war on drugs is a war with human costs and very real casualties. When this American civilian death captured public attention, the U.S. Department of State suspended the aerial interdiction program in Peru during an investigation into the accident, which

U.S. DRUG POLICY DIRECTOR BARRY MCCAFFREY HOLDS UP A COPY OF PLAN COLOMBIA, THE PROJECT DESIGNED TO END GUERRILLA WARFARE AND DRUG TRAFFICKING IN COLOMBIA. MCCAFFREY VISITED COLOMBIA IN FEBRUARY 2000 TO PRESENT THE PLAN TO GOVERNMENT OFFICIALS. *(Reuters NewMedia Inc./Corbis. Reproduced by permission.)*

revealed that both the United States and Peru had failed to follow rigorous procedures to avoid civilian casualties. U.S. officials have yet to determine whether or not they will resume the programs to force or shoot down suspected drug-trafficking flights, though there is significant pressure from Andean governments and other proponents of the policy to continue the program. They claim that targeting the "air bridge" of drug trafficking between Peru and Colombia isn't crucial to anti-drug efforts, noting that the price of coca has already risen in Peru and some farmers are returning to coca cultivation since this interdiction program was suspended.

The United States is likely to continue a high level of cooperation with Latin American governments to attempt to curb the flow of illicit drugs. Colombia continues to be the number one source of cocaine to the United States, while the supply from Bolivia and Peru has dropped in recent years. Mexico and Colombia provide over 70 percent of the heroin used in the United States today. The White House Office on National Drug Control policy indicates that cocaine and heroin use in the United States are on the decline, though they report that the price of those drugs is

cheaper than a decade ago, and that cocaine is readily available in most metropolitan areas in the United States.

The United States' international anti-drug efforts are focused primarily on Colombia due to the country's significant role in the drug trade— and the debate regarding the best approach to take in Colombia is likely to continue for years to come. Government officials state that the United States has made a five-year commitment to financing Plan Colombia—though many caution that the Colombian conflict and the drug trade will likely wear on for years to come, and the United States does not have an "exit-strategy" to determine when efforts have been successful and when U.S. financial support should end. The outcome of Colombia's presidential elections in May 2002 may have some bearing on the United States' confidence in Colombia as a partner in the war.

As U.S. involvement in Colombia escalates, there has been increased media attention to the Colombian situation and to diverging views on drug policy. In recent years there has been a shift in public opinion about the effectiveness of drug policy. A March 2001 report by the Pew Charitable indicates that 74 percent of Americans polled believed that "the Drug War is being lost," and that many are skeptical about providing anti-drug aid to foreign nations such as Colombia and Peru. In particular the 2000 Steven Soderbergh movie *Traffic* (U.S.A. Films), which highlighted tough questions regarding drug abuse and the violence of the illicit drug trade, spurred many viewers to question whether or not the war on drugs is actually winnable.

Recognizing the shift in public opinion, in 2001 the Bush administration promised a $1.6 billion increase in funding for drug treatment over the next five years. This increase will provide a much-needed boost to drastically under-funded treatment programs, though it will not close the treatment gap. In 2001, there were nearly 3,000,000 hard-core drug users in the United States who did not have access to drug treatment.

## BIBLIOGRAPHY

Acción Andina (Bolivia). Available online at www .cedib.org (cited September 14, 2001).

Andean Information Network (Bolivia). Available online at http://www.scbbs-bo.com/ain/ (cited September 14, 2001).

Amatangelo, Gina, and Peter Clark. *U.S. International Drug Control Policy; A Guide for Citizen Action.* Washington, DC: Washington Office on Latin America, 2001.

Bagley, Bruce M., ed. *Drug Trafficking Research in the Americas: An Annotated Bibliography.* Miami: University of Miami, North-South Center, 1997.

Bertram, Eva, Morris Blachman, Kenneth Sharpe, and Peter Andreas. *Drug War Politics: The Price of Denial.* Berkeley: University of California Press, 1996.

Center for International Policy. Available online at www.ciponline.org (cited September 14, 2001).

*Coca Mama: The War on Drugs,* film, January 2001. Available online at www.journeyman.co.uk/ (cited September 14, 2001).

Common Sense Drug Policy. Available online at www.cspd.org (cited September 13, 2001).

Council on Foreign Relations. *Rethinking International Drug Control Policy: New Directions for U.S. Policy: Report of An Independent Task Force.* New York: Council on Foreign Relations, 1997.

Criminal Justice Policy Foundation. Available online at www.cjpf.org (cited September 14, 2001).

Drug Enforcement Administration. Available online at www.doj.org/dea (cited September 14, 2001).

Drug Reform Coordination Network. Available online at www.drcnet.org (cited September 17, 2001).

Farthing, Linda, and Mary Jo Dudley. *Five Day High School Curriculum on the Drug War in the Americas.* Cornell University Latin American Studies Program, 2001. Available upon request: contact 607-255-9532 or latinamericanprg@cornell.edu.

Finlayson, Reggie. "Teacher's Guide: War on Drugs." PBS Frontline, 2001. Available online at http://www.pbs.org/wgbh/pages/frontline/teach/american/drugs/ (cited September 14, 2001).

Foreign Policy in Focus. Available online at www.foreignpolicy-infocus.org (cited September 13, 2001).

Frontline's "Drug Wars." Available online at www.pbs.org/wgbh/pages/frontline/shows/drugs/ (cited September 14, 2001).

Institute for Policy Studies. Available online at www.foreignpolicy-infocus.org (cited September 14, 2001).

Latin America Working Group. Available online at www.lawg.org (cited September 14, 2001).

Lindesmith Center-Drug Policy Foundation. Available online at www.dpf.org (cited September 14, 2001).

MacKay, Lesley, "The Coca Wars," *Ms.* August/September 2001.

Office of National Drug Control Strategy. Available online at www.whitehousedrugpolicy.gov (cited September 14, 2001

Rand Corporation's Drug Policy Research Center. Available online at www.rand.org/center/dprc (cited September 14, 2001).

Transnational Institute (Netherlands). Available online at www.worldcom.nl/tni (cited September 14, 2001).

United Nations, International Drug Control Programme. Available online at http://www.undcp.org/index.html (cited September 14, 2001).

U.S.-Colombia Coordinating Office. Available online at www.igc.org/colhrnet (cited September 14, 2001).

U.S. State Department, Bureau for International Narcotics and Law Enforcement Affairs. Available online at www.state.gov/www/global/narcotics_law/index.html (cited September 14, 2001).

U.S. Department of State. *International Narcotics Control Strategy Report, 2001.* Washington, DC: The White House, The National Drug Control Strategy, 2001.

Washington Office on Latin America. Available online at www.wola.org (cited September 14, 2001).

*Gina Amatangelo*

# HARD TO SAY SORRY: INDIGENOUS AUSTRALIA'S RECONCILIATION MOVEMENT

## THE CONFLICT

Beginning in the nineteenth century Australia had assimilation policies under which aboriginal children (the "Stolen Generation") were separated from their parents, to be raised in institutions or foster homes. Although the practice of separating children from their families ended in the 1970s the devastation to the indigenous individuals and communities has continued. The reconciliation movement was established in the early 1990s to familiarize Australia with this aspect of its own history, to ensure honest and equal relations in the future. Prime Minister John Howard, elected in 1996, has refused to offer an official apology to the aboriginal people and reconciliation has not been achieved.

### Political

- Australia is the only former British colony that never signed a treaty with its native peoples. Because of this, many feel that aboriginal rights are at the whim of each elected administration.

- Among Australians striving to advance indigenous rights, some believe that the symbolic gestures of reconciliation—such as the official apology and public awareness of history—will pave the way for the more substantial changes in legislation that are needed.

### Economic

- Aboriginal and Torres Islander Australians, forced from their traditional lands and marginalized from European society, have been impoverished, and live in conditions well below those of non-indigenous Australians.

- Many believe that John Howard refuses to apologize for the stolen generations from a fear that such an apology could lead to compensation payments to all the people who were victimized by the governmental policy.

### Ethnic

- Assimilation for Australia's aboriginal children and children of mixed descent was expressly seen to involve the destruction and elimination of the cultural heritage, languages, traditions, and family history of aboriginal peoples. In attempting to stamp out all traces of the aboriginal cultures, the Australian government was committing genocide.

On December 15, 2001, in Canberra, Australia, a large group of indigenous Australians and supporters gathered to protest the government's new US$2.9 million monument commemorating aboriginals and Torres Strait Islanders in Australia. Some aboriginal peoples of Australia reject the terms that are used to identify them, such as "natives," "aborigines," and "indigenous peoples." Most aboriginal groups refer to themselves in native language words referring to their own specific group. The word "Koori" is often used to mean all aboriginal peoples, but the term used by the government and most journalists and academics is "aboriginals and Torres Strait Islanders." Torres Strait Islanders live in islands to the northeast of Australia, and have a distinct culture and language. The commemorative monument, Reconciliation Place, had been built in the midst of federal government buildings in Canberra to "acknowledge the history of the nation's first peoples, our shared history, and our desire as a nation to move forward together and share a harmonious future," in the official words of the government. It was built just in time for the November elections, in which Australian Prime Minister John Howard won another term in office.

The protestors believe the monument whitewashes the history of the "Stolen Generation," the estimated 50,000 to 100,000 aboriginal children separated from their families by force under an Australian assimilation policy that ended in the 1970s. Many believe the Australian government's past actions constituted genocide; they were aimed at the extermination of a culture, and the long-term effects are still devastating to the victims and the aboriginal communities. The monument's display of the separation policy, however, depicts happy children in comfortable and facili-

# CHRONOLOGY

**1770** Captain James Cook claims the east coast of Australia for the British, naming the territory New South Wales. There are an estimated 300,000 aborigines in about 250 tribal groups at this time.

**1788** The first British settlers arrive in Australia.

**1850s** With the gold rush and natural resources to be mined in Australia there is a great influx of European immigrants. The non-indigenous population reaches over one million people.

**1860s** The Board for the Protection of Aborigines is established with the power to remove aboriginal children from families.

**1901** Six states of Australia federate under the new Federal Constitution of Australia, which excludes indigenous people as part of the new nation. The states control aboriginal people and each institutes its own forced separation program.

**1910–70** Efforts at assimilating indigenous children are stepped up; it is believed that somewhere between 50,000 and 100,000 children are taken from their families in this period.

**1937** The first national referendum on aboriginal affairs, the Commonwealth-State Native Welfare Conference, resolves that children of mixed aboriginal and European descent be "absorbed" into the white community.

**1940s** The states begin to use an assimilationist-welfare model in their efforts with indigenous children, under which the removal of children is handled by state welfare departments, and a cause for removal, such as neglect or abuse, has to be determined.

**1948** The Universal Declaration of Human Rights is adopted by the United Nations. Australia supports the bill.

**1949** The Convention on Genocide, which specifies "forcibly transferring children of [a] group to another group with the intention of destroying the group" as an act of genocide, is ratified by Australia.

**1967** A national referendum amends the federal constitution, allowing for indigenous people to be counted as part of the population. The federal government is given the power to legislate on aboriginal issues and establishes the Office of Aboriginal Affairs.

**1989** The government orders an investigation of suicides committed by aboriginal people in jail.

**1991** Royal Commission into Aboriginal Deaths in Custody reports that of the 99 deaths it investigated, 43 were people who had been separated from their families as children.

**1991** The Council for Aboriginal Reconciliation is created to promote harmony between indigenous and non-indigenous Australians with a specific mission to make the public aware of the history of the stolen generations.

**1992** In the Mabo case, the High Court of Australia determines that native title to land did in fact exist in 1788 and could still exist if it has not been extinguished by later acts of the government, overturning the doctrine of terra nullius.

**1993** The International Year of the World's Indigenous Peoples.

**1994** Representatives from all states meet in Darwin, Northern Territory, for the Going Home Conference, to discuss the plight of the Stolen Generation and the avenues available to connect the Australian public with the history of the assimilation policies.

**1995** Australia's Attorney General commissions "The National Inquiry into the Separation of Aboriginal and Torres Strait Islander Children from Their Families," to be conducted by the Human Rights and Equal Opportunity Commission.

**1996** John Howard of the Liberal Party is elected prime minister.

**May 1997** *Bringing Them Home*, the 700-page report of the inquiry into the separation of indigenous children from their families, is tabled in the Australian Parliament.

**December 2000** The Council for Aboriginal Reconciliation finishes its ten-year term.

**November 2001** John Howard is reelected as prime minister.

**December 15, 2001** A group of indigenous Australians and supporters gather to protest the government's new US$2.9 million monument commemorating aboriginals and Torres Strait Islanders in Australia.

MAP OF AUSTRALIA. (© *Maryland Cartographics. Reprinted with permission.*)

tating environments, either with foster families or in schools.

The demonstration protesting the monument is just one indication of the deep conflict between the Australian government and the country's growing reconciliation movement, which strives to elicit significant symbolic as well as practical changes in future relations between aborigines and the government. The belief behind reconciliation is that the past wrong must be officially acknowledged and repented—history must be accepted, and then the nation can move on.

It has only been in recent years that the practice of taking aboriginal children away from their parents—which began in the late nineteenth century and peaked from about 1910 to the late 1960s—has openly been reviled by those in power in Australia. For decades the policies were generally regarded as charitable efforts to provide aboriginal children with better homes and opportunities. In August 1995 Australia's Labor government commissioned an investigation into the "Stolen Generation." In May 1997 the human rights commission report *Bringing Them Home* was tabled in Parliament after a lengthy and emotional investigation headed by Sir Ronald Wilson and Mick Dodson. The 680-page report concluded that the assimilation policy was not just wrong but genocidal, with an aim to eliminate aborigines as distinct groups. The report included hundreds of first-hand reports and was widely read throughout Australia. A passionate argument that an apology was due to the victims of the government's past crimes and that reparations were in order was part of the report:

> The actions of the past resonate in the present and will continue to do so in the future. The laws, policies and practices which separated Indigenous children from their families have contributed directly to the alienation of Indigenous societies today .... That devastation cannot be addressed unless the whole community listens with an open heart and mind to the stories of what has happened in the past and, having listened and understood, commits itself to reconciliation.

The native inhabitants of Australia number about 400,000 people in a total population of 19 million. It is said that almost every aboriginal family in Australia today has suffered from the forced separation of children from their parents. Indigenous communities, too, have experienced tremendous disruption to health, education, and economic development because of the assimilation policies, adding one more obstacle to the recovery of an already severely disadvantaged group. Poverty and unemployment among aboriginal peoples are rampant. Life expectancy is 15 to 20 years lower than for non-indigenous Australians. Family breakdowns, drug and alcohol abuse, and the highest suicide rate of Australia plague modern-day aboriginal society. Aboriginal juveniles are 30 times more likely to be jailed than non-indigenous youth.

Like that of the United States, Australia's colonial history is one of devastation for the indigenous people. Disease and violence at the hands of the mainly British settlers wiped out vast numbers. Those who survived most often lost their traditional lands and were treated as second-class citizens or worse. Australia was slow to grant basic rights to the indigenous groups, who did not gain the rights of citizenship until the 1960s.

For some Australians, viewing history through the light of "white guilt," rather than the rugged heroism of legend, is uncomfortable. Former Australian Prime Minister Malcolm Fraser in a 2000 speech sums up the struggle in store for the non-indigenous Australian public in grappling with its national history:

> It is hard to realise that the history we were taught of a great empty land being settled by brave explorers was largely false. It is hard for us to understand that the real history of Australia was quite different from that which we were taught as children. It might be harder still for some of us who have known people of influence and respect, who participated in policies

which today we regard as outdated, barbarous, cruel and racist.

John Howard, elected prime minister in 1996, has been an outspoken opponent of what he calls the "black-armband view of history," in which the heroic deeds of white settlers are forgotten in the process of viewing the damage they did. Howard does not believe that shame can attach from one generation to the next and will not apologize for the acts of Australian governments before him. He does not support compensation for the sufferings imposed by a past government. Many observers believe that he equates an official apology with an admission of guilt, and fears that the government of Australia could be held financially accountable for the theft of life, family, and income for the "Stolen Generation" if he were to make an apology. In fact, Howard, his Aboriginal and Torres Islander Affairs Minister John Herron, and other members of his coalition government have denied that the Stolen Generation exists.

Howard has expressed his preference for "practical reconciliation." Some steps were planned within his government to advance living conditions for aborigines, particularly in terms of helping separated families to find lost members, get counseling, and participate in oral history projects. In 1997 Howard promised $63 million in funding for these and other projects, but critics later claimed that only a small portion (in 2000, about $13 million) of these funds were put to use. Howard and many of his ministers have remained steadfast in their refusal to grant special awards or treaties to the indigenous for any past events.

## HISTORICAL BACKGROUND

Scientists believe that aboriginal occupation of Australia reaches back to about 50,000 BCE or earlier, the longest continuous cultural history known to humankind. Before the eighteenth century there were hundreds of distinct groups of people living on the continent, speaking as many as 200 different languages. All of the groups had their own customs, but there were many shared traits among Australia's first peoples as well.

The traditional life style was nomadic, and most lived as hunter-gatherers. Social networks among the various groups demanded a certain amount of multilingualism. Tribes held their own traditional lands, and territorial boundaries were respected. Among the many aspects of art and culture in the pre-contact indigenous societies, knowledge of The Dreaming or the Dreamtime stands out. The rules for living were set down in The Dreaming: relationships, law, spirituality, history, and caring for the land. It was and still is a central social feature of aboriginal groups in Australia.

When the first Europeans arrived in Australia from Portugal and Holland, there were an estimated 300,000 aborigines in about 250 tribal groups. In 1770 British explorer Captain James Cook (1728–79) landed in Botany Bay, a short distance from the location of the city of Sydney today. He named the land New South Wales and claimed it for Britain. The British then decided to make Botany Bay a penal settlement. In January 1788, a fleet of eleven ships landed there with a mission to colonize the land and a strange group of settlers: 759 unwilling convicts from England, along with guards and crew and provisions. There were almost immediate conflicts between the indigenous groups and the settlers. The aborigines had no immunity to diseases brought by the Europeans, and epidemics swept through the tribes, bringing many near extinction.

In the 1850s gold was discovered in Australia and a tremendous influx of Europeans arrived in the ensuing rush. At the same time, the industrial revolution was increasing England's demand for Australia's natural resources, and more colonists arrived to make their fortunes. The colonists did not honor the aboriginal territories, declaring the continent to be *terra nullius,* or free and uninhabited by humans. The aboriginal groups resisted, but the Europeans took most of the fertile lands and forced the indigenous groups into Australia's harsh interior. Deprived of their traditional means of subsistence and finding few alternatives, many aboriginal people were impoverished. They suffered from hunger, disease, alcoholism, and the continuing violence of the settlers.

## "Protectionist" Measures

To the settler population in the mid- to late nineteenth century the sick and hungry aborigines who often dwelt on the fringes of towns were an uncomfortable sight. As the United States had done, the government set aside reserves for aborigines to live in. Because the indigenous people had been decimated by violence and disease, it was easy for the European population to forecast their ultimate extinction. Under the then-popular principles of social Darwinism the law of the "survival of the fittest" was at play, and the colonial theory was that the weak—the aboriginal people—would simply die out within decades. A significant number of settlers were more than willing to help them

go: the massacres and atrocities toward aboriginal people in the nineteenth century were appalling. One of the practices of the early colonists was to abduct aboriginal children from their mothers. A profitable trade in children arose. Among settlers, stockmen, drovers, and teamsters, there were significant numbers who bought young boys or girls to serve them and sometimes to provide sexual services as well.

In 1837 the British investigated the treatment of indigenous people in all British colonies and found the Australian colonies to be particularly abusive. The British recommended that the Australian government appoint protectors of aborigines. Accordingly, in the 1860s the Board for the Protection of Aborigines was established to look after the interests of indigenous Australians. This board had the power to remove aboriginal children from families, generally to place them in reformatories or industrial schools where they were trained in skills considered useful to European settlers.

At the turn of the twentieth century six states of Australia (New South Wales, Victoria, Queensland, South Australia, Western Australia, and Tasmania) federated under the new Federal Constitution of Australia. The constitution excluded the indigenous population from being counted as part of the new nation. It also excluded the federal government from enacting laws in regard to the indigenous population, thereby shifting the governing of aboriginal people to the state governments.

Within ten years all of the states except Tasmania had a form of what was called "protectionist legislation." Chief protectors in each state had extreme control over indigenous people, in some states becoming the legal guardian of all aboriginal children. In New South Wales, for example, the Aborigines Protection Act was passed in 1909, giving the chief protector power to take custody of an aboriginal child if neglect was determined. In 1915 the Aborigines Protection Amending Act in New South Wales gave the chief protector the power to remove children from their homes and families without any determination of neglect. One by one, the states adopted similar measures.

As forecast, the aboriginal people were indeed dying out under the harsh conditions they were forced to endure. There was a growing population, however, of mixed-descent children of indigenous mothers and European fathers. This group was troubling to the European-based population. Over time the states formulated policies of assimilating the children of mixed descent and forever disconnecting them from aboriginal traditions. *Bringing Them Home* provides a quote from the May 1937 Brisbane *Telegraph* describing the policies' intent. It begins by noting that Auber Octavius Neville, the Chief Protector of Western Australia, believed that the "pure black" would be extinct in one hundred years. Half-castes, however, were increasing every year. The idea behind the policies, then, was to segregate the pure blacks and take the half-castes into the white Australian population. "Sixty years ago," the paper noted, "[Neville] said, there were over 60,000 full-blooded natives in Western Australia. Today there are only 20,000. In time there would be none. Perhaps it would take one hundred years, perhaps longer, but the race was dying. The pure blooded Aboriginal was not a quick breeder. On the other hand the half-caste was. In Western Australia there were half-caste families of twenty and upwards. That showed the magnitude of the problem."

## The Commonwealth-State Native Welfare Conference of 1937

The first national referendum on aboriginal affairs, the Commonwealth-State Native Welfare Conference of 1937, resolved that "the destiny of the natives of aboriginal origin, but not of the full blood, lies in their ultimate absorption by the people of the Commonwealth, and it therefore recommends that all efforts be directed to that end." From that time the Director of Native Welfare was the legal guardian of all aboriginal children. According to *Bringing Them Home,* this marked a turning point in Australian policy. Assimilation was the national goal for the "aboriginal problem," and the new destiny of the children of mixed descent was expressly seen to require the destruction and elimination of the cultural heritage, languages, traditions, and family history of aboriginal peoples. It was clearly assumed by the white Australian policymakers that there was nothing of value in the aboriginal culture.

Australia's former assimilation policies have been defended in modern times by the belief that those who carried them out were well intentioned and did not know of the potential harm in what they were doing. Many historians point out that this was not the case. From the early 1800s many spoke out on the cruelty and injustice of separation policies. The Human Rights and Equal Opportunity Commission notes, "From as early as 1874 warnings were sounded about the threat to family structures and systems; the links were clearly identified between the removal of young girl children for domestic work, and slavery; about the lack of

AN ABORIGINAL WOMAN IS ARRESTED BY POLICE IN A SYDNEY SUBURB KNOWN AS "THE BLOCK." MANY ABORIGINES LIVE IN POVERTY. *(A/P Wide World. Reproduced by permission.)*

responsibility, authority and supervision of those involved in the forcible removal of children, and about the repressive conditions in which children were held."

The children of mixed descent were by far the most targeted for separation. The states differed on the most optimal ages to take the children from their mothers. Some felt it was best at birth, some at four years old, and many children were taken at older ages. Mothers were often deceived into giving up their children, or the children were just forcibly taken from them. The children were, when possible, taken far from home and further contact was usually not allowed or strongly discouraged.

Poor or no records were kept of the separated families, so that finding one's family after separation could be nearly impossible. Many of the children were told that their parents were dead. The children were taken to schools run by churches or charitable organizations, or to foster homes. Overall, the institutions that cared for removed children were grossly lacking in funding and could not adequately care for the children. Although there are reports of children ending up in loving homes and being well cared for, there are many reports of terrible abuse: malnutrition, neglect, forced servitude, sexual assault, physical abuse, and much more.

Children from full aboriginal families were less targeted for removal, but frequently taken from their parents as well. They were more often sent off to schools where they could learn to perform cheap labor for the European-based society of Australia.

From 1910 to 1970 it is believed that somewhere between 50,000 and 100,000 children were taken from their families. Because records were not kept, the true figures will never be known. The official figure is that 10 percent of aboriginal children were removed, but many estimate that it was as high as 30 percent. Somewhere between 1 in 3 and 1 in 10 indigenous children were taken from their families. Some communities were harder hit than others; in some places, the number of aboriginal children taken from their parents approached 100 percent.

In the 1940s the states began to use an assimilationist-welfare model in their efforts with indigenous children. The removal of children began to be handled by state welfare departments, and a cause for removal, such as neglect or abuse, had to be determined. But it was evident that aboriginal children were being taken away from their families under very different circumstances, and far more frequently, than non-aboriginals. A third Native Welfare Conference held in 1951 reaffirmed the national mission to assimilate the aboriginal children. During the 1950s and 1960s children removed from their families overflowed the institutions. More and more were placed with white foster families and some were even adopted at birth. Many of these children would never know their family name, the language or traditions of their parents, or even where they came from.

Because of strong racial discrimination in Australia, many aboriginal children who grew up in institutions and foster homes were to find a world that was unwilling to accept them, no matter how much of their culture had been erased from their memory. As adults they found themselves alienated from both the white and the black social worlds.

### 1967—Part of the Population

In 1967 a national referendum amended the federal constitution. For the first time, indigenous people were to be counted in the census. The fed-eral government was given the power to legislate on aboriginal issues, and established the Office of Aboriginal Affairs. Soon the term "assimilation," which was losing favor as it became clear that aboriginal people and their culture were not going to simply disappear, was replaced with the word "integration." Removal of indigenous children from their families continued. By the early 1970s various groups had begun to represent aboriginal families in court to challenge the removal of their children. Once it became apparent that the removals might have to be answered for in court, they decreased significantly. Although removal continued into the 1980s, a new surge of activism on the part of the aboriginal population that had begun in the 1960s was having a positive effect.

### Connecting with the Past

By the end of the 1970s Australian policies slowly turned away from full-scale attempt to eliminate the cultures of the indigenous populations by the removal and reeducation of children, but the Australian public remained largely unaware of the magnitude of what had happened to the stolen generation and their families. Hundreds of thousands of aboriginal people had gone through the disruption of being separated from parent, child, or sibling without acknowledgement from the public or the government that something terrible had been done to them. The trauma experienced by several generations of indigenous families became cyclical, as psychological turmoil created in the past crossed into new generations.

Indigenous activists spoke out on the issue of the stolen generation and by the late 1980s the Australian government finally heard them. In 1991, through a unanimous agreement of Parliament, the Council for Aboriginal Reconciliation was created to promote harmony between indigenous and non-indigenous Australians with a specific mission to make the public aware of the history of the stolen generations. One of the council's goals was to achieve reconciliation by 2001, the Australian centenary.

In 1992 the eight-year-old Mabo case brought international attention to Australian aborigines, when the High Court of Australia determined that a man named Eddie Mabo owned his own land—land that his family had been on for generations. The ruling was historical in that it overturned the doctrine of terra nullius, which had been clearly established in Australian law. The new judgment found that a native title to land did in fact exist in 1788 and could still exist if it had not been extinguished by later acts of the govern-

THE 2000 OLYMPICS IN SYDNEY HIGHLIGHTED THE GROWING RECONCILIATION MOVEMENT IN AUSTRALIA. EVENTS SUCH AS THIS PASSING OF THE TORCH TO AN ABORIGINE IN NATIVE DRESS WERE OFTEN CONTRASTED BY DEMONSTRATIONS CALLING FOR RECONCILIATION. *(A/P Wide World. Reproduced by permission.)*

ment. "Native title" describes the interests and rights of indigenous inhabitants in regard to the land under the traditional laws of the indigenous inhabitants, and was a very large advance in aboriginal affairs in Australia.

After this important decision, the year 1993 was made the International Year of the World's Indigenous Peoples. Prime Minister Paul Keating launched the Australian celebration of the year with words that paved the way for the reconciliation movement: "Mabo is an historic decision—we can make it an historic turning point, the basis of a new relationship between Indigenous and non Aboriginal Australians. The message should be that there is nothing to fear or to lose in the recognition of historical truth, or the extension of social justice, or the deepening of Australian social democracy to include Indigenous Australians."

### Bringing Them Home

In the early 1990s the government ordered an investigation on suicides committed by aboriginal people in jail: it turned out that 43 out of 99 sui-

cides examined had been aborigines removed from their families as children under the government's assimilation policy. This was a startlingly clear indication that the psychological repercussions of the governmental policy were by no means over.

In 1994 representatives from all Australian states met in Darwin, Northern Territory, for the Going Home Conference, to discuss the plight of the stolen generation and the avenues available to connect the Australian public with the history of the assimilation policies.

In 1995 Australia's Attorney General, spurred on by the investigations into the suicides, commissioned a formal inquiry entitled "The National Inquiry into the Separation of Aboriginal and Torres Strait Islander Children from Their Families" to be conducted by the Human Rights and Equal Opportunity Commission. The inquiry had a four point objective: (1) "to examine the past and continuing effects of separation of individuals, families and communities"; (2) "to identify what should be done in response, which could entail recommendations to change laws, policies and practices, to re-unite families and otherwise deal with losses caused by separation"; (3) "to find justification for, and nature of, any compensation for those affected by separation"; and (4) to examine "current laws, policies and practices affecting the placement and care of Indigenous children."

Two men took charge of the inquiry, the commission president, Sir Ronald Wilson, and the Aboriginal and Torres Strait Islander Social Justice Commissioner, Mick Dodson. They appointed indigenous staff and advisors to help them. The two-year investigation throughout Australia was to bring in evidence from indigenous organizations, state and church representatives, non-government agencies, and mission and government employees, as well as confidential evidence taken in private from hundreds of members of the stolen generation through oral and written testimony.

For many of the members of the Stolen Generation who were asked to share their most painful memories, providing testimony was traumatic, and the commission had a counselor at hand to help them through the experience. As much as they suffered, though, many of the witnesses expressed relief at finally being able to tell their tale, as this letter of thanks from a participant indicates: "There is some good news I would like to pass on to you. Everyone I have spoken to has said it is like the world has been lifted off their shoulders, because at last we have been heard. For me I have grown stronger and now am able to move forward. You have played a significant part in my journey back ..."

In 1996, during the two years while the investigation took place, John Howard of the Liberal Party was elected prime minister. From the start he took a harder line on aboriginal issues than the Labor Party administration before him. In May 1997 *Bringing Them Home* was tabled in the Australian Parliament. It provided nearly 700 pages of testimony, analysis, and recommendations for the future. The report firmly stated that the past government policy of separating children from their parents had constituted genocide: its aim was to eliminate the aborigines as a distinct group of people, in clear violation of the 1949 Universal Declaration of Human Rights.

Australia ratified the Convention on Genocide in 1949, which specified "forcibly transferring children of [a] group to another group with the intention of destroying the group" as an act of genocide. *Bringing Them Home* recommended many measures for remedy, including an apology from the federal government. For months Howard's administration did not respond.

The Australian public, however, was very interested. Tens of thousands of copies of an abridged edition of the report sold throughout the country and the media took up the subject in force. Sir Ronald Wilson, a former Justice of the High Court, is quoted in *For a Change* magazine describing the highly emotional content of the report: "This Inquiry was like no other I have undertaken....for these people to reveal what had happened to them took immense courage and every emotional stimulus they could muster.... We heard the story, told with that person's whole being, reliving experiences which had been buried deep, sometimes for decades. They weren't speaking with their minds, they were speaking with their hearts. And my heart had to open if I was to understand them."

Their testimony was to provoke deep and painful self-scrutiny among Australians. Sir Ronald goes on to describe his own reaction to what he was hearing: "I was Moderator of the Presbyterian Church in Western Australia at the time we ran Sister Kate's home, where 'stolen children' grew up. I was proud of the home, with its system of cottage families. Imagine my pain when I discovered, during this Inquiry, that children were sexually abused in those cottages."

### Sorry Day

As a direct result of the report, *Bringing Them Home*, Australia celebrated the first National Sorry Day on May 26, 1998. The day was set aside for apologies, and they were plentiful. As church bells rang and children prayed, church leaders, state governments, and institutions publicly and often tearfully apologized for past mistreatment of aboriginal people. Communities staged a variety of events and activities. Thousands of people signed Sorry Books. Schools focused on aboriginal issues. National attendance at the Sorry Day activities estimated to be over a million. Howard, however, held out; no apology was heard from the federal government.

On Friday May 26, 2000, Australia celebrated its third Sorry Day (also called Journey of Healing Day), and thousands of indigenous and non-indigenous marchers flowed through cities throughout Australia. The next day "Corroboree 2000," a conference sponsored by the Council for Aboriginal Reconciliation, was held in Sydney. The council presented a Declaration for Reconciliation and proposals for future action to the fed-

# PATRICK AND MICHAEL (MICK) DODSON

*1947– and 1950–* Indigenous activists, statesmen, and brothers Patrick (1947–) and Mick Dodson (1950–) have worked tirelessly on the reconciliation movement in their efforts to raise awareness and promote change. They are members of the Yawuru peoples of the Broome area of Western Australia. Patrick was born in Broome; Mick was born in Katherine, a small town in the Northern Territory. Their family history, like most indigenous Australians', revolves around Australia's removal policies.

Their grandmother was the daughter of an Irish man and an aboriginal woman. Under assimilation policies she had been taken from her home and placed in a mission. Around the time of her grandsons' births she applied for citizenship under the Native Citizen Rights Act of Western Australia. Despite her enforced education she was denied citizenship, the judge telling her that she "had not adopted the manner and habits of civilized life."

The Dodsons' mother and later two older sisters were also placed in the same mission, and the sisters went to an orphanage, although their parents were still alive. When the Dodsons' parents died in 1960, Patrick was made a ward of the state. An aunt and uncle successfully battled in court to keep Mick out of state guardianship, having been brought up in the mission themselves and wishing to spare him. Both brothers got scholarships and went on to successful university careers. Patrick studied to become a Catholic priest, but left the church in 1981 because it did not allow for his belief that aboriginal and Christian rites celebrated the same spiritual force. Mick got his law degree.

Both brothers then went to work on indigenous issues. Mick worked with the Victorian Aboriginal Legal Service from 1979 to 1981. He served as senior legal adviser for the Northern Land Council in 1984, becoming its director in 1990. Patrick worked for the Central Land Council in Alice Springs and then became the chair of the Royal Commission into Aboriginal Deaths in Custody in 1989. Mick worked with his brother as counsel to this commission from 1988 to 1990. He then became an active participant in drawing up the

1993 Native Title Act. Patrick went on to become the Chairman of the Council for Aboriginal Reconciliation in 1991. Because of his advocacy, he is known as the "father of reconciliation."

In 1993 Mick became Australia's first Aboriginal and Torres Strait Islander Social Justice Commissioner with the Human Rights and Equal Opportunity. The same year he was named Co-Deputy Chair of the Technical Committee for the 1993 International Year of the World's Indigenous People. The job that he said affected him most, however, was to come in 1995, when Australia's Attorney General commissioned a formal inquiry entitled "The National Inquiry into the Separation of Aboriginal and Torres Strait Islander Children from Their Families" to be conducted by the Human Rights and Equal Opportunity Commission. In 1997 he and Sir Ronald Wilson had completed the landmark investigation and released the report *Bringing Them Home.*

As chair of the Reconciliation Council, Patrick was a long-time proponent of a treaty enshrining indigenous peoples' rights in Australia. The Council was a federally supported organization, and after John Howard was elected prime minister, it became clear to Patrick that the administration would oppose him on almost all fronts, so he stepped down from his position in 1997. Mick, in the meantime, served his 5-year term as Aboriginal and Torres Strait Islander Social Justice Commissioner, and was not appointed to a second term. He went on to work with the United Nations, helping to determine international standards for indigenous rights in the Draft Declaration on the Rights of Indigenous Peoples.

Patrick continues to be involved in issues relating to the maintenance of Yawuru culture and language. Both brothers, though disgusted with the setbacks that have occurred under the current administration, have continued traveling through the nation and speaking on aboriginal rights and reconciliation. The Dodson brothers are charismatic and insightful commentators and have made a tremendous difference in keeping the urgent issues and plight of aborigines in the public eye.

eral government. On Sunday more than 250,000 people in Sydney took the "Walk for Aboriginal Reconciliation," crossing the Harbour Bridge to show their support for the council's proposals. It was the largest march of its kind in Australian history. Again, the prime minister did not make an appearance. Later in the year the city of Melbourne held a similar walk.

## AUSTRALIAN DECLARATION FOR RECONCILIATION

We, the peoples of Australia, of many origins as we are, make a commitment to go on together in a spirit of reconciliation.

We value the unique status of Aboriginal and Torres Strait Islander peoples as the original owners and custodians of lands and waters.

We recognise this land and its waters were settled as colonies without treaty or consent.

Reaffirming the human rights of all Australians, we respect and recognise continuing customary laws, beliefs and traditions.

Through understanding the spiritual relationship between the land and its first peoples, we share our future and live in harmony.

Our nation must have the courage to own the truth, to heal the wounds of its past so that we can move on together at peace with ourselves.

Reconciliation must live in the hearts and minds of all Australians. Many steps have been taken, many steps remain as we learn our shared histories.

As we walk the journey of healing, one part of the nation apologises and expresses its sorrow and sincere regret for the injustices of the past, so the other part accepts the apologies and forgives.

We desire a future where all Australians enjoy their rights, accept their responsibilities, and have the opportunity to achieve their full potential.

And so, we pledge ourselves to stop injustice, overcome disadvantage, and respect that Aboriginal and Torres Strait Islander peoples have the right to self-determination within the life of the nation.

Our hope is for a united Australia that respects this land of ours; values the Aboriginal and Torres Strait Islander heritage; and provides justice and equity for all.

*The Declaration was produced by the Council for Aboriginal Reconciliation after an extensive consultation process amongst the Australian people, and was handed to national leaders and to the Australian people as a whole on May 27, 2000, at Corroboree 2000. Australian Declaration for Reconciliation: Council for Aboriginal Reconciliation. Available on online at http://www.austlii.edu.au/au/other/IndigLRes/car/2000/12/ [cited 2-03-02].*

In July 2000 the United Nations Committee for the Elimination of Racial Discrimination issued a formal censure to Australia and the Howard administration for its handling of the issues involved in the Stolen Generation controversy. In November 2001 Pope John Paul II issued a formal apology from the Vatican for the past actions of members or organizations of the Catholic Church in connection with the stolen generation. By that time all of Australia's state governments had offered official apologies for past abuses as well. Howard offered regrets, but still refused to make an official apology. Although he faces strong opposition from the large reconciliation movement and its supporters nationwide, Howard was reelected for another term in 2001.

## RECENT HISTORY AND THE FUTURE

There are two prominent strains within the indigenous campaign for reconciliation. Since 1997 and the release of *Bringing Them Home* there has been strong support for the symbolic gestures of healing: apologies, support, public awareness, and righting history. The many proponents of reconciliation between the indigenous and the non-indigenous believe that the knowledge of history and the spirit of apology, forgiveness, and acceptance, will pave the way for more substantial changes in the form of legislation or treaties.

Other indigenous activists, however, have repudiated the symbolic or spiritual nature of the reconciliation movement and want to work on the practical issues at hand. The indigenous population of Australia is impoverished and faces tremendous hurdles of racial discrimination, violence, drug and alcohol addiction, disease, and welfare dependency. Having lost their traditional manner of survival and having been marginalized out of the mainstream occupations for more than a century, many aboriginal people have lost the skills and structures of self-reliance. Rather than dwell on what some call "liberal guilt," some indigenous activists would prefer to concentrate on economic, community, and political change that will remove the barriers to self-sufficiency.

The need for solid change is agreed upon by both groups of activists. The centenary of the Australian Federation came and went without reconciliation; John Howard never relented in his refusal to apologize. As soon as Howard came into office, he pledged to undo some of the Mabo decision on native title. The results were his Native Title Act Amendments, which extinguished significant indigenous rights to traditional lands in favor of Australian farmers. In March 1999 the United Nations Committee on the Elimination of All Forms of Racial Discrimination (CERD) sharply criticized the Australian government for these amendments, saying that they discriminated against indigenous landholders in favor of the non-indigenous in a variety of ways. Thus, the steps forward for aboriginal communities have been at the mercy of the elected leaders and can be reversed with a change in administration.

AUSTRALIA'S ABORIGINAL PEOPLE WOULD LIKE THE GOVERNMENT TO APOLOGIZE FOR ITS TREATMENT OF THE STOLEN GENERATION. *(A/P Wide World. Reproduced by permission.)*

Australia is unusual in that it was the only British colony that never signed a treaty with its native peoples. Most native rights activists agree that a treaty between the government and the indigenous people is now in order, one that would specify indigenous rights to land, culture, language, self-determination, social justice, and equity. Further, it could stipulate that indigenous people be represented in Parliament, provide for reparation and compensation for cultural dispossession, and establish conditions for independent law and economic structures. Besides the lack of a treaty, Australia operates under a constitution that lacks acknowledgement of the special status and rights of indigenous people. The constitutional amendment of 1967, according to some, is not compelling in ruling against discrimination against aboriginal people. Many would like to see an amendment or a Bill of Rights.

Because the Howard government has been so oppressive in its dealings with indigenous affairs, many indigenous rights leaders and spokespeople have felt obliged to step down from prominent positions, notably including the two brothers Patrick Dodson, the chair of the Council of Aboriginal Reconciliation (known to some as the "father of reconciliation") and Mick Dodson, the first Aboriginal and Torres Strait Islander Social Justice Commissioner with the Human Rights and Equal Opportunity, who co-chaired the *Bringing Them Home* investigation and report with Sir Ronald Wilson. As the Council of Aboriginal Reconciliation finished its 10-year term, it left behind a report recommending a treaty or other legislation to enshrine aboriginal rights in Australia—despite knowing that Howard opposed the idea of a treaty. After 2000, however, there was no longer a federally sanctioned reconciliation agency.

There are many issues to be resolved over the next years in connection to the reconciliation movement. The first court cases in regard to compensation for damages inflicted on children who were removed from their families by the government have been tried. In 1991 the courts ruled against the stolen generation, finding the government not responsible to pay reparations, but more cases will be brought before the courts. Land reforms for indigenous people will continue to be sought. Organizations have formed to help victims of the separation policy in a variety of ways; others strive to restore indigenous arts, languages, and cultures that have long been pushed aside.

There is a strong international effort to advance the interests of indigenous peoples worldwide. The United Nations Draft Declaration on the Rights of Indigenous Peoples, developed by indigenous peoples from around the world, should advance the rights and interests of indigenous people. But the conditions of life among Australia's aboriginal people remain far below the Australian standard. Along with coping with the grief and loss that lie behind, many challenges clearly lie ahead.

## BIBLIOGRAPHY

Aboriginal and Torres Strait Islander Commission (ATSIC). Available on online at http://www.atsic.gov.au/default_ie.asp [cited 2-08-02].

Austin, Tony. *I Can Picture the Old Home So Clearly: The Commonwealth and "Half-caste" Youth in the Northern Territory, 1911–1939.* Canberra: Aboriginal Studies Press, 1993.

"Australian Reconciliation," Australian Department of Foreign Affairs and Trade. Available online at http://www.dfat.gov.au/facts/reconciliation.html [cited 2-04-02].

"Bringing Them Home: Report of the National Inquiry into the Separation of Aboriginal and Torres Strait Islander Children from Their Families," Australasian Legal Research Institute, Reconciliation and Social Justice Library. Available online at http://www.austlii.edu.au/au/special/rsjproject/rsjlibrary/hreoc/stolen/ [cited 2-06-02].

"Bringing Them Home: The Stolen Children Report," Australian Human Rights and Equal Opportunity Commission, Aboriginal and Torres Strait Islander Justice. Available online at http://www.hreoc.gov.au/social_justice/stolen_children/ [cited 2-7-02].

Edwards, Coral, and Peter Read, eds. *The Lost Children: Thirteen Australians Taken from Their Aboriginal Families Tell of the Struggle to Find Their Natural Parents.* Sydney: Doubleday, 1989.

Haebich, Anna. *For Their Own Good; Aborigines and Government in the Southwest of Western Australia, 1900—1940.* Nedlands, W.A., Australia: University of Western Australia Press, 1988.

"Out of the Shadows, Paul Keating Speaks," *HoriZons, the Journal of Community Aid Abroad,* Vol. 1, 3, 1993, p. 10. Available online at http://www.caa.org.au/publications/reports/MABO/shadows.html [cited 2-06-02].

The Past We Need to Understand: Malcolm Fraser's Vincent Lingiari Memorial Lecture. *Sydney Morning Herald.* August 25, 2000. Available online at http://www.smh.com.au/news/0008/25/update/news3.html [cited 2-06-02].

Read, Peter. *The Stolen Generations: The Removal of Aboriginal Children in New South Wales, 1883 to 1969.* Sydney: Ministry for Aboriginal Affairs, 1983.

Reconciliation Australia. Available online at http://www.reconciliationaustralia.org/home.html [cited 2-01-02].

Reynolds, Henry. *Aboriginal Sovereignty.* London: Allen and Unwin, 1996.

"Stolen Generation," *Wikipedia: The Free Encyclopedia.* Available online at http://www.wikipedia.com/wiki.phtml?title=Stolen_Generation [cited 2-05-02]

"Sir Ronald Wilson," *For a Change,* January 1998. Available online at http://www.austlii.edu.au/au/special/rsjproject/sorry/status.htm [cited 2-02-02]

*Sonia Benson*

# THE EURO VERSUS THE POUND: BRITAIN AND THE EUROPEAN SINGLE CURRENCY

Imagine a United States without a single, common currency. Imagine flying from New York to Dallas and having to change your wallet-full of "bigapples" into "texes." And then flying on to Los Angeles where your texes would buy you nothing, and would have to be changed into "sunnies." Imagine up to 50 currencies covering the huge landmass that is the United States. Think of the commission on each currency exchange, and the diminishing value of your money as you traveled on, changing your bank notes in each state of the union.

Imagine the effects on the internal market in the United States, the additional costs of bringing one commodity from one state to another, of moving raw materials from one state to another for manufacture. Yes, there are variable taxes between states that affect the price the consumer pays for some goods; but at least the currency is common. The dollar is the dollar wherever you go. But then the United States is politically a federation, a group of states bound together by a central government and a common currency.

Think of another landmass called Europe. When Americans cross the Atlantic to visit the old world they are renowned for the intensity of their tourism. Five countries in two weeks is not at all unusual. As these peripatetic Americans "do" Europe, and move from France to Italy to Germany to Spain to Greece and to the United Kingdom (UK), they change their dollars, or the currency of the country they are departing, at every frontier or airport. They move from French francs to Italian lira to German deutschmarks to Spanish pesetas to Greek drachmae to UK pounds. Paying commission every time. No wonder they always

## THE CONFLICT

From March 1, 2002, forward, 12 European countries—Austria, Belgium, Finland, France, Germany, Greece, Holland, Ireland, Italy, Luxembourg, Portugal, and Spain—are to have one currency, the euro. The United Kingdom has never made the decision to abandon its own currency, the pound sterling, for the euro. Some within the voting population question the way the European Union is developing, what political union could mean to the national sovereignty of the member states, and how common policies across the European Union covering agriculture, defense, competition, and social policy will affect the UK. But for the most part, the question of the euro has just been repeatedly deferred, and along with it, the possible advantages in trade and foreign relations.

### Political

- After years of the "little Englander" Conservative party viewpoint that opposed entering into a single currency, the new Labour Party still hesitated to take the risk of joining the euro. It was not a popular issue for either party, since there was no widespread approval for the euro and its opponents had carried center stage for many years. British leader Tony Blair was known to be pro-euro. A referendum on the issue, if it brought in negative results, would have been like an anti-Blair vote. It has been easier to defer the decision than to educate the public on a difficult and not very glamorous issue.

### Economic

- With all trade conducted in euros, costs should be reduced and efficiency increased for British businesses trading with countries in the eurozone.

- There is risk involved in joining the euro, since the resilience of the eurozone and the ability of the single currency, the central bank, and common interest rates to handle economic crisis have not yet been tested.

# CHRONOLOGY

**1951** "The Six"—France, Germany, Italy, Belgium, Luxembourg, Holland—sign a treaty setting up European Coal and Steel Community (ECSC), precursor of the European Economic Community (EEC). ECSC comes into existence in 1952.

**1957** Treaties of Rome establishing EEC of The Six are signed. EEC comes into existence in 1958.

**1961** The United Kingdom, together with Ireland and Denmark, and the following year Norway, apply to join EEC.

**1963** French President Charles de Gaulle vetoes UK attempts to join the community.

**1967** The UK, along with Ireland, Denmark, and Norway, renews its application to join the EEC.

**1971** The UK decimalizes the pound; 240 pennies become 100.

**1972** Paris EEC summit sets 1980 as target date for monetary union; this doesn't happen.

**1973** The UK (and Denmark and Ireland) joins the EEC.

**1975** A UK referendum endorses membership of the EEC.

**1979** Exchange Rate Mechanism (ERM) is set up to bind exchange rates of currencies of EEC member states.

**1981** Greece becomes the tenth member of EEC.

**1985** European states agree to complete single market by 1992.

**1986** Spain and Portugal bring EEC membership up to 12.

**1990** The UK joins the ERM.

**1992** The Maastricht Treaty is signed, establishing the European Union (as opposed to the EEC) and committing member states to join the single currency by 1999. Britain's negotiators opt out.

**1992** The pound is forced out of the ERM on "Black Wednesday."

**1993** The Maastricht Treaty comes into force, setting up the European Union (EU).

**1995** Austria, Finland, and Sweden join the EEC, making 15 members.

**1997** The single currency launch is postponed because too few countries have achieved entry criteria.

**January 1, 1999** The single currency—the euro—becomes the official currency (alongside national currencies) of 11 member states: Austria, Belgium, Finland, France, Germany, Holland, Ireland, Italy, Luxembourg, Portugal, and Spain.

**2001** Greece joins the euro.

**January 1, 2002** Euro notes and coins are introduced in 12 countries joining the euro.

**February 28, 2002** All national notes and coins withdrawn from circulation. Only the euro remains throughout the 12 countries.

---

try to pay in dollars, which may work at the Hilton but seldom at the small pension.

But now Europe is changing, and as of March 1, 2002, in 12 countries, there was one currency, the euro. Those countries are: Austria, Belgium, Finland, France, Germany, Greece, Holland, Ireland, Italy, Luxembourg, Portugal, and Spain. Note the crucial absentee: the United Kingdom, or Britain as she is often referred to.

And therein lies a huge political story, one that has dominated UK politics for nearly 50 years, more intensely for the past 30 years. It is an issue that has destroyed prime ministers and seriously damaged political parties. It has ruined

political careers and brought leading politicians into acrimonious conflict with other leading politicians in the same party. It has divided the most influential commentators and opinion formers. It has distorted elections. It has in the best sense produced profound and worthwhile debate about the position of Britain and Europe in the world in the twenty-first century, and in the worst sense revealed pettiness and small-mindedness sometimes approaching racial prejudice.

For a debate so profound in its implications and consequences, generating such passion and so many millions of spoken and written words, it stirs the British public very little. Mention Europe, and particularly the euro, to all but the obsessed political classes, and eyes glaze, yawns are stifled, bars empty. Read opinion poll data about the issues that preoccupy the British electorate, and health, education, transport, and crime are up there at the top, every time. You have to wander far down the list to find Europe. Yet in the last British general election, June 2001, the leader of the opposition Conservative Party, William Hague, made the euro his central, at times only, theme. He was heavily defeated. So Britain had decided? The euro question had been dealt with, in favor of its supporters? End of 50 years' wrangling? No. The British electorate had simply said to the politicians, "Don't tell us that this general election is about one issue that concerns us little. We will decide on the basis of policies about health, education, transport, and crime."

That does not alter the centrality of the issue. It will not go away. It has been deferred and deferred, and will remain high on the agenda despite the electorate, until it is resolved. It is at one level simple, a decision as to whether the UK should join the other 12 (of the 15 member states of the European Union—Sweden and Denmark have also decided not to join the euro yet) in abandoning its own currency, the pound sterling, for the single common currency, the euro. But it is also immensely complicated, because the basic question about whether it is in Britain's economic self-interest to join the euro is bound up with deeper and more far-reaching questions about the way the European Union is developing, about political union—in extremist speak federalism—and the national sovereignty of the member states, about common policies across the European Union covering agriculture, defense, competition, and social policy.

These are questions that absorb the politicians and the campaigners on each side. The single currency is seen by some as just the tip of the iceberg, an easily portrayed totem covering an irresistible move to greater and greater integration of Europe. There are those who would not want to resist it. There are those who believe the single currency is an issue, and a decision that can be separated from the grander political integration issues. There are those who believe that in the medium-to-long-term, staying outside the single currency will condemn the UK to marginal status and influence in Europe, and thus the world. There are those who believe the UK's future is bound up more with ever-closer ties with North America and the UK does not "need" Europe. There are those who believe in the need for Europe to be a bloc, much expanded beyond the present 15 members of the EU. And those who believe the "Brussels bureaucrats" (the Belgian capital is where the main European institutions and the bureaucratic apparatus that runs the EU are located) have a master plan to create a 'United States of Europe' of a power and influence to challenge that of the United States of America.

It could reasonably be asked whether the 12 countries that with little angst have signed up to the euro have similar concerns. And the answer is that by and large they do not. So what is this peculiarly British problem, and why do the British peculiarly have it? As is so often the case, the answer lies in history and geography.

From Greece in the far southeast of the European mainland to Portugal in the far west, with the major economies of Germany and France in the middle, the doubts and divisions over the European project have been small compared with those of Britain. It is not sufficient to say that Britain is a former colonial power, because so too were the French, the Dutch, the Spanish, and the Portuguese, to name but four. Perhaps it is true to say that Britain has found it harder to come to terms with post-colonialism, still has a sovereign who still "reigns" over a Commonwealth, still regards itself as having disproportionate influence in the world, and still regards itself as America's closest ally.

But less contemporary history is more significant. Britain has fought and won wars for hundreds of years. Britain has not been invaded for hundreds of years.

Then, linked with the history is the geography, or one narrow strip of water referred to in Britain as the English Channel. You cross at its narrowest point in 45 minutes by ship and 30 minutes through the tunnel. But in significance it is so much wider. Britain remains the offshore island to the north of mainland Europe. If Britain and the United States are connected by a common language, then Britain and France are separated by a narrow strip of water, and a cultural chasm.

Those who support British entry into the euro, and scorn the objections of the opponents—who say that increased integration of European countries can only lead to the dilution of national characteristics and creeping uniformity—point to the 12 countries that have entered the eurozone and are committed Europeans. Has this made France more like Germany, they ask? Do the French now drink beer and eat sausages? Have the Spanish abandoned their paella, the Italians their

# EURO GLOSSARY

**Brown's five tests:** The tests the British government, and particularly its chancellor (finance minister) Gordon Brown, say have to be met before the UK can move forward to a decision on joining the euro (see sidebar).

**CAP:** Common Agricultural Policy.

**Convergence Criteria:** Economic conditions which must be met before a country can join the single currency (see sidebar).

**Ecu:** European Currency Unit, the "shadow currency" that became the euro after monetary union. It was based on a basket of national currencies.

**Euro:** The denomination of the single European currency, used exclusively by the members of the EMU after February 2002. It is broken down into 100 cents.

**European Coal and Steel Community (ECSC):** Original postwar initiative to form an economic association of European countries to build a lasting peace through common trade interests. Led to the EEC and then the EU.

**European Economic Community (EEC):** Created in 1958 by the six members of ECSC as a trading bloc free of internal tariffs, and with many aspirations to closer economic and political ties.

**European Monetary Union (EMU):** The policy of the European Union to bring the currencies of the member states together in a single currency called the euro.

**European Union (EU):** Created by the Maastricht Treaty of 1963, which paved the way for the euro.

**Eurozone:** The countries that have joined the single currency. Sometimes called Euroland.

**Exchange Rate Mechanism (ERM):** System used in the preparation for the single currency to maintain exchange rates between different currencies in Europe within narrow bands.

pasta or the Greeks their dolmades? Of course not. Is a trip through the 12 a tour of homogenous countries progressively taking on similar national characteristics? No.

But there is a belief among many of these opponents that Brussels and the European Commission of unelected bureaucrats are set on standardization in the name of harmonization, of destroying the essence of European diversity. All

of this is the subtext of the debate in which the UK is engaged, and which should be resolved in the next few years.

# HISTORICAL BACKGROUND

## The Evolution of the European Project

A little history will put the debate in context. The genesis of Europe as more than a geographical continent, instead a trading community, came in the aftermath of World War II (1939–45). It was based on the lofty ideal that after two world wars involving Germany there must be no more. In May 1950 the French foreign minister Robert Schuman made his famous statement at the setting up of the European Coal and Steel Community (ECSC), the precursor of the modern European organization. Its result would be, said Schuman, that "any war between France and Germany" would be "not merely unthinkable, but materially impossible."

The basis of the European project was the creation of a free trade area, a lifting of tariff barriers between nations joining in the new alignment, and common tariffs for trading with countries outside it. The goal in some minds was much more than that, but the original stated aims were all about free trade. In the first half of the 1950s the original six members of the ECSC, Belgium, France, Germany, Holland, Italy, and Luxembourg, moved towards setting up this broader free trade area. The Treaty of Rome, signed in 1957, brought into being the following year the European Economic Community (EEC, often referred to as the Common Market).

Within two years Britain had declared her desire to join, but met continuing opposition—and the formal veto—from the then French president, Charles de Gaulle (1890–1970). The most nationalist of Frenchmen, he disliked what he considered the federalist aspirations of some members of the EEC. In that way he echoed the feelings of many of the present-day Euroskeptics in Britain who see every step forward, including monetary union, as another step towards federalism. It was to take another 14 years, and the passing of de Gaulle, for Britain to be accepted. The negotiations, with the by-then-established EEC, with policies, particularly agricultural policies, favorable to the original members, particularly France, were led by then British prime minister Edward Heath. He was one of the most committed Europeans ever to sit in the British parliament, something he remained until he left politics in the

BRITISH CITIZENS IN WESTERN ENGLAND DEMONSTRATE THEIR FRUSTRATION WITH THE EUROPEAN UNION. MANY BRITISH CITIZENS HAVE RESERVATIONS ABOUT EU MEMBERSHIP AND ARE AGAINST ADOPTING THE EURO AS BRITAIN'S CURRENCY. *(A/P Wide World. Reproduced by permission.)*

election of 2001. He also made Europe the decisive and divisive issue it has remained in Britain ever since. His commitment to the European project was ideological and total. It was his vision and he never wavered from it.

## Joining the Common Market

Heath was a Conservative, and the opposition Labour Party of that time included views ranging from outright antipathy to joining the EEC to considerable doubts about its desirability. Heath was portrayed as the prime minister who took Britain into the EEC—in 1973—without the "full-hearted consent of the British people." In 1974 Heath lost the general election, in which the Common Market was an issue, but not the main one, to Labour, and Harold Wilson became prime minister.

Wilson steered round the divisions in his own party, divisions every bit as strong as those in the Conservative Party today, by announcing that he would hold a retrospective referendum on the decision to join. This was a device alien to British

politics, and Wilson went further in allowing his own cabinet ministers to campaign against continued membership if that was their personal position. Wilson recommended voting for continued membership, but some cabinet ministers did not. The British people voted in 1975 in favor of staying in the Common Market, but there remained many Labour politicians who were opposed. Future Labour leaders like Neil Kinnock campaigned against the EEC.

For the next few years membership of the EEC seemed uncontroversial in Britain. The referendum endorsement had been overwhelming, and now Europe seemed to be democratizing with the first direct elections to the European Parliament being held in 1979.

The British Labour politician Roy Jenkins became president of the European Commission in 1977, and was responsible, together with the French and German leaders, for pushing the idea of closer economic integration and eventually monetary union. The European Monetary System (EMS) was the result, producing the exchange

CONSERVATIVE LEADER WILLIAM HAGUE STANDS IN FRONT OF AN ANTI-EURO BILLBOARD. THE UNITED KINGDOM IS ONE OF THE EU-MEMBER COUNTRIES OPPOSED TO A SINGLE EUROPEAN CURRENCY. *((c) AFP/Corbis. Reproduced by permission.)*

rate mechanism (ERM), which linked member states' exchange rates—requiring central banks to intervene in the currency markets to control their own exchange rates between narrow agreed bands. The EMS also introduced the European currency unit (ecu), used only technically rather than as a currency. It was, however, the acorn from which the euro oak grew.

The EMS was set up in 1979, with all but one of the EEC member states joining—all but Britain, where Labour's hostility to the EEC had continued to grow. It was the first, but not the last, of the opt-outs that were to feature so strongly in Britain's relations with the EEC.

### Opinion Hardens Against Europe

In the 1980s the EEC expanded, to include Greece in 1981 and Portugal and Spain in 1986. Development of the Common Market set in train the measures that are so controversial in Britain today. Margaret Thatcher, prime minister throughout the decade, set the tone of semi-detachment from Europe that was later to divide and almost destroy the Conservative Party. She brought her style of combative politics to the European stage, initiating or supporting a Euroskepticism that dominated British politics, and European attitudes to Britain, for many years.

She did, however, subscribe to the next stage of European development, the single market, which was the final realization of the abolition of all tariffs and quotas. She was after all a passionate free marketer in her attitude to economics.

The next stages of European development, however, building on the momentum of the success of the single market and the stability brought about by the ERM, increased her Euroskepticism and that of the Conservative Party acolytes who surrounded her. A newly confident Europe, particularly the French, wanted to drive on towards the single currency. Thatcher was opposed.

The Soviet bloc collapsed in 1989, opening the way for potential expansion of the EEC to the east to include some of the former soviet republics, and for reunification of Germany. The end of the Soviet superpower was to have a massive effect on the development of Europe. Mutual interests between the German leader Helmut Kohl and the French leader, François Mitterand, brought those countries even closer at the center of Europe.

The Maastricht Treaty solidified that alliance, and paved the way for the single currency, the euro, the European Central Bank, and a variety of other reforms covering social and employment policy. These critical moments came at the end of the Thatcher era. She was still prime minister when in the middle of 1990 she allowed her chancellor of the exchequer (finance minister), John Major, to take Britain into the exchange rate mechanism (ERM). It was 11 years after the other member states joined ERM, and it was not a success. Britain entered at too high an exchange rate, at the wrong stage of the economic cycle, and with a prime minister who was increasingly hostile to the European project. Thatcher was driven from office by her senior colleagues at the end of 1990, to be succeeded by John Major. He inherited a party already riven by Europe, but pledged his desire to place Britain at "the heart of Europe."

Major was quickly engaged in the Maastricht negotiations. He emerged with opt-outs for Britain over both the single currency and the social chapter (covering employment measures). The other member states tolerated this position from a country seeking to be at the heart of Europe because it was the only way to get the treaty. Major returned to Britain having kept his own party together through the opt-outs. The Maastricht Treaty was signed in March 1992. Britain was forced out of the ERM in June of the same year, unable to defend sterling's exchange rate against other European currencies. The Maastricht Treaty came into force at the end of 1993. With this the EEC became the European Union, the EU.

From then on UK domestic politics were much affected by European politics, as the euro became the center of debate, and the 18 years of Conservative rule under Thatcher and Major came to an end. Labour, which had long been hostile to Europe, lost the 1992 general election, under its Euroskeptic leader Neil Kinnock, who promptly resigned (and paradoxically later became a European Commissioner working in Brussels.) Tony Blair became Labour leader (following the death of John Smith, who succeeded Kinnock) and set about the wholesale modernization of a party many considered to be close to death.

New Labour shed the old party's solid links with the trade union movement, moved away from class-based, socialist politics, to become a social democratic party on the European model, believing firmly in the mixed economy, with the mix very much weighted in favor of the private sector. This had consequences for European policy too. Tony Blair, the architect of New Labour, together with Gordon Brown, his designated chancellor of the exchequer, saw attitudes to Europe as crucial to the difference between traditional (now unelectable) Labour and his re-launched party.

John Major, the Conservative prime minister, was approaching the 1997 election with a party more divided than ever over Europe. The anti-Europeans were in the ascendancy, near to dominating the party against the old pro-European senior figures like Michael Heseltine and Ken Clarke. The infighting was bitter. The party was portrayed by the media and seen by the public as sleazy, with various scandals hitting the headlines. The Conservatives were trounced at the general election, with Tony Blair becoming prime minister with one of the great landslides of modern times.

## A Pro-Euro Government Comes to Power

The Conservatives went away to nurse their wounds, elected the very young, and very Thatcherite, William Hague, as leader, and became the most anti-European mainstream British political party since the birth of the EEC. New Labour, however, despite its formidable mandate, did not immediately commit to the single currency. Tony Blair made it plain that he intended to be a player in the EU, and a major one. But contrary to some expectations he did not jump at once. There were reasons.

Labour had had 18 years in opposition. Many commentators, and indeed many Labour supporters, had doubted whether Labour would ever return to power. The expression "unelectable" was used. Labour over the opposition years was identified with a series of policies that would never capture the center ground so essential for election victory. Labour was variously and at various times opposed to the independent nuclear deterrent, in favor of extending nationalization, of giving greater powers to the trade unions, and, most significantly in this case, of further distancing itself from the European Union, in some cases even of leaving altogether.

Now Labour was in power, with a new party, a new leader, a landslide victory. It was fresh, it was young, and it had shed the baggage that associated it with the old heavy industries and conservative trade unionism. It used the adjective "new" like it had invented it. It had seized middle-income, middle-Britain, Conservative votes. It had dumped ideology and persuaded the electorate that is was a modern party for a modern Britain.

Part of that modernity was to be European. The modern British voter had enjoyed late twentieth-century affluence, taken European holidays, and traveled through Europe on business and pleasure. Numerous British businessmen were regular commuters to the European mainland, so that

## GORDON BROWN'S FIVE TESTS TO BE MET BEFORE THE UK MOVES TO MEMBERSHIP OF EURO

- Are business cycles and economic structures compatible so that the UK and others could live comfortably with Euro interest rates on a permanent basis?

- If problems emerge is there sufficient flexibility to deal with them?

- Would joining the EMU create better conditions for firms making long-term decisions to invest in Britain?

- What impact would entry into the EMU have on the competitive position of the UK's financial services industry, particularly the UK's wholesale market?

- Will joining the EMU promote higher growth, stability, and a lasting increase in jobs?

Brussels airport on a Friday night was as busy as Waterloo station. Britain had voted in a referendum 25 years earlier to be committed members of the EEC. The general election had seen off the "little Englander" Conservative party of Thatcher and Major—or so it had been portrayed. Surely New Labour, newly elected to govern a new Britain, would move quickly to put the old Euro-negativism behind it. The most obvious way to do that would be to join the single currency, the euro, and stop being the reluctant European partner always seeking its opt-out. Britain did not proceed in that way.

The economy Labour inherited in 1997 was very strong. All the indicators were positive: inflation, interest rates, growth, exchange rates, investment, and particularly inward investment from outside the EU. Labour was determined not to repeat the errors of its predecessors, so widely predicted by its opponents. Former Labour governments had come to power with a series of commitments involving substantial public spending and quickly run into inflationary pressures bringing rising interest rates and then tax increases. This new Labour government was pledged to maintain direct tax rates and the public spending plans of its Conservative predecessor.

The new chancellor of the exchequer Gordon Brown immediately set out to portray himself as prudent and devoted to keeping Britain on the economic straight and narrow. Joining the euro implied risk. Why disturb the economy when everything was going so well? Brown and others around him remembered the short and unsuccessful participation in the ERM. The single currency was a much bigger commitment, and effectively an irreversible one. As Labour settled in to government Brown would mention the euro less and less, happy to preside over an economy that was doing very well. It worked. Why fix it?

Brown made one significant policy change within a few days of Labour coming to power. He granted independence to the central bank, the Bank of England, taking the setting of interest rates out of his control. Government would set inflation targets. The Bank of England, without influence from government, would set interest rates to deliver those targets. To some observers this action by Brown so soon after taking office was a sure sign that joining the euro would follow quickly. It was not to be, not for the whole of the 1997–2001 Labour government.

And where did the new prime minister stand? Tony Blair was quickly active on the European stage, attending a succession of meetings with fellow heads of government, seeking quickly to row back the distance the previous Conservative government had created. Blair set out to be at the heart of Europe, talking of expansion, greater democratic accountability, less bureaucracy, and more looking out to the less fortunate world. But Blair too said little about the euro. And all the while, preparations were continuing for the 12 to adopt the single currency. A year after Labour came to power, in May 1998, the EU decided that 11 were ready to move ahead to the euro in 1999. Greece was not considered to have met the criteria, and so was not ready.

The following month the European Central Bank, which would determine interest rates within the single currency zone, was set up. On January 1, 1999, after Labour had been in power for 18 months, the euro became the official currency of the 11. All goods were priced in both the national currency and the euro. Greece joined in January 2001. And on January 1, 2002, euro notes and coins were in circulation throughout the 12 members of the eurozone, with national currency notes and coins finally withdrawn two months later. Still silence from Britain about her plans to join.

Blair always seemed more positive about Europe than Brown, the man he had beaten to the leadership of the party, but he had a tendency to defer to Brown over matters economic, and thus said little about the euro. A full government term was passing, with the single currency being adopted on the European mainland, with a new, supposedly pro-Europe, British government in power, and the anticipated moves towards the euro were not coming. It was as though delaying tactics, or silence, were being deliberately deployed.

## Save the Pound Campaign Develops

The government silence on the euro left the stage free for the opponents of the single currency. It was an opportunity they seized with enthusiasm. The anti-euro press in Britain is confident and articulate, and accounts for considerable circulation. The biggest-selling tabloid, Rupert Murdoch's *Sun* (towards four million copies a day), is vigorously anti-euro. So is Lord Rothermere's *Daily Mail* (2.5 million), and Conrad Black's *Daily Telegraph* (1.1 million). The *Sun* supported Labour in both their landslide election victories, but always with the qualification that it would continue to campaign strongly against the euro and further European integration. Both the *Mail* and *Telegraph* are Conservative newspapers, and thus in line with Conservative policy over the euro. Far from keeping a low profile in the light of the Conservatives' electoral humiliations, both papers saw the European fight as bigger than that, the issues fundamental, historic, and requiring a fight to the last. All weapons were brought to this fight, many of them crude and unsophisticated.

The period towards the end of the first (1997–2001) New Labour government saw the argument conducted in a way that reinforced the "little Englander" image of many of the British. It was the fault of the government, which chose not to engage, and of the pro-European media, such as the *Guardian, Independent,* and *Daily Mirror* (the *Financial Times* was a distinguished exception) which gave little coverage, leaving the field clear for an anti-European view. The problem is that there is much about the EU, its institutions, policies, and procedures, which is technical and often quite boring. Not the stuff of daily newspapers. Whereas, the antis could seize on superficially (and usually actually) trivial issues, and inflate them to make the point that they were indicative of the way Europe was going, and the way Britain would go if it became closer to Europe.

Towards the end of 2000 the EU was developing the idea of a Rapid Reaction Force, a military capability for certain peacekeeping activities where NATO chose not to be involved. To the critics this rapidly became the "Euro army." The

---

### EU CONVERGENCE CRITERIA TO BE MET BEFORE BEING ALLOWED TO JOIN EURO

- Stable exchange rate

- Inflation and interest rates in line with other countries in the euro

- Low budget deficit and national debt. Annual budget deficit must be less than three percent of gross domestic product, and total national debt must be moving towards 60 percent of GDP

---

*Daily Mail* screamed: "EU picks German to lead 'forerunner of a new Euro army.'" The emotive implications of that headline to British of a certain generation do not need elaborating.

"Millions died for Britain only for Blair to surrender," wrote the *Daily Telegraph* on the same issue. And in another edition: "Euro army is a threat to NATO."

The *Daily Mail,* the British newspaper with the most xenophobic tendencies, was outraged to discover the flag of the EU would fly over 10 Downing Street to mark Europe Day. To the *Mail* this represented sovereignty ceded. The paper is as strong on food as it is on tradition. "The scandal of why cod has had its chips. The death of Britain's favorite food is a devastating indictment of the European Union," was the headline right across a double page spread.

The Daily Telegraph took up the case of the "metric martyr," the English greengrocer who insisted on challenging the law that goods must be priced in metric (kilo) measures as well as pounds.

And in the run-up to the 2001 general election the *Sun* echoed the mantra of William Hague: "Last chance to save the pound."

This drip, drip diet of anger and ridicule towards any policy emanating from the EU had its effect, which could be seen in the opinion polls. And when the counterarguments are not being aired, and the government is not seeking to lead or inform opinion, then one side makes all the running. And when that is conducted at a trivial level—there is a serious case against the euro that

---

is often swamped by the sort of examples quoted above—political debate is devalued. That was the situation through much of Labour's first term.

### Heading for the Referendum—And the Euro?

Gordon Brown's contribution to the debate on joining the euro was the "five tests." The government would consult the British people in a referendum about whether the UK should join the euro when it was satisfied that the five tests had been passed. These tests (see sidebar) covered the convergence of the British economy with the other economies of the eurozone; the retention of the flexibility to deal with national economic problems once interest rates and devaluation had been removed as weapons; the encouragement of investment in Britain; the maintenance of the financial services sector through the City of London; and the impact on the British economy in terms of growth and employment of membership of the euro.

The impression was given that these tests were continuously under consideration, continuously being applied, and that one morning Brown would announce that they had been passed and the referendum could go ahead. In reality, they were announced and put to one side. The decision as to whether the tests had been passed lay with the Chancellor. It was both subjective and political. Most economists agreed that it was perfectly possible to present the tests as met at any time during the first Labour government. Taking the next step towards joining the euro was really a political decision.

Of all the reasons put forward for the delay—many outlined above—the critical one was public opinion. The Conservative opposition, in deep disarray after its election defeat, despite the election of the new leader, William Hague, still seemed to strike a chord with the public on just one issue, the euro, or as they put it, "saving the pound." The party was now more anti-euro than at any time, with the pro-Europeans marginalized as never before. Poor Edward Heath, the "father" (longest-serving member) of the House of Commons, sat smoldering on the green bench as his life's work was challenged day after day.

The British public was regularly asked the question "Do you think Britain should replace the pound with the single European currency?" And they regularly told the ICM pollsters "No, we do not think Britain should do that." The figure moved steadily upwards. In October 1998, 56 percent answered "No." In September 1999 the figure

was 64 percent. In September 2000 it was 66 percent, and in March 2001 it was 67 percent. Only 22 percent answered "Yes, Britain should join the single currency." When those figures are broken down by political party, the March 2001 poll gives Conservatives voting 86 percent "No" and 8 percent "Yes." Perhaps surprisingly, in view of Labour's pro-European stance in the election that brought it to power, Labour voters divided 55 percent "No" to the euro, and 29 percent "Yes, let's have the single currency."

On the basis of those figures the Labour leadership's reluctance to drive ahead with joining the euro seems a little more understandable. Labour is committed to holding a referendum on euro entry, but to hold a referendum in which the government recommended a vote in favor of joining the euro, and then lost, would be a massive blow to the government. After its second landslide victory in 2001, and the further collapse of the Conservatives (who then changed their leader again, for an equally anti-euro figure in Ian Duncan Smith), a negative result on a referendum would be unlikely to destroy the government. It would nevertheless weaken it, and particularly the prime minister.

So it is reasonable to assume that Labour would not hold a referendum unless it was confident it would win. Shortly before the 2001 general election the prime minister pledged a decision on whether to hold a referendum—an assessment of the five Gordon Brown tests—in the first two years of the new government. This looked like a move towards the euro, except that such an assessment of the five tests could always have been made at any time, and the promise could be fulfilled and the referendum avoided simply by saying that one of the tests had been failed. They are imprecise enough to allow that.

## RECENT HISTORY AND THE FUTURE

So it all comes down to determination and will. Does the government care deeply about euro entry? Does it believe Britain's future prosperity depends on full membership of Europe, which means membership of the single currency? Does the government subscribe to the present version of the European vision, embracing further integration in the areas of defense, tax harmonization, laws, and other areas? These questions have new urgency, because of the momentum running. The new Europe, with its single currency, will be less and less willing to hang around waiting for Britain, ever reluctant, to catch up.

A COUNTDOWN CLOCK IN A LONDON SUBWAY STATION MARKED THE AMOUNT OF TIME LEFT UNTIL THE EURO BEGAN TRADING IN JANUARY 1999. THE UK HAS DELAYED SWITCHING TO THE EURO BECAUSE IT DOES NOT WANT TO LOSE THE ABILITY TO SET ITS OWN MONETARY POLICY. *(A/P Wide World. Reproduced by permission.)*

The real question is whether Tony Blair holds all these views. His power after the September 11, 2001, terrorist attacks in the United States was complete, his ambitions apparently more on the international than national stage. It seemed clear that Blair wanted to drive ahead with the European project, despite faint hearts within his own cabinet, a stubborn refusal to commit on the part of his chancellor, and an enduring ambivalence/antipathy to Europe and the single currency on the part of the electorate.

It was on September 11 that Blair abandoned giving a speech to the Trade Union Congress in order to rush back to London to deal with the terrorist crisis. But the text of that speech was released, and it contained a stronger commitment to the euro than he had shown in public for a long time. He pointed out that from January 2002 there would be 12 countries in the euro, that of the other three, Sweden was considering joining, Denmark, although it had rejected the euro, had its currency tied to the euro, and then there was Britain. A successful euro was in Britain's national interest, said Blair. So, provided the economic conditions were met, it was right that Britain should join.

He went further four weeks later, at the conference of the Labour Party. In a speech deeply influenced by the New York and Washington atrocities and the subsequent "war on terrorism," he spoke of a new world order in which Europe, with Britain fully engaged, would play a major part. It was clear that rather than consigning such matters as the euro to the back burner, Blair saw the new world crisis as an opportunity for internationalist measures, such as pressing on with the euro.

Britain needed to forego isolationism and instead gain greater strength through the European alliance. Britain had a unique opportunity to build economic and political bridges between Europe and the United States.

"If the economic conditions are met," said the prime minister, "we should join (the euro), and if met in this parliament we should have the courage of our argument to ask the British people for their consent in this parliament. Britain needs its voice strong in Europe, and bluntly Europe needs a strong Britain, rock solid in our alliance with the USA yet determined to play its full part in shaping Europe's destiny."

After much foot-dragging and reluctance to take on the euro issue, suddenly the government seemed ready to commit, to campaign, to move towards the resolution of the issue that had dominated British politics for so long. Technically

Blair's speech represented no change of policy. But it was a significant change of tone.

The route ahead suddenly took on some clarity. The assessment of whether Gordon Brown's five tests had been passed would be taken by the summer of 2003. Before then the government would start talking about the euro—"selling" the euro. There were signs of that by the autumn of 2001, as the European minister Peter Hain toured the country making speeches about the positive side of joining the euro.

Large numbers of the British take their vacations on the European mainland, mainly in Spain, France, Italy, and Greece. From the summer of 2002 they will be buying their drinks and presents, their ice creams, and their Euro Disney entry tickets with euros. They will get used to the euro, the politicians believe, and this will help to dismantle their objections to it. Those who drive through Europe—passing through several countries, as many do—will see the advantages of using the same currency throughout, not having to take several different currencies with them. The same theory insists that once the British have seen that Spain and France using the same currency has had no effect on the national character or culture of those countries, that they are still completely different, the British will lose the objection that single currency means single character.

At the same time all trade will be conducted in euros, thus reducing costs and increasing convenience for British businesses trading with countries in the eurozone. This will change attitudes of the business community, who will speak positively of the benefits of the euro, influencing others. Or so the theory goes.

Then, in this projection, in 2003 the Brown tests will be declared passed and the government will announce a referendum the following year, two years before another general election has to take place. Intense campaigning, selling the euro and its benefits, clear government commitment, two years of experience of the euro in operation, and the British people will vote to join. Britain enters the euro in 2005. That is the Euro-optimist theory, and appears to be where the government is at the end of 2001.

The Euro-skeptic prognosis runs rather differently. The government's decision to run with the euro brings the issue center stage. This allows the "save the pound" faction endless space to put across their message of loss of sovereignty, loss of economic independence, and subservience to some central bank in Germany. With a firm opinion poll base of antipathy to the euro, they see this growing through a referendum campaign so that ultimately the referendum result is "No" to the euro.

And there is one other imponderable. Unforeseen economic circumstances— perhaps brought about by the war on terrorism—could test the resilience of the eurozone and the ability of the single currency, the central bank, and common interest rates to handle economic crisis. If that test failed, then the prospects for British entry into the euro would take a serious downturn. But, on balance, towards the end of 2001, British entry seems more likely than not. In matters European she is always late, always reluctant, but gets there in the end.

## BIBLIOGRAPHY

Browne, Anthony. *The Euro: Should Britain Join?* Cambridge: Icon Books, 2001.

European Commission on the Euro. "EMU." Available online at http://www.cec.org.uk/info/pubs/bbriefs/ (cited January 25, 2002).

*Financial Times* Special Report, "Europe Reinvented." Available online at http://specials.ft.com/europereinvented1/index.html (cited January 25, 2002) .

*Financial Times* on the Euro. Available online at http://specials.ft.com/euro/index.html (cited January 25, 2002).

*Guardian Unlimited.* "Special Report: Economic and Monetary Union." Available online at http://www.guardian.co.uk/EMU/ (cited January 25, 2002) .

Pinder, John. *The European Union: A Very Short Introduction.* London, New York: Oxford University Press, 2001.

Rosenbaum, Martin, ed. *Britain and Europe: The Choices We Face.* London, New York: Oxford University Press, 2001.

Siedentop, Larry. *Democracy in Europe.* London, New York: Penguin, 2000.

*Peter Cole*

# READING, WRITING, AND WARFARE: CHILDREN IN ARMED CONFLICT

On a Tuesday in June of 2000, almost 1,700 boys and girls who had been abducted, forced to serve in the rebel army, and trained to kill by rebel armies in Sierra Leone were released to the United Nations Children's Fund (UNICEF). Only a few days later, UNICEF reported the release of 2,500 child soldiers in Sudan in similar conditions. Then, in October of the same year, as the Palestinian-Israeli conflict again turned violent, images of wounded children who had thrown rocks at Israeli soldiers appeared nightly on world news programs. In February 2001, the same international humanitarian organization found almost 200 children soldiers in Uganda. In August, fighting in Rwanda between the Rwandan Patriotic Army (RPA) and rebels from the Democratic Republic of Congo (DRC) escalated. As the RPA took control of the situation, it liberated several hundred children fighting for the DRC. These cases are only a few of the horrendous stories of children becoming not only victims, but also active participants in warfare.

In the last ten years an estimated two million children have been killed in armed conflicts. Increasingly, though, the international public is hearing about it. As this story repeated itself in country after country, the violence experienced by children in war shocked the world and became an international affair. On one hand, there has been a triumph—the international community has exposed governments and rebel armies who use children in combat. Yet, at the same time, these events highlight a growing problem and reflect the worldwide failure to protect children from the atrocities of war.

What has come to light is that in many places throughout the world, instead of making mud

## THE CONFLICT

More than two million children have been killed as a result of warfare during the last ten years. Children under the age of 18—sometimes much younger—are used in warfare by 41 countries throughout the world, by governments and rebel groups. They are denied basic human rights and are often abused terribly, and the practice of training young children to destroy and kill perpetuates cycles of violence in war-torn countries. Rehabilitation of former child soldiers has been beyond the resources of many nations that use children as fighters. Enforcement of international, national, and regional laws against the use of children in warfare is very difficult.

### Political

- The increase of long and turbulent civil wars within countries has escalated the problem of children being used as soldiers. Ethnic conflicts, revenge for family killed, and state or rebel propaganda can draw children into the violence, and the shortage of adult fighters after years of violence makes them necessary. International forces are less likely to be able to help in internal conflicts.

- Despite international attention to the problem, issues such as the international sale of small arms and the existence of millions of land mines in places where children will be killed or maimed by them have not received enough attention to be corrected.

- When countries demobilize the child soldiers, they often lack the resources to help them through the transition. Trained in war, children are psychologically damaged and need rehabilitation. They are often ostracized by their own families or communities. They will often return to violence unless they receive help.

### Economic

- The children from families with the lowest incomes are most vulnerable to military recruiters and abductors. Lack of education, the inability to pay off the recruiters, being orphaned, the need of the family for income from the military, and many other factors of poverty make a child easy prey to harsh and dangerous military servitude and a very uncertain future after demobilization.

# CHRONOLOGY

*1924* The League of Nations' Declaration of the Rights of the Child declares that "mankind owes to the child the best it has to give."

*1949* The Geneva Convention sets guidelines for war, prohibiting rape and requiring that enemy sides provide adequate food, shelter, and medical supplies for civilian captives. The document does not refer specifically to children.

*1977* The UN adopts General Protocols I and II, proclaiming that children "shall be the object of special respect and shall be protected against any form of indecent assault."

*1989* The Convention on the Rights of the Child is adopted by 191 countries. This document sets 15 as a minimum age for participation in hostilities, compulsory recruitment, and recruitment by nongovernmental armed groups.

*1990* A United Nations report reveals that children as young as ten years old are being used as soldiers throughout the world. The UN hosts a World Summit for Children to improve international awareness and initiates an international research project, naming Graça Machel its chair.

*November 11, 1996* Graça Machel releases her report, "The Impact of Armed Conflict on Children," drawing international attention to the issue.

*1999* The UN Security Council unanimously adopts Resolution 1261, which "condemns the targeting of children in situations of armed conflict including killing and maiming, sexual violence, abduction and forced displacement, recruitment and use of children in armed conflict in violation of international law and attacks on places that usually have a significant presence of children such as schools and hospitals—and calls on all parties concerned to put an end to such practices."

*May 25, 2000* The Optional Protocol to the Convention on the Rights of the Child prohibits the forced recruitment of all children under 18, yet still allows a government to accept volunteers at 16.

*Spring 2001* Rebel forces in Sudan release 3,500 children to UNICEF.

pies, playing with toy trucks and baby dolls, many children carry weapons, act as spies, decoys, and assassins. In addition to traditional warfare, children clear minefields, act as suicide bombers, and serve as messengers and sex slaves. Almost 5,000 children are still in military groups within Sierra Leone, and Myanmar, also known as Burma, holds an estimated 50,000 child soldiers. Some researchers guesstimate that half a million children are involved in war activities. Despite the fact that many humanitarian organizations like UNICEF and CARE (Cooperative for Assistance and Relief Everywhere) have focused on this issue for decades, it is only in the last few years that international media organizations started sending pictures of eight-year-old children carrying AK-47s in the jungle of Sudan to the living rooms of people in the United States and Europe.

Sudan, the largest country in Africa, with more than 10,000 children serving in military organizations, clearly illustrates all of the issues facing children in warfare. The Juvenile Care Council Sudanese, an official government agency, often takes children into custody directly off the street. Children out running errands or playing are scooped up and quickly forced into military camps. The government does not attempt to notify a child's family, who may not see the child again for several years. If a child manages to escape the clutches of the military, he or she is at risk of being picked up by the other side, Sudan's rebel army—the Sudan People's Liberation Army (SPLA).

Children's rights while they are serving as soldiers in Sudan are violated in a number of ways. Beyond the forcible capture, reports indicate that while in government custody children are denied their rights of religious freedom and forced to take a Muslim name and to convert to Islam. On the other side, the SPLA rebel organization often recruits with promises of food and then forces its new recruits to walk hundreds of miles from their homes. In 1994 one particularly desperate case was reported. Famine had triggered the United Nations to provide food rations for the children in the rebel army, but, tragically, the rebels stole the food. A few months later, UNICEF reported that 47 boys under the supervision of the SPLA died from lack of food and medical care.

The problems in Sudan are deep rooted. The government denies any use of children and instead points to a Sudanese law that prohibits the recruitment of anyone under the age of eighteen into the military. Furthermore, the rebel group SPLA is hidden in the shadows of the country and out of the control of the government, international observers, and aid workers. It is in prolonged conflicts within countries like Sudan that most child soldiers appear.

No continent is immune from the practice of using children as soldiers. Children are weapons and instruments of war in more than 41 countries, including Afghanistan, Colombia, Indonesia, Iraq, Kosovo, Lebanon, Liberia, Myanmar, the Philippines, and Sri Lanka. Children are found in national armies as well as in paramilitary rebel groups, including the Tamil Tigers in Sri Lanka and extremist Palestinian groups in Israel. One report in the *International Journal of Psychology* claims that almost 70 percent of Palestinian children have, at one time, been involved in acts of violence against Israeli troops. In the developed world children are fighting in the streets of Belfast, Northern Ireland. Some also point to the U.S. military, which sends people at age seventeen into combat; others accuse the British, who recruit soldiers at sixteen.

Unfortunately, the problem of child soldiers does not recognize gender barriers. Within Sri Lanka, girls are commonly part of the Tamil Tiger operations, and one report found that before the civil war in Ethiopia ended in 1991, approximately 25 percent of the opposition army in that country were young girls. One particularly tragic report in the *Los Angeles Times* on Christmas Day, 2000, described how the Sri Lankan government had killed 18 Tamil Tigers rebels—14 of whom were girls. Both official armies and rebel forces use girls in noncombatant roles, and girls are often sexually abused by soldiers.

## HISTORICAL BACKGROUND

As far back as ancient Greece and Rome, there exist accounts of young people in battle. During the Middle Ages children were close to the frontlines of war. A boy who wanted to become a knight served as a squire and shadowed his master on the battlefield. Later, during the Napoleonic Wars and throughout the eighteenth and nineteenth centuries, children loaded artillery, engaged in espionage, and acted as drummer boys leading the charges. In the historical drama, *Henry V*, William Shakespeare describes the Battle of

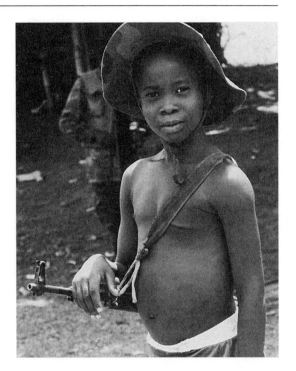

YOUNG CHILDREN, FROM AFRICA TO ASIA AND LATIN AMERICA, ARE FIGHTING IN WARS AND BATTLES AROUND THE WORLD. *(AP/Wide World Photos. Reproduced with permission.)*

Agincourt and the brutal massacre of the young pages and drummer boys in the British army by French soldiers. Within the American tradition, many youth fought in the Revolutionary War and historical documents are filled with testimony from soldiers as young as ten. George Washington himself was only 20 years old when he served as a major in the Virginia Militia.

Even in more contemporary wars like World Wars I (1914–18) and II (1939–45) there are romantic stories of young boys lying about their age to enlist in combat forces to fight for their country. One glaring example is found in the notorious story of German leader Adolf Hitler's young 12th SS-Panzer Division, which was made up entirely of boys who would not retreat against the British even under orders to do so. During the war 60 percent of the children in Germany were part of Hitler's youth forces. A five-chapter report on the Hitler Youth in the History Place web site describes the intensity of these child warriors: "The shocking fanaticism and reckless bravery of the Hitler Youth in battle astounded the British and Canadians who fought them. They sprang like wolves against tanks. If they were encircled or outnumbered, they fought on until there were no survivors. Young boys, years away from their first

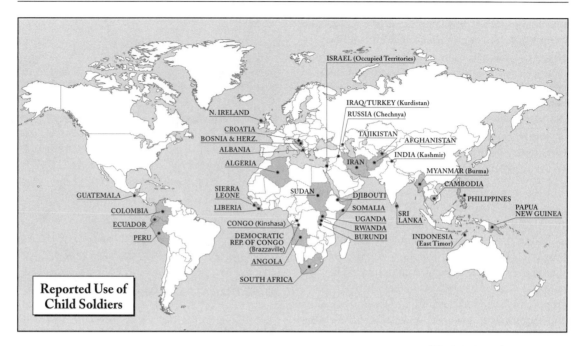

MAP DOCUMENTING THE REPORTED USE OF CHILD SOLDIERS AROUND THE WORLD. *(The Gale Group.)*

shave, had to be shot dead by Allied soldiers, old enough in some cases, to be their fathers."

Despite the long history of children on or near the battlefield, it is only in the last 50 years that the world has viewed this as a humanitarian issue demanding its attention. The presence of children in war is not new; however, the extent and the type of incorporation is. As more of the world's conflicts are internal and remain within one country, children are more frequently both the victims and the agents of war. When internal civil strife continues for years and even decades, adults available for fighting can become short in supply. In addition, children in war-torn areas are more vulnerable to abduction and persuasion to join military organizations because the conditions at home are often disturbed by war. At the same time, the modern world brings with it changing social values that honor and uphold childhood as something that is innocent and should be cherished and protected, and it is therefore more shocked by the use of child soldiers.

## Recruiting, Training, and Demobilization

**Forced Recruitment:** As the story of children in Sudan illustrates, the practice of forced recruitment is a particularly brutal aspect of the use of children in warfare. Schools become a source of military manpower, and government forces as well as rebel forces often snatch children right from

their desks. The countries most often cited for such practices include Myanmar/Burma, Guatemala, El Salvador, Ethiopia, Mozambique, Angola, Sri Lanka, and Sudan. Although this kind of abduction is a common tactic, it is seldom documented and therefore difficult to regulate. Usually, there is no formal process; children are simply collected from playgrounds and public areas.

During their "recruitment" children often experience extreme brutality, such as being forced to witness or participate in their parent's executions, or suffering beatings from their captors. Some are forced to attack their own families and neighbors in an attempt to isolate them from any normal future within their community. Tragically, in addition to losing their families, many lose their identity as they are forced to forget their names, ages, and the towns or villages they came from. The child soldier is a lost child and may remain so for much of his or her life.

**Volunteers:** Not all children combatants are abducted. Although many are kidnapped, others volunteer. As the increase in civil wars and internal conflicts takes its toll on civilian populations, there are more orphans who may find little alternative but to relinquish their childhood to a local militia or paramilitary group. Many argue that even those who go willingly into war are in actuality forced by the circumstances of their underprivileged situation.

The problem of child volunteers is most severe in underdeveloped countries. In areas that experience the devastation of war there may be no roads, no way for a family to eke out subsistence, and no schools. Without opportunities for education or work, enlisting in a local army or joining a guerrilla group may give an adolescent a sense of community, purpose, and honor.

Lack of education is another determining factor. One central study, Rachel Brett and Margaret McCallin's *Children: The Invisible Soldiers* (1996), states that "educational deprivation is the hallmark of the child volunteer." Idealism increases when opportunities are limited—a child can become a true believer going off to fight and protect his or her family and community. In some cases, as with the Hitler Youth discussed above, the culture legitimizes violence as an appropriate and honorable strategy to obtain a better life. Brett and McCallin observe that "a weapon provides access to food, and is better than staying home afraid and helpless."

**Obedience:** Once captured, drafted, or volunteered, a child undergoes training that is often incredibly brutal and intended to desensitize him or her to violence and ensure compliance. Reports in Central America found that children are forced to kill animals and drink their blood. They are burned with cigarettes, beaten, verbally abused, and even killed if they resist. Children are also taught to abuse and kill each other for insubordination. It is also common practice in Sierra Leone and parts of Central America for children to be forced to use drugs and alcohol to increase susceptibility, heighten aggression, and create dependence on their captors.

Attempts to escape are met with brutality; those who try to flee often lose an ear or a limb. Since a child's home community may associate such injuries with brutal militias and therefore reject the child, these scars in themselves can prevent children from attempting to flee in the future. In addition to facing rejection from their community, child combatants often suffer from posttraumatic stress and may continue their violence outside of war, withdraw from social interactions, and suffer from nightmares and hallucinations.

**Demobilization:** The demobilization of children and their reintroduction into society as noncombatants is another complex and controversial issue. In times of war it is likely that a child's family has been killed or his or her community wiped out. As discussed above, a community may also reject a child who has been a soldier, and then there is no one to provide for his or her essential needs. Girls who are forced into sexual service are commonly cast off by their families. These problems are exacerbated by the fact that in many African countries, children who are recruited for sexual services are exposed to HIV/AIDS and have extensive health needs.

In addition to practical considerations children face emotional challenges in their transition into civilian lifestyles. The trauma of warfare often remains with them; some commit suicide. Children who are trained to be violent may continue to pose a threat to their community and their country as they mature. A child who has witnessed violence and brutality may need assistance in healing from guilt, anger, fear, and hatred to lessen the chances that he or she will return to violence. Together, these needs often entail more than a country can provide. In many cases child soldiers have been written off as a lost generation with no hope of emotional and physical rehabilitation.

## Debating the Numbers

One of the most challenging aspects of this issue involves identifying exactly who is a child. Child soldiers can be as young as six, or in some eyes, anyone under the age of eighteen. Because of the lack of consensus on when a child becomes an adult, there is controversy in tallying the number of children actively participating in warfare and in the figures used to establish long-term trends. Within western societies the tendency is to view eighteen as the cutoff point. For example, the United States government defines all persons under the age of eighteen as minors in the legal sense, in issues such as criminal prosecution, voting, marriage, and signing legal contracts. Yet, in many cultures throughout the world, particularly those with lower life expectancies, adulthood is defined at an earlier age. Religious and cultural traditions may also place the age of maturity much lower. For example, within Judaism the age of maturity begins with puberty; in some African societies marriage can occur as early as twelve. At fourteen, a boy may be regarded as a man and a good candidate for military work.

This debate about childhood spills into discussions about what age is too young to fight in combat. In Cambodia one author describes the army's criteria for drafting as when an individual is as tall as a rifle. Most argue that the rule of thumb should be when an individual is mature enough to

## GRAÇA MACHEL

*1945–* Graça Machel has been an outspoken advocate of education and children's rights in her native country of Mozambique and internationally. She was born Graça Simbine in 1945 in Mozambique, then a colony of Portugal. Her father, a Methodist minister, died three weeks before she was born but arranged for her education. In 1968 Machel began her studies at Lisbon University with a major in romance languages. There she became involved in anti-colonial politics and in 1972 was forced to flee to Switzerland to escape the Portuguese secret police. In Europe she joined the Marxist-based Mozambican Liberation Front (FRELIMO) in the struggle against colonialism. She returned to Africa and served FRELIMO in Tanzania, until Mozambique was freed from Portuguese rule in 1975.

In 1975 she married Samora Machel, the Marxist president of newly independent Mozambique. She was appointed Minister of Education and worked tirelessly to reduce the high rate of illiteracy and to alleviate the terrible toll that years of upheaval had caused to the educational system in Mozambique.

On the night of October 19, 1986, Samora Machel was killed when his airplane mysteriously crashed into a hillside while returning from a meeting in Zambia. Machel believed that the pro-apartheid groups her husband had been fighting for years were responsible. Devastated by his loss, she resigned her post as Minister of Education. Machel later went on to serve in increasing international positions in education and child welfare.

In 1990 a United Nations report revealed that children as young as ten years old were being used as soldiers throughout the world. The UN initiated an international research project, asking Machel to be its chair. Her report, "The Impact of Armed Conflict on Children," was published by the UN on November 11, 1996. The report's findings were shocking and gruesome, but the results were positive. It laid out effective measures to protect or rehabilitate children who were victims of armed conflicts and had a tremendous impact on international awareness of the atrocities suffered by child soldiers.

GRAÇA MACHEL IS A STRONG ACTIVIST IN CHILDREN'S RIGHTS. *(A/P Wide World. Reproduced by permission.)*

*BBC News Online* writer Josephine Hazeley called Machel's report "a cry from the heart." In a personal note that introduces the report, Machel wrote:

In the two years spent on this report, I have been shocked and angered to see how shamefully we have failed in this responsibility... In some countries, conflicts have raged for so long that children have grown into adults without ever knowing peace. I have spoken to a child who was raped by soldiers when she was just nine years old. I have witnessed the anguish of a mother who saw her children blown to pieces by land-mines in their fields, just when she believed they had made it home safely after the war. I have listened to children forced to watch while their families were brutally slaughtered. I have heard the bitter remorse of 15-year-old ex-soldiers mourning their lost childhood and innocence, and I have been chilled listening to children who have been so manipulated by adults and so corrupted by their experiences of conflict that they could not recognize the evil of which they had been a part."

In July 1998 Machel married former president of South Africa Nelson Mandela and has continued her work as an advocate for the rights of women and children.

understand the consequences of certain actions. A common definition was established by child rights activist Graça Machel in her benchmark 1996 United Nations Report, which defines child soldiers as anyone "under the age of 18 who is compulsorily or voluntarily recruited or otherwise used in hostilities by armed forces, paramilitaries, civil defense units, or other armed groups."

Overall, the lack of agreement on the age of majority poses an obstacle for counting the number of children soldiers and also for establishing international guidelines to prevent child militias. Depending on how you count and whom you include as a child soldier, estimates on the numbers of children active in some capacity of war range from 87 countries with close to one million children in combat, to 30 countries with 300,000 children active in war. The challenge in determining the numbers are exacerbated by the fact that governments and rebel groups are seldom forthcoming about their use of children. Child warriors are often stashed in jungles and forests, far from the eyes of international media and human rights organizations.

## Why Children? Causes and Consequences

Why are children such a prevalent component of modern warfare? There are several reasons, including political factors, economic conditions, and cultural values. Furthermore, the source of the problem comes from both national and international politics. Local economic conditions, political crises, increases in civil strife overall, and the international sales of small weapons to countries in conflict all contribute to the presence of children in combat zones.

**Economic Conditions:** At the local level economics can be a key contributor to a child's becoming a soldier. Children who grow up in poverty without clean water, safe shelter, and education are the most vulnerable. Forced recruitment tends to target poorer children. While poverty-stricken families have few resources and little recourse for finding and retrieving a child taken by a military organization, wealthier families can send their children out of the country for educational purposes, bribe authorities to release their child, or buy out their child's obligation to a military operation. In addition, when local economies fail, children become hungry. The appeal of looting, and therefore eating, draws them into war. Again, in Sudan, the SPLA provides grand illusions of food and safety, causing parents to relinquish their children freely because they believe their lives may actually be better in a militia.

On the other side, children appeal to military groups who are strapped for resources. They tend to be more economical, since they eat less and demand lower wages, if they are even paid. If a child is paid he may earn an important salary and contribute to the well-being and continued existence of an entire family. Within Western developed countries that have educational systems and employment opportunities the thought of children serving as military personnel is very disturbing. In areas without these resources a child in the military may be viewed as a blessing. Ironically, efforts to discontinue the use of children in the military may be viewed as threatening, leaving both child and family without income.

**Political Situations:** Political instability also contributes to childhoods lost to warfare. In the last decade the world has seen an increase in civil war. In areas with unrelenting ethnic violence, like Rwanda, Israel, Sri Lanka, East Timor, Kosovo, and Bosnia, children are more likely to be included in the fighting. Children may be caught up in wars of ideology and manipulated for political purposes to support the agendas of certain groups. This can be extremely damaging, as it teaches intolerance and extremist solutions that can then lead to cycles of reoccurring violence. Children become pawns in a dangerous political game.

Government publicity actions in times of war can be an additional source of the problem as they glamorize war and hold soldiers up as heroes. The use of parades, propaganda, rallies, and even anthems and pledges teach children that war is an honorable activity and that soldiers have exciting and rewarding duties. With the use of slogans, flags, and songs children become vulnerable to suggestion and manipulation. For example, within Hamas (an extremist Palestinian group), children who fight against Israel are told they are guaranteed access to heaven for fighting in defense of their religion. Another example of wartime propaganda was found in the Khmer Rouge in Cambodia, a government that killed two million of its own people. The Khmer Rouge used textbooks to train children in warfare, complete with lessons in land mine detonation and instructions on constructing a deadly poisonous bamboo spike.

Children also respond to the idea of revenge. Some recruits have relatives who have died in civil war and family members may pressure a them to avenge the death of a loved one by joining the military or an opposition force.

## Good Things Come in Small Packages

Unfortunately, the very nature of children—not being fully grown either physically or emotionally—plays a contributing factor. Tragically, physical size often contributes to capture; kids are easier to transport than adults. Children are also malleable and less prone to question authority. As one Congolese official, quoted in a July 10, 1999, article in the *Economist* describes, children "make very good soldiers... they obey orders; they are not concerned about getting back to their wife or family; and they don't know fear." They are often perceived as more reckless than adults and, unfortunately, more suited to extreme missions.

Children are also less likely to attract suspicion and can easily plant bombs and engage in intelligence-gathering operations. If apprehended, children often face less harsh punishments from the law than do their adult counterparts. According to a report by the Coalition to Stop the Use of Child Soldiers, children are "cheap, expendable and easier to condition in fearless killing and unthinking obedience." An additional benefit for a military or rebel group is that adult soldiers of the other side may not fire on child soldiers.

## The International Arms Trade

The international trade in small arms is intricately tied to the issue of children in warfare. Technology has in recent years created smaller guns, plastic explosives, hand grenades, and overall lighter weapons. Children are more able to handle the new instruments of warfare. For example, assault rifles like the Russian-built AK-47 and the American M-16 are easy to carry and to use. Brett and McCallin explain: "The medieval squire could not hope to don his master's armour until he had reached physical maturity and even a generation ago battlefield weapons were heavy and cumbersome." These new weapons are also less expensive. The United Nations Research Institute for Social Development found that in some African countries the guns sell for US$6 apiece.

Some observers argue that countries that sell these weapons aggravate the problem as they continue their very profitable sale of small arms to governments or groups supported by governments who employ children as combatants. The contentious aspects of the arms trade and warfare are highlighted by Jo de Berry, who, in the article "Child Soldiers and the Convention on the Rights of the Child" (2001), describes how the United Kingdom faced considerable international embarrassment when images of a 14-year-old Sierra Leone soldier—dressed in British fatigues and carrying a British weapon—appeared across the front page of international newspapers in May 2000. Berry writes that the child's "gun thus came to him through the world of international politics, a world that is framed by the global history of colonialism and organizations such as the United Nations, of international intervention or nonintervention." A recent report on global arms sales in the *New York Times* estimated that the international arms trade grew by 8 percent in 2000, and that the United States has about 50 percent of the market share. Of the $34 billion dollar industry, the United States sold $18 billion in weapons, with almost 70 percent of those sales going to developing countries.

## Preventions: Crime without Punishment

Despite the fact that popular international attention is only beginning to focus on children in armed conflict, efforts to prevent children from participating in warfare are more than 70 years old. Although most agree that children should not become pawns of violent adult power struggles, the prevention of such activities is riddled with controversy. The issues revolve around what rights children have, if these rights compete with the rights of parents, and what rights countries have to form and recruit their own militaries. There are three layers of legal protections for children: international laws and treaties, regional laws such as those passed by the Organization of African Unity, and laws within a country.

Within the legal codes of most countries, there are laws that set age restrictions on many activities associated with war. In addition to laws dealing directly with children in conflict there are regulations prohibiting child slavery, ensuring freedom of religion, and offering protections from sexual abuse. For example, in the United States there are extensive provisions preventing child abduction, labor, prostitution, and the sale of weapons to minors. Similar laws are found in other countries and often tie the age of maturity to voting, criminal prosecution, and conscription. On the other hand, many of the countries where we find children involved in war are plagued by internal conflict and are fighting illegal rebel organizations, like the SPLA in Sudan and the Tamil Tigers in Sri Lanka, which exist outside the parameters of law. A country's laws cannot protect young recruits into the rebel groups because they are by nature outside the realm of law.

**International Protections of Children** The now obsolete League of Nations passed one of the first international laws protecting children in combat zones. The opening paragraph of the 1924 Declaration of the Rights of the Child declared, "mankind owes to the child the best it has to give." Another important document protecting all persons involved in warfare is the 1949 Geneva Convention. This document sets guidelines against rape and requires that enemy sides provide adequate food, shelter, and medical supplies for civilian captives. Interestingly, although it is considered the cornerstone of international laws protecting human rights, the document does not refer specifically to children.

To address the issue of children directly, in 1977 the UN adopted General Protocols I and II, proclaiming that children "shall be the object of special respect and shall be protected against any form of indecent assault." Later it declares that "all human beings under fifteen" be treated as children. Within these documents additional provisions explicitly state that families are the most important aspect of a child's physical and emotional well-being, and children who are displaced by war should be expeditiously reunited with their parents. Unfortunately, countries can get around these guidelines since the conventions largely deal with conflict between countries and not within them.

In the last decade of the twentieth century many international treaties and regulations were put into place. In 1989, 191 countries adopted the Convention on the Rights of the Child. This document set 15 years old as a minimum age for participation in hostilities, compulsory recruitment, and recruitment by non-governmental armed groups. Only two countries have not ratified the convention—Somalia and the United States. Somalia's government is only beginning to take shape after it fell apart a few years ago. The United States is reluctant to sign; the U.S. military, specifically the Pentagon, does not want to be limited in its recruiting so it can assure a certain level of preparedness.

In 1999 the UN Security Council added more weight to these guiding principles when it unanimously adopted Resolution 1261. The document "condemns the targeting of children in situations of armed conflict including killing and maiming, sexual violence, abduction and forced displacement, recruitment and use of children in armed conflict in violation of international law and attacks on places that usually have a significant presence of children such as schools and hospitals—and calls on all parties concerned to put an end to such practices." This measure holds particular significance as the Security Council can strictly enforce its provisions (if it chooses to do so).

Many applaud another recent move, by the UN General Assembly on May 25, 2000, to raise the minimum age for combat to 18. The Optional Protocol to the Convention on the Rights of the Child prohibits the forced recruitment of all children under 18, yet still allows a government to

CHILD SOLDIERS LIKE THIS YOUNG CAMBODIAN, CENTER, FIGHT AND DIE ALONGSIDE THEIR OLDER COMRADES. MANY ARE NOT RECRUITED WILLINGLY. *(A/P Wide World. Reproduced by permission.)*

accept volunteers at 16. Although the United States—along with 84 other countries—signed the document, it has not ratified the treaty. Despite these edicts, 17 year olds participated in U.S. military operations in the Persian Gulf War, Somalia, and Kosovo. The United States, like most countries, argues that it is its sovereign right to form an army of its choosing. Six countries legally adopted the Optional Protocol—Bangladesh, Sri Lanka, Andorra, Canada, Iceland, and Panama.

In addition to these documents the United Nations Secretary-General has established a Committee on the Rights of the Child and appointed a Special Representative for Children and Armed Conflict. Ugandan attorney Olara Otunnu held this position in 2001. His duties included visiting the troubled spots of the world, preventing armies and militias from recruiting children, assisting in the demobilization of minors, and encouraging

# OPTIONAL PROTOCOL TO THE CONVENTION ON THE RIGHTS OF THE CHILD ON THE INVOLVEMENT OF CHILDREN IN ARMED CONFLICT: EXCERPTS

**Article 1:** States Parties shall take all feasible measures to ensure that members of their armed forces who have not attained the age of 18 years do not take a direct part in hostilities.

**Article 2:** States Parties shall ensure that persons who have not attained the age of 18 years are not compulsorily recruited into their armed forces...

**Article 4:**

- 1. Armed groups that are distinct from the armed forces of a State should not, under any circumstances, recruit or use in hostilities persons under the age of 18 years.

- 2. States Parties shall take all feasible measures to prevent such recruitment and use, including the adoption of legal measures necessary to prohibit and criminalize such practices.

- 3. The application of the present article shall not affect the legal status of any party to an armed conflict...

**Article 6**

- 1. Each State Party shall take all necessary legal, administrative and other measures to ensure the effective implementation and enforcement of the provisions of the present Protocol within its jurisdiction.

- 2. States Parties undertake to make the principles and provisions of the present Protocol widely known and promoted by appropriate means, to adults and children alike.

- 3. States Parties shall take all feasible measures to ensure that persons within their jurisdiction recruited or used in hostilities contrary to the present Protocol are demobilized or otherwise released from service. States Parties shall, when necessary, accord to such persons all appropriate assistance for their physical and psychological recovery and their social reintegration.

**Article 7**

- 1. States Parties shall cooperate in the implementation of the present Protocol, including in the prevention of any activity contrary thereto and in the rehabilitation and social reintegration of persons who are victims of acts contrary thereto, including through technical cooperation and financial assistance. Such assistance and cooperation will be undertaken in consultation with the States Parties concerned and the relevant international organizations.

- 2. States Parties in a position to do so shall provide such assistance through existing multilateral, bilateral or other programmes or, inter alia, through a voluntary fund established in accordance with the rules of the General Assembly.

peace agreements to include provisions for the demobilization of children. In addition, the United Nations appoints child protection advisers who both monitor and assist in interagency coordination and work to provide basic necessities. Both these offices spend much of their time educating the international public about the countries using children in conflict and their extensive abuses. Another important movement towards increasing awareness and international support has come through international conferences. In 1990 the UN hosted a World Summit for Children to improve international awareness about countries and rebel groups who use children to fight their wars. Again, these meetings are intended to fight an important barrier—lack of public awareness.

## Implementation

Although there is an extensive body of international law, treaties, and statutes prohibiting the use of children in armed conflict, these resolutions and treaties are seldom enforced. In a UN Press Release, Olara Otunnu acknowledged the difficulty in enforcing these guidelines and observed, "Words on paper cannot save children in peril." The problem is that the people who agree to

CHILD SOLDIERS SET DOWN THEIR ARMS AND WALK AWAY FROM THE REBEL GROUP SUDAN PEOPLE'S LIBERATION ARMY. THEY RANGE IN AGE FROM EIGHT TO EIGHTEEN. *(A/P Wide World. Reproduced with permission.)*

enforce international protocols are often the very same people who violate their statutes.

Enforcement of international law is often like asking wolves to watch the chicken coop. Countries that may not even enforce their own laws are asked to enforce international law against their own military. Furthermore, rebel and guerrilla groups are not parties to international treaties and agreements and therefore hold no obligation to obey the rules. There are further barriers to successfully implementing these guidelines. Many countries do not keep adequate birth and death records, making it difficult to know how old a soldier is or to prove a child was abducted. For the governments who use children in the military, and for the children themselves, there are very few legal consequences.

An area of much controversy in recent years is whether children who participate in violence, human rights abuses, and war crimes should be punished for their deeds. There are calls from the international community to prosecute these children as war criminals. Supporters of this position argue that regardless of age, whoever violates international law and commits war crimes must be brought to justice. In addition, many argue that prosecuting children may deter future youth violence in warfare. UN Secretary-General Kofi Annan supports this position and wants 15 to 18

year olds to be tried for war crimes in Sierra Leone. At the same time, human rights campaigners argue that punishing juvenile offenders will only prolong their suffering and possibly push them to more violence.

## RECENT HISTORY AND THE FUTURE

### The Future of Children in Combat: Good News and Bad

Depending on where you look, the future for preventing the involvement of children in warfare is encouraging. A global report on child soldiers published in 2001 notes that the situations in Latin America, the Balkan regions, and the Middle East are improving. Unfortunately, the report cautions that children in African countries face increased risk. Yet, even within Africa, areas of success are visible. In the spring of 2001 the SPLA in Sudan released 3,500 children to UNICEF, and in August 2001 all but 70 returned to their homes. The United Nations has been successful in requiring demobilization of children in cease-fire and peace agreements and most countries using children in combat are coming under stricter scrutiny by human rights organizations.

Another area of accomplishment comes in the form of international awareness. Because the headlines are full of stories about children in warfare, it has become an important international issue. A recent poll of Americans found that 75 percent of people surveyed felt that child survival should be both an American and an international priority. Furthermore, there are hundreds of international organizations and non-governmental organizations working on monitoring the use of children in warfare, negotiating their treatment while in combat, and assisting in their reintroduction to civilian life. Organizations like UNICEF, UNHCR (United Nations High Commissioner for Refugees), the International Committee for the Red Cross, the World Food Program, and the International Rescue Committee, as well as private groups like Save the Children and CARE, employ hundreds of doctors, counselors, and researchers to address this problem. The Deputy Director of UNICEF is cautiously optimistic, "Protection of children has finally made its way onto the global agenda... we have much more work to do to fully achieve it."

Just as the causes occur at many levels, so must the solutions. Attempts to eliminate this type of suffering are needed at the most local levels, as well as internationally. When children are taught warfare, it can become the only thing they know how to do. Unfortunately, their training can undermine cease-fires and youth can continue the violence. Michael Wessells writes in *The Bulletin of the Atomic Scientist* (November/December 1997), "A society that mobilizes and trains its young for war weaves violence into the fabric of life, increasing the likelihood that violence will be its future."

Children often prove themselves very adaptable. With medical attention, counseling, and vocational training, many former soldiers return to a normal life. In Sierra Leone, one representative from Amnesty International reports that "the majority of them have really improved... they are back in schools. Once they are in the right environment, we start to see the change very quickly."

Despite the increased awareness and development of legal instruments to ensure that children are not exploited by war, efforts fall short in several areas. The most discouraging element is the fact the many of the root causes of this issue are not being addressed. Poverty, hopelessness, lack of educational and professional opportunities, fear and hatred, ethnic suspicion, and the international sales of small arms are all part of the problem, and their eradication would contribute to the solution. As long as internal conflict continues to escalate in areas like the Middle East, Northern Ireland, and Sudan, the likelihood that children will be part of the violence remains high. Without attention at the source of internal warfare the cycle of violence that pulls children into battle and robs them of their innocence will continue.

# BIBLIOGRAPHY

Brett, Rachel, and Margaret McCallin. *Children: The Invisible Soldiers.* Vaxjo, Sweden: Swedish Save the Children, 1996.

Cairns, Ed. *Children and Political Violence.* Oxford: Blackwell, 1996.

"Child Soldier: A Global Report," 2001, The Coalition to Stop the Use of Child Soldiers. Available online at http://www.child-soldiers.org/ (cited December 29, 2001).

*Children of Sudan: Slaves , Street Children and Child Soldiers.* Human Rights Watch Children's Rights Project, 1995.

"Children of War: A Newsletter on Child Soldiers," from Rädda Barnen, Swedish Save the Children. Available online at http://www.rb.se/chilwar/ (cited October 15, 2001).

"Children Under Arms: Kalashnikov Kids," *Economist,* July 10, 1999, pp. 19–21.

Cockerill, A. W. *Sons of the Brave: The Story of Boy Soldiers.* London: Leo Cooper with Martin Secker & Warburg Ltd., 1984.

de Berry, Jo. "Child Soldiers and the Convention on the Rights of the Child," *Annals of the American Academy of Political and Social Science 575,* May 2001, pp. 92–105.

Farley, Maggie. "The World: Child Soldiers Used Widely," *Los Angeles Times,* June 13, 2001, p. A3.

"14 Girls Are Among 18 Tamil Rebels Slain in Sri Lanka," *Los Angeles Times,* December 25, 2000, p. A42.

Goodwill-Gill, Guy, and Ilene Cohn. *Child Soldiers: The Role of Children in Armed Conflicts.* Oxford: Clarendon, 1994.

Hazeley, Josephine, "Graca Machel: Children's Champion," *BBC News Online,* August 28, 2001. Available online at http://news.bbc.co.uk/hi/english/world/africa/newsid_1513000/1513267.stm (cited October 10, 2001).

Hick, Stephen. "The Political Economy of War-Effected Children," *Annals of the American Academy of Political and Social Science 575,* May 2001, pp.106–121.

"Hitler Youth," The History Place. Available online at http://www.historyplace.com/worldwar2/hitleryouth/index.html (cited December 28, 2001).

Jett, Dennis. "Ratify the Global Ban on Child Soldiers," *Christian Science Monitor,* June 4, 2001, pp. 9–10.

Kuper, Jenny. *International Law Concerning Child Civilians in Armed Conflict.* Oxford: Clarendon Press, 1997.

Machel, Graça. UNICEF, Information on "Report on the Impact of Armed Conflict on Children," United Nations General Assembly: A/51/306 Available online at http://www.unicef.org/graca/ (cited October 15, 2001).

Machel, Graça. "Report on the Impact of Armed Conflict on Children." Available online at http://www.un.org/rights/introduc.htm (cited October 10, 2001).

Masland, Tom. "Growing Up in Africa's Cruelest War Zone; How the School of Drugs, Rape and Terror Turns Young Kids into Fighters," *Newsweek,* July 9, 2001, p. 28.

McDowell, Robin. "Khmer Rouge Children's Text Has Lessons in War," *Seattle Times,* May 22, 1998. Available online at http://seattletimes.nwsource.com/news/nation-world/html98/altbook_052298.html (cited October 15, 2001).

Quato, Samir, Raija Punamaki, and Eyad el-Sarraj, "The Relations Between Traumatic Experiences, Activity, and Cognitive and Emotional Responses Among Palestinian Children," *International Journal of Psychology* 30, 1995, p. 291.

"Security Council Strongly Condemns Targeting of Children in Situations of Armed Conflict," United Nations Security Council Press Release SC/6716, 4037th Meeting, August 25, 1999.

Shanker, Thom. "Global Arms Sales Rise Again, and the U.S. Leads the Pack," *New York Times,* August 20, 2001, p. A3.

UNICEF, "Convention on the Rights of the Child." Available online at http://www.unicef.org/crc/crc.htm (cited October 15, 2001).

War Child, "Helping the Innocent Victims of War." Available online at http://www.warchild.org/aims.html (cited October 15, 2001).

Wessells, Michael. "Child Soldiers," *Bulletin of the Atomic Scientists,* 56 November/December 1997, pp. 32–40.

*Alynna J. Lyon*

# THE SANXIA (THREE GORGES) PROJECT IN CHINA: A CRISIS IN THE MAKING?

## THE CONFLICT

On the site of Sanxia (the Three Gorges) in western Hubei province China is in the process of building the largest and most powerful dam ever to be built. Proponents of the dam point out that it will bring a great deal of clean energy into many parts of China more cheaply than other means and that it will aid in preventing severe flood damage along the Chang (Yangtze) River. Opponents point out that the dam will eventually displace well over a million people, destroy majestic natural beauty that draws tourists to China, cost a great deal in time, money, and effort, and may not be effective in some of its primary functions. Since the project is already underway and probably will not now be stopped, opponents hope to convince the authorities to scale back on some of the dam's proportions and to use other technology along with the dam to achieve the best ends.

### Political
- Within China the Sanxia Dam has been seen as another attempt to rapidly catch up with developed nations and solve problems with a single grand project.

- It is almost impossible for public opinion in China to block a project if the leadership is in favor of it.

- Today forced relocations are the most sensitive issue connected with this mega-project.

### Economic
- Government estimates suggest that electricity generated by the dam will be cheaper than what could be generated from coal-fired plants but the method of measuring efficiency and costs are very limited and ignore essential elements.

- Although foreign media are able to publish the opposition's arguments, foreign governments are not trying to restrict investment in the project. With acid rain and global warming very much a concern of the developed nations, a hydroelectric dam begins to look more attractive.

- Sanxia is scheduled to cost about US$24 billion and could create greater economic strain.

On August 27, 2001, hundreds of migrants displaced by the giant Sanxia Dam clashed with police during a two-hour protest in Yongzhou city, Hunan province, China. A batch of newly arrived migrants displaced from the dam's reservoir area took to the streets to protest resettlement subsidy payments. Scuffles broke out when police were brought in to control them. Several police officers were injured when a handful of protesters became violent, although no arrests were reported and train service was not disrupted. Thus, this was just a small event in the big picture of life in China and the huge problems surrounding the Sanxia Dam.

"Sanxia" is often directly translated as the Three Gorges. The name refers to three separate gorges that extend for 200 kilometers (124 miles) along the Chang (Yangtze) River in western Hubei province. The Three Gorges are internationally renowned for their scenic beauty and have been a major draw to tourists for many years. The Chang is China's longest river—the third longest in the world. At completion, the dam that is being built there will be the largest hydroelectric station in the world, capable of generating 17,680 megawatts of electricity (as compared to the current largest hydroelectric plant, the Brazilian Itaipu Dam, which can produce 12,600 megawatts of power). Construction of the Sanxia includes building a 400-mile-long (645 kilometers) reservoir that will submerge cities and villages and displace well over a million people. This project will take approximately 20 years and cost upwards of US$24 billion.

The scale of the dam is remarkable in size and effort. The Sanxia will become the world's largest dam in terms of volume of concrete work, which,

# CHRONOLOGY

*1911* The Republic of China is founded.

*1921* The idea of building a dam in the Sanxia appears in *The International Development of China* by Sun Yat-sen.

*1933* Huanglingmiao near Sandouping is selected as an ideal location for a hydroelectric project.

*1944* The chief design engineer of the United States Bureau of Reclamation, John L. Savage, organizes a Chinese and American joint research group, which concludes that the Sanxia area would be ideal for a multipurpose dam.

*1949* The People's Republic of China is founded when the communists win their war against the nationalists.

*1953* Chairman Mao Zedong states: "After expending so much effort constructing reservoirs on tributaries and still not reaching our goal of stopping floods, why not concentrate all our efforts and block it at Sanxia?"

*1954* Major floods occur on the Chang River.

*1955–57* A Chinese-Soviet joint survey of the Chang River valley takes place.

*1958–60* Mao Zedong and his administration initiate the Great Leap Forward, an attempt to spur the economic and technical development of the country at a rapid pace, which results in mass starvation and the collapse of the economy.

*1966–74* Mao initiates the Cultural Revolution, his mass movement to cleanse Chinese communism, eliminate bourgeois values, punish those who have criticized his policy, and fortify his own power base in China. Half a million people are estimated killed.

*1979* The site for the Sanxia Dam is reconfirmed as Sandouping.

*1985* A preliminary design report for the dam is completed and the project is scheduled to begin in 1986.

*1988* Controversial research reports are submitted to the State Council.

*1989* The Sanxia Dam project is shelved after heated debate in the National People's Congress.

*1991* Major floods on the Chang River kill thousands and displace millions.

*1992* The Sanxia project is formally approved.

*1996* The Sanxia Airport and major transport links are opened.

*1997* Chongqing City is split off from Sichuan province and the Chang River is cut for construction.

*August 27, 2001* Hundreds of migrants displaced by the dam clash with police during a two-hour protest in Yongzhou city, Hunan province, just one of many such protests by the displaced.

*2002* The reservoir is scheduled to begin filling.

*2003* The first generator is to be in place.

*2009* The dam is to be completed.

at completion, will be 185 meters (607 feet) high and 1,983 meters (6,500 feet) wide, with a final reservoir surface area of 1,060 square kilometers (409 square miles), a capacity of 39,300 million cubic meters (51,365 cubic yards), and a maximum flow rate of 100,000 cubic meters per second. The work is already well along in progress. In autumn 1997 the walls rose to 90 meters high and severed the Chang River. The reservoir is scheduled to begin filling sometime in 2002; the first generator is to be in place in 2003; and the dam is to be completed in 2009, with reservoir water reaching its final level in 2010 and all debts repaid by 2012.

The protests and opposition to the dam, such as that in Hunan province, have become increasingly common as construction of the dam has proceeded since 1994. Today, forced relocations of people living in the vicinity of the construction are among the most sensitive issues connected with this mega-project. Although corruption cases related to the project remain a taboo in the mainland Chinese media, accounts still appear about

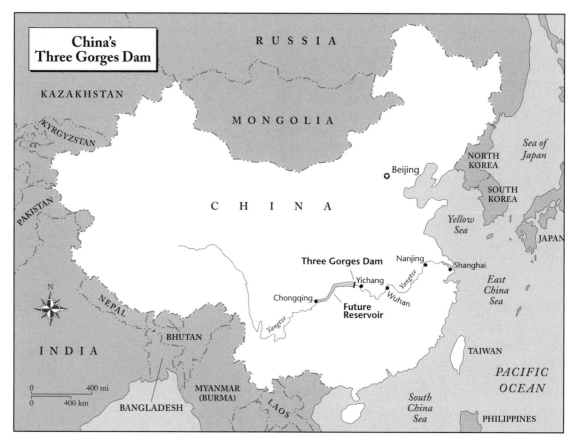

MAP OF THE AREA AFFECTED BY THE THREE GORGES DAM IN CHINA. *(The Gale Group.)*

protests by disgruntled migrants. They often focus on migrants finding themselves cheated after arriving at their new homes. Many have found the compensation far less than promised and they suspect the resettlement funds have been pocketed by local officials.

In China, public argument over the building of the Sanxia Dam has been limited by the lack of a free press and the possibility of censure. Thus most of the opposition has been centered overseas. Within China the Sanxia Dam can be seen as another attempt to rapidly catch up with developed nations and solve problems with a single grand project, as occurred during the Great Leap Forward of the late 1950s and early 1960s. That attempt to industrialize China overnight ended in failure, environmental degradation, and famine. Scholars have referred to China's mega-scheme drive as a "Great Wall mentality"—a Chinese and a communist fascination with making risky gambles in planning decisions out of desperation. Opponents argued that, with the possibilities for irreparable damage due to natural causes and/or

mismanagement so great, it was dangerous to proceed with this huge project.

Along with the great issue of resettlement, opponents have many concerns about the technical feasibility of the project regarding flood control, energy supply, navigation, water supply, and environmental damage. The Chinese leadership of the early 1990s, however, proceeded with the long-debated project, preferring to appear to be doing something spectacular about flooding and energy shortages and in giving China something they felt would be a positive legacy than to err on the side of caution.

## HISTORICAL BACKGROUND

The idea of building a dam in the Sanxia first appeared in *The International Development of China* by Sun Yat-sen (1866–1925), one of the founders of the Republic of China. Since the 1930s the Sanxia area was surveyed by Chinese, Soviet, and American engineers, and arguments about whether or not to develop the dam have been continuous.

Intensified investigations into building the dam at Sanxia have often been triggered by major floods that occur in the area from time to time. This appeared to be the case when massive flooding in the Chang River valley in 1931 was responsible for the deaths of 140,000 people. The ensuing investigation resulted in a 1933 team finding Gezhouba and Huanglingmiao to be the best locations on the Chang River for hydroelectric projects because of steep gorges and their central location. Gezhouba is the site of the current Gezhouba Dam, 24 miles downstream from the Three Gorges, and Huanglingmiao is only a few kilometers to the east of the current Sanxia Dam site.

In 1944 Chief Design Engineer of the United States Bureau of Reclamation John Lucian Savage organized a Chinese and American joint research group that concluded that the Sanxia area would be ideal for the world's largest multipurpose dam. An American economic adviser, G.R. Passhal, also urged construction of a hydroelectric project at the site. After the communist victory in the Chinese Civil War in 1949, the Chinese unit that had been involved in the investigative work with Savage went on to become the Chang River Valley Planning Office. This office was the primary think tank for dam development along the river.

## The New People's Republic of China and the Dam

After flooding on the Chang River in 1949 the central government ordered research to begin on a dam in 1951. In 1953 Communist Party Chairman and Chinese leader Mao Zedong (1893–1976) stated: "After expending so much effort constructing reservoirs on tributaries and still not reaching our goal of stopping floods, why not concentrate all our efforts and block it at Sanxia?" After more floods in 1954 the pace of research accelerated, and the government decided to devise a comprehensive plan for the river. Between 1955 and 1957 a team surveyed the Chang River valley with Soviet help. The debate on whether the dam should be built had appeared in the press by 1956, with the vice minister of electric power, Li Rui, leading the opposition to the dam and the head of the Chang River Valley Planning Office taking the position of leading advocate.

The project was actually accepted as a long-term planning goal in the mid-1950s. In March 1958 the Communist Party, under the guidance of Zhou Enlai (1898–1976), decided to proceed with preliminary design work on a 190- to 200-meter dam. Instead of pushing ahead with Sanxia, Mao Zedong decided to proceed with the smaller Danjiangkou Dam on the Han River, a tributary.

## Lengthy Delays in the Mega-Project

From 1960 onwards, efforts to begin construction of the Sanxia Dam were halted by China's economic collapse in the aftermath of Mao's Great Leap Forward (1958–60) and the Cultural Revolution (1966–74). Sino-Soviet military tension in 1969–70 also affected plans for the dam because it was thought that the Soviets would make it a target should war break out. Reservoir siltation (a build-up of sediment that can block or clog or otherwise damage the dam or its proper functioning) of the Sanmenxia Dam on the Huang River, ecological problems caused by the Aswan Dam on the Nile River, and lower-than-planned power generation rates from both dams also discouraged the Chinese from taking up the Sanxia project.

The decision to build the Gezhouba Dam 24 miles downstream, however, did go forward in order to appease pro-Sanxia interests in Hubei. Because of the Cultural Revolution and problems with design, the Gezhouba Dam was not begun until 1970 and not finally completed until 1989. Coming in at a cost close to twice what was originally projected, the Gezhouba Dam did not set a good precedent.

## Renewed Interest under Deng Xiaoping

With the return to emphasis on economic development after 1978, the Sanxia project again came to prominence after close to two decades of obscurity. In 1979 the site for the dam was reconfirmed as Sandouping, and proponents almost succeeded in launching the project, with work scheduled to begin within two or three years. Again, however, government leaders urged caution.

In the summer of 1980 Chinese leader Deng Xiaoping (1904–97) visited the site and encouraged research on Sanxia. Various foreign groups, particularly the Americans, began to become involved in the project. Brazil tried to promote its skills from the Itaipu Dam and the Chinese government attempted to get both Japan and Canada actively involved. In 1986 the Canadian International Development Agency helped finance a feasibility study. The terms of reference for this study indicated that its main purpose was to secure foreign financial support. Delegations from Sweden, Belgium, Singapore, and Hong Kong also visited the site and held discussions on the project. Securing of loans was as important in these efforts to involve foreigners as was obtaining expertise.

In 1984 a meeting was called that concurred with a report written by the Chang River Valley Planning Office stating that a dam at Sanxia with a reservoir height of 150 meters (492 feet) was feasible. The State Council made Li Peng (1928–; later premier of China and chair of the National People's Congress) responsible for the Sanxia Dam. By 1985 a preliminary design report was completed. The project was to be included in the Seventh Five-Year Plan (1986–90) with construction to begin in 1986. But an internal document from 1985 recommended that construction of the dam be excluded from the Seventh Five-Year Plan because it would not be cost effective and might cause natural or military disasters. Despite final exclusion from the plan, high-rise worker housing was built, along with a road linking the south bank of the Sandouping site to Gezhouba.

The urgency for construction was again felt in November 1986 after the State Council issued a directive for further discussion of the project and set up the Sanxia Construction Discussion Leading Group to write reports on aspects of the project. When these research reports were submitted to the State Council in 1988, 10 out of the 412 specialists involved in research for the Leading Group had refused to sign their reports largely for environmental reasons. The project was shelved in the spring of 1989 after heated debate in the National People's Congress.

### 1991 Floods Prod Action

In July 1990 the State Council set up a special committee to study the issue. Then, in June 1991 devastating floods left 10 million people homeless along the Chang River and brought the issue to the fore. At the time of the floods an article appeared in the Communist Party ideological magazine by a former Minister of Water Conservancy praising the accomplishments of the party in water management. This article came under attack in the Taiwan and Hong Kong press, which placed the blame for the floods on the Communist Party. Party Secretary Jiang Zemin's statement made during his late June 1991 visits to the flood districts—"If we rely on the party's leadership, if we rely on the socialist system, then we certainly can defeat natural disasters"—also came under particular criticism.

Using the 1991 floods as a case in point, hydraulic engineers in mainland China were able to suggest that there was a need for investment in all sorts of water conservancy projects including large dams. Hard-line proponents strengthened their stance and those sitting on the fence came

over to their side. In July 1991 the project was probably approved at a key meeting held in Beijing.

While there was considerable debate within the bureaucracy, in general Chinese leaders have been behind the dam, whereas much of the opposition has come from technical experts and intellectuals. The arrest of dissidents in the aftermath of the Tiananmen incident of the summer of 1989, in which the army brutally crushed a pro-democracy demonstration, helped to reduce open opposition to the project. Since that time the press favored articles promoting the dam whereas negative opinions appeared less often. Opposition to the dam from abroad virtually never appears in the Chinese press. By the late 1990s the opposition movement had cooled, although reports of problems with construction and resettlement continue to appear in the foreign press and groups have effectively worked to block foreign loans for construction.

### A Controversial Approval of the Project

The formal beginning for the project was on April 3, 1992, when the Chinese National People's Congress passed the Sanxia Key Water Control Project. Although slightly over two-thirds of the delegates voted for the project, the record-breaking number voting against or abstaining represented far greater opposition than the ratio suggests, especially when one considers that the prior function of the congress had been to automatically approve all that was put before it. Thus even the approval of the project was controversial. Open opposition at the National People's Congress included the unprecedented walk-out by two delegates.

From the founding of the People's Republic in 1949 to the time the dam received approval, the Chang River Valley Planning Office, the Ministry of Water Conservancy, State Planning Commission, and downstream provinces have generally supported the Sanxia project. The Ministry of Electric Power, the Ministry of Communications, and Sichuan province have generally opposed it. Sichuan, which used to include Chongqing Municipality, was always cool towards the Sanxia project because it was to receive only 10 percent of the hydroelectric output, even though it was home to 85 percent of the people to be relocated, whereas downstream provinces will receive a considerable amount of the power and Hubei only has to move 15 percent of the reservoir population. Problems resolving these various bureaucratic differences helped make it difficult for the central government to come down firmly in favor of the project prior to the 1990s.

# LI PENG

*1928–* Probably more than any other modern-day figure, Li Peng, the Chinese premier from 1987 to 1998 and then leader of the National People's Congress, has been the Sanxia Dam's primary advocate. Either success or failure of the dam will probably be credited more to him than anyone else, and this association has added to the politicization of the construction of the dam.

Li was born in 1928 in Sichuan province. Three years after Li's birth, his father was executed by Chiang Kai-shek's nationalist government for participating in a communist uprising. Li was then adopted by communist leader Zhou Enlai (1898–1976; later premier, foreign minister, and leading statesman in the People's Republic of China). Li joined the Communist Party in his late teens. In 1948, just before the communists drove the nationalists out of mainland China, Li was sent to Russia (then the Soviet Union) to study at the Moscow Power Institute, where he specialized in hydroelectric engineering. When he returned to China in 1955, he went to work as the deputy director of a hydroelectric plant. He went on to other managerial positions in power projects throughout China.

In 1976 Zhou Enlai, Li's adoptive father, died, but Zhou's widow maintained influence in the party and used it to help promote Li. In 1979 he became deputy minister of the power industry and two years later he became its minister. In 1982 Li joined the Communist Party Central Committee. He was elected to the Politburo and became the Party Secretariat in 1985. In 1988 Chinese President Deng Xiaoping (1904–97) chose Li as prime minister of China, to take the place of Zhao Ziyang, who resigned from the post to become party general secretary. By this time, Li was already known for taking the orthodox communist hard line on most issues, supporting a strong centralized government and economy. He also supported Deng's desire to see the mammoth dam at Sanxia underway.

As Li took his position as premier, student protests had begun to erupt throughout the country. In May 1989, more than a million people gathered in Tiananmen Square in Beijing in a student-led demonstration seeking political reform. China's leaders debated about taking action for three weeks, with the party secretary Zhao Ziyang sympathizing with the students. Li, on the other hand, called for martial law on May 20. When the demonstrators continued, he advocated a military strike to clear Tiananmen Square. President Deng went along with Li. The Chinese army's brutal massacre of demonstrators took place on June 4, with thousands of casualties. Zhao Ziyang was dismissed from his position as party secretary and arrested.

On the heels of Tiananmen, the decision whether or not to move forward on the dam at Sanxia arose again. Public debate on this issue had been banned after the Tiananmen incident, but there was a great deal of disagreement among Communist Party leaders. In spite of strong opposition, Li Peng pushed the decision through. When it finally came to a vote in 1992 in the National People's Congress, one-third either abstained from voting or voted against building the dam.

Li served two five-year terms as premier. In 1998 Zhu Rongji, a reform-oriented leader, replaced him in that position and became responsible for the Three Gorges Dam. Li became the leader of the National People's Congress, the number two position under President Jiang Zemin. Although Li Peng is viewed with distrust by many Chinese people, he remains a powerful leader representing the hard-line communists who oppose the globalization and Westernization taking place under Zhu.

In 1998, flooding once again beset the Yangtze River, and Zhu, either as a political attack on his predecessor or out of real concern about the potential for disaster, publicly raised his concerns about the dam. Zhu fired 100 officials for alleged corruption and called in foreign experts to monitor the dam. Since then, more criticism of the project has arisen in public forums, but the work continues. President Jiang Zemin allows the two factions, the hard-liners under Li and the reformers under Zhu, to play against each other in this as in many other Chinese issues.

---

Some bureaucratic changes accompanied the construction efforts after 1992. In 1994 the State Council approved the establishment of a Sanxia Open Economic Zone with all the priorities given to special economic zones, which to that point had all been located on the east coast. Several cities along the river were designated as "open cities." Preliminary transport links into the area were completed in mid-1996 and China opened the Sanxia Airport, located about 30 miles, or 48 kilo-

# DAI QING: OUTSPOKEN OPPONENT OF THE SANXIA DAM PROJECT

In 1986 a group of Chinese scientists traveled to the Three Gorges to examine the site for dam construction. After their inspection, all of these scientists opposed the building of the dam. They organized a meeting in Beijing to voice their findings, but the Chinese government told the media not to cover it. By chance, journalist Dai Qing with the Communist Party-operated *Guangming Daily* was the only reporter there. At that time she knew nothing about the project at Sanxia and had not been assigned to cover the meeting, but the words of the scientists were deeply compelling to her. Later she traveled to Hong Kong and learned much more about the Three Gorges Dam project and from that time she began to receive all articles written about the dam in the Hong Kong papers. As the Chinese government convened to decide whether or not to begin construction on the dam, Dai was greatly concerned that almost no one in China had ever heard about the potential disadvantages of the dam that were well known in other countries.

Dai felt that the public should have all sides before a decision was made on Sanxia. She and several other respected journalists interviewed the opposing scientists and then tried to publish the 22 resulting essays and interviews in Chinese magazines. None would touch the interviews. After much difficulty, the interviews she had compiled were published as the book *Yangtze! Yangtze!* in March 1989. The book immediately made a very big splash. Even though the press had been instructed not to report on it, more than a dozen Chinese newspapers, including *People's Daily*, *Guangming Daily*, and the *World Economic Herald*, did so. The book, quickly running through several printings, played a large hand in influencing the decision then made by government ministers to delay the project at Sanxia. Despite its huge readership, *Yangtze! Yangtze!* was banned by the government that same year.

At that time, pro-democracy sentiments were simmering throughout China. Student protests had been going on for several years. In June 1989 came the infamous military assault by the Chinese government on demonstrators in Tiananmen Square in Beijing. Dai resigned from the Communist Party and shortly afterward was arrested and spent 10 months in prison. She believes this was because of her book. After Tiananmen Square, the government allowed no public debate on the dam.

After her release from prison in 1990, Dai studied at Harvard University, Columbia University, and the Australian National University. She then returned to China, where she continues to write. A second work on Sanxia, *The River Dragon Has Come,* was published in 1998. She has been blacklisted by the Chinese government and lives under police surveillance, but has committed herself to a relentless campaign to stop—or at least to reduce the scale of—the ongoing construction of the dam at Sanxia. In her second book she calls the dam "the most environmentally and socially destructive project in the world." Although the cause she has taken up is an environmental one, Dai did not start out with that orientation. In an interview with the Environmental News Service, she said: "I always thought of myself as a human rights activist, particularly a free speech activist. Had there been free press, the opinions of the scientists who were opposed to the Three Gorges Dam would have been made public without my involvement."

meters, from the dam, on December 29, 1996. In 1997 Chongqing City was split off from Sichuan province and turned into China's fourth national-level municipality. This was done to appease Chongqing, as well as to give the central government more leverage in local affairs.

In December 1998 Premier Zhu Rongji visited the dam site and made a speech in which he said: "We must adopt effective measures and use any and all means to ensure its engineering quality, and we must not relax our efforts in the slight-est degree." Zhu also stated: "We may hire well-known, reputable, and experienced foreign supervision and inspection corporations to take part in supervising and inspecting certain important segments of the project." These statements were made in light of slip-shod construction on several projects, including a bridge in the Chongqing area that had collapsed due to corrupt building practices.

Most opponents of the project knew that the National People's Congress approval was an auto-

CHINA'S THREE GORGES DAM, OR SANXIA, ON THE YANGTZE RIVER, IS SET TO BE COMPLETED IN 2009, AT A COST OF $24.5 BILLION. *(A/P Wide World. Reproduced by permission.)*

matic affair. It has been suggested that the project had been approved in all but name before the congress met and that the decision was made solely by the Ministry of Water Conservancy. The former vice minister of electric power, many senior scientists, and some journalists spoke out against the project prior to approval. Despite this, the ambition to build a super dam on the Chang River is deeply rooted in the psyche of those wishing to rapidly develop China. This group includes many government officials, engineers, and scientists.

The arguments opposing construction of the dam concentrated on several key technical questions: flood control, energy supply, navigation, and water supply. Since construction began there has been much debate over the feasibility of resettlement of population out of the area to be flooded and whether the reservoir height should be lowered.

### Flood Protection

The Sanxia Dam will provide flood protection for people living downstream of it. On account of the serious flooding in 1991, this became the official main reason for launching the project. Flooding has been costly to China throughout the ages and it is suggested that the dam will be able to control all but the most serious of flood conditions below the dam. Prior to 1950 flooding in the Chang River valley was less frequent than in the

Huang River (Yellow River) valley in northern China. Chang River flooding, however, became quite serious during the 1980s.

Flood control in the valley is not easy. When waters rush through tributary catchments they transport large amounts of eroded granite rubble, which is deposited on the streambeds that become prone to flooding. As a result the lower Chang River bed has risen, and lakes throughout the valley saw their navigable area shrink due to siltation from their tributary rivers and from misguided policy which forced peasants to fill in lakes and create crop land during the Maoist period (1950–76). This reduced the river system's flood control capacity.

Moreover, the level of flooding during the summer of 1991 was made more severe by the acceleration of human-induced deforestation, soil erosion, silt deposition, and lack of investment in agricultural infrastructure and flood control in the 1980s. In 1991 the Minister of Water Conservancy and Electric Power said that one-third of the large and medium-sized reservoirs in China had problems caused by siltation and lack of proper management.

From late June to mid-July 1991, heavy rains fell in the central Chang River valley on three occasions. Flooding in central portions of the valley got worse as water seemed to be backing right

MANY TOWNS AND SIGHTS OF HISTORIC AND CULTURAL VALUE, SUCH AS THE GHOST TEMPLE IN FENGDU, SICHUAN, WILL BE FLOODED ONCE THE THREE GORGES DAM IS COMPLETE. (© AFP/Corbis. *Reproduced by permission.*)

up the river. Tributaries burst their banks while reservoirs and lakes overflowed. The official death toll reached 3,074 by mid-September. Direct loss estimates from the flooding by mid-September totaled a figure equal to about one-quarter of the total Chinese budget for 1991. The situation on the Chang River has continued to be serious, with major flooding in 1995, 1996, and 1998.

While opponents to the Sanxia Dam do not often argue against the dam's having flood control potential, they note that flood control would only be relevant to the area directly below the dam because there are a considerable number of tributaries that enter the Chang River in the middle and lower reaches. Therefore, what occurred downstream in the summer of 1991 would repeat itself even with the dam. In addition, major rainstorms upstream could fill the reservoir and lead to a flooding of Chongqing.

It has been noted that clear water releases from the dam could lead to undercutting of dikes downstream, in turn leading to an increased bur-

den of dike maintenance. Thus it has been suggested that raised dikes on lower portions of the river combined with several dams on tributaries would be a far more effective means of flood control.

Opponents of the Sanxia project continue to point out that there is a degree of mutual exclusion between a flood-prevention dam and a power-generating dam. A dam used for hydropower generation should have its reservoir largely full of water, whereas one used mostly for flood control should be kept close to empty. Flood prevention capabilities could be sacrificed for hydroelectric power despite statements that over half the reservoir capacity is earmarked for flood prevention.

### Hydroelectric Power Generation

The Sanxia Dam is expected to have a 17,680 megawatt generating capacity, making it the world's largest hydroelectric generating plant. Two turbines are slated to begin generating electricity in 2003. When completed, 26 turbines would generate 84,000 million kilowatt hours, the equivalent of fourteen 1,200 megawatt thermal power plants. Estimates of the government suggest that electricity generated by the dam will be cheaper than what could be generated from coal-fired plants.

While the coal reserves of China are significant, supporters stressed that China would find it virtually impossible to meet its future planned energy needs simply by expanding coal production or nuclear power. It was thought that other plans for hydropower generation would not provide enough electricity to meet targets without the Sanxia Dam. The dam site in Hubei is seen as a good one for distribution of electricity up and down the valley as well as north to Beijing and south to Guangzhou and has been part and parcel of China's plans to develop the interior by expansion westward along the Chang River valley.

Most supporters favored building a dam at Sanxia first and then building a series of dams on the tributaries. Supporters believed that building a large dam at Sanxia was more cost effective than building a series of small dams on tributaries upstream. Efficiency was measured solely in terms of cost per kilowatt hour of power versus excavation and concrete costs. The projections that suggest that one large dam will generate electricity more economically, ignore many positive aspects of building smaller dams, particularly in terms of ecological and aesthetic losses. Furthermore, as the construction time for smaller dams is much shorter than for the Sanxia Dam, China could recoup costs more quickly.

Opponents of the Sanxia Dam have doubts about its cost effectiveness in terms of electricity potential. Power will be transmitted over great distances to reach the energy-deficient east coast. Considerable amounts of power will be lost in transmission. For the electricity to be used locally or upstream, the upper valley must quickly develop to the same economic level as the lower valley, which seems highly unlikely despite preferential policies.

## Navigation and Siltation

The Chang River contains many rapids from its central reaches upstream, so it is possible only for small cargo boats to reach Chongqing. Between 1950 and 1985 work was done on over 110 shoals and rapids to increase the water depth in the Chongqing area to allow larger boats access, but it remains quite limited. With the Sanxia Dam reservoir pool's normal level at a 175-meter (574-foot) elevation, the large tows will be able to travel the 400 miles (644 kilometers) upstream to just beyond the city of Chongqing for more than half of the year and many other tows carrying significant loads will be able to get there year-round. In addition, ships will need to use less fuel going to Chongqing in the reservoir rather than fighting their way up a river.

Downstream of the Sanxia Dam there will be navigation benefits, as boats will be able to go upstream to the dam site in the dry season. The navigation factor came into play in late June 1992 when it was announced that all administrative units along the Chang River, including those in Sichuan, would be opened to foreign trade for the first time since 1949. Thus, the potential for additional domestic traffic upstream to Chongqing is also great.

But there are major concerns about the siltification—the building up of sediments that will change water levels, causing flooding and severe damage. Supporters of the project know that worries about the dam's reservoir silting up are justified. This is especially true in the location between the dam and Chongqing, where the water level changes often, the river meanders, and movement of the silt is complex. The official view, however, is that siltation will not be a problem with the Sanxia reservoir because the water level in the reservoir can be altered to flush out much of the silt buildup by keeping the water level at 145 meters (476 feet) during high-water and silt-depositing season (June–September).

Once the high waters have passed, the reservoir can begin to be filled for the coming dry season. In the following April, towards the end of the dry season, the water level can attain at least 155 meters (509 feet) and then be dropped ten meters (33 feet) in order to flush the silt that has built up over the winter. After a century or so, when the silt load reaches its dead storage volume, the depth of water at the tail-end of the reservoir should still be three meters, which will allow shipping to continue to reach Chongqing as planned. This solution is subject to the incoming silt load remaining more or less stable.

Opponents of the dam suggest that if the silt loads in the Chang River continue to increase, a reservoir on the order of 175 meters will not keep bed load sediments low in the Chongqing area, even with the flushing techniques proposed. The buildup of silt upstream would lead to increased flooding above the dam. There are also worries of silt building up where tributaries flow into the reservoir, which increases flood problems along the tributaries, and of fine silt piling up in the locks. If silt piles up at the base of the dam, opponents claim that the accumulated pressure could cause the dam to burst. Aside from siltation worries upstream in the reservoir and at the dam site, there is also the potential of siltation downstream. Even if much of the silt is deposited upstream, the slower flow of the river might lead to silt being deposited in places downstream where it previously wasn't deposited or in being lifted in places where it used to be deposited.

Again, the siltation arguments are largely conjecture which depend on various factors not directly connected with the dam construction at Sanxia, such as the conservation and deforestation rate upstream and construction of smaller dams on tributaries. While supporters place confidence in the models of siltation done for Sanxia and point out that models for some other major dams built in China were roughly accurate, one must doubt the ability of such models to predict siltation levels, given all the unknown factors involved.

Also, the project has built five sets of locks for ships to be get past the Sanxia Dam. With five sets of locks, the chances of a lock failure are significantly increased. There is no existing dam in the world with such a complex set of locks.

## Water Supply

Those arguing for the dam also note the 16,500 million cubic meters of water storage capacity of the reservoir will facilitate plans for further south-north water transfers from the middle Chang River valley to the North China Plain and thus allow for irrigation of an additional 10 million acres of farm land. The 175-meter reservoir height will allow water to flow northeast under the central China water diversion plan, which has been approved. In addition, downstream pumping of water along the Grand Canal to the North China Plain along the eastern China diversion route, which has also been approved, will be steadier in the dry season as the dam releases stored water. Opponents of the Sanxia Dam tend to be equally opposed to any long distance water transfers on ecological and cost efficiency grounds.

### Population Transfers

Resettlement of the reservoir population will be the key to the political success or failure of the Sanxia project. It is estimated that 1.13 million people will have to be relocated by 2008 (although, as of 2001, the project is far short of this goal). A total of 19 county-level units including 140 market towns, 11 county seats, and the county-level municipalities of Wan Xian and Fuling, hundreds of factory and mining sites and power stations as well as 600 miles (966 kilometers)of roads are to end up under water. Proponents had argued that the Sanxia area was the most ideal site for a dam along the river from the point of view of population transfers. Since the future reservoir is in a deep gorge, they say, this site involves minimal movement of people. It is said by opponents, on the other hand, that the choice of the reservoir was not good, as this area is the most densely populated portion of China's hilly area.

Opposition to the dam today concentrates on trying to get the reservoir height reduced, since the project as a whole is already underway. The smallest sized dam considered just prior to approval was 140 meters (459 feet). Such a dam would have only required displacement of about 200,000 people, but the idea was abandoned because it would have a far lower hydroelectric generating potential, an increased unit cost of production, and a lowered flood control capacity.

As rural incomes rise, so have compensation costs. Opponents point out that of the ten million people who have been relocated due to dam construction in China since 1950, approximately one-third are still extremely poor and short of food—dam construction has not helped them at all. The addition of another million-plus relocated people from the Sanxia reservoir area could add as many problems as it solves.

Population transfer experiments began in 1985 before the dam was approved. Traditionally Chinese peasants resist moving and identify with place. Such attachment has made movement of large numbers of ever more vociferous peasants very difficult.

### Landslides and Earthquakes

One contention connected with the project is that it could induce landslides and earthquakes in the reservoir area. Landslides or earthquakes induced by the large reservoir could threaten the dam directly or through wave surges. Some pro-Sanxia scientists have stated that even multiple landslides into the reservoir could not cause a serious enough wave surge to damage the dam. They also claim that areas where landslides are likely to occur are far away from the dam. Supporters had gone so far as to say that, without the wide Sanxia reservoir, the threat of landslides blocking the river were greater. One can find papers stating that the geological conditions at Sanxia are very good.

Opponents note that landslides have been common in the reservoir area. It has been postulated that a rise in the water table caused by the reservoir could trigger landslides. Some say there is remote sensing data to suggest that further rockslides are likely. Contrary to what some supporters say, opponents point out that there are three geological fault belts near the reservoir area and that earthquakes greater than 4.75 on the Richter scale have been recorded in the reservoir area 21 times, with the greatest reaching 6.5. It is said that increased pressure upon the bottom of the new reservoir could cause stronger earthquakes and there is evidence to suggest that more than 80 large and medium reservoirs around the world have induced this type of earthquake.

### Ecological, Agricultural, Historical, and Tourism Issues

Supporters and opponents of the dam make only modest attempts to base their case around ecological issues, in part because the facts are not known and hard to quantify. However, supporters confidently note that environmental research on the project began in the 1950s with further studies conducted down to today. They point out that the amount of water being stored in the reservoir is only 4.5 percent of the total river flow through the Sanxia area, thus suggesting the environmental impact will not be that great. Air pollution along with water pollution from slag that would have been generated by coal-fired power plants will be avoided. Proper management of water releases should eliminate any worries about salinization (the water becoming full of salt) at the river's mouth. Although ecological damage will occur, according to the official government view, other ecological benefits will outweigh that damage.

In addition, supporters say that as only four percent of the land to be flooded is plains, the loss of good agricultural land will not be as serious as it could be elsewhere. Losses to downstream agriculture due to reduction of nutrient-rich silt loads would be minimal as most irrigation water downstream comes from tributaries. From the public health point of view there is little evidence to suggest that the reservoir will create many new shallow bays that could serve as breeding grounds of snails or mosquitoes so that worries of increased parasitic diseases are unfounded.

Both supporters and tour guides today state that the new landscape formed by the reservoir will be just as beautiful as the current one. The reservoir would have great commercial fish-raising potential and might increase the aquatic wildlife variety. The increased size of the water body will also have a positive effect on microclimate. Some of the peaks within the reservoir area will become islands with possibilities for tourism. Many historical artifacts, which are now located underneath the new water level, can be moved to such higher locations adding to the tourism potential of the remaining area.

In contrast, opponents of the project feel it will have an overall negative effect on local agriculture and fishing. It is estimated that nearly 59,000 acres of cropland and over 12,000 acres of orange groves will be under water. Opponents point out that losses from rich alluvial fields to be flooded cannot easily be compensated for by the new, less fertile lands proposed for settlement. Resettled peasants are farming on steeper slopes higher up the hillsides where there is considerable potential for increase of soil erosion. If the water level in the Chang River is raised during the winter and spring, soils, especially in central Hubei, could become swamp-like and gleyed (forming a sticky clay-like soil under the waterlogged surface), leading to reduced agricultural production in waterlogged fields. Irrigation with colder water from the reservoir could affect crop growth. Fish-breeding grounds will also change along the river, probably for the worse.

Much of the negative impact cannot be measured in economic terms. Unique scenery, habitats of animals, and historic sites are being destroyed. Economically speaking, opponents feel the reservoir will destroy more tourist attractions than it will create. There are also worries about the effect of the dam on climate, the creation of disease-favorable habitats, especially for malaria and schistosomiasis, pollution from submerged mines, industrialization, and slowed flow in the reservoir

THE THREE GORGES DAM IS DESIGNED TO CONTROL THE FLOODING OF THE YANGTZE RIVER. UPON COMPLETION, IT WILL BE THE LARGEST DAM IN THE WORLD. *(A/P Wide World. Reproduced by permission.)*

area, and other impacts on ecosystems along the river's course and in the East China Sea.

In particular there are worries about the future of some forms of wildlife—including 18 special types of upstream fish as well as the Yangzi sturgeon (*Acipensel sinensis*), the Yangzi dolphin (*Lipotes vexillifer*), the Chinese sucker (*Myxocyprinus asiaticus*), the grenadier or samli fish (*Macrura reevesii*) and the Siberian crane (*Grus leucogeranus*). The colder water temperatures in the reservoir are sure to affect fish breeding. An increase in boats brought on by improved navigation, blockage of migration routes for fish upon which they feed, or changes in the riverbed could further reduce their small numbers. Some marine life that prefer the current semi-saline environment at the mouth of the river could be harmed by the flow rate and nearby fishing banks could be affected.

No one knows for sure how serious environmental damage will be. For example, a slowed flow rate should also reduce natural oxidation of the river water and the ability of the Chang River to flush out pollutants. It could also result in land being lost through coastal erosion, although the counter argument suggests that considerable silt from downstream tributaries will still reach the river's mouth. As experiments cannot predict exactly what will happen there is no way the supporters can assure the opposition that such negative ecological consequences will not occur.

### Strategic Concerns

At the time of the Persian Gulf War in 1991, a famous Chinese scientist, Qian Weichang, stated that the Sanxia Dam should not proceed until the international world order was stable enough to insure that no foreign power would try to blow it up. Although Geneva protocols prohibit destruction of dams, they still remain a common military target. Opponents feel such issues have been generally neglected in favor of direct economic benefits such as power generation and irrigation water storage.

Supporters say the dam is safe from attack provided necessary precautions are taken. The Chinese government has conducted tests on models of the dam at their Lop Nur nuclear testing site since the 1950s. In official sources it was stated that the reinforced concrete used for the dam will have properties that help it to resist damage in an attack, and all that will be necessary is to lower the reservoir level to 145 meters at times of military tension and channel a certain amount of the waters into flood diversion paths. In such a scenario, the government predicts flooding will be restricted to areas above the city of Shashi in Hubei with the lower courses of the river protected. They contend that the narrowness of the gorges will reduce the level of damage expected from a burst.

## RECENT HISTORY AND THE FUTURE

Although the Sanxia Dam would be the largest dam ever constructed in the world, proponents see the technological aspects as within China's grasp and have been attempting to assure people that the dam will be safe with no possibility of mishap.

Opponents point out that results from the Gezhouba Dam, as well as other dams in China, do not necessarily inspire confidence in the Sanxia project. After Gezhouba had been under construction for two years, the project was stopped and replanned. Instead of taking five years to complete as originally planned, Gezhouba took 18 years to finish at a cost close to four times the original estimate. Opponents suggest that the high cost of the Gezhouba project put a strain on the Chinese economy and led to inflation. The Sanxia project will create an even greater economic strain. New

technical problems could make the Sanxia project far more difficult, although so far this does not appear to have been the case.

The political situation in the People's Republic of China is such that it is almost impossible for public opinion to block a project if the leadership is in favor of it. As is often the case, political decisions rather than a careful look at the evidence determine a project's future. The Sanxia Dam went ahead on the basis of a political decision. With so many technical matters unclear and in light of the difficulties of costing the project, ultimately the politicians are using the Sanxia Dam to fulfill political goals they feel are important.

The project's future could still be thrown into question if the current government is toppled or there is a massive leadership shake-up resulting in the removal of Li Peng and other pro-Sanxia leaders. More likely is the possibility of funding constraints stalling the project or resulting in a lower reservoir level.

As the dam is going ahead, foreign governments are listening to their business constituents and not trying to restrict investment in the project to a rigorous degree. With acid rain and global warming very much a concern of the developed nations, a hydroelectric dam begins to look more attractive. Opposition groups now are trying to get the height of the reservoir reduced since it is virtually impossible to stop construction of the dam as a whole.

Within the comprehensive plans for the Sanxia project, however, there are many subsidiary measures that actually are more suitable for sustainable river management than construction of the dam itself. These tried and tested, less spectacular measures include: soil conservation and afforestation, reservoir construction on tributaries, improvement of the central and lower course dykes, expansion of flood water retention districts, dredging of the river and adjoining lake beds, improving flood warning systems, and educating the local populace. If faithfully carried out, these efforts will go a long way towards amplifying and helping China to fulfill the stated goals of the Sanxia project.

## BIBLIOGRAPHY

Barber, Margaret, and Gráinne Ryder, eds. *Damming the Three Gorges: What Dam Builders Don't Want You to Know*. 2nd ed. London: Earthscan and Probe International, 1993.

Boxer, B. "China's Three Gorges Dam: Questions and Prospects." *China Quarterly*. 1988: 113, pp. 94–108.

Childs-Johnson, Elizabeth, et al. "The Three Gorges Dam and the Fate of China's Southern Heritage" *Orientations,* Hong Kong, July/August, 1996, and *Archaeology* October 1996.

"Chinese Environmentalist Dai Qing Speaks Out on Three Gorges Dam," Environmental News Service May 26, 1999. Available online at http://ens.lycos.com/ens/may99/1999L-05-26-01.html (cited January 02, 2002) .

Dai Qing, "Sandouping: Building the Three Gorges Dam, 1992: A Battle Against Nature on the Yangtze River," TIMEasia.com, September 27, 1999. Available online at http://www.time.com/time/asia/magazine/99/0927/sandouping.html (cited January 02, 2002)

Dai Qing, ed. *Yangtze! Yangtze!* English edition edited by Patricia Adams and John Thibodeau, translation by Nancy Liu, Wu Mei, Sun Yougeng, and Zhang Xiaogang. London: Earthscan and Probe International, 1994.

"Dam Politics: How Three Gorges Plays in Beijing," Stratfor.com's Global Intelligence Update, Asia Times Online, May 4, 2001. Available online at http://www.atimes.com/china/BE05Ad01.html (cited January 05, 2002).

Edmonds, Richard Louis. "Recent Developments and Prospects for the Sanxia (Three Gorges) Dam." In *China's Economic Growth: The Impact on Regions, Migration, and the Environment,* pp. 161–83. Terry Cannon, ed. Basingstoke: Macmillan, 2000.

Fearnside, Philip M. "The Canadian Feasibility Study of the Three Gorges Dam Proposed for China's Yangzi River: A Grave Embarrassment to the Impact Assessment Profession." *Impact Assessment* 12–1, 1994: pp. 21–53.

Hajari, Nisid. "Some Cracks in the Façade," TIME.com, June 21, 1999. Available online at http://www.time.com/time/magazine/printout/0,8816,27581,00.html (cited January 03, 2002).

Heggelund, Gørild M. *Moving a Million: The Challenges of the Sanxia Resettlement.* Oslo: Norsk Utenrikspolitsk Institutt, October 1994. Research Report No. 181.

Jackson, S., and A. Sleigh. "Resettlement for China's Three Gorges Dam: Socio-economic Impact and Institutional Tensions." *Communist and Post-Communist Studies,* 33–2, May 2000: pp. 223–41.

Jing Jun. "Rural Resettlement: Past Lessons for the Three Gorges Project." *China Journal* 38, 1997: pp. 65–92.

"The Man Who Took on the Dissidents," CNN.com. Visions of China, 1999. Available online at http://www.cnn.com/SPECIALS/1999/china/profiles/li.peng/ (cited January 05, 2002).

Ronning Topping, Audrey, "Dai Qing, Voice of the Yangtze River Gorges," Earth Times News Service. Available online at http://weber.ucsd.edu/dmccubbi/chinadaiqingjan11_97.htm (cited January 02, 2002) .

Wang Z. "Navigation on Yangtze River and the Three Gorges Project." *Bulletin of the Permanent International Association of Navigation Congresses / Bulletin de l'Association Internationale Permanente des Congrès de Navigation* 70, 1990, pp. 86–96 (in English with French résumé).

Whitney, Joseph, and Luk, eds. *Megaproject.* London: M.E. Sharpe, 1992.

Zhai, Yushun; Harrison, Steve; Xu, Q. "Sustainable Land Use in the Three-Gorges Area of China." In *China's Economic Growth and Transition: Macroeconomic, Environmental and Social/Regional Dimensions,* Clement A. Tisdell and Joseph C. H. Chai, eds. Commack, NY: Nova Science Publishers, 1997, pp. 317–32.

*Richard Louis Edmonds*

# THE SPY PLANE INCIDENT: CHINA-U.S. RELATIONS

## THE CONFLICT

Although China and the United States have been making moves toward diplomacy, some real and unresolved friction continues to exist between the two states. China has emerged from a century and a half of devastation at the hands of the industrial nations; its future stance toward the United States and the West is not certain. Incidents such as the spy plane collision may indicate hard-line policies and a fierce competitor in world power as well as the world market.

### Political

• Taiwan remains a long-standing and unresolved issue between the two nations. China will not accept it as an independent nation, and the United States will not allow China to use force to reclaim it.

• China has joined the World Trade Organization and was highly supportive of Washington after the September 11, 2001, terrorist attacks. There are several strong points of agreement and cooperation between China and the United States.

### Economic

• In order to modernize, China has had to import foreign capital, technology, and specialists; these have produced a foreign cultural influence that did not always mesh with Communist Party policy.

• As China grows wealthier and more powerful it becomes a truly significant military competitor to the United States. Some observers see another Cold War-like balance of powers as the possible outcome.

On April 1, 2001, an American Navy EP-3E surveillance plane on patrol along the China coast in international airspace collided with a Chinese F-8 fighter. The fighter crashed into the sea and the pilot, Wang Wei, was killed, while the severely damaged surveillance plane, code name "Peter Rabbit," made an emergency landing on Hainan Island. American pilot Lieutenant Shane Osborn followed international rules by making a distress call and attempting to contact the Chinese airfield on Hainan for permission to land, but got no response. Chinese officials then detained Osborn and his crew of 23 for 11 days, while the aircraft was taken apart. The intelligence-gathering plane was returned in pieces to the United States on Russian cargo planes after being inspected by Chinese officials.

The Chinese leadership in Beijing insisted from the outset that its airspace had been violated when the American plane landed on Hainan without permission. It demanded an apology for the incursion and for the death of pilot Wang. President George W. Bush (2001–) expressed "sorrow" for the loss of life, and the American government announced its "regret" over the incident, but refused to use the word "apologize."

In China Wang Wei became a symbol of national pride, his widow and child prominently positioned in the various media, while in the United States the returning air crew received a well-publicized hero's welcome. Although there are many possible explanations for the collision and the way the Chinese government responded to it, near the top of any list of causes has to be the humiliation China has experienced until recently at the hands of the industrial nations. Whether

# CHRONOLOGY

**1912** The Manchu/Qing dynasty collapses and the Republic of China is founded by Sun Yat-sen.

**1931–45** Japan conquers and occupies Manchuria.

**1937–45** As World War II begins in China, the nationalists and the communists join forces once again to battle against the invading Japanese.

**1945–49** With the Japanese defeated, the nationalists and communists fight each other in a civil war.

**1949** Chiang Kai-shek's defeated nationalist forces flee to Taiwan and form the Republic of China. Mao Zedong's forces establish the People's Republic of China on the mainland.

**June 25, 1950** When communist North Korea attacks non-communist South Korea, the United States sends the Seventh Fleet into the Taiwan Straits to prevent the communist forces from invading the nationalist-occupied island of Taiwan.

**September 1954** The Mutual Defense Treaty provides that the United States could use force to counter an attack on Taiwan from the communist mainland.

**1958** Mao initiates the Great Leap Forward, a disastrous attempt to spur China's economic and technical development that results in mass starvation and economic collapse.

**1966–76** The Cultural Revolution is launched in China, a mass movement to revitalize Chinese communism that becomes violent and oppressive.

**1971** When U.S. President Richard Nixon announces he will visit mainland China, the United Nations immediately recognizes the People's Republic of China as the official government of China.

**1976** Mao Zedong dies.

**1978** Deng Xiaoping takes power and the Chinese Communist Party moves toward more moderate economic programs.

**January 1, 1979** U.S. President Jimmy Carter recognizes the People's Republic of China after promising not to "sacrifice" Taiwan.

**March 1979** The U.S. Congress passes the Taiwan Relations Act, which acknowledges the existence of only one China, but which also suggests that the United States might intervene militarily if the communist mainland attempts to reunify China by force.

**1987** The nationalists in Taiwan usher in democratic, multi-party elections for the first time.

**June 1989** The Chinese military brutally crushes a large pro-democracy/pro-reform demonstration at Tiananmen Square.

**February 1997** Deng Xiaoping dies and Jiang Zemin takes his place as China's leader.

**May 7, 1999** U.S. planes bomb the Chinese Embassy in Belgrade during NATO's air war against Yugoslavia, killing three, wounding others, and causing serious damage to U.S.-China relations.

**July 13, 2001** China wins the nomination to stage the 2008 Olympics.

**November 10, 2001** China officially becomes the 143rd member of the World Trade Organization.

**2000** In Taiwan, the presidential election produces a peaceful transfer of power from the Nationalist Party to the Democratic Progressive Party.

**April 1, 2001** A U.S. surveillance aircraft on patrol along the China coast in international airspace collides with a Chinese fighter plane. The fighter crashes into the sea and the pilot is killed, and the severely damaged surveillance plane makes an emergency landing on Hainan Island.

**April 11, 2001** The Chinese release the U.S. plane's crew.

one agrees with Beijing's grievances, they serve as a foundation of Chinese foreign policy today.

Part of that sense of grievance has to do with Taiwan, an estranged part of China maintaining a separate existence by virtue of foreign—that is, American—protection. The surveillance plane was, among other possible things, monitoring Chinese troop activities in provinces adjacent to Taiwan. Beijing viewed this as foreign intervention in an ongoing civil war between the legitimate government of China on the mainland and the

DIPLOMACY BETWEEN CHINA AND THE UNITED STATES WAS STRAINED IN THE AFTERMATH OF A COLLISION BETWEEN A U.S. AND CHINESE MILITARY PLANE, WITH CHINA DEMANDING AN APOLOGY, AND THE UNITED STATES UNWILLING TO ADMIT SOLE RESPONSIBILITY. *(Kevin Kallaugher (Kal), Baltimore Sun, Cartoonists & Writers Syndicate. Reproduced by permission.)*

renegade province of Taiwan. The last remnants of the foreign invasion and dismemberment of China that began in the early nineteenth century were apparent once again, revealing a long-term friction in need of resolution. By examining China's earlier relationships with the outside world we might better understand China's thinking about its international relations today.

## HISTORICAL BACKGROUND

### China's Traditional Approach to International Relations

In order to understand contemporary China's interaction with the outside world, one needs to grasp its past century-and-a-half struggle with the industrial nations—chiefly Britain, France, Russia, and Japan—and, most recently, the United States.

China's turbulent encounters with these nations featured numerous wars, most of which China lost, and resulted in national humiliation and the surrender of territory, the payment of reparations, and the relinquishing of control over foreigners in the Middle Kingdom, as China is known. Contrasted with China's heritage of greatness and its earlier position at the top of the hierarchy in its international relations, the confrontations China experienced during the nineteenth and twentieth centuries seemed marked by ineptitude, impotence, and indecision.

Until the early nineteenth century China's relations with the outside world were largely a product of Chinese design. In those periods when it was unified and strong China imposed the tributary system on all nations wishing to do business with it. This universal system assumed not an equal relationship between nations, but a hierarchical one, with China at the top of the cultural pyramid and other states holding inferior positions. For its part China, at the center, *in theory* maintained order by installing rulers in Vietnam, Korea, Japan, and among the nomadic tribes, and protected those territories from aggressors. In return these vassal states sent tributary missions to the Middle Kingdom to offer gifts to the Chinese emperor and receive the ruler's endowments, acknowledging his moral authority to order the terrestrial sphere, a mandate conferred on him by heaven. *In practice* the territories of East Asia suffered Chinese pretensions in exchange for access to the Middle Kingdom, which enhanced a ruler's legitimacy and a businessman's advantage.

Such was the system the Europeans encountered in the sixteenth century and to which they submitted, for most of the same pragmatic reasons and with the same warranted reservations that the Asians had. Before the industrial revolution in England in the seventeenth century, no nation proved powerful enough to force China to change its conduct of foreign affairs. During those times in history when China had been occupied by nomadic intruders—such as the Uighurs, Mongols, or Manchus, which occasionally governed all or part of China for brief or lengthy periods—the occupying groups typically embraced most Chinese cultural practices, including the tributary system.

In the early nineteenth century, however, opium, free trade, and industry intervened to establish another, this time European, universal system of international relations. Until that time the Canton system had been in place, an offshoot of the tributary system that required Western nations doing business with China to do so only in Canton and only with approved Chinese merchants. But the Canton system had deteriorated, due in part to the need for two-way trade. Europeans had purchased much from China, but China did not reciprocate, instead claiming to be self-sufficient. Consequently Europeans began to run out of the gold and silver necessary to sustain ongoing commercial activity.

Finally Westerners, realizing that a demand for opium existed in China, began to import large quantities of the narcotic into the country. Soon silver flowed out of China, due to the addiction of millions of subjects. The drug trade flourished partly because it served as an alternative to the monopolistic trading system between China and the West that had excluded the vast majority of Chinese and Western merchants, allowing only

European East India companies and government-approved Chinese merchants to operate. In protest, and illegally, non-favored merchants plied their trade in opium and other commodities. The First Anglo-Chinese War, also known as the Opium War, commenced in 1839 when a Chinese official burned contraband opium of the British East India Company. In the ensuing conflict, industrial Britain soundly defeated pre-modern Confucian China.

### China in Revolution, 1840–1976

The collision between China and the West proved to be both chronic and shattering well into the mid-twentieth century. Within the span of one hundred years China was invaded and defeated in: the First Opium War (1839–42); the British and French Second Opium War (1856–60); the Sino-French War (1880–84); the First Sino-Japanese War (1894–95); the Boxer Rebellion (1899–1900); Japan's conquest of Manchuria (1931–45); and the Second Sino-Japanese War (1937–45). Lost wars resulted in many hardships for China. It was forced to cede territories, such as Hong Kong, Taiwan, Manchuria, and the maritime provinces in what is now eastern Russia. It was also forced to lease some territories, including Liaodong, Qingdao, and the New Territories adjacent to Hong Kong. More than 200 treaty ports were established, where foreigners possessed extraterritorial rights akin to diplomatic immunity. Foreigners gained control over Chinese customs and the tariff, and numerous indemnity payments were imposed upon the Chinese. Although technically not a colony, China was left with little control over how it dealt with the outside world and not much more mastery over domestic events.

As persistent foreign incursions weakened China's last dynasty (the Qing or Manchu, 1644–1912), ruinous internal rebellions and domestic discord further undermined the social order. The Taiping Rebellion (a large and violent uprising by anti-Qing rebels, 1850–64) and lesser insurrections of the mid-nineteenth century were followed by the Boxer Rebellion (a powerful anti-foreigner uprising mainly in northern China, from 1898–1900), and finally the collapse of the Manchu Qing dynasty in 1912.

Political questions in China revolved around if, and then how, the Middle Kingdom would change to confront the outside challenge. Even after its lopsided defeat in the First Opium War, consensus among China's elite seemed to be to stick with the Confucian system—which included absolutist government, a bureaucratic elite recruited through an examination system which tested a narrow curriculum, agrarian economics, and a hierarchical social order of subjects, not citizens. Most believed the system was basically good but that it needed to be revitalized with more virtuous leadership.

After the reversal in the Second Opium War, a small but noticeable questioning of the Confucian system emerged, producing minor systemic reforms, such as the introduction of some Western diplomatic, educational, military, industrial, and business techniques. This "self-strengthening movement" of the last third of the nineteenth century proposed to maintain the essence of Confucian China while adopting the more practical techniques of the industrial world. China suffered dramatic defeat by Japan in 1895, which further eroded faith in the Confucian way and led to calls for radical reform, including a constitutional monarchy, even revolution, and especially the idea of republican government.

The collapse of the last dynasty and the creation of the Republic of China in 1912 seemed to offer some hope of progressive change, but alas, the original revolutionary, Sun Yat-sen, was pushed aside when Yuan Shikai (1859–1916) became premier and then president of the republic. Yuan, who had little appetite for or faith in power-sharing, set out to establish himself as a dictator. His death in 1916 ushered in more than a decade of warlordism, as high-ranking military officials divided the nation among themselves into numerous satrapies (individually ruled territories).

In order to crush the warlords and drive the imperial powers from China, two emerging parties temporarily united. The Nationalist Party under the leadership of Sun Yat-sen (1866–1925) and later his protégé Chiang Kai-shek (or Jiang Jeshi, 1887–1975), joined forces with the Communist Party, eventually under the control of Mao Zedong (1893–1976), to form the First United Front (1923–27), which proved to be short-lived and eventually resulted in large-scale civil war between the two parties. The Japanese incursions of the 1930s produced another united front (1937–45) between the nationalists and the communists, but after the allied defeat of Japan, renewed conflict between the two parties ensued (1945–49), resulting in a divided China that continues to today. Chiang Kai-shek's defeated nationalist forces fled to Taiwan, where multiparty governments have since administered the Republic of China. Mao Zedong's forces established the People's Republic of China in October 1949 on the mainland, where the Communist Party continues to monopolize political power.

The showdown between Chiang and Mao promised to produce China's ultimate path to the future. Chiang's early defeat of the communists and the establishment of his nationalist government (1927–49) seemed to indicate that the nationalist route to modernization, known as "soft" authoritarianism today, would vanquish the communist model of development. The communist defeat of the nationalists in 1949 appeared to signify just the opposite. Mao had unified the nation, driven out the foreigners, and promised speedy and efficient economic development.

But the story did not end with the communist victory. In the 27 years between the creation of the People's Republic in 1949 and Mao's death in 1976, yet another reversal of fortunes occurred, this time on the economic, not the military, field of battle. Communist China's economy experienced tremendous convulsions during this period. Mao initiated the Great Leap Forward in the late-1950s, a disastrous attempt to spur China's economic and technical development; and the Cultural Revolution between 1966 and 1976, a mass movement to revitalize Chinese communism that became violent and oppressive. The result of these programs was what can most generously be described as developmental stagnation. At that time, on the other hand, the Republic of China on the island of Taiwan recorded impressive economic advances.

With the ascendancy of Deng Xiaoping in 1978, the Communist Party substantially abandoned Stalinist and Maoist prototypes of economic development in favor of the more successful Chinese economic models in freer Singapore, Hong Kong, and Taiwan. Politically, China appeared to know where it did not want to go, but it had yet to settle on where it did want to proceed. Meanwhile, mainland China and Taiwan continued to compete with each other for legitimacy among the Chinese, and also among foreign nations for diplomatic and less formal recognition. At this time the United States became intimately involved in some parts of the competition. Let us now look at the relationship that has developed between the United States and China.

### American Relations with Revolutionary China, 1840–1976

United States relations with China began with U.S. independence and the new nation's search for markets. As a colony, America had access to the perquisites of the British mercantile system. Upon achieving its independence, however, the former colony had to establish its own diplomatic and economic ties with the nations of the world. In its dealings with China, until the time of the Opium War, this meant operating officially within the Canton system. Unofficially it involved a great deal of illicit commercial activity, a small percentage of which included opium trafficking.

After the Opium War, for the remainder of the nineteenth century, the United States took advantage of the special rights the industrial nations had acquired in China. For business this meant gaining access to the "China market," then a fanciful world of 400 million potential customers as well as a realistic source of cheap labor. For Christian missionaries this represented an opportunity to convert those millions of souls. For Washington the relationship entailed keeping China intact, thus permitting continued U.S. accessibility. The vast majority of the Chinese, however, viewed foreigners, including Americans, at best neutrally and usually negatively, while that small percentage of Chinese merchants, students, or converts who benefited directly from foreign contact tended to be seen as collaborators with the "barbarians."

As the nineteenth century closed, however, foreign nations' relationship with China began to change. Under the earlier Canton system all foreign nations had equal access to the country, and this remained true even under the radically different system of treaties China signed after the Opium War. Since 1844 all industrial nations had had "most favored nations" clauses included in their treaties with Beijing, which provided them with the same best treatment as any other nation. But when the First Sino-Japanese War ended with a treaty that ceded Taiwan to Japan, the imperial powers began scheming to carve China up into spheres of influence. England, France, Germany, Austria, Italy, Japan, and Russia claimed exclusive trading rights to a portion of the nation, and many went on to more or less colonize their "sphere of influence" in China.

The United States had no desire to establish a sphere of influence in China and feared that with other countries forming exclusive trading rights, there would likely be a full or partial closure of the China market to Americans. To keep this from happening the Open Door policy was proclaimed by the United States. First enunciated by Secretary of State John Hay in 1899, the Open Door policy stipulated that China should remain in one piece and all nations should have equal access to the Middle Kingdom. In Chinese eyes, the U.S. policy of open foreign access remained preferable to the likely annexation of significant parts of the country by the other foreign nations. By the turn of the twentieth century, then, the United States had a more positive image in Chinese eyes than the other imperial powers, which had forcibly leased or outright seized Chinese territory.

Until the founding of the People's Republic of China in 1949 the United States' reputation remained clearly above those of the other industrial nations because of numerous actions by Washington that tended to help China in its struggle to survive dynastic decline and foreign assault. So, although the United States continued to be associated with harmful imperial policies, it also came to be regarded as the nation that most often stood with China when significant international issues arose. After the Boxer Rebellion in 1900 the United States took its share (roughly seven percent) of the indemnity China had to pay to several industrial nations (a total of £67.5 million) for the Boxer attack on their legations, missions, and citizens, but used the funds to educate deserving Chinese students in the United States.

The United States also got behind the Chinese government's nearly successful attempt to eradicate opium during the first decade of the twentieth century. It was also America that encouraged Yuan Shikai, the first president of the newly created Republic of China, to promote the democratic ideals of the 1911 Revolution. When, during World War I (1914–18), Japan issued the infamous Twenty-One Demands in 1915, the core aim of which was Tokyo's control of China, Washington refused to recognize Japan's right to make such demands. Later, at the Washington Conference of 1921–22, and with U.S. encouragement, Japan agreed to return Qingdao—which the Germans had leased from China and which Tokyo had taken from the Germans during World War I—to China. A decade later, when Japan invaded Manchuria in 1931, the United States attempted to rally world opinion against this aggression and again issued a statement of non-recognition. And when World War II (1939–45) began in China in July 1937, Washington openly supported China. After Japan bombed Pearl Harbor, Hawaii, on December 7, 1941, the United States, entering into the war, provided China with soldiers and war material.

## U.S. Alliance Remains with Chiang Kai-shek

The United States' intimate involvement with China during World War II included support for the nationalist government headed by Chiang Kai-shek. When civil war between the nationalists and communists re-erupted in 1946, Washington sided with the existing nationalist regime. With the communist military victory and the subsequent nationalist retreat to Taiwan it appeared that the Chinese civil war would shortly end. The United States had withdrawn its financial support from Chiang when it became clear that he and his nationalist regime had lost popular favor as well as military strength. When communist North Korea attacked non-communist South Korea on June 25, 1950, however, the United States sent the Seventh Fleet into the Taiwan (Formosa) Straits to prevent Mao Zedong's communist forces from invading the island of Taiwan.

For the next two decades Washington supported Chiang's government with diplomatic, economic, and military aid, as well as with U.S. troops and a military alliance. With U.S. support the Republic of China on Taiwan held China's seat at the United Nations and received the diplomatic recognition of most nations. Moreover, the Mutual Defense Treaty of December 2, 1954, in part a consequence of the communist September 1954 bombardment of Quemoy (Jinmen), a small nationalist-held island, provided that Washington could use force to counter a communist attack from the mainland. Again in 1958 communist artillery attacks on Quemoy and Matsu (Mazu) islands along with troop buildups in Fujian province brought quick promises of U.S. support for Chiang. Nor did the 1960s usher in a thawing in Sino-U.S. relations. During the Sino-Indian War of 1962, the United States assisted India, while the Vietnam War found Beijing and Washington on different sides as well.

As unlikely as it might have seemed in the 1960s, the communist People's Republic of China and the anti-communist United States came to realize that they had one large common interest: checking the power and influence of the Soviet Union. In the late 1950s Russian advisers in China withdrew, signaling the onset of the Sino-Soviet split. Meanwhile the convulsive Cultural Revolution in China championed the Maoist model of socialist development for the emerging third world over the old Stalinist formula. By the late 1960s border clashes between the two competing communist giants seemed to confirm deep-seated, perhaps irreconcilable differences that the United States could exploit.

In 1971 President Richard Nixon (1969–74) created a "China card" to play by announcing he would visit mainland China the following year, a statement that immediately led to the recognition of the People's Republic of China as the official government of China by the United Nations, as well as to greater access to the mainland by American business and students. Even though the United States still recognized Chiang's government on Taiwan, the end of the Cultural Revolution and the death of Mao Zedong in 1976 seemed to promise closer ties between Washington and Beijing.

## China Since the Cultural Revolution, 1976–

Mao's death brought an end to the more radical politics and impractical economic policies that had exemplified communist rule since 1949. After a brief period of political jockeying, China's new "paramount leader," Deng Xiaoping (1905–97), emerged with a plan for economic development, the Four Modernizations, which included modest political liberalization. This movement was symbolized by a wall in Beijing, called the Democracy Wall, on which from 1978 to 1979 people were encouraged to hang posters of protest or criticism of the government. When an essay was posted on the wall calling for the Fifth Modernization, or democracy, in 1979, however, the poster's creator was imprisoned and that same year Deng had the wall razed.

The democracy movement in China reflected the delicate balance the Communist Party had to maintain in order to preserve its monopoly of political power. In order to modernize, China needed to import foreign capital, technology, and specialists, but these produced a foreign cultural influence that did not always mesh with party policy. Thus Chinese attraction to democratic ideas, McDonald's fast food, Hollywood motion pictures, or American pop music had to be countered lest the party lose even more control than the modernizing technicians, foreign and Chinese, had already appropriated to generate economic growth. Consequently the party launched crusades aimed at these putative sources of unrest, beginning with a campaign against bourgeois liberalism and spiritual pollution, and culminating in the crushing of the democracy movement in the spring of 1989, most visibly at Tiananmen Square.

At this point many problems had to be confronted. Obviously the party had to deal with those who directly challenged it, and the democracy movement leadership either fled abroad or found itself in prison. The socio-economic consequences of rapid economic development also had to be acknowledged. These included massive unemployment, perhaps as high as 100 million people at any one time by the end of the twentieth century; the potential for trouble as a result of spiritual despair, as best evidenced by the Falun Gong religious movement; and party corruption, particularly the nepotism associated with most large joint ventures China established with the outside world.

Another obstacle China faced as Deng approached 90, was the transition of power, which required the grooming of a loyal successor. Deng's previous heirs apparent (Hu Yaobang and Zhao Ziyang) did not measure up, desiring either too rapid or too liberal a modernization, so in the wake of the Tiananmen Square bloodbath Deng selected Jiang Zemin. By the time of Deng's death in February 1997, Jiang had consolidated his position in the party, but neither he nor his likely successor will ever possess the stature of Mao or Deng. Accordingly party factions and civilian interest groups have come to play much more important roles in policy making. Potential party leaders must stake out popular political positions, and the most important of these likely revolves around the issue of Taiwan. And when we speak of Taiwan after 1950, we also need to insinuate the United States into the discussion.

## U.S. Relations with China, 1976–

When the Vietnam War ended in 1975 the United States departed Indochina, replaced by the Soviet Union. Yet even as Beijing denounced Yankee imperialism, it did not seek a total U.S. withdrawal from Asia. Such a power vacuum would almost certainly be filled by Moscow, which already held substantial influence in North Korea and India, and to which southeast Asian leaders journeyed to revamp relationships in light of the American defeat. Beijing's interests would be best served by a continued U.S. presence in Asia.

But China did not want a U.S. presence in Taiwan. Mao, Deng, and Jiang all uncompromisingly demanded a reunification of separated Chinese territories with the motherland: Hong Kong, Macao, and Taiwan. Great Britain negotiated a return of Hong Kong in 1997; Portugal handed back Macao in 1999; only Taiwan remained separated as the twenty-first century began. Taiwan represented a much more difficult problem since the rulers of Taiwan are Chinese, not foreigners. Nonetheless, it is clear to all that a separate Taiwan would not exist without United States protection.

U.S. PRESIDENT BILL CLINTON SPEAKS TO AN AUDIENCE OF STUDENTS AT BEIJING UNIVERSITY, STRESSING THE IMPORTANCE OF HUMAN RIGHTS. (*A/P Wide World. Reproduced by permission.*)

Richard Nixon's efforts in Chinese-American relations left a number of issues unresolved. The United States established a relationship with Beijing, but Washington continued to recognize Chiang Kai-shek's government in Taiwan. The Shanghai Communiqué of February 28, 1972, proclaimed that there was only one China, but Washington did not indicate—and Beijing did not insist that Washington indicate—which government, the one in Beijing or the one in Taipei, constituted the legitimate Chinese government.

Political momentum strongly suggested that Beijing was in fact the Chinese capital, and in the 1970s the United States agreed to gradually eliminate its military presence in Taiwan. The Watergate scandal in the United States in the early 1970s, however, undermined Nixon's ability to normalize relations with Beijing. Gerald Ford, who also desired to establish diplomatic relations with China, lost the necessary political capital when he pardoned Nixon. When President Jimmy Carter (1977–81) finally recognized the People's Republic of China on January 1, 1979, he did so only after promising not to "sacrifice" Taiwan. The U.S. Congress went further, passing in March 1979 the Taiwan Relations Act, which acknowledged the existence of only one China, but which also suggested that Washington might

## WHAT IS AN EP-3E SURVEILLANCE PLANE?

The United States has been flying surveillance planes over China for decades. In the aftermath of the collision in April 2001, some observers have noted that the Chinese military must have been delighted to have the American Lockheed Martin EP-3E Aries II SIGINT (Signals Intelligence)–a four-engine, low-wing, electronic warfare and reconnaissance aircraft—practically delivered to their door for them to take apart and examine as they wished. The electronic surveillance devices they found on board were state-of-the-art. According to the U.S. Navy the role of the EP-3E is to provide "the Fleet Commander with a real-time assessment of the tactical posture of potentially unfriendly military forces." It can pick up radio, radar, ship-to-shore messages, satellite transmissions, telephone, e-mail, and fax signals. The surveillance system is operated by a skilled mission crew able to make an immediate analysis of the signals received, and it has the capacity to directly relate its findings to commanders. The aircraft costs about US$36 million.

The United States was probably seeking information about China's military capacity along its southern border on April 1, 2001, when the Chinese fighter plane collided with the EP-3E. It is possible that when the aircraft came into its possession, China was able to determine how much the United States knows about its (China's) military operations as well as getting a good picture of the U.S. intelligence capabilities in general.

intervene militarily if the communist mainland attempted to reunify China by force.

So long as Taiwan remained a one-party state under a nationalist government dominated by mainland politicians, the question of Taiwan's status was not much of an issue. Every significant player—the Chinese Communist Party, the Nationalist Party, and the United States—agreed that Taiwan was part of China. In 1987, however, the nationalists under Chiang Kai-shek's son, Chiang Ching-kuo, ushered in democratic, multi-party elections. This opened the door to Taiwanese political power, heretofore insignificant in light of the mainland Chinese monopoly. Upon the death of the younger Chiang, Lee Teng-hui, the Taiwan-born vice-president, became the president of the Republic of China, as well as leader of the Nationalist Party. Increasingly Taiwanese-Chinese,

not mainlanders, called the political shots. Moreover, radical Taiwanese formed a viable political opposition with the creation of the Democratic Progressive Party, which favored a Taiwan declaration of independence from the mainland.

The new political establishment on Taiwan presented a threat to Beijing. In the presidential election of 1996, the People's Republic attempted to intimidate Taiwanese voters by carrying out military exercises in the Taiwan Straits. In response the United States sent a carrier battle group into the straits with another standing nearby. The mainland also conducted military maneuvers during the 2000 presidential election, which produced a peaceful transfer of power from the Nationalist Party to the Democratic Progressive Party and its successful candidate, Chen Shuibian.

## RECENT HISTORY AND THE FUTURE

### Why the Spy Plane Incident?

When the American EP-3E flew through international airspace along the coast of the Chinese mainland on April 1, 2001, Chinese aircraft pursued. A number of explanations for the fatal collision have been offered. One asserts that the American plane crashed into the Chinese jet intentionally, a not-so-subtle statement by Washington that it intends to contain China. Another maintains that the Chinese pilot flew too aggressively and misjudged the distance between his F-8 fighter and the EP-3E. Still others assert that this collision did not result from the reckless behavior of an individual pilot but represented the policy of a significant part of the Chinese military, flexing its muscle in its struggle with civilian leadership. Yet others argue the struggle is between the hardliners and softliners in Beijing or those in Washington—those who favor containment of China and those who seek engagement.

Perhaps it was Beijing testing an inexperienced American president, or conceivably it was President George W. Bush upholding the right to fly in international airspace, or possibly it was Washington testing Chinese electronic capabilities. We can not say with a high degree of confidence the extent to which Taiwan was an issue, whether it was a proximate cause or mainly a pretext. To be sure, the mainland will not permit Taiwan to declare independence, and the United States will not likely allow Beijing to use force against Taiwan. But within that context, all sorts

CHINESE MEN VIEW AN AMERICAN U2 SPY PLANE AT THE MILITARY MUSEUM IN BEIJING. THE SAME DAY, U.S. TECHNICIANS ARRIVED TO INSPECT A NAVY SURVEILLANCE PLANE THAT COLLIDED WITH A CHINESE FIGHTER JET AND WAS FORCED TO LAND ON THE CHINESE ISLAND OF HAINAN. *(© AFP/Corbis. Reproduced by permission.)*

of other controversies can be generated, the resolutions of which are far from unclouded.

### Before and After 9/11

The spy plane incident was just winding down on September 11, 2001, when terrorists attacked New York and Washington D.C. Prior to the attacks, the United States' relationship with China had remained rocky and, except in superficial ways, will likely continue to remain somewhat strained. While it is true that Beijing and Washington have forged strong economic ties and now seem to share a common threat from Muslim extremists, there are as well significant disagreements that will continue into the foreseeable future. Chief among the differences is Taiwan, which the United States will likely defend if attacked. Moreover, many of the states surrounding China, especially in the former Soviet republics but also in both India and Pakistan, have become quite friendly with the United States. China will not want to push those nations, most of which are Muslim, closer still to the United States by being perceived as too anti-Muslim, especially in light of Beijing's harsh handling of its Turkish-Muslim population in Xinjiang province.

From the U.S. point of view, one large source of tension results from China selling weapons to nations with questionable reputations, especially Iran. But the larger issue deals with the future, when a wealthier and more powerful China will be the United States' significant military competitor. Even as the U.S. business and academic communities applaud closer ties with the People's Republic, security specialists fret that the United States is helping to create not little dragons, as in South Korea, Taiwan, or Singapore, but a gigantic creature capable of great harm. Put another way, was the spy plane incident one of the last Chinese attempts to resolve past international troubles, or was it a harbinger of a militant China that needs to be contained?

## BIBLIOGRAPHY

Alford, William P. *To Steal a Book Is an Elegant Offense: Intellectual Property Law in Chinese Civilization.* Stanford: Stanford University Press, 1995.

Bernstein, Richard, and Ross H. Munro. *The Coming Conflict with China.* New York: Knopf, 1997.

Chang, Gordon G. *The Coming Collapse of China.* New York: Random House, 2001.

Cohen, Warren I. *America's Response to China: A History of Sino-American Relations,* 4th ed. New York: Columbia University Press, 2000.

"Dangerous Straits." *PBS Frontline.* Aired October 18, 2001. Available online at http://www.pbs.org/wgbh/pages/frontline/shows/china/ (cited January 10, 2002).

Kitts, Charles R. *The United States Odyssey in China, 1784–1990.* Lanhan: University Press of America, 1991.

Nathan, Andrew J., and Robert S. Ross. *The Great Wall and the Empty Fortress: China's Search for Security.* New York: Norton, 1997.

Pearson, Margaret M. *China's New Business Elite: The Political Consequences of Economic Reform.* Berkeley: University of California Press, 1997.

Shambaugh, David, ed. *Is China Unstable?* Armonk, NY: M.E. Sharpe, 2000.

*Thomas D. Reins*

# CÔTE D'IVOIRE: A COSMOPOLITAN SOCIETY DESCENDS INTO POLITICAL CHAOS AND VIOLENCE

On October 26, 2000, Laurent Gbagbo was sworn in as president of Côte d'Ivoire (the Ivory Coast). The week preceding his inauguration had been violent, and included both the overthrow of a military junta and a sectarian conflict that had cost at least 200 lives. This followed a year of violence and instability that shattered the image of stability in Côte d'Ivoire, which had long been viewed as sub-Saharan Africa's political and economic success story.

## The 1999 Coup

This period of instability began on December 24, 1999, when a military coup led by General Robert Gueï overthrew the government of Henri Konan Bedié, the anointed successor to the founding father of Ivorian politics, Félix Houphouët-Boigny (1905–1993; pronounced *hoo-foo-AY BWAH-nyee*). The coup started as a protest by soldiers over lack of pay but General Gueï, a former Army Chief of Staff who had been forced into early retirement by Bedié, quickly took advantage of the uprising.

On taking over the government, Gueï appointed civilian ministers and promised an early return to democracy. The coup was initially viewed with some relief by many Ivorians who saw it as a liberation from the corrupt and divisive politics that had characterized the Bedié era. It soon became clear, however, that Gueï was willing to play the same games to hold onto power as Bedié had. While elections were announced for October 2000, he eliminated most of his opponents—most notably former Prime Minister Alassane Ouattara—through legalisms in much the same way that Bedié had marginalized opponents in the past. This time Gueï used his handpicked Supreme Court to eliminate Ouattara on the

## THE CONFLICT

Côte d'Ivoire, once considered the African model of economic and political success after independence, has experienced political instability, continuous economic tailspins, and violent confrontations along ethnic and religious lines in the last decade. In this time, political leaders seeking to bolster their fragile positions have exacerbated ethnic hostilities, pitting Christians against Muslims, natives against immigrants, and the various ethnic groups against each other. With people thus divided, the election system and embryonic party system are either being circumvented or are ineffective, and the threat of chaos looms.

### Political

- The 33-year presidency of Félix Houphouët-Boigny had been marked by solid economic growth and a peaceful multiethnic society. When he died in 1993 Prime Minister Alassane Ouattara, a Muslim from the north, and Henri Konan Bedié, the speaker of the General Assembly and a Baoule Christian, both believed they had a right to the presidency, but neither enjoyed the widespread support of the societal and ethnic groups that Houphouët-Boigny had had.

### Religious

- Roughly, Christian and Muslim populations account for slightly more than one-third of the Côte d'Ivoire population each, with the animist communities making up the remainder. The Muslim community has grown considerably in recent decades—primarily through immigration—and has become the target of hostility from the other groups.

### Ethnic

- Côte d'Ivoire has four major ethnic groupings. The Akan are largely Roman Catholic Christian and occupy the southeastern part of the country. The Kru are also largely Roman Catholic and occupy the southwestern part of the country. The Muslim Mandé and largely animistic Voltaic peoples occupy the northwest and northeast of the country respectively. For almost all of the independent history of Côte d'Ivoire, the Christian Baoule, a tribe of the Akan, have ruled the country.

# CHRONOLOGY

*1960* Côte d'Ivoire achieves independence from France; Houphouët-Boigny becomes president.

*1988* The Front Populaire Ivoiren (FPI) is formed and Laurent Gbagbo is elected chairman.

*1990* Houphouët-Boigny allows the first multi-party elections and appoints Allasane Ouattara prime minister.

*December 1993* Houphouët-Boigny dies and Bedié becomes acting president.

*September 1994* The Rassemblement des Republicains (RDR) is formed.

*October 1995* Bedié wins a boycotted presidential election after having Ouattara barred due to claims of non-residency.

*December 24, 1999* Bedié is overthrown in a military coup led by General Robert Gueï.

*January 2000* Gueï forms a government with many civilian ministers.

*June 2000* The FPI joins the Gueï government.

*September 2000* The Supreme Court declares both Ouattara and former president Bedié ineligible for the presidency.

*October 22, 2000* Gbagbo apparently wins the presidency but Gueï attempts to void the result; violent protests ensue.

*October 26, 2000* Gueï flees; Gbagbo is sworn in as president but refuses to hold a new election with the participation of Ouattara. Fresh violence erupts with hundreds dying.

*December 2000* With Gbagbo refusing to hold another presidential vote, the RDR boycotts legislative elections.

*January 7–8, 2001* In an attempted coup, someone tries, and fails, to seize the national radio station.

*January 2001* In the wake of the failed coup, thousands flee anti-Muslim violence.

*March 2001* Gbagbo and Outarra meet in Lomé, Togo, under the auspices of the Togolese president, Gnassingbe Eyadema.

*March 28, 2001* The RDR makes significant gains in municipal elections.

*June 2001* Côte d'Ivoire significantly strengthens its border presence along the border with Burkina Faso after rumors of pro-RDR rebels training there.

grounds that Ouattara was not of Ivorian parentage and hence not a citizen under restrictive new citizenship laws.

## *The Contested Election: October 2000*

After failing to have himself declared the candidate of former President Bedié's Parti Democratique de Côte d'Ivoire (PDCI) party, Gueï decided to stand under his own banner in the October polls. After early election results showed that Gueï was losing heavily to the candidate of the Front Populaire Ivoiren (FPI), Laurent Gbagbo, Gueï attempted to have the election voided.

This action brought massive groups of protesters into the streets, forcing Gueï to flee the country. Gbagbo, a longtime opposition leader and perennial also-ran, suddenly found himself the victor of the elections and was declared president. Supporters of Ouattara, however, demanded new

elections on the grounds that he had been unfairly excluded from the poll of October 22.

When Gbagbo refused to conduct new elections, former allies in protests against the military government—Gbagbo's FPI supporters and Ouattara's supporters from the Rassemblement des Republicains (RDR)—began to fight each other in the streets. Protests rapidly turned xenophobic in nature as Muslims, the primary supporters of the RDR and Ouattara, found themselves the targets of attacks. Muslim immigrants were also targeted and many fled to neighboring Burkina Faso.

Both Gbagbo and Ouattara appealed for calm and the violence slowly subsided. In protest to Gbagbo's decision not to hold a new presidential poll, however, the RDR boycotted legislative elections held in December and the situation remained unsettled. On January 7, 2001, there was an attempted coup by unknown forces that failed

MAP OF CÔTE D'IVOIRE. (© *Maryland Cartographics. Reprinted with permission.*)

to take the national television station. General Gueï has denied any involvement but suspicions circle around him and possible foreign allies, including President Charles Taylor of Liberia.

In the wake of the coup attempt thousands fled to neighboring Burkina Faso, Mali, Ghana, and Niger as security forces and civilian FPI supporters launched a series of attacks on those they perceived to be enemies of the new regime, according to the Associated Press. These attacks targeted in particular Muslim northerners and foreigners, including those born in Côte d'Ivoire to foreign parents.

Another threat to the Gbagbo government was the suspected training of insurgents in neigh-

boring Burkina Faso and Mali. The trainees in exile allegedly supported the RDR and Ouattara, who was in exile in France during much of this period. During the summer of 2001, representatives of Côte d'Ivoire repeatedly sought assurances from Burkinabe President Blaise Campaore that he would not support the training of rebels in his country. Côte d'Ivoire also strengthened its border patrols in the area.

The background of both the coup and rebels supposedly training across the border remain somewhat murky and the details may be—at least partially—an attempt by the Gbagbo government to shore up its shaky domestic support by associating its political enemies with both violence and

# FÉLIX HOUPHOUËT-BOIGNY

*1905–* The son of a wealthy Baoule chief, Félix Houphouët was born in Yamoussoukro in Central Côte d'Ivoire in 1905. Educated at Ecole Ponty in Dakar, Senegal, Boigny practiced medicine in Côte d'Ivoire from 1925 to 1940. At the age of 35 he inherited his father's vast coffee and cocoa plantations and becomes chief of his tribe, leaving his career in medicine.

In 1944 Houphouët began his political career by helping to form the African Agricultural Union (AAU), an anti-colonial movement. At the time, Côte d'Ivoire was governed by France. A year later, in 1945, Houphouët was elected to the French National Assembly as a member of the Democratic Party of the Côte d'Ivoire (PCDI), formerly the AAU.

As a member of the French National Assembly from 1945-1960, his party formed close links with prominent leftist politicians such as François Mitterand. Houphouët forged close personal ties with Charles de Gaulle and adds the political name Boigny, which means "irresistible power." During that time he was instrumental in founding the Rassemblement Démocratique Africain (RDA), a transnational group of African delegates to the French National Assembly.

During the struggle for independence that would follow, Houphouët-Boigny opposed a federation of all West African states and with the Support of de Gaulle Côte d'Ivoire votes for a separate independence.

Houphouët-Boigny became the first President of Côte d'Ivoire in 1960, and insured that PDCI controlled the legislature throughout his 33-year tenure. He oversaw considerable economic expansion and cooperated closely with Western economic advisors, particularly those from France. In 1963–64 Boigny defeated several attempts made to wrest power from the PDCI through alleged coup plots and arrests.

Boigny was an influential force in Ivorian politics and initiated several series of dialogues between various groups in Ivorian society. While serving, though, Boigny refused to hold multiparty elections until 1990 when he defeated Laurent Gbagbo handily, retaining his post. The campaign, however, was short and restricted.

In 1993 Félix Houphouët-Boigny died, and Henri Konan Bedié, then President of the Ivorian National Assembly, assumed the presidency.

foreign support. Ouattara has studiously avoided any association with violent action and has pursued a course of reconciliation that has led to several meetings with Gbagbo over the course of 2001. The RDR has also shown a political resurgence. After boycotting the legislative elections of December 2000, the RDR polled very strongly in local and municipal elections in March 2001, taking mayoralties in several cities previously held by either the FPI or the FDCI.

## HISTORICAL BACKGROUND

### In the Times of Houphouët-Boigny

As with most French African colonies, independence for Côte d'Ivoire came rather suddenly in 1960. France viewed its colonies in a somewhat different light than Britain, which always thought in terms of eventual independence for its colonial possessions. In contrast, France assumed that most of its colonies would eventually become part of metropolitan France. Local politicians were there-

fore groomed in French political institutions, according to Robert H. Jackson in his book *Quasi-States: Sovereignty, International Relations and the Third World* (1990). Côte d'Ivoire's first president, Félix Houphouët-Boigny, served as a minister in Paris for several years prior to Ivorian independence and counted French president Charles de Gaulle (1890–1970) as a personal friend.

As a result, when it achieved independence, Côte d'Ivoire maintained a very close relationship with Paris. Houphouët-Boigny encouraged a strong foreign influence in the running of the country, particularly the economy. Partially as a consequence of this intensive relationship, the first 30 years of Ivorian independence were marked by considerable economic growth and stability.

From a political standpoint, Houphouët-Boigny maintained a deft hand over the complex politics of this country with dozens of competing ethnic groups. He was noted for being a dictator who did not allow others to make decisions. But he was also viewed almost as a father figure in his

MEN IN THE ADJAME SECTION OF ABIDJAN, CÔTE D'IVOIRE, WHICH WAS DEVASTATED BY ETHNIC AND POLITICAL VIOLENCE FOR TWO DAYS IN DECEMBER 2000, RESCUE WHAT THEY CAN FROM THE RUBBLE. *(A/P Wide World. Reproduced by permission.)*

country: a popular leader who never resorted to brutality to maintain his one-man rule. Houphouët-Boigny justified his way of ruling on the grounds that a multiparty system would create rivalries among the 60 different ethnic groups in the country. After 1990, however, the stability he had built was proving increasingly difficult to sustain. At his death in 1993, Houphouët-Boigny left behind a very precarious political situation for his successor, Henri Konan Bedié.

Historically, Côte d'Ivoire is divided roughly into four major ethnic groupings. The Akan are largely Roman Catholic Christian and occupy the southeastern part of the country. The Kru are also largely Roman Catholic and occupy the southwestern part of the country. The Muslim Mandé and largely animistic Voltaic peoples occupy the northwest and northeast of the country respectively. In the four decades since independence there has been a considerable influx of Muslims from both Mandé territories as well as Mali and Burkina Faso into the more industrialized south of the country, particularly Abidjan. This Muslim influx has been a key catalyst for the recent unrest in the country. Currently, according to various estimates, Christian and Muslim populations account for slightly more than one-third of the population each, with the disorganized animist communities making up the remainder.

Houphouët-Boigny was Baoule, the largest of the Akan tribes. Bedié, his successor, also hailed from the same group and so, for almost all of the independent history of Côte d'Ivoire, the Christian Baoule have ruled the country. Houphouët-Boigny, however, pursued a policy of inclusiveness toward the increasing Muslim population. None of his successors have followed his lead in that area.

Houphouët-Boigny, the son of a Baoule chief, was educated in Senegal before returning to Côte d'Ivoire as a doctor. He seemed to have an instinctive grasp of how to balance the competing forces within his country. It also didn't hurt that his 33-year tenure in office was marked by almost constant economic growth through which he was able to keep most of the elites within the country relatively satisfied. Among Houphouët-Boigny's politically astute institutions were his "dialogues"—forums over which he presided that were designed to give voice to the diverse populations represented in the National Assembly. Barbara Lewis explains:

> The dialogues were enthusiastically and sincerely acclaimed as transforming a climate of anxiety into one of security under the president's sharp and benevolent eye. The dialogues were a catharsis; men and women spoke frankly of widely recognized economic and political wrongs and problems, and the president reprimanded the guilty and rewarded the

# THEORIES OF ETHNIC IDENTITY

As the recent turmoil in the Ivory Coast amply demonstrates it is not always easy to determine what makes up an ethnic group or why they come into conflict with other groups. Most ethnic groups coexist in harmony. Indeed, in many cases it is hard to determine what makes up an ethnic group. Some would like to see themselves defined as religiously, tribally, racially, or linguistically distinct from other groups, but in fact no one of these conditions are actually pre-conditions for ethnic identity.

Ethnic identity is a learned behavior. It is in no way innate. You may be taught that you were born Bété or Baoule or American but more importantly, you are taught what it means to be a part of that group. This teaching goes on formally as well as informally. You can be taught it in school, by family, or by friends. Every person learns to be part of his or her society and that society has a certain set of shared beliefs.

Ivorians lived in relative harmony for decades—both within their internal divisions and with the large immigrant population. This all changed in the 1990s. Why? Mainly because political and other elites decided it was to their benefit to promote division rather than unity. This fed upon the general tension bred by economic uncertainty that already existed in the country. Unfortunately, once these passions are stoked to a certain point, they are hard to undo—especially when they have led to killing.

The same situation has occurred over and over again from Bosnia to Indonesia to Russia (to name but a few) as nationalisms and ethno-nationalisms have been used by elites seeking power who have no positive way of holding on to it. In some cases ethnic identity has come as a surprise to people. At the beginning of the Bosnian war, for example, thousands flocked to genealogists to determine whether they were Croat, Muslim, or Serbian.

The confused nature of Ivoirité is another example of this. Who is the enemy to the Christian groups in the south: the Muslim Mandinké people who have lived in what is now the Côte d'Ivoire for generations, or the new immigrants from Burkina Faso, Mali, and other neighboring countries? The controversy around the citizenship of Alassane Outtara centers around this very issue.

For a comprehensive look at this problem that is affecting many groups in the world today, see the following sources of information: "What Is Nationalism Really?" by Thomas Haymes in the December 1997 issue of *Nations and Nationalism*; *Imagined Communities* by Benedict Anderson (Verso Press, 1983); *Ethno-nationalism: The Quest for Understanding* by Walker Connor (Princeton University Press, 1994); *Nations and Nationalism Since 1780: Programme, Myth, Reality* by E.J. Hobshawm (Cambridge University Press, 1990); and Professor Thomas Hylland Eriksen's Web site at: http://folk.uio.no/geirthe/.

meritorious. Thus Houphouët-Boigny placed himself above the government, hearing complaints in person as an Ivorian rendition of the *cahiers de doléances* (list of grievances) of French kings. He assumed the role of teacher as well as student, lecturing his subjects on the need for dedication to work, to family and to country. These dialogues provided relief from the routine distance and formality of Ivorian administrative authoritarianism.

In other words, while his administration was overwhelmingly Baoule in composition, Houphouët-Boigny was able give other groups a feeling that they had a voice in the administration of the country.

## New Lines of Division

Economic times became more difficult in the latter half of the 1980s. Houphouët-Boigny,

advancing in age, felt that his personal vigor was in question (he was well into his eighties at this point). The president took action by drawing a more diverse political spectrum into his administration. One of the new people was Alassane Ouattara, a Muslim from the north of the country who was appointed by Houphouët-Boigny to the newly created post of prime minister in the wake of Côte d'Ivoire's first multiparty elections in 1990. With this action, Houphouët-Boigny unwittingly set up a political conflict between Ouattara and Bedié, who both thought they had a legitimate right to the presidency after his death in December 1993.

A third political actor began emerging at this time in the personage of Laurent Gbagbo, who ran against Houphouët-Boigny in the 1990 presidential and legislative elections as head of the Front Populaire Ivoirien (FPI). The FPI is nominally a social-democratic party but more specifically it has come to represent the interests of the Bété people, the most significant sub-grouping of the Kru. As the other main Christian ethnic grouping in Côte d'Ivoire, the Bété had generally cooperated with the Baoule in the administration of the country. The Library of Congress country report on the Côte d'Ivoire, however, reported in 1988:

> In the twentieth century the Bété have been recognized for their success in cash cropping and for their widespread acceptance of Christianity. They have a strong ethnic consciousness despite these foreign influences and have been active both within the government and in antigovernment dissent groups since independence. They also have a long history of resistance to foreign domination and strong beliefs in their own cultural superiority.

The Bété quickly pushed much of their leadership into opposition to PDCI rule. The FPI was one of the first parties formed in opposition to the PDCI and Gbagbo returned from exile in 1988 to lead it. Gbagbo, a former history professor, makes an unlikely political figure, but his persistence has made him a factor in all Ivorian elections since 1990. As recently as 1998, the *Economist* theorized that Gbagbo would never come to power. While eclipsed by Ouattara during much of the 1990s as the chief opposition figure, however, he was the only major political figure left standing against General Guëi in the disputed 2000 presidential election.

## The Death of the President

Even before Houphouët-Boigny's death in December 1993, the stability of Côte d'Ivoire was being undermined by international economic conditions such as the precipitous fall of world commodity prices. Côte d'Ivoire depends on cocoa and coffee exports for much of its capital and when these commodities began to fall, the country suddenly found itself in serious economic trouble. This situation was not helped by the rampant corruption within the government—a legacy of Houphouët-Boigny's policies of patronage. In his times, with excess capital, corruption was not a serious drain on the economy, but with the downturn in Côte d'Ivoire's economic fortunes, it became a significant problem that has only gotten worse.

One of the reasons that Houphouët-Boigny brought Ouattara into the government in 1990 was for his economic expertise. He had been Director of the African Department of the International Monetary Fund. During his time as prime minister, Ouattara was able to reform the

## HENRI KONAN BEDIÉ

1934– A member of the Baoule ethnic group, Henri Konan Bedié was born in Dadiékro, Côte d'Ivoire in 1934. He was educated in France and received his Ph.D. in Economics from the Université de Poitiers. In 1960, while Côte d'Ivoire was still under French colonial rule, Bedié entered the Côte d'Ivoire Civil Service. He served as the First Ivorian ambassador to the United States from 1961 to 1966. Shortly after his diplomatic service, Bedié served as Côte d'Ivoire's Minister of Finance from 1966 to 1977 under the first president after independence, Félix Houphouët-Boigny. He was also the Governor of the International Monetary Fund and an administrator for the International Bank for Reconstruction and Development, which is part of the World Bank group.

In 1977 Bedié was dismissed from his position as finance minister after six state-owned sugar factories failed under suspicious circumstances. He was then appointed as Special Advisor for African Affairs to the President of the International Finance Corporation of the World Bank, and served in that capacity until 1980, when he became the President of the National Assembly of Côte d'Ivoire.

President Houphouët-Boigny died in 1993, and Bedié, as President of the National Assembly, became the acting President of Côte d'Ivoire. He was officially elected President in 1995 after excluding most of his challengers from the election. He was President for nearly five years until December 24, 1999, when he was ousted in a military coup.

economy somewhat and secure additional funding from international donors, mainly because of his economic expertise and the international perception that he had not been affected by the corruption that characterized the rest of the government. The strict economic measures that he imposed on Côte d'Ivoire in order to achieve this success, however, angered many groups within the country.

With Houphouët-Boigny's death, Bedié, as speaker of the General Assembly, assumed the role of acting president as set out in the Ivorian constitution. Ouattara was quickly forced out of the government and Bedié worked to marginalize him before the presidential elections of 1995. In September 1994, reformist members of the PDCI founded the Rassemblement de Republicains (RDR) in the hopes of running Ouattara for the presidency in 1995. Despite the controversy over

# LAURENT GBAGBO

*1945–* Laurent Gbagbo was born in Gagnoa, Côte d'Ivoire in May of 1945 as a member of the Bété ethnic group. Gbagbo was educated in both Côte d'Ivoire and France. In 1969 he received a Teaching Certificate in History from the Université d'Abidjan, and later received a Doctorat de Troisième Cycle from the Université de Paris VII in 1978.

Gbagbo's career as a teacher had a tenuous beginning. In 1970 he was appointed professor of History and Geography at the Lycée Classique d'Abidjan. A year later, he served two years in prison for subversive teaching. In 1974 he began advanced academic studies. In 1980 Gbagbo returned to the field of education and was appointed Director of the Institut d'Histoire, d'Arte, et d'Archéologie (Institute of History, Art, and Archaeology) at the Université d'Abidjan. From 1980 to 1982 Gbagbo also served as the leader of the Syndicat National de la Recerche et de L'Enseignement Supérieur (SYNARES), a union of teachers.

In 1982 Gbagbo began his political career, founding the Front Populair Ivoirien (FPI) to which he is also elected secretary. The party is banned by President Houphoët-Boigny, who refused to hold multiparty elections.

Gbagbo spent the next six years in self-imposed exile in France. It was during that time that he wrote several books and participated in socialist political activities as a representative of the FPI. In 1988 he returned to the Côte d'Ivoire after the FPI is legalized and returned to his teaching career. But soon after he would challenge President Houphoët-Boigny for the

CÔTE D'IVOIRE'S PRESIDENT, LAURENT GBAGBO, CASTS HIS VOTE IN THE 2000 PARLIAMENTARY ELECTIONS, WHICH WERE BOYCOTTED BY BACKERS OF FORMER PRIME MINISTER ALASSANE OUATTARA. *(© Reuters NewMedia Inc./Corbis. Reproduced by permission.)*

presidency. Gbagbo received 17 percent of the vote in his bid against President Houphoët-Boigny in the first multiparty elections in the Côte d'Ivoire. From 1990 to 2000 he was the FPI Deputy in the Ivorian National Assembly. Gbagbo finally was able to win an election in 2000, though it was disputed, when he was elected president of the Côte d'Ivoire.

his economic policies, Ouattara remained a popular figure, particularly among the Muslim community.

Bedié, who never seemed sure of his own popularity and certainly lacked the charisma of Houphouët-Boigny, worked to eliminate potential opposition candidates for the upcoming presidential elections. In order to eliminate Ouattara, he required all candidates to have resided in Côte d'Ivoire for five years prior to the election, effectively disqualifying the former prime minister from the election. As a result, both the RDR and FPI boycotted the subsequent poll held in October 1995.

## Ivoirité

Perched precariously in the faltering economy and lacking the political skills of his predecessor, Houphouët-Boigny, Bedié began playing the various groups within Ivorian society against one another. His method of excluding Ouattara from the elections was indicative of the policy of *Ivoirité* adopted by Bedié during his administration. Ivoirité refers to an attempt to clarify the ethnicity of "true" Ivorians. Côte d'Ivoire has an immigrant population—encouraged to migrate during the presidency of Houphouët-Boigny—that numbers as high as 40 percent of the population. During the years of economic downturn, ethnic and national

## TESTIMONY CITED IN "THE NEW RACISM: THE POLITICAL MANIPULATION OF ETHNICITY IN CÔTE D'IVOIRE," A HUMAN RIGHTS WATCH REPORT

The testimony below, from an elderly Malian man in Côte d'Ivoire, is one among many first-hand accounts of the escalating and systematic violence and ethnic abuses in the country. This man was apparently the only survivor out of 14 men gunned down in October 2000. His testimony was verified by other eyewitnesses.

On Thursday October 26, at around 2:00 PM. I left my house to do an errand. On my way I saw the gendarmes were all around. A minute later they saw me and ordered me to come to them. They said they were going to kill me because I'm a Dioula, because I'm a Muslim. I was wearing my bobo [robe] and slippers so they knew I was a Muslim. After hearing that I took off running across the railway line but was unfortunately caught by another gendarme. I begged them to forgive me—I shouldn't really have to ask forgiveness for anything but I figured my life was more important than my pride.

The gendarme who'd caught me told me to lie down on the railway and then the others said, no, I should join another group of prisoners nearby. As I was led to this place I saw there were thirteen prisoners; even though I'm old my mind is sharp and I took time to count. The gendarmes were all around and they kept pointing their guns at us. When I arrived they told me to take off my bobo and lay down on the grass with the others.

While lying there the gendarmes asked our nationality, which is how I came to know there was also one Burkinabé and one Mauritanian among us. One of them said, 'all of you are RDR, all of you are Dioula.' They beat us for about thirty minutes. They kicked and beat us with the thick iron buckles of their red belts. They were especially tough on the younger men but left me alone because I'm old. We were asking pardon and telling them we were sorry. One gendarme came by and said, "haven't you killed these people yet?"

*Human Rights Watch, Human Rights News, August 28, 2001. Available online at http://www.hrw.org/press/2001/08/cote-testimonies-0828.htm.*

identities became lines of division, and Ivoirité became the buzzword of those who felt victimized by the Muslims from the north. Ouattara, a Muslim, formed a convenient target for government accusations against his group as a whole.

With Bedié unable to sustain the economic resurgence produced by Ouattara's austerity measures and his ability to generate foreign capital, Ivoirité formed a convenient outlet for public resentment. In Côte d'Ivoire as elsewhere, in times of economic downturn the immigrant community is often seen as taking jobs away from the native community, and becomes a convenient target for public animosity. Bedié encouraged this kind of xenophobia in order to distract the population from his own administration's corruption and incompetence.

Muslims from within the borders of Côte d'Ivoire were soon lumped in with immigrants, thus the Mandé community members who migrated from the northern part of the country to the commercial center of Abidjan became targets of hostility. Bedié used this trend to cast aspersions on the nationality of Ouattara's parents and thereby question his rights to citizenship—and the presidency.

### A Coup and an Election

Bedié's inefficiency and corruption finally resulted in his overthrow by General Gueï in December 1999. The inability to pay parts of the army was the direct impetus for the coup, but the general economic malaise that the country had fallen into provided much-needed support to the general in the weeks following the coup. Both Gbagbo and Ouattara initially expressed their support for the army's action. Gbagbo and the FPI eventually joined Gueï's government.

By the summer of 2000, however, Gueï was unable to find a new basis of support in an increasingly fragmented country and fell back on the xenophobic policies of his predecessor. With few prospects for a strong economic recovery, xenophobia seemed to be the only card that Ivorian politicians, particularly those of the increasingly hard-pressed Christian south, had left to play. Gueï decided that he should be the candidate for the next presidential elections due in October 2000 and set in motion machinations very similar to those Bedié had used before him in order to make sure he was the only realistic candidate. In a series of decisions, his handpicked Supreme Court eliminated 15 of 19 candidates for the presidency, including both Ouattara and Bedié.

# ALASSANE OUATTARA

*1942*– Alassane Ouattara was born January 1, 1942, in Dimbroko, Côte d'Ivoire. Ouattara pursued higher education in the United States and received his Ph.D. in Economics from the University of Pennsylvania in 1972. From 1968 to 1973 Ouattara was on staff as an economist at the International Monetary Fund (IMF). In 1973 Ouattara became a representative at the Bank of West African States (BCEAO), and in 1975 became the Governor and Director of Research at the BCEAO and served in that position until 1983. In 1984 Ouattara worked as Deputy Governor of the BCEAO. Ouattara became Director of the African Department and Advisor to the Director-General of the IMF in 1984 and remained there until 1988 when he returned to the position of Governor of the BCEAO.

In 1990 Alassane Ouattara began his career in the government of the Côte d'Ivoire. President Houphouët-Boigny selected Ouattara to head a cabinet-level commission on the Ivorian economy. Shortly thereafter he became the first Prime Minister of the Côte d'Ivoire. During his tenure he launched unpopular austerity measures and was ousted upon the death of President Houphouët-Boigny in 1993.

After being forced out of office Ouattara returned to the IMF as Deputy Managing Director. In 1995 he was selected as the presidential candidate of the new Rassemblement des Republicains (RDR). President Bedié, however, barred him from the election on the grounds that he failed to meet residency requirements. Ouattara would remain at the IMF until 1999, and in 2000 he again attempted a run for the presidency of Côte d'Ivoire as the RDR's candidate. Again he was barred from running by the military dictator of the country, General Robert Gueï, on the grounds that his parentage was not Ivorian and he was not qualified for citizenship. Since that time, Alassane Ouattara has been living in exile in France.

Gueï apparently did not take Gbagbo's candidacy particularly seriously as the FPI had never had terribly strong polling numbers and the Bété group, from which it drew its primary support, only makes up about six percent of the population. Gbagbo's candidacy, however, apparently attracted the support of a wide range of disaffected Ivorians who saw him as the only viable alternative with Ouattara out of the picture. When early returns showed Gbagbo polling more than 50 percent of the vote to Gueï's 40 percent, the general attempted to circumvent the results, leading to the wave of violence that shook the country in October 2000. After much of the army apparently turned against him, Gueï fled, leaving Gbagbo the first non-Baoule to assume the Ivorian presidency.

## RECENT HISTORY AND THE FUTURE

While clearly a break from the past, in some ways Gbagbo's ethnic and political base among the Bété put him in a far weaker position than any of his Baoule predecessors. He is still a Christian in an increasingly Muslim country and his ethnic grouping makes up an even smaller percentage of the population than the Baoule. There is still no clear way out of the economic morass in which Côte d'Ivoire currently finds itself. Partially as a result, Gbagbo has not abandoned his predecessors' policy of Ivoirité.

In an August 2001 report Human Rights Watch severely criticized the policies of the Gbagbo government for failing to right the wrongs of previous administrations and continuing to support violence and repression of political and ethnic opponents. Police and soldiers involved in brutalities during the disturbances of October 2000, most notably the massacre of 57 RDR supporters in a forest outside of Abidjan, have been let off very lightly, while RDR supporters have spent months in jail on charges of inciting violence during the riots.

While many of these opposition supporters have since been released, the government apparently still countenances violence against Muslims and immigrants. Its light treatment of abuses by the security forces sends a strong signal that such activity will be tolerated in the future, creating a high level of tension and undermining prospects for reconciliation and recovery.

In addition to these domestic concerns there are suspicions of foreign activity in destabilizing

DURING VIOLENT PROTESTS AGAINST CÔTE D'IVOIRE PRIME MINISTER ALASSANE OUATTARA, A RALLY OF REPUBLICANS PROTESTER BRANDISHES A STICK IN FRONT OF BURNING BARRICADES. (© *AFP/Corbis. Reproduced by permission.*)

the government. Some within the Gbagbo regime and the press that supports it have theorized that Liberian President Charles Taylor was in some way involved in the January 2001 failed coup attempt. The Baoule political leadership enjoyed close relations with Taylor during Liberia's long civil war, in which Côte d'Ivoire acted as a transit point for arms shipments. Taylor has considerably less influence over Gbagbo and none over Ouattara. Accordingly, he is seen as having an interest in seeing either Gueï or Bedié reinstalled in office and is perfectly willing to foment unrest in pursuit of that goal.

Another interesting foreign connection involves Blaise Campoare, the president of Burkina Faso and also a close associate of Taylor's. Large portions of Côte d'Ivoire's immigrants are Burkinabe and they have been particularly targeted in anti-immigrant violence. Coincidentally, these Muslim Burkinabe are often lumped in with Ouattara's RDR supporters, creating a useful synergy of foreign enemies for the government to target in its efforts at maintaining popular support. Rumors of armed RDR supporters training in Burkina Faso have aroused a great deal of concern among the non-Muslim population and have resulted in a strengthening of Ivorian military presence on the border.

Gbagbo is clearly in a difficult position if he wants to continue as president. There are no signs that the Ivorian economy will come out of its slump anytime soon and the continuing unrest undermines any attempts at attracting new foreign investment. He has embarked on a course of partial reconciliation with Ouattara, but it is clear that he can only pursue this course so far before he risks the policy of Ivoirité upon which he has increasingly been forced to base his power.

The one ray of hope in this situation has been the continued moderation of Ouattara and the senior elements of the RDR leadership. One thing that could exacerbate the situation would be the radicalization of the Muslim elites. But with his continued moderation it is possible that at some time in the future Ouattara could peacefully come to power in a free and fair election. At this point, however, there are few signs that this will actually take place. In the current circumstances it is just as likely, if not more so, that radical elements will take advantage of the situation and the country will experience more chaos like that of October 2000.

## BIBLIOGRAPHY

Associated Press. "Thousands Stream into Burkina Faso to Escape Attacks in Ivory Coast," January 20, 2001.

Handloff, Robert E. ed. *Ivory Coast/Côte d'Ivoire: A Country Report.* Washington: Library of Congress, 1988.

Human Rights Watch. "The New Racism: The Political Manipulation of Ethnicity in Côte d'Ivoire," Vol. 13, No.6 (A); August 2001. Available online at http://www.hrw.org/press/2001/08/cote-testimonies-0828.htm (cited October 15, 2001).

Jackson, Robert H. *Quasi-States: Sovereignty, International Relations and the Third World.* Cambridge: Cambridge University Press, 1990.

Lewis, Barbara. "Félix Houphouët-Boigny," in Harvey Glickman ed., *Political Leaders of Contemporary Africa South of the Sahara:* Westport, CT: Greenwood Press, 1992, pp. 87–93.

"Why Things Fall Apart; A Slow, Preventable March in Crisis," *New York Times,* October 29, 2000, Section 4, p. 1.

*Thomas Haymes*

# POST-COLD WAR ESPIONAGE BETWEEN THE UNITED STATES AND RUSSIA: HOW HAS THE MISSION CHANGED?

On February 18, 2001, the Federal Bureau of Investigation (FBI) arrested Robert Philip Hanssen, one of its own counter-intelligence agents, in a park in Vienna, Virginia, shortly after Hanssen had left a package under a small footbridge. The area was known to the FBI as a drop point for the illicit exchange of information with Russian agents and, indeed, Hanssen's arrest was the result of a lengthy FBI investigation into his activities as a spy for the Soviet Union, and after 1991, the Russian Federation.

Robert Hanssen was a 25-year veteran of the FBI; the bureau alleges that 16 of those years were spent spying for Russia. Hanssen himself, in the plea agreement reached in July 2001, admits that his activities stretch back even further, to 1979. In return for pleading guilty to 15 counts of espionage and conspiracy charges, Hanssen was spared the death penalty. In addition to requiring Hanssen to serve a life sentence in prison, the plea agreement orders him to cooperate with the FBI and the Central Intelligence Agency (CIA) and be fully debriefed, in order for those agencies to ascertain the exact scope of the damage Hanssen caused to U.S. intelligence. News of Hanssen's activities has hit the headlines after his February 2001 arrest, not because it is a unique story, but because a number of high-profile cases of American intelligence officers caught spying for Russia have come to light in the past few years.

From 1945 to 1991, when the political culture of the Cold War draped U.S.-Soviet relations in an icy shroud of mutual mistrust and antagonism, espionage was a critical, if obviously underpublicized, game of learning the enemy's secrets before the enemy learned yours. But with the collapse of the Soviet Union in 1991, the Cold War

## THE CONFLICT

The ideological conflict between capitalism and communism sparked the Cold War, fought by the two countries that emerged most powerful from World War II—the United States and the Soviet Union. Espionage between the two superpowers was a major component of the Cold War. When the Soviet Union collapsed in 1991 and the Cold War ended, the nature of espionage between the United States and Russia changed dramatically.

### Political

*   Since 1991, Russia has been more concerned with its own internal situation, particularly its economy, than with acquiring U.S. military secrets. The United States, meanwhile, has made new enemies in the Middle East, and focuses its espionage on this region more than on Russia. Despite the high-profile arrests of Russian spies such as FBI agent Robert Hanssen, espionage since 1991 is very different from what it was during the Cold War, and neither the United States nor Russia is a prime target of each other's spy activity.

*   Even during the Cold War, the nature of espionage changed noticeably. U.S. spies for the Soviet Union in the early days of the Cold War were generally motivated by ideology, whereas in the 1980s and 1990s they were generally motivated by personal gain.

*   After the collapse of the Soviet Union, most U.S.-Russian spying was for security purposes. The United States did not always trust the Russian reports on the poorly guarded sites of weapons of mass destruction in Russia and politically unstable former Soviet republics. Russia has concerns about the expansion of the North Atlantic Treaty Alliance (NATO) along Russia's borders and the United States's use of its power around the world.

# CHRONOLOGY

*1920s–1930s* While communist parties gain strength in Western Europe, governments in the United States and Canada act to restrict the activities of local communists in their countries.

*1939* The outbreak of war between Britain and Germany leads to an increase in espionage between the two countries, as well as counter-intelligence efforts to combat it.

*1941* The German invasion of the Soviet Union and the Japanese attack on Pearl Harbor bring the United States and the Soviet Union into the war as allies. Publicly, both countries shelve their ideological differences in order to work together to defeat fascism.

*1941–45* Despite the outward façade of cooperation, the United States and the Soviet Union begin operating extensive espionage networks against each other.

*1945* The United States drops the world's first atomic bombs on Japan, ending World War II and signaling the dawning of the nuclear era.

*1947* The United States government begins to realize the extent of Soviet espionage during the war, prompted by the testimony of former agents Elizabeth Bentley and Igor Gouzenko. President Harry S. Truman creates the Central Intelligence Agency (CIA) in response.

*1949* The Soviet Union successfully tests its own atomic bomb. The United States realizes that Soviet spies in the American atomic bomb program (code-named the Manhattan Project) facilitated the Soviet feat.

*1950* Extensive U.S. counter-intelligence investigations lead to the arrests of Julius and Ethel Rosenberg. They are later convicted and executed.

*1950–54* The McCarthy Era, in which Senator Joseph McCarthy conducts a zealous war against communism in the United States, destroys much of the American Communist Party.

*1953* Soviet dictator Joseph Stalin dies, and in the next few years the scale of his crimes against the people of the Soviet Union is revealed. Support for the American Communist Party continues to dwindle.

*1962* The Cuban Missile Crisis brings the world to the brink of nuclear catastrophe, underlining for both superpowers the importance of reliable intelligence information.

*1968* The Prague Spring, as the popular uprising in Czechoslovakia is known, is crushed by Soviet tanks. Very few Soviet spies in the United States are still motivated by ideological commitments to communism; for the remainder of the Cold War, most will be mercenaries.

*1972* A new era of détente lessens tensions between the superpowers; ironically, espionage activity increases.

*1985* Mikhail Gorbachev comes to power in the Soviet Union; his reformist policies of *glasnost* (openness) and *perestroika* (restructuring) initiate the demise of the Soviet Union.

*1989* Communist governments throughout Eastern Europe crumble along with the Berlin Wall. The Soviet Union is left standing alone behind the Iron Curtain, though not for long.

*1991* An attempted coup against Soviet leader Gorbachev fails, but leads to the collapse of the communist government. The Cold War is suddenly over, the Soviet Union breaks into 15 independent states, and a solitary Russia tries to recover economically, politically, and culturally.

*1994* CIA counter-intelligence officer Aldrich Ames is arrested for spying for the Soviet Union and Russia. The highly publicized case shows that despite the end of the Cold War, espionage between the former superpowers continues.

*1999* The use of NATO force against the Serbian military in Kosovo increases Russian suspicion of the alliance, particularly as it encroaches on Russia's borders and in its former spheres of influence.

*2001* FBI agent Robert Hanssen is arrested for spying for Russia, sparking a reevaluation of the nature and meaning of espionage between the United States and Russia in the post-Cold War era.

came to an abrupt end. Espionage between the former enemies, as evidenced by the arrest of Hanssen and others since 1991, clearly did not end with the Cold War. It did, however, change course. Priorities for both countries were suddenly quite different from what they had been during the nearly half-century of bipolar hostility and East-West alignment.

The United States became less interested in Russia and more concerned with security threats from rogue states such as Iraq and Afghanistan, while Russia became less interested in security against American espionage and more concerned with encouraging much-needed investment from American companies in the disastrous post-Soviet economy. The result of these shifting priorities has been a marked decrease in U.S.-Russian espionage activity, despite what the high-profile arrests of Hanssen and others might indicate. It has not completely stopped, and likely never will, but the mission has drastically changed on both sides, and the current state of espionage between the United States and Russia is far removed from the frenzy of intelligence activity that characterized the Cold War years.

## HISTORICAL BACKGROUND

### The Cold War Begins

Although some historians have argued for an earlier date, most agree that the Cold War began in 1945, with the end of World War II, and with it, the end of the strategic alliance of convenience between the United States and the Soviet Union against Nazi Germany. So named because it was a war of ideology rather than a "hot" military conflict, the Cold War, at its basic level, pitted capitalist economics and political democracy, as embodied by the United States, against the centrally planned economy and communist political system represented by the Soviet Union. Each sought to prove to its own citizens, each other's citizens, and political leaders in other parts of the globe that its system represented a model for the rest of the world to follow. Each developed a sphere of influence, by which countries of geographical or ideological proximity to the United States or the Soviet Union aligned themselves with one of the superpowers.

This created a bipolar world system that paralyzed action on a number of conflicts and deadlocked many issues in the United Nations and other international bodies. Fuelling this ideological war of attrition was the threat of nuclear catastrophe, which hung over global politics after 1949

when, with the successful testing of an atomic bomb, the Soviet Union joined the United States as the second country in the world to possess nuclear weapons. Proof of the bomb's destruction had already come in 1945, when the United States dropped two atomic bombs on Japan as a means of forcing the Japanese to surrender and end the war.

After the Soviet Union joined the nuclear club in 1949, the two superpowers held the rest of the world hostage to their interests, using the threat of another nuclear attack to control global politics. While the Cold War went through periods of "freeze" and "thaw," owing mostly to changes in the political leadership of one or another of the superpowers, it essentially maintained its form as a period of heightened paranoia and global tension until its sudden end in 1991.

A logical outcome of the mistrust and paranoia that characterized the Cold War was the increased use of espionage between the United States and the Soviet Union. The intelligence-gathering techniques of both countries, as well as Britain, Germany, and others, were honed during World War II (1939–45), when intelligence information could—and did—shape the outcome of the war. Perhaps the most famous story of wartime espionage is that of the code-breakers at Britain's Bletchley Park, who cracked the German Enigma code without German knowledge, allowing Britain and its allies to collect critical information about the German war effort and to organize its counter-efforts accordingly.

Wartime intelligence efforts were not only directed against the enemy, however; espionage activity between the United States and the Soviet Union existed prior to the outbreak of the war and continued throughout the war years, despite the façade of Allied cooperation. During the war, and continuing into the early Cold War years, Soviet espionage in the United States focused on obtaining technological secrets in order to thwart American technical superiority. A major part of these operations was the Soviet attempt, through spying, to learn American atomic secrets in order to achieve its own nuclear capabilities. These efforts were in fact largely successful; the Soviet Union's 1949 detonation of an atomic bomb is generally agreed to have occurred earlier than would have been possible without the information gleaned from its intelligence agents at sites for U.S. atomic weapons development.

### The Manhattan Project and the Rosenbergs

Soviet infiltration of the Manhattan Project, the code name for the United States's wartime

THE AMERICAN FLAG FLIES OUTSIDE THE U.S. EMBASSY IN MOSCOW, JUXTAPOSED WITH A RUSSIAN REVOLUTION-ARY MONUMENT. FIFTY-ONE RUSSIAN DIPLOMATS WERE EXPELLED FROM THE UNITED STATES IN MARCH 2001. *(A/P Wide World. Reproduced by permission.)*

atomic weapons project based at Los Alamos, New Mexico, is one of the most high-profile examples of the stakes involved in espionage activity during the Cold War. A decade ago the scope of Soviet penetration of the American atomic program was less understood than it is now, thanks to the release of previously unknown documents such as the Mitrokhin Archive (a collection of papers brought to Britain during the 1992 defection of KGB officer Vasili Mitrokhin) and the Venona files (a secret American code-breaking operation to be further discussed below). It is now evident that the Soviet Union successfully penetrated the most inner secrets of the Manhattan Project, by recruiting Klaus Fuchs and Theodore Hall, two key physicists, as well as technician David Greenglass as spies.

Perhaps the best known of the atomic spies were the Rosenbergs and their extended family members. Julius Rosenberg was not himself involved in the Manhattan Project, but he was a major recruiter of Soviet spies in the United States. By the time of his arrest in 1950, Rosenberg had become a key link between the Soviet Union and many top-level spies in American industry and government. When his brother-in-law, David Greenglass, was hired as a machinist at the Manhattan Project, Rosenberg notified the KGB, the Soviet Union's intelligence agency, and recruited Greenglass into the fold of Soviet espionage.

While Greenglass did not have access to information as secretive as that which physicist Theodore Hall passed on to the Soviets, his efforts were nonetheless useful to Russian atomic development. The complicity of Ruth Greenglass and Ethel Rosenberg, both Communist Party members, in their husbands' subversive activities led to their implication as enablers when the FBI caught up with their husbands in 1950.

The case of the Rosenbergs cannot be discussed without noting its influence on American public discourse on espionage and anti-communism. The Rosenbergs' trial and subsequent execution for treason sparked an outcry of public antagonism towards what was seen as increasingly authoritarian and unfairly overzealous anti-communist tactics on the part of the American government. The Rosenbergs came to represent the liberal argument that the government's anti-communist drive had gone too far, to the point of targeting—and indeed executing—innocent people, whose only crime was having the wrong political affiliations.

These pervasive views about the probable innocence of the Rosenbergs were facilitated by the rather weak case with which the government brought them to trial. Based almost entirely on circumstantial evidence, corroborated by the testimony of David Greenglass, the public was particularly incensed by the government's lack of solid evidence against the Rosenbergs. In truth, the government had plenty of evidence against the pair but was unable to use it in court, lest the secrecy of its counterintelligence operations be compromised. With the 1995 release of the files gathered by the Venona code-breaking operation, the evidence against the Rosenbergs was finally made public. It showed, indisputably, that the Rosenbergs were indeed guilty of the crimes for which they were executed.

### Cold War Espionage after the 1970s

The quest for technological information appears to have motivated U.S.-Soviet espionage for much of the Cold War, particularly its early years as the so-called "arms race" and "space race" heated up, and it became increasingly clear that a technological lag by either country could spell disaster in the event of war. While this main goal of espionage between the superpowers remained constant during the Cold War, the operation did go through changes between 1945 and 1991. Ironically, espionage between the two countries increased with the onset of détente in 1972, although it arguably became more covert. With détente came a flurry of new diplomatic, cultural, and commercial enterprises between the Soviet Union and the West, which enabled intelligence officers to enter enemy territory under the guise of journalism, trade interests, or diplomacy.

Late Cold War espionage had a different character, however. Motivated in the early years chiefly by ideological convictions—an overwhelming majority of early Soviet spies were members of the American Communist Party—by the 1970s most were simply mercenaries seeking to augment their government salaries. In this way, although numerically there may have been more spies in the later years of the Cold War, historians of the period seem to agree that the true height of Soviet espionage in the United States had occurred during World War II and in the early years of the Cold War. This was the period when highly sensitive atomic material and other technological secrets were passed to the Soviets, and a complex spy network operated not only in the technology sector, but in senior offices of government and industry as well.

These networks, of which Julius Rosenberg and eventual defector Elizabeth Bentley were among the most prominent leaders, were comprised of not only the spies themselves, but recruiters, middlemen, and covering agents. After McCarthyist zeal, which sought to root out communists in the United States, destroyed most of these networks in the late 1940s and early 1950s, espionage in the United States consisted mostly of independent agents who sought only financial compensation for procuring sensitive material.

### Post-Cold War Espionage

In 1989, a series of political, economic, and social events in communist Eastern Europe resulted in both the physical and metaphorical crumbling of the Berlin Wall. The unification of communist East Berlin and capitalist West Berlin reflected a turning point in history—the approaching end of the Cold War. The Soviet Union, after withdrawing in defeat from a ten-year war in Afghanistan, watched as the Communist Party collapsed in Eastern Europe. The Party's power within Russia rapidly weakened, especially after the extent of damage caused by the nuclear accident at Chernobyl—and the government's cover-up of the situation—were known. When political and economic pressure points reached a climax, the result was the dissolution of the Soviet Union. The Cold War abruptly ended, prompting many (Western) observers to crudely label the United States the "winner." Regardless of the accuracy of that declaration, it was clear that the international system of bipolarity that had defined global politics for a half-century was no more.

The United States and Western Europe scrambled to offer financial aid to the struggling economies of former communist countries. Trade and investment opportunities opened up, and many observers applauded the end of the Cold War power games which, buttressed by the threats of nuclear warfare, had held the world hostage for so long. As the twentieth century gave way to the twenty-first, many said the much-anticipated global village would finally come about with the nations of the world working together, across ideological lines, for global peace and prosperity. Unfortunately, this was not to be the case.

## RECENT HISTORY AND THE FUTURE

As the Soviet Union teetered on the brink of collapse in early 1991, the Gulf War (1991) was already giving the world—especially the United States—a hint of what was in store for the post-Cold War age. Anti-Americanism in states formerly supported by the Soviet Union was unleashed anew. The number of states possessing nuclear capabilities increased, and the world real-

# ELIZABETH BENTLEY

*1908–1963* Elizabeth Terrill Bentley, the "Red (or Blond) Spy Queen," became a public figure in the mid-1940s when she quit her career of spying for the Soviets and became an informant to the Federal Bureau of Investigation (FBI), reporting on KGB operations that were ongoing within the American government. Born in New England, Bentley graduated from Vassar College in 1930 and received a master's degree from Columbia University. She then studied in Florence, Italy, returning to New York City in 1934. There she joined the Communist Party and took a job at the Italian Library of Information. The library was an agency of the fascist government of Italian dictator Benito Mussolini (1883–1945) and Bentley used her position to inform about the fascists to the Italian Communist Party. Her contact with the Communists was Jacob Golos, a party officer and Soviet secret-police agent, who was soon to become her lover as well.

By 1941 Bentley (code name "Good Girl") was a regular courier between Golos in New York and a group of Communist agents employed in the federal bureaucracy in Washington, a spy ring that included Klaus Fuchs, Whittaker Chambers, and David Greenglass. She made regular trips to the capital to relay instructions from Moscow and to collect the material the agents had taken from government offices. Golos died in 1943. In 1945 Bentley had apparently tired of espionage and took her story to the FBI. She appeared before a grand jury in 1946.

In August 1948 Bentley testified before the House of Representatives Committee on Un-American Activities, naming dozens of government officials who had supplied her with secret military and political information. She had no physical evidence and none of the people Bentley named were ever indicted for espionage. Her testimony, though, helped to convict William W. Remington, an economist in the Department of Commerce, of perjury. It was also involved in the conviction Julius and Ethel Rosenberg for spying for the Soviet Union.

ON AUGUST 9, 1948, ELIZABETH T. BENTLEY SAT BEFORE THE HOUSE UNAMERICAN ACTIVITIES COMMITTEE. SHE WAS THE LEADING WITNESS OF THE CONGRESSIONAL "RED SPY" HEARINGS. *(A/P Wide World. Reproduced by permission.)*

Bentley had become a something of a celebrity as an ex-Communist. She published an autobiography, *Out of Bondage* in 1952. After that she worked for a time as a consultant and lecturer on communism. From 1958 until her death, she taught at a state correctional institute in Middletown, Connecticut.

For many years, Bentley's testimony was treated with skepticism. Fifty years later in 1995, the United States released the Soviet messages that had been decoded in the VENONA project. The Venona translations confirmed that Bentley's confessions were accurate and that the government officials she had implicated had in fact been working as agents for the Soviets.

ized that these weapons were now in the hands of unpredictable leaders of politically unstable countries. Further, the Gulf War introduced biological warfare as a new threat in the 1990s. Conventional warfare has in many places been replaced by rogue terrorism, in which enemies are not only unpredictable, but often unknown. Meanwhile, technology, led by the historically incomparable revolution brought about by the Internet, has forever changed the nature of war, diplomacy, and, of course, espionage. Spies in the digital age are operating in ways entirely different from their predecessors: wireless communications systems, satellite imagery, even simple e-mail have all become a major part of a spy's world, creating new headaches for counter-intelligence agents who must devise new ways of tracking the enemy's activities.

Perhaps this new technology has helped the FBI to discover the activities of post-Cold War Russian spies. Since 1991, the United States has seen the high-profile capture of a number of them, most notably former CIA counter-intelligence officer Aldrich Ames, who was arrested in 1994 as a Russian spy. Walking into the Soviet embassy in Washington in 1985 to volunteer his services, a cash-strapped Ames acted not out of any anti-American or anti-capitalist ideological convictions, like his early Cold War predecessors had, but simply for money. He asked for, and received, US$50,000 for the first piece of information he offered the Soviets; by the time of his arrest he had reportedly earned $2.7 million for his activities, and was owed a further $1.9 million. While Ames betrayed a significant amount of sensitive material during his ten years on the KGB payroll, he is best known, and publicly reviled, for revealing to the KGB the names of 25 Russian agents working for the CIA. Ten of those spies, including some of the most valuable agents the CIA had ever recruited, were later recalled to Moscow and shot. Ames is currently in prison, serving a life sentence for his crimes.

## The Venona Project

The 1990s thus saw a number of changes in the ways in which espionage was both practiced and uncovered. The post-Cold War years have also seen one archive after another open in Russia and the United States alike as the governments of both countries decide that much of their Cold War information can be declassified. This new information has been a gift to academics, particularly historians seeking to reconstruct the early period of Cold War espionage. In 1995, for example, historians were delighted when the National Security Agency (NSA) finally released the Venona files. Venona was the code name of one of the United States government's most covert—and effective—code-breaking projects, which targeted Soviet-coded messages during World War II and in the early Cold War years.

Project Venona was initiated in 1943, when United States military officials feared that Stalin and Hitler were preparing to conclude a secret peace on the Eastern front, leaving the Western front to stand alone against the German army. In order to ascertain whether this fear had foundation, the Venona project began intercepting cables

to and from the Soviet embassy in Washington. Once the intensely complex code was finally broken, in 1946, the war was over, the Allies had won, and it was clear that the Soviet Union had not attempted a secret peace with Germany.

When the Venona code-breakers started sifting through the cables they had amassed, however, they quickly realized that the content was not related to diplomacy at all, but espionage. For example, they learned that the Soviet Union was receiving atomic secrets from American sources—the first clue the U.S. government had received about the egregious security breach at Los Alamos. Eventually, through analysis of the cables and a long investigation into deciphering the code-names used in them, analysts would identify hundreds of Americans—including the Rosenbergs, Elizabeth Bentley, Klaus Fuchs, Theodore Hall, David Greenglass, and others—engaged in espionage activity on behalf of the Soviet Union.

In the late 1940s, the KGB heard about Venona's existence from a number of sources, including Kim Philby, the famous British spy. Philby continued to have access to Venona information until 1951, when suspicion fell on him and he was ordered out of the British intelligence service. Faced with mounting evidence against him, Philby fled to Moscow in 1963.

Historians and other intelligence experts began hearing rumors about the existence of the Venona project and its files in the 1980s, after the NSA had officially closed the operation. In 1995, U.S. Senator Daniel Patrick Moynihan of New York spearheaded a drive to reverse some of the United States' secrecy laws, arguing that they were too severe for the post-Cold War climate, and that Americans deserved to know at least some of their government's activities. Among the examples mentioned when historians were brought in to testify before Senator Moynihan's commission was the continued classification of the Venona files. While information on Venona was available at that time in Russian archives, the files themselves remained closed in the United States.

Partly as a response to the commission, partly because it had been debating the idea itself anyway, the NSA declassified the Venona files—over 3,000 decrypted messages—in 1995. Since then, historians have been rushing to fit this new, essential information into the picture they already had of espionage in the 1940s. Some have even gone so far as to assert that American history as a whole in this era will have to be reevaluated in light of the new information that the Venona files provide. For example, the files include decrypted messages clearly implicating Julius Rosenberg in a series of espionage activities. These messages could not be introduced as evidence at his trial because the very existence of the Venona operation could not be publicized. The public reaction against his execution, therefore, might have been very different had the Venona files been known at the time.

Similarly, Venona cables show that Manhattan Project physicist Theodore Hall was also a Soviet spy, offering the KGB highly sensitive atomic information. He was never prosecuted, however, because the Venona cables were the only evidence against him, and as with Rosenberg, that evidence could not be used in court without compromising the security and secrecy of the Venona project. The information historians have taken from these files since their post-Cold War release has therefore been invaluable, and has shown another side to espionage, and how we discuss it, in recent years.

### Into the Twenty-first Century

Since the end of the Cold War, the arrests of Aldrich Ames and Robert Hanssen, as well as a number of others, indicate that espionage activity between the two former enemies did not collapse along with the Berlin Wall. The spy mission in the 1990s, however, was quite different from that of the early Cold War period, and indicators suggest that the twenty-first century will see further changes in the nature of espionage activity between the United States and Russia.

First, as we have already seen, the early Cold War spies were primarily motivated by ideology. An overwhelming majority of them were members of the American Communist Party, and they believed that the Soviet Union was entitled to all information available in the United States. This was particularly true for the technological and atomic secrets that were passed to the Soviets. These spies believed ideologically in communism as an economic system, Stalin as a great leader, and the Soviet Union as an ideal country. They also believed that the United States should not have a monopoly on nuclear secrets, espousing a traditional view of science as beyond political borders and actions, something that should be openly shared around the world.

After this initial wave of spies, however, the political situation in both countries changed the espionage climate. The death of Soviet leader Joseph Stalin in 1953 led to the gradual revelation of the scale of his crimes against the people of the Soviet Union during his rule. Further, Soviet intervention to crush popular uprisings in Hungary in 1956 and Czechoslovakia in 1968 caused widespread disillusionment among communists in the United States and Western Europe. Domestically, the McCarthy era of anti-communism in the United States in the early 1950s, combined with the staunch political rhetoric that the Soviet Union was no longer a wartime ally but an evil enemy, decreased the fervor of American communism. These factors did not stop espionage between the United States and the Soviet Union, of course, but they did help change the political climate enough that Soviet spies recruited in the United States no longer acted out of an ideological commitment to communism.

By the 1970s, Soviet spies were largely acting simply for the money they could earn in the endeavor, and this trend continued into the 1980s and 1990s. Aldrich Ames and Robert Hanssen both began spying in the 1980s, and both did so essentially for money. When looking at the future of U.S.-Russian espionage, then, it is significant to consider the motivation of potential spies. With the continued decline of ideology as a defining force in world affairs, it seems safe to assume that spies will continue to operate primarily for financial gain.

Second, when analyzing espionage changes since the end of the Cold War, it is significant to consider that both Ames and Hanssen, as well as many other spies caught in the 1990s, did not begin their activities in the 1990s. While there may well be active spies as we speak who started in the post-Cold War years, the majority of those who have been caught and have thus come to public attention were leftovers from the Cold War, perhaps working with Russian handlers who were similarly displaced in the post-Cold War structure. Spies starting out since 1991 would most certainly have a different agenda (and motivation) than those who were in place prior to the fall of the Soviet Union.

That said, what is the current state of espionage between the United States and Russia? For both countries, security concerns have simply changed since the Cold War. While Russia occasionally spouts brave rhetoric in the face of U.S. intrusions into what it sees as a Slavic sphere of influence—as we saw during the 1999 crisis in Kosovo—the United States is not really a Russian enemy any longer. Nor is Russia a genuine American enemy at the beginning of the twenty-first century. We have seen Russia recently included in the G-8 group of the world's largest industrial

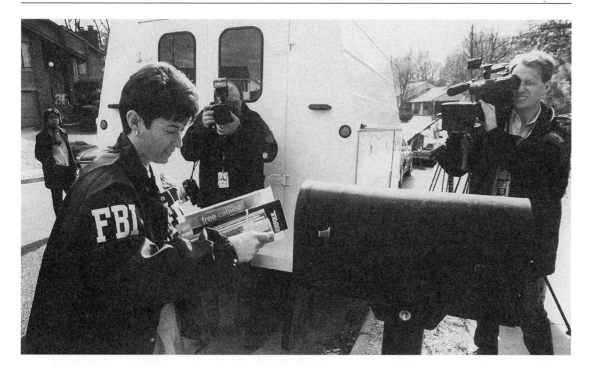

AN FBI AGENT CONFISCATES MAIL FROM THE HOME OF FBI SPECIAL AGENT ROBERT PHILIP HANSSEN, ACCUSED OF SPYING FOR THE SOVIET UNION FOR MORE THAN 15 YEARS. *(A/P Wide World. Reproduced by permission.)*

economies, for example, and a continuing dialogue—politically, economically, and culturally—between Russia and the West has decreased the residual feelings of animosity that remained for many years as fallout from the Cold War.

Russia's main concerns as it enters the new century are domestic. Politically, its system still suffers the communist legacy of excessive bureaucracy, an aged elite that struggles to grasp Western-style partisan democracy, and a lack of public faith in elections. Economically, the state cannot support its civil servants, the taxation system is riddled with problems, and general recovery from the damage wrought by central planning remains a struggle. Furthermore, Russia continues to face a military nightmare in Chechnya, a southern Islamic republic that has been fighting for independence since 1994. It faces not only a security threat from Chechen terrorists, who have already allegedly detonated explosives in Moscow shopping centers and apartment buildings, but the possibility of the Chechen rebellion spreading to other republics, or gaining the support of Islamic states outside Russia's borders. Espionage efforts would surely be better advised against this more immediate threat than against the United States.

Yet the United States is not completely off the hook from the Russian point of view. Russia remains fearful of American hegemony in the world, and to a degree bemoans the collapse of the bipolar system. It will certainly continue to employ espionage as a means of keeping tabs on American strength and ensuring that the United States does not abuse its position as the world's most powerful country. Furthermore, a major concern of Russia in the post-Cold War years has been the expansion of the North Atlantic Treaty Alliance (NATO) to include several countries in Eastern Europe that formerly fell within the Soviet Union's sphere of influence. Russian espionage motivated by a concern over future NATO expansion along Russia's borders is a strong possibility.

From the American side, it is clear that the world is no longer divided so easily between East and West. Looking back ten years to the collapse of the Soviet Union and the Gulf War, it is clear that both events helped usher in a new age of global politics, in which the United States has continued to be a major player, and also a major enemy. With the collapse of East-West bipolarity, however, the new threats faced by the United States multiplied. As demonstrated by the Gulf War, a major U.S. concern today is the activities of rogue states such as Iraq. Ruled by unpredictable dictators or extremist religious councils, armed with an array of biological and chemical weapons, known to sponsor terrorism as a means

## RECENT U.S. SPY CASES

**1984: Richard William Miller.** An FBI agent based in Los Angeles, Miller was arrested for passing sensitive material to two Soviet immigrants, who were later also arrested and charged with conspiracy. Miller maintained his innocence, claiming that he was in fact trying to infiltrate the KGB. After three trials, he was convicted and sentenced to 20 years in prison in 1991. That sentence was later reduced, and he was released in 1994.

**1985: Edward Lee Howard.** Howard was a new CIA recruit who was fully debriefed on intelligence issues before being sent to Moscow. Before his mission began, however, he was dismissed for alleged drinking. Angry with the CIA for its actions, Howard began telling the KGB what he had learned in his initial debriefing sessions. He fled to Moscow when he fell under FBI suspicion, and has never been charged.

**1985: Walker family.** A naval officer, John A. Walker Jr. was charged with selling classified documents to the Soviet Union for 18 years. After he retired from the navy, he recruited his son, Michael Walker, and his brother, former naval commander Arthur James Walker, to continue accessing sensitive information for Walker to pass to the Soviet Union. All three were arrested after Walker's ex-wife informed the FBI of their activities. Walker was sentenced to two life terms plus ten years; his son was sentenced to 25 years, and his brother to life in prison.

**1985: Robert Pelton.** Pelton worked at the National Security Agency (NSA) between 1966 and 1980 as a communications specialist. He was arrested in 1985 and convicted in 1986 of selling secret information to the Soviet Union. He is best known for informing the KGB of the American operation to attach listening devices to the Soviet Union's undersea communication lines.

**1994: Aldrich Ames.** Known as one of the most damaging spies in CIA history, Ames was the head of the CIA's Soviet counter-intelligence division when he began selling secrets to the KGB in 1985. Motivated by money, he supplied the KGB with at least 25 names of their agents on the CIA's payroll. At least ten of those agents were later executed in Moscow. Ames was sentenced to life in prison without parole, while his wife, Rosario, was sentenced to five years for co-conspiracy.

**1996: Edwin Earl Pitts.** A veteran FBI agent, Pitts began spying for the Soviet Union in 1987, and continued to pass secret information to Russia until 1992. An American spy in the KGB tipped off the FBI about Pitts, and he was caught in a sting operation in which FBI agents posed as Russian handlers and paid him $65,000 for classified FBI documents. Pitts pleaded guilty to espionage charges and was sentenced to 27 years in prison.

**1996: Harold Nicholson.** Arrested in Washington in 1996 while trying to board a flight to Switzerland, Nicholson was found carrying classified documents and coded messages intended for his Russian handlers. The highest-ranking CIA official ever to face espionage charges, Nicholson pleaded guilty in 1997 and was sentenced to 23 years in prison after cooperating with prosecutors.

**1998: David Boone.** Boone was a former analyst at the NSA, arrested for selling secrets to the Soviet Union between 1988 and 1991. Among the information he passed to the KGB was a list of Russian targets for U.S. nuclear weapons. Like many others, Boone was motivated by money, and first volunteered his services at the Soviet Embassy in Washington in 1988. In 1999 he was sentenced to 24 years in prison.

**2000: George Trofimoff.** A retired Army Reserve colonel, Trofimoff is the highest-ranking military officer ever charged with espionage in the United States. Born in Germany to Russian parents, Trofimoff began spying for the Soviet Union in 1969, while he was chief of the U.S. Army Element of the Nuremberg Joint Interrogation Center in Germany. He continued to pass sensitive information to the KGB until 1994, and managed to elude capture until 2000, when an FBI sting operation led to his arrest in Florida.

**2001: Robert Philip Hanssen.** A 25-year veteran of the FBI's counter-intelligence division, Hanssen was a Russian spy from 1985 until his arrest in 2001. Apprehended after dropping a package off for his Russian handlers in a Virginia park, Hanssen pleaded guilty in return for the government's promise not to pursue the death penalty against him. The exact scope of the damage Hanssen caused to U.S. operations is not yet known; as part of his plea agreement in July 2001, he was required to undergo a full debriefing by the FBI and CIA, in order to ascertain how much classified information he disclosed to the Russians.

RETIRED ARMY RESERVE COL. GEORGE TROFIMOFF, ACCUSED OF SPYING FOR THE SOVIET UNION FOR OVER 25 YEARS WHILE WORKING IN GERMANY, WAS CONVICTED OF CONSPIRACY TO COMMIT ESPIONAGE IN JUNE 2000. (A/P Wide World. Reproduced by permission.)

of achieving political goals, and harboring a hatred of America—not capitalist ideology, but the real, tangible country of America—these states threaten the United States in a way the Soviet Union never did. Accordingly, U.S. espionage efforts since the end of the Cold War have been targeted less towards Russia, and increasingly towards safeguarding the United States and its allies from the unpredictable actions of rogue states.

The United States has not completely cancelled its intelligence concerns regarding Russia, however. Foremost among its concerns are the poorly guarded sites of weapons of mass destruction in Russia and politically unstable former Soviet republics. Russia is embarrassed by the weakness inferred by its lack of control over this situation, and is thus prone to assure the United States and the world that its nuclear weapons are safely guarded. American espionage will undoubtedly be useful in the years to come in ascertaining the truth of those assurances. Finally, Russia remains important to the United States simply because of its key geopolitical location. With its

proximity to Europe, East Asia, and the Middle East, Russia remains a major player in all these areas, and the United States understands the danger of undervaluing the importance of Russia's position. Espionage in Russia could assist the American pursuit of geopolitical strategies in neighboring regions.

### Conclusion

The Cold War was a unique period in history. It resembled an intense chess match more than it did a traditional war. Each move was calculated, and the chess pieces manipulated by the two players were essentially unable to move independently. In this high-stakes game, with the threat of nuclear catastrophe hanging overhead, the practice of covertly peering into the opponent's head to detect his next move, before he made it, was almost more important than actually playing the game. Thus espionage between the United States and the Soviet Union deeply influenced relations between the two countries, and the repercussions of that are still felt ten years after the end of the Cold War, despite the professed fraternity of the former antagonists. These repercussions are appearing in the form of continued espionage activity between the United States and Russia, as evidenced by the arrest of Robert Hanssen as a Russian spy in 2001.

While activity has not ceased, however, motivations have changed, and U.S.-Russian spy missions have charted a new course in the twenty-first century. No longer each other's prime enemy, priorities have shifted for both countries: Russia is under pressure from both its own citizens and its foreign investors to look inward and address its domestic problems; the United States, meanwhile, faces a new threat from a faceless enemy in the form of terrorist warfare. Intelligence resources in the immediate future will have to be directed towards fighting an exceedingly difficult and taxing war with stateless terrorists. As the twenty-first century dawns, and the line between friend and foe is often blurred and changes quickly, both the United States and Russia face new challenges to global order in the post-Cold War world.

## BIBLIOGRAPHY

Andrew, Christopher, and Vasili Mitrokhin. *The Mitrokhin Archive: The KGB in Europe and the West.* London: Penguin Press, 1999.

Central Intelligence Agency. Available online at http://www.cia.gov/cia/index.html (cited November 16, 2001).

Cold War International History Project. Available online at http://cwihp.si.edu (cited November 16, 2001).

Federal Bureau of Investigation. Available online at http://www.fbi.gov (cited November 16, 2001).

Federal'naya Sluzhba Bezopasnosti (Federal Security Service). Available online (in Russian language only) at http://www.fsb.ru (cited November 16, 2001).

Fried, Richard M. *Nightmare in Red: The McCarthy Era in Perspective.* Oxford: Oxford University Press, 1990.

Grose, Peter. *Operation Rollback: America's Secret War Behind the Iron Curtain.* Boston & New York: Houghton Mifflin, 2000.

Haynes, John Earl, and Harvey Klehr. *Venona: Decoding Soviet Espionage in America.* New Haven & London: Yale University Press, 1999.

Hunter, Robert W. *Spy Hunter: Inside the FBI Investigation of the Walker Espionage Case.* Annapolis MD: Naval Institute Press, 1999.

Intelligence Resource Program (from the Federation of American Scientists). Available online at http://www.fas.org/irp (cited November 16, 2001).

Maas, Peter. *Killer Spy: The Inside Story of the FBI's Pursuit and Capture of Aldrich Ames, America's Deadliest Spy.* New York: Warner Books, 1995.

Murphy, David E., Sergei A. Kondrashev, and George Bailey. *Battleground Berlin: CIA vs. KGB in the Cold War.* New Haven & London: Yale University Press, 1997.

Sluzhba Vneshnei Razvedki (Foreign Intelligence Service) (cited November 16, 2001). Available online at http://www.svr.gov.ru (Russian language only).

Venona Project. Available online at http://www.nsa.gov/docs/venona (cited November 16, 2001).

Weinstein, Allen, and Alexander Vassiliev. *The Haunted Wood: Soviet Espionage in America—the Stalin Era.* New York: Random House, 1999.

*Erica Fraser*

# INDIA'S CASTE SYSTEM UNDER ATTACK: THE DALIT MOVEMENT

The World Conference Against Racism, Xenophobia and Related Intolerance, a United Nations (UN) convention held in Durban, South Africa, from August 31 to September 7, 2001, stirred a hornet's nest in India. The Dalit activists and their supporters demanded that India's 2000-year-old caste system be included in the deliberations at the conference and that the United Nations (UN) should pass a resolution condemning the inherent social gradation of the system. The demand to bring this issue before an international forum was countered vociferously by the Indian government, which maintains that the caste system and caste-related discrimination are internal affairs that should be fought within the country.

"Dalit" literally means downtrodden or oppressed, and is a term used in place of the word "untouchables" to identify the lowest caste categories. In modern times, though laws have forbidden discrimination against Dalits, the stigma of untouchability continues to isolate millions of members of this group. They are still associated by many upper caste members with a sense of pollution—as having been the workers in charge of functions like disposing of animal carcasses, digging graves, and cleaning latrines and therefore polluted. Despite India's modern democratic government and a 50-year-old constitution that abolishes the caste system and provides for the rights of the lowest caste, there is much work left to do in order to wipe out the discriminatory practices still prevalent in no small measure.

Dalits, who comprise 16 percent of India's population and number about 160 million, suffer disproportionately from poverty, segregation, lack of education, discrimination, and physical abuse.

## THE CONFLICT

Although India's Constitution of 1947 abolished the practice of untouchability, the Dalits continue to experience discrimination, segregation, and violence. The laws providing for the welfare of Dalits are often ignored. The government of India maintains that the problems should be handled internally and do not represent a form of racism, while the sections of Dalit intelligentsia seek international attention to the problems they face.

### Political

- The Dalits, mostly landless agricultural laborers or menial laborers, need greater political voice and participation in political processes to break free from the age-old socio-culturally imposed bondage, segregation, and discrimination. Despite the advances brought about by the reservation system, customs and other social practices continue to hinder rapid and all around social emancipation of Dalits.

### Economic

- As landless laborers who depend upon the landlord farmers for their livelihood, the Dalits continue to suffer from the traditional caste equations and the landlords continue to profit from it. This system provides fertile ground for atrocities. Only economic empowerment of Dalits, providing them with land and the related wherewithal, can mitigate the social tensions.

### Religious

- The caste distinction has not only social but religious sanction. It is based on the Hindu idea that a person's positioning in the social hierarchy is ordained by his or her deeds in the previous life, since Hindus believe in rebirth. The current social status of an individual depends on the good or bad deeds committed by that individual—his or her Karma—and is therefore immutable in this real world.

# CHRONOLOGY

**1400–1000 BCE** The caste system in India begins when Indo-Aryans conquer all of northern India enslaving the Dravidians—the present day Scheduled Castes, or the Dalits.

**1757–1947** The British rule India as a colony.

**1927** Bhim Rao Ambedkar organizes the Dalits to draw water from the public tanks, although it is not allowed by members of the upper castes. Ambedkar pursues equality for the Dalits through courts, education, and politics.

**April 1942** Ambedkar establishes a political party, the Scheduled Caste Federation, which is considered the beginning of the Dalit-based political parties and movements.

**1947** India achieves independence from Britain.

**January 26, 1950** A new constitution is written, which provides for the abolition of the untouchable system and fair representation of Dalits in public jobs and education systems.

**1955** The Untouchability (Offences) Act, 1955, later amended and re-titled as the Protection of Civil Rights Act, provides penal measures against untouchability.

**1989** The Scheduled Castes and the Scheduled Tribes (Prevention of Atrocities) Act, provides punishments for those who commit atrocities against Dalits.

**1993** The Employment of Manual Scavengers and Construction of Dry Latrines (Prohibition) Act, prohibits employment of manual scavengers in an attempt to assure the dignity of the individual.

**1997** India celebrates its Golden Jubilee, celebrating its fiftieth year of independence. The Dalits find they have less to celebrate than the rest of the country and many join the campaign to end the caste system in India.

**August 31–September 7, 2001** At the World Conference Against Racism, Xenophobia and Related Intolerance, a United Nations (UN) convention held in Durban, South Africa, representatives of the Dalit movement demand that India's caste system be included in the deliberations at the conference and that the United Nations (UN) should pass a resolution condemning the hierarchical social system.

The caste system that has kept the Dalits downtrodden is an ancient social malice, and there has been an unsatisfactory and tardy implementation of the existing constitutional provisions to eliminate it.

The government of India, although acknowledging the harmful aspects of the caste system, believes that caste discrimination is not the same as racial discrimination and that internationalizing the issue will be of no use in resolving the age-old problem. In opposition to the government's position are academicians, jurists, other sections of the intelligentsia, and representatives of nongovernmental organizations (NGOs), mostly from Dalit communities, who have demanded debate on caste in the World Conference Against Racism. These groups believe that international scrutiny would expose the failure of the Indian State to implement constitutional safeguards for victims of caste-based oppression or to eliminate this ancient social evil.

# HISTORICAL BACKGROUND:

## The Origins of the Caste System

In the millennia before the Christian era, the population in the area that is now India was mixed. The Negroids or Negritos were early inhabitants, followed by the Australoids and the Mongoloids. At least two of the present-day Scheduled Tribes or "Adivasis" as they are called, the Santhals and the Bhils, came from Australoid origin. Dravidians were the fourth and the most numerous group to inhabit ancient India. The Dravidians came from the eastern Mediterranean region in the third millennium BCE, founding an advanced culture and civilization. By 1400 BCE the Dravidians are said to have extended their civilization throughout the country. In the second millennium BCE, Indo-Aryans migrated from central Asia and exterminated and enslaved the indigenous Dravidians, calling them "Dasyus" or slaves. The Indo-Aryans finally conquered all of

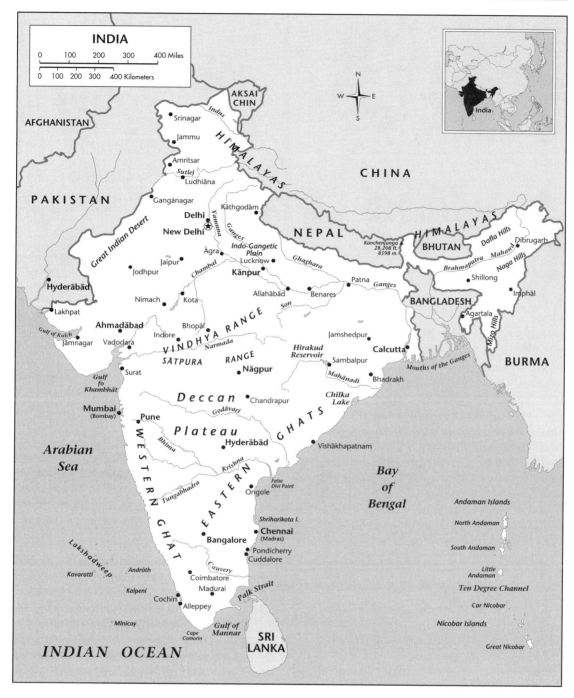

MAP OF INDIA. (© *Maryland Cartographics. Reprinted with permission.*)

northern India by 1400–1000 BCE Those enslaved by them are the present-day Scheduled Castes, or the Dalits.

India's caste system, which emerged with the advent of Aryans in India, was a unique social institution in which the society was stratified in a hierarchical or quasi-hierarchical social order. This was not a merely social but an economic distinction: the upper castes represented the well-off

economic classes, whereas the lower castes represented the poorer sections of society.

Even today, there are thousands of castes, or *jatis,* in India. A person is born into a particular caste and remains in that caste until death. Within the caste, members are severely restricted as to their occupation and their social participation. The caste distinction has not only social and economic but also religious sanction, based on the

INDIAN MEN VIEW A POSTER OF PHOOLAN DEVI, THE FORMER "BANDIT QUEEN" WHO BECAME A MEMBER OF INDIAN PARLIAMENT AND FOUGHT FOR LOWER CASTE RIGHTS. DEVI WAS MURDERED IN JULY 2001. *(A/P Wide World. Reproduced by permission.)*

Hindu idea that a person's positioning in the socio-economic hierarchy is ordained by his or her deeds in the previous life, since Hindus believe in rebirth. The current social status of an individual depends on the good or bad deeds committed by that individual—his or her Karma—and is therefore immutable in this real world. Society in India is further classified in social sub-groups traditionally based on the concept of ritual purity and its opposite, the pollution.

Along with the system of *jati*, the two thousand-year-old caste system divides the Hindu religion and society into four broader idealized categories, called *Varnas* (literally "color.") These are:

- Brahmins: Priests and teachers believed to originate from the head of the God, who served the functions of learning, teaching, and performing sacrifices.

- Kshatriyas: Warriors skilled in the martial arts and educated to be leaders, whose task was to protect the people and fight their enemies.

- Vaisyas: The merchant class.

- Shudras: Laborers not entitled to an education, who generally served as servants to the other three classes.

A fifth category, which falls outside the Varna system, was the "untouchables" or Dalits. Untouchability stems from a cultural notion of "ritual pollution." Dalits were excluded from the classified social hierarchy and undertook the polluting tasks.

The major castes or jatis (there are 3,000 according to one estimate) correspond to one or the other of the four varna, and constitute varna-Hindus. The Dalits are, in accordance with this classification, "varna-Sankara," or external to the system of varnas, since they are considered polluting and untouchable. Dalits too are divided into several sub-castes. During British colonial rule of India (from 1757 to 1947), the British created lists of the different Indian communities. They used the word "castes" to refer to the jatis and varnas, and the word "tribes" to denote the communities that isolated themselves from Indian society and culture, usually by living in the most remote areas. The British called the untouchables the "Depressed Classes" and the "Scheduled Castes" in the Scheduled Castes Act of India of 1935. The terms Scheduled Castes and Scheduled Tribes continue to be used under the Indian Constitution today.

The term "Dalit" was coined by Marathi social reformer Jyoti Rao Phule (1826–1890) to

# DR. BHIM RAO (OR BHIMRAO; ALSO BABASAHEB) RAMJI AMBEDKAR

*1891–1956* Bhim Rao Ambedkar was born in Mhow, Central India, into the "untouchable" Mahar caste. Both his father and grandfather served in the British Army, and since all Army personnel and their families were educated in government schools, Ambedkar, unlike most Dalit children, received a good education. It was in school, however, that he began to feel the sting of discrimination against untouchables. His teachers would not touch his books or papers, and he was forced to sit on the floor in one corner of the classroom. He was not allowed to drink from the public fountain and was once beaten for doing so.

In 1913 the Maharajah of Baroda sponsored Ambedkar in a scholarship at Columbia University, where he received a Ph.D. Upon graduating in 1916, he went on to the London School of Economics, where he was awarded a doctorate in economics and a law degree. He returned to India and was hired to teach economics at the Sydenham College of Commerce, but was forced to leave his post because his colleagues would not associate with a member of his caste.

From 1923 until his death in 1956 Ambedkar fought a hard and constant battle for the rights of the Dalits of India. In the 1920s he founded a newspaper and an educational institution. In 1927 he led a renowned demonstration at a public water tank, in which Dalits drank from the tank used by the upper castes. They were beaten. In another demonstration, Ambedkar burned the book of Hindu code that gave rise to the caste system. At the same time, he worked to educate the Dalits, believing that for the Dalits "salvation lies in their social elevation."

In the early 1930s Ambedkar worked with the British in trying to form a new Indian government. He insisted that the downtrodden in India needed a separate electorate in order to protect themselves as India went to the polls in provincial elections. In this, he was in extreme opposition to Indian leader Mahatma Gandhi (1869–1948), who went on a fast to prevent this separation of elections. They finally agreed on a reservation system instead. In 1935 Ambedkar shocked the Indian nation when he called on all Dalits to convert to any religion but Hinduism, which he held responsible for the caste system. He went on working for his people into the 1940s, founding a political party, taking their plight through India's court system and winning his case, and representing them in the discussions about independence.

In 1947, India became an independent state and Ambedkar joined the cabinet as the Minister of Law and also became the chair of the drafting committee for the constitution of the new Republic of India. The Constitution of India abolished all forms of untouchability. He was responsible, also, for the Fundamental Rights passages of the constitution, which provide for freedom, equality, and enforcement remedies to ensure fair distribution of wealth and equal living conditions. For several years after the constitution was put into effect, Ambedkar worked on in frustration, as he saw the continued oppression of his people.

In 1956, less than two months before his death, Ambedkar announced that he had converted from Hinduism to Buddhism.

---

describe the untouchables and the outcasts. Later, Dr. Bhim Rao Ambedkar (1891–1956), often called the founding father of the Indian Constitution and the most significant leader of the Dalit community, popularized the term. In the 1930s Indian leader Mahatma Mohandas Gandhi (1869–1948) called the Dalits "Harijans" or "the children of God," and that term was used until the 1980s. Dalits have been derisively called Dasa, Dasyu, Rakhshasa, Asura, Avarna, Nisada, Panchama, Chandala, Chura, Bhangi, Mahar, Mala, Paraiya, and Pulayam in different regions and languages. The deep derision inherent in these terms is clearly reflected by their literal meaning. For instance Dasa means "slave"; Dasyu means "brigand"; Rakshasa and Asura mean "demon," and Avarna refers to someone who is external to the acknowledged social gradation of the varna system or is an outcast and is the opposite of Savarna, which refers to those who are included.

## The Scheduled Tribes or the "Adivasis"

According to the 1981 census, there are 53 million people or approximately eight percent of India's population and one-fourth of the world's

# DALITS AND THEIR RELIGION

Dalits in India belong to various religions, including Hindu, Sikh, Buddhist, and Christian. Dalits constitute more than 60 percent of India's 21 million Christians. A large number of Dalits converted to Buddhism. The Neo-Buddhist movement started under the leadership of Dr. Ambedkar in Nagpur in 1956, when he converted to the religion along with his half million followers.

Religious groups as percentages of the total Dalit population of India were as follows in 2001:

- Hindus: 140 million (70 percent)

- Muslims: 15.5 million (7.75 percent)

- Christians: 19 million (9.5 percent)

- Sikhs: 15 million (7.5 percent)

- Buddhists: 7.5 million (3.75 percent)

- Jains and others: 3 million (1.5 percent)

indigenous population who are called Scheduled Tribes or "Adivasis," which means aboriginal. Scheduled tribes were groups that did not accept the social hierarchy, but preferred to live remote from civilization. The greatest geographical concentration of Scheduled Tribes is in central India extending from West Bengal to Gujarat, Maharashtra, Bihar, Orissa, and Madhya Pradesh. Ninety percent of the Scheduled Tribes depend on subsistence agriculture, with about 30–40 percent of their income coming from the collection and sale of minor forest products like honey, seeds, nuts, and tendu leaves. They are the poorest of India's communities, with 85 percent living well below the official poverty line. Compare this with the average figure of 40 percent for the total population of India. Low agricultural productivity and massive deforestation have contributed to the further pauperization of the Scheduled Tribes. Eighty-four percent of them are illiterate. They thus find it difficult to participate in the labor market and are exploited to a great extent. Low incomes, ill-health due to poor availability of health facilities, and malnutrition is endemic among them.

## Dalits in the Twentieth Century

In 1913, a young student from the "untouchable" caste, Bhim Rao Ambedkar, was granted a scholarship to go study at Columbia University in New York, where he received a Ph.D., and then went on to obtain further degrees at the London School of Economics. When Ambedkar returned to India, he was appointed Professor of Economics at the Sydenham College of Commerce. Because of his caste status, most of his colleagues at the university refused to speak to him, so he was unable to do his job. He had no choice but to move to Bombay. In 1924 Ambedkar founded an organization with a mission to abolish the caste system. He started a free school and ran reading rooms and libraries.

Ambedkar then took the grievances of the untouchables to court. In 1927 he organized the Dalits to draw water from the public tanks in protest, although the upper castes did not allow it. Ambedkar established a political party, the Scheduled Caste Federation, in April 1942, which is considered the beginning of the Dalit-based political parties and movements.

When India gained independence from Britain in 1947, Ambedkar was appointed the Law Minister and as such he was one of the authors of the Constitution of Independent India. The new constitution abolished the untouchability system, and provided for a significant percentage of government jobs for the Scheduled Castes and Scheduled Tribes. The jobs were "reserved" for Dalits, and this was called the reservation system.

## Legal-Constitutional Provisions since Independence

Along with abolishing the untouchable system and reserving government jobs for Dalits, the new Indian Constitution contained articles that provide for defending the dignity of Dalits. Article 15 prohibits discrimination on grounds of religion, race, caste, sex, or place of birth. Article 16 enjoins that no citizen shall, on grounds of religion, race, caste, sex, descent, place of birth, or residence, be ineligible for or discriminated against in respect of any employment or office under the State. Article 17 provides for the abolition of untouchability and forbids its practice—making it an offence punishable by law. Article 46 enables the State to promote the educational and economic interests of the weaker sections of the people, and, in particular, of the Scheduled Castes and the Scheduled Tribes, and enjoins it to protect them from social injustice and all forms of exploitation.

Article 243D of the Indian Constitution reserves seats for the Scheduled Castes and the Scheduled Tribes in every rural body of government, or Panchayat, of which not less than one-

# POPULATION OF SCHEDULED CASTES AND TRIBES*

|  | *Number of People* | *Percent of Total Population* |
|---|---|---|
| Scheduled Castes | 138,223,277 | 16.48% |
| Scheduled Tribes | 67,758,380 | 8.08% |

\* excluding Jammu and Kashmir

### *Scheduled Castes*

| State with highest proportion of Scheduled Castes | Punjab, 28.3% |
|---|---|
| State with lowest proportion | Mizoram, 0.1% |
| Union territory (UT)† with highest proportion | Delhi, 19.1% |
| UT with lowest proportion | Dadra and Nagar Haveli, 2.0% |
| District with highest proportion | Koch Bihar, 51.8% (West Bengal) |
| District with lowest proportion | Tamenglong, 0.0% (Manipur) |
|  | West Khasi Hills, 0.0% (Meghalaya) |

### *Scheduled Tribes*

| State with highest proportion of Scheduled Tribes | Mizoram, 94.8% |
|---|---|
| State with lowest proportion | Uttar Pradesh, 0.2% |
| UT with highest proportion | Lakshadweep, 93.1% |
| UT with lowest proportion | Andaman and Nicobar Islands, 9.5% |
| District with highest proportion | West Khasi Hills, 98.1% (Meghalaya) |
| District with lowest proportion | 46 districts in Uttar Pradesh, 0.0% |
|  | 11 districts in Bihar, 0.0% |
|  | 1 district in Himachal Pradesh, 0.0% |

† Union territories, though not states, are a part of India and are administered for tourism.

INDIA'S STATES, UNION TERRITORIES, AND DISTRICTS VARY IN COMPOSITION BETWEEN SCHEDULED CASTES AND TRIBES. *(The Gale Group.)*

third of the total number of reserved seats are for women. According to the Article 243T, seats are reserved for the Scheduled Castes and the Scheduled Tribes in every municipality or urban body of government. Of these not less than one-third of the total number are reserved for women. Article 330 enables reservation of seats for Scheduled Castes and Scheduled Tribes in the House of the People or the Central Legislatures, the Lok Sabha and the Rajya Sabha. Article 332 provides for the reservation of seats for Scheduled Castes and Scheduled Tribes in the Legislative Assemblies of the States. Article 335 provides that the claims of the members of the Scheduled Castes and the Scheduled Tribes shall be taken into consideration in the making of appointments to services and posts in both the Central or Federal and State or Provincial governments.

The implementation of these provisions has never been complete, however, and social discrimination against Dalits has continued. Consequently, a series of further laws was enacted in an attempt to defend the honor and dignity as well as the physical well-being and safety of the Dalits. The Untouchability (Offences) Act, 1955, later amended and re-titled as the Protection of Civil Rights Act, 1955, provides penal measures against untouchability. The Scheduled Castes and the Scheduled Tribes (Prevention of Atrocities) Act, 1989, provides punishments for those who commit atrocities against Dalits. The Employment of Manual Scavengers and Construction of Dry

A HIGH CASTE LANDOWNER POSES WITH HIS WEAPON. HIGH CASTE MEMBERS SUCH AS THIS MAN FORMED A PRIVATE ARMY TO FIGHT COMMUNISTS, WHO WERE ENCOURAGING DALIT FARM HANDS TO DEMAND HIGHER WAGES. *(A/P Wide World. Reproduced by permission.)*

Latrines (Prohibition) Act, 1993, prohibits employment of manual scavengers (people who remove human waste from latrines and dispose of it, historically a job given to the Dalits), in an attempt to assure the dignity of the individual.

### Dalits in Contemporary India

The ancient social institution of untouchability continued despite the remedial measures that were initiated in post-colonial India. The Dalits, mostly landless agricultural laborers or those engaged in menial jobs, were for the most part unable to break free from the age-old socio-culturally imposed bondage, segregation, and discrimination. Despite the advances brought about by the reservation system, in modern times the changes in social norms, culture, and customs leave much to be desired.

It is painfully apparent to most observers that the Dalits have continued to suffer abuse of all kinds. Socially, they suffer discriminatory practices. In many Indian villages, there are separate living areas for Dalits, often with different water sources. In schools, Dalit students may be forced to sit at the back of the classroom and they are often taunted. In some places, they may not be allowed to worship in the same temples as the higher castes or to use same cremation grounds.

Economically, despite some small progress owing to the reservation policy, more than 77 percent of Dalits continue to depend on what they can get from the land, according to the 1991 census; 25 percent of these are marginal and small farmers and 50 percent are the landless laborers. There are 0.8 percent or 1.1 million Dalits working in service sector through the reservation system. The majority of the remaining Dalits have to fend for jobs, primarily in urban areas.

In India, the increase in the prices of basic food items in the last decade as a consequence of liberalization and the free market, has meant that poorer sections have been forced to cut down on consumption. Dalit households, particularly in rural areas, have experienced a significant reduction in the calories taken in and thus were more frequent victims of malnutrition. As in other countries, the poor are most affected in shaky economic times, with unemployment hitting them hardest.

In India's educational institutions, the reservation system and financial assistance in the form of scholarships are granted to Dalits. In the era of economic reforms at the end of the twentieth century, however, the grants to many institutions were stagnating, if not reduced. The free market ethos has entered the educational sphere in a big way. Schools are increasingly commercialized and offer specialized education that should help the underprivileged. But along with these new avenues, the job market has become intensely competitive, and others are entering into these programs. Dalits, handicapped by socio-economic deprivation, find themselves increasingly alienated from the system of education. Moreover an increasing Dalit dropout rate from the schools points out their immediate need to supplement very low family incomes, as well as a lack of confidence that education will deliver them a decent life.

The reservation policy provides for the employment of a proportionate representation of Dalits in all the public jobs in the government, public sector, autonomous bodies, and institutions receiving grant-in-aid from the government. Over 50,000 Dalits could get governmental jobs as a result of reservations. This gives them hope for the future and prevents alienation from the nation and the society. The private sector, on the other hand, provides very limited scope for the absorption of Dalits.

Similarly, there is representation of Dalits at high governmental levels. The highly regarded

DALITS DEMONSTRATE AGAINST THE SHOOTING OF 12 DALITS WHO RIOTED IN BOMBAY. THE DEMONSTRATORS BURNED AN EFFIGY OF THE POLICE OFFICER FOUND RESPONSIBLE FOR ORDERING THE SHOOTING. *(A/P Wide World. Reproduced by permission.)*

president of the Republic of India and the speaker and the deputy speaker of the Lower House of the Parliament, as well as several Parliamentary ministers hail from the Dalit community. One hundred twenty-two members of Parliament belong to the Dalit community out of a total strength of five hundred forty-five in the Lower House of the Parliament or Lok Sabha, thanks primarily to the statutory reservations.

## The Dalits and Indian Politics

Since independence, the Dalits have, to greater and lesser degrees, had a political voice. Dr. Ambedkar, long regarded as an icon of the Dalit movement by all involved in it, brought together several organizations and groups to help the Dalits find empowerment and fight discrimination. Dalits traditionally supported the Congress Party, which was perceived as having granted them numerous concessions like the reservation system, although there has been a consensus on this issue across the political spectrum in the country. A large majority of Dalits continued as the Congress Party's captive vote-bank, supporting it election after election. With the decline of the Congress Party in 1980s and 1990s, and the increasing awareness of a separate Dalit political identity, numerous groups and political parties,

MARTIN MACWAN, AN ADVOCATE AGAINST
"UNTOUCHABILITY" AND THE ABUSES AGAINST DALITS
IN INDIA, RECEIVES THE ROBERT F. KENNEDY
MEMORIAL HUMAN RIGHTS AWARD FOR HIS WORK.
*(A/P Wide World. Reproduced by permission.)*

such as the Bahujan Samaj Party in the north, started emerging and anchoring their politics on the Dalit vote-base. These parties always had regional basis, however, and no single pan-Indian political party could ever emerge based on Dalit identity. Several groups and societies comprised of Dalit intellectuals, activists, youth, government employees, and missionary organizations have emerged from time to time and tried to highlight the issues facing the Dalit community.

## RECENT HISTORY AND THE FUTURE

### Dalits and Social Oppression

Violence against the Dalits in India continues in shocking numbers. Atrocities are a common occurrence as far as Dalits are concerned, particularly in rural areas where vestiges of feudal socio-economic-cultural order are still strong. The abuse occurs despite a host of constitutional and legal provisions to prevent it. According to the latest statistics, every day nearly 50 atrocities are registered throughout the country. Over three Dalit women are raped and six are disabled *each day*. The National Commission analyzed the causes of each of the atrocities in a sample of 45 cases and

found that 13 are clearly attributable to economic factors. The majority of Dalits are landless laborers or small and marginal farmers who are compelled to supplement their incomes through additional wage labor. They are therefore in an adversarial relationship with landlords, most of who belong to the higher castes, who exploit them not only socially but economically as well. The resultant socio-economic conflict becomes the source of tensions and atrocities.

Among social factors is the Dalits' resistance to socio-political dominance—their growing assertiveness and refusal to accept the indignities heaped on them for centuries. The atrocities continue despite the strong laws that should prevent such violence. There is much to be desired as far as law enforcement and delivery of justice to the victims is concerned. Several national and international social organizations, human right agencies, and sections of media have consistently highlighted the atrocities committed on Dalits, often at risk to themselves.

The economic situation of most Dalits will keep the old hierarchies strong. Only economic empowerment of Dalits, providing them with land and the related wherewithal, can mitigate the social tensions. This ancient wound will continue to trouble modern India unless economic and political empowerment of this vital section of the Indian society is implemented to put a decisive end to this type of exploitation and oppression.

## BIBLIOGRAPHY

Alte, I.D. *Rural Employment of Scheduled Castes.* New Delhi: Deep & Deep Publications, 1992.

Ambedkar, B.R. *Annihilation of Caste.* Jalandhar: Bheem Patrika Publications, 1933.

Appasamy, P., S. Guhan, R. Hema, M. Majumdar, and A. Vaidyanathan, eds. *Social Exclusion from a Welfare Rights Perspective in India.* Geneva: IILS/UNDP, 1996.

"Awards for Indian Human Rights Campaign," Christian Aid. Available online at http://www.christian-aid.org.uk/news/media/pressrel/001122.htm (cited November 19, 2001).

Biswas, Swapan Kumar. *Gods, False-Gods and the Untouchables.* London: Orion Books, 1998.

Briggs, George Weston. *The Chamars.* Delhi: A Venture of Low Price Publications, 1920, 1990.

Chaurasia, B.P. *Scheduled Castes and Scheduled Tribes in India.* Allahabad, Chugh Publications.

The Dalit Solidarity Forum in the USA. Available online at http://www.dalitusa.org/ (cited January 2, 2002).

Dalitstan Organization. Available online at http://www.dalitstan.org (cited January 2, 2002).

Das, Ganga. *Who Worships False Gods?* New Delhi: S. K. Associates.

"Dr. Babasaheb Ambedkar and His People," A Dalit-Bahujan Media. Available online at http://www.ambedkar.org (cited November 19, 2001).

Kabra, Lalitha. *Scheduled Caste Girls.* New Delhi: Mittal Publications, 1991.

Knowles, Marco. "The Development of Indigenous People: What Can India and Mexico Learn from Each Other's Policy Approaches to the Development of Indigenous People?" Dissertation, University of Bath, United Kingdom, October 1996–September 1997.

Kshirsagar, R.K. *Political Thought of Dr. Babasaheb Ambedkar.* New Delhi: Intellectual Publishing House, 1992.

Mendelsohn, Oliver, and Marika Vicziany. *The Untouchables.* Cambridge: Cambridge University Press, 1998.

Nagar, V.D., and K. P. Nagar. *Economic Thought and Policy of Dr. Ambedkar.* New Delhi: Segment Books.

Narula, Smita. *Broken People: Caste Violence Against India's "Untouchables."* Human Rights Watch, March 1999. Available online at http://www.hrw.org/reports/1999/india/ (cited January 2, 2002).

National Campaign on Dalit Human Rights, "Atrocities." Available online at http://www.dalits.org/ (cited September 9, 2001).

Parvathamma, C. *Scheduled Castes and Tribes: A Socio-economic Survey.* New Delhi: Ashish Publishing House, 1984.

Rao, Hemlata, and M. Devendra Babu. *Scheduled Castes and Tribes.* New Delhi: Ashish Publishing House, 1993.

Seenarine, M. "Dalit Female Education and Empowerment." Published in *Dalit International Newsletter,* Vol. 2, No. 1, February 1997.

Seenarine, Moses. "Dalit Women: Victims or Beneficiaries of Affirmative Action Policies in India: A Case Study," a paper presented at a lecture the Southern Asian Institute, Columbia University, April 10th, 1996. Available online at http://saxakali.com/Saxakali-Publications/dalit1.htm (cited January 2, 2002).

Sharma, Kusum. *Ambedkar and Indian Constitution.* New Delhi: Ashish Publishing House, 1992.

Srinivas, M.N. "The Caste System in India" (1952). In Béteille, A., ed. *Social Inequality.* London: Penguin, 1969, pp. 265–272.

"Statement by Women's Voice and National Federation of Dalit Women," Asian Women's Electronic Network Training. Available online at http://www.aworc.org/bpfa/gov/escap/wv_nfdw.html (cited January 2, 2002).

Teltumbde, Anand. "'Ambedkar' In and For the Post-Ambedkar Dalit Movement." (A paper presented in the seminar on the Post-Ambedkar Dalit Movement organized by the Department of Political Science, University of Pune on 27–29 March, 1997), Sugawa Prakashan, Pune.

——— "Impact of New Economic Reforms on Dalits in India." (A paper presented in the seminar on Economic Reforms and Dalits in India, organized by the University of Oxford, Oxford, England, on November 8, 1996.)

World Conference Against Racism, Racial Discrimination, Xenophobia, and Related Intolerance, Durban, South Africa, UN Office of the High Commissioner for Human Rights, 31 Aug–7 Sept 2001. Available online at http://www.unhchr.ch/html/racism/ (cited November 19, 2001).

*Vinayak N. Srivastava*

# INTERNATIONAL MILITARY TRIBUNALS: BRINGING THE WORLD'S WORST TO JUSTICE

## THE CONFLICT

When violent conflicts in the former Yugoslavia and in Rwanda went beyond the pale of human endurance—involving the torture, rape, and massacre of groups of people—the international community, under the auspices of the United Nations, felt obliged to intervene. Creating ad hoc tribunals in the Hague and Tanzania, this international court system has tried individuals for their war crimes and held them accountable. A permanent international war crimes court is being established at the Hague, which, if successful, should handle war crimes more quickly and efficiently than the temporary tribunals.

### Political

- The Fourth Geneva Convention, agreed upon by the UN General Assembly in 1949 and known formally as the Convention on the Protection of Civilian Persons in Time of War, required UN nations to enact laws that made it illegal to commit or order others to commit "grave breaches" of the Convention and to actively seek to bring such offenders to trial. This Convention, however, did not establish a formal, international judicial system to address these crimes. Tribunals have been established, but there are no hard and fast rules for a permanent solution to prosecuting war crimes.

- In the ethnic fighting in the former Yugoslavia and in Rwanda, the international community was slow to become involved, costing thousands of lives and allowing countless atrocities to take place.

### Ethnic

- In ethnic or religious conflicts a domestic court is likely to be staffed by people connected with one or the other of the conflicting ethnic groups, and therefore may be unable to offer a partial trial.

For as long as there have been international relations between states, there have been tensions between them. Long before the development of international organizations like the United Nations, states had ways of settling disputes between them, using both peaceful and violent methods. As rulers fought for control over territory or the dominance of one society over another, the people most often hurt were innocent civilians. Although they had no role in the conflict, they were often the first to die.

During the 1990s the international community stood up and took notice of the fact that thousands of innocent victims, many of whom were women and children, ended up being the casualties of a war that they neither understood nor wanted. The atrocities committed in the "ethnic cleansing" campaigns in the former Yugoslavia, which sought to eliminate Serbian Muslims from territory in Bosnia, Croatia, and Kosovo, solely on the basis of their race, created a situation of urgency, and a reminder to the world that war crimes on a large scale can and do occur in the modern world. In Bosnia, the world witnessed the tearing apart of families, the destruction of cities, and the disenfranchisement of thousands of innocent Bosnian people. The same was true in the 1990s in an African context, as the genocide in Rwanda attracted the attention of the world. While the leaders of the world delayed, hundreds of thousands of Tutsi people were slaughtered.

The international military tribunals for Yugoslavia and Rwanda were established to bring the people behind the war crimes to justice when it was beyond the capacity or desire of their nation to do so. They represented at least a temporary solution to bringing relief to helpless victims and starting the process of healing and reconciliation in their nations. With the tribunals, the international community can intervene within nations to hold individuals responsible for criminal acts such as crimes against peace, war crimes, crimes against humanity, and genocide.

The international community, through the League of Nations and then the United Nations, has developed mechanisms of ensuring that the innocent are protected, and that the perpetrators of war crimes pay the price on a global scale. The world has stood by in horror as entire communities of people have been driven from their homes, massacred, raped, or tortured with no protection from their own government. International military tribunals, from Nuremberg to Rwanda, have served as a means to capture and try those responsible for some of these grave atrocities.

## HISTORICAL BACKGROUND

### Nuremberg: The First Attempt at International Military Justice

*"The most effective means to combat... distortions is to make the facts accessible, and, with them, expose the statements for what they are. At Nuremberg, General Telford Taylor, the prosecutor of more war criminals than any other man, said: 'We cannot here make history over again. But we can see that it is written true.'"*—Robert E. Conot, in *Justice at Nuremberg* (1983).

At the end of World War I (1914–18) in 1918 the Allied Powers established a commission to investigate action on war crimes committed by the defeated Central Powers. The Allies concerned themselves with crimes against peace (which related to waging war in the first place), crimes against humanity (which involved the murder of innocent people in connection with war), and war crimes (which focused on violations of the laws of war). Although the Treaty of Sevres (1920) and the Treaty of Versailles (1919) provided for the prosecution of Turkish and German war criminals, no tribunal was established in order to achieve this. In addition, the worst offenders, including Kaiser Wilhelm (William II, 1859–1941, emperor of Germany and king of Prussia) were given protection by other countries, including the Netherlands. As a result the prosecution of offenders often occurred in domestic courts. In the case of the German war criminals only 12 were put on trial, and of these, only six were given sentences. Despite the efforts by the Allied leaders to bring the offenders to justice, no real action was taken, and they were left unsatisfied.

## CHRONOLOGY

*1945* As World War II ends, the Allies seek to bring German and Japanese war criminals to justice.

*1946* The Nuremberg Tribunal is established. In Germany more than 22 violators are convicted, and many are sentenced to death by hanging.

*1946* The International Military Tribunal for the Far East is established to deal with Japanese war criminals.

*1949* The United Nations (UN) drafts the Geneva Conventions on the Laws of War and the Protection of War Victims.

*1949–1993* The International Law Commission works to draft the statute of the International Military Tribunal/International Criminal Court.

*1993* The UN Security Council adopts resolution 808 to enact the International Criminal Tribunal for Yugoslavia.

*1995* The Security Council adopts Resolution 827 to enact the International Criminal Tribunal for Rwanda.

*1998* UN member states pass the statute of the International Criminal Court.

*September 2, 1998* The Rwandan Tribunal convicts a Hutu leader of genocide.

*1999* Former Yugoslav leader Slobodan Milošević is indicted for crimes against humanity in Kosovo.

*August 14, 2000* The UN Security Council investigates setting up a special court to prosecute war crimes in Sierra Leone.

*June 2001* The Yugoslav government hands over Milošević to the court at The Hague.

*January 3, 2001* The Cambodian government requests the United Nations to set up a tribunal to prosecute top leaders of the Khmer Rouge for atrocities committed there in the late 1970s.

*October 2001* A second indictment against Slobodan Milošević charges him with 32 counts of persecution, torture, murder, plunder, unlawful imprisonment, destroying religious institutions and schools, and other "inhuman acts" in a Serb campaign of ethnic cleansing in Croatia in 1991–1992.

*November 2001* Milošević is indicted for genocide in Bosnia.

## THE GENEVA CONVENTIONS (ON THE LAWS OF WAR)

- 1. Convention (II) for the Amelioration of the Condition of Wounded, Sick and Shipwrecked Members of Armed Forces at Sea. Geneva, 12 August 1949.

- 2. Convention (III) relative to the Treatment of Prisoners of War. Geneva, 12 August 1949

- 3. Convention (IV) relative to the Protection of Civilian Persons in Time of War. Geneva, 12 August 1949.

- 4. Protocol Additional to the Geneva Conventions of 12 August 1949, and relating to the Protection of Victims of International Armed Conflicts (Protocol I), 8 June 1977.

- 5. Protocol Additional to the Geneva Conventions of 12 August 1949, and relating to the Protection of Victims of Non-International Armed Conflicts (Protocol II), 8 June 1977.

At the end of World War II (1939–45) the Allies discovered the extent of the Nazis' brutality as they liberated concentration camps. Six million Jews and millions of others had suffered and died in the camps. The killings were not the same as the deaths of millions of civilians during the war, who were victims of gunfire or bombing. These deaths were genocide, the deliberate and systematic attempt to destroy an entire ethnic or national group. It was clear to many Allied leaders that the atrocities that had occurred in the death camps could not go unpunished.

In October 1943 the Allies had set up the United Nations Commission for the Investigation of War Crimes. At the same time, they issued the Moscow Declaration, which said that German and Japanese political and military leaders responsible for war crimes and crimes against humanity would be brought to trial for their crimes. In August 1945 the governments of France, the United Kingdom, the United States, and the former Soviet Union concluded an agreement establishing the International Military Tribunal at Nuremberg. It was designed to try high-level German officials accused of crimes against peace, crimes against humanity, and war crimes. A similar tribunal was set up in Tokyo, to try Japanese war criminals.

The rules of procedure for the Nuremberg tribunal were somewhat different than the rules in domestic courts. While defendants were entitled to certain rights guarantees there were many rules that served to limit those rights. A conviction and sentence issued by the tribunal could only be imposed on an accused person by a guilty vote by at least three out of four members of the tribunal. In addition, there were no technical rules of evidence, and prosecutors were allowed to admit any evidence they thought had value to the case. The tribunal also had the power to interrogate defendants, and to try people without them being present (known as trial in absentia). The judges of the Nuremberg tribunal also had the authority to order any punishment they considered just, and there was no right of appeal.

Many people criticized the Nuremberg tribunals for a lack of neutrality. For instance, some suggested that because this justice system was established by the countries that won the war and imposed on the countries that had lost, neutrality was all but impossible. The advocates of the tribunals believed that the personal views of the judges would not stop them from carrying out a fair trial.

Despite the criticisms many consider the Nuremberg process to be one of the most important developments in international law. Of the 22 German officials who were tried at Nuremberg, 19 were found guilty; of those, 12 were sentenced to death by hanging. The Nuremberg tribunal was the first time that the international community had brought people to justice for war crimes. It laid the foundation for over one thousand subsequent war crimes trials in Germany and in the Allied nations.

During the war the Japanese military had slaughtered hundreds of thousands of Chinese civilians in the Chinese city of Nanking (Nanjing). In Tokyo after the war, an 11-member tribunal brought to trial some of the Japanese officials who were responsible for the massacres in Asia. Seven were sentenced to death. The Tokyo trials, like the Nuremberg trials, were firsts in international law. The judges had no precedents to follow and were basically forced to write the book on how it should be done.

### The Development of International Humanitarian Law and the Geneva Conventions

In the years following the Nuremberg and Tokyo trials the United Nations set out to establish "the laws of war." The UN Charter made it clear that war was not an acceptable means of settling disputes against states, but recognized that there are sometimes situations where states need to defend themselves against attacks that threaten their independence or their territory. As a result, a framework of laws that would govern situations of conflict was created. The body of law that developed is known as humanitarian law.

International humanitarian law does not question the lawfulness of war, but aims to limit the unnecessary suffering that war can cause. It demands respect for human beings during times of war, and aims to protect ordinary citizens. International humanitarian law consists of a set of rules designed to limit the effects of war on people. In order to ensure that these protections would be respected, the United Nations drafted conventions that can be grouped in four categories: (1) treaties on the protection of victims of war; (2) treaties on the limitation of different types of arms; (3) treaties on the protection of certain objects (like hospitals and ambulances); and (4) treaties governing international jurisdiction. These treaties apply to both international and non-international conflicts. Collectively, they are known as the Geneva Conventions.

The main message of the Geneva Conventions is that people who are not directly involved in conflict should not be subject to attack, and that weapons that cause damage to the environment or unnecessary suffering should not be used. These treaties represent the minimum treatment that is required in situations of conflict. Breach of these rules constitutes a war crime and is punishable by the international community. When the United Nations drafted these conventions, they did so in the hopes that they would set a standard for conduct during hostilities. Enforcement of these standards was another question altogether. The international community has had to find ways bring about justice when individual countries could not do it themselves.

## Yugoslavia: A Renewed Need for International Intervention

In the early 1990s longstanding ethnic tensions in the former Republic of Yugoslavia erupted. In 1991 the republics of Croatia and Slovenia declared their independence from the republic. Serbia then invaded Croatia, proclaimed a new Federal Republic of Yugoslavia, and started savage ethnic warfare when it incited Serbs—especially those in Bosnia-Herzegovina—to violence against non-Serbs. In 1992 Bosnian Serbs seized territory inhabited by Bosnia's Muslim

## LOUISE ARBOUR

*1947* Justice Louise Arbour was born in Montreal, Canada, in 1947. After completing her law degree, she taught at Osgoode Hall Law School, and in 1987 was appointed trial judge for the High Court of Justice for the Supreme Court of Ontario. She then received an appointment to serve on the Court of Appeal for Ontario. In 1995 the United Nations Security Council named her a prosecutor for the International Criminal Tribunals for Yugoslavia and Rwanda to bring to justice those responsible for genocide and war crimes in the former Yugoslavia and Rwanda. She regarded the tribunal as "the most important chapter in the history of criminal and international humanitarian law." During her term, which spanned October 1996 to September 1999, she was responsible for the indictment and prosecution of countless political leaders, including the first indictment of the prime minister of the former Yugoslavia, Slobodan Milošević. In 1999 she left the tribunal to assume a seat on the Supreme Court of Canada.

population. They began a campaign of systematic violence, known as "ethnic cleansing," intended to eliminate the Muslims from the region. In the summer of 1992 the world learned of the existence of Serb-run concentration camps in Bosnia-Herzegovina, which was a painful reminder of Nazi-run camps of World War II. These concentration camps were accompanied by "rape camps," in which Serbian fighters brutalized Muslim women. While the Bosnian Serbs murdered and raped the Bosnian Muslims, the Serbs simultaneously starved and bombed the people of Sarajevo. The conflict had transformed the city of Sarajevo, once host to the Winter Olympics and a symbol of harmony, to the site of mass murders. Although the West dispatched humanitarian aid, none of the UN member nations initially wanted to get involved in military conflict.

As it became increasingly clear that genocide was taking place in Bosnia on a grand scale, support for intervention, both in the United States and around the globe, increased swiftly. As the conflict progressed, the international community began to demand a response from the UN Security Council. Finally, they were prepared to give one.

On October 6, 1992, the United Nations Security Council unanimously adopted a resolution establishing a commission to investigate the atrocities committed in the former Yugoslavia in the ongoing war there. On February 22, 1993, by Resolution 808, the Security Council called for the setting up of an international criminal tribunal for the prosecution of crimes against humanity including murder, torture and "ethnic cleansing."

Unlike the Nuremberg and Tokyo tribunals, which were formulated by the drafting of numerous treaties, the Yugoslav tribunal was established by a resolution of the UN Security Council, acting under its ability to take measures to maintain peace or restore international peace and security, following a determination of the existence of a threat to or breach of peace. This is known as the Chapter VII power.

On May 25, 1993, the Security Council adopted Resolution 827, which established the format of the Yugoslavia tribunal. It was called the International Tribunal for the Prosecution of Persons Responsible for Serious Violations of International Humanitarian Law in the Territory of the former Yugoslavia since 1991. The International Tribunal was set up to achieve three fundamental goals: "ending war crimes, bringing the perpetrators to justice and breaking an endless cycle of ethnic violence and retribution." Some of the notable features of the resolution are:

1. Location of the tribunal: the Hague (the Netherlands)

2. Working languages: English and French

3. Election of 11 judges, no two from the same country, for a four-year term

4. Independent Prosecutor's Office

5. Two Trial Chambers (3 judges each), one Appeal Chamber (5 judges; this differs from the Nuremberg tribunal, which offered no right of appeal)

6. Penalty: Imprisonment Only (this also differs from the Nuremberg tribunal, at which many of the convicted were sentenced to death by hanging. International opposition to capital punishment led to the exclusion of this sentencing option from the Yugoslavia and Rwanda tribunals.)

The tribunal was given a strict responsibility: it was to prosecute only those persons responsible for serious violations of international humanitarian law committed in the territory of the former Yugoslavia since 1991. Unlike the Nuremberg tribunal, which was carried out by the four Allied nations that had won World War II, the International Criminal Tribunal for the former Yugoslavia (ICTY) was an independent body created by the world community in response to a situation of crisis. As a result, the tribunal had a higher degree of impartiality than Nuremberg. Prosecutors, judges, and other participants were selected from countries all over the world. Interestingly, four of the eleven judges elected by the General Assembly upon the nomination of the Council came from states with predominantly Muslim populations. This is striking because the battle for control of Bosnia was, to a large extent, a war between Bosnian Muslims and Bosnian Serbs.

In contrast to Nuremberg the statute of the Yugoslavia Tribunal protects defendants against being tried in an international court, and then again at the national level (called "double jeopardy") by prohibiting national courts from retrying persons who have been tried by the International Tribunal. The ICTY's protections for the rights of defendants is a vast improvement over Nuremberg.

In addition, article 12 of the statute states that there will be three judges in each Trial Chamber and five judges in the Appeals Chamber, and Article 14(3) expressly states that a judge shall serve only in the chamber to which he or she is assigned. This prevents the possibility of the same judge hearing a trial and appeal for the same defendant.

Third, the statute of the Yugoslav tribunal prohibits trials in absentia, another change from Nuremberg. The accused person must be present, it was determined, in order to receive a fair and impartial hearing and have a full opportunity to present a defense.

At first, the government of Yugoslavia did not agree with the Security Council's actions in setting up the tribunal. It challenged the ability and authority of the Security Council to do so before coming to accept and comply with the tribunal.

In the years of its operation the Yugoslav tribunal has been an important fixture in the development of international humanitarian law. Working on a global scale it has made a considerable number of judgements, and has brought some of the most violent offenders to justice, as illustrated below.

### Tadic: The Trial of The Century

The most famous judgement of the ICTY is the first decision it made, in the case of Dusko Tadic. Tadic was arrested in February 1994 on suspicion that he committed offenses, including

CLOCKWISE FROM LEFT, BOSNIAN SERBS MIROSLAV KVOCKA, MILOJICA KOS, MLADO RADIC, AND ZORAN ZIJIC DURING THEIR TRIAL AT THE INTERNATIONAL WAR CRIMES TRIBUNAL AT THE HAGUE. THE MEN WERE CHARGED WITH VIOLATIONS OF THE RULES OF WAR AND OTHER CRIMES. *(© Reuters NewMedia Inc./Corbis. Reproduced by permission.)*

torture and genocide, in the former Yugoslavia. His indictment included 132 charges of grave breaches of the Geneva Conventions and countless crimes against humanity, including murder, torture, rape, inhumane treatment, and persecution. He pleaded not guilty to all charges.

Before the outbreak of conflict in Yugoslavia, Tadic was the owner of a café. He became involved with nationalist politics and helped to implement a policy of "ethnic cleansing," which meant killing, torturing, and otherwise abusing Muslims and Croats, many of whom were his life-long friends.

The prosecutors at the ICTY managed to collect a substantial body of evidence against Tadic, and a number of credible witnesses were able to testify to his presence at the site of the crimes, as well as his participation in them. In total, the prosecutors had 125 witnesses and 473 exhibits. They proved beyond a reasonable doubt that Tadic had

brutally assaulted prisoners, participated in mass beatings, and had tortured innocent people.

The trial lasted seven months. When the judges made their decision, they wrote a 300-page judgement to explain their interpretation of all the evidence and the result of the case. Tadic was sentenced to 20 years imprisonment. He appealed his conviction, but lost. He is now serving his sentence. The Tadic trial, the first time the courts recognized the crime of "ethnic cleansing," created international support for the Yugoslav tribunal.

### The Indictment of Slobodan Milošević, Prime Minister of the Former Yugoslavia

On June 29, 2001, the initial indictment of Slobodan Milošević, the prime minister of the former Yugoslavia, was amended and confirmed. The indictment alleged that, between January 1, 1999, and June 20, 1999, Milošević ordered the armed forces and the police forces of the Federal

# The Types of Crimes Addressed by International Military Tribunals

**Crimes Against Peace:** planning, preparation, initiation or waging of a war of aggression, or a war in violation of international treaties, agreements or assurances, or participation in a common plan or conspiracy for the accomplishment of any of the foregoing.

**War Crimes:** violations of the laws or customs of war. Such violations can include murder, ill-treatment, or deportation for slave labor or for any other purpose of civilian population of or in occupied territory: murder or ill-treatment of prisoners of war; killing of hostages; plunder of public or private property; and destruction of cities towns or villages.

**Crimes Against Humanity:** murder, extermination, enslavement, deportation, and other inhumane acts committed against a population before or during a war, or persecutions on political, racial or religious grounds, in execution of or in connection with any crime within the jurisdiction of the tribunal, whether or not in violation of the domestic law of the country where perpetrated.

Republic of Yugoslavia to execute a campaign of terror and violence directed at Albanian civilians in Kosovo.

The indictment alleges that Milošević gave orders targeting the Albanians in Kosovo with the objective of eliminating a large portion of the Kosovo Albanian population. This was in order to protect Serbian control over the Kosovo province in the former Yugoslavia. The indictment describes a series of well-planned and coordinated operations, all of which were employed to achieve this objective.

Approximately 740,000 Kosovo Albanian civilians were expelled from the province by forced removal and subsequent looting and destruction of their homes, or by the shelling of villages. Surviving residents were sent to the borders of neighboring countries. Many were killed en route, others were abused and had their possessions and identification papers stolen. Massacres took place in many cities within and surrounding the Kosovo province.

Specifically, Milošević and other leaders have been charged with:

- Violations of the laws or customs of war (Article 3: murder; persecutions on political, racial, or religious grounds)

- Crimes against humanity (Article 5: deportation; murder; persecutions on political, racial, or religious grounds).

The trials of Milošević and other leaders are scheduled to begin during 2002.

## The International Military Tribunal for Rwanda: Peace and Reconciliation

On April 6, 1994, the president of Rwanda was killed when his plane was shot down. The country was embroiled in severe ethnic conflict, most of which had been brewed up by politicians. Even before the president's death, close associates in his majority-Hutu administration were planning a massive extermination of the minority Tutsi tribe. A group of soldiers and the presidential guard went into action immediately after the president's death, setting up roadblocks throughout the country and killing both Tutsis and moderate Hutus in their homes. Thousands were killed that first day. By April 11, the International Red Cross estimated that tens of thousands of Rwandans had been killed. Ten days later their estimates rose to hundreds of thousands. The United Nations withdrew most of its aid missions from the country. Hundreds of thousands of Tutsis also fled to neighboring countries like Tanzania. Finally, in just 100 days, the Hutus, sanctioned by their own leadership, had killed somewhere between 500,000 and 800,000 Tutsis, frequently torturing their victims before killing them.

The UN had an ongoing mission with about 2,500 people in Rwanda, but they were not authorized to intervene. Many UN forces stood by and witnessed the killings. In April and May, discussions on Rwanda within the United Nations tended to avoid the word "genocide," because it would have obligated military action. Genocide is defined in the Geneva Convention as those acts committed "with intent to destroy, in whole or in part, a national, ethnical, racial or religious group."

On November 8, 1994, the UN Security Council recognized that serious violations of humanitarian law were being committed in Rwanda and that a situation of genocide did exist within the nation. The government of Rwanda appealed to the Security Council to end the civil war and return peace to the country. Acting under Chapter VII of the United Nations Charter, the

UN SECRETARY GENERAL KOFI ANNAN SPEAKS WITH A JUDGE FROM THE UN'S INTERNATIONAL CRIMINAL TRIBUNAL FOR RWANDA. THE TRIBUNAL HAS BEEN ESTABLISHED TO PROSECUTE THE ORGANIZERS AND LEADERS OF THE 1994 RWANDAN GENOCIDE, IN WHICH 800,000 TUTSIS WERE KILLED. *(A/P Wide World. Reproduced by permission.)*

Council created the International Criminal Tribunal for Rwanda (ICTR) by passing resolution 955.

The purpose of the tribunal is to contribute to the process of national reconciliation in Rwanda and to the maintenance of peace in the region. The tribunal was established for the prosecution of persons responsible for genocide and other serious violations of international humanitarian law committed in the territory of Rwanda between January 1, 1994, and December 31, 1994. On February 22, 1995, the Security Council decided that the seat of the tribunal would be located in Arusha, United Republic of Tanzania.

After the Security Council passed the resolution to create the tribunal, there was some opposition from the Rwandan government regarding the structure of the court. The first reason for opposition was that the court did not include capital punishment as a sentencing option. The Rwandan government wanted to include capital punishment as a possible sentence. The second cause for concern was that, like the Yugoslav tribunal, the Rwandan tribunal had a mandate to try only those issues that had occurred during a very limited period.

The Rwandan government was concerned that there were many important events that took place both before and after 1994 that would not be addressed by the tribunal. Finally, the government was concerned that none of the judges on the panel would be Rwandan, arguing that judges from other countries would not be able to understand and appreciate the particular culture and history of the country. Despite these concerns the Rwandan government realized that the international tribunal was the nation's best chance to bring those responsible for atrocities to justice, especially those that had left the country. After discussion, Rwanda agreed to cooperate with the United Nations and the tribunal.

Like the Yugoslav tribunal, the Rwanda tribunal has the authority to prosecute and try four clusters of offenses:

- Grave breaches of the 1949 Geneva Conventions (Article 2)

- Violations of the laws or customs of war (Article 3)

- Genocide (Article 4)

- Crimes against humanity (Article 5)

The Rules of Procedure for the ICTR were also modeled after those of the tribunal for the former Yugoslavia. They incorporate the fundamental

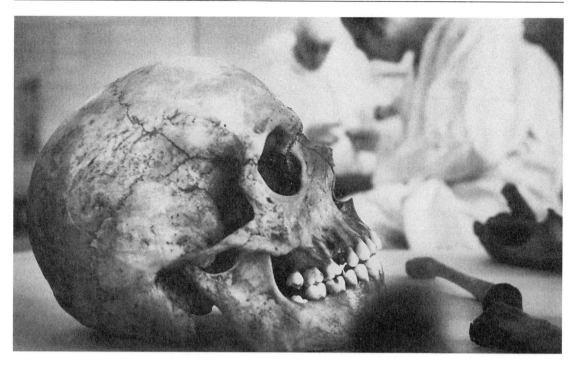

THE INTERNATIONAL WAR CRIMES TRIBUNAL WAS FORMED TO PROSECUTE THOSE RESPONSIBLE FOR PERPE-
TRATING ACTS IN VIOLATION OF THE GENEVA CONVENTION. THIS SKULL WAS FOUND IN A GRAVE OF BODIES SUS-
PECTED TO BE THOSE OF BOSNIAN MUSLIMS KILLED BY SERBS IN 1992. (© *Reuters NewMedia Inc./Corbis. Reproduced by
permission.*)

due process guarantees to a fair and speedy trial found in Article 14 of the United Nations International Covenant on Civil and Political Rights (ICCPR). Consequently, the Rwanda Tribunal, like its Yugoslavian counterpart, has the potential to assume a significant role in the enforcement of international human rights standards. It includes the same guarantees to a fair trial and to the presumption of innocence that characterize the ICTY, and also provides for the right of appeal.

There is one significant difference between the statutes of the Yugoslav and Rwanda tribunals. In the case of the Yugoslav tribunal, the court is only allowed to consider acts that took place in the former republic of Yugoslavia. In contrast, the mandate of the Rwandan tribunal states that it has the power to prosecute violations of international humanitarian law in Rwanda, as well as Rwandan citizens responsible for violations in the territory of neighboring states. As a result, the statute gives the tribunal both personal and territorial jurisdiction in Rwanda as well as limited personal and territorial jurisdiction in surrounding states.

The Rwanda Tribunal is also important for its objectivity. In Rwanda, where the source of the problem relates to ethnic groups and their exercise

of power, the tribunal is vital because it represents a neutral, outside intervention, which presumably does not hold an ethnic connection within the community and can bring impartiality and justice to the process.

The Organization of African Unity (OAU), a federation of 32 independent African states formed in 1963 in order to promote unity and to defend the sovereignty of its members, provides for non-interference in the internal affairs of member states. The Rwanda Tribunal places the international rules of war over and above those of the OAU, with the United Nations assuming a higher authority.

## RECENT HISTORY AND THE FUTURE

### *The International Criminal Court: The Future of Military Justice*

"*For nearly half a century—almost as long as the United Nations has been in existence ... the General Assembly has recognized the need to establish such a court that can prosecute and punish persons responsible for crimes such as genocide.... Our time ... has shown us that man's capacity for evil knows no limits.*"—Kofi Annan, United Nations Secretary-General

In spite of the effectiveness of the ad hoc tribunals, meaning a tribunal set up for a specific occasion, established in Nuremberg, Tokyo, Yugoslavia, and Rwanda, there has been an ongoing interest in the establishment of a permanent international criminal court. Following the Nuremberg and Tokyo tribunals the United Nations and the International Law Commission worked for many years to draft the statute (the enabling document) of an International Criminal Court. Widespread opposition resulted in several breakdowns in the process and disagreement about the types of issues that would be addressed. For instance, there was much dissention about whether drug trafficking would be included as an offence within the mandate of the tribunal.

The outbreak of hostilities in Yugoslavia, and the ad hoc tribunal that was created in response to the problems provided a great deal of international support for the International Law Commission to firmly establish the court. The Commission therefore completed its work on the draft statute of the court and submitted it to the United Nations General Assembly in 1994. Between 1995 and 1998 a committee composed of various countries met to discuss and draft the statute for the international criminal court.

In August 1998 the statute of the International Criminal Court was approved by a vote of 120 in favor and 7 against, with 21 abstentions. It will enter into force after 60 countries have ratified it. As of September 2001, 37 countries had ratified the statute and 139 had signed it, showing their intent to seek ratification. The court will be located at The Hague, in the Netherlands, but it will be authorized to try cases in other locations when appropriate and necessary.

In order to appreciate the value and importance of the International Criminal Court, it is necessary to understand the role it will play. National courts will always have jurisdiction over their citizens. Under the principle of "complementarity," the International Criminal Court will act only when national courts are unable or unwilling. Unfortunately, in some countries, in times of conflict or social and political confusion, there may be no courts capable of dealing with war crimes, genocide, or crimes against humanity. The government in power may be unwilling to prosecute its own citizens, especially political officials. Since those who commit crimes included in the statute of the International Criminal Court often cross borders, it is necessary for states to be able to cooperate to capture and punish them. The International Criminal Court would provide this option and ensure that necessary prosecutions take place.

It is useful to distinguish the International Criminal Court from other international bodies. The International Court of Justice, based in The Hague, is an international court with which many are familiar. In comparison to the International Criminal Court, however, the International Court of Justice only handles cases between states, not those that involve individual actors. Without a court to respond to the crimes of individual persons, many crimes including genocide, war crimes, and crimes against humanity have gone unpunished. During the 1970s, for instance, an estimated two million people were killed by the Khmer Rouge. Similar atrocities were committed in El Salvador, Liberia, and the Great Lakes African region, including Burundi, Rwanda, and Democratic Republic of the Congo, to name a few. When ratified, the International Criminal Court will thus act as a specialized court, to deal with these types of crimes, and bring the actors to justice.

In contrast to the ad hoc tribunals that have been established, the International Criminal Court is a permanent, standing facility that can be relied on quickly and effectively. While in the case of Yugoslavia and Rwanda the world had to wait for the Security Council to draft a statute for each tribunal, the International Criminal Court statute will be permanent and the court will be fully operational. The rules will be set out clearly. Without the delays associated with setting up a tribunal, which can lead to the destruction of evidence and the disappearance of accused persons, the International Court will be able to act more efficiently than tribunals.

Ad hoc tribunals are also subject to certain limitations. Thousands of refugees from the ethnic conflict in Rwanda were murdered after 1994, but the mandate of that tribunal is limited to events that occurred during that year only. Crimes committed since that time are not covered. A permanent court is not confronted with these types of limitations and will be able to concentrate on bringing those accused of war crimes to justice.

Finally, while the International Military Tribunals had to make a lot of decisions regarding procedure as they went along, the International Criminal Court will have a formal set of procedures in place well before it starts operating. This gives the court a higher degree of legitimacy in the eyes of the international community and should lead to widespread acceptance and participation.

# BIBLIOGRAPHY

Ackerman, John, and Eugene O'Sullivan. *Practice and Procedure of the International Criminal Tribunal for the Former Yugoslavia, With Selected Materials from the International Criminal Tribunal for Rwanda.* The Netherlands: Kluwer Law International, 2000.

Clifford, J. Garry. "Bosnia-Herzegovina." *Dictionary of American History, Supplement.* Charles Scribner's Sons, 1996. Reproduced in History Resource Center. Gale Group. Farmington Hills, MI: 2001.

Conot, Robert E. *Justice at Nuremberg.* New York: Harper Publishing House, 1983.

David, Eric, Pierre Klein, and Anne-Marie La Rosa, eds. *International Criminal Tribunal for Rwanda: Reports of Orders, Decisions and Judgements, 1995–1997 / Tribunal pénal international pour le Rwanda: recueil des ordonnances, décisions et arrêts, 1995–1997.* Brussels, Belgium: Bruylant Publishers, 2000.

Hugh M. Kindred et al. *International Law Chiefly as Interpreted and Applied in Canada.* 5th ed. Toronto: Emond Montgomery Publications, 1993.

International Committee for the Red Cross. Available online at http://www.icrc.org (cited October 25, 2001).

International Criminal Tribunal for the Former Yugoslavia. Available online at http://www.icty.org (cited October 25, 2001).

International Criminal Tribunal for Rwanda. Available online at http://www.ictr.org (cited October 25, 2001).

Morris, Virginia, and Michael Sharf. *An Insider's Guide to the International Criminal Tribunal for the Former Yugoslavia.* Ardsley, NY: Transnational Publishers Ltd, 1995.

Steiner, Henry J., and Philip Alston. *International Human Rights in Context-Law, Politics, Morals.* 2d ed. New York: Oxford University Press, 2000.

Taylor, Telford. *The Anatomy of the Nuremberg Trials : A Personal Memoir.* New York: Knopf Publishers, 1992.

United Nations. Available online at http://www.un.org (cited October 25, 2001).

"War Crimes Tribunals: An In-Depth Analysis," *Facts on File.* Available online at http://www.facts.com/icof/warintro.htm (cited November 16, 2001).

*Sapna Butany-Goyal*

# AFRICA'S IVORY TRADE:
# FIGHTING FOR THE BEARERS
# OF "WHITE GOLD"

Elephants have been revered as gods and feared as fighters; they have been adored in movies and have inspired awe in the wilderness. Throughout the ages these majestic animals have aroused many emotions. During the month of April 2000 these sentiments were threatening to divide Africa.

One hundred fifty-one delegates from governments worldwide gathered in Nairobi, Kenya, at that time, to decide what degree of protection would be afforded to the African elephant under the United Nations Convention on International Trade in Endangered Species of Wild Fauna and Flora (CITES). Elephant tusks, also known as ivory or "white gold," have been prized for centuries. Between 1979 and 1989 the demand for ivory reached such a feverish pitch that over half a million elephants were killed. In an effort to protect the disappearing elephant a complete ban on the international trade in ivory was put in place during the CITES meeting in 1989.

In the spring of 2000, 11 years after the ban, the southern African countries of Botswana, Namibia, Zimbabwe, and South Africa all requested that the ivory ban be lifted. Not all countries with elephant populations agreed with this proposal. East African countries led by Kenya along with India not only rejected the idea of lifting the ivory ban—they were calling for stricter regulations to make sure that resumption of the ivory trade in the future was even more unlikely.

Kenya and other East African countries, along with some conservation groups such as Save the Elephants, the International Fund for Animals, and Born Free, argued that the future of the elephant hung in the balance; to allow a lifting of the 1989 ban on the ivory trade would mean extinc-

## THE CONFLICT

In 1989, realizing that poaching was out of control, that over half of Africa's elephants had been killed, and that their nations were losing a tremendous resource, eight African countries (Tanzania, Kenya, Somalia, Gambia, Zaire, Chad, Niger, and Zambia) agreed to support an international ban on the ivory trade to begin in January 1990. This measure has been called into question by some southern African countries after a decade of the ban. East African nations, however, support the ban.

### Political

- Some who oppose the ban on the ivory trade perceive it as a form of "ecological colonialism"—that decisions as to how land in Africa should be used is being dictated by external groups in much the same manner as in colonial times.

- Pro-ivory trade ban groups argue that ivory must be banned entirely, worldwide. The existence of legitimate ivory makes illegal sales easier, since the ivory from elephants killed in one country can be smuggled across the border to a country where ivory sales are allowed.

- As long as there is an ivory market, poachers will remain a problem. Poachers not only kill elephants illegally and in ways that decimate the population, but they also bring arms into African nations, causing significant security problems, and they are very difficult to regulate.

### Economic

- The countries that oppose the ban on the ivory trade argue that it is prohibitively expensive as it stands now. Not only do some very poor nations lose the income from the vast ivory business, but they also have to pay for expensive conservation programs. In the meantime, the growing population of elephants destroys valuable crops.

- The anti-ban faction promotes the theory that unless the elephants are economically self-sufficient, there will not be enough interest in the long run to save them.

- The pro-ban group argues that elephants are just as profitable alive as they are dead. Wildlife tourism can generate as much income as the ivory trade.

# CHRONOLOGY

*1976* The Asian elephant is put on Appendix I (most protected) of the CITES Convention.

*1977* The African elephant is recognized as needing some degree of protection and put on Appendix II (not necessarily threatened with extinction, but in need of trade controls) of the CITES Convention.

*1979* The African elephant population is 1.3 million.

*1986* Quotas for ivory exports are introduced for African range states.

*1989* The elephant population is estimated at around 600,000.

*July 18, 1989* Kenya's president, H.E. Daniel arap Moi sets ablaze a stockpile of several thousand tusks valued at approximately US$3 million in an effort to gain Western countries' support for the ivory ban.

*1989* Ivory's price reaches a high of $140 a pound on the international market.

*1989* A complete worldwide ban on the ivory trade is passed overwhelming by at the CITES conference in Switzerland.

*1990* The ivory market collapses—the price of ivory falls to $5 per pound.

*1992* The CITES conference takes place in Kyoto, Japan; the ban on ivory is maintained.

*1992* Namibia, Malawi, Botswana, and Zimbabwe announce that they will prepare to set up a southern African ivory trade but do not commit themselves outright to an immediate resumption of the trade.

*1997* After eight years of campaigning for a lift on the ban of the ivory trade, Zambia switches sides and declares that lifting the ban will lead to "senseless slaughter."

*1997* At a CITES Conference, elephant populations of Botswana, Namibia, Zimbabwe are downgraded to Appendix II, and each country is given permission to make one experimental sale of existing ivory stocks. These sales will take place in Japan in 1999 and are controlled by CITES.

*1999* Poaching increases five times in Kenya.

*2000* At a CITES Conference, South Africa's elephant population is downgraded to Appendix II. No sales of ivory stocks are allowed for any country. The ban on the ivory trade is continued.

---

tion for the elephant. On the other hand, Botswana, Namibia, Zimbabwe, and South Africa, supported by different conservation groups including the World Wildlife Fund, argued that in order to preserve their elephant populations as well as save their people from grinding poverty, lifting the ban on the ivory trade was vital. Both sides were passionate and the debates were heated.

East African countries claimed that if their southern African neighbors resumed the ivory trade it would mean an extra burden for the rest of Africa, and the certain loss of their elephant populations in the east, because they were not wealthy enough to protect their elephants from illegal poaching. In essence, the countries in East Africa were accusing the countries in the south of selfishly pursuing their own economic interests to the detriment of their poorer neighbors. In turn, southern African countries accused the East of mismanaging their elephant populations, and

claimed that they should not be blamed for their mistakes.

Conservation groups weighed in on both sides of the debate. Those groups supporting the East African anti-ivory trade position argued that the greed of poachers knew no bounds, and that the elephant would be wiped out entirely should the ban be lifted. South African officials viewed much of the animal rights lobby as extremely biased and accused them of wanting Africa to be preserved as a giant national park for others to be able to come and visit like a zoo.

Given the growing hostility between the two sides, it came as a surprise when on April 17, 2000, Botswana, Namibia, South Africa, and Zimbabwe withdrew their request for quotas to sell ivory. Likewise, Kenya and India withdrew their request for stricter protection standards. An agreement was made to spend the next two and a half years working to build a continent-wide consensus on a long-term conservation strategy for elephants. Finding such consensus will be an enormous challenge. There are multiple political, economic, and environmental considerations, each with their own merits.

For the time being the ban on international trade in ivory will continue, but in 2003 the debate will start again. The arguments on both sides of the table are compelling, particularly in view of the history of elephants as they came to be a threatened species and the different perspectives that exist on how to protect the world's largest land mammal.

## HISTORICAL BACKGROUND

### The History of the Ivory Trade and the Disappearing Elephant

There was a time when elephants lived on practically every land area of the world, from the shores of the Arctic Ocean to the Gulf of Mexico. There were once more than 300 different branches of elephants. Now there are only two. The African elephant and the Asian elephant are all that survive.

Elephants have been mankind's helpmate from at least as early as 1200 BCE. They have been employed as laborers; they have been used to transport troops; they have been part of royal pageantry; and they have played a key role in determining the success or failure of a nation in war. Elephants were considered so valuable that they were sometimes offered as gifts of friendship between countries (see sidebar).

Almost as valuable as the elephant itself, and perhaps more so, are its upper incisor teeth, or tusks, which are made of ivory. Prized for its color, its texture, and its strength, ivory is considered one of the most beautiful animal products. Ancient kings and magistrates of Rome sat upon ivory seats. Traditional carvers in Japan carved ivory as a fine art, often working on a single tusk for an entire year. In more recent times, ivory has been used to make billiard balls, piano keys, knife handles, jewelry, and many other articles of luxury.

The trade in ivory is considered responsible for the fact that the North African elephant was wiped out nearly 1,000 years ago. During the 1800s the elephant population in East Africa was also plummeting as the slave and ivory trades fed one another. Men and women from East Africa were captured and forced to carry ivory tusks to the coast for shipment. They were then sold into

### ELEPHANTS IN AMERICA?

In the Far East, elephants were considered so valuable that inhabitants wondered how Americans and others could carry on their daily work without them. In 1861, the King of Siam (now Thailand) sent a friendly letter to the president of the United States, Abraham Lincoln, offering to send a number of young elephants of both sexes to the United States in order to begin developing an elephant population there. It was felt that the elephants could be raised in the United States in much the same way as ostriches are now raised in some states like California. This generous offer was declined with thanks by the authorities in Washington.

slavery, according to Cynthia Moss in *Elephant Memories: Thirteen Years in the Life of an Elephant Family.* By the early 1900s some colonial administrators in Africa became alarmed by the decreasing elephant population and decided to establish reserves to protect the animal, and instituted laws banning the killing of elephants.

As a result of these protections, the elephant populations in central, southern, and eastern Africa began to recover. During the first 50 years of the 1900s the trade in ivory shifted from mainly European destinations to Asia; however, the volume continued at a relatively low pace.

In the late 1960s the price of ivory began to rise, starting at around US$2.45 a pound and soaring to over $140 a pound in the late 1980s, writes Moss. As the value of elephant ivory increased, so too did the number of elephants killed. From 1963 to 1989, 86 percent of all the elephants in Africa were shot for their ivory, skin, tails, and feet, according to Delia and Mark Owens in *The Eye of the Elephant: An Epic Adventure in the African Wilderness.* Some people predicted that at that rate the African elephant would be extinct by 2000.

### Why the Sudden Growth in the Ivory Trade?

During the 1960s many countries in Africa gained their independence after many years of colonial rule. In an article in *Environment and History* K.A. Hill observes that over the course of the colonial period, wildlife preservation came to be negatively associated with white rule and

KENYAN PRESIDENT DANIEL ARAP MOI SPEAKS AT THE 11TH CONVENTION ON INTERNATIONAL TRADE IN ENDANGERED SPECIES. ONE MATTER DISCUSSED AT THE CONVENTION WAS WHETHER THE PARTIAL TRADE IN IVORY SHOULD CONTINUE. *(AP/Wide World Photos. Reproduced by permission.)*

oppression. Some people were killing elephants as part of a backlash against symbols of colonialism such as the reservations, which had protected the lives of animals sometimes at the expense of the human population in the country.

The post-colonial period was also a very politically unstable time and arms flowed into the continent. The increased availability of weapons played a key role in the increased numbers of elephants being killed. Poachers, often armed with AK-47 rifles, chain saws, and even rocket-propelled grenades, were able to decimate elephant populations in a way that would not have traditionally been possible.

The rocketing price of oil during this period is also believed to have played a role in the increased demand for ivory. Compared to the unstable oil markets, ivory was seen as a relatively stable and valuable commodity on the international market.

During this period the popularity of personal seals, or *hankos*, was also growing. In Japan hankos are used by individuals and companies instead of written signatures. Ivory is used because it absorbs and transfers ink well. In the past only the face of the seal was made of ivory. Gradually, however, it became a status symbol to have a hanko made entirely out of solid ivory. Rather than one carver working on one tusk for an entire year—the advent of mechanized carving meant that a single hanko-making factory could work its way through one ton of ivory in a single day. According to Allan Thornton and Dave Currey in their 1991 book, *To Save an Elephant: The Undercover Investigation into the Illegal Ivory Trade*, for that single day's work, 100 elephants must be killed.

### Trying to Protect the Elephant: The UN Convention on International Trade in Endangered Species of Wild Fauna and Flora.

The United Nations Convention on International Trade in Endangered Species of Wild Fauna and Flora, commonly referred to as CITES, protects wildlife from the exploitation often found in the international wildlife trade. Every two or three years the countries who are members of CITES gather to evaluate and make any changes necessary to the level of protection granted to animals listed under the convention. In 1989, realizing that poaching was out of control—that over half of Africa's elephants had been killed, and that their nations were losing a tremendous resource—eight African countries (Tanzania, Kenya, Somalia, Gambia, Zaire, Chad, Niger, and Zambia) agreed to support an international ban on the ivory trade to begin in January 1990. This push to protect the elephant was helped by the fact that in March 1989 the United States imposed an immediate ban on the importation of ivory. Canada, the European Community, Switzerland, and the United Arab Emirates followed the U.S. lead.

As a result, during the 1989 CITES conference, parties voted overwhelmingly to place the African elephant on the convention's Appendix I, which grants an endangered species most protected status. Consequently, the elephant was declared an endangered species and all trade in elephant products was effectively banned. This convention and the degree of protection afforded to the African elephant has become a critical source of conflict in Africa.

### The Ivory Debates

While most agreed that the elephant needed the utmost degree of protection, a minority of the 37 African range states who had wild elephant populations did not agree that the ban should be universally applied. In particular, six southern African states, including Botswana, Malawi, Mozambique, South Africa, Zambia, and Zim-

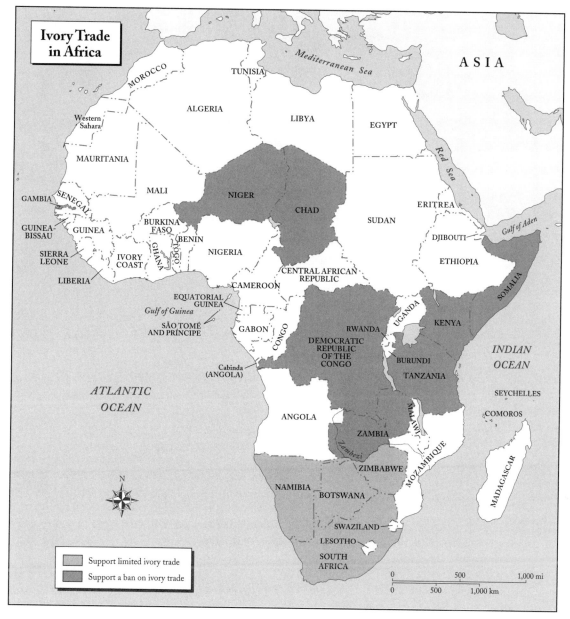

MAP OF AFRICA DETAILING NATIONS IN SUPPORT OF LIMITED TRADE IN IVORY AND NATIONS SUPPORTING A FULL BAN ON THE TRADE. *(The Gale Group.)*

babwe, whose elephant populations were not in immediate danger, felt the ban would mean not only significant economic losses in general but also that there would be less funds to invest in conservation efforts. While the number of countries objecting to the ban was relatively small in number, collectively they did represent 40 percent of Africa's elephants.

Meanwhile, for countries in East Africa and many Western countries, the 1989 ban in ivory was an important step in saving the elephant. Countries such as Kenya had lost the vast majority

of their elephants and a ban meant that there might still be a chance to rescue them. These hopes were not misguided. Once a ban on the international trade in ivory was in place, the ivory market collapsed from US$140 a pound in 1989 to less than $5 per pound a year later. Poaching rates also decreased dramatically. There was renewed hope that the African elephant would survive.

The debate between those supporting a ban on the ivory trade and those who want it to be lifted has raged in Africa for over a decade and promises to continue. Since 1989 each time

WILDLIFE RANGERS IN KENYA STACK IVORY AT THE KENYA WILDLIFE HEADQUARTERS. KENYA OPPOSES A PROPOSED LIFT OF THE BAN ON IVORY SALES, FEARING THAT THE SALES, INTENDED TO REDUCE STOCKPILES, WILL ENCOURAGE RENEWED POACHING. *(AP/Wide World Photos. Reproduced by permission.)*

CITES has reconvened, heated debates have erupted between those countries who wish to continue the ban on ivory by keeping the elephant under Appendix I and those who wish to see the elephant moved to Appendix II, which allows trade through a system of permits.

### Pro-Ivory Trade

The main group of countries that have consistently called for a lift of the ivory ban and a resumption of limited trade include the southern African countries of Botswana, Namibia, and Zimbabwe. Other countries, such as Malawi and South Africa, have also taken a stand against the ban, with the latter occasionally taking a leadership role in the debates. This group has found some support among conservation groups like the World Wildlife Fund. For those who support the ivory trade there are four main sets of arguments. First, elephants are a necessary form of income; second, in order to preserve the elephant population, there needs to be an economic benefit; and third, these countries argue that they have too many elephants. Finally, many of those supporting the trade in ivory argue that the ban on ivory was a form of eco-colonialism.

**A Necessary Form of Income.** The ivory trade is big business. For poor countries struggling with crippling poverty, ivory represents an important way to generate income, to invest in local communities, and to become less reliant on foreign aid. It is viewed like other natural resources as a commodity that should be used to improve the living standards of people.

In addition to the money earned from selling ivory internationally, local ivory carving businesses create much needed employment. Other parts of the elephant, such as its hide, are also sold on the international market and the meat can be used to feed local populations. Hunting licenses, purchased for tens of thousands of dollars by wealthy foreigners so that they can shoot elephants, lions, leopards, and buffalo, have also been an important source of income. A ban on killing elephants means that many people lose a very important source of income—a source that can, at times, mean the difference in survival.

**Killing Elephants in Order to Preserve Them.** "For much of emergent Africa the only long-term hope for the big mammals of the savannahs depends in part on a new line of thought: you either use wildlife or you lose it. If it is not economically self-sufficient there is little point in saving its space. If it pays its own way some of it will survive, it if can't, it won't," said British ecologist

Norman Myers, as quoted in Irven O. Buss's *Elephant Life: Fifteen Years of High Population Density*. One of the most important arguments of groups supporting the ivory trade is that the people living next to the elephants need to have a stake in the animal's preservation. Hours and hours of work dedicated to growing crops for a family's survival can be trampled in moments by a herd of elephants.

For many farmers the elephant is a 5-ton garden pest, a threat to their livelihood and potentially to their life. Unlike the small bugs that might eat a few leaves in a North American garden, one elephant can eat its way through 300 kilograms of vegetable matter a day, according to V. Campbell in a World Wildlife Fund article. In addition, people are occasionally killed by elephants; between 1990 and 1993, 100 people were killed in Kenya alone. Given these reasons, it is not surprising that sometimes people who must share living space with elephants do not object if a few are killed.

Unless individuals feel there is some direct benefit for preserving the elephants' natural habitat, people will likely choose to convert land into livestock ranges and agricultural land. This decision is significant. Next to the illegal trade in ivory, the loss of habitat is the greatest danger to elephants. According to the World Wildlife Fund (which supports a limited ivory trade) it is necessary for local people to be involved in order to protect the elephant over the long term. In essence, those who support a regulated ivory trade argue that a total ban is misguided. Unless it is possible to sell the elephant's ivory, the elephant itself will only be seen as a nuisance—and if this nuisance is threatening a family's food, their children's education, or their survival—long-term interests like "saving the elephant" will seem irrelevant.

One example of a program that allows local communities to have a stake in conserving elephants is the Communal Areas Management Programme for Indigenous Resources (CAMPFIRE), which was started in Zimbabwe during the early 1990s. This program, often mentioned by pro-trade countries as a model, gives control and a substantial share of profits from animals hunted on communal lands back to the communities. Wealthy tourists from the United States, Spain, and Germany pay thousands of dollars to shoot animals according to a quota determined by the Department of National Parks. Using proceeds from animals hunted on their land, notes L. McGregor in a *Mail and Guardian* article, communities participating in CAMPFIRE have been

## ELEPHANT POPULATION IN MILLIONS

| Year | Estimated Numbers |
|------|-------------------|
| 1900 | 10 million |
| 1979 | 1.3 |
| 1989 | 600,000 |
| 2000 | 400,000 |

DROPPING FROM 10 MILLION TO A MERE 400,000 IN ONE HUNDRED YEARS, THE ELEPHANT POPULATION CONTINUES TO FACE THREATS FROM THE IVORY TRADE. *(The Gale Group.)*

able to build medical clinics, community halls, sink wells, and purchase necessities for local schools.

In addition to individuals and communities needing to have a stake in elephant conservation, southern African governments such as Zimbabwe, Namibia, and South Africa have also argued that they need the funds from the sales of ivory to maintain well-managed national level conservation programs. In 1997 Namibia's Environment and Tourism Minister, Gert Hanekom, argued that "reinvesting the money through the conservancy programme would help Namibia move closer to sustainable management and conservation without encouraging illegal killing of elephants or illegal trade in ivory" (as quoted in a 1997 article by E. Koro, L. Mooketsi, and T. Moyo, in *Africa Information Afrique/Misa*.)

Without the money from ivory and other elephant parts, protecting elephants and preserving their habitat becomes very expensive. Indeed, after the ivory ban went into force, Zimbabwe claimed that because of this loss of revenue, it was not able to properly fund park enforcement programs. Consequently, the number of elephants that were illegally killed rose from 10 to 100 in one year.

**The Cost of Too Many Elephants.** One of the other key arguments put forward by pro-trade groups is that some countries, such as Botswana, Namibia, and Zimbabwe have too many elephants. By 1997 the elephant population in countries such as Zimbabwe was growing at a rate of 5 percent a year. If left unchecked, these groups argued, not only would the elephants trample crops and physically threaten the people living close to them, but they would also destroy their own environment and the vegetation on which other animal species depend.

In order to keep an ecological balance it was necessary to cull some of the elephants, meaning the elephants were selectively killed. Without being able to recoup some of the costs from selling the ivory, the process becomes very expensive. Indeed, for some southern countries with growing elephant populations, not only was managing elephant populations not cost effective, it was becoming a liability. Zimbabwean economist Dr. Brian Child has estimated the ban is costing the country a minimum of $4 million a year (as quoted in I. Matheson's 1999 article for the BBC News).

In the past, governments were able to sell the ivory from elephants that died naturally, or, as mentioned above, were culled due to large elephant populations. Once the ban was put in place, storing the ivory became a necessity. This created two problems. First, it was essential to protect the ivory from theft so that it would not get onto the black market and be sold illegally. Second, in order to ensure that the ivory did not dry out and shrink (as it tends to do over time), it was necessary to pay to store the ivory in certain conditions in order to preserve it. For developing countries, the protection and preservation of ivory can be excessively expensive, particularly when contrasted with many of the other pressing concerns of the state.

Considerable efforts had been made towards other types of sustainable management, but with limited success and considerable expense. For example, in some instances where the elephant population became too large for a particular area, some were moved to other parks. What was discovered, however, was that the cost of moving a group of elephants from one area of a country to another prohibitively expensive, and some elephants appeared to be traumatized by the experience. After being forcibly moved some elephants would become extremely aggressive towards humans or become extremely fearful. Contraception methods for female elephants have also been attempted, but these are controversial and have met with limited success.

Essentially the pro-trade groups have argued that not being able to trade in ivory is an economic liability, and to date no alternative method of sustainable management has been shown to be cost effective. These countries further argue that because they have done an effective job of managing their elephant conservation programs, they should not be punished for what they saw as inef-

ficiency and corruption in the East African countries that were demanding a sustained ban.

**Eco-Colonialism.** Another reason that the ban on ivory sales was deeply resented by some is that it was perceived as "ecological colonialism," notes K. A. Hill in a 1995 article in *Environment and History.* During the colonial period in Africa, the best lands were given to whites, while the more marginal regions were designated for the indigenous people. In regard to the issue of the conservation of elephants, once again it seemed that decisions as to how land in Africa should be used were being dictated from external groups in much the same manner—that comfortably well-fed Europeans and North Americans were insisting on strict environmental policies for poor countries who were struggling to feed their populations. Indeed to some, as McGregor observes, it seemed that the African elephant was more valued than the African people.

## Anti-Ivory Trade

The other side of the debate is led by Kenya and supported by up to 35 other African countries along with Western conservation groups and governments. The anti-ivory trade group's arguments follow four main lines: fear of extinction, an increase in poaching and black market operations, the benefits of wildlife tourism, and a fundamental disagreement on how many elephants there are at this time.

**The Loss of a Species.** By 1989 the elephant population was at risk of extinction due to large scale poaching. The anti-ivory trade group has argued that unless a ban is maintained, the elephant will once again be at risk of extermination. This group argues, quite simply, any lifting of the ban will seriously put the future of the elephant in danger.

**Problems with Poaching.** For the anti-trade groups the key argument is that even a limited trade in ivory would spark an upsurge in elephant poaching. There is evidence that even a possibility that the ban might be lifted leads to an increase in the amount of ivory poached and then stockpiled. Poaching, or the illegal killing of elephants, is a significant danger for multiple reasons. Prior to the ban on the international ivory market, it was estimated that 90 percent of the ivory entering the international market was from poached elephants. In other words, most of the elephants were shot illegally and sold on the black market or the illegal tusks were "laundered" by using false documents.

PROTESTERS AGAINST A PROPOSED LIFT ON THE BAN OF IVORY TRADE DEMONSTRATE IN KENYA PRIOR TO A MEETING OF THE CONVENTION ON INTERNATIONAL TRADE IN ENDANGERED SPECIES. *(© AFP/Corbis. Reproduced by permission.)*

Countries such as Kenya have argued that the existence of legitimate ivory makes illegal sales easier. The ivory from elephants killed in one country would be smuggled across the border to a country where ivory sales are allowed. When in 1997, Botswana, Zimbabwe, and Namibia were permitted by CITES to sell their ivory on a "one-off," or one-time only, basis, poaching increased five-fold in Kenya alone, notes M. Wilson in a 2000 article in BBC News Online. While CITES tried to ensure that these one-time sales were highly regulated and controlled, the presence of some legal ivory on the market led to a flood of illegal tusks as well. As a result, the number of elephants killed illegally soared, and under-funded and overworked wildlife department officials in elephant range countries were stretched beyond their limits by having to combat the immediate rise in poaching.

Poachers are not only considered a serious problem because of the number of elephants they kill, but because of the way that they kill them. Part of the reason that the elephant population dropped so dramatically before the ban was because poachers were first targeting the larger, older male elephants with the larger tusks, according to S. Njumbi in a chapter in *A Week with Elephants*. Consequently, the breeding patterns of the elephant population was disrupted. Fewer older male elephants meant a decreasing number of female elephants becoming pregnant. Once the numbers of the older male elephants began to fall, poachers would begin to target the older female elephants. Loss of female elephants often resulted in the death of some of the younger orphaned elephants because of starvation and lack of protection.

Another significant problem with poaching is the security threat that it poses. Campbell notes that the funds from the sales of illegal ivory have sometimes been used to fund civil wars, such as the one in Angola, and to pay for weapons that threaten the security of the people in the region. As poachers became a serious threat to the survival of the elephant populations in some countries, governments enacted policies to shoot poachers on sight. Unfortunately the government "anti-poaching forces" were often powerless against the much better armed poaching gangs. Not surprisingly, the well-armed poachers shot back. Both people and elephants have been killed in the wars over the ivory trade.

The problems presented by poaching have been fairly widely recognized and some of the southern countries that support the ivory trade

ELEPHANTS AT A WATERING POND IN ZIMBABWE, ONE OF THE COUNTRIES THAT WANTS THE ABILITY TO TRADE IN IVORY. KENYA AND ITS SUPPORTERS WANT THE BAN AGAINST THE IVORY TRADE TO REMAIN IN PLACE. *(A/P Wide World. Reproduced by permission.)*

have promised to institute a poaching monitoring system in order to help effectively crack down on poachers. Unfortunately this system has not yet been put into place and as a result there is no real system to track and stop poachers. Without such a system in place, anti-ivory trade parties argue, there is no way to protect elephants against poaching, and without a good protection system the elephant, quite simply, will not survive.

**Worth More Alive Than Dead.** While those wishing to resume the trade in ivory argue that they need to sell the ivory to ensure the protection of the elephant, the pro-ban group argues that elephants are just as profitable alive as they are dead. Wildlife tourism can generate as much income as the ivory trade. Kenya's elephants, for example, bring in $20 million a year through tourism, according to Thorton and Currey. Indeed, for Kenya and other countries that depend on tourism for a substantial amount of their income, the illegal killing of elephants is considered a form of economic warfare.

These groups argue that funds generated from tourism benefit many people while money from poached elephants falls into only a few hands. According to Marianthy Noble of the David Shepherd Conservation Fund, a British conservationist group, Zambia has lost almost 90 percent of its elephants since the 1970s, but neither Zambia nor its people have benefited from the ivory. The big money she says, has been made by the consumer countries and the ivory cartels.

Another significant benefit of elephants is their important role in the ecological balance of the environment. They disperse seeds, expand grasslands for other animals, and reduce the incidence of the tsetse fly. It is estimated that as many as 40 species of plants depend on the elephant for survival, writes R. L. Brahmachary, in a chapter in *A Week with Elephants.* These plants can only begin to germinate after they have passed through an elephant's digestive system.

Others have argued that it is important to think of elephants not merely as consumable economic resources but rather as a priceless part of African, and indeed humanity's, heritage. The African elephant should be preserved in its natural habitat for future generations.

**Counting Elephants.** Pro trade/anti-trade groups also disagree on numbers. While some of the southern African countries have been arguing that the numbers of their elephants is actually too high, other groups insist that there is a real problem in determining which elephants belong to which country. Elephants are migratory and do not stay within the borders of one country. Elephants have been crossing the Zambezi River for centuries, a river that serves as a border between Zambia and Zimbabwe, and Botswana and Namibia. Groups such as the Environmental Investigation Agency have alleged that many of these countries that are sharing borders are in fact counting the same elephants. The result can be an inflated picture of the elephant population in a particular area.

Another reason that the numbers of elephants sometimes appear to be high is that the southern African countries have crowded the elephants into small parks, either because of outside poaching pressures or loss of habitat from human development. In these cases, the conservation groups argue, it is not that the numbers are too high but that the spaces are too small and the threats too great. If the poaching was eliminated or if elephants were allowed to inhabit a greater portion of their ranges, they would no longer be overcrowded.

In sum, the anti-ban groups argue that in order to ensure that the African elephant species survives in its natural habitat and remains more than just a rare animal in a zoo, it is important to consider the economic value of the elephant beyond the short-term gains from the ivory. It is also important to look at how elephants are counted and protected. Perhaps most importantly, they argue, unless significantly stronger controls on poaching are developed, it is infinitely better to ban the trade in ivory completely than to attempt a limited regulated trade. Poaching could drive the African elephant to extinction.

## Recent History and the Future

There will be no legal ivory trade between 2000 and 2003. After that, however, the future is uncertain. "It leaves the door open. There will be no ivory sales for the time being, but the principle of possible sales in the future is accepted," said Zimbabwe's Department of National Parks Representative at the CITES meeting in Nairobi.

**Initiatives Over the Coming Years.** Currently, there are projects being piloted in a few central African and southeast Asian countries to try to prove that poaching levels are not a threat to elephant security, and that trade can start again. It can be expected that during the next CITES conference, southern African countries will submit proposals using evidence from these projects to suggest ways as to how ivory can be traded without endangering the elephant, according to the Born Free Web site.

Along a similar vein, during the 2000 meeting, it was agreed that the CITES system to monitor illegal killing of elephants, known as MIKE, is ineffective. Over the next three years, work will be done to revise the system so that it might be used as a tool to effectively monitor ivory trade and poaching trends.

It is also likely that between now and the next CITES meeting, countries and groups will further explore potential elephant conservation methods, such as elephant contraception, which may present African range states some new possibilities.

One rather disturbing trend emerging in Asia will need to be monitored closely for its potential impact on the African elephant. In some parts of the Indian sub-continent, nine out of ten male Asian elephants no longer grow tusks. Conservationists believe that because poachers have systematically killed those elephants with tusks that only those elephants without tusks have been left to breed. The trait is believed to be spreading

### WHAT IS CITES AND HOW DOES IT WORK?

CITES (the Convention on International Trade in Endangered Species of Wild Fauna and Flora) is an international agreement between governments. Its aim is to ensure that international trade in specimens of wild animals and plants does not threaten their survival.

CITES works by subjecting international trade in specimens of selected species to certain controls. These require that all import, export, re-export, and introduction from the sea of species covered by the Convention have to be authorized through a licensing system. 'Re-export' means export of a specimen that was imported.

Because the trade in wild animals and plants crosses borders between countries, the effort to regulate it requires international cooperation to safeguard certain species from over-exploitation. CITES was conceived in the spirit of such cooperation. Today, it accords varying degrees of protection to more than 30,000 species of animals and plants, whether they are traded as live specimens, fur coats, or dried herbs.

The species covered by CITES are listed in three Appendices, according to the degree of protection they need.

- Appendix I includes species threatened with extinction. Trade in specimens of these species is permitted only in exceptional circumstances.

- Appendix II includes species not necessarily threatened with extinction, but in which trade must be controlled.

- Appendix III contains species that are protected in at least one country, which has asked other CITES Parties for assistance in controlling the trade.

*CITES Secretariat: Convention on International Trade in Endangered Species of Wild Fauna and Flora Web Site. Available online at http://www.cites.org (cited December 10, 2001).*

through Asia and it is thought that it will eventually affect Africa if the poaching continues.

While the debates about how best to protect the African elephant have many layers and angles, in essence, there are two main points of view. There are those who take a preservationist perspective—essentially, the elephant is not a resource to be exploited and there should be absolutely no trade; and there are those who take a socio-economic approach—in order to preserve the elephant it is essential to be able to trade its ivory and earn an income from it.

Despite the forcefulness of the arguments on both sides and the nuances of the debate, there is at the root a common desire on the part of all countries with elephant populations to ensure that the African elephant survives. It is this common ground and the willingness on the part of the African countries with elephant populations to make compromises, as was demonstrated during the last CITES meeting, which holds out the best hope for the future of the elephant.

At an international level it is in the interest of all countries to support the collaborative efforts being made in Africa. The burden of responsibility for a species cannot be borne only by those who are most directly affected and least financially equipped. If wealthier countries wish to see the elephant survive, they will need to participate by lending support, financial and otherwise, to the African-led initiatives.

It tends to be a peculiar habit of humanity, that when a valuable natural resource is discovered, it is exploited until it exists no more. Elephants, bearing their tusks of white gold, are deemed to be one such valuable resource. The range states of Africa are making a concerted effort to ensure that the elephant is not driven to extinction—and that they, as a continent, are not driven apar    t. Whether they will be successful is as yet unknown.

## BIBLIOGRAPHY

African Wildlife Foundation. "Critical Species: Elephants." Available online at http://www.awf.org (cited December 1, 2001).

Barbier, E., J. Burgess, T. Swanson, and D. Pearce. *Elephants, Economics and Ivory.* London: Earthscan Publications Ltd., 1990.

Bate, R. "Culling To Be Kind," Institute of Economic Affairs, 1997: United Kingdom. Available online at http://www.iea.org.uk (cited December 5, 2001).

Born Free Foundation Web Site, http://www.bornfree .com. This nongovernmental organization believes the situation facing African's elephants is far worse than official statistics suggest.

Born Free Foundation. "No Ivory: Last Minute Deal Takes Bloody Ivory Off the Agenda." April 17, 2000. Available online at http://www.bornfree.org.uk/ stoptheclock/petition.htm (cited December 10, 2001).

Brahmachary, R. L. "Seed Dispersal Through the Elephant," in *A Week with Elephants.* J.C. Daniels and Hemant S. Datye, eds. Bombay: Oxford University Press, 1993, pp. 389–93.

Bulte, E., and C. van Kooten. "Economic Efficiency, Resource Conservation and the Ivory Trade Ban," *Ecological Economics,* 1999, Vol. 28 (2) pp. 171–81.

Buss, Irven O. *Elephant Life. Fifteen Years of High Population Density.* Ames, Iowa: Iowa State University Press, 1990.

Campbell, V. "Elephants in the Balance: Conserving Africa's Elephants," World Wildlife Fund, 1998. Available online at http://panda.org/resources/ publications/species/elephants/ (cited December 10, 2001).

Convention on International Trade in Endangered Species (CITES), official website. http://www.cites.org.

Hill, K.A. "Conflicts Over Development and Environmental Values: The International Ivory Trade in Zimbabwe's Historical Context." *Environment and History,* 1995, 1(3) pp. 335–49.

Holder, F.C. *The Ivory King. A Popular History of the Elephant and Its Allies.* New York: Charles Scribner's Sons, 1886.

International Fund for Animal Welfare, http://www .ifawct.org/education/shared.htm. This group believes that the ivory trade cannot be effectively controlled and that any resumption of the trade will encourage illegal poaching and further accelerate the decline of elephant populations worldwide.

Khanna, J., and J. Harford. "The Ivory Trade Ban: Is It Effective?" *Ecological Economics,* 1996, 2 (19) pp. 147–55.

Kirby, Alex. "Shoot an Elephant, Save a Species" BBC World News, March 18, 1999. Available online at http://news.bbc.co.uk/hi/english/sci/tech/newsid_ 275000/275273.stm (cited December 10, 2001).

———. "Analysis: What Price Sustaining a Species?" BBC World News, April 10, 2000. Available online at http://news.bbc.co.uk/hi/english/world/newsid_ 708000/708172.stm (cited December 10, 2001).

Koro, E., L. Mooketsi, and T. Moyo. "Zimbabwe Wants Compensation for Lost Ivory Trade," *Africa Information Afrique/Misa,* Feb. 3, 1997.

Matheson, Ishbel. "A Jumbo-Sized Dilemma in Zambia," BBC World News, September 8, 1999. Available online at http://news.bbc.co.uk/hi/english/world/ africa/newsid_441000/441951.stm (cited December 10, 2001).

McGregor, L. "The Great Ivory Debate" *Mail and Guardian,* May 23, 1997.

Moss, Cynthia. *Elephant Memories: Thirteen Years in the Life of an Elephant Family.* New York: William Morrow, 1988.

Mulenga, M. "Africa Splits Over Ivory Trade," *Mail and Guardian,* May 23, 1997.

Njumbi, S. (1993) "Effect of Poaching on the Elephant Population: A Case Study of the Elephants of the Meru National Park," in *A Week with Elephants.* J. C. Daniels and Hemant S. Datye, eds. Bombay: Oxford University Press, 1993, pp. 509–22.

Noble, Marianthy. "Zambia's War on Poaching Continues," David Shepherd Conservation Foundation,

2000. Available online at http://www.dscf.demon.co.uk (cited December 14, 2001).

Otieno, B. "African Nations Sustain Ban on Ivory Trade," *Environmental News Service,* April 17, 2000, Nairobi, Kenya.

Owens, Delia, and Mark Owens. *The Eye of the Elephant: An Epic Adventure in the African Wilderness.* Boston: Houghton Mifflin, 1993.

Padgett, B. *The African Elephant, Africa, and CITES: The Next Step.* Bloomington: Indiana University Law School, 1995.

Robinson, Simon. "Kenya: Dying for Ivory," *Time Europe,* April 17, 2000.

Save the Elephants, http://www.save-the-elephants.org. STE believes the greatest threat to elephants is the ivory trade and strongly supports a total ivory trade ban.

*Talking Point: Forum—Quiz the Experts on the Ivory Trade,* BBC News Online, April 14, 2000. Available online at http://newsvote.bbc.co.uk/hi/english/talking_point/forum/newsid_712000/712551.stm (cited December 10, 2001).

Thornton, Allan, and Dave Currey. *To Save an Elephant: The Undercover Investigation into the Illegal Ivory Trade.* London: Doubleday, 1991.

UNEP. "No Early Renewal of Ivory Trade Agree Governments," 11th Meeting of the Conference of the Parties to CITES, United Nations Environment Programme, April 17, 2000. Available online at www.unep.org (cited December 1, 2001).

Watson, J. "Giants Born without Their Tusks" *The Scotsman,* June 17, 2001.

Wilson, Martin. "Ivory Trade: Horns of a Dilemma," BBC News Online, April 4, 2000. Available online at http://news.bbc.co.uk/hi/english/world/africa/newsid_700000/700103.stm (cited December 11, 2001).

World Wildlife Fund, http://www.panda.org. The Fund is guided by a single objective: ensuring the long-term future of elephants in the wild and supports a limited ivory trade.

World Wildlife Fund, "Threats to the African Elephant," 2000. Available online at http://www.panda.org (cited December 10, 2001).

*Colleen Hoey*

# Japanese Voters Seek Change as Their Economy Deteriorates: New Prime Minister Vows to Break Political Logjam

## The Conflict

Japan's economy, which had achieved an almost miraculous rise in the decades after World War II, has been in a prolonged period of slow or no growth since the early 1990s. Some of the same factors that led to its success have led to its failures, particularly the close ties between government and business and the conglomerates of businesses that defy open competition on the market. To correct the situation, the voters have elected a reformer, Koizumi Junichiro. His administration is faced with the daunting task of shutting down the crony system that is carrying some of Japan's financial institutions and businesses in order to, in the long term, make Japan over into a free market economy. It promises to be a painful process, with Japan's entire economy, at least in the short-term, in grave jeopardy.

### Political

- In order to reform the economy, Koizumi will have to defy long honored traditions and an old guard in Japan that is used to taking care of its own. Reforms could also result in huge layoffs and the demise of small businesses. It could be difficult to rely even on those who elected him president hoping for reform, if those very reforms further destabilize the Japanese economy.

### Economic

- Japan's national deficit now stands at 1.3 times the amount of its gross domestic product. Banks are burdened with more than a trillion dollars worth of bad loans, and normal lending can no longer carry on. The Japanese people, lacking confidence in their economy, are saving their money. In order to clear the way for growth in Japan's economy, its very foundations will have to be shaken.

When the wildly popular prime minister of Japan, Koizumi Junichiro, was elected in April 2001 he promised the Japanese people that he would once and for all rescue the country's ailing economy, then going into its second decade of slow or negative growth. In stark contrast to the soothing but meaningless assurances of previous leaders, Koizumi repeated that the reforms necessary to rescue the economy from its ten years of stagnant performance would require deep sacrifices by everyone. Voters applauded Koizumi's fresh candor and said they were willing to accept such sacrifices. But the wealthy businessmen and old guard politicians to whom they're beholden may very well stymie Koizumi's good intentions.

Koizumi, who is known familiarly as Junchan, knew all of this, and yet he seemed determined to push ahead and implement the necessary reforms. This made him the most popular leader in 30 years, even though he admitted that Japan's economic situation would get worse—a lot worse—before it got better. "No pain, no gain," he told the Japanese public. Even so, expectations were high. It was those entrenched party bosses Koizumi would have to fight. And it could get nasty. The question was, could Koizumi do it?

Time was not on his side. As of September 2001, the $5.6 trillion public debt was nearly 130 percent of the gross domestic product (GDP, the total value of all goods and services), the highest ratio in the industrialized world. Nonperforming loans, at one time over $250 billion worth, continued to drive down banks' balance sheets. Nonperforming loans are loans that are not being paid back. Fear that the state pension program might not be solvent drastically cut consumer spending. Unemployment remained near record

# CHRONOLOGY

*1591* Sumitomo Masatomo develops a copper refining process and opens a copper mine, laying the foundation for the later Sumitomo zaibatsu.

*1673* The Mitsui zaibatsu begins when Mitsui Takatoshi opens a group of textile shops.

*1825* An edict to drive foreign vessels from Japan is issued.

*1853* American Commodore Matthew Perry arrives in Tokyo Bay demanding that the Tokugawa leaders trade with the United States.

*1854* The Treaty of Kanagawa is signed between the United States and Japan, opening Japan to the United States.

*1868* A new government is established in Japan with Tokyo (Edo) its new capital.

*1873* Iwasaki Yataro buys out a government-operated shipping line to lay the foundation for the Mitsubishi zaibatsu.

*1894–95* Sino-Japanese War.

*1904–05* Russo-Japanese War.

*1914* Japan enters World War I, declaring war on Germany.

*1932* Japan withdraws from the League of Nations.

*1937* War breaks out between Japan and China.

*1940* Japan enters the Tripartite Alliance with Germany and Italy, entering World War II.

*December 7, 1941* Japan attacks Pearl Harbor.

*August 15, 1945* Japan surrenders after the United States drops atomic bombs on the cities of Hiroshima (August 6) and Nagasaki (August 9).

*1945* The Allied Occupation of Japan begins under U.S. General Douglas MacArthur.

*1947* Under a new constitution, Japan passes a law disbanding the zaibatsu.

*May 1947* When a union coalition calls for a nationwide general strike, more than five million workers pledge to stay away from their jobs in a total work stoppage that could paralyze the entire country. General Douglas MacArthur intervenes at the last moment to stop the strike.

*1948* Joseph Dodge, a Detroit banker, calls for a balanced budget and an end to subsidies in order to halt Japan's inflation and strengthen Japan's economy.

*1950* The Korean War breaks out, giving a huge boost to Japanese economy.

*1952* The Allied Occupation in Japan ends.

*1953* A union strike against Nissan results in limited union activity but gains workers the promise of "lifetime employment."

*1990* Japan's economic surge causes a "bubble economy," with inflated values of Japanese real estate and businesses.

*1993* The Liberal Democratic Party (LDP) loses its ruling position after 38 years of control.

*1996* New prime minister Hashimoto Ryutaro pledges to reform Japan's pro-business economy and bureaucracy. He's out of office in less than a year.

*2000* Japan enters its tenth year of low-growth, or recessionary economy.

*2001* Koizumi Junichiro is elected prime minister. He vows to turn Japan around but warns that the transition will be painful.

---

highs, officially around five percent but more likely double that. Bankruptcies kept on rising. In addition, in mid-September 2001 the Tokyo stock exchange fell to its lowest point since 1984.

All of this led Moody's, the U.S. credit-rating agency, to judge Japan's credit as risky as Portugal's. In its *Global Trends 2015* report, the U.S. Central Intelligence Agency (CIA) predicted that Japan would have "difficulty maintaining its current position as the world's third largest economy [after the United States and Europe]," to be replaced by China. In contrast, as recently as 1990 Japan was the world's second largest economy and fast gaining on the United States.

Everyone knew what had to be done. Big banks, long tied to the government's apron strings through receiving virtually interest-free loans, would have to be allowed to go bankrupt when their outstanding loans no longer performed satisfactorily. The Japanese farmers—long pampered by powerful politicians who lobbied to keep out foreign agricultural imports—had come to grow the most expensive rice in the world. Clearly they would have to compete with world markets. And the umbilical cord between inefficient public-works construction companies and entrenched bureaucrats who provide funds for building highways that go nowhere needed to be cut. In other words, Japan had to stop doing "business as usual."

Unless and until Japan is able to deal satisfactorily with these and other problems (such as the rapidly aging population, which will go from a 4:1 to a 2:1 ratio of workers to retirees by 2025), this once leading economy will continue to deteriorate and possibly pull down all of Asia with its implosion. American and European officials are holding their breath in hopes that the world's number two powerhouse won't create a world depression. There has been no shortage of advice and promises of support from abroad, but the problem was Japanese, and only Japan could solve it. Koizumi needed to pull off a tough balancing act between a popular desire for change and the vested interests in his party and the bureaucracy.

## HISTORICAL BACKGROUND

### The Meiji Challenge

For more than 200 years, beginning in the early seventeenth century when the new shogun (a military dictator), Tokugawa Ieyasu, proclaimed a new dynasty, Japan purposely locked itself away and refused any contact with outsiders in the hope that this would assure a peaceful and stable country. The plan seemed to work: during most of that time Japan was relatively free of conflict. The problem lay in the fact that Asia was being picked apart by Western imperialist powers engaging in a very lucrative trade there. It was only a matter of time before Japan would begin to feel the pressure to open up. By the mid-nineteenth century the foreigners were knocking on her door, threatening to break it down.

On the afternoon of July 8, 1853, American Commodore Matthew Perry's flotilla of four ships steamed into Tokyo Bay and demanded that the Tokugawa leaders trade with the United States. The Japanese found themselves in a dilemma. In order to open up, the policy of *sakoku*, or self-imposed isolation, had to be changed and to change that policy required the emperor's agreement. When the de facto ruler of Japan, the shogun of the Tokugawa clan, explained that he could never stand up to American naval firepower, he was rebuffed by His Majesty the emperor. This left the shogun in an impossible situation: he could not oppose both the emperor and the Americans. Japan resisted, but America insisted. Perry said that he'd be back in six months for an answer.

When Perry did return early in 1854 the shogun could not but give in to a superior power and signed the Treaty of Kanagawa. This gave the Americans certain preferential rights in Japan, including the opening of two ports to trade, the guarantee of low customs duties, and the principle of extraterritoriality by which U.S. residents in Japan were subject to American, not Japanese, law. This accommodation was seen correctly by the Japanese as a humiliating concession. Even worse was the fact that the treaty had been signed against the emperor's wishes. This opened the door for anti-Tokugawa forces to take the upper hand.

After several years of civil war between pro- and anti-Tokugawa samurai (elite warriors), in 1868 the shogun was ousted by a coalition led by the Satsuma and Choshu clans, two groups that had long harbored anti-Tokugawa sentiment. But instead of putting themselves in power, they enthroned the young emperor. Under the slogan of *sono joi* ("revere the emperor and expel the barbarian") they proclaimed him the true leader of Japan, rather than the figurehead that all emperors under the Tokugawa dynasty had been. It must be noted, however, that this was only a pretext. Those who elevated the emperor made sure that they controlled his seals and in fact ruled in his name. The period of his reign was dubbed Meiji, "Enlightened Rule."

From the fall of the Tokugawa in 1868 until 1890, when a new constitution was put into effect, Japan would experience a thoroughgoing restoration that laid the foundation for the political-commercial relationships that are today besetting the nation. Having learned to appreciate the superior weaponry of the Westerners, Japan's young revolutionaries agreed that it was better to learn from them than be annihilated by them. As one samurai put it: "We have swords but they have cannons; they'll mow us down!"

In order to resist the Western powers and to assure that Japan not be colonized by them as

Southeast Asia had been—or carved up into concessions as China had been—Japanese leaders knew they had to strengthen the country. Under the slogan *fukoku kyohei* ("rich country, strong military") they set about to create a favorable climate for economic growth as well as to build a powerful army and navy.

From the outset the government played a prominent role in Japan's economic development by first creating a financial and educational framework, and then a technological physical infrastructure. A system of universal education was adopted, patterned after the French and American forms. Japan was the first country in the world to implement mandatory schooling. A national banking system was implemented, and the tax system standardized. The government took the lead in building shipyards, mines, armories, textile mills, railways, and telegraph communications. It did all of these things with foreign loans and government subsidies, and relied on foreign advisers and technicians to train ex-samurai warriors until the advisors could be replaced by skilled Japanese.

By the 1880s the government had run out of money. Inflation, a trade deficit, and overextended capital expenditures had depleted the treasury. In order to continue the building program and to further the economy, the government auctioned off most of its enterprises to private businessmen, usually friends of government leaders, at bargain prices. Buying these businesses at steep discounts and then doing business with the government led to the appearance of huge industrial-financial combines known as *zaibatsu,* the core of the Japanese economy until the end of World War II (1939–45). By the end of the nineteenth century the association of business with government became the dominant characteristic of Japan's commerce and trade.

A zaibatsu, a business combine or cartel, was more than just an enormous business enterprise. It was a network of corporate alliances of various manufacturers organized around a common bank and trading company called a *sogo shosha*. It wasn't a single business but a group of separate companies, each of which owned parts of the others through interlocking shares, all of which were financed by their central bank. A zaibatsu, such as Mitsubishi, Mitsui, or Sumitomo, might have controlled a railroad, a shipping line, coalmines, department stores, a construction company, a trading firm, and above all a central bank. It is as if the Bank of America also controlled General Motors, American President Lines, Alcoa copper mines, the Union and Pacific Railroad, and K-Mart.

## THE PROPENSITY TO SAVE

The Japanese have the highest rate of personal savings as a share of gross domestic product ever recorded by any market economy in peacetime. Does the explanation lie deep in cultural roots—for instance in the traditional frugality of the samurai? Maybe, but other external factors have also been noted. Consider:

- The high cost of education, both secondary and university level

- An inadequate social security system

- Inflated housing prices, which require large down payments

- Interest on home mortgages not being tax deductible

- A wage system that includes large, semiannual bonus payments

- An underdeveloped consumer credit system

- The government-run postal savings system with guaranteed competitive rates

- The lack of alternatives to personal savings

- The exemption from income taxes for interest earned on savings accounts

**Sources:** Borthwick, Mark. *Pacific Century: The Emergence of Modern Pacific Asia*, 2nd ed., Boulder, CO: Westview Press, 1998; Boyle, John Hunter. *Modern Japan: The American Nexus*. San Diego: Harcourt Brace Jovanovich, 1993.

From the end of the Meiji period, which ended in 1912 with the death of the emperor, until the late 1930s Japan refined and solidified its industrial structure. The partnership between government and business epitomized by close collaboration between state officials and corporate elites continued to develop into what has come to be known as a "developmental state" or more colloquially, "state-guided capitalism." This describes neither a capitalist economy, where there is a relative separation of government and business in favor of market-driven forces, nor a command economy, wherein the government controls all factors of production.

According to Japanese specialist Chalmers Johnson, who is credited with coining the phrase,

# A Few Key Figures in Japanese Economic History

**Tokugawa Ieyasu (1542–1616):** Became the founder of the Tokugawa shogunate (1603) after winning one of the most famous military engagements in Japanese history, the Battle of Sekigahara (1600). The Tokugawa shogunate would last until 1867.

**Fukuzawa Yukichi (1835–1901):** Perhaps more than anyone else in Japanese history, Fukuzawa was successful in introducing Western learning and institutions to the Japanese public. In many respects ahead of his time, especially in his views about the oppression of women and the need for self-fulfillment, his later philosophical convictions took on an increasingly nationalistic tone.

**Ito Hirobumi (1841–1909):** Japan's first prime minister (1885–1888), Ito was perhaps *the* symbol of the new Meiji era: given to modernization and open to the West, yet a diehard nationalist.

**Hirohito (1901–1989):** Japan's 124th emperor, whose reign was marked by rapid militarization and wars of aggression against China in the 1930s. Under the Allied Occupation of Japan, he renounced his divinity. His reputation remains under a cloud as research continues concerning his role vis-a-vis the more radical generals in the onset and continuation of the war.

**Douglas MacArthur (1880–1954):** U.S. general who became commander-in-chief of all army forces in the Pacific during World War II. MacArthur was appointed Supreme Commander of the Allied Powers (SCAP) during the Occupation of Japan (1945–52). He also led the UN forces in the Korean War, but was ultimately relieved of command by President Harry S. Truman.

**Yoshida Shigeru (1878–1967):** Twice prime minister (1946–47, 1948–54), Yoshida played a key role in shaping Japan's post-war economy by positioning Japan as an anticommunist bulwark of democracy. This stance, which led to considerable American diplomatic and financial aid, and his resistance to any new military buildup (the Yoshida Doctrine), enabled Japan to begin its economic advance.

**Ikeda Hayato (1899–1965):** Prime minister (1960–64) instrumental in Japan's phenomenal economic growth due to his "income doubling" plan, in which he proclaimed to see every Japanese family double its income in ten years. With minor exceptions, the policy was successful.

**Nakasone Yasuhiro (1918–):** The first prime minister (1982–87) to attempt to replace the Yoshida Doctrine (see Yoshida Shigeru), Naksone believed that Japan's pacifist stance was no longer relevant in the new world order. This led him to call for more overseas investment and aid and an increase in imports. These and other policies (such as reduced working hours) were highly unpopular with the same interests that, in 2001, Koizumi must contend with.

**Koizumi Junichiro (1942–):** Elected prime minister in April 2001 on a platform promising to radically reform and restructure Japan's economic institutions.

the "capitalist developmental state" combined private ownership of property with goals set by the state. The government did not displace the market as it does under socialism, but the bureaucrats created incentives for businesses to operate in the market. In other words, according to Johnson, as quoted in Mark Borthwick's *Pacific Century: The Emergence of Modern Pacific Asia* and paraphrased here, the government blurred the public and private sectors to the point that achievements of privately owned and managed enterprises were regarded as national achievements, but any profit that resulted was treated as private property.

This incestuous old-boy network helped to prolong Japan's war effort during World War II

(1939–45). The great zaibatsu were the core of the armament industry and turned out everything from rifles and hand grenades to bombers and battleships. These giant business cartels were not the primary reason for the war, they weren't responsible for its onset, but they almost certainly enabled the Japanese military machine to carry on as brutally and as long as it did.

## The Occupation: MacArthur's Free Market Vision

The United States believed that the ultra-nationalist leaders of Japan had been responsible for the war with their aggressive policies that had cost so much loss of life and destruction throughout Asia. The Occupation forces, primarily U.S. forces overseeing Japan's surrender, therefore decided to render the Japanese military state unable to wage war ever again. The way to assure this was to destroy the very foundation of the war-making machinery. The United States intended to impose its own form of democracy—and its economic concomitant, free-market capitalism—on the defunct Japanese fascist government. This meant that market forces, not government–business cronyism, were to direct the economy.

It was with that in mind that U.S. Army General Douglas MacArthur, otherwise known as Supreme Commander of the Allied Powers (SCAP), the head of the Allied Occupation of Japan from 1945 to 1952, set out to break the zaibatsu, whom MacArthur referred to as "merchants of death," and put its leaders behind bars. In what came to be known as "the purge," some 200,000 "warmongers"—government officials, military officers, business leaders, even teachers and academics—were accused of carrying out Japan's aggressive policies. They were removed from their positions and barred from returning to their former stations; many were also imprisoned. In addition, MacArthur ordered that all zaibatsu be dismantled and abolished and replaced by small business and light industry.

The shares of these multi-industrial combines were placed on the open market, forcing the components of each combine to carry on as independent companies. A newly enacted anti-monopoly law prohibited all cartel activities. Japan was suddenly a country of cottage industries and corner manufacturing plants that catered to the needs of the time, primarily providing inexpensive consumer items. Neither U.S. nor Japanese visionaries saw any need for large-scale projects, at least for the near future.

In addition, in his design to democratize Japan MacArthur released from prison all political prisoners. Many of these prisoners were members of the outlawed Japan Communist Party, the only major group that had consistently opposed the militarists. Others were labor leaders, many of whom were also communists. Immediately they began to organize unions to assure that business management would meet their demands.

This resurgence of union activity quickly led to a growing conflict between labor and business. The political left soon gained influence over the workers' movement and demanded better pay and work conditions. The leftist militants wanted far more than higher wages. They sought worker con-

trol of the factories and real political power. In May 1947 a union coalition called for a nation-wide general strike. The response was overwhelming: more than five million workers pledged to stay away from their jobs in a total work stoppage that would paralyze the entire country, which is exactly what the unions hoped for.

MacArthur was forced to intervene just hours before the strike was due to begin. According to John Hunter Boyle in his book *Modern Japan: The American Nexus*, a communiqué from MacArthur's headquarters flatly forbade any action on the grounds that "the paralysis ... would produce dreadful consequences upon every Japanese home." MacArthur had had in mind a moderate labor union activity, not communist-led nationwide strikes that threatened chaos.

### The Cold War Influence on American Policy in Japan

By 1948 the Occupation was facing two growing problems. The fear of an increasing Communist presence in Japan's labor movement was paralleling the ominous signals emanating from both the Soviet Union and China, where the beleaguered Nationalist Party of Chiang Kai-shek (or Jiang Jeshi) was daily losing ground to Mao Zedong's communists. Related to this was a second problem: the dissolution of the zaibatsu had removed the very concentration of power that provided the foundation upon which to build an economy and create jobs. It would simply take too long for a nation of small businesses to develop to that point; in the meantime labor, and the communists, were losing patience.

Several factors prompted the United States to concentrate on reviving the Japanese economy rather than reforming it, that is, making it over into a free-market capitalist economy. The most obvious was the deteriorating state of the economy. Three years into the Occupation, industry remained stagnant and production was below even that of the 1930s. Moreover, such a wretched economy created labor unrest and runaway inflation. This led to a flourishing black market that brought on crime, corruption, and demoralization. A third problem was that the United States was paying for most of Japan's economic activity, a burdensome relief expense that showed no signs of abating. American Congressmen worried about how long U.S. taxpayers would have to foot the bill.

What was soon seen as the most important issue in Japan's unsteady situation was the onset of the Cold War in Europe and the rising tide of communism in China. Washington's Far East policy had been pinned on a stable and prosperous noncommunist China, a "strategic anchor" in the Pacific. But by mid-1949 Mao Zedong's communist armies had swept Chiang's Nationalist troops from the mainland to their exile on the island of Taiwan. When Mao stood at the rostrum in Tiananmen Square in October and proclaimed the new People's Republic of China, America's foreign policy abruptly shifted gears. The United States needed a strong ally to replace the defeated Chinese Nationalists. Japan would become that ally—the centerpiece of resistance to communism in Asia.

Led by Cold War diplomat George Kennan, many conservative U.S. officials wondered if MacArthur had not taken Japan too far to the left in trying to implement a capitalist democracy. Kennan and his ilk were all for building up Japan in order to "immunize" the region against communism, just as the United States was building up Germany in Europe as a bulwark against a rising Soviet Marxism there. To them it seemed the only thing to do was to resurrect the zaibatsu and rebuild the economy as quickly as possible lest it become a hotbed of communist activity attracting poor and unemployed workers.

MacArthur strongly disagreed. According to Walter LaFeber in *The Clash: U.S.-Japanese Relations throughout History*, MacArthur saw his conflict with Kennan as one "between a system of free competitive enterprise ... and a socialism in private hands." But backed by a group of Old Japan Hands known as the "Japan Lobby," Kennan's position held the day. The Japan Lobby pressured Truman and the Congress, in a move known as the "reverse course," to turn Japan around by allowing the former zaibatsu to recover their holdings. Conservative Washington officials argued that Japan needed the infrastructure that the zaibatsu could provide in order to finance construction and provide employment. Their dissolution, says Boyle, came to be seen as a dead end and "nothing less than a declaration of war on capitalism." In the end only nine of the more than a hundred businesses slated to be dismantled were in fact dissolved.

The reverse course may have solved the political issue of communist influence, but it failed to address the growing problem of inflation. Expensive war reparation payments and poor currency controls caused severe stagnation in the Japanese economy. In order to jump-start the new economy, Washington sent Detroit banker Joseph Dodge to Japan with instructions to halt the infla-

tion, remove government controls on trade, and revitalize the economy. The measures he proposed were draconian: balance the budget, end government subsidies, and fix the exchange rate for the yen. Inflation was stopped but Japan was plunged into recession and labor unrest grew.

### The Korean War Lifts the Economy

It began to appear that Dodge's cure was worse than the disease as the economy continued to spiral downward and more people were put out of work. But suddenly Japan received a "gift from the gods." In June 1950 the Korean War (1950–53) broke out. This proved to be a tremendous shot in the arm for the floundering Japanese economy because nearly US$3 billion worth of goods and supplies were contracted by the American government—equal to two-thirds of all Japanese exports during the early 1950s—in what was called the "procurement boom" (*tokuju bumu*).

How important was this? The following example from Boyle is instructive. The president of a Japanese company that made gunnysacks was invited by the U.S. Army Procurement Office to stop by for contract talks just after the Korean War began. The officer in charge informed the company president that the army needed all of the gunnysacks the company had, whether they were new or not. The company, barely managing an existence prior to this by making sacks for rice, jumped at the opportunity, which ultimately netted them an order for more than 200 million sacks.

Japanese companies lost no time in exploiting this wonderful opportunity. They modernized and expanded production, employing the excess labor and stabilizing the economy well beyond the end of the war. By 1952 the conflict accounted for more than 60 percent of all Japanese exports. The Korean War proved to be an unexpected windfall for the Japanese economy, just as the Vietnam War would be 15 years later.

### From Zaibatsu to Keiretsu

The Allied Occupation of Japan ended in 1952, and the Japanese government quickly took steps to support industrial reconstruction. For instance, government-funded banks supplied state funds to strategic industries in long-term, low-interest loans. The government also gave priority to heavy industry such as electric power, coal, shipping, and steel, over light industries. One of the biggest changes was to modify the anti-monopoly laws to allow the formation of cartels and to permit companies to hold interlocking shares. This was the final step in the

最近の動き（過去9ヶ月）
日経平均　13664.10　-250.33

A JAPANESE BUSINESSMAN LOOKS AT A GRAPH DEPICTING THE PLUMMETING NIKKEI STOCK AVERAGE. IN DECEMBER 2000, THE NIKKEI AVERAGE REACHED ITS LOWEST POINT IN ALMOST TWO YEARS. *(A/P Wide World. Reproduced by permission.)*

comeback of the zaibatsu, although in the post-war reorganization they became known as *keir-etsu,* or "linked chain."

The links were very tight, indeed. Vera Simone, in her book *The Asian Pacific: Political and Economic Development in a Global Context* has shown how each group (not company) in a keir-etsu is itself a network of corporate alliances orga-nized around a single bank and trading company. Each group exercises control over its subsidiaries through its monopoly of credit. Take, for example, Sumitomo, which is not a single manufacturer but a group of distinct companies. Each of these com-panies owns parts of the others through mutual share-holding. They also do business with each other rather than with outsiders. Just as important are their relations with subcontractors, the compa-nies that make parts for the keiretsu groups' prod-ucts. These relations are not contractually based on competitive pricing. Instead, the individual enterprises in a keiretsu incorporate suppliers and subcontractors into the network based on loyalty and personal relationships. This means that in return for the keiretsu guaranteeing to contract with a certain supplier because of personal rela-tions, that supplier will provide a part at an agreed-upon price outside the normal rules of free-market competition.

Borthwick explains that because keiretsu shares are not publicly traded but instead held by other companies in the link, they are not subject to the opinions of small or foreign shareholders. This means that the keiretsu companies can, and do, cooperate (Western free-marketers might prefer the word "collude") to leverage and dominate buying and selling their products and thereby overwhelm any "go it alone" small firms. In other words, they have changed the rules of free competition.

Given this situation it should be obvious that the Japanese business world does not operate in a competitive environment. It never has. How, then, did Japan manage to do so well beginning in the 1950s and continue without a break for over 30 years to create such a powerful economy? And how does all this relate to Koizumi Junichiro? There are as many answers to this as there are experts to answer it. Setting aside any arguments about how "unique" the Japanese are, Japan's for-mer success and its current malaise rest on three major factors: technology transfer, export markets, and the corporate-government relationship.

## Technology Transfer

Recall that the United States and its allies saw Japan as the new anti-communist bulwark in Asia after the communists took over China. At that

# "SECRETS" TO THE JAPANESE ECONOMIC MIRACLE

How did Japan rise from a devastated war-torn country to the world's second largest economy in forty years (1945–85), which is exactly the same time it took to go from an isolated feudal state to a leading Asian power (c. 1853–95)?

- Japan's high savings rate means low or no-interest loans to businesses.

- Not having to worry about anxious stockholders, Japanese companies can take a longer range view of business strategy—up to 20 years longer.

- In Japan there is much greater investment in new capital projects because of low research and development funding, especially compared to the United States.

- Japan's scarcity of raw materials has required it to be more innovative in compensating with lower cost production.

- Because Japan started from nothing after World War II, it was able to rebuild with the latest technology.

- The Japanese decided to build high-quality products rather than those with "built-in obsolescence" as in the United States.

- Japan has had good access to open markets—had it not been for its exports to America, Japan's post-war economic boom might not have occurred.

- In Japan, government and business collaborate closely, forming a kind of "Japan, Inc."

time, in the late 1940s and 1950s, the United States' economy was clearly number one. There was no question about this, and there was no competition to concern her. Therefore, the United States' largesse rolled long and strong to any government that professed to be anti-communist, especially to Japan, its hand-picked Asian ally.

In this enthusiastic and patronizing environment the United States was only too happy to provide the new technologies that Japan needed for its industrial development, technologies that were being advanced primarily in America. By the 1950s Japan was catching up with other advanced countries by importing the innovations and know-how already developed in the United States. This

cheap or even free access to key American technologies was an essential ingredient in Japan's economic resurgence. Chalmers Johnson, however, argues that we miss the point if we think that Japan's acquisition at low cost of Western technologies was a "free ride." In fact, it was the heart of the matter. Technology transfer was for Japan a central component of its postwar industrial policy. Had it not been for this technology transfer, companies such as Kawasaki Steel, Matsushita Electric, and the Sony Corporation would likely have had a much more difficult time of building their businesses, and may have never gotten off the ground at all.

## The World Export Market

Another instrumental factor in Japan's miraculous economic rise was the world export market, primarily that of the United States. Many countries, especially those in Asia, have developed their economies in a similar process. Following World War II most manufacturing plants in Asia were destroyed and many Asian countries were forced to import the majority of their products until they were able to begin producing some of their own.

This stage of "import substitution" enabled these countries, including Japan, to substitute some of their own manufactures for those that might otherwise have to be brought in from outside, thus saving a good deal of hard currency. As the economies grew to a higher level of technology, they were able to produce more items for export. "Export oriented" economies are those that have reached a mature level whereby their economy is able to produce goods to be consumed by other countries. This not only saves money at home, it earns profits through the exports.

And so it was with Japan. The economy shifted from the high tariffs of its import-substitution policies to lower tariffs that promoted exports of labor-intensive manufactured goods. This led eventually to the production of electronic equipment such as TVs, radios, and VCRs. By the time other Asian countries were starting to compete at this level, the Japanese moved on to high-tech information equipment. But because Japan was the leader, all the other economies were to various degrees dependent on Japanese imports (of both technology and capital). This turned into what has become known as the "flying geese" formation, with Japan as the lead goose and the other developing Asian economies ranked behind it in a spreading "V" of decreasing levels of technical sophistication. For instance, Walter LaFeber has shown in *The Clash: U.S.-Japanese Relations throughout History* that as Japan moved into cutting-edge, profitable electronics at home, it passed auto and steel production down to lower-waged countries, such as Taiwan and South Korea.

### The Relationship between Business and Government

Following technology transfer and an export-oriented economy, a third factor also accounts for Japan's phenomenal economic growth—what is at the very core of her success and what accounts for her problems today. This is the special relationship between big business, party officials, and government bureaucrats.

Nearly 20 years ago in his landmark study of the Japanese economy, *MITI and the Japanese Miracle* (1982), Chalmers Johnson showed how Japan's economic development was not the result of a free-market laissez-faire environment, but rather "an authoritarian state's active intervention in shaping business decisions," as quoted by Vera Simone in *The Asian Pacific: Political and Economic Development in a Global Context.* According to Johnson, ever since the Meiji period (1868–1912) Japan enjoyed a market economy that benefited from the conscious direction of a bureaucratic authoritarian state. The organization that has controlled the strings is the Ministry of International Trade and Industry (MITI).

The Japanese bureaucracy, especially MITI and the Ministry of Finance (MOF) have various means of obtaining compliance in their planning priorities. The Japanese enjoy a very high savings rate, generally between about 14 and 20 percent of disposable income, compared to the 1 to 4 percent in the United States. These huge pools of funds, found mostly in the national postal savings system, allow MITI to provide low or no-interest loans to banks and other institutions. In late 2001 the official interest rate was near zero—approximately .25 percent. MITI also enjoys the authority to set interest rates, as well as currency exchange rates, tax bases, and some prices of strategic goods. MITI negotiates and arbitrates a consensus among private businesses to assure there will be no undue competition among Japanese firms as well. This does not mean that there is no competition. Often Japanese companies go head-to-head when seeking to introduce a new product, but once a company establishes a position with a product it has virtually a free ride from then on.

There are two ways in which this special relationship between government bureaucracy and private business is so tight: what Vera Simone has called (1) the "institutional interlocking" of government, financial, and production organizations; and (2) the "cultural interlocking" of lifetime employment, the tightly integrated educational system, and the public conception of the "market."

The "institutional interlocking" of government, financial, and production organizations, as epitomized by the keiretsu, is at the core of Japan's economy, and has three main consequences for the economy. Supply and demand are created through member groups, who buy and sell amongst themselves. Since these organizations own each other through the keiretsu, hostile takeovers are difficult to nonexistent. Additionally, the pressure to achieve short-term profits is lessened by the fact that stock shares are typically held by other firms within the group, giving management more freedom to pursue long-term planning goals.

Additionally, lifetime employment, the tightly integrated educational system, and the public conception of the "market" all, through personal and professional relationships, create a complex "cultural interlocking" within the keiretsu. An individual who retires from a government post and takes a new position in private industry is commonly expected to use any connections from the preceding job to further the interests of his current employer. This practice is called *amakudari*, translated as "descent from heaven."

Finally, Japan's education system reinforces the "company culture" by providing the personnel for the bureaucracy. The scores one receives on high school and university exams determine which university or ministry one will be assigned to. For instance, the top scorers in high school will be admitted first to Tokyo University, then Waseda University, then down the line. Similarly, Tokyo University graduates with the highest grades will join MITI, then the MOF, and so on. This also serves to assure a close-knit "old boy" network atmosphere.

It is this network that has woven such a tight web around the Japanese business environment that Koizumi has to untangle in order to breathe new life into the economy. In order to assess his chances of success we will consider what needs to be done and the consequences of making those changes.

## RECENT HISTORY AND THE FUTURE

### Sacred Cows: Koizumi and Reform

When he came into office, Koizumi and his advisors laid out three major reforms they had to tackle: (1) generating greater consumer spending; (2) taking on the banks' huge piles of debts; and (3) opening up Japanese business to real competition. First, let's look at the consumer. The Japanese are well known for their penchant for saving, as noted above. This is reinforced through the postal savings system, a quasi-government institution that takes in billions of yen every year from private citizens investing in its tax-free (admittedly very low) interest-bearing accounts. This very strong savings tradition has enabled Japan to provide low-interest loans to big business.

The problem was, and remains, that very little of this money goes directly into the economy. To create a metaphor: money is the oil that lubricates the economic engine. Without oil the engine stops. Because the Japanese people are fearful of a continuing recession they are, like anyone else, holding onto their money. Again, fine for bank loans but bad for generating economic activity.

If the government does succeed in loosening people's purse strings, however, there will be that much less for banks to rely on for their loans, thus slowing down the economy, which is already in a recession. If people continue to hang on to their money, the nation is faced with the current problem, that of a slowdown in the economy. It's a lose-lose situation.

The second problem that Koizumi must deal with is that of the banks' nonperforming loans, meaning loans that are no longer being paid back. The numbers are frightening. The government itself admits that the banks have ¥150 trillion (US$1.23 trillion) in bad or doubtful loans. Even in Japan that is a magnitude that cannot be easily dealt with. Until these bad loans are eliminated, the normal lending that sustains any economy cannot take place, and neither consumers nor companies will regain the confidence needed to start spending again.

In a recession, doing nothing exacerbates the weakness in the economy. When prices fall, lower prices make the real value of the debt grow so that businesses that have over-borrowed have even greater debts. This makes it harder for them to pay back their loans to banks, and thereby decreases earnings of both the lending banks and the borrowing corporations. Furthermore, when there is slow growth, the government gets less tax revenue. In order to raise money to meet expenses it must sell more bonds to cover a bigger deficit, but Koizumi has declared a cap on bond issues (at ¥30 trillion, or US$245 billion) citing the already over-burdened government deficit of 1.3 times the amount of Japan's gross domestic product. If the cap is lifted the deficit grows. If the cap remains the recession grows.

The third problem facing Japan's economic crunch is the lack of open competition in the building industry, particularly in highway and infrastructure construction. Koizumi has vowed to review the public works budget that has long been a source of largesse from politicians to private business. This review would include scrapping the laws that reserve gasoline and vehicle tax revenues exclusively for road building. Just the idea of tampering with a long-honored tradition of pork-barrel politics—the government patronage system where public funds benefit a specific locale and a legislator's constitutents—however, sends howls of dismay from all sides.

Koizumi's vow to cap the issuance of government bonds, noted above, will squeeze public-works spending that has been the lifeblood of many construction firms. David Kruger of the *Far Eastern Economic Review* notes that "the construction industry accounts for about 10 percent of all jobs in Japan and bankruptcies would mean large numbers of layoffs."

There is also talk of deregulating the economy, meaning that the government will no longer be the safety net ready to protect smaller businesses from larger companies. This would likely lead to greater competition in the long run, but in the meantime cottage industries would be negatively affected. Those same groups have benefited from government protection and in return have been faithful supporters of the ruling Liberal Democratic Party (LDP).

Another sacred cow that Koizumi wants to kill is the vast postal savings system, which he wants to privatize. Again, in the long run this will probably benefit more people. But getting there will likely mean layoffs. It will also cut into some of the sources of funds that have been at the heart of the LDP's power structure. If implemented it would undermine its traditional support base—money given away by politicians to industry.

So where do we go from here? What's the bottom line? The short answer, and the easy one, is that it's too early to tell. Koizumi has yet to provide *specific* information on how he intends to go about chopping, cutting, and replacing. No specialist yet has gone public to predict what will happen. It's a "wait and see" situation. Having said that, there is a general consensus among the experts that nothing short of a miracle will be able to turn Japan around any time soon. It's not for want of wishing

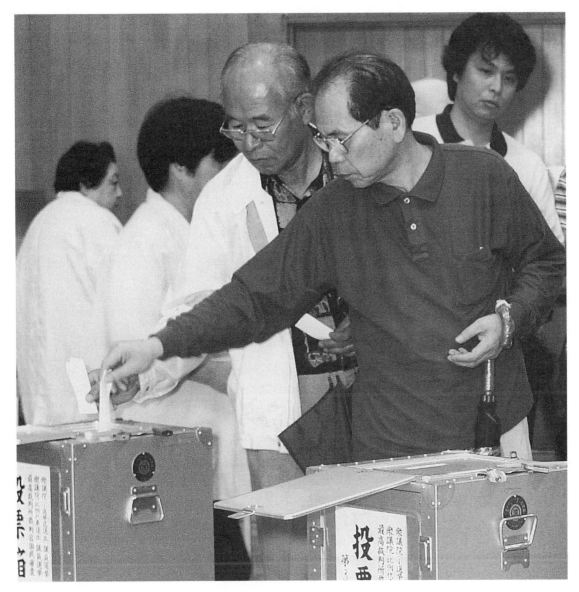

VOTERS IN JAPAN CAST BALLOTS IN THE 2000 LOWER HOUSE ELECTIONS. PUBLIC DISCONTENT WITH THE GOVERNMENT HAS INCREASED AS ECONOMIC TROUBLES HAVE CONTINUED. *(A/P Wide World. Reproduced by permission.)*

and trying—everyone wants Koizumi to succeed. But there are many toes to step on and much pain to feel before his plans will work.

Koizumi must deal with the Big Three: big business, big politicians, and big bureaucrats. They have enjoyed a cozy arrangement for years and like vested interests anywhere, they all want to protect their own turf. Koizumi is operating within a consensus-oriented society where nothing much gets done without unanimous approval. No one bets that that will happen. So the onus is on him to force through programs that will certainly be unpopular somewhere along the line, bucking the age-old tradition that everyone has to

agree. It will also run against the grain of the very core of the "capitalist developmental state." The prime minister, who for now has the people on his side, will have to hope that they'll be in it with him for the long haul. If not, the needed reforms won't happen and Japan will continue to muddle along, perhaps going to negative growth.

And if that happens the whole world will probably feel the shock waves. Even in such dire straits as Japan is in now, its economy is still number two in the world and is still so huge that the repercussions of a continuing recession will be felt around the world, from the rest of Asia to Europe to America. The income that Japan generates, the

AFTER JAPAN'S ECONOMIC SLOWDOWN IN 2000 THE HOMELESS POPULATION ROSE DRAMATICALLY TO 1.7 TIMES MORE THAN 1995 LEVELS. *(A/P Wide World. Reproduced by permission.)*

loans and investments it makes globally, the exports it sends abroad, and the markets it opens up to other countries are so vast that any retraction will have immediate and direct effects. Foreign direct investment that so many Asian economies have relied on will dry up. The high levels of trade between Japan and the United States and Japan and Europe will plummet, which could lead to layoffs and bankruptcies in all these areas. Even the funds that Japan expends to provide for U.S. service personnel will decline.

As if that were not bad enough, the September 11, 2001, bombing of New York's World Trade Center and the Pentagon in Washington, DC, will only exacerbate the problem. Although the long-term effects are impossible to know, analysts agree that the situation in the immediate future will only worsen if simply because the entire industrialized world will likely feel the impact. With the slowdown in air travel, the steep fall in major stock markets, including Japan's, the tendency for people around the globe to reduce their purchases of nonessential items, and the falling yen/dollar exchange rate (which makes Japanese imports more expensive), there seems little likelihood that any stimulus to jolt the Japanese economy will become available to Koizumi.

With nowhere to turn, Koizumi Junichiro and Japan seem forced into a corner from which there is little possibility of escape.

## BIBLIOGRAPHY

Anchordoguy, Marie. *Whatever Happened to the Japanese Miracle?* Cardiff, CA: Japan Policy Research Institute (Occasional Paper No. 80), September 2001.

Arnold, Wayne. "Japan's Electronics Slump Takes a Toll on Southeast Asia." *The New York Times,* September 1, 2001, B.1.

"The Axe Falls in Japan." *The Economist Global Agenda.* August 28, 2001. Available online at http://www.economist.com/agenda (cited September 3, 2001).

Bai Gao. *Japan's Economic Dilemma: The Institution of Prosperity and Stagnation.* New York: Cambridge University Press, 2001.

Bevacqua, Ronald. "Japan's Old Guard vs. the Internet Revolution." *Asian Wall Street Journal,* March 1, 2000.

Borthwick, Mark. *Pacific Century: The Emergence of Modern Pacific Asia,* 2nd ed. Boulder, CO: Westview Press, 1998.

Boyle, John Hunter. *Modern Japan: The American Nexus.* San Diego: Harcourt Brace Jovanovich, 1993.

Carlile, Lonny E., and Mark C. Tilton, eds. *Is Japan Really Changing Its Ways? Regulatory Reform and the Japanese Economy.* Washington, DC: Brookings Institution Press, 1998.

Christensen, Clayton, et al, "The Great Disruption," *Foreign Affairs,* 80, no. 2 (2001), pp. 80–95.

Garran, Robert. *Tigers Tamed: The End of the Asian Miracle.* Honolulu: University of Hawaii Press, 1998.

Gibney, Frank. "Reinventing Japan _ Again." In Dean W. Collinwood, ed., *Japan and the Pacific Rim,* 6th ed. Guilford, CT: McGraw-Hill/Dushkin, 2001 (reprinted from *Foreign Policy,* Summer 2000), pp. 145–50.

Gluck, Carol. *Japan's Modern Myths: Ideology in the Late Meiji Period.* Princeton, NJ: Princeton University Press, 1985.

Hatch, Walter, and Kozo Yamamura. *Asia in Japan's Embrace: Building a Regional Production Alliance.* Cambridge: Cambridge University Press, 1996.

Helweg, Diana. "Japan: A Rising Sun?" *Foreign Affairs,* 79, no. 4 (2000), pp. 26–39.

Howe, Christopher. *The Origins of Japanese Trade Supremacy.* Chicago: University of Chicago Press, 1996.

Huber, Thomas M. *Strategic Economy in Japan.* Boulder, CO: Westview Press, 1994.

Jameson, Sam. "Japan's Amoeba Politics." *Asian Perspective,* 24, no. 4, pp. 17–35.

"Japan: Economy Stuck in a Whirlpool of Trouble." *Asia Times Online.* Available online at http://www.atimes.com/japan-econ/CH04Dh01.html (cited August 6, 2001).

"Japan: Pain and No Gain?" *Asia Times Online.* Available online at http://www.atimes.com/editor/CH02Ba01.html (cited August 1, 2001).

Johnson, Chalmers. *Japan: Who Governs? The Rise of the Developmental State.* New York: W. W. Norton & Company, 1995.

———. *Japanese "Capitalism" Revisited.* Cardiff, CA: Japan Policy Research Institute (Occasional Paper No. 22), August 2001.

———. *MITI and the Japanese Miracle: The Growth of Industrial Policy, 1925–1975* Stanford: Stanford University Press, 1982.

Katz, Richard. *Japan: The System That Soured: The Rise and Fall of the Japanese Economic Miracle.* Armonk, NY: M.E. Sharpe, 1998.

Kruger, David. "'Change the LDP! Change Japan!'" *Far Eastern Economic Review,* May 3, 2001, pp. 14–16.

———. "The Heavy Cost of Winning Big." *Far Eastern Economic Review,* June 21, 2001, pp. 16–19.

——— and Ichiko Ruyuno. "Power Struggle Saps Reform." *Far Eastern Economic Review,* April 19, 2001, pp. 21–22.

LaFeber, Walter. *The Clash: U.S.-Japanese Relations Throughout History.* New York: W. W. Norton & Company, 1997.

Landers, Peter. "Arthritic Nation." In *Japan and the Pacific Rim,* edited by Dean W. Collinwood, 6th ed. Guilford, CN: McGraw-Hill/Dushkin, 2001 (reprinted from *Far Eastern Economic Review,* July 16, 1998), pp. 169–171.

Magnier, Mark. "Japan Eases Policy to Jump Start Economy." *Los Angeles Times,* August 15, 2001, sec C.

———. "Koizumi's Budget Seen as Risky." *Los Angeles Times,* August 11, 2001, sec C.

Mann, Jim. "'Trouble' with Japan? U.S. Advice." *Los Angeles Times,* February 14, 2001, sec A.

Morris-Suzuki, Tessa. *Re-Inventing Japan: Time, Space, Nation.* New York: M. E. Sharpe, 1998.

Mulgan, Aurelia George. "Japan: A Setting Sun?" *Foreign Affairs,* 79, no. 4 (2000), pp. 40–52.

Norris, Floyd. "Japan's Budget Deficit Has Soared. It's Time for a Tax Cut." *New York Times,* August 17, 2001, sec B.

Porter, Michael, and Hirotaka Takeuchi. "Fixing What Really Ails Japan." *Foreign Affairs,* 78, no. 3 (1999), pp. 66–81.

Schoppa, Leonard J. "Japan, the Reluctant Reformer." *Foreign Affairs,* 80, no. 3 (2001), pp. 76–90.

Simone, Vera. *The Asian Pacific: Political and Economic Development in a Global Context,* 2nd ed. New York: Addison Wesley Longman, 2001.

Tabb, William K. *The Postwar Japanese System: Cultural Economy and Economic Transformation.* New York: Oxford University Press, 1995.

Tamamoto, Masaru. "The Privilege of Choosing: The Fallout from Japan's Economic Crisis." In Dean W. Collinwood, ed., *Japan and the Pacific Rim,* 6th ed. Guilford, CT: McGraw-Hill/Dushkin, 2001 (reprinted from *World Policy Journal,* fall 1998), pp. 158–162.

———. "Japan and Its Discontents: A Letter from Yokohama." *World Policy Journal,* 17, no. 3 (2000): pp. 41–49.

Tilton, Mark. *Restrained Trade: Cartels in Japan's Basic Materials Industries.* Ithaca, NY: Cornell University Press, 1996.

Tsuru, Shigeto. *Japan's Capitalism: Creative Defeat and Beyond.* Cambridge: Cambridge University Press, 1993.

"The Voters Give Koizumi a Chance. Will the LDP?" *Economist,* August 4, 2001, pp. 21–23.

Wei, Peh T'i. *East Asian History.* Hong Kong: Oxford University Press, 1981.

Woo-Cumings, Meredith, ed. *The Developmental State.* Ithaca, NY: Cornell University Press, 1999.

Woodall, Brian. *Japan Under Construction: Corruption, Politics, and Public Works.* Berkeley, CA: University of California Press, 1996.

*Allen Wittenborn*

# QUITTING THE KYOTO PROTOCOL: THE UNITED STATES STRIKES OUT ALONE

## THE CONFLICT

The huge international effort to reduce greenhouse gas emissions and counter global warming experienced a major setback at its conference in Bonn, Germany, in May 2001, when the United States pulled out of the conference and refused to sign the revised Kyoto Protocol. What could be done when the producer of 25 percent of the world's greenhouse emissions refused to participate, possibly threatening the rest of the world with its emissions? The Bonn conference forged ahead in its negotiations, attempting to create an effective international agreement despite the loss of U.S. participation.

### Political

- U.S. President George W. Bush challenged the fundamental assumption of Kyoto: that global warming had been demonstrated to be a real event, and that it could be traced to human activity. Bush also believed that the Kyoto Protocol put undue responsibility on industrialized nations without requiring the participation of developing nations.

- With concessions made in compromise, the revised protocol featured loopholes, such as a trading system for emissions reductions and credits for tree-planting. To some critics these features were unfair and could render the accord ineffective in decreasing greenhouse emissions in the future.

### Economic

- An 8 percent reduction in the United States' greenhouse gas emissions would require a substantial revision in the way American industry operated. Lobbyists cited the massive economic and employment dislocations that could occur if such a reduction were made.

- While the protocol requires governments to reduce emissions, the problem of emissions lies with private industries, institutions governments might not be able to coerce into reducing emissions. Large multinational corporations facing costly emissions controls might simply move their production facilities to nations that allow higher $CO_2$ emissions.

In May 2001, 179 nations met in Bonn, Germany, to hammer out an historic environmental accord aimed at reducing the amount of greenhouse gas emissions entering the atmosphere each year. The goal of the conference was to stave off "global warming" or the "greenhouse effect" by requiring different nations to reduce their output of these gases and chemicals by different amounts. Greenhouse gases, such as carbon dioxide, methane, nitrous oxide, halogenated fluorocarbons, ozone, perfluorinated carbons (PFCs), and hydrofluorocarbons (HFCs) are gases that absorb infrared radiation in the atmosphere. The greenhouse effect occurs when greenhouse gases allow incoming infrared radiation into the earth's atmosphere, but prevent it from escaping, thus keeping the earth warm. While the greenhouse effect is a natural event that sustains life, increased emissions of greenhouse gases due to human activities, particularly industrial processes, are thought to be causing present and future global warming, a gradual rise in the earth's surface temperature, and other potentially harmful climate changes.

The Bonn conference was an effort to ratify and give force to an agreement signed in 1997 called the Kyoto Protocol on Greenhouse Gases. Despite the fact that President Bill Clinton (1993–2001) had signed the protocol, newly elected U.S. President George W. Bush (2001–) announced that he found the protocol to be fatally flawed and indicated that unless it was dramatically revised, the United States would not participate in the Bonn conference. Efforts by several nations, including Great Britain, France, and Germany, to alter Bush's thinking failed, and in June 2001, the president indicated that he would not sign the protocol.

# CHRONOLOGY

*1972* The first Earth Summit convenes at Stockholm, Sweden, where world leaders decide to meet every ten years to discuss environmental issues. (The 1982 summit, scheduled to take place in Nairobi, Kenya, never takes place).

*1979* The National Academy of Scientists (NAS) releases a report warning that steps should be taken at once to avoid human-caused climate change.

*1988* The Intergovernmental Panel on Climate Change (IPCC) is established by the United Nations Environmental Programme (UNEP) and the World Meteorological Organization (WMO). The panel brings together scientists from all over the world to discuss and analyze current scientific information on human-induced climate change.

*1990* Two documents bring climate change to public attention. An appeal signed by 49 Nobel prize winners and 700 members of the National Academy of Scientists asserts "broad agreement among the scientific community that amplification of the Earth's natural greenhouse effect by the buildup of various gases introduced by human activity has the potential to produce dramatic changes in climate." An IPCC report by a panel of 170 scientists from 25 countries concludes the same thing, saying that greenhouse gas emissions will result in "an additional warming of the Earth's surface."

*1992* The second Earth Summit meeting is held at Rio de Janeiro, Brazil, to address various environmental concerns from deforestation to the loss of usable croplands, but focuses particularly on the problem of global warming.

*May 1992* At the Rio Earth Summit, 160 nations adopt a program called the United Nations Framework Convention on Climate Change, promising to find ways to reduce their production of greenhouse gases to the amounts each nation produced in 1990 by the year 2000. They agree that in 2000, they will examine ways to reduce the production of these gases even further.

*October 15, 1992* The Framework Convention passes in the U.S. Senate.

*1993* The Framework Convention on Climate Change is ratified by more than 50 nations, putting it into effect.

*December 1997* A conference to create a stronger protocol outlining how each participating nation could reduce its production of greenhouse gases is held in Kyoto, Japan. It draws delegates from nearly 170 nations, including the United States.

*November 1998* Clinton signs the Kyoto Protocol, but with Senate confirmation unlikely, he can do little to move the protocol ahead.

*November 2000* The Sixth Conference of Parties (COP 6) to the United Nations Framework Convention on Climate Change is held at the Hague, Netherlands, but ends without accord, to be continued in 2001 in Bonn.

*November 2000* George W. Bush, who opposes participation in the Kyoto Protocol, is elected president of the United States.

*February 19, 2001* IPCC's Third Assessment Report is released, with stronger warnings about human-induced climate change.

*March 28, 2001* Christine Todd Whitman, head of the U.S. Environmental Protection Agency, confirms that the United States will not implement the Kyoto Protocol.

*May 2001* The conference in Bonn, Germany, begins, with 179 nations participating in revising the Kyoto Protocol on Greenhouse Gases.

*June 2001* President George W. Bush announces that the Kyoto Protocol is "fatally flawed" and he will not sign it, withdrawing the United States from the Bonn conference.

*July 28, 2001* A new accord is reached at Bonn, without the participation of the United States.

The United States' withdrawal from the Bonn conference seemed to deal a fatal blow to any hope of its success. First, any international agreement that excluded U.S. participation was less likely to be consistently enforced. Second, the United States produces about 25 percent of the key greenhouse gas carbon dioxide ($CO_2$), and its production of $CO_2$ is increasing. Any accord that failed to curb U.S. production of $CO_2$ was likely to be ineffective in combating global warming.

## THE INTERGOVERNMENTAL PANEL ON CLIMATE CHANGE

In 1988, the United Nations Environmental Programme (UNEP) and the World Meteorological Organization (WMO) created the Intergovernmental Panel on Climate Change (IPCC), bringing together scientists and governmental officials from more than one hundred nations to develop a consensus on the issues of climate change and the possible global warming trend. The IPCC has since released three reports, all with increasing urgency in warnings about climate change.

In 2001, the IPCC released its Third Assessment Report. This report stated that "there is new and stronger evidence that most of the warming observed over the last 50 years is attributable to human activities" and that "emissions of greenhouse gases and aerosols ... continue to alter the atmosphere in ways that are expected to affect the climate system." Among its findings were: the global average surface temperature has increased over the twentieth century by about 0.6°C; snow cover and ice extent have decreased; global average sea level has risen, and ocean heat content has increased.

The IPCC estimated that, unless emissions were limited, during the twenty-first century global warming would increase by 1.4°C–5.8°C (2.5°F–10.4°F). The group warned that warming of between 1°–2°C would lead to extreme climate events and jeopardize endangered ecosystems. The report also noted that changes in the climate system were already taking place, particularly in severe storms seen throughout the globe.

Moreover, Japan, another heavy producer of $CO_2$, indicated that if the United States would not participate in the Bonn treaty, it might not participate either.

Despite this major setback, 178 nations continued to work on the protocol, and by July 28, 2001, had hammered out a modified agreement. This agreement was a substantial departure from the agreement first drafted in 1997, but many people believed it was an important first step in dealing with the challenge of climate change. Others believed that the compromises made at Bonn only undermined the accord, making future efforts to address man-made environmental problems more difficult. The critics argued that the withdrawal of the United States allowed industries in many industrialized nations to avoid serious efforts to curb greenhouse gas emissions.

U.S. policy on climate change had been in place since the international environmental conference in Rio de Janeiro, Brazil, in 1992. To withdraw from the work in progress was seen by many as an extreme reversal. Was the Kyoto Protocol fatally flawed, as Bush claimed? President Bush rejected the Kyoto Protocol because he believed it placed an unfair burden on industrialized nations while allowing underdeveloped nations to develop and pollute at a much greater degree. Bush also continued to challenge the fundamental assumption of Kyoto: that global warming had been scientifically demonstrated to be a real event, and that it could be traced to human activity.

## HISTORICAL BACKGROUND

### Rio de Janeiro Conference, 1992

The roots of the Kyoto Protocol to Control Greenhouse Gases are found in the Rio Conference of 1992. Representatives of the United States and over 160 other nations met in Rio de Janeiro, Brazil, for the second "Earth Summit." (The first Earth Summit, held in Stockholm, Sweden, in 1972, ended with a decision to hold conferences every decade to discuss international environmental issues. In 1982 a planned Earth Summit in Nairobi, Kenya, failed to come together.) The 1992 summit was a multinational effort to address various environmental concerns, from deforestation to the loss of usable croplands to the problem of global warming. Global warming was a topic of particular importance. Scientific evidence since the mid-1970s indicated that the earth's atmosphere and oceans were getting warmer. Many scholars traced this increase in temperature to human use of fossil fuels such as coal and oil. These fuels produce an enormous amount of carbon dioxide (as well as other gases), which gets into the atmosphere and traps sunlight energy. Much as in a greenhouse, this trapped energy has to go somewhere, so it goes into the ground and into the oceans, raising the temperature of the earth (see figure on the greenhouse effect). The effect is that the world gets hotter, polar ice caps begin to melt, ocean levels rise, and people become sick from sun exposure, insect-borne illnesses, and increased molds.

The Earth Summit at Rio de Janeiro included a program called the United Nations Framework Convention on Climate Change, which set out to achieve "stabilization of greenhouse gas concentra-

DUTCH ENVIRONMENT MINISTER JAN PRONK AND BELGIAN SECRETARY OF STATE OLIVIER DELERIZE TAKE A TOUR OF THE ICE HOTEL IN SWEDEN, WHICH IS THREATENED BY GLOBAL WARMING. EUROPEAN UNION ENVIRONMENT MINISTERS MET IN SWEDEN IN MARCH 2001 TO REEVALUATE THE KYOTO PROTOCOL. (© AFP/Corbis. *Reproduced by permission.*)

tions in the atmosphere at a level that would prevent dangerous anthropogenic [human-caused] interference with the climate system." In other words, the 160 signers of the Framework Convention promised to find ways to reduce their production of greenhouse gases and avoid causing new changes in weather patterns. In May 1992, the United States and other nations promised to attempt to reduce their production of these gases to the amounts each nation produced in 1990 by the year 2000. They also agreed that in 2000, they would examine ways to reduce the production of these gases even further.

It is important to understand that while President George H. Bush (1988–92) signed the Framework Convention in May 1992, it would not be enforceable as a treaty until the U.S. Senate ratified it—67 senators out of 100 would have to vote for the Framework Convention. Members of Congress soon found that the directors of the United States' largest industries were bitterly opposed to ratification of the Rio Framework. They argued that reducing greenhouse gas emissions would cost money and jobs, and it would reduce U.S. competitiveness worldwide. Despite strong opposition, the convention passed Congress on October 15, 1992.

### The Road to Kyoto

The Rio Conference and convention has been called a milestone in efforts to curb global warming. The Rio convention was in reality, however, only a promise to work more on the issue of global warming. Shortly after the conference ended, the conferees determined that a stronger protocol outlining how each participating nation could reduce its production of greenhouse gases would be necessary. They decided to meet in Kyoto, Japan, in 1997 to draft that accord.

In the meantime, debate over the core assumptions of the Rio Convention emerged. In the United States, many scholars debated the reality of global warming and, if it was indeed a reality, whether human activity was its source. Moreover, leaders of the United States' largest industries had begun to study ways to reduce their greenhouse gas emissions and had concluded that such activity would indeed be very costly. These corporations engaged in a substantial lobby and media effort to change members of Congress's (and the public's) minds about the necessity of drastic control efforts. In this environment, conferees convened in Kyoto, Japan, in 1997.

AMERICAN STUDENTS DEMONSTRATE IN SUPPORT OF U.S. PRESIDENT GEORGE W. BUSH'S REFUSAL TO SUPPORT THE KYOTO PROTOCOL. (© *Reuters NewMedia Inc./Corbis. Reproduced by permission.*)

### The Kyoto Conference

The December 1997 Kyoto conference drew delegates from almost 170 nations, including the United States. This meeting was designed to set realistic time frames for reducing greenhouse gas emissions and specific emission reduction goals for each participating nation. The discussion, however, quickly became embroiled in controversy. The conferees were divided into two groups, or "annexes." The first group, Annex I, was composed primarily of industrialized nations such as the United States, many of the Russian republics, and the nations of western Europe. These nations were supposed to make serious efforts to reduce emissions of greenhouse gases such as $CO_2$ that are released in the process of industrial production. The Annex II nations, including China, India, the nations of Africa, and most of the Middle East, were not required to reduce emissions because their industrial development had not reached the stage in which dangerous levels of emissions were being produced. Instead, Annex II nations were required to implement population control measures. Many scholars believed that large populations use more resources than smaller ones. Since those nations in Annex II all had substantial population growth patterns, it was believed that they should help solve global warming by reducing their populations. Neither the industrialized nations nor the developing nations were happy with the arrangement. Many of the industrialized nations argued that setting targets for greenhouse gases would come at the expense of jobs and growth in their countries. They were concerned that these limits would eventually give the Annex II nations a competitive advantage over Annex I nations once Annex II nations began to develop. The Annex II nations, on the other hand, argued that there is no scientific link between population growth and greenhouse gases, and that limiting their populations was in effect a way for the Annex I nations to prevent them from becoming economically competitive.

Despite these disagreements, the participants were committed to addressing the problem of global warming. By the end of the Kyoto conference, the delegates had hammered out a protocol by which signatory nations could begin to reduce their production of greenhouse gases. The protocol contained several key provisions:

1. **Differentiated Reduction Targets.** Each Annex I nation received a "quantified emissions reduction limitation commitment" that limited that nation to some percent of its 1990 greenhouse emissions.

2. **Commitment Periods.** The protocol defined several commitment periods, generally in five-year intervals, to show significant progress in meeting reduction targets.

3. **Greenhouse gases.** The protocol included six greenhouse gas emissions nations were to seek to reduce: carbon dioxide, methane, nitrous oxide, hydrofluorocarbons (HFCs), perflourocarbons (PFCs), and sulfur hexafluoride. All of these are byproducts of industrial production.

4. **Demonstrable Progress.** Annex I nations were required to make measurable reductions by 2005.

5. **Land Use and Forestry.** The Kyoto Protocol allow nations to count reforestation efforts (often called carbon sink credit) toward their reduction targets. In simple terms, a national tree-planting program is considered an effort to reduce greenhouse gases, and may help a nation meet reduction targets.

6. **Flexible Reduction Methods.** Perhaps the most controversial component of the Kyoto Protocol was the inclusion of several creative methods by which Annex I nations could spread out and reduce the "costs" of their

emissions. For example, a nation that already reduced its emissions below 1990 levels would be granted emission "credits," which it could trade or sell to another nation. That nation could then count those credits as part of their emissions reductions. Annex I nations could also implement reduction policies in conjunction with other nations, and thus both nations would use the average emissions reduction figure instead of the individual ones. Nations could also form larger coalitions. Finally, nations could receive emissions credits by engaging in emissions reduction projects in Annex II (and perhaps nonprotocol) nations.

The protocol was approved by a majority of the 160 nations attending, but several components were strongly debated. The most controversial was the flexible system by which polluting nations could "trade" their emissions with other nations. In simple terms, if a nation's reduction target is 5 percent, but that nation could only reduce emissions by 3 percent by 2000, that nation could "buy" credits from another nation that had exceeded its target reductions. Since the specifics of the trading system were not established in the Kyoto conference, many people criticized it as a huge "loophole" for polluter nations to use. The process was supposed to be resolved at a conference scheduled in Buenos Aires, Argentina, in 1998, but that conference met with delays.

Although a majority of Kyoto attendees voted for the protocol, most observers considered U.S. participation as critical. The reason was simple: the United States was at the time responsible for 25 percent of carbon dioxide emissions. The Clinton administration approved of the protocol, but, because it was clear that the U.S. Senate would never ratify the protocol, the president never submitted it to the Senate.

The Senate's objection was simple: reducing greenhouse gases was more than an industrial nations issue. Unless the Kyoto Accord required similar reductions among developing nations, the United States would not sign the treaty. Led by Senators Robert Byrd (D-WV) and Chuck Hagel (R-NE), the Senate passed a resolution refusing to join any environmental protocol that did not apply to developing nations as well as industrialized nations. This action effectively barred U.S. participation in the Kyoto accords unless modifications were made. Clinton signed the protocol in November 1998, but that action was largely ceremonial. With Senate confirmation extremely unlikely, Clinton could do little to move the protocol ahead.

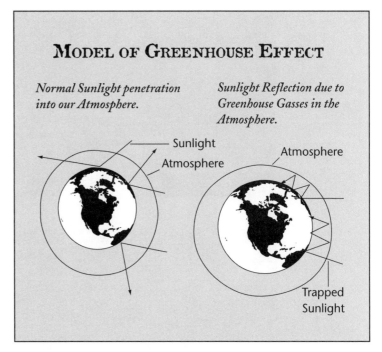

NORMAL SUNLIGHT PENETRATION INTO THE ATMOSPHERE IS ABLE TO ESCAPE AS EASILY AS IT ENTERS, BUT GREENHOUSE GASES CAUSE SUNLIGHT REFLECTION, WHICH CAN TRAP SUNLIGHT WITHIN THE ATMOSPHERE. *(The Gale Group.)*

## RECENT HISTORY AND THE FUTURE

### A New U.S. Administration Comes to Bonn, Germany

The U.S. election of 2000 brought George W. Bush to the White House. Bush had stated a number of times during the campaign that he opposed ratification or participation in the Kyoto Protocol because it was a bad deal for American businesses and it threatened U.S. autonomy. Despite his campaign rhetoric, Bush did send delegates to the Bonn Convention in May 2001. Early in the negotiations, however, Bush withdrew his support for the convention and recalled U.S. delegates. The immediate reaction from the other participants was that Bush had essentially doomed the protocol, because without U.S. participation the remaining nations could not address the single largest source of greenhouse gas production. The remaining 178 nations forged ahead, however, and in July 2001, announced that they had negotiated a redrafted accord. This accord reflected many U.S. demands, such as longer target dates to meet emission standards, fewer international penalties for individual nations, and most importantly, the new protocol allowed a nation to claim greenhouse credits if that nation were to engage

**Aerial view of Martha's Vineyard**

**Computer-enhanced view**

THE FIRST VIEW, ABOVE, IS AN AERIAL IMAGE OF MARTHA'S VINEYARD AS IT APPEARS TODAY. THE SECOND IMAGE IS A COMPUTER-ENHANCED VIEW OF THE ANTICIPATED GLOBAL WARMING IMPACTS ON THE REGION IN 100 YEARS. *(AP/Wide World Photos. Reproduced by permission.)*

in a tree-planting program specifically designed to absorb greenhouse gases.

These provisions did little to pacify the Bush administration, which refused to consider the protocol or submit it to the Senate. Bush still considered the bill dangerous to U.S. businesses, and flawed in its failure to resolve the issue of developing nation's emissions.

The Senate's resistance to the Kyoto Protocol was two-fold. First, and perhaps most importantly, the United States was required to reduce its greenhouse gas emissions by 8 percent, although some scientists wanted the U.S. to reduce emissions by 30 percent. Such a reduction would require a substantial revision in the way American industry operated. Lobbyists pressured Congress, citing the massive economic and employment dislocations that would occur if such a reduction were to be made.

Moreover, scientists believe that very soon, the developing nations of the world will become the leading group of greenhouse polluters, so that any accord that does not affect them will have the dual effect of allowing them an industrial advantage and while doing little to reduce greenhouse gases.

### The Kyoto Controversy: Problems with the Protocol

The Kyoto Protocol has generated a great deal of controversy and debate. The debate over Kyoto centers on several key issues: the science underpinning the global warming hypothesis; the economic impacts of meeting specific reduction targets; the failure to apply emissions limits on developing nations; the unusual trading system allowing nations to trade emissions credits; and the tremendous emphasis the Kyoto Protocol places on controlling carbon dioxide emissions as opposed to other greenhouse gases.

**The Science of Global Warming.** The evidence for global warming is based on complex mathematical models of ocean temperatures, atmospheric temperatures, measurements of northern and southern ice fields, and estimates of the amounts of greenhouse gases in the atmosphere. One point upon which all scholars agree is that the largest and most important "greenhouse gas" is actually water vapor, a gas humans can do little to affect. Depending on how one estimates the impact of man-made gases, and how one constructs the mathematical model, there is either a substantial problem, a small problem, or no real problem at all. Moreover, historical data about average temperatures provide few clues about whether the current rise in temperatures (a point that most scholars concede) is part of a cycle or something new.

**The Economics of Greenhouse Gas Emissions.** Many members of Congress worried that committing to the Kyoto Protocol would have a negative impact on businesses without any real assurance that the problem being addressed was worth the effort. Other critics of the protocol point out that while the protocol requires governments to reduce emissions, the problem of emissions lies with private industries, institutions governments might not be able to coerce into reducing emissions. This is particularly true of the large multinational corporations, who might simply move their production facilities to nations that allow higher $CO_2$ emissions. Interestingly, this complaint has led to a new type of enterprise, companies that sell or buy $CO_2$ emission credits. One such company,

## GREENHOUSE GASES AND GREENHOUSE GAS INDEXES

| Gas | Lifetime in Atmosphere | Direct Effect on sunlight, 20 years |
|---|---|---|
| Carbon Dioxide | Variable | 1 |
| Methane | 12 ± 3 years | 56* |
| Nitrous Oxide | 120 | 280 |
| *HFCs, PFCs, and Sulfur Hexafluoride* | | |
| HFC-23 | 264 | 9,200 |
| HFC-125 | 33 | 4,800 |
| HFC-134a | 15 | 3,300 |
| HFC-152a | 2 | 460 |
| HFC-227ea | 37 | 4,300 |
| Perfluoromethane | 50,000 | 4,400 |
| Perfluoroethane | 10,000 | 6,200 |
| Sulfur Hexafluoride | 3,200 | 16,300 |

*Methane is 56 times more reflective than CO

**Data Source:** Energy Information Administration Publication, "Emissions of Greenhouse Gases in the United States, 1999."

GREENHOUSE GASES CAN LINGER IN THE ATMOSPHERE FOR A FEW YEARS TO A FEW THOUSAND YEARS. *(The Gale Group)*

based in the United States, is $CO_2$-e, an e-commerce enterprise buying and selling greenhouse credits. The economic impact of compliance might actually increase the amount of $CO_2$ in the atmosphere as corporations move into Annex II nations and continue business in nations not restricted by the protocol. If industries chose to move to Annex II nations, Annex I nations would see both rising unemployment and a loss of competitiveness. On the other hand, supporters of the protocol argue that once an Annex II nation industrializes or substantially increases its $CO_2$ outputs, the protocol would simply be renegotiated.

**Annex II Nations and Greenhouse Gases.** Other observers criticize the Kyoto Protocol because it does not place limits on greenhouse emissions from Third World countries now or in the future. While the United States currently produces about 25 percent of greenhouse gases, and Western democracies account for over half of all these emissions, projections indicate that in the next 20 years, the greatest producers of greenhouse gases will likely be China and India. Neither country currently faces limits under the Kyoto Protocol. Both nations protest that until they are sufficiently industrial, such limitations would only inhibit their development into sustainable economies, and that Western nations prefer to limit them precisely to keep them from competing in the global market.

**The Credit Trading System.** The most important criticism of the Kyoto Protocol is probably aimed at the credit-trading and the tree-planting allowances. For example, France had been engaged in a tree-planting program for several years before the Bonn conference. Despite clear evidence that the program had not been initiated as part of a greenhouse strategy, France is permitted to count this program as a credit against its own emissions. Thus, France is more likely to meet its reduction targets without undue economic hardship.

# THE FINAL NEGOTIATIONS AT BONN

The final negotiations session of the conference at Bonn, Germany, in 2001 lasted 31 hours, through the night and into the next day, with the continued participation of 178 nations. During these long and difficult hours there was a strong and successful effort to keep Japan, Canada, Australia, and New Zealand from following the United States out the door. At the earlier sessions in the Hague in 2000, there had been three major obstacles to agreement: the idea of carbon sinks (getting credit for forests); flexibility mechanisms—particularly the trading of emissions reduction credits; and enforcement. A split had formed between the European Union—which disapproved of carbon sink credits and flexibility mechanisms and urged enforcement guidelines—and a coalition of countries called the "Umbrella Group" that included the United States, Japan, Australia, Canada, New Zealand, and the Russian Federation that urged some or all of these measures. At Bonn, the European Union finally gave in to the pressure and accepted carbon sink credits and emissions reduction credits and left the matter of enforcement largely unsolved. In the Bonn negotiations, Japan was particularly concerned that penalties would be placed on nations that did not meet the reduction requirements. It also wanted to be able to use the carbon sink credits to help it reach its goal. Once these compromises were reached, Japan said it would try to convince the United States to join into the accord.

To the negotiators, there may have seemed little choice but to concede to many of the requests of these nations once the United States had withdrawn. If more nations were lost, the accord would have lost its international mandate. Most of the remaining nations wished to show that they could succeed even without the United States' participation, and at the same time felt it imperative that they create an agreement that the United States could join at a later time. There was a strong general desire not to end in a stalemate again, as had happened the year before at the Hague. The result of this drive to achieve accord was, in the view of some, a general watering down of the Kyoto Protocol. The environmental group Greenpeace, for example, called the revised accord "Kyoto Lite." To others, though, it was a valiant effort of compromise.

With the compromises, the cut in emissions is only about a third of the original goal. While the initial Kyoto Protocol required industrialized countries (Annex I) to cut greenhouse emissions by an average of 5.2 percent below their 1990 levels over the next 11 years, under the Bonn agreement emissions would be cut only to about 2 percent below the 1990 level. Japan and the European Union agreed to cut their emissions by 8 percent. (In 2001, Japan's emissions level was about 2.7 percent above its 1990 level, while the European Union's was about .5 percent higher than in 1990. By contrast, in 2001, the United States was 13 percent above its 1990 emissions level.) Under the terms of the treaty finalized at Bonn, only the 30-odd most developed nations would be required to cut emissions.

After the crew of delegates at Bonn finally agreed on the treaty, Paula J. Dobriansky, the U.S. delegate at the summit, relayed the United States' position. "Although the United States does not intend to ratify that agreement," she told the exhausted group, "we have not sought to stop others from moving ahead, so long as legitimate U.S. interests were protected." Dobriansky went on to reiterate that the United States believed that the Kyoto Protocol was "not sound policy." "Among other things, the emissions targets are not scientifically based or environmentally effective, given the global nature of greenhouse gas emissions and the Protocol's exclusion of developing countries from its emissions limitation requirements and its failure to address black soot and tropospheric ozone. The decisions made today with respect to the Protocol, in addition, reinforce our conclusion that the treaty is not workable for the United States." Dobriansky was booed loudly by the delegates of other nations. Later, a negotiator from the European Union, Olivier Deleuze expressed a prevailing sentiment at the conference: "Almost every single country stayed in the protocol. There was one that said the protocol was flawed. Do you see the Kyoto Protocol flawed?"

The process by which nations may trade emissions credits is even more criticized. In the years following the collapse of the Union of Soviet Socialist Republics (USSR), the Russian republics actually reduced their greenhouse emissions substantially. This was due in part to the widespread economic collapse and unemployment that followed the breakup of the USSR, but the practical consequence is that Russia is now a net greenhouse creditor and the United States a net debtor.

## GREENHOUSE GAS EMISSIONS

*Per Capita CO$_2$ Emissions, in thousand metric tons*

| *Less than 2.11* | *2.11 – 4.20* | *4.21 – 8.42* | *More than 8.42* |
|---|---|---|---|
| Algeria | Argentina | Austria | Australia |
| Brazil | Chile | France | Bahrain |
| Colombia | China | Greece | Belgium |
| Peru | Cuba | Hungary | Bulgaria |
| Ecuador | Iran | Ireland | Canada |
| Egypt | Iraq | Israel | Former Czechoslovakia |
| India | Malaysia | Italy | Denmark |
| Indonesia | Mexico | Libya | Finland |
| Morocco | Portugal | New Zealand | Germany |
| Nigeria | Syria | North Korea | Japan |
| Pakistan | Turkey | Oman | Kuwait |
| Philippines | | South Africa | Netherlands |
| Thailand | | South Korea | Norway |
| Tunisia | | Spain | Poland |
| Vietnam | | Sweden | Qatar |
| Zimbabwe | | Switzerland | Romania |
| | | Venezuela | Saudi Arabia |
| | | FR Yugoslavia | Singapore |
| | | | Former Soviet Union |
| | | | United Kingdom |
| | | | United States |

NATIONS WITH GREENHOUSE GAS EMISSIONS OF MORE THAN 8.42 ARE GENERALLY INDUSTRIALIZED, DEVELOPED COUNTRIES, WHEREAS LESSER DEVELOPED NATIONS EMIT FEWER GREENHOUSE GAS EMISSIONS. *(The Gale Group.)*

The United States was required to reduce emissions by 8 to 9 percent, and many nations anticipated that it would be unable to do so. In order to make up the difference in real reductions and targets, the United States would have to purchase greenhouse credits. Since the United States would likely buy up most of the credits available, Russia and other creditor nations anticipated a very high price for their credits. When the United States withdrew from the protocol, there was a substantially reduced demand for credits, and nations like Russia soon found that they could not sell their credits as easily or as expensively as they had anticipated. Private corporations have assisted in selling these credits, but the economic impact to Russia and other nations still remains. Most importantly, the withdrawal of the United States and the excessive Russian credits means that Britain and France can, as a practical matter, increase their emissions up to 30 percent and still purchase enough credits to meet their reduction targets. In other words, the credit trading system, in effect, could contribute to a net increase in global greenhouse gases without the United States' participation.

**Reducing the Right Greenhouse Gases.** Many scholars and scientists criticize the Kyoto Protocol's focus on CO$_2$ gases, as opposed to other greenhouse gases. While it is true that 80 to 85 percent of greenhouse emissions are in the form of carbon dioxide, this gas is not necessarily the correct target in correcting the greenhouse effect. Carbon dioxide is a small, short-lived, naturally occurring molecule, readily broken apart by rain or a thunderstorm, and as a consequence, it is not particularly successful at reflecting the sun's rays. Of greater importance to the greenhouse effect are the man-made gases such as the fluorocarbons and sulfur compounds. These gases have much longer lifetimes (some will last thousands of years) and have a greater ability to reflect and trap sunlight. The standard greenhouse gas measure is to compare

U.S. PRESIDENT BUSH, FLANKED BY VICE PRESIDENT DICK CHENEY, LEFT, AND SECRETARY OF STATE COLIN POWELL, RIGHT, REMARKS ON GLOBAL WARMING. BUSH BELIEVES THE KYOTO PROTOCOL IS FLAWED. *(A/P Wide World. Reproduced by permission.)*

one kilogram of gas to one kilogram of carbon dioxide (a kilogram is equal to 2.2 pounds). Thus, the greenhouse index for $CO_2$ is 1, while the index for sulfur hexafluoride (used in plastics production) is 16,300 in 10 years, and 23,900 in 100 years. In other words, sulfur hexafluoride gas is 16,000 times more reflective than $CO_2$. Yet the majority of the Kyoto Protocol is aimed at controlling carbon dioxide emissions. (See the graph for other gases and their indices).

## Enforcement of the Protocol

The Kyoto Protocol has several enforcement mechanisms to ensure that participating nations make progress in meeting target emissions reductions. For example, if a nation misses its target reductions, it must meet those reductions and more at the next target point. Enforcement, however, remains problematic, as there are no international organizations with sufficient force and moral authority to compel cooperation. Moreover, if a nation-state believes that the protocol is causing economic harm, there is little other nations can do to prevent that nation from simply withdrawing. It is important to remember that the Kyoto Protocol is a voluntary system among member nations, not enforced by the United Nations or any other inter-

national body. Consequently, if a nation, such as the United States, chooses not to participate, there is little other nations can do to compel compliance.

## Conclusion

The fact that 178 nations were able to produce a negotiated agreement without U.S. participation indicates that there is a world consensus about the importance of addressing global warming. Such international agreement may be used to bring international moral pressure on the United States and other nonparticipant nations. Since the issue of global warming is both a survival issue and a moral one, an international consensus provides the Kyoto Protocol with a kind of moral force that may in the long run override national or domestic concerns. In the end, most scholars agree that the likelihood of success of international agreements depends on international commitments like this one.

Many nations see human-induced climate change as the most important global challenge of the twenty-first century. Whether global warming is a reality or not, such a uniform commitment by such a diverse list of nations cannot be ignored. It seems likely that the United States will eventually participate in some form of agreement to reduce greenhouse emissions. If the United States fails to do so, it potentially jeopardizes its moral authority in other arenas as well. In the end, the Bush administration has shown a propensity towards caution and prudence. It would appear to most observers that the prudent course is to treat greenhouse gases as a potential harm and to act accordingly. This seems to be the dominant position among the Kyoto Protocol signatories, and it seems unlikely that the United States can long stand alone on this matter.

## BIBLIOGRAPHY

"Climate Change, Bonn 2001 Summit," CNN.com. Available online at http://europe.cnn.com/SPE-CIALS/2001/climate.change/ (cited September 8, 2001.

Congressional Quarterly Researcher. Available online at http://wysiwyg://97/http://library.cqpress (cited August 15, 2001).

*Emissions of Greenhouse Gases in the United States 1999.* Energy Information Administration: Washington, DC, 1999.

"In President's Words: 'A Leadership Role in the Issue of Climate Change,'" *New York Times,* June 12, 2001; A12.

Official Website, Conference of the Parties, Sixth Session, Part 2, 16–27 July 2001, Bonn, Germany. Available online at http://www.unfccc.int/cop6_2/ (cited September 8, 2001).

Penkava, Melinda. "Analysis: Bush Administration's Rejection of Global Treaties." National Public Radio's *Talk of the Nation.* Transcript, 2001.

Philips, Melanie. "The Myth of Global Warming Endangers the Planet," *Sunday Times* (London), April 15, 2001.

Pianin, Eric. "Emissions Treaty Softens Kyoto Targets; Environmentalists' Euphoria over Global Pact Gives Way to Debate on Concessions," *Washington Post,* July 29, 2001, A23.

"Profile of the Kyoto Protocol," Facts on File electronic archives Available online at http://www.2facts.com (cited August 15, 2001).

Revkin, Andrew C., 2001. "178 Nations Reach Climate Accord: U.S. Only Looks On," *New York Times,* July 24, 2001; A1.

Victor, David G. "Global Warming: Bogus Rescue," *Los Angeles Times,* August 19, 2001; A1.

Zengerle, Jason. "Hagelianism," *New Republic,* February 8, 2001, 10–12.

*Michael P. Bobic*

# LIBYA, QADHAFI, AND THE AFRICAN UNION

## THE CONFLICT

Colonel Muammar al-Qadhafi, after having been isolated as a leader of an alleged terrorist nation for years, returned to the international arena as a spokesperson strongly pushing the unity of African nations. He deftly brought about the unanimous decision of the African states to form the new African Union in 2001. With Africa's current political configuration as 53 distinct nation-states with diverse markets, civil wars, and individual health measures, there is less hope for progress than there would be as a strong union of nations. There are many obstacles to federation, not least of which are suspicions about Qadhafi himself.

### Political

- Many suspect Qadhafi, who was not long ago the primary advocate of Arab unity, of attempting to amass power for himself and for anti-Western, anti-Israeli causes.

- Qadhafi's vision of a United States of Africa entails changing the concepts of national identity within the African nations.

- Some people in the nation of Libya rose up against their leader's mission to unite Africa because of its high cost to the Libyan people. The country is accustomed to seeing itself as Arab before African.

### Economic

- Libya and Qadhafi receive a disproportionate amount of international attention due in part to the vast oil resources of the country. Qadhafi is using Libya's oil income to help finance the African Union campaign, drawing many poor African nations to support Qadhafi and tipping the normal scales that balance power.

### Ethnic

- Before the arrival at the end of the 1990s of more than one million African immigrants from many countries, Libya's population was very homogeneous, with 97 percent of the population Sunni Muslims of Berber and Arab descent. Introducing new groups within the country resulted in violence. Eliminating borders between the nation-states of Africa, many of which have strong cultural and ethnic identities, could require careful attention to the possibilities of ethnic conflict.

In 1999 Libyan leader Colonel Muammar Abu Minyar al-Qadhafi (also Gaddafi, Kadhafi, Gadafy, and various other spellings) called a meeting of all African heads of state to discuss the creation of a new union of African states. The new union Qadhafi proposed was to be far stronger than the existing Organization of African Unity (OAU), which had been formed by 32 independent African states in 1963 in order to promote unity and to defend the sovereignty of its members and eradicate all forms of colonialism on the continent. Following several meetings and a two-day summit of 40 African heads of state in Sirte, Libya, in March 2001, Libya announced the creation of a new African Union, to be roughly modeled on the European Union.

Upon the announcement of the new pact, established by a unanimous decision of all 53 member states of the OAU, Colonel Qadhafi flashed a victory sign. "Africans will no longer accept to be treated like animals and Africa has the right to take the place that is hers in the world," Qadhafi said, as quoted by Paul Ejime in a March 2, 2001, *Panafrican News Agency* article. Qadhafi declared the formation of the African Union a major turning point in modern African history. "Today marks the crowning of the dozens of steps taken by Africa on the road to freedom and unity" Qadhafi pronounced, as quoted in an article in the *Middle East News Online*. For Qadhafi too, the creation of African Union was a turning point in his long struggle to bring about worldwide changes as a legitimate statesman.

The African Union that was voted in will actually be a watered-down version of Qadhafi's original proposal to create a federated super-nation similar to the United States of America,

# CHRONOLOGY

**1951** With British and American backing, the United Nations approves independence for Libya under King Idris.

**1963** Egyptian President Gamal Abdul Nasser and Kwame Nkrumah, president of Ghana, call a meeting of all African leaders in Cairo, Egypt, to discuss the union of African nations into a single state headed by one ruler. The Organization of African States that emerges is a much weaker institution than its creators had envisioned.

**September 1, 1969** Muammar al-Qadhafi engineers a bloodless military coup in which a group of about 70 military officers depose King Idris.

**1970** Qadhafi announces his intention to pursue a federation of Arab nations and begins to work with Egypt on plans for a union.

**1976** The first volume of Qadhafi's *The Green Book,* setting out his revolutionary theory of a socialized Islamic people's government, is published.

**1977** The General People's Committee (GPC) proclaims the new Socialist People's Libyan Arab Jamahiriya.

**1978** Egyptian leader Anwar Sadat concludes a peace agreement with Israel, infuriating Qadhafi, who then organizes other Arab nations in opposition to Egypt.

**1979** A mob sets fire to the U.S. embassy in Tripoli. Staff members were withdrawn from the country. The U.S. government declares Libya a "state sponsor of terrorism."

**1980s** Oil prices begin to fall and Libya's economy deteriorates. Tens of thousands of foreign workers are expelled. Opposition to Qadhafi's rule increases.

**1984** Qadhafi attempts to form a regional union with Morocco, but then accuses Morrocan King Hassan II of "Arab treason" for meeting with Israel's Prime Minister Shimon Peres.

**1986** Libya is accused of the Berlin discotheque terrorist bombing; the United States launches an air strike against targets near Tripoli and Benghazi in April.

**1988** The explosion of Pan Am Flight 103 over Lockerbie, Scotland, claims the lives of 259 passengers and crew. The United States imposes sanctions on Libya as the "prime suspect" in the bombing, and the UN imposes an air embargo on Libya, severely damaging Libya's already shaky economy.

**1997** Despite air embargoes, South African President Nelson Mandela visits Qadhafi in Libya and publicly expresses his appreciation of Qadhafi's support in the fight against apartheid in South Africa.

**1997** Qadhafi declares that Libya is African and no longer part of the Arab world.

**1997** Qadhafi opens Libya to foreigners by easing travel and visa restrictions. Hundreds of thousands of African immigrants annually begin to enter the country seeking work.

**1999** Qadhafi surrenders the two men accused of blowing up PanAm Flight 103 for trial in Scotland.

**1999** The UN sanctions against Libya are suspended.

**1999** Qadhafi convenes a summit at Sirte with the leaders of all African states to discuss a union of African nations.

**2000** An estimated one million African immigrants reside in Libya, coming in primarily from Nigeria, Ghana, Chad, Niger, Gambia, and Sudan. Unemployment rises.

**September 2000** Libyan youth gangs rise up against the African workers in their country, killing 130 Africans and injuring thousands more. Hundreds of thousands of African immigrants are expelled from Libya.

**March 2001** After a two-day summit of 40 African heads of state in Sirte, Libya, the creation of a new African Union is announced.

**September 11, 2001** Qadhafi condemns the terrorist attacks on the United States and offers to send aid to the American people.

MAP OF LIBYA. *(© Maryland Cartographics. Reprinted with permission.)*

with a president and a congress. The new African Union will have a Union executive council, a parliament, court of justice, a monetary union, a peacekeeping force, and financial institutions, including a common currency, central bank, and investment bank. The Union should be a forum to foster greater cooperation among African nations, end wars, and promote prosperity. Member nations hope eventually to form a single political body that can compete among the global powers on an economic, political, and military basis.

United Nations (UN) Secretary-General Kofi Annan has given the African Union his blessing, and the new Union has brought a ray of hope and promise to some African nations. But there are those in Africa and in the West who have grave concerns, and some confusion, about Qadhafi's motivations. The controversial Libyan leader is thought to have sponsored state-organized and financed terrorism aimed at select Western targets in the past; many fear that he is building up to create worse havoc in the future.

Qadhafi rules 5,445,500 Libyans. His country by itself has too small a population to pose a substantial military threat to the West. But under Qadhafi, Libya has played an international role more appropriate to a far larger nation. The new African Union would give Qadhafi access to some 680,000,000 Africans—a tremendous power base.

No less concerned are the people of Libya, who experienced a tremendous shift in their nation's population when their leader shifted his orientation from Arab countries in the Middle East to the federation of African nations.

### Arab or African?

Qadhafi adopted the mantel of "Mr. Africa" in the late 1990s, after a long career as a spokesperson for the Middle East. When asked by a Reuters reporter if he was detached from the Arab world, Qadhafi replied, "Libya is a very dynamic country. Libya's territory is *African*. The Arab countries can catch up with the African countries."

Despite their leader's words, Libyans, as North Africans, are probably more accustomed to thinking of themselves as Arab than as African. For many the idea of being part of Africa and the African Union is a novel concept. When Libya's economy plunged in 2000, there were public riots and terrible violence against the African immigrants in Libya, ending with the deportation of hundreds of thousands back to their native lands. It will take time for Libyans to accept Africans from countries such as Nigeria, Chad, and Ghana as "brothers" in any meaningful sense. Yet, with Libyan television broadcasting local divas singing "Africa, our father, our mother" (according to the March 12, 2001, *Time*), perhaps the idea of being African will eventually take hold among Libyans.

### Suspicions about Qadhafi and Libya

Qadhafi had been politically isolated from the international world before he stepped into his new role of statesman for Africa. The West has accused Qadhafi of being involved in acts of terrorism for many years. Libya is one of seven governments that the United States designated as state sponsors of international terrorism. Qadhafi has gone to great lengths to change the image. He has notably been a major advocate of peace in the war-torn nations of Africa. He has repeatedly condemned terrorism, and on September 11, 2001, he condemned the "terrible" terrorist attacks on the United States and offered to send aid to the American people. The West, however, has not been quick to forget the past.

The government of Libya was suspected of involvement in the 1988 bombing of Pan Am Flight 103 over Lockerbie, Scotland, killing more than 200 innocent civilians. Qadhafi's minions were also suspected of bombing a disco in Germany and killing two U.S. soldiers stationed there, and they have been associated with a number of other terrorist attacks that have targeted Westerners. It was widely reported that Qadhafi offered a US$5 million payout to anyone who could provide him with fissionable material and the know-how to make an atomic weapon of mass destruction, according to Patrick Lyons in his article "Gaddafi's African Union Is a Fraud, *Part II:* Would You Trust This Man with Nukes?"

Libya has huge internal sources of uranium, which Russia used under a 1985 agreement to build a nuclear power plant in Qadhafi's hometown of Sirte. This plant currently produces 880 megawatts of electricity. Some are concerned that it could also create bomb-grade material. A German-built pharmaceutical complex near Rabta was suspected of producing mustard gas; it was destroyed in a "mysterious" fire. Suspicion has also been focused on an enormous underground tunnel being built through Tarhuna Mountain, south of Tripoli, as a possible chemical weapons plant, especially since Libya has refused to sign the 1993 UN Convention outlawing chemical weapons and has also refused to open Tarhuna to international inspection.

On November 24, 1999, British authorities seized a consignment of Scud missile parts at Gatwick Airport near London that was bound for Libya. The boxes were marked "automotive spare parts," but they contained parts of North Korean Nodong-1 advanced ballistic missiles. These missiles have a range of 600 miles (966 kilometers), which would allow Libya to target sites in Athens and Rome. Continuing signs that Qadhafi is seeking to build or acquire weapons of mass destruction have led some analysts to question whether he is the right person to lead a new African Union.

African leaders have their own complaints, also based on the Libyan leader's past. Qadhafi's support of the brutal and inhumane Ugandan tyrant Idi Amin Dada in the early 1970s made Tanzania suspicious of Qadhafi's motives. A senior Nigerian official quoted by MacLeod complained that Qadhafi, "wants to be the driver, with all of us (African nations) in the back seat." In Kenya John Githongo, also recorded by MacLeod, noted that Qadhafi "has backed some nasty little regimes across Africa, so there is suspicion of his motives."

Despite this, other leaders of great stature, such as former South African president Nelson Mandela, support Qadhafi. During its many years of struggle against apartheid the African National Congress Party (ANC) received support from Qadhafi, along with Cuban leader Fidel Castro and one or two other leaders who supported the South African fighters without hesitation or reservation. Qadhafi is also sought out for the great oil revenues his country has enjoyed in recent decades. Poor African nations, such as Gambia, Cape Verde, the Central African Republic, Equatorial Guinea, Ethiopia, Lesotho, Madagascar, Malawi, Mali, and Niger, which are saddled with debt, poverty, and disease, hope to gain financial help from Libya. The allure of Libya's money is obvious, and the poorest African nations were the first to ratify the new union to curry favor with Qadhafi.

Incidents of anti-African violence in Qadhafi's own country, Libya, demonstrate that it could be a long time before the people of the nations of Africa are prepared to take on a Pan-African identity. Many Africans do not know a lot about the people of their own country, much less their continent-mates. For ordinary Africans, joining a continent-wide union will require re-education as well as a tremendous leap of imagination and faith.

## HISTORICAL BACKGROUND

W.E.B. DuBois (1868–1963) coined the term "Pan-Africanism" to capture the desire to unite all people of African descent worldwide. He believed that all nations on the continent of Africa should unite and form a United States of Africa. In 1957 Kwame Nkrumah (1909–72), a student of Dr. DuBois and a Pan-Africanist, became the first head of an independent black African nation, Ghana. In 1963 Gamal Abdel Nasser (1918–70), president of Egypt, and Nkrumah called a meeting of all African leaders in Cairo, Egypt. Nkrumah wrote a book entitled *Africa Must Unite* to sell these leaders on the need for a United States of Africa that would unite all African nations into a single super-state headed by one ruler.

There was opposition to an African union. Julius Nyerere (1922–96), president of Tanzania and a highly respected statesman, and other African leaders argued that Africa needed first to form viable regional unions that could later be united into a United States of Africa. Because of the strong opposition, the Organization of African States that eventually emerged from the Cairo

meetings was a much weaker institution than its creators had advocated. Nyerere successfully later regretted his opposition to the union, saying "We lost a lot of time."

Member states of the OAU pledged to consider the inherited boundaries of the colonial states sacred. Thus, today Africa remains divided into 53 nation-states and the disputed Western Sahara territory.

Qadhafi was an unlikely champion of Pan-Africanism. He had long been associated with the Middle East and with the drive for Arab unity, as well as with alleged terrorist acts. In recent years, however, he set out to revive the ideal of a unified African federation with determination. That Libya should have become such a leader in the African Union—or for that matter, that Africa is even entering into a union at this point at all—is largely the result of this one man's idiosyncratic, but powerful, brand of revolution.

### Libya's Early History

Until recent history Libya had no separate identity. What is now the country of Libya had almost always been part of some other nation or empire. Even the early inhabitants, the Berbers, were allegedly foreign invaders who came to Libya in 3000 BCE. Repeated conquests followed by long periods of foreign dominance created a notable absence of internal unity in Libya.

The foreign influences differed within Libya, which is comprised of three regions—Tripolitania, Cyrenica, and Fezzan—each cut off from the others by desert. Tripolitania province has always looked seaward and north for trade and cultural ties with Europe. Cyrenica province has always looked east for trade and cultural ties with Egypt and the Arab world. The Fezzan province looks south to Africa. Before the 1969 revolution these provinces looked outward more than inward.

Of all Libya's invaders, however, the Arabs had the most enduring influence by grafting their religion onto Libyan culture. Libyan culture is held together by Islam. The Arabs invaded Libya in waves beginning in the Middle Ages, intermarrying and trading with the resident Berber families. In this way Islam spread and the Berbers became arabized. The Ottoman Turks conquered the country in the sixteenth century and after that Libya remained, at least nominally, a part of the Ottoman Empire until the early twentieth century.

Beginning in the nineteenth century the Sanusiya movement unified eastern Libya. This was a movement dedicated to purifying and reforming Muslims and leading them back to a simple community of faith ruled by just leaders. The Grand Sanusi, its founder, was from Algeria. When European colonial powers began seizing North African territory, the Sanusi became warrior-monks and fought the foreign invaders.

### Europeans in Libya

In 1911 Italy began to conquer Libya, and after World War I (1914–18) it began settling people there. The Italians met fierce resistance from the Sanusi warriors. Libyans fought hard because they believed that the Italians intended to exterminate them to make room for Italian settlers. The Italians used brutal means to suppress the resistance and treated Libyans as inferiors once in control.

Libya became the battleground during World War II (1939–45) on which German General Erwin Rommel and his Italian allies were defeated in a major turning point in the war. Libya's Grand Sanusi put the Sanusi warrior-monks under British command; thousands fought bravely and died. When the war ended the British military officers who served with Libyans supported them in their case for independence. A British military administration occupied northern Libya. The French occupied the Fezzan, and the United States built a major air base at Wheelus Field near Tripoli. After the war Italy, Russia, and France all wanted some portion of Libya under their control. The United States joined England in supporting independence for Libya under the leadership of the pro-British Grand Sanusi. In 1951, with British and American backing, the United Nations General Assembly approved independence for Libya under King Idris, the Grand Sanusi.

### Idris's Kingdom

King Idris established a constitutional monarchy, which ruled Libya from 1951 until 1969. At the time of independence, Libya was comprised of three separate provinces with different identities. For most Libyans loyalty was to one's family, clan, village, tribal confederation, and certainly to Islam, but it was not to the king or the country. Tripolitanians openly talked of abolishing the monarchy. Only the Cyrenicans strongly supported King Idris.

In 1951 the per capita income in Libya was US$30 per year. By 1960 the king had lifted the per capita income to $100 per year, but most economists considered Libya a lost cause. It depended on income from Wheelus Air Field and on foreign aid for survival. The United States Agency for International Development (USAID)

AN ENORMOUS BANNER OF MUAMMAR QADHAFI IS DISPLAYED AT A SUMMIT ON AFRICAN UNITY. QADHAFI SUPPORTS THE FORMATION OF A UNITED STATES OF AFRICA. (© *Reuters NewMedia Inc./Corbis. Reproduced by permission.*)

gave Libya $42 million each year because Libya's airfields were a vital part of U.S. Cold War strategy for containing the Soviet Union. Wheelus was Libya's largest single employer.

King Idris did not encourage political development in Libya; in fact, he outlawed all political parties, which he distrusted. This was to prove a mistake; he simply drove opposition underground. Despite his ban of parties, elections were held every four years. Only property-owning adult males could vote. The same legislators were re-elected repeatedly. Discontent brewed, and several factions began plotting coups.

### The Coup

On September 1, 1969, the charismatic and mercurial young Qadhafi engineered a military coup in which a group of about 70 military officers under his direction deposed King Idris. It was a bloodless coup, readily accepted by most of the Libyan population. After the coup, Qadhafi, then a captain in the military, announced to Libyans

## Excerpt from a Speech by President Nelson Mandela at a Banquet Hosted by Colonel Qadhafi

South African president Nelson Mandela offered his support to Qadhafi in a speech in Libya on October 22, 1997. At the time, Libya was under a United Nations-sponsored air embargo, which Mandela ignored in order to travel to Libya. The full text of the speech is available through the Office of the President: African National Congress. Entitled "Mandela Speaks," it is located on the World Wide Web at http://www.anc.org.za/ancdocs/history/mandela/1997/sp1022.html (cited February 1, 2002).

> Our visit to your country, brief as it has had to be, has proved a moving experience. The people of Libya shared the trenches with us in our struggle for freedom. You were in the front ranks of those whose selfless and practical support helped assure a victory that was as much yours as it is ours....
>
> The suffering of the people of any single country affects all of us no matter where we find ourselves. That is why it is so important that multilateral bodies assume collective responsibility for finding fair and just solutions to problems in the world, taking into account equally the considerations of the weak and the mighty; the rich and the poor; developed and developing nations alike.
>
> As Africans, especially as those who have benefited from African solidarity, we cannot be unmoved by the plight of African brothers. We should all redouble our efforts to have Africa's collective voice heard in the councils of the world in finding such fair, just and even-handed solutions.
>
> We look forward keenly to the time when this great country can again take its rightful place in the community of nations....
>
> We ... share, as a priority, the welfare and development of the continent of Africa. This should indeed be so, as this is our continent; as we are the children of Africa.

over the radio, "People of Libya . . . your armed forces have undertaken the overthrow of the reactionary and corrupt regime . . . . From now on Libya is a free, sovereign republic, ascending with God's help to exalted heights."

For a time after the coup the Revolutionary Command Council (RCC) governed, with Qadhafi serving as the de facto head of Libya. Islam was proclaimed the nation's state religion. Though the new leadership espoused a form of Arab socialism based on Islamic principles, it utterly rejected communism as atheistic. Among the first acts of the new government was to request the United States and Britain to remove their

troops from the country. The Americans complied by June 1970.

### The Revolutionary Un-Leader

Qadhafi said from the beginning that Libya would not be governed by an individual leader, but rather by the people. In 1973 he initiated a popular revolution, beginning by redistributing some of the country's oil wealth among the largest possible number of Libyans. He also provided Libyans with many social services. Industry in Libya began to thrive, with many new plants and factories opening.

With Libya prospering Qadhafi took some time away from actively governing to work on his revolutionary theory, which he called the Third Universal Theory. Set out in his two-volume *The Green Book* (1976 and 1978), the Third Universal Theory is an attempt to get beyond communism and capitalism, to find a natural form of socialism and direct democracy. It was his idea to place government, business, and military in the hands of the people. Qadhafi sought to make "workers partners in their enterprise [and] to give them a voice in management and control of their work." He encouraged Libyans to take over the companies they worked for. He also urged that they take over the organs of the government and to form people's committees for local rule. In 1977 the General People's Committee (GPC) proclaimed the new Socialist People's Libyan Arab Jamahiriya (the official name of the country: Jamahiriya can be translated roughly as "state of the masses" or "people's government").

To meet the rising movement toward Islamic fundamentalism and the ideal of a pure Islamic state, Qadhafi empowered the General People's Committee to apply *sharia,* or Islamic law, for marriage and divorce, wills and inheritance, crimes of theft and violence, and apostasy, meaning renunciation of faith in Islam. Despite this adherence to Muslim traditions, Qadhafi avidly supported women's rights. His social welfare programs offered free medical care, free education, and low-cost housing. Libya in Qadhafi's early days prospered well beyond expectations, largely because of its oil resources.

Libya is the largest producer of oil in Africa and one of the largest producers in the world. In the past few decades, oil income has transformed Libya from a poor nation into a rapidly developing nation, with one of the highest per capita incomes in Africa. The Libyan economy is still very vulnerable to price fluctuations, since the country does not have substantial agriculture or industry to sus-

# MUAMMAR ABU MINYAR AL-QADHAFI

*1942–* Muammar Qadhafi was born in Sirte, Libya, in 1942, the son of a poor Berber family. His political views began to take shape while he was in his teens, attending school in the Fezzan province. Great changes were taking place at that time in Egypt, where Gamal Abel Nasser, the Egyptian president, was calling for Arab unity. Inspired by the ideas and political actions of Nasser, Qadhafi organized student demonstrations in Libya. He was expelled from school but continued his education near Tripoli while organizing a secret revolutionary movement. After graduation in 1963, Qadhafi joined the Military Academy in Benghazi and helped to create the nucleus of the Free Unionist Officers Movement, an organization aimed at overthrowing Libyan King Idris and taking over power in the country.

After graduating from the Military Academy in 1965, Qadhafi was sent to an army school in Britain. On his return to Libya he enrolled at the University of Benghazi and majored in history. Commissioned in the army in 1966, he never finished his studies.

On September 1, 1969, Qadhafi instructed a group of young officers to seize power of Libya. After a bloodless coup, he proclaimed the Libyan Arab Republic. On September 10 Qadhafi was named the president of the Revolutionary Command Council (RCC), the chief organ of the new regime.

Qadhafi's first years in power were remarkable for his persistent attempts to bring about the union of Arab countries. Despite his enthusiasm, Qadhafi failed to achieve Arab unity, and went on to work out his political theory, an unusual blend of Islamic fundamentalism and socialism. *The Green Book* appeared in 1976, which advocated some drastic political and economic policies, in which Libyan workers were encouraged to take over the businesses they worked for and citizens were to take over local governments.

Between 1980 and 1987 oil prices fell. Economic and transportation sanctions on Libya were imposed by the United States and the United Nations for Qadhafi's alleged involvement with international terrorist groups. Libya's economy eroded quickly. By 1988 there was

LIBYAN LEADER COL. MUAMMAR QADHAFI AND THEN SOUTH AFRICAN PRESIDENT NELSON MANDELA STAND TOGETHER IN A POSE OF UNITY. SOUTH AFRICA AND LIBYA ARE BOTH MEMBERS OF THE ORGANIZATION OF AFRICAN UNITY. *(A/P Wide World. Reproduced by permission.)*

strong opposition to Qadhafi's policies and there were many attempts to overthrow him. To survive politically Qadhafi began to change course. In 1988–89 he set free a number of political prisoners and invited members of the opposition living abroad to come home.

As acts of international terrorism became more frequent in 1980s, Qadhafi was perceived to be the source of training and financing of such activities. In 1986 the United States carried out a retaliatory bombing raid on Libya, killing nearly 100 people. Qadhafi claimed that he was innocent and said that one of his children had been killed during the raid. But the United States and the UN continued to isolate the leader and his country for many years. In the late 1990s, Qadhafi altered international perceptions of him to some degree when he began to appear on the scene once again as a leading proponent of African Unity.

tain it during times of low oil prices. In the 1970s, with the greatly increased income brought in by oil, many Libyans revered Qadhafi as the leader who ushered in an era of unprecedented prosperity.

In 1980 oil prices began to fall. Throughout the decade Libya's economy deteriorated. By the mid-1980s the government began to expel tens of thousands of foreign workers, whom it could no longer pay. In 1984 opposition to Qadhafi within Libya grew. There was a coup attempt against him that he managed to stop. Qadhafi's reprisals were very harsh. Thousands were imprisoned and many were executed. Since that time he has periodically called for the death of his opponents who have fled to other countries.

Since the 1970s Qadhafi had been accused by the West of harboring terrorist groups in Libya. In 1986, when an explosion in a German discotheque killed two American soldiers, the United States retaliated against Libya with air strikes near Tripoli and Benghazi. During this time Libya was in intermittent war with Chad. These were not good times for Libyans and many grew discontent with their leader. By 1988 Qadhafi began to reverse the harshest of his policies and released political prisoners. But he began to severely oppress Islamic fundamentalists in Libya, believing they threatened his power base. He held onto power despite opposition.

## Arab Unity

In his first years as a leader in Libya, Qadhafi took a very active role in Arab affairs, and was the foremost champion of Arab unity in the Middle East. He advocated a single military, legal system, business infrastructure, and foreign policy for all Arab nations. Most Arab leaders in the early 1970s did not believe there was much possibility that the nations of the Middle East would put aside differences to join in one union, at least not without years of preparation and change. Qadhafi, though, was determined. He even offered his own country to be the first to give up its individual borders and identity, to join with Egypt as the start of a league of Arab nations.

Qadhafi was deeply devoted to the support of Palestinians in their struggles against Israel. He worked to undermine Arab leaders he considered "reactionary," unfriendly, or undemocratic, and particularly those who were willing to negotiate with the Israelis. Although he had worked on Arab unity issues with Egyptian President Anwar Sadat (1918–81), after Sadat forged a peace treaty with Israel in 1978–79, Qadhafi began to organize other Arab nations in opposition to Sadat and Egypt. Qadhafi did not believe that any Arab nation should negotiate with the Israelis.

Qadhafi then tried regional unions with Arab countries. His attempt at union with Morocco ended in 1984 when Qadhafi accused Morrocan King Hassan II of "Arab treason" for meeting with Israel's Prime Minister Shimon Peres. He tried a union with Algeria, but this too failed. In 1988

Libya joined the Arab Maghreb Union that linked Mauritania, Morocco, Algeria, Tunisia, and Libya in a grouping modeled on the European Union.

At the same time that he was pressing for Arab unity, however, Qadhafi was working against it. He funded various groups throughout the Middle East that were planning coups in Arab countries, setting up guerrilla armies, or even conspiring to assassinate other leaders that Qadhafi wanted out of the way.

## From Arab Unity to African Unity

In 1988 an explosion on Pan Am Flight 103 flying over Lockerbie, Scotland, claimed the lives of 259 passengers and crew and 11 people on the ground. The United States imposed sanctions on Libya, calling the nation the "prime suspect" in the bombing. The UN then imposed an air embargo on Libya. Western sanctions crippled Libya's economy and blighted the everyday lives of ordinary Libyans. To Qadhafi's horror, other Arab nations willingly upheld the UN embargo, despite his call to disregard it. Many African leaders, however, did violate the embargo and visited Libya in defiance of it, risking severe consequences. In 1997, despite strenuous U.S. objections, South African President Nelson Mandela visited Qadhafi in Libya and publicly expressed his appreciation of Qadhafi's support in the fight against apartheid in South Africa. At an OAU summit meeting the next year, African leaders decided to ignore the UN air embargo on Libya.

In the late 1990s Qadhafi began to distance himself from his former Arab allies and grew closer to his new African allies. Qadhafi declared in 1997 that Libya was African and no longer part of the Arab world. Shortly afterward, the Libyan leader began his push for the creation of the African Union. After years of isolation from the international stage, he came back to the fore with a whole new set of issues on behalf of another continent. Libya, once offered up as a pawn in the quest for Arab unity, was suddenly thrust into a new role as a potential leader of a united Africa.

## The African Leader

As Qadhafi re-entered the international spotlight, it was clear to all that he wished to change his image considerably. He began by turning over the suspects in the Lockerbie explosion for trial. He became a prominent advocate of peace in Africa. In an interview with the French newspaper *Le Figaro*, quoted in a *BBC News* article, he said that for Africa: "the time for wars is over.... An army is costly and has nothing to do but

# CONSTITUTIVE ACT OF THE AFRICAN UNION, ARTICLES 2–4

The Constitutive Act of the African Union was adopted in Lomé, Togo, on July 11, 2000. The act required ratification by a two-thirds majority of member nations. The 36th and final ratification was entered on April 26, 2001, and the Constitutive Act was entered into force on May 26, 2001, establishing the African Union. At the July 2001 Lusaka Summit the OAU Secretary-General announced that all member states had signed, and that the number of countries that had ratified the act had reached 51 in total.

Thirty-three articles comprise the Constitutive Act of the African Union, which sets forth guidelines for the establishment and government of the Union. A summary of the contents of Articles 2–4 follows.

Article 2 explicitly establishes the African Union. The remainder of the articles outline various issues common to most constitutions such as objectives, procedures, and legislative processes to which the member states of the African Union will adhere, as well as setting forth the ruling bodies of the African Union.

Article 3 describes the objectives of the African Union. There are fourteen objectives outlined within Article 3. The African Union seeks to unify the countries and people of the continent of Africa and protect the boundaries and independence of each of the member nations. Article 3 also addresses unity in common interests within the continent and the promotion of political and economic integration of African countries. International relations are also addressed, as Article 3 proposes cooperation with such international agreements as the Charter of the United Nations and the Universal Declaration of Human Rights. In accord with these agreements the African Union seeks to further the cause peace and security within Africa, encourage governments to adhere to democratic ideals, such as citizen participation in government, and the defense of human rights.

Economic issues are also a focus of Article 3, which sets forth the intention of improving Africa's economic standing on a global level through development and integration of the continent, improving the standard of living, and coordinating of the policies of the Regional Economic Communities within Africa to assure the realization of the economic goals established in the Constitutive Act. The article also declares that the African Union will work with international bodies in improving the health of Africans and encourage research to advance science and technology. In essence Article 3 lays out the African Union's plan for improving African society.

With the establishment and objectives of the African Union firmly in place, Article 4 delineates the principles of the African Union. The majority of the principles address mutual cooperation and peace among the member nations. The respect of boundaries, non-intrusion in the internal affairs of one member nation by another, and peaceful solutions to conflict between member nations are all laid out within Article 4. A policy of non-aggression is also included.

The African Union also establishes its ability to function as a peacekeeping force if asked by a member nation or if it is deemed that a conflict cannot be solved without the African Union's intervention. The article also reiterates the objectives of human rights and equality laid out in Article 3, specifically referring to gender equality, promotion of democracy and social justice, respect for human life, and denunciation of terrorism and other acts against humanity.

Through the Constitutive Act, the African Union apparently is attempting to bring the continent of Africa together as one community and align itself with international bodies such as the European Union and the United Nations in the hopes of improving and advancing the interests of the African people.

---

coups. As for me, if a neighboring state wants to invade Libya, I'll scatter flowers on its way. Let it come to help me face Libya's problems." He worked rigorously with other African leaders to hasten the end of violent conflict in the Democratic Republic of the Congo, in the war between Ethiopia and Eritrea, and in the many civil wars that plagued Africa. Qadhafi was suc-

cessful in changing the way he was viewed in Europe, and the UN sanctions were removed.

Beginning in 1997 Qadhafi began his all-out campaign for the African Union, skillfully courting the nations of Africa to drum up support for the idea. He was quite successful in his campaign, due in part to his charismatic presence and in part

A BILLBOARD SUPPORTING AFRICAN UNITY IS INSTALLED IN SIRTE, LIBYA, IN PREPARATION FOR A TWO-DAY SUMMIT OF THE ORGANIZATION OF AFRICAN UNITY, MADE UP OF 40 AFRICAN HEADS OF STATE, IN FEBRUARY 2001. (© *AFP/Corbis. Reproduced by permission.*)

to his financial backing. He used his nation's oil resources to sponsor the summit of the Organization of African Unity and to pay a significant part of the back OAU membership dues owed by several of the poorer African countries. Part of his promise was to open his own country's doors to Africans who wished to work there. He eased travel and visa requirements in Libya accordingly.

## Libya Reacts to the New African Immigrant Population

For several years, hundreds of thousands of Africans flocked to Libya annually to find work. By the year 2000 an estimated one million (some estimates have claimed the number exceeded two million) African immigrants resided in the country, coming in primarily from Nigeria, Ghana, Chad, Niger, Gambia, and Sudan. Libya's population had only been 5 million to start, so the newcomers presented a significant population change; trouble soon began to brew. Unemployment rose to 30 percent and crime and drug trafficking erupted in a country where they had been almost nonexistent. An article in the *Economist* summarizes the bitterness and hostility that arose among the native Libyans. Noting that anti-black violence was on the rise and given impetus by Libya's economic crisis that made times harsh for the gen-

eral public while the country's oil business drew in $11 billion, the article stated that "… Libyans, feeding their families on monthly salaries of $170, see the money squandered on foreign adventures, the latest of which is the colonel's pan-African policy. As billions flowed out in aid, and visa-less migrants flowed in, Libyans feared they were being turned into a minority in their own land."

In 2000, with growing pressure from the Libyan people, the government in Libya decided to crack down on the employment of foreigners and even to forcibly deport them. Many Africans were gathered as "illegal immigrants" and placed in detention centers. In September 2000, newspapers reported that 130 Africans in Libya had been killed in street violence. Thousands more were injured and forced from their homes. The *Economist* reported the experience of Nigerian welder Emeka Nwanko, "one of hundreds of thousands of black victims of the Libyan mob. He fled as gangs trashed his workshop. His friend was blinded, as Libyan gangs wielding machetes roamed the African townships. Bodies were hacked and dumped on motorways. A Chadian diplomat was lynched and Niger's embassy was put to the torch."

The Libyan government said the reports of violence were exaggerated and that only four people were dead. But before the anti-African violence there had been about a million Africans in Libya, and afterwards there were very few to be seen. Libya deported hundreds of thousands of Africans (unfairly blaming them for the violence) and held thousands more in detention camps, nominally for their own protection. Ghana's President Jerry Rawlings, concerned for the safety of Ghanaians in Libya, flew to Tripoli in early October to see what was going on with his countrymen who were being held in a detention camp. He brought 250 Ghanaians home with him that day.

For Qadhafi the attacks on African immigrants must have been the source of embarrassment in view of his Pan-African mission. He tried to blame the attacks on outsiders who wanted to damage his African unity campaign. But those who fled Libya told quite a different story. They said they had been attacked by youth gangs and that they believed the Libyan state forces were behind the attacks. They had experienced a great deal of hostility from Libyans before being attacked and forced to leave. In the end Qadhafi agreed to pay $20 million in retribution to ten thousand of the Africans who were deported. Unfortunately, many of the deportees never received the money and believe their governments pocketed it. Some of the African governments, notably Nigeria, wished to remain in Qadhafi's favor and have played down the incident.

# RECENT HISTORY AND THE FUTURE

## The Advantages of the African Union

Qadhafi's plan to go ahead with the African Union was not spoiled by the violence in Libya, and it appears in 2001 that the overall mission he pushed through could be beneficial to Africa on a number of different fronts. The economics of a large unified region are stronger than those of many small, poverty-ridden countries. It will be more effective to fight the AIDS/HIV epidemic and save millions of lives as a unified base. There is also the fact that 15 of the 53 countries of Africa are at war. While at war, Africa cannot advance economically or otherwise. An all-African peacekeeping force could intervene in these wars, restoring peace and settling ethnic conflicts without recourse to the United States or the United Nations. Qadhafi feels that if only for this reason, the United States should support the African Union, in order to avoid future U.S. or UN casualties.

In 1994 many African leaders were infuriated when the OAU stood by helplessly while 800,000 Tutsi were slaughtered by the Hutu majority in Rwanda, despite the fact that there had been advance warning of the genocidal plans. While a mere ten thousand African troops could probably have prevented the slaughter of innocent people, the old OAU rules tied the hands of those who wanted to act. The OAU had no army, no money, and no mandate to intervene in the affairs of member nations. Its main objective was to liberate the continent of Africa, a worthy goal that has been achieved. The president of the OAU was a figurehead. The president of the AU, on the other hand, will have the power to intervene with a continent-wide army as well as a mandate to act on behalf of Africa.

In a world headed toward increasing globalization the AU makes good sense economically. Small banks are merging with larger ones everywhere, so why not create a continent-wide financial institution? Just as Europe now has the euro, a new currency, Africa will also have a single currency, which will make it easier and cheaper to do business across the entire continent. There are 680,000,000 people in Africa, forming a huge and potentially lucrative market for African products.

It will not be easy for powerful heads of state in the individual nations of Africa to sacrifice power, prestige, and influence for the sake of the continent. Will African nations put aside their current power structures and alliances to rally to the banner of the African Union?

## Where Will This Lead?

Qadhafi has an impulsive and whimsical personality. He seized power in a military coup d'état in 1969 and began to attempt to play a role in international relations. Clearly wanting to cast himself as a major world actor, he turned to the Arab world and tried to unite all Arabs behind him. After this failed he shifted his attention to Africa, where he now uses diplomacy and economic leverage to act as a regional power. The 1999 African summit at Sirte was his first foray into this new area. After 30 years of experimentation and impractical political theories Qadhafi has, at least temporarily and in some place, achieved some success in remaking himself as a regional statesman. It should be noted, however, that his position in his own nation of Libya is somewhat precarious, with a strong Islamic movement opposing him. In Libya Qadhafi is under fire for his oppression of the Islamists and has been the target of several assassination attempts in the late 1990s.

Qadhafi's dream of a future United States of Africa faces many obstacles, not the least of which is the prevailing image of Qadhafi himself as a troublemaker and manipulator, not to mention the quixotic world revolutionary leader. He will also need to overcome the doubts that were cast when his own nation, Libya, rose up to attack the African immigrants he invited to his country as a part of his Pan-African campaign. Qadhafi has the capacity to make changes for the good in Africa. Suspicions about his motivations linger internationally and can only be dispelled if he stays the course.

# BIBLIOGRAPHY

Abdrabboh, Bob, ed. *Libya in the 1980's: Challenges and Changes.* Washington, DC: International Economics and Research Incorporated, 1985.

"African Development Forum to Focus on Defining Priorities for Regional Integration." *Addis Tribune* (Addis Ababa), August 6, 2001, pp. 1–2. Available online at http://allafrica.com/stories/200108060153 .html. (cited January 11, 2002).

"African Summit Closes; No Union Yet," *BBC News, World: Africa,* p. 1. Available online at http://news .bbc.co.uk/hi/english/world/africa/newsid_1198000/1 198337.stm. (cited November 5, 2001).

"African Union Established in a Historic Summit," *Middle East News Online Reporter,* March 2, 2001, pp. 1–2. Available online at http://www.middleeastwire.com/ newswire/stories/20010302_2_memo.shtml (cited January 11, 2002).

Aidi, Hisham, "Libyans Are Africans: Race and Identity in North Africa." Africana.com. Available online at http://www.africana.com/DailyArticles/index_ 20001102.htm (cited November 30, 2001).

Ajaja, Dele. "Beware of Ghadafi." *Africa News,* August 3, 2000.

Al-Kurdi, Husayn, "Why America Hates Qadhafi," Mathaba.Net. Available online at http://mathaba.net/ info/kurdi/htm (cited January 11, 2001).

Bearman, Jonathan. *Qadhafi's Libya.* New Jersey: Zed Books, 1986.

Castle, Stephen. "EU Leaders Seek Talks with Gaddafi at Africa Summit." *The Independent* (London), March 29, 2000, p. 15.

Constitutive Act of the African Union, Organization of African Unity. Available online at http://www .oau-oua.org/LOME2000/Africa%20Union %20Constitutive%20Act%20ENG.htm (cited January 11, 2001).

Cooley, John. *Libyan Sandstorm: The Complete Account of Qadhafi's Revolution.* New York: Holt, Rinehart, and Winston, 1982.

Dawoud, Khaled, "Gaddafi Hopes Africa–E.U. Summit to End Isolation," *Deutsche Presse-Agenteur,* April 3, 2000.

Ejime, Paul, "African Union Proclaimed," *Panafrican News Agency,* March 2, 2001. Available online at http:// allafrica.com/stories/200103020362.html (cited January 11, 2001).

El-Khawas, Mohamed A. *Qaddafi: His Ideology in Theory and Practice.* Beltsville, MD: Amana Books, 1986.

"Ethiopia Ratifies Constitutive Act of African Union," *Xinhuanet,* Xinhua News Service, August 6, 2001, p 1. Available online at http://news.xinhuanet.com/ english/20010314/384890.htm (cited January 11, 2001).

Fisk, Robert, "Profile: Moammar Gaddafi—A Very Weird Leader." *The Independent* (London), August 20, 2000, p. 5.

Graves, David, "West Should Pay Us for Sanctions, Says Gaddafi." *The Daily Telegraph* (London), February 1, 2001, p 6.

Gumede, William Mervin, "Mbeki Moves to Steer Union Out of Gaddafi's Clutches," *Financial Mail* (South Africa), April 27, 2001, p. 32.

Harris, Lilllian Craig. *Libya: Qadhafi's Revolution and the Modern State.* Boulder, CO: Westview Press, 1986.

Hawley, Caroline, "Gaddafi Comes Back in from the Diplomatic Cold." *The Independent* (London), December 1, 1999, p. 16.

IMF. *African Development Indicators, 2000.* Washington, DC: International Bank for Reconstruction and Development, IMF Publication, 2000.

Jehl, Douglas, "Libya's Maverick Leader, 30 Years in Power, Makes a Bid for Respectability," *The New York Times,* September 6, 1999, p. 10.

Lemarchand, Rene. *The Green and the Black: Qadhafi's Policies in Africa,* Bloomington: Indiana University Press, 1988.

"Libya" Ethnologue.com. Available online at http://www.sil.org/ethnologue/countries/Liby.html (cited November 5, 2001).

"Libya," *The World Factbook,* Central Intelligence Agency (CIA). Available online at http://www.cia.gov/cia/ publications/factbook/geos/ly.html (cited November 7, 2001).

Lyons, Patrick, "Gaddafi's African Unity Is a Fraud, Part I: Could Africa Really Unite Under a Man Who Says Black People Are 'Backwards?'" *Arab Culture,* pp. 1–4. Available online at http://arabculture.about.com/ library/weekly/aa073001a.htm (cited January 11, 2001).

———, "Gaddafi's African Union Is a Fraud, Part II: Would You Trust This Man with Nukes?" *Arab Culture,* pp. 1–3. Available online at http://arabcul- ture.about.com/library/weekly/aa073001b.htm (cited January 11, 2001).

MacLeod, Scott, "A New Dawn for Africa?" *Time,* March 2, 2001. Available online at http://www.time.com/ time/world/article/0,8599,101184,00.html (cited November 3, 2001).

———, "Welcome to the USA." *Time Europe,* March 12, 2001, Vol. 157, No. 10, pp. 1–3. Available online at http://www.time.com/europe/af/magazine/

0%2C9868%2C101319%2C00.html (cited November 3, 2001).

"Mandela Speaks," Office of the President: African National Congress. Available online at http://www.anc.org.za/ancdocs/history/mandela/1997/sp1022.html (cited November 5, 2001).

Mudzengi, Earnest, and Paul Nyakazeya, "United States of Africa: A Pipedream?" *Africa News*, July 30, 2000.

Mupuchi, Speedwell, "AU Cannot Succeed Without Peace," *The Post* (Lusaka), August 6, 2001, pp. 1–2. Available online at http://allafrica.com/stories/200108060137.html (January 11, 2001).

Nkrumah, Kwame. *Africa Must Unite*. London: Panaf, 1963.

———. *Revolutionary Path*. London: Panaf, 1973.

"North Africa: Sweet Unity." *Economist*, July 16, 1988, Vol. 308, No. 7559, pp. 38–42.

Osman, Khalil, "Qaddafi Makes Slow Progress Towards a Pan-African Confederation," *Crescent International*, March 16, 2001, pp. 1–4. Available online at http://www.middleeatwire.com/commentary/stories/20010316_6_meno.shtml (cited January 11, 2001).

"Pogrom," *Economist*, October 12, 2000.

Peterson, Scott, "Qaddafi's New Role as Peacemaker," *Christian Science Monitor*. September 21, 1999, p 6.

Quist-Arcton, Ofeibea "From OAU to AU—Whither Africa?" Available online at http://allAfrica.com (cited January 11, 2002).

Reuters, "Leaders Agree to An African Union," CBS News Reuters, pp. 1–2. Available online at http://cbsnews.com/now/story/)%2C1597%2C214554-412%2C00.shtml (cited January 11, 2002).

Sadler, A., and Paul Winter, eds. *Urban Terrorism*. San Diego, CA: Greenhaven Press, 1996.

Simons, Geoff. *Libya: The Struggle for Survival*. London: Macmillan, 1996.

Spencer, William. *The Middle East: Global Studies*. Guilford, CN: Dushkin/Mcgraw-Hill, 2000.

*Statistical Yearbook: Forty-Fourth Edition*. Paris: UNESCO, 2000.

Takeyh, Ray, "The Rogue Who Came in From the Cold," *Foreign Affairs*, May 2001, p. 62.

Teng, Fan Yew. *The Continuing Terror Against Libya*. Kuala Lumpur: Egret Publications, 1993.

UNESCO. *1999 Statistical Yearbook*. Lanham: UNESCO Publishing, 1999.

"Zimbabwe Ratifies Act of African Union." *China News Service*. March 2, 2001, pp. 1–2. Available online at http://www.chinatopnews.com/xh/-03-0DAAxHaWtJ.html (cited January 11, 2002).

*Dallas L. Browne*

# THE LOCKERBIE TRIAL ON TRIAL: WAS JUSTICE SERVED?

## THE CONFLICT

When Pan Am Flight 103 exploded over Lockerbie, Scotland, in 1988, the United States and the United Kingdom joined forces to track down the guilty parties. They determined that two Libyan men were responsible and ordered Colonel Qadhafi, the leader of Libya, to turn them over to be tried in the United States or the United Kingdom. When he refused, sanctions were instituted against Libya by the United Nations Security Council, despite Libya's attempt to gain protection from the International Court of Justice. Almost 12 years after the crash, a compromise deal was reached and the suspects brought to trial in a neutral location (the Netherlands). Nonetheless, questions continue to linger about the case and the way it was handled.

### Political

- Libya, the United States and the United Kingdom all claimed jurisdiction over the investigation. Libya, because the suspects were Libyan nationals; the United States, because the majority of the crash victims were American and the plane was registered in the United States; and the United Kingdom because the crash occurred in that country.

- Some argue that the distinction between law and politics became blurred in the drive to bring the Lockerbie suspects to trial.

### Economic

- Libya maintains that the extensive economic and political sanctions imposed by the United Nations have brought about significant harm to the country as a whole.

The trial of the two Libyan men accused of bombing Pan Am Flight 103 began on May 3, 2000. Over the course of the following nine months, the prosecution sought to prove that Abdelbaset Ali Mohmed al Megrahi and Al Amin Khalifa Fhimah were guilty of infiltrating a suitcase containing a bomb onto Air Malta Flight KM180 out of Luqa Airport, Malta. The suitcase traveled, unaccompanied, from Malta to Frankfurt, then from Frankfurt to London, and finally onto the ill-fated Pan Am flight from London to New York City, which exploded over Lockerbie, Scotland on December 21, 1988.

The fact that this was no ordinary trial is undeniable. It was held in Camp Zeist, a former U.S. Air Force base in the Netherlands, yet was presided over by a panel of three Scottish judges. The material presented at the proceedings was the result of a vast investigation involving police forces from both sides of the Atlantic Ocean. The trial itself was the culmination of 12 years of legal and political maneuvering by the governments of the United States, the United Kingdom (UK), and Libya, among others. The United Nations Security Council and the International Court of Justice (also known as the World Court) became actively involved in the case, coming into potential conflict with each other. Extensive and controversial sanctions were imposed on Libya by the United Nations in an effort to force it to turn over the two suspects for trial.

As a whole, the case provides a window into the complex world of international law and politics, and the possibilities and pitfalls awaiting any attempt to bring international crimes to justice. Even now, with the trial concluded and the sanctions suspended, questions remain about the case

# CHRONOLOGY

*December 21, 1988* Pan Am Flight 103 explodes over Lockerbie, Scotland, killing 259 passengers and crew, as well as 11 Lockerbie residents.

*September 19, 1989* French UTA Flight 772 explodes over Niger.

*November 14, 1991* The United States and the United Kingdom issue an indictment against two Libyan men.

*November 27, 1991* The United States and the United Kingdom issue a joint statement calling on Libya to surrender the two accused men for trial in Scotland or the United States. Libya refuses to give up the suspects, announcing instead that it was placing them under house arrest.

*January 21, 1992* The UN Security Council passes Resolution 731, urging Libya to comply with U.S. and U.K demands to turn over the accused for trial.

*March 3, 1992* Libya initiates proceedings at the World Court against the United States and the United Kingdom.

*March 31, 1992* The UN Security Council passes Resolution 748, accusing Libya of threatening international peace and security.

*April 14, 1992* The World Court denies provisional measures that Libya had requested, based on the Security Council resolution.

*April 15, 1992* In accordance with Resolution 748, all members of the United Nations are called upon to enforce sanctions on Libya, including reduced diplomatic relations, an embargo on all air travel to and from Libya, and a prohibition on any arms trade with Libya.

*November 11, 1993* The UN Security Council passes Resolution 883, condemning Libya for not complying fully with the two previous resolutions. Sanctions against Libya are tightened.

*August 24, 1998* The United States and the United Kingdom agree to a trial to be held in the Netherlands.

*April 5, 1999* Two Libyan men accused of the bombing surrender for trial. The UN sanctions against Libya are suspended.

*May 3, 2000* The trial of Abdelbaset Ali Mohmed al Megrahi and Al Amin Khalifa Fhimah begins in the Netherlands.

*January 31, 2001* After 84 days of the Lockerbie trial, in which the prosecution called 232 witnesses, and at a cost of approximately $90 million, a verdict is delivered. Megrahi is found guilty of murder and Fhimah is acquitted.

and how it was handled, keeping the Lockerbie tragedy in the public eye.

## HISTORICAL BACKGROUND

### The Bombing of Flight 103

On December 21, 1988, Pan American (Pan Am) Airliner Flight 103 departed London's Heathrow airport for New York. Just over 30 minutes later, the plane plummeted to the ground, crashing into the town of Lockerbie, Scotland. All 259 passengers and crew were killed, as well as 11 Lockerbie residents. The plane was registered in the United States and the passengers were predominantly American, yet the incident had occurred in the United Kingdom. Therefore, the two countries would work closely together to prosecute the crime in the ensuing years.

A vast investigation was immediately launched in order to determine the cause of the disaster. Within a week, it was established that the plane had crashed as a result of an explosion on board. Local law enforcement officers combined forces with personnel from British and American intelligence services to sift through, catalogue, and analyze tens of thousands of pieces of debris. The aircraft itself was reconstructed from its scattered remains. By studying the type of fractures found in the structure and the remains of cargo bay containers, it was determined that the damage was caused by the detonation of an explosive device within a suitcase, which was housed in a cargo container located next to the plane's fuselage.

THE NOSE AND COCKPIT OF PAN AM FLIGHT 103 LIES IN A FIELD IN LOCKERBIE, SCOTLAND. THE PLANE, WHICH EXPLODED AS THE RESULT OF A BOMB PLANTED BY LIBYAN TERRORISTS, WAS CARRYING 259 PASSENGERS, ALL OF WHOM DIED. (© *Bryn Colton; Assignments Photographers/Corbis. Reproduced by permission*)

In a further feat of forensic and detective work, investigators were able to pinpoint exactly in which suitcase (a brown hard-shell Samsonite) the bomb had been placed, based on the type and amount of damage to it. They also uncovered that the charge for the explosion had been hidden inside a Toshiba radio cassette player in that suitcase. Finally, they figured out what clothes had likely been in the suitcase, based on how burnt they were, and the fact that they had pieces of the explosive device and the suitcase's inner partition imbedded in them.

Even as these specifics—which would prove essential to the trial 12 years later—were being worked out, other questions continued to be hotly debated. Who had committed this act of international terrorism, and why had they done it?

At the outset, suspicion focused on the governments of Iran and Syria. Many believed that the bombing was carried out by the Popular Front for the Liberation of Palestine-General Command (PFLP-GC), an Iranian-backed Syrian-based terrorist group. It was argued that the bombing was in retaliation for the accidental destruction of an Iranian passenger plane by a U.S. Navy warship, the USS *Vincennes*, in July 1988. The ship, on duty in the Persian Gulf, mistakenly believed that the plane was an F-14 fighter and shot it down, killing all 290 on board. While, as will be seen, many continue to believe this version of events, official American and British suspicion switched to Libya.

As Walter Laqueur explains in *The New Terrorism*, Libya, under Colonel Muammar al-Qadhafi, was one of the leading sponsors of international terrorism throughout the 1970s and 1980s. Support—in the form of both money and training—was given "primarily to Arab terrorist groups, but also to a variety of Central and West African groups, and eventually to terrorists from Ireland to the Philippines." Libya also sponsored terrorist attacks against Libyan political emigrants, American and European targets, and moderate Arab states. In April 1986 La Belle Discotheque in Berlin (known to be frequented by American military personnel) was bombed, killing three, including two American soldiers, and injuring more than 200. In response to this and other terrorist attacks believed to have been perpetrated by Qadhafi's regime, the United States launched an air strike against targets in Libya (including the capital, Tripoli). Thirty-seven died as a result of the U.S. bombing raid, reportedly including Qadhafi's adopted child.

In his book *Inside Terrorism*, Bruce Hoffman argues that, "far from stopping Libyan-backed terrorism, the U.S. air strike goaded the Libyan dictator to undertake even more serious and heinous acts of terrorism against the United States and its citizens. Indeed, after a brief lull, Libya not only resumed but actually increased its international terrorist activities." Many believe that the bombing of the flight over Lockerbie was one such retaliation for the air strike.

The following year, Libya was associated with yet another downed plane. French UTA Flight 772, travelling from Brazzaville, Congo, to Paris, France, exploded over Niger in September 1989, killing all 171 on board. It was thought that Libya perpetrated the attack as part of its ongoing territorial war in Chad, where French and Libyan forces had fought repeatedly throughout the 1970s and 1980s. The similarities between this attack and the one on Pan Am Flight 103 encouraged France to join forces with the United States and the United Kingdom to pressure Libya to cooperate with the investigations and renounce terrorism.

## The Indictment

After almost three years of sifting through the evidence, on November 14, 1991, the Lord Advocate of Scotland and a Grand Jury of the United States District Court for the District of Columbia issued simultaneous indictments against Megrahi and Fhimah, who were said to be officials of Libyan Arab Airlines and part of Libya's intelligence service. Both the United States and the United Kingdom made it clear that they considered the Libyan regime directly responsible for the attack. Libya denied the charges and began its own inquiry into the accusations. This was not acceptable to the two Western governments. On November 27, the United States and the United Kingdom issued a joint statement calling on the government of Libya to "surrender for trial all those charged with the crime; and accept responsibility for the actions of Libyan officials; disclose all it knows of this crime...[and] pay appropriate compensation."

Libya refused to give up the suspects. Instead, it announced that they were being placed under house arrest and the Libyan judge in charge of the inquiry offered to work with British and American officials to review evidence and conduct an investigation. Legally, Libya was not compelled to extradite, or hand over, the two Libyan nationals. As Marcella David explains in an article in the *Harvard International Law Journal*, under international law, a country is not required to extradite its citizens unless it is obligated to do so under a relevant international agreement or through an extradition arrangement with another state. Libya had no such arrangement with either the United States or the United Kingdom.

The only international agreement relevant to the case at hand was the *Convention for the Suppression of Unlawful Acts Against the Safety of Civil Aviation* (commonly known as the "Montreal Convention"). Under this convention, extradition is only required if the law of the extraditing state allows it. Libya, however, maintained that its domestic law forbade it from extraditing its nationals under any circumstances. In such a case, the Montreal Convention requires that the state prosecute the suspects in its own courts. This is what Libya proposed to do.

## The United Nations Security Council and the International Court of Justice

Unwilling to consider the possibility of a fair trial in Libya for what they believed to be an act of state-sponsored terrorism, the United States and the United Kingdom proceeded to take an unprecedented step. With the help of France, which was busy investigating Libya's involvement in the bombing of its flight over Africa, they began to gather support within the United Nations Security Council for sanctions against Libya. Their diplomatic efforts bore fruit on January 21, 1992, when the Security Council unanimously adopted Resolution 731. The Resolution "strongly deplore[d]" Libya's noncooperation with American, British, and French requests to establish responsibility for the terrorist attacks on the Pan Am and UTA flights. It further "urge[d]" the government of Libya to "immediately provide a full and effective response to those requests so as to contribute to the elimination of international terrorism." In essence, the Security Council was stating that it supported the demand that Libya turn over the accused for trial in the United States or Scotland, and cooperate fully with the investigation.

The Resolution was noteworthy for many reasons, not the least of which was that it "... represented the first time that the Security Council had been asked to call for the extradition of the citizens of one country to stand trial in another. It also marked the first occasion that the Security Council had given implicit support to accusations of state-sponsored terrorism against a member government of the United Nations," according to Angus M. Gunn Jr. in his 1993 article "Council and Court: Prospects in *Lockerbie* for an International Rule of Law."

# CONVENTION FOR THE SUPPRESSION OF UNLAWFUL ACTS AGAINST THE SAFETY OF CIVIL AVIATION (THE MONTREAL CONVENTION)

### Article 1

- 1. Any person commits an offence if he unlawfully and intentionally. . . .

- c. places or causes to be placed on an aircraft in service, by any means whatsoever, a device or substance which is likely to destroy that aircraft, or to cause damage to it which renders it incapable of flight, or to cause damage to it which is likely to endanger its safety in flight; or. . . .

### Article 6

- 1. Upon being satisfied that the circumstances so warrant, any Contracting State in the territory of which the offender or the alleged offender is present, shall take him into custody or take other measures to ensure his presence. The custody and other measures shall be as provided in the law of that State but may only be continued for such time as is necessary to enable any criminal or extradition proceedings to be instituted.

- 2. Such State shall immediately make a preliminary enquiry into the facts. . . .

### Article 7

The Contracting State in the territory of which the alleged offender is found shall, if it does not extradite him, be obliged, without exception whatsoever and whether or not the offence was committed in its territory, to submit the case to its competent authorities for the purpose of prosecution. Those authorities shall take their decision in the same manner as in the case of any ordinary offence of a serious nature under the law of that State. . . .

### Article 8

- 1. The offences shall be deemed to be included as extraditable offences in any extradition treaty existing between Contracting States. Contracting States undertake to include the offences as extraditable offences in every extradition treaty to be concluded between them.

- 2. If a Contracting State which makes extradition conditional on the existence of a treaty receives a request for extradition from another Contracting State with which it has no extradition treaty, it may at its option consider this Convention as the legal basis for extradition in respect of the offences. Extradition shall be subject to the other conditions provided by the law of the requested State. . . .

### Article 14

- 1. Any dispute between two or more Contracting States concerning the interpretation or application of this Convention which cannot be settled through negotiation, shall, at the request of one of them, be submitted to arbitration. If within six months from the date of the request for arbitration the Parties are unable to agree on the organization of the arbitration, any one of those Parties may refer the dispute to the International Court of Justice by request in conformity with the Statute of the Court.

While the validity of Resolution 731 (and subsequent Resolutions) seems to have been accepted without question in most news reports, it rang warning bells within the legal community. In an article in the *European Journal of International Law*, Bernhard Graefrath argues that, by condemning Libya for not responding effectively to the requests for cooperation put forward by the United States and the United Kingdom (with the support of France), "... the Security Council simply decided the dispute in favor of the United States and the United Kingdom, without giving any explanation as to why Libya would be obliged to surrender its nationals or pay compensation for an act which, at that point, had not been attributed to Libya by any legal procedure." Graefrath and others have also raised questions about the legitimacy of the voting procedure (as parties to the dispute, it has been argued that the United States and the United Kingdom should have abstained from voting) and the absence of any attempt by the Security Council to work with the parties to settle the dispute by peaceful means (as the UN Charter instructs).

In February 1992 Libya responded with proposals aimed at establishing responsibility for the bombing. According to Marcella David these included allowing the suspects to be questioned at the UN offices in Tripoli and, if probable cause was found by a committee of judges chosen by the Secretary-General of the UN, turning the suspects over to be tried in a neutral state. On March 3, 1992, they took a further step and initiated a court case at the United Nations International Court of Justice (ICJ) against the United States and the United Kingdom.

As summarized in a recent *Press Communiqué* from the ICJ (September 13, 2000), the case Libya brought against the two Western countries was concerning "Questions of Interpretation and Application of the 1971 Montreal Convention arising from the Aerial Incident at Lockerbie." Libya argued, as it had from the start, that under the Montreal Convention it was allowed to try the two suspects itself, and under no obligation to extradite them. It accused the United States and the United Kingdom of breaching their obligations under the Convention by attempting to force Libya to comply with their demands and not assisting it in conducting its own investigation. Meanwhile, Libya also asked the court for "provisional measures to prevent further action by the United Kingdom and the United States to compel it to surrender the alleged offenders before any examination of the merits of the cases."

On March 31, 1992—after the Court had heard the case but before it issued a ruling—the Security Council passed Resolution 748. This resolution was far more strongly worded than the first. It stated that the failure of Libya to demonstrate in a concrete fashion that it had renounced its terrorist activities and responded to the requests in Resolution 731 constituted "a threat to international peace and security." Thus, as of April 15, all countries were called upon to enforce sanctions on Libya. These included significantly reduced diplomatic relations, an embargo on all air travel to and from Libya, and a prohibition on any arms trade with Libya.

Like the previous resolution, Resolution 748 was by no means free of controversy. As Graefrath explains, it "... was adopted even though several members expressed reservations. It was felt that the resolution was too early or hasty, that it was not really justified, that it would interfere with an ongoing Court procedure, or that it should not be passed when peaceful means had not been exhausted."

This Security Council resolution did indeed have a profound impact on the ongoing proceedings at the World Court. As Gunn recounts, on April 14 the Court ruled (by 11 votes to 5) that it was denying the provisional measures that Libya had requested. It argued that all members of the United Nations are required to comply with Security Council Resolutions. Therefore, Resolution 748 had to be carried out. If the ICJ had ruled that (based on the Montreal Convention) Libya should be protected from being forced to surrender the two accused, then it would have directly countered Resolution 748. This would have implied that obligations under an international agreement like the Montreal Convention took precedence over the obligation to carry out Security Council decisions. The UN Charter specifically states that this cannot be the case. In essence, Resolution 748 was exactly what Libya had asked the ICJ to protect it from. The fact that the Resolution was issued before the Court reached its decision effectively served to nullify the power of the Court. This has disquieting implications for the balance of power between politics and law on the international stage.

## 1992–99: Negotiations and Resolutions

The seven-year period between the original Security Council Resolutions and the eventual surrender of the suspects was marked by continued pressure on Libya to send the two men to the United States or Scotland for trial. It was obviously not completely without result. In September 1993, according to the Lockerbie Trial website set up by the University of Glasgow, Libya stated "that it has no objection to the two suspects standing trial in Scotland but that the decision is for them to take." It could not force them to go, but it was willing for them to make the decision on their own.

In October 1993, Professor Robert Black, a Scottish law professor who had become involved with the case, was present at a meeting with the two suspects and their defense team in Libya's capital, Tripoli. He described in "From Lockerbie to Zeist (via Tripoli, Tunis and Cairo)" (2000) why the accused were unwilling to stand trial in Scotland. Black stated that it was "their belief that, because of unprecedented pre-trial publicity over the years, a Scottish jury could not possibly bring to their consideration of the evidence in this case the degree of impartiality and open-mindedness that accused persons are entitled to expect and that a fair trial demands."

On November 11, 1993, the Security Council passed Resolution 883 which, while noting that

AN ARTIST'S DEPICTION OF THE COURTROOM DURING THE TRIAL OF ABDEL BASET AL MEGARAHI, LEFT, AND AL AMIN KHALIFA FHIMAH, RIGHT, TWO LIBYANS CHARGED IN THE 1988 BOMBING OVER LOCKERBIE. (© *AFP/Corbis. Reproduced by permission.*)

"Libya stated its intention to encourage those charged with the bombing of Pan Am 103 to appear for trial in Scotland and its willingness to cooperate with the competent French authorities in the case of the bombing of UTA 772," nonetheless condemned Libya for not complying fully with the two previous resolutions. Sanctions were therefore tightened, freezing Libyan financial assets abroad and prohibiting the sale of equipment for its crude oil industry.

In early 1994 Black came up with a proposal to break the deadlock. He suggested to Dr. Ibrahim Legwell, the head of the Libyan defense team, that the trial be held in a neutral location (ideally the Netherlands) under Scottish criminal law but before a panel of judges, instead of a jury as was the norm. While Legwell agreed to the plan, the British and American governments would not, stressing that the Security Council Resolution called for the trial to be held in Scotland or the United States, nowhere else.

This impasse continued relatively unchanged until 1998. In March the League of Arab States, in consultation with the Organization for African Unity and the Organization of the Islamic Conference, proposed that the trial be held in a neutral country or at the World Court with Scottish judges or at a special tribunal in The Hague. Then, finally, on August 24, the United States and the United Kingdom reversed their total opposition to the idea of a trial anywhere other than in one of their two countries and announced to the UN that they would agree to a trial by Scottish court, under Scottish law, but held in the Netherlands.

Through the intervention of Nelson Mandela, Kofi Annan (the Secretary-General of the UN), and Saudi Arabian and Egyptian officials, among others, Qadhafi and the suspects were convinced that such a trial would be both safe and fair. The two accused surrendered for trial on April 5, 1999.

### The Trial

Almost 12 years after Pan Am Flight 103 plunged from the sky, the relatives of the 270 dead finally saw somebody brought to trial. The trial of Abdelbaset Ali Mohmed al Megrahi and Al Amin Khalifa Fhimah began on May 3, 2001, with both pleading not guilty to the charges of either conspiracy to murder, murder, or contravention of the 1982 *Aviation Security Act*. From the start, the defense tried to have the conspiracy charges dropped on the grounds that the bombing was not planned in Scotland, so no conspiracy occurred there, and thus a Scottish court had no jurisdiction over this matter. The judges dismissed this argument. In the end, however, the prosecution itself dropped all charges except murder in its closing submission. This was likely done in the hope that a pared down list of charges would have a greater chance of leading to a guilty verdict.

The trial itself lasted 84 days and cost approximately $90 million. During that time, the prosecution called 232 witnesses, while the defense called only three. Of the prosecution's witnesses, one of the most damning for Megrahi was Tony Gauci, the owner of Mary's House, a clothing store in Malta. Investigators had determined that the clothes contained in the suitcase that housed the bomb had been purchased in that store. Gauci was able to identify Megrahi as being the man who bought the clothing in early December 1988.

Two other key witnesses for the prosecution provided equally damaging—but not as trustworthy—evidence. The testimony of a Libyan secret service agent, who had been providing information to the U.S. Central Intelligence Agency (CIA) since 1988 and definitively linked the two accused to the bombing, was largely discounted on the grounds that he was an unreliable witness. Similarly, the judges only conditionally accepted the evidence provided by Edwin Bollier, on the basis that his testimony was, at times, untruthful. Before the trial, it was believed that he would be the prosecution's star witness since he was the head of the Swiss electronics firm that allegedly made the circuit board for the MST-13 timer used in the bomb, and supplied it to the Libyan government.

Lawyers for the two defendants countered by blaming the Syrian-backed Popular Front for the Liberation of Palestine-General Command (PFLP-GC) and the Palestinian Popular Struggle Front (PPSF)—some of the initial suspects of the bombing—for the terrorist act. Toward the end of the proceedings, the trial was adjourned for one month while the defense attempted to procure a document from Syria that they said would have supported this counter-charge. Syria, however, refused to hand over the evidence. While the judges considered the defense's claims in their verdict, they concluded that they had no doubt, given the evidence presented, that the crime was Libyan in origin.

In the end, despite some remaining uncertainties, Megrahi (the first accused) was found guilty of murder and sentenced to life in prison in a Scottish jail, eligible for parole after 20 years.

The judges based their decision on several factors, including the clothing purchased in Malta and present in the primary suitcase, which was then conveyed from Malta to London, as well as the identification of Megrahi, his movements under a false name, and his associations with other individuals implicated in the crime. Taken together, the judges felt that these factors created a "real and convincing pattern."

In contrast, Fhimah (the second accused) was acquitted. This, despite the fact that two damning entries in his 1988 diary specifically referred to taking luggage tags from Air Malta. The prosecution maintained that these were taken for Megrahi, who used them to infiltrate the unaccompanied suitcase containing the bomb onto the Air Malta flight from Luqa to Frankfurt. Further, they argued that Fhimah had used his experience as an airline employee in Luqa to get around the security features in that airport. Interestingly, however, in their closing submission, the prosecution changed their assessment of him, accepting that he was not a member of the Libyan intelligence service, only an employee of Libyan Arab Airlines.

The judges ruled to acquit Fhimah on the grounds that, while the diaries may have allowed for "sinister inference," there was not enough acceptable evidence to support the conclusion that Fhimah was involved, particularly in regards to whether "the second accused was aware that any assistance he was giving to the first accused was in connection with a plan to destroy an aircraft by the planting of an explosive device."

## RECENT HISTORY AND THE FUTURE

### Responses to the Verdict—Libyan State Guilt

The verdict, while seemingly marking the end of a long and torturous road, raised almost as many questions as it answered. It did nothing to unequivocally prove or disprove Libyan state complicity in the terrorist act, or to bring any higher-ranking Libyan officials, including Qadhafi himself, to justice. Yet, as a relative of one of the victims stated (as quoted by Ian Black in *The Guardian*): "It was made quite clear that he [Megrahi] was acting as an agent for Libyan intelligence. That means we have to go after Libya as a state sponsor of terrorism." He is certainly not alone in this presumption. In the article, "Lockerbie: What happens next?" CNN reports that relatives of the victims continue to

# AN EXTRACT FROM UN SECURITY COUNCIL RESOLUTION 748

Determining in this context that the failure by the Libyan Government to demonstrate, by concrete actions its renunciation of terrorism and in particular its continued failure to respond fully and effectively to the requests in resolution 731 (1992), constitute a threat to international peace and security. . . .

Acting under Chapter VII of the Charter of the United Nations,

1. Decides that the Libyan Government must now comply without any further delay with paragraph 3 of resolution 731 (1992) regarding the requests contained in documents S/23306, S/23308 and S/23309;

2. Decides also that the Libyan Government must commit itself definitively to cease all forms of terrorist action and all assistance to terrorist groups and that it must promptly, by concrete actions, demonstrate its renunciation of terrorism;

3. Decides that on 15 April 1992 all States shall adopt the measures set out below, which shall apply until the Security Council decides that the Libyan Government has complied with paragraphs 1 and 2 above:

4. Decides that all States shall:

- (a) Deny permission to any aircraft to take off from, land in or overfly their territory if it is destined to land in or has taken off from the territory of Libya, unless the particular flight has been approved on grounds of significant humanitarian need. . .

- (b) Prohibit, by their nationals or from their territory, the supply of any aircraft or aircraft components to Libya. . .

5. Decides further that all States shall:

- (a) Prohibit any provision to Libya by their nationals or from their territory of arms and related material of all types. . .

- (b) Prohibit any provision to Libya by their nationals or from their territory of technical advice, assistance or training related to the provision, manufacture, maintenance, or use of the items in (a) above;

- (c) Withdraw any of their officials or agents present in Libya to advise the Libyan authorities on military matters;

6. Decides also that all States shall:

- (a) Significantly reduce the number and the level of the staff at Libyan diplomatic missions and consular posts and restrict or control the movement within their territory of all such staff who remain. . .

- (b) Prevent the operation of all Libyan Arab Airlines offices;

- (c) Take all appropriate steps to deny entry to or expel Libyan nationals who have been denied entry to or expelled from other States because of their involvement in terrorist activities;

7. Calls upon all States, including States not Members of the United Nations, and all international organizations, to act strictly in accordance with the provisions of the present resolution, notwithstanding the existence of any rights or obligations conferred or imposed by any international agreement or any contract entered into or any licence or permit granted before 15 April 1992.

campaign for justice, and the U.S. and British governments will seek monetary compensation from Libya to affected families, which could reach more than US$10 billion.

Clearly, Libya's isolation is not yet at an end. Nonetheless, the mood of the international community is changing. In August 1998, after the United States and the United Kingdom accepted that the trial could be held in the Netherlands, the UN Security Council passed Resolution 1192 stating that sanctions against Libya would be suspended when the two accused arrived in the Netherlands and "the Libyan Government has satisfied the French judicial authorities with regard to the bombing of UTA 772." On April 5, 1999, the UN sanctions against Libya were suspended because the conditions set forth in Resolution 1192 had been met.

The question that remains is whether the UN sanctions will stay in their state of suspension or be officially removed. They could also be reimposed if it is decided that Libya has not cooperated fully in the aftermath of the verdict. With many countries, however, tired of the sanctions and willing to believe that Libya is not the purveyor of terrorism it once was (and many companies eager to invest in its lucrative oil and gas trade), this would be difficult to bring about. In contrast, the United States' own unilateral sanctions against Libya (first imposed by the Reagan administration in January 1986) were extended for an additional five-year period in the summer of 2001. According to a *BBC News* report of August 4, 2001, the reasons for the extension were Libya's continued involvement in international terrorism, its drive to develop weapons of mass destruction, and its unwillingness to accept responsibility for the Lockerbie bombing and pay compensation to the relatives.

## Responses to the Verdict—A Miscarriage of Justice

While many see the verdict as simply the first stage in an all-out attack on Libyan state-sponsored terrorism, others see it as nothing more than a total miscarriage of justice. In a compelling article in the British newspaper *The Guardian* (June 27, 2001), Ian Ferguson and John Ashton argue that there has been a top-level cover-up of the real facts of the case. As was originally believed by many, they maintain that it was the Syrian-backed Popular Front for the Liberation of Palestine-General Command (PFLP-GC) that committed the bombing, hired by Iran in retaliation for the Iranian passenger plane that was shot down by the United States. This version gets more interesting (and, some might add, more fantastical) when it describes how the bomb got on the plane.

> Two PFLP-GC insiders and many western intelligence sources claim it was planted in the luggage of Khalid Jaafar, a Lebanese-American mule in a heroin trafficking operation. The whistle-blowing spooks say elements within the CIA were allowing Middle Eastern dealers to ship drugs to America in return for help in locating and releasing U.S. hostages. In allowing the suitcases containing heroin to bypass security procedures, the CIA handed the dealers' terrorist associates a failsafe means of getting the bomb on the plane.

The article goes on to suggest that Pan Am Flight 103 was targeted in part because a U.S. intelligence specialist was on board. He had found out about the CIA's open-door drug policy and was going to "blow the whistle" in Washington, so his travel plans were leaked to the terrorists.

While their arguments are mainly circumstantial, and sound at times like a spy novel rather than real life, Ferguson and Ashton are not alone in their refusal to go along with the official line of Libyan guilt. Many were surprised in 1991 when suspicion switched from Syria and Iran to Libya. At the time, it was cynically suggested that the shift had more to do with closer political ties between Syria, Iran, and the United States in the wake of the 1990 Gulf War than any proof of Libyan guilt. As for Megrahi's conviction, a high-profile international team of lawyers—including renowned U.S. criminal lawyer, Alan Dershowitz—have signed on to work on his appeal on the basis that the wrong man was convicted.

## Did the End Justify the Means?

Questions regarding the verdict are not the only ones that remain. Doubts as to the legitimacy of the process that got the accused to trial continue to linger. From a legal standpoint, it seems clear that there were definite irregularities in U.S., U.K., and Security Council actions. Two very different interpretations can be made of this, however.

One version of events is that the power of politics prevailed when international law was too weak and would have allowed a terrorist state to hide behind the letter of the law. Under this interpretation, the Security Council actions were necessary because they were the only way that the criminals could be brought to justice and terrorist activity halted. Qadhafi was negotiating in bad faith, cynically buying time with his proposals and the World Court proceeding. He "did not want to surrender the pair for fear of offending their tribes, undermining his own standing as a paragon of anti-western defiance and exposing his more unsavoury activities," summarized the April 10, 1999, *Economist*. The idea that a head of state as powerful as Qadhafi did not have enough clout to persuade two of his citizens (at least one of whom worked within his intelligence agency) to surrender themselves for trial is laughable. Thus, he was simply stalling when, in the early years of the case, he pronounced himself willing to see them tried in Scotland, but argued that he could not convince them to give themselves up.

In this version, the trial only took place because the UN sanctions forced Libya to cooperate. For that matter, as Yoram Schweitzer argues, this case should become an example for dealing with other terrorist regimes. "The primary lesson to be learned from the outcome of this tragic affair is that the only effective strategy against international terrorism—especially state-sponsored terrorism—is by means of an international coalition working in close cooperation." He goes on to say

## THE UNITED NATIONS (UN)—
## SOME BASIC FACTS

- Established October 24, 1945, by 51 countries. Today 189 countries are members—almost every country in the world.

- The **General Assembly** is "a kind of parliament of nations which meets to consider the world's most pressing problems." Every Member State of the UN—whether big or small—has one vote and decisions on "important matters" need to be agreed to by a two-thirds majority.

- The **Security Council** has primary responsibility for the maintenance of peace and security. It has 15 members—five of these (the United States, the United Kingdom, France, China, and the Russian Federation) are permanent members and (other than in votes on procedural matters) they have the right to veto any Council decision. The other 10 members are elected to the Security Council for two-year terms by the General Assembly. Council decisions require nine "yes" votes (and no veto by any of the permanent members) to pass. All Members States of the UN are required to carry out Council decisions.

- The **International Court of Justice** (World Court) is the main judicial organ of the UN. Its 15 judges are elected by the General Assembly and the Security Council. Its mandate is to decide disputes *between countries*. States can voluntarily decide whether or not to participate in a Court proceeding, but once they decide to participate, then they must comply with any decision made by the Court.

that only a coalition has the extensive means—economically and politically—to effectively deter those who would support or carry out terrorist acts.

The other perspective sees the events leading up to the trial in a very different light. In this version, there remains some uncertainty as to whether Libya—and its agents—were even responsible for the bombing. The only thing that is clear is that that country was railroaded by the United States and Britain, who used the United Nations Security Council to push through their own agenda. They did so either because they believed, in good faith, that Libya was responsible and had to be brought to justice, or as part of a wider cover-up of what

really happened. Regardless, in so doing, they weakened the very fabric of international law by not working within existing treaties to find justice and by undermining the World Court. In contrast, Qadhafi and the Libyan defense team made repeated attempts to compromise and work to discover a fair and legal way to bring the case to trial. They were rebuffed at every turn. It is this situation that Professor Black describes when he details his repeated failure to get the British government to agree to a trial in a neutral location.

### The Problems and Prospects of International Law

Of course, these are two extreme scenarios and there is little likelihood that either is completely true; the answer probably lies somewhere between the two perspectives. What is evident is that nothing is clear-cut in international law or international politics, largely because the two tend to be so closely intermingled. In this matter, it will be interesting to see what happens with the ongoing case before the World Court. Despite denying the protection of provisional measures, the Court agreed to hear the case initiated by Libya against the United Kingdom and the United States. While the trial of the two accused—the basis for the sanctions and these proceedings—has since come and gone, the case at the World Court continues. Therefore, there remains the possibility that the court could rule in Libya's favor, agreeing that American and British efforts to force Libya to extradite its citizens were in conflict with international law. Though it might seem ridiculously after the fact, this could still have far-reaching implications by calling into question the actions of the UN Security Council.

This intricate dance between law and politics most often hinges upon strongly held principles of state sovereignty—the right of countries to exclusive control over affairs within their own borders. While this principle is starting to erode in an increasingly interconnected world, states continue to hold it up as a shield to guard themselves from interference by outside powers. Without any international police force or judiciary to enforce it, international criminal law can do nothing to get around this shield. Instead, it is reliant on the cooperation of states and the international agreements they sign. Yet negotiated treaties are, by their very nature, weak instruments. They depend on compromise and the goodwill of countries for their development and execution. Thus, they are often diluted in order to gather support from the widest possible range of nations.

LIBYAN LEADER MUAMMAR QADHAFI AND AL AMIN KHALIFA FHIMAH APPEAR BEFORE THE PRESS IN TRIPOLI AFTER FHIMAH'S ACQUITTAL OF THE LOCKERBIE BOMBING CHARGES. QADHAFI CALLED THE TRIAL "POLITICAL." (© *AFP/Corbis. Reproduced by permission.*)

In this case, the United States and the United Kingdom had to depend on the cooperation of Libya to bring its citizens to trial. But Libya was not confident that a fair trial could be had in either of those countries (and the Western countries were not confident a fair trial could be held in Libya). Without a neutral international court to send the suspects to, a deadlock ensued. Libya turned to the Montreal Convention, which protected state sovereignty and state laws by not forcing a country to extradite its nationals. The United States and the United Kingdom turned to the United Nations Security Council, exerting political pressure when legal pressure was unavailable.

Another possible route was that taken by France. Unlike British and American law, French law allows trials to be held *in absentia*—without the presence of the accused or anyone representing them. After many years of investigating the 1989 bombing of the UTA flight over Niger, six Libyan secret service agents (including Qadhafi's brother-in-law) were tried in absentia, convicted, and each given life sentences in March 1999. While Qadhafi eventually awarded $25.7 million to France in compensation, he continues to deny responsibility and it seems unlikely that the six men, who remain in Libya, will ever be sent to jail. This case was resolved marginally faster than the

Lockerbie trial and compensation has already been paid, nonetheless, it is unclear whether trials in absentia are the answer to the pitfalls of international criminal justice. As the March 13, 1999, *Economist* explains, without the presence of the six accused, "no light was shed on the motive for the UTA attack. And while the life sentences may have brought some psychological relief to the families of the victims, it provided no guarantee that the court's decision will actually be carried out."

Recognizing all of these problems, the international community has been working to strengthen international criminal law. In 1998 the *Rome Statute of the International Criminal Court* (ICC) was adopted. Since then 37 of the 139 signatories have ratified it; it will be formally established once it has 60 ratifications. One of the most notable absences in making the ICC a reality is the United States, surprising given its drive to bring international criminals to justice in the Lockerbie case. In the words of Republican Senator Orrin G. Hatch (as quoted by Robin Oakley in her CNN article, "Why Not an International Court?"): "We do not like war crimes but nor do we like subjecting Americans to decisions of judges appointed by 139 nations many of whom may not like America." Many within the American administration are afraid that the creation of

A TOMBSTONE STANDS IN THE MEMORIAL GARDEN OF LOCKERBIE CEMETERY. THE MEMORIAL WAS CON-STRUCTED IN REMEMBRANCE OF THOSE WHO DIED IN THE BOMBING OF PAN AM FLIGHT 103. (© *Reuters NewMedia Inc./Corbis. Reproduced by permission.*)

the ICC will bring about a deluge of politically motivated charges against Americans, and are unwilling to trust the impartiality of foreign judges.

Yet, the entire purpose of the ICC is to provide a neutral international criminal court made up of a panel of judges from around the world—exactly what the makeshift Scottish court in the Netherlands tried to provide, after 12 years of negotiations. The existence of this new court would negate the problem of sending the accused to be tried in a national court that may be hostile to them and ease the process of extradition. Unfortunately, the ICC will not have jurisdiction over international terrorism. It will only hear cases regarding genocide, crimes against humanity, war crimes, and aggression.

While "treaty crimes," such as those in the Montreal Convention, were listed in the Annex of the Draft Statute, they were not included in the final 1998 Statute. John Dugard, in a 1997 *Cambridge Law Journal* article notes that some countries were against their inclusion on the grounds that, "such crimes are not part of customary international law and therefore qualify as international crimes only for state parties to the treaties in question. It is also argued that these crimes will overburden and trivialise the court." In addition, at the

final negotiations in Rome, countries could not agree on a definition of terrorism, a touchy subject at the best of times.

The matter has not been completely laid to rest, however. As the UN Web site explains, a consensus resolution was passed in Rome, recommending that the inclusion of crimes such as terrorism be considered at a future review conference. There is therefore still hope that the ICC—once established—could have jurisdiction over cases like the terrorist attack on Flight 103 over Lockerbie. This should minimize the possibility of another 12-year pursuit of justice; a pursuit, which, in the Lockerbie case, many would argue, continues still.

## BIBLIOGRAPHY

Ashton, John, and Ian Ferguson. "Flight from the Truth." *Guardian,* June 27, 2001.

Black, Ian. "Old Brutality Catches Up with 'New' Gadafy." *Guardian,* February 1, 2001.

Black, Robert. "From Lockerbie to Zeist (via Tripoli, Tunis and Cairo)," Available online at http://www .thelockerbietrial.com/from_lockerbie_to_zeist.htm (cited September 21, 2001).

*Convention for the Suppression of Unlawful Acts Against the Safety of Civil Aviation.* Signed at Montreal on September 23, 1971. Entered into force on January

26, 1973. Available online in United Nations Treaty Collection at http://untreaty.un.org/English/Terrorism.asp.

David, Marcella. "Passport to Justice: Internationalizing the Political Question Doctrine for Application in the World Court." *Harvard International Law Journal* 40, Winter 1999, pp. 81–150.

"Deadlock Broken." *Economist*, April 10, 1999, pp. 44–45.

Douglas, Lynn Margaret. "A Primer on Scots Law and the Pan Am 103 Bombing Trial," *CNN Interactive*. Available online at http://europe.cnn.com/LAW/trials.and.cases/case.files/ 0010/lockerbie/procedure.html (cited September 21, 2001).

Dugard, John. "Obstacles in the Way of an International Criminal Court." *Cambridge Law Journal* 56, July 1997, pp. 329–42.

"Forensic Doubts." *Economist*, May 27, 2000, p. 47.

Graefrath, Bernhard. "Leave to the Court What Belongs to the Court—the Libyan Case." *European Journal of International Law* 4, 1993, pp. 184–205.

Grant, John. *The Charges.* University of Glasgow School of Law Lockerbie Trial Briefing Site. Available online at http://www.ltb.org.uk/backgroundsummary.cfm (cited September 21, 2001).

Gunn Jr., Angus M. "Council and Court: Prospects in *Lockerbie* for an International Rule of Law." *University of Toronto Faculty of Law Review* 52, Fall 1993, pp. 206–58.

International Court of Justice. *Press Communique 2000/27.* September 13, 2000.

Lacquer, Walter. *The New Terrorism.* Oxford: Oxford University Press, 1999. pp. 168–72. Cited in David Whittaker. *The Terrorism Reader.* London: Routledge, 2001.

*Letter dated 24 August 1998 from the Acting Permanent Representatives of the United Kingdom of Great Britain and Northern Ireland and the United States of America to the United Nations addressed to the Secretary-General.* S/1998/795.

Leveque, Thierry. "French Court: Gaddafi Can Be Prosecuted for Bombing." Reuters, October 20, 2000.

"Libya and the Bombed Airliners." *Economist*, March 13, 1999, pp. 55–56.

"Libya and Iran Hit by New Sanctions." *BBC News.* August 4, 2001.

"Libyan Bomber Sentenced to Life." *CNN.com* January 31, 2001. Available online at http://europe.cnn.com/LAW/trials.and.cases/case.files/ 0010/lockerbie/procedure.html (cited September 21, 2001).

"Lockerbie Lawyers Sum Up." *CNN.com* January 9, 2001. Available online at http://europe.cnn.com/LAW/trials.and.cases/case.files/ 0010/lockerbie/procedure.html (cited September 21, 2001).

"Lockerbie: What Happens Next?" *CNN.com* January 31, 2001. Available online at http://europe.cnn.com/LAW/trials.and.cases/case.files/ 0010/lockerbie/procedure.html (cited September 21, 2001).

Lord Sutherland, Lord Coulsfield, and Lord MacLean. *Lockerbie Verdict.* Case No. 1475/99. 31 January 2001.

Lustig, Robin. "Analysis: The Whole Story?" *BBC News.* January 31, 2001.

McDougall, Dan, and John Robertson. "Top Team to Fight Lockerbie Appeal," *Scotsman.* August 8, 2001.

Oakley, Robin. "Can Libya Come in from the Cold?" *CNN.com.* January 31, 2001. Available online at http://europe.cnn.com/LAW/trials.and.cases/case.files/ 0010/lockerbie/procedure.html (cited September 21, 2001).

———. "Why Not an International Court?" *CNN.com.* January 31, 2001. Available online at http://europe.cnn.com/LAW/trials.and.cases/case.files/ 0010/lockerbie/procedure.html (cited September 21, 2001).

Schweitzer, Yoram. "The Lessons of Lockerbie." International Policy Institute for Counter Terrorism. December 21, 1998. Available online at http://www.ict.org.il (cited September 21, 2001).

*Statement Issued by the Government of the United States on November 27, 1991, Regarding the Bombing of Pan Am 103,* UN Doc. S/23308 (1991).

United Nations. *1998 Rome Statute of the International Criminal Court.* July 17, 1998.

United Nations Security Council. *Resolution 731* (1992). S/RES/731 (1992). Adopted by the Security Council at its 3033rd meeting on January 21, 1992.

United Nations Security Council. *Resolution 748* (1992). S/RES/748 (1992). Adopted by the Security Council at its 3063rd meeting on March 31, 1992.

United Nations Security Council. *Resolution 883* (1993). S/RES/883 (1993). Adopted by the Security Council at its 3312th meeting on November 11, 1993.

United Nations Security Council. *Resolution 1192* (1998). S/RES/1192 (1998). Adopted by the Security Council at its 3920th meeting on August 27, 1998.

*Jessica Blitt*

# MACEDONIA FACES DIVISION AND VIOLENCE

## THE CONFLICT

Tensions between the Macedonian and Albanian communities in the Republic of Macedonia have been high since the 1980s; in 2001 the hostilities have descended into violence and mass flight.

### Political

- Albanian rebels are demanding increased civil rights in terms of education, language, employment, and expression of national identity. Most Albanians agree with these demands, but many do not agree with the use of violence.

- Macedonians fear that ethnic Albanians will attempt to form a separate nation if they are granted too much autonomy, resulting in the state fragmenting and falling prey to hostile neighbors.

- Macedonians strongly resent international intervention and are reacting against it.

### Ethnic

- Macedonians claim that Albanians are not committed to a multiethnic Macedonian state and hope to separate western Macedonia from the rest of the country to create a "Greater Albania."

- The war in Kosovo divided Macedonia along ethnic lines. Ethnic Macedonians felt sympathies for the Serbs, while ethnic Albanians sympathized with the KLA.

### Economic

- The war in Kosovo weakened the already unstable economy in Macedonia. With the country gripped by continued stagnation, hostilities have risen and meaningful reform has been impeded.

- Ethnic Albanians in Macedonia are not as well off as ethnic Macedonians. The chiefly Albanian-inhabited areas in the west remain poorer, with less funding for hospitals, schools, roads, and infrastructure than other parts of the country.

In February 2001, ethnic Albanian guerrillas of the National Liberation Army (NLA) rebelled in western Macedonia. The country had been the only part of the former Yugoslavia to gain independence without bloodshed. Since 1991, agreements between the majority ethnic Macedonian population and the minority ethnic Albanians had created an uneasy peace. Although the government included representation from the major ethnic Albanian parties, in the first decade of independent rule it delayed taking steps against what Albanians considered systematic discrimination. The result was anger—and finally, armed action.

Upon hearing of the NLA uprising, the government, dominated by Slavic Macedonians but including ethnic Albanian ministers in the cabinet, vowed to crush the rebels. Both sides proved reluctant to press the conflict, and casualties were light in the first six months—perhaps one hundred dead—but tens of thousands of refugees fled western Macedonia as the fear loomed that ethnic cleansing would be used by either side, driving out the enemy by murder, rape, or other violence, as had so recently occurred in regions of the former Yugoslavia. The escalating conflict prompted Western intervention. Several cease-fires were arranged, but it is unsure if and for how long peace will hold.

Tension in Macedonia is largely a product of domestic ethnic relations and politics. The NLA claims that the government discriminates against Albanians, a claim shared even by the Albanian political parties in the current unity government. Many ethnic Macedonians, on the other hand, claim that Albanians are not committed to a multiethnic Macedonian state and hope to separate western Macedonia from the rest of the country to create a "Greater Albania."

# CHRONOLOGY

*1912–13* The Balkan Wars divide Ottoman territory, leaving Macedonians divided between three states and large Albanian populations in Kosovo and Macedonia. Both Albanians and Macedonians rebel against Belgrade.

*1946* Federal People's Republic of Yugoslavia is created, with a constituent Macedonian Republic.

*November 1968* Widespread protests are staged by Albanians in Kosovo, demanding greater rights. Some Albanians in Macedonia join the protests.

*November 1990* The first multiparty elections are held in Macedonia.

*June 1991* Croatia and Slovenia declare independence, signaling the breakup of Yugoslavia.

*September 1991* Macedonia declares independence from Yugoslavia. A moderate government takes power.

*April 1992* Albanian extremists declare a separate Albanian "Republic of Illyria."

*November 1992* Macedonia requests a UN mission to help maintain the border with Serbia and Kosovo. The mission remains through March 1999.

*February 1994* A Greek embargo against Macedonia, in effect until October 1995, weakens the economy.

*February 17, 1995* An Albanian university in Tetovo opens; the police intervene to shut it down.

*1997–98* The Kosovo Liberation Army begins attacks.

*June 9, 1997* Macedonian special police forces confront protesters in Gostivar over the flying of the Albanian flag.

*October 1998* Parliamentary elections result in a new coalition government that includes a nationalist Macedonian party and an activist Albanian party.

*March 24–June 10, 1999* War ensues between NATO and Serbia.

*April–May 1999* Hundreds of thousands of Albanian refugees flee Kosovo. Many go to Macedonia.

*April 2000* The Liberation Army of Preševo, Medvedja and Bujanovac attacks Serb positions, attempting to unite the region (in Serbia proper) with Kosovo. Fighting continues until May 2001.

*February 2001* Fighting breaks out in western Macedonia between the Albanian NLA and police.

*March 15, 2001* Rebels move to within 12 miles of Skopje, the capital.

*April 28, 2001* The NLA ambushes and kills 8 Macedonian soldiers, escalating the conflict.

*May 13, 2001* A National Unity government is formed, including Albanian parties.

*May 22, 2001* Leaders of DPA and PDP meet with NLA rebels, angering Macedonians. Partly because of this, the Macedonian government launches a new offensive against rebels.

*June 5, 2001* A temporary cease-fire is brokered by foreign diplomats, setting off anti-Albanian rioting in Bitola.

*June 25, 2001* Ethnic Macedonian rioters, including many army reservists, attack the parliament building in protest over the new cease-fire.

*July 5, 2001* European and American diplomats arrange new a cease-fire between Albanian and Macedonian political parties to end the violence.

*July 22–24, 2001* Heavy fighting around Tetovo escalates the conflict; foreign embassies are attacked by protesters in Skopje.

*August 13, 2001* A peace accord is signed, but scattered fighting continues.

What set off the recent violence in Macedonia (as well as in the Preševo valley of Serbia) was the apparent success of the Kosovo Liberation Army (KLA; the rebel Albanian Kosovar group that fought the Serbs in Yugoslavia). The possibility that Kosovo may achieve independence in some form spurred conflict in other Albanian-inhabited regions of the former Yugoslavia. With the NLA seemingly successful at obtaining reform through rebellion, it may encourage other attempts to gain ethnic rights through violence—particularly in Bosnia among the Croat and Serb communities, or in Greece among the Albanian minority there.

MAP OF MACEDONIA. (© *Maryland Cartographics. Reprinted with permission.*)

# HISTORICAL BACKGROUND

## Ottoman Macedonia

At the dawn of the twentieth century Macedonia was a geographic concept but not a state—and, some argue, not a nationality. Macedonians today sometimes claim descent from the ancient Macedonian empire of Alexander the Great (356–323 BCE). But that empire collapsed upon his death and the region was dominated by outside states for two thousand years; Romans, Byzantines, Bulgarians, Serbs, and Ottomans each ruled in turn. The constant flux of borders and migration of peoples created an ethnic diversity that remains today. The Republic of Macedonia comprises only part of this "geographic Macedonia" that also includes southwestern Bulgaria (Pirin Macedonia) and northern Greece (Aegean Macedonia).

Perhaps the most significant event in this history was the Ottoman Empire's conquest of Macedonia in the late fourteenth century. Ottoman rule is often reviled in Macedonia (and in the

Balkans as a whole) and all manner of problems blamed on the "Turkish Yoke." This overstates the case, since some aspects of early Ottoman rule, such as religious freedom, were more advanced than in the contemporary early modern kingdoms of western Europe. But by the nineteenth century Ottoman rule had become brutal and corrupt.

One of the Ottoman rule's most profound influences on later ethnic relations in the region of Macedonia was that it served to retard the growth of ethnic identity. Under Ottoman rule, identity was confessional (religious) in nature. The chief "nations" of the empire were the Muslims, the Orthodox Christians, and the Jews. Though ethnic identities did exist, *religious* identity was far more important when it came to such issues as taxation, law, and military service. The Ottoman system divided most Albanians and Macedonians into two different worlds of religious identity— Albanians generally lived in Muslim communities and Macedonians in Christian communities (although there were Christian Albanians and Muslim Macedonians). Despite some interaction, the communities fundamentally lived apart.

The question of whether or not a strong Macedonian *national* identity existed before the turn of the century is a controversial one. Most likely, a portion of the more educated population was attracted to the idea of a local, Macedonian identity, while some preferred a Bulgarian identity, and the peasant majority identified themselves as Christian Slavs. The history of the Ilinden Uprising of 1903, a crucial event in Macedonian national historiography, shows the confused nature of national identity: in the uprising, some revolutionaries sought Macedonian autonomy while others hoped to unify the region with Bulgaria.

At the same time, Albanians were slowly developing their own national identity. The process was slower than for the Christian peoples of the empire, probably because Muslim Albanians enjoyed certain benefits from their religious status and had less reason to resent Ottoman rule. National identity was also hindered by the fundamental differences among the ethnic Albanians. Family and clan identity was, and still is, very important to the Albanians. With family/clan priority, the identity of an abstract national law did not fully take hold.

Across Macedonia, religious divisions were deep between Orthodox, Catholic, and Muslim communities, since under Ottoman law the three groups didn't intermarry, used different churches,

IN A VILLAGE NORTHEAST OF SKOPJE, MACEDONIA, AN ETHNIC ALBANIAN WOMAN STANDS IN ANGUISH IN FRONT OF HER HOME. THE HOUSE WAS DESTROYED DURING ESCALATING ETHNIC CONFLICT IN THE AREA. *(A/P Wide World. Reproduced by permission.)*

and were subject to different laws. A large linguistic and regional difference existed between north and south. Scholars are uncertain how important this difference has been, but it is notable that Tosk politicians, for example, tended to deal with other Tosks and not with Ghegs. Many Albanians continued to see themselves primarily in terms of clan, religion, and region since there was limited interaction across these lines.

In 1878, however, the Treaty of San Stefano (though later revoked) provided part of Albanian-inhabited Kosovo to Serbia, which sought to liberate the Serb population in the province from Ottoman rule. It was clear that the decaying Otto-

man Empire could not or would not protect the Albanians any longer. Albanian leaders increasingly called for autonomy in a "Greater Albanian" province within the empire, at first peacefully and later through violence.

## The Macedonian Question and Partition

The root of the current problem in Macedonia lies in this growth of ethnic identity in the Balkans in the nineteenth century. Over time, independent states arose in Serbia, Greece, and Bulgaria, and each sought to expand its territory and influence. Each state was founded as a *national* state: its inhabitants would all be the same nationality, with

# POLITICAL PARTY GLOSSARY

The plethora of Macedonian political parties can cause confusion—particularly since acronyms are sometimes from English translations and sometimes (here given in parentheses) from the Macedonian original. The largest parties include:

- **DA:** The Democratic Alliance is chiefly a vehicle for the political ambitions of its leader. Politically, billed as an alternative to previous incompetent political parties.

- **DPA (DPSh):** The Democratic Party of Albanians was a 1997 merger of more radical members of the Party for Democratic Prosperity (PDP) and the People's Democratic Party (NDP). The result is an exclusively Albanian party. Though the NDP acted in partnership with the PDP on many issues, the new DPA claimed an exclusive role as the "voice of the Albanians." Party members publicly supported independence for Kosovo and flirted with creating a "Greater Albania" in the past but condemned the violence in 2001. Arben Xhaferi, widely quoted by the foreign media, leads the party.

- **IMRO-DPMNU (VMRO-DPMNE):** The Internal Macedonian Revolutionary Organization–Democratic Party for Macedonian National Unity is an ethnic Macedonian party and one of the largest in the country. The party initially in 1990–91 took a firm nationalist line with hints of irredentism toward Greece. Both President Boris Trajkovski and Prime Minister Ljubtsjo Georgjevski are members.

- **LDP:** The Liberal Democratic Party is a centrist party formed by the merger of the Liberal and Democratic Parties. The party is liberal, not formally ethnically based, and focuses on economic and political reform.

- **PDP:** The Party for Democratic Prosperity was initially the largest Albanian political party, but splits between "hard" and "moderate" wings led to much of the former splitting off. The party calls for reform and change, but not violent action. Since the formation of the DPA, the PDP diminished in importance and size.

- **SDUM (SDSM):** The Social Democratic Union of Macedonians is one of the most influential parties. The party is not ethnically based and supports a multiethnic state. SDUM dominated the government after independence. The first president of Macedonia, Kiro Gligarov, was a member.

- **SPM:** The Socialist Party of Macedonia is now the standard-bearer of socialism. Small but influential, the party is not ethnically based and has supported a multiethnic, semi-socialist state.

---

minorities either assimilated or encouraged to emigrate. This was not a particularly "Balkan" trait; the same process took place in western Europe over a period roughly from 1700 to 1900. What led to problems in the Balkans was the degree of ethnic mixture (and the greater differences between cultures) in a small area. When new governments attempted to quickly create "ethnically pure" states, they eventually turned to short-cuts such as ethnic cleansing.

The Russo-Turkish War of 1877 and the treaties ending the war revealed the vulnerability of the declining Ottoman Empire and posed the "Macedonian question": who would obtain the territory of Macedonia by proving that the inhabitants belonged to their own, claimant, nation? The local Slavic inhabitants were of uncertain national character. Although there were similarities between Slavic Macedonians and Bulgarians in terms of language, Serbia and Greece also made claims that these Slavs were Serb or Greek in character. At the same time, the "Albanian question" arose: what would happen to the territory inhabited by Albanians? Would they obtain their own state or would Albanian-inhabited areas be annexed by the neighboring states?

Bulgaria, Greece, and Serbia each had their own aspirations for the remaining lands of the Ottoman Empire in Europe, at this point consisting of Albania, Kosovo, geographic Macedonia, and Thrace. Macedonia, was the largest territory and central to the others, and each state sought to obtain it. "Regaining" Macedonia was the focus of Bulgarian foreign policy—it had been promised to Bulgaria in the Treaty of San Stefano in 1878, but the later Treaty of Berlin returned the region to "Ottoman slavery."

Bulgaria claimed Macedonians as co-nationals, pointed to the region's role in the medieval Bulgarian empires, and sought to promote a Bulgarian identity. The Serbian government was stymied to the west by the Austro-Hungarian occupation of Bosnia-Herzegovina in 1878. It shifted its own territorial designs south to Kosovo and Macedonia, claiming both regions as integral to the medieval Serbian empire and that Macedonians were "South Serbs." The Greek government, after conquering Thessaly and southern Epirus in 1881, saw inclusion of Macedonia's Greek population (and Hellenization of its Slavic population) as a step toward the fulfillment of the *megale idea*, creating a new Greek empire to unite all Greek lands. In each case, an aggressive, expanding state saw Macedonia as its only opportunity for expansion.

The three states collaborated in the First Balkan War of 1912, attacking the Ottoman Empire and planning to divide Macedonia between them. Failure to reach an agreement among them led to the Second Balkan War in 1913, in which Serbia and Greece took the lion's share of the spoils—the present Republic of Macedonia is formed out of Serbia's gains in the war. Kosovo—and its Albanian population—was acquired by Serbia at the same time, and Greece acquired an Albanian minority in Epirus. Both wars were noted for their brutality on all sides toward local inhabitants.

Each state's gains included large minority populations. Although demographic statistics for Macedonia are inexact in this period, the last Ottoman census of 1912 recorded that in geographic Macedonia as a whole (what would become Serb, Greek, and Bulgarian territories) only about half of the total population was Slavic—sizeable Turkish, Albanian, Roma, and Vlach minorities existed in the north, Greeks were in the south, and a large Jewish community resided in the city of Thessaloniki. Large minorities hindered control over the region, and in each state the goal became to assimilate or expel the minorities. Greece and Bulgaria embarked on population exchanges with each other and with Turkey and assimilated as much of the remaining minority population as possible.

## Yugoslav Macedonia

Assimilation in Serbia, however, proved difficult. After World War I (1914–18) a new Kingdom of Yugoslavia united Bosnia, Croatia, Montenegro, and Slovenia with Serbia under a Serbian king. While a multiethnic state, Royal Yugoslavia was dominated by Belgrade, and ethnic tensions were high. In Kosovo and Macedonia the new state had minority populations of over 480,000 Albanians and 630,000 Macedonians. Neither ethnicity was officially recognized by the government in Belgrade.

Tensions between the new central government and the people of Macedonia abounded from the start. Macedonians and Albanians rebelled against Serb rule in 1913 and sided with Serbia's enemies in World War I, leading to new repressive measures following the war. Tens of thousands of Albanians revolted in the *kaçak* rebellion of 1918–24 against Belgrade; thousands of Macedonians participated in the Internal Macedonian Revolutionary Organization's (IMRO) terrorist attacks against Serbian officials. The government put down both rebellions harshly, banning expression of national identity by both groups, settling Serbs in Macedonia and Kosovo, and further alienating local inhabitants.

During World War II (1939–45) Belgrade's policies helped lead to the collapse of the country in 1941 in the face of the German invasion. Army units of conscripts from the minorities deserted, and Yugoslavia was quickly overrun. Croatians, Hungarians, Albanians, and Macedonians welcomed the invaders as liberators. Their collaboration with the Germans contributed to further ethnic tension; for Yugoslavia World War II became a civil war in which hundreds of thousands were killed in interethnic conflict. Among the groups that successfully resisted the Germans were the communist partisans led by Josip Broz Tito (1892–1980). The partisans ultimately drew support from each ethnic group, and by the end of the war Tito's army was a powerful multiethnic force.

The Federal People's Republic of Yugoslavia created in 1945 by the communist partisans had to resolve the dual legacy of the Royal Yugoslav state and World War II. The new communist state was a federation formed by six republics: Bosnia-Herzegovina, Croatia, Macedonia, Montenegro, Serbia, and Slovenia. The principle of ethnic equality became enshrined in Yugoslav communism. It was an attempt to heal past scars and encourage a "common Yugoslav spirit."

Macedonia benefited from Tito's policy. In order to obtain the loyalty of the Macedonians, an "official" Macedonian national identity was recognized and encouraged. A Macedonian republic was created with Macedonian as the official language, the Macedonian Orthodox Church was established, and Macedonian culture in general

YUGOSLAV PRESIDENT VOJISLAV KOSTUNICA, LEFT, TURKISH PRIME MINISTER BÜLENT ECEVIT, RIGHT, AND MACEDONIAN PRESIDENT BORIS TRAJKOVSKI MET AT THE BALKAN SUMMIT IN FEBRUARY 2001. (© *Reuters NewMedia Inc./Corbis. Reproduced by permission.)*

was supported by the federal government. As one of the poorest republics, Macedonia received extensive grants from the federal government for economic development and recorded gradual gains in growth and industry from the 1950s to 1970s. Skopje and other cities grew rapidly as rural Macedonians flocked to factory jobs.

Ethnic Albanians were less fortunate, and their failure to obtain an Albanian republic would ultimately lead to discontent and violence. Because Albanians lacked a republic, they were not able to address ethnic issues in Yugoslavia on an equal footing with Macedonians and Serbians and would, after 1991, be left as unwanted minorities instead of a majority in a republic of their own.

Though conditions were better in Tito's Yugoslavia than in the inter-war period, the federal secret police headed by Aleksandar Ranković; harshly repressed the Albanian population. By the late 1960s Tito moved to decentralize power in Yugoslavia and, following widespread rioting by Albanians in 1968, to address Albanian discontent. An Albanian-language university was founded in Priština in 1969, greater expressions of Albanian nationalism were allowed, and in 1974 Kosovo was granted autonomy and representation in the federal government through a new Yugoslav constitution. Economic growth, however, lagged and many

of the graduates of new Albanian-language high schools and the university were not able to find jobs. Serbs in Kosovo left rural villages for better jobs in Serbia proper, reducing the Serb population in the province and creating the fear that Albanians would overwhelm the historic Serb presence in Kosovo.

Ethnic Albanians in Macedonia developed close ties with their co-nationals in Kosovo during this period. The Macedonian provincial government limited some expression of Albanian nationalism and granted only limited ethnic rights. But as Albanian institutions such as the University of Priština were created in Kosovo, Albanians from Macedonia could attend them—providing interaction existed between Albanians in both parts of Yugoslavia. Increasingly, common cause was perceived between the groups.

In 1968 ethnic Albanians protested across western Macedonia to support their co-nationals in Kosovo and demanded the union of western Macedonia with Kosovo to create a seventh, Albanian republic in Yugoslavia. Such demonstrations created unease among the Macedonian leadership and led to policies in Skopje aimed at limiting Albanian national expression, lowering their birth rate, and preventing the possibility that Kosovo and western Macedonia might unite.

Although Tito's government in Belgrade was successful in neutralizing the memories of the war, by the 1970s tensions in Yugoslavia seemed to be on the rise. From 1967 to 1972 Slovene, Croatian, and Serbian regional party leaders pressed for economic reform. Tito refused and the dissidents were suppressed, but the economic problems remained. The republics reacted, each demanding increased funding for its own economic projects and agendas. With limited funding for improvement, political debates slowly became issues of "us versus them" and economic issues were recast along republican—and ethnic—lines. With Tito's death in 1980, his stabilizing influence was lost. Inter-republican squabbles increased, leading to the rise of nationalists such as Slobodan Milošević.

As real incomes began to decline across Yugoslavia in the 1980s, ethnic tensions in Kosovo and Macedonia increased. A growing Albanian population in both areas worried Serbs and Macedonians, who saw their own rural population declining and formerly Serb- or Macedonian-inhabited villages now populated by Albanians. The Serbian Academy of Arts and Sciences issued a memorandum in 1986 that called for Kosovo to be brought under direct control by Belgrade to protect the region's Serbs. The Macedonian republican government further sought to limit Albanian national expression and in some cases chipped away at existing rights.

In 1987 Serbian nationalist Slobodan Milošević; rose to power as the Serbian Communist Party leader by stirring up hostile feelings within the federation, promoting a vision of a "Greater Serbia" that included Kosovo as well as large Serbian-inhabited areas of Croatia, Bosnia and Herzegovina, and even Macedonia. Many Slovenes and Croats increasingly wanted to secede from the federation, for a variety of reasons. They were angry that the central government taxed their republics to support poorer regions, attracted to their own nationalist leaders, or concerned over Milošević's growing power. By 1991, the Yugoslavian federation was breaking apart. Ethnic tensions had destroyed Tito's dream of "brotherhood and unity."

### Albanian-Macedonian Relations after Statehood

Macedonia seceded from Yugoslavia on September 17, 1991, not long after Bosnia and Croatia's bids for independence led to fighting in both countries. The breakup of Yugoslavia seemed inevitable. In a referendum that summer, 68 percent of ethnic Macedonians voted for independ-

## THE CENSUS QUESTION

The status of Albanians is connected to the censuses taken in 1991 and 1994. Ethnic Albanian political leaders argue that both censuses undercount the Albanian population due to deliberate manipulation by the government. Although the government agreed to a second census in 1994 with international monitoring, many Albanians feel neither census is accurate—and place their percentage of the population in the 30 to 40 percent range.

Macedonian political leaders, in turn, argue that the Albanian figures include tens of thousands of ethnic Albanians from Kosovo and Albania who have flooded into the country, and have accused Albanians of attempts to coerce other Muslims in the country, such as Turks and the Torbeshi, ethnic Macedonians who practice Islam, into officially registering as Albanian. The government holds to the official figure of a 23 percent ethnic Albanian population in Macedonia. This figure does not include resident Albanians who are non-citizens, however; including them might well increase the Albanian percentage close to 30 percent.

The census debate is sometimes used to mask another issue: the difference in birth rates between ethnic Albanians and ethnic Macedonians. Ethnic Albanians, predominantly rural, have a much higher rate than that of the predominantly urban Macedonians, and their share of the country's population has steadily grown since the 1950s. If this rate of growth were to remain constant, it would create an Albanian majority by the middle of the twenty-first century. As in Kosovo, many rural villages in the country once inhabited by Macedonians have come to be inhabited mainly by ethnic Albanians, leading some Macedonians to fear that they are slowly being driven out of the country and enclosed in a few small pockets.

dence, but ethnic Albanians boycotted the voting, and in an independent referendum 74 percent supported the creation of an autonomous "Republic of Illyria" in the west. The new Republic of Macedonia was nevertheless formed, and its constitution guaranteed ethnic rights for minorities. Though tensions did exist—Albanians boycotted the 1991 census—Macedonia was spared the ethnic fighting experienced in Croatia and Bosnia. The new government invited Albanian participation and accepted Albanian ministers into the cabinet.

Though the Yugoslav National Army left the republic without bloodshed in a negotiated

## COMPOSITION OF POLITICAL PARTIES IN MACEDONIAN GOVERNMENT, 1992–2001

| | Government Composition | | | | |
| Political Parties | 1992 | 1994 | 1996 | 1998 | 2001 |
|---|---|---|---|---|---|
| Democratic Alliance (DA) | | | | ◊ | ◊ |
| Democratic Party of Albanians (DPA) | | | | ◊ | ◊ |
| Internal Macedonian Revolutionary Organization —Democratic Party for Macedonian National Unity (IMRO-DPMNU) | | | | ◊ | ◊ |
| Liberal Democratic Party (LDP)* | | ◊ | | | ◊ |
| People's Democratic Party (NDP)† | ◊ | | | | ◊ |
| Party for Democratic Prosperity (PDP) | ◊ | ◊ | ◊ | | ◊ |
| Social Democratic Union of Macedonians (SDUM) | ◊ | ◊ | ◊ | | ◊ |
| Socialist Party of Macedonia (SPM) | | ◊ | ◊ | | ◊ |

\* In 1994 government as the Liberal party
† Later merges into DPA.

THE COMPOSITION OF THE MACEDONIAN GOVERNMENT CAN INCLUDE VARIOUS POLITICAL PARTIES, WHICH OFTEN JOIN TOGETHER TO FORM A COALITION TO RULE THE COUNTRY COOPERATIVELY. *(The Gale Group.)*

withdrawal, fear of spreading violence led Macedonian President Kiro Gligorov to request a United Nations (UN) mission, the United Nations Preventative Deployment (UNPREDEP) later renamed the UN Protection Force (UNPROFOR) to observe the border with Serbia. Macedonia's position in terms of the rest of the world was made awkward by the Greeks, who blocked international recognition of Macedonia as a nation because of a Greek claim to the Macedonian name.

Of more importance to most Macedonians, the republic's economy declined further after independence. Most of the population in 2001 remained worse off than it was before 1990, and as much as one-third of the workforce was unemployed (60 percent among Albanians). Corruption was widespread, and much of the economy functioned as a "gray market," unreported to the government. The UN placed embargoes against Serbia in the 1990s that caused a devastating blow to Macedonia's economy—direct transportation links to central Europe were cut off, as was the Serbian market that had purchased a fifth of Macedonia's export. The Greeks set up a blockade in 1994–95 that cut off the rest of the transportation links and plunged the economy into crisis.

With the country in danger of economic collapse and invasion, many ethnic Macedonian voters were not receptive to Albanian protests. Moreover, members of the Macedonian intelligentsia felt betrayed by the Albanians. Many who believed in the ideal of a multiethnic state had reached out to support Albanians in their political and cultural struggles and joined in the fight against right-wing, exclusive Macedonian nationalism only to find that ethnic Albanian leaders themselves were seemingly encouraging Albanian nationalism and refusing to commit to a multicultural state. For other Macedonians, the old fear of a high Albanian birthrate was bolstered by a surge of illegal immigrants from Kosovo. Increasingly, many Macedonians began to express anti-Albanian sentiments, even among the intelligentsia.

Ethnic Albanians in Macedonia felt themselves to be second-class citizens due to systematic government discrimination. The censuses of 1991 and 1994 were widely regarded as deliberate underestimates of the Albanian population. Education was another point of conflict. Ethnic Albanian students from Macedonia could no longer attend the University of Priština, given the conflict in Kosovo and Macedonian independence from Serbia. The national university in Skopje, the University of Ss. Kiril and Metodij, only taught in the Macedonian language, and the Albanian student population there was small. Accordingly, ethnic Albanians attempted to create a private university in the western Macedonian town of Tetovo in 1995. The government closed the university on its opening day, February 17, 1995; one ethnic Albanian was killed and some 50 students and professors were arrested. In the face of protests, the government tacitly allowed the university to function but refused to recognize degrees awarded. Schools in the west received little funding, and other forms of infrastructure, such as roads, hospitals, and public works, decayed. Economic problems and the loss of Yugoslav aid after 1991 have resulted in decay throughout the country. Albanian leaders accuse the government of deliberate policies to starve the western regions of funds; this may be true, in part, since Macedonian politicians would naturally try to obtain as much of the limited budget as they could for their own constituencies.

Albanians also felt the government persecuted them for expressing ethnic identity. Tensions peaked in the summer of 1997 when the Albanian mayors of the Macedonian towns of Tetovo and Gostivar flew the Albanian and Turkish flags alongside the Macedonian flag in front of the city halls in both towns. Ruling that flying the flag of a foreign country in such a fashion was illegal, the government sent in police units to remove the flags. Confrontation between police and protesters on July 9, 1997, led to the deaths of three protesters. More then 200 people were wounded, including nine police officers. The mayor of Gostivar, Rufi Osmani, a member of the Democratic Party, was sentenced to 13 years and 8 months in prison under legislation dating back to the Ranković's leadership of the secret police in the 1960s, and other Albanian leaders received lesser sentences. Although amnesties were later given to Osmani and others, Albanians, as well as international human rights groups, accused the government of using excessive force.

Overall, the situation in Macedonia in the 1990s was mixed. Albanians enjoyed protected ethnic rights under the constitution, and each government since 1990 has included four or five ethnic Albanian ministers. Albanians sit on the Constitutional Court and Supreme Court, serve as ambassadors, are mayors in 26 towns and cities, and hold the rank of general in the army. Opportunities in the public sector improved in 1998 when a coalition government including the Democratic Party of Albanians (DPA) took power.

Due to the cronyism and corruption in the Macedonian government, however, improvements at this level may not have benefited all ethnic Albanians equally. The number of Alba-

## FOUR WOLVES OR FOUR FRIENDS?

The fear that if western Macedonia was lost, the country itself would not survive is seen in the history of "the four wolves"—the belief that, given a chance, Macedonia's neighbors—Serbia, Bulgaria, Albania, and Greece—would carve up the country between themselves. This belief is rooted in part in the history of the Balkan Wars and is a major theme in Macedonian historiography. But is it likely today?

Serbia officially recognizes Macedonia's borders; only extreme Serbian nationalists have proposed redrawing the border. There is only a small Serb population in Macedonia, and Belgrade and Skopje were able to agree on the latter's secession from Yugoslavia.

Bulgaria was one of the first governments to recognize the new state—if not the national identity. Though disagreements remain between Macedonia and Bulgaria, Bulgaria provided military equipment in 1999 to Macedonia and might intervene against the Albanians if conditions in Macedonia deteriorate badly.

Though in the early 1990s the government of Sali Berisha in Albania flirted with ethnic Albanian nationalists in Macedonia, since 1997 the republic's government in Tirana has generally supported the current borders and called for reform rather than revolution. Even if full-scale civil war broke out, Albania can do little to intervene.

Of the "four wolves," only Greece has been openly hostile to the Macedonian government. But since this is chiefly in regard to the use of national symbols, Greece is unlikely to invade. Greece has concerns regarding its own Albanian minority, and any intervention might well be to limit the flight of Albanian refugees into Greece.

The fear among western analysts is not that Macedonia's neighbors will invade, but that if Macedonia implodes each may be pulled into the war seeking to intervene on behalf of one side or the other.

nians in the officer corps overall, in the police, and among university students remained low. With tensions high, both Albanians and Macedonians drew their own conclusions from the events to the north in Kosovo, as Albanian-Serb ethnic conflict led to guerrilla warfare and international intervention.

## In the Shadow of Kosovo

Slobodan Milošević rose to power by exploiting Serbian nationalism and promising to regain control over Kosovo. In March 1989 Kosovo was stripped of its autonomy and integrated into Serbia. In response, in 1990 the Albanian members of the former provincial assembly declared the existence of the Republic of Kosovo—within Yugoslavia, not as an independent state. Within the next two years, Belgrade assumed control over local government, police, economy, and education, while Albanians created their own "shadow" government, declared the full independence of Kosovo in 1991, and refused to participate in official public life. Despite, or perhaps because, of this, there was little violent conflict in the province even as war raged in Croatia and Bosnia from 1991 to 1995. The leader of the Kosovar Albanians, Ibrahim Rugova, stressed the importance of nonviolent and passive resistance to Serb policies. International mediation was considered to be inevitable given the degree of Serb violence elsewhere.

By the mid-1990s many within the Albanian community gave up hope for peaceful change after five years of Serb rule. In 1996 the United States finally recognized the Federal Republic of Yugoslavia (the remaining union of Serbia and Montenegro), and Kosovars felt that mediation was a dim hope. Isolated terrorist attacks had already begun in 1993, and the Kosovo Liberation Army (KLA) slowly formed over 1996–97.

In 1997 and 1998 fighting between the KLA and Serbian police broke out. By mid-1998 the KLA held as much as 40 percent of the province, but Serb offensives in August hard-pressed the KLA and targeted civilians suspected of supporting the rebels. Increasing violence led to international demands for mediation and to the unsuccessful talks in Rambouillet, France, in March 1999, where American and European diplomats attempted to force the Serbian government and KLA to cease fighting. Milošević's refusal to allow foreign observers in Kosovo resulted in the North Atlantic Treaty Organization's (NATO) air campaign against Serbia from March 24 to June 10, 1999. This was countered with Serb reprisals against the Albanian population. Hundreds of thousands of Albanians fled, many to Macedonia. But with the occupation of Kosovo by United Nations troops in 1999 and the subsequent flight of Serbs from the province (encouraged by KLA attacks on civilians), many Albanians saw themselves as having won *de facto* independence.

Macedonia was weakened by the war in Kosovo. Transportation and economic links were cut off again, the economy weakened, and the state burdened with 350,000 Albanian refugees, who were reluctantly admitted by the government. The government's decision to allow NATO to use the country as a staging area for UN troops was not entirely popular among Slavic Macedonians, but accepted as part of the price of international affairs. Despite the sacrifices and cooperation the country made, many Macedonians thought that international aid was small, grudgingly given, and in the interests of international donors rather than Macedonia's needs.

The Republic of Macedonia was divided along ethnic lines by the war in Kosovo. Macedonians felt sympathies for the Serbs, particularly since many Macedonians had relatives or friends in the Serbian cities being bombed by NATO. Ethnic Albanians, many providing shelter to refugees, sympathized with the KLA. Both saw the conflict in Kosovo as representative of the conflict in Macedonia. The Albanians equating the Macedonian government's bias to Serbian oppression, and the Macedonians seeing Albanians in both countries as separatists. Kosovar Albanians during the war expressed sympathy for ethnic Albanians in Macedonia and called for the creation of a "Greater Albania" that might include western Macedonia. Since the war in Kosovo, however, moderation has prevailed, and Kosovar political parties such as the Democratic Party and the Alliance for the Future have, in 2001, stated that Macedonia's current borders should remain inviolable.

## The NLA Rebellion of 2001

In March 1997, the Republic of Albania collapsed into anarchy. Order was restored over time, but in the furor police and military armories were looted and hundreds of thousands of assault rifles were stolen along with ammunition and other military equipment. An AK-47 assault rifle could be purchased on the black market for as little as $50, and much of the KLA's armory was purchased from looters. Ethnic Albanians in Macedonia availed themselves of the same opportunity to build up stockpiles for future use. The UN embargo against Serbia, combined with porous borders, made border smuggling a lucrative practice, and the Albanians in Macedonia certainly engaged in it—possibly including drug trading, an important source of financing for the KLA.

During the year 2000, feeling that there was no room for peaceful reform and seeing the success that violence brought the KLA in Kosovo, the National Liberation Army (NLA) began to organize and enlist among the ethnic Albanians of Macedonia, particularly among veterans who had volunteered with the KLA. Kosovars joined the NLA in turn—perhaps as much as 40 percent according to NLA statements, though the Macedonian government claimed the number of Kosovars was even higher.

In late February 2001 the NLA launched its rebellion, catching the Macedonian government by surprise and quickly occupying several villages in western Macedonia. The government responded by forming a "unity coalition" including all political parties in the country. International pressure kept President Boris Trajkovski from declaring a state of war, but the government called up reserves and reinforced troops in the west. The pattern of conflict was established in March: rebels would occupy a village, and the government would contain them and attempt to drive them out without resorting to storming the village.

The conflict escalated in late April, when eight soldiers were ambushed and killed by NLA guerrillas, the worst action to date. The Macedonian Army, now armed with helicopter gunships, tanks, and heavy artillery, began bombarding rebel-held villages in an attempt to drive out the rebels. Albanian villagers were increasingly caught between the NLA and the Macedonian army, raising fears of massacres and mass flight. The Democratic Party of Albanians (DPA) and the Party for Democratic Prosperity (PDP) continued to support the unity government, but pressed for peace talks to resolve the fighting. The discovery that the leaders of both parties met with the NLA on May 22, however, led to a backlash by the ethnically Macedonian parties and public and led to a new series of government offensives.

At this point, the international community intervened. The United Nations, the United States, and the European Union pressed both rebels and the government to agree to cease-fires. But the cease-fires were seen by many Macedonians as favoring the Albanians. Riots erupted in protest, mostly targeting Albanians, but on June 25 Macedonian protestors—including Army reservists—attacked parliament in protest. The international community also attempted to limit the rebels; the United States placed Albanian groups on its list of proscribed terrorist organizations. UN troops began to cut off collaboration

AN ETHNIC ALBANIAN BOY AND MAN LOOK OUT THE WINDOW OF A BUS TRANSPORTING REFUGEES INTO MACEDONIA. BUSLOADS OF ETHNIC ALBANIANS ESCAPED THE VIOLENCE IN SERBIA AND KOSOVO BY CROSSING THE BORDER INTO MACEDONIA, EXACERBATING ETHNIC TENSIONS THERE. *(A/P Wide World. Reproduced by permission.)*

between the Albanian Liberation Army of Preševo, Medvedja and Bujanovac (LAPMB) and the NLA, and cut off NLA supply lines that ran through Kosovo. Among other things, NATO forged an agreement with Serbia to allow Serb troops to reoccupy demilitarized zones in the south to help suppress the rebellion in Serbia. Fighting continued through May and June, with two dozen villages being taken or retaken by the rebels and government.

By July 2001, the United Nations Refugee Agency estimated that more than one hundred thousand had fled their homes, about half remaining in Macedonia and the other half having fled to Kosovo. Most of these were Albanians, but some were Macedonians; on July 1 and 2 there were reports that the NLA was driving Macedonian villagers out of the west. On July 5, 2001, international diplomats brokered a cease-fire in the hope that the fighting could be halted and a 3,000-strong NATO force, comprised of British,

CANADIAN SOLDIERS GIVE A SIGN OF THEIR SUCCESS IN NATO'S OPERATION ESSENTIAL HARVEST, WHICH COLLECTED MORE THAN 3,400 WEAPONS FROM ETHNIC ALBANIANS IN AN ATTEMPT AT PEACE IN MACEDONIA. *(A/P Wide World. Reproduced by permission.)*

French, Greek, and Turkish troops, but no U.S. troops, would be put in place to disarm the rebels.

Both sides agreed to talks, but the obstacles were great. Questions of language rights and public funding for Tetovo University were problematic, as were suggestions by European representatives that Albanians, and other minorities, have virtual veto power in the parliament over any legislation that affects them. Prominent Macedonian political figures, including President Trajkovski, refused to consider the more extreme measures that Albanian leaders such as Arben Xhaferi claimed were "essential" to any peace agreement.

The fighting between the ethnic Albanians and the Slavic Macedonians further alienated each side from the other. Alarmingly, there was unprecedented discussion by members of Macedonia's Academy of Arts and Sciences on the possibility of an exchange of population and territory with Kosovo and Albania. In these discussions, it was suggested that portions of Albanian-inhabited areas in the west, including Gostivar, Tetovo, and Debar be transferred to Albania, while Albania would cede territory near lakes Ohrid and Prespa. Several hundred thousand Albanians and over 50,000 Macedonians would be resettled. Such an arrangement was implausible since Macedonia would gain far more than Albania would, trading poor, mountainous territory for fertile agricultural land. Such an exchange has been widely condemned in both countries. But if ethnic tensions remain and both sides remain intransigent, will such a policy of ethnic cleansing look more appealing?

The "Macedonia Paramilitary 2000 Order," issued anonymously and reported in late June by Human Rights Watch, threatened to kill one hundred illegally resident Albanians for every police officer or soldier killed and to burn shops owned by Albanians. Other reports suggest that ethnic Macedonian paramilitary organizations such as the "Lions" had formed that could take action outside of government control. Albanian guerrillas, in turn, threatened to shell government installations in Skopje and were likely to retaliate against Macedonians. If fighting continued, the possibility of an all-out war could not be discounted, with the Albanians in Kosovo and Albania aiding the NLA in its struggle.

## RECENT HISTORY AND THE FUTURE

On August 12, 2001, a cease-fire agreement was reached that promised to end the violence in Macedonia. The NLA would disarm to a 3,500-strong NATO force. In return the Macedonian government would address rebel concerns. Specifically, the constitution would be changed to define the country as a civic multiethnic society. Albanian would become an official language in areas where 20 percent of the population speak it, and higher education would be offered in Albanian in all such regions. Ethnic Albanian participation in the Constitutional Court and police would be increased. A new census would be taken later in the year 2001. Broader authority would be granted to local governments. And checks and

# THE CONSTITUTION

Many of the grievances held by Albanians stem from the status provided for minorities in the 1991 Constitution of the Republic of Macedonia. Ethnic Macedonian leaders point to guarantees for minority status, while ethnic Albanian leaders argue that Macedonians enjoy a privileged position. Some of the key sections in question include:

**The preamble:**

> ... Macedonia is established as a national state of the Macedonian people, in which full equality as citizens and permanent coexistence with the Macedonian people is provided for Albanians, Turks, Vlachs, Romanies, and other nationalities living in the Republic of Macedonia...

**Article 7**

- (1) The Macedonian language, written using its Cyrillic alphabet, is the official language in the Republic of Macedonia.

- (2) In the units of local self-government where the majority of the inhabitants belong to a nationality, in addition to the Macedonian language and Cyrillic alphabet, their language and alphabet are also in official use, in a manner determined by law.

- (3) In the units of local self-government where there is a considerable number of inhabitants belonging to a nationality, their language and alphabet are also in official use, in addition to the Macedonian language and Cyrillic alphabet, under conditions and in a manner determined by law.

**Article 48**

- (1) Members of nationalities have a right freely to express, foster and develop their identity and national attributes.

- (2) The Republic guarantees the protection of the ethnic, cultural, linguistic and religious identity of the nationalities.

- (3) Members of the nationalities have the right to establish institutions for culture and art, as well as scholarly and other associations for the expression, fostering and development of their identity.

- (4) Members of the nationalities have the right to instruction in their language in primary and secondary education, as determined by law. In schools where education is carried out in the language of a nationality, the Macedonian language is also studied.

---

balances in parliament would insure that Albanians and Macedonians could protect their ethnic interests. Despite the fact that leaders on both sides endorsed the plan, scattered violence continued. Splinter factions on both sides may attempt to continue the violence.

Enforcement of such an agreement is another matter. Previous provisions by the Macedonian government for ethnic rights have been enforced sporadically. If agreements are not kept, then the NLA or an organization like it will likely rise again and begin another rebellion.

The chance for a backlash against the agreement on the part of Macedonians is a real concern. The riots in Bitola and Skopje against cease-fires were both sparked by internationally brokered cease-fires, which were widely unpopular among Macedonians. Many Macedonians resent the extreme influence that the European Union and United States exert when they use economic aid as "leverage" to influence domestic policy. And finally, many Macedonians see the government as being on the brink of victory, and a NATO task force as a pretext to aid Albanian rebels. This is not true—the Macedonian Army lacks well-trained troops for house-to-house fighting and has relied on artillery bombardment to flush out rebels rather than risk conscripts. A Macedonian victory will take time, time to train enough troops and prepare for a thorough reconquest of the west. Still, if Macedonian popular opinion deems settlement agreements as a "stab in the back" supported by the United States and the European Union, these feelings will provide political leaders with a popular, anti-Albanian platform in the future.

Probably the most difficult problem to solve in Macedonia at this time is how to reform state rule. Macedonia not only needs improved economic growth to recover the losses of the past two decades, but must establish an efficient government, eliminate corruption, and create a sense of "civil society" in which people can trust their political leaders. No matter the outcome of the current rebellion, the basic structural problems of the state will foment tension.

# BIBLIOGRAPHY

Ackerman, Alice. *Making Peace Prevail: Preventing Violent Conflict in Macedonia.* Syracuse, NY: Syracuse University Press, 2000.

Albanians in Macedonia Crisis Center. Available online at http://www.alb-net.com/amcc/ (cited July 26, 2001).

The Albanian American Civic League. Available online at http://www.aacl.com (cited July 26, 2001).

Banac, Ivo. *The National Question in Yugoslavia.* Ithaca, NY: Cornell University Press, 1984.

Barker, Elizabeth. *Macedonia: Its Place in Balkan Power Politics.* Reprint. Westwood, CT: Greenwood Press, 1980.

Brailsford, H. N. *Macedonia: Its Races and Their Future.* London: Methuen, 1906.

Carnegie Endowment. *The Other Balkan Wars: A 1913 Carnegie Endowment Inquiry in Retrospect.* Washington, DC: Carnegie Endowment Book, 1993.

Dzambazovski, Klimet, "Macedonia on the Eve of the Balkan Wars." In *East Central European Society and the Balkan Wars,* eds. Bela Kiraly and Dimitrije Djordjevic. New York: Columbia University Press, 1987.

Government of Macedonia. Available online at http://www.gov.mk/English/index.htm (cited July 26, 2001).

Human Rights Watch, "Conflict in Macedonia." Available online at http://www.hrw.org/campaigns/macedonia (cited July 26, 2001).

Judah, Tim. *Kosovo: War and Revenge.* New Haven, CT: Yale University Press, 2000.

Karakasidou, Anastasia, *Fields of Wheat, Hills of Blood: Passages to Nationhood in Greek Macedonia, 1870–1990.* Chicago: University of Chicago Press, 1997.

Kofos, Evangelos. *Nationalism and Communism in Macedonia.* New York: A. Caratzas, 1993.

Kosova Liberation Army. Available online at http://www.kosovapress.com (cited July 26, 2001).

Lampe, John. *Yugoslavia: Twice There Was a Country.* 2nd ed. New York: Cambridge University Press, 2000.

Macedonia.org. Available online at http://www.macedonia.org (cited July 26, 2001).

Macedonian Information Agency. Available online at http://www.mia.com.ml/webang.asp (cited July 26, 2001).

MAK-NEWS (Macedonia). Available online at http://www.maknews.com/ (cited July 26, 2001) .

Manchevski, Milcho. *Before the Rain.* Film, 112 min; Polygram Video, 1999.

Palmer, Stephen, and Robert King. *Yugoslav Communism and the Macedonian Question.* Hamden, CT: Archon Books, 1971.

Perry, Duncan. *The Politics of Terror: The Macedonian Revolutionary Movements, 1893–1903.* Durham, NC: Duke University Press, 1998.

Pettifer, James. *The New Macedonian Question.* New York: St. Martin's Press, 1999.

Poulton, Hugh. *Who are the Macedonians?* Bloomington: Indiana University Press, 1995.

Ridgeway, James, and Jasminka Udovicki, eds., *Burn this House: The Making and Unmaking of Yugoslavia.* Durham, NC: Duke University Press, 1997.

Ritovski, Blazhe. *Macedonia and the Macedonian People.* Skopje, Macedonia: Magnat, 1999.

Rossos, Andrew. "Macedonians and Macedonian Nationalism on the Left," in Ivo Banac and Katherine Verdery, eds., *National Character and National Ideology in Interwar Eastern Europe.* New Haven, CT: Yale Center for International and Area Studies, 1995.

Stavrianos, L.S. *The Balkans Since 1453.* 2d. ed. London: C. Hurst & Co., 2000.

Sugar, Peter F., ed. *Eastern European Nationalism in the Twentieth Century.* Lanham, MD: American University Press, 1995.

———. *Southeastern Europe Under Ottoman Rule.* Seattle, WA: University of Washington Press, 1977.

Todorova, Maria, "The Balkans From Discovery to Invention," *Slavic Review* 53 (1994): 453–482.

Vickers, Miranda, and James Pettifer. *Albania: From Anarchy to a Balkan Identity.* New York: New York University Press, 1997.

*James Frusetta*

# DEFENDING AGAINST THE INDEFENSIBLE: CREATING A NATIONAL MISSILE DEFENSE IN THE UNITED STATES

The warning could come out of the blue—a missile launch has been detected, and the likely target is the West Coast city of Los Angeles. Or, a possible nuclear missile strike could be used as a bargaining chip, committing the United States to respect a blackmail offer that threatens the annihilation of one of its larger cities. The George W. Bush administration argues that either of these scenarios is a possibility in the near future and is, therefore, constructing a missile defense shield designed to destroy incoming missiles during three separate phases: immediately after launch, during the "boost" phase in which the missile climbs in the atmosphere, and during its descent immediately before impact.

Bush's proposed missile defense initially intends a 60 percent (or $3 billion U.S.) increase in missile defense efforts in the first year, bringing total missile defense outlays to $8 billion U.S. annually. The specifics of the National Missile Defense (NMD) plan remains vague, but most of the additional appropriations appear to be dedicated to short-range or theater missile defenses dedicated to protecting battlefield personnel. A significant sum, however, is being allocated to long-range missile defense systems, which are those systems designed to protect entire cities and targets from intercontinental strikes. In all, the plan suggests that the Defense Department would deploy at least 1,000 defensive interceptors capable of destroying long-range missile warheads, and many Bush administration officials have expressed very publicly their hopes of limited deployment within three to four years.

The Bush administration's pursuit of NMD has encountered much criticism, both at home and abroad, in the key areas of its feasibility, cost, and

## THE CONFLICT

The George W. Bush administration has pushed ahead with plans for a U.S. National Missile Defense (NMD) program to be deployed in about 2005 at tremendous cost and with questionable feasibility. Critics say that deployment of the NMD could threaten the world security environment by fueling an arms race and make enemies out of current allies.

### Political

- With "rogue states" such as North Korea and Iraq developing nuclear arsenals, those in favor of developing the NMD argue for the system as insurance against nuclear terrorism. Opponents favor diplomacy and engagement and point to the infeasibility of the program.

- The United States and the Soviet Union limited themselves in the 1972 Anti-Ballistic Missile treaty to two anti-ballistic missile sites, later cut to one each. Breaking the treaty could mean instigating other states to build up nuclear arsenals. Russia has not agreed to withdraw from the treaty, even at the urging of the Bush administration.

### Economic

- NMD would cause a 60 percent increase in the missile defense budget in its first year alone. With such a huge outlay of funds for missile defense, other kinds of military expenditure will be neglected.

# CHRONOLOGY

*1939–45* Germany develops the first guided missiles, the V-1 and V-2 rockets, during World War II.

*1956–63* The United States establishes the Nike-Zeus program, with interceptor missiles to carry to high altitudes and explode nuclear warheads designed to destroy incoming missiles.

*1957* The Soviet Union develops an intercontinental ballistic missile, with the successful launch of the *Sputnik* satellite. The United States soon follows with its own and the "arms race" in nuclear weapon delivery systems is on.

*1961–67* Nike-X program replaces Nike-Zeus, and advances missile technology.

*1967* Sentinel program, introduced by Defense Secretary Robert McNamara, pursues a limited shield. An attempt stop the anti-ballistic system program from further advance is made.

*1969* A close vote in the Senate results in the deployment of the Sentinel system.

*1972* At the Strategic Arms Limitation Talks (SALT) negotiators discuss limiting antiballistic missile technology. The Antiballistic Missile (ABM) treaty is signed.

*1974* SALT II results in further limitations on anti-ballistic missile systems.

*March 23, 1983* Ronald Reagan delivers his "Star Wars" speech, launching his Strategic Defense Initiative (SDI).

*1985* The Pentagon proposes a $4 billion system, capable of defending 3,500 targets against Soviet

attack, but many elements prove to be technologically not feasible.

*1991* George Bush Sr. launches Global Protection Against Limited Strikes (GPALS) system, which includes a limited number of offensive ballistic missiles.

*1991* Iraqi "Scuds" launched against Israel and the coalition forces in Saudi Arabia cause the first U.S. combat casualties due to missiles. Congress enacts the Missile Defense Act (MDA), calling for a deployment of a ground-based system of interceptors by 1996.

*1996* The secretary of defense transitions NMD program from a technology development effort to an acquisition effort with a mission to develop a deployable system within three years by 2000.

*September 2000* National Missile Defense Independent Review Team reports that the United States is not capable of fielding an NMD within the next five years. President Bill Clinton defers authorizing the Pentagon to proceed with the system.

*June 16, 2001* U.S. President George W. Bush and Russian President Vladimir Putin meet to discuss the 1972 Antiballistic Missile Treaty, but fail to reach agreement.

*July 14, 2001* After many unsuccessful defense technology tests, a new missile defense weapon launched from the Marshall Islands achieved success when it collided with the targeted decoy missile and destroyed it.

---

impact upon the world security environment—all familiar criticisms in the history of missile defense. No such system has ever been created, and critics are highly skeptical that any defense system could ever advance more quickly than missile technology itself. The cost of developing a missile defense system could preclude developments in other areas of defense, and expanding development of an antiballistic missile (ABM) system, and the consequent withdrawal from an ABM treaty signed with the Soviet Union in 1972, could lead to the proliferation of nuclear missiles in other states. The Bush administration, however, has argued

that the danger of rogue missile attacks is great enough, and the fear of nuclear attack strong enough, to warrant the pursuit of an antiballistic system in the United States.

## HISTORICAL BACKGROUND

### *The History of Missile Defense*

The modern missile arose with the invention of the V-1 and V-2 rockets by Germany during World War II. Both rockets were used as weapons against England following the Nazi capture of

TWO MEN EXAMINE THE MIRROR OF THE REFLEXICON LASER, WHICH WAS CONSTRUCTED AS PART OF THE STRATEGIC DEFENSE INITIATIVE UNDER PRESIDENT RONALD REAGAN'S ADMINISTRATION IN THE 1980s. (© *Roger Ressmeyer/Corbis. Reproduced by permission.*)

most of Western Europe. The V-1 was relatively noisy and slow and was, therefore, also easy to counter, but there was virtually no defense against the quiet, fast, and relatively accurate V-2 rockets. Fortunately for the British and the rest of the allies, use of the V-2 reached its peak immediately prior to the conclusion of the war and had little impact on the overall outcome of the conflict.

The initial nuclear arms race between the United States and Soviet Union in the early 1950s concentrated on increases in the number and quality of aircraft-delivered bombs. Both governments virtually ignored missile and antimissile capacity because the technology for long-range missiles was not well developed. This soon changed, however, with the successful launch of the *Sputnik* satellite by the Soviets on October 4, 1957, and the launching pad failure of the U.S.-constructed *Vanguard* rocket a few weeks later. By January 1958, the United States had successfully launched its *Explorer I* satellite into orbit, and both countries began a push to develop offensive and defensive long-range missile capabilities.

In the United States, antimissile defenses began with the Nike-Zeus program in 1958. This program called for interceptor missiles to carry and explode nuclear warheads at very high altitudes (60 miles, 96.56 kilometers, or more above the earth's surface). These explosions were designed to destroy incoming missiles. Rocket technology was capable of producing these interceptor missiles, but the radar technology dedicated to tracking the missiles was ill-equipped to deal with large numbers of missiles and counter-measures like decoys and was also physically vulnerable to attack. Another concept that reached beyond existing technological capabilities was the Ballistic Missile Boost Intercept (BAMBI) program. This concept called for satellite-based missiles containing huge wire mesh arrays—giant nets much like those used by the butterfly enthusiast—designed to kill offensive missiles in the first five minutes of flight. The cost of the technological leaps necessary to make this feasible was prohibitive in the context of an escalating nuclear arms race, however.

The Nike-Zeus program was replaced by Nike-X in 1961. This program made several important advances, including improved missile technology, a new short-range interceptor with a nuclear tip named Sprint, and electronically guided radar capable of handling a large number of incoming missiles. The advances made by Nike-X were carried on by its successor program, Sentinel, in 1967. In introducing this program, Defense Secretary Robert McNamara by then recognized the dangers of ballistic missile defense. He and

# WHAT IS A MISSILE DEFENSE SYSTEM?

Missile Defense is any system—on land, at sea, or in space—designed to detect, intercept, and destroy missiles before they hit their targets. There are several kinds of proposed missile defense systems that function, or may someday function, in different ways.

One of the basic current models of U.S. missile defense works with satellites that orbit the earth in space, serving as sensors, combined with tracking radars and an early warning system at work on the earth. If a missile is launched toward the United States, the early warning detectors and the sensors in space detect it and track its movement. Then interceptor rockets are launched, which hit the missile's warhead (the part that causes the explosion) at tremendous speed—approximately 16,000 miles an hour—destroying it in space.

Another kind of missile defense system is set up on rigs on land or in the sea near the enemy. Because they are close to the enemy missile launch sites, these defense missiles can intercept enemy missiles in the "boost phase," while they are on their way up. A third kind of missile defense system is called the Theatre High Altitude Air Defense (THAAD). This is a ground-based system, in which computer-guided missiles seek out and destroy incoming missiles in space.

In 2001 President George W. Bush proposed a fixed, land-based, non-nuclear missile defense system with a space-based detection system. He would like to develop a "shield" protecting all 50 states and possibly even U.S. allies.

To a large extent, the missile defense system is still in the idea stage only. Technology is not yet in place to deploy such a system. Testing of aspects of the missile defense systems began in the Clinton administration in 1998 and was stepped up by the Bush administration in 2001. On July 14, 2001, after a series of failures, a test of the NMD system was pronounced successful by the administration. A target missile set up with one large balloon as a mock warhead was launched from Vandenberg Air Force Base in California. Then an interceptor missile or "kill vehicle" was launched from the Kwajalein Atoll in the Marshall Islands, 4,800 miles away in the Pacific. The kill vehicle hit the warhead, and both the target and kill vehicle exploded high above the earth.

Critics of the test say that the ability of the kill vehicle to discriminate between the warhead and a dummy or decoy—a crucial factor that had failed in past tests—was not in fact tested, since the target was equipped with a global positioning satellite beacon that guided the kill vehicle toward it. Other critics of the missile defense tests warn that there are so many different factors that need to work together within one system, the ability to test the systems in a situation even remotely simulating reality is not yet feasible.

Each defense missile test has been said to cost approximately $100 million. If the Bush administration attempted to test the various kinds of defense systems: ground-based interceptors, sea-based systems, airborne laser, and space-based lasers, many observers estimate the development program will cost about $100 billion.

---

President Lyndon B. Johnson's administration (1963–69) believed that the United States would probably never be able to defeat an all-out attack by the Soviet Union, so only a limited shield, dedicated to protecting major cities, was to be pursued by Sentinel. Foreshadowing the current debate over NMD, McNamara also argued that attempts to deploy a comprehensive antiballistic missile system would only fuel an offensive arms race designed to thwart advancing technologies. In 1969, under the Richard M. Nixon administration (1969–74), the Sentinel system was deployed after a tie-breaking vote was cast in the Senate by then-Vice President Spiro Agnew.

Limited shields in place to defend major cities against the limited threats of small arsenals (such as China's at the time) became the guiding concept for United States-based antiballistic missile defenses for the next 15 years. Intellectually and perhaps empirically, both the United States and the Soviet Union had reached a period of what scholars have termed nuclear deterrence. Both countries were capable of withstanding a crippling initial nuclear attack and of responding to the first attack with a similarly crippling counter-strike. The survivability of the first attack was thought to logically ensure that no rational leader would ever attempt his or her own country's destruction by

CRITICS OF A NATIONAL MISSILE DEFENSE SYSTEM IN THE UNITED STATES QUESTION ITS EFFECTIVENESS IN LIGHT OF THE CHANGING THREATS TO NATIONAL SECURITY. *(By Daryl Cagle for Slate.com. Reproduced by permission.)*

escalating a dispute to the point of nuclear war. Mutually Assured Destruction (MAD), as it came to be called, was therefore thought to ensure an incredibly tense peace between the world's superpowers. This led both countries to pursue technologies that made their nuclear arsenal defensible against any imaginable type of first strike. It also led both countries to eschew technologies that rendered second-strike capabilities ineffectual.

The conceptual framework of MAD led negotiators in 1972 to focus their Strategic Arms Limitation Talks (SALT) to limiting the pursuit of antiballistic missile technology. The Antiballistic Missile (ABM) treaty, signed by representatives from both the United States and the Soviet Union,

limited each country to two antiballistic missile interceptor sites, and these two were subsequently reduced to one site each by a 1974 protocol. The Soviet Union chose to defend Moscow while the United States focused its defenses on the Minuteman missile site in Grand Forks, North Dakota. Within one year, however, Congress voted to close the Grand Forks site after it became apparent that a Soviet move to equip their missiles with multiple independent reentry vehicles (MIRVs) would easily overwhelm the interceptor site. This, and the fact that most experts agreed that the radar systems would be blinded with the first electromagnetic pulse of a nuclear explosion over the site, led to the demise of the system less than four months after it became operational.

# THE 1972 ANTIBALLISTIC MISSILE TREATY: BUSH'S ARGUMENT FOR ABROGATION

President George W. Bush's proposal for a National Missile Defense has as its mission the protection of all 50 states of the union. To try and raise a "shield" over the whole nation is not legal under the 1972 Antiballistic Missile (ABM) Treaty signed by U.S. President Richard M. Nixon and Soviet President Leonid Brezhnev when the two nations were enemies in the Cold War. The treaty, which forbids either nation to build antimissile systems covering more than two (later changed to one) areas within their borders, is designed to balance the powers. Since both nations are vulnerable and both nations have the capacity to retaliate should the other attack with missile forces, neither side is likely to engage in missile warfare. In 2001, President Bush argued for breaking the treaty, saying that with the Cold War over, the treaty no longer makes sense.

An excerpt from Bush's Speech on Missile Defense Development at National Defense University, May 1, 2001 (available on the World Wide Web at http://www.whitehouse.gov/news/releases/2001/05/20010501-10.html):

> [During the Cold War] the security of both the United States and the Soviet Union was based on a grim premise that neither side would fire nuclear weapons at each other, because doing so would mean the end of both nations.
>
> We even went so far as to codify this relationship in a 1972 ABM Treaty, based on the doctrine that our very survival would best be ensured by leaving both sides completely open and vulnerable to nuclear attack....
>
> In that world, few other nations had nuclear weapons, and most of those who did were responsible allies, such as Britain and France. We worried about the proliferation of nuclear weapons to other countries, but it was mostly a distant threat, not yet a reality.
>
> Today, the sun comes up on a vastly different world. The Wall is gone, and so is the Soviet Union. Today's Russia is not yesterday's Soviet Union....

> The Iron Curtain no longer exists. Poland, Hungary and Czech Republic are free nations and they are now our allies in NATO, together with a reunited Germany. Yet, this is still a dangerous world; a less certain, a less predictable one.
>
> More nations have nuclear weapons and still more have nuclear aspirations. Many have chemical and biological weapons. Some already have developed a ballistic missile technology that would allow them to deliver weapons of mass destruction at long distances and incredible speeds, and a number of these countries are spreading these technologies around the world.
>
> Most troubling of all, the list of these countries includes some of the world's least-responsible states. Unlike the Cold War, today's most urgent threat stems not from thousands of ballistic missiles in the Soviet hands, but from a small number of missiles in the hands of these states—states for whom terror and blackmail are a way of life.
>
> They seek weapons of mass destruction to intimidate their neighbors, and to keep the United States and other responsible nations from helping allies and friends in strategic parts of the world. When Saddam Hussein invaded Kuwait in 1990, the world joined forces to turn him back. But the international community would have faced a very different situation had Hussein been able to blackmail with nuclear weapons.
>
> Like Saddam Hussein, some of today's tyrants are gripped by an implacable hatred of the United States of America.
>
> They hate our friends. They hate our values. They hate democracy and freedom, and individual liberty. Many care little for the lives of their own people. In such a world, Cold War deterrence is no longer enough to maintain peace, to protect our own citizens and our own allies and friends.
>
> We must seek security based on more than the grim premise that we can destroy those who seek to destroy us. This is an important opportunity for the world to rethink the unthinkable and to find new ways to keep the peace. Today's world requires a new policy, a broad strategy of active nonproliferation, counter-proliferation and defenses.

Further research into NMD was not seriously pursued until President Ronald Reagan's (1981–89) famous "Star Wars" speech on March 23, 1983. The Strategic Defense Initiative (SDI) began as a way of making "nuclear weapons impotent and obsolete" according to Reagan. His critics charged that the "Star Wars" plan, which envisioned satellite-based lasers and missiles striking incoming warheads, was actually an excuse for large increases in defense spending. In 1985, the Pentagon proposed a system that would be capable of defending 3,500 targets against Soviet attack at a cost of $4 billion U.S., but many antimissile concepts were soon abandoned as technologically not feasible. This, however, did not stop the subsequent George H. Bush administration, after the collapse of the Soviet Union, from calling for a grand Global Protection Against Limited Strikes

(GPALS) system designed to thwart tactical, theater, and a limited number of offensive ballistic missiles.

As with most concepts, technology and theory followed events, and the Iraqi missile strikes that inflicted the first-ever U.S. combat casualties caused by missiles led Congress to enact the Missile Defense Act (MDA) of 1991. The MDA was a response to the early (and much exaggerated) reports of the successes achieved by Patriot missiles in knocking down Iraqi Scud missiles. It called for deployment of a ground-based system of interceptors by 1996. The Pentagon later pushed this deployment date back to 2002 because the initial date was, again, not technologically feasible.

The election of the first Democratic president in more than 12 years, President Bill Clinton (1993–2000), gave rise to a new skepticism regarding defense spending. However, estimates soon surfaced that the Iraqis were, prior to the Gulf War in 1991, within six months of having a nuclear weapon and would, therefore, be capable of blackmailing the United States or of attacking any of its neighbors. This, and the eventual Republican ascension to leadership in both houses of Congress, led to a new push for a National Missile Defense (NMD) system deployable by 2003. Technological setbacks, including "misses" in two out of three tests of the early system, pushed the deployment date back to 2005— a year in which most experts estimated that the North Koreans would be capable of hitting the U.S. mainland with a ballistic missile of their own. In 1999, the North Koreans agreed to a moratorium on further development of these long-range missiles in exchange for increased aid, but the North Koreans could still likely field such a long-range missile by 2006.

In September 2000, based on the report of the National Missile Defense Independent Review Team that argued that the United States would not be capable of fielding an NMD by 2005, President Clinton announced his decision not to authorize the Pentagon to proceed with the system. The NMD system, according to Clinton, was technologically infeasible and deployment would significantly threaten the world security environment—Russia, China, and even close allies in Europe had all expressed doubts about pursuit of the system. Clinton's refusal to authorize came only four months after then-Texas Governor George W. Bush called for an ambitious program of NMD.

A PROTOTYPE U.S. AIR FORCE MISSILE WITH AN INTERCEPTOR ON BOARD IS LAUNCHED FROM MECK ISLAND. A MODIFIED INTERCONTINENTAL BALLISTIC MISSILE WAS LAUNCHED AS AN INTERCEPT TARGET, BUT THE ATTEMPTED INTERCEPTION FAILED. (© *Reuters NewMedia Inc./Corbis. Reproduced by permission.*)

## RECENT HISTORY AND THE FUTURE

### The Current Imbroglio: The Rogue State Threat

The *raison d'être* of President Bush's calls for NMD has been the possible existence of "rogue states" whose interests do not conform to the rational expectations of Mutually Assured Destruction, and who would possibly risk their own survival in confrontations with the United States—the likely list of such states includes at least Iran and Iraq in the Middle East, as well as North Korea in Asia. Critics have assailed the rationale behind the NMD plan, however, by arguing that engagement rather than isolation is the best method of protection against these so-called rogue states. Money used in diplomatic efforts, through mutual aid and confidence-building measures, is better at pacifying and, hopefully, satisfying the leaders of these states. Adherents of the "democratic peace," which argues that democracies are more peaceful than other types of governments, further argue that diplomatic efforts could lessen tensions and provide the political environment necessary for a peaceful transition to democracy; isolation of these states has only seemed to intensify the political hold of their leaders—witness Iraq and Cuba.

If diplomatic efforts fail, as they often do, critics further charge that the real threats from these states would not be missile based. Instead, state-backed terrorist groups or the rogue states themselves are much more likely to smuggle the nuclear or biological warheads into the United States than to try to acquire the technology necessary to reach their targets through the air. NMD would be incapable of stopping this threat, and pursuit of the costly program would greatly reduce or prevent the development of advancements in anti-terrorist capabilities.

## Cost and Feasibility

Nevertheless, the main obstacle to NMD is, as it always has been, the cost and feasibility of national antiballistic missile defense. The National Missile Defense Independent Review Team in 2000 argued that ever-increasing offensive technological advances would forever outstrip any technological gains in defense capabilities. In other words, the antiballistic missile race could never be won, and in dollars, it would be a costly race to pursue (currently at $8 billion U.S. annually).

## Cost to International Security

Critics contend that the costs of the program would also be felt in a more hostile world environment. The Bush administration has courted Russia, its cosignatory of the 1972 ABM Treaty, to allow a mutual withdrawal from the antiballistic missile treaty regime. The destruction of this treaty regime, which is often credited with limiting international tensions among nuclear powers, could, however, lead to large increases in the nuclear arsenal of China. Of course, because of the interconnectedness of the current political environment, increases in China's arsenal would also probably lead to increases in the arsenals of India and Pakistan—bitter rivals for more than 50 years.

Russia has consistently used the ABM Treaty, which it calls "the cornerstone of strategic stability" (but which in all likelihood was violated several times during the 1980s by both sides), to try to control the United States and deter its pursuit of a system capable of destroying an errant or intentional nuclear first strike. Only significant concessions, such as like much-needed development assistance, assurances on NATO expansions, etc., would convince Russia to alter its stance against a system that could potentially render its nuclear arsenal obsolete.

The NATO allies of the United States fear that the pursuit of NMD by the United States would lead the United States even further down a path of international isolationism. Following World War II (1939–45), the United States has played an active role in Europe and the rest of the world, fearing that the rise of small instabilities can lead to greater conflicts eventually affecting the United States homeland. If the United States were removed from the threat of attack at home, Europeans fear that it may retreat to its historically (pre-World War II) isolationist ways. In the first seven months of President George W. Bush's administration, the United States has either threatened to abrogate or has withdrawn from five major international treaties and protocols (including the ABM Treaty), so the European fear of a renewed was not unfounded.

## The Future of NMD

In spite of mounting criticisms at home and abroad, the Bush administration seems likely to continue and even succeed in deploying a rudimentary NMD within the next several years. At home, an increasingly larger portion of the budget dedicated to defense masks the significant outlays for this one project. The shifting control of the Senate has not seemed to stop the pursuit of more tests of rudimentary antimissile systems, and the first successful shoot-down of a missile by another a missile has led Bush administration officials to contemplate breaking ground for deployment in Alaska before the end of 2001—well ahead of the most optimistic technological reports.

Abroad, the United States faces a Europe that is rhetorically hostile to the concept of missile defense but which is also pursuing joint weapons design programs. Significant among these are the development of a short-range missile defense system with Germany and Italy and the discussion of a sophisticated radar system with Britain. Among non-European allies, the United States is working on both a medium-range theater defense and a high-energy laser with Israel and has signed an agreement with Japan for research on advanced missile components. The Bush administration is even set to begin talks on technology-sharing with Russia. The Russians are reported to have constructed a considerable laser infrastructure that may be applicable to the envisioned NMD, and they would likely trade this technology for information regarding U.S. advances in "hit-to-kill" missile technology. The technology gains for both sides plus the added incentive of increased revenues for Russia could make an agreement possible.

REPRESENTATIVE BARNEY FRANK (D-MASS.) ADDRESSES AN ANTI-MISSILE DEFENSE RALLY IN WASHINGTON, DC. OPPOSITION TO PRESIDENT GEORGE W. BUSH'S NATIONAL MISSILE DEFENSE PLAN HAS GROWN, WITH DEMOCRATS LEADING THE RESISTANCE. *(A/P Wide World. Reproduced by permission.)*

These agreements and possible agreements could leave China increasingly isolated, even though it signed an accord with Russia in July 2001 condemning the pursuit of NMD. The Chinese arsenal of 20 intercontinental ballistic missiles (ICBMs) could be increased fivefold with relative ease, and increasing tensions with the United States would make this choice likely. Still, such a move on China's part would not seem to hinder the pursuit of an NMD that could make China's arsenal impotent against the United States; instead, given the history of U.S. foreign policy, it could create a greater incentive for deployment.

The deployment of an NMD does not mean that the system would actually work. Much like MAD, an NMD would hopefully go significantly untested against the threat it is designed to thwart—a missile attack by a "rogue" state. It would also be impossible to know how a NMD would respond to an attack of 100 or more mis-

siles aimed at the United States, and it would obviously be ineffectual against non-missile chemical, biological, or nuclear attacks. A failure in any of these cases would be devastating, but without the NMD system, there would be no protection from these attacks at all.

The post-Cold War security environment is paradoxically more peaceful and more difficult for defense planners. The pursuit of NMD is a conscious effort by the Bush administration to grapple with the complexities of uncertain threats in an uncertain future. If the threat of missile-based nuclear weapons could be eliminated, the security of the United States would be dramatically improved. Unfortunately, previous attempts to acquire this security have not worked, and it is unclear whether current outlays will produce programs that will work in the future. Add to this the inherent costs, at home and abroad, of a move to an NMD system, and the Bush administration is taking a risky, expensive gamble. Whether that gamble is successful remains to be seen, but a rudimentary system of NMD seems likely to be deployed.

## BIBLIOGRAPHY

"Ballistic Missile Defense Organization Link." Available online at http://www.acq.osd.mil/bmdo/bmdolink/html/nmd.html (cited September 12, 2001).

Durch, William. *The ABM Treaty and Western Security.* Cambridge, MA: Ballinger, 1988.

Krass, Allan. *The United States and Arms Control.* Westport, CT: Praeger, 1997.

"National Missile Defense," *Washington Post.com.* Available online at http://www.washingtonpost.com/wp-dyn/nation/specials/nationalsecurity/nationalmissiledefense/ (cited September 4, 2001).

Sauer, Tom. *Nuclear Arms Control.* New York: St. Martins, 1998.

Stutzle, Walther, Bhupendra Jasani, and Regina Cohen. *The ABM Treaty: To Defend or Not to Defend?* New York: Oxford University Press, 1987.

"Weapons of Mass Destruction," Federation of American Scientists. Available online at http://www.fas.org/index.html (cited September 4, 2001).

*Douglas M. Gibler*

# NORTH KOREA: THE HERMIT KINGDOM IN THE GLOBAL ERA

In November 2001 U.S. President George W. Bush (2001–) issued a warning to the Democratic People's Republic of Korea (DPRK or North Korea) and Iraq that they would be "held accountable" if weapons of mass destruction designed for use in terrorism were being developed within their borders. He told North Korea that it should allow inspectors to determine whether there has been continued production of weapons of mass destruction in that county. Since the September 11, 2001, terrorist attacks on the World Trade Center and the Pentagon, the United States had been making it clear that it would take the "war on terrorism"—at the time being actively fought in Afghanistan—out to any other nations that it believed was sponsoring terrorism, and North Korea was on the U.S. list of seven countries that sponsor terrorism. Along with his warning Bush said that the United States would not negotiate with the North Koreans until they reduced their military forces—a new demand that infuriated North Korea.

In response the North Korean newspaper *Rodong Sinmun,* reporting that the United States was planning an attack on North Korea, stated that it would find the "Korean people to be in full combat preparedness to lay down their lives for their country," according to Doug Struck in the December 19, 2001, *Washington Post.* The paper claimed that the North Korean military was building itself up to meet the "strong-arm policy" of the United States.

There was plenty of antagonism preceding the September 11 terrorist attacks in the United States. When Bush came into office in 2001 he took a hard-line policy and quickly labeled North Korea a "rogue state," often pointing to

## THE CONFLICT

The Democratic People's Republic of Korea (DPRK or North Korea) has been isolated from relations with the United States and Europe since the Korean War ended in 1953. During those years it has engaged in the arms trade and developed capabilities with weapons of mass destruction. It was also suspected of sponsoring terrorist activities for several decades. By the late 1990s North Korea had lost its two major supporters in trade and aid, the former Soviet Union and China, as the Cold War ended. At the same time, the North Korean economy collapsed and famine struck the country. It seemed like a good time to end its isolation. But with its background of Cold War animosity, hard-line communism, and alleged terrorist activities it is difficult for the DPKR to take the steps to reintegrate and it is difficult for some world leaders to accept the DPKR as a legitimate nation.

### Political

- In the United States, political and military leaders agree that it is in the country's best interest to attempt to stop North Korea from producing or exporting any more weapons of mass destruction. Leaders disagree, however, regarding negotiating with the North Korean government: whether it should be through engagement and diplomacy or through economic sanction and isolation.

- While the leaders of North Korea have engaged with South Korea in its "sunshine policy," there is still a very long way to go to breach the tremendous differences that developed between the two nations. It is likely that they will never be able to reunite—as both sides wish—because the differences in government are so great. Alternative relations need to be considered.

### Economic

- Long-time economic sanctions against North Korea, the loss of China and Russia as trading partners, drought, and faulty agricultural policies have led the country into a long-lasting and devastating famine and the collapse of its economy. The last Stalinist communist system left in the world has been forced to look into entering the world market in order to survive.

# CHRONOLOGY

*1905–45* Japan occupies Korea and begins a colonial rule there.

*1945* The United States drops atomic bombs on Hiroshima and Nagasaki, Japan; Japan surrenders unconditionally and World War II ends. As Japan leaves Korea, the Soviet Army occupies its northern part; the United States occupies the southern part.

*1948* A UN-sponsored election takes place in the southern part of Korea. South Korea forms a government and elects a president. North Korea quickly holds its own elections and Kim Il Sung becomes the leader of the country.

*1950–53* The Korean War breaks out between North and South Korea and ends in stalemate.

*1950s* With the help of the Soviet Union, North Korea develops chemical weapons.

*1953–59* North Korea, assisted by the Soviet Union, hones its skills in spying, intelligence gathering, and other covert activities.

*1960s* North Korea begins to develop biological weapons.

*1960s–1980s* South Korea and other countries report kidnappings by North Koreans.

*1974* The first of four known tunnels across the demilitarized zone between North Korea and South Korea is found, with evidence that it was dug by the North Koreans.

*1980s* North Korea's economy falters; the country defaults on international loans and domestic production drops.

*Early 1980s* The DPRK begins producing Scud missiles domestically.

*October 9, 1983* North Korean terrorists make an attempt to assassinate South Korean President Chun Doo Hwan.

*1985* A small reactor is put into operation at a large nuclear complex in North Korea for the purpose of producing weapons-grade plutonium. Two larger reactors are built there later.

*November 28, 1987* A Korean airliner on its way from Baghdad to Bangkok explodes in mid-air, killing 115 people on board. A woman arrested for planting the bomb is a North Korean agent.

*1989* The Soviet Union dissolves, leaving North Korea without its accustomed sponsor and major trading partner.

*1990* North Korea is reported to have provided military training to groups in 62 countries.

*Early 1990s* The DPRK develops the Nodong, a missile believed to have a range of 1,000 to 1,300 kilometers with a large enough diameter in the missile body to accommodate an early generation nuclear warhead.

*1994* The so-called "Agreed Framework" effectively halts North Korean production of weapons-grade fuel and commits both the United States and North Korea to working towards normalizing relations, making the Korean peninsula free from nuclear weapons, and strengthening the international non-proliferation regime.

*1994* Kim Il Sung dies. A political struggle takes place before his son, Kim Jong Il, assumes power.

*1996* Famine hits North Korea.

*1996* A North Korean submarine runs aground in South Korea. It is suspected to have been on a terrorist mission targeting South Koreans.

*1998* The DPRK launches a Taepodong 1 missile directly over Japan.

*1998* South Korean President Kim Dae Jong announces the "sunshine policy" of détente between North and South Korea.

*1999* The Perry Report finds that any nuclear program in North Korea must be stopped, but rather than using sanctions and isolation to achieve this end, it suggests diplomacy and engagement.

*June 2000* The first summit between leaders of the DPRK and ROK takes place in South Korea in a meeting between President Kim Dae Jung and Kim Jong Il.

*June 19, 2000* The United States eases its economic sanctions against North Korea.

*October 6, 2000* The United States and North Korea issue a joint statement rejecting terrorism in any form.

*November 2001* U.S. President George W. Bush issues a warning to the DPRK it would be "held accountable" if weapons of mass destruction designed for use in terrorism were being developed within its borders.

North Korea as a major reason for developing a national missile defense in the United States. With a history of terrorist attacks, known nuclear capabilities, and its traditional cold war animosity, North Korea has been isolated from the Western world for a half century, since the end of the Korean War in 1953. There is little certainty about what goes on in North Korea. Intelligence shows that there may be underground activity in nuclear and missile development, and it is possible that the country has amassed large quantities of biological and chemical weapons as well. Yet North Korea's last known terrorist act was in 1987, and there is no conclusive evidence that it has reneged on its 1994 agreement to stop processing nuclear fuel.

As the twenty-first century began, progress—through diplomacy rather than threats—had been made in negotiations with North Korea. Discussions took a positive tone, particularly after the successful summit meeting of South Korean President Kim Dae Jung (1998–) and North Korean leader Kim Jong Il (1994–) in June 2000, the first meeting between leaders of the two nations since the Korean War (1950–53). Indeed, it appeared that the "hermit kingdom," as North Korea is known, would come out of its shell. This last bastion of Stalinist-type communism faced nearly complete isolation after losing its sponsors and trading partners, the former Soviet Union and China, in the 1990s. With its economy in a state of collapse and with millions of people dead from prolonged famine North Korea was making moves to end its 50-year isolation. The renewed verbal attacks in November 2001 were a step backward in what appears to be a long and difficult reintegration process. The conflict can best be understood by a review of the background of the DPRK's relationship to the international community.

## HISTORICAL BACKGROUND

Up to the end of the nineteenth century the people of Korea led a reasonably peaceful, agrarian life in a territory about the size of the U.S. state of Mississippi. For thousands of years, despite part of their country being conquered by the Chinese or Japanese, Koreans managed to thrive in an environment that was not particularly hospitable—a land of formidable mountains, rocky soil, a short growing season, and few harbors. Efforts to invade Korea generally failed to endure because the costs outweighed the gains; Korea was poor. Because it was bordered in the north by China, which exercised a strong influence on its political and economic well being, Korea was much influenced by Chinese philosophy and language, especially by Confucianism. Korean daily life reflected the Confucian ideals of orderliness and correct relations between government and citizens, family relations, and social customs. And because they had almost no contact with cultures outside China and Japan, other than with a few missionaries from the West and some American "gunboat diplomacy" (diplomacy backed by the use or threat of military force), Koreans viewed outsiders as barbarians.

From the end of the nineteenth century to the end of World War II (1939–45) Korea, along with China, was tyrannized and terrorized by Japanese occupation. The Japanese colonial government held tremendous power over the Korean people, maintained by a powerful police force. Koreans were told that they could not even speak their own language at home, their newspapers were closed down, and they were compelled to change their names to Japanese names. During World War II women were forced into prostitution and men into slave labor. Resistance against the Japanese was brutally put down.

The best known Korean guerrilla fighter against Japan's empire, from the 1930s onward, was Kim Il Sung (1912–94). When, in 1945, the Japanese unconditionally surrendered to the Americans following the first and only use to date of atomic bombs on Hiroshima and Nagasaki, the U.S. and Soviet allies began a "proxy fight" for control of the Korean peninsula. While the United States wanted to be sure that the Soviet Union and the forces of communism did not take over the Korean peninsula, the Soviets, too, wished to prevent an American military presence on continental Asia that could pose a future threat. Korea, always a single country, was divided in two by these foreign powers, with the Soviets occupying the northern part of the country above the 38th parallel and the Americans occupying the south.

In 1948 an American-backed United Nations (UN) team arrived in Korea to set up elections for a Korean government. The Russians and the North Koreans refused to cooperate. The UN-sponsored election was then held in the south without the input of northern Korea. The election of a government in the south was quickly followed by an election sponsored by the Soviet Union and held in the north. Kim Il Sung, who had become the *de facto* leader in the north with the help of the Soviets, was elected. By early 1949 the military

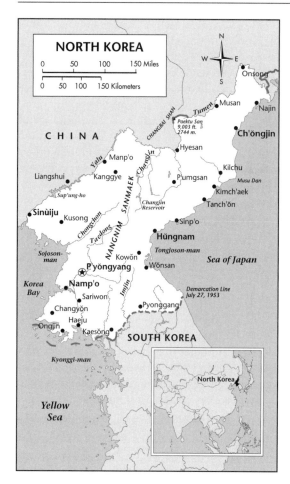

MAP OF NORTH KOREA. (© *Maryland Cartographics. Reprinted with permission.*)

governments, and most of the Soviet and U.S. troops, had left Korea, but both countries left behind a core of military advisors. Thus the two Korean governments that exist to this day were created.

### The Two World Wars

To understand what happened next—the Korean War of 1950–53—and why that set the path of both North and South Korea to the present day, we must broaden the context past even China, Japan, and the United States. The first half of the twentieth century was racked by two world wars, both begun by Germany. Germany was the last of the great European military and economic powers to try to carve out a world empire for itself. For centuries European technological progress, fueled by the great innovations of science and the wedding of military and industrial might, enabled governments to expand their control over other cultures and their governments. The United King-

dom, French, and Russian empires had managed to reach a rough equilibrium with each other and lesser European colonizers such as the Dutch and the Belgians. But they had not found a balance with the Germans, who had twice proceeded to expand through intimidation and conquest into territories controlled by other empires. Similarly, the Japanese, adopting German constitutional structure, law, and military strategy, proceeded to colonize China, carrying out more forcefully what had already been started by the Europeans half a century earlier—effectively exercising suzerainty, meaning the control of foreign relations and other matters, over large areas of China.

After World War II the American public was fed up with war. The 12-million-man U.S. military was reduced to about 300,000 in only two years; the 40 percent of the U.S. economy that had been engaged in military production was reduced to one percent. By 1947 the United States had all but disarmed, leaving only token occupation forces in Germany and Japan. This was not, however, true of the Soviet Union. The Soviets retained a 12-million-man military, with 3 million in Europe alone. The leadership tried to expand the Union of Soviet Socialist Republics (USSR, or Soviet Union) into all of Eastern Europe and, indeed, wherever it could find a government willing to become communist or be taken over in revolution by a communist faction.

The reason for this behavior was not hard to see, communist ideology aside. Three times in the first half of the twentieth century they had been victims of vicious attacks from Western powers: first the "White Wars" following the communist revolution of 1917, then World War I (1914–18), and then World War II. The Soviets had been occupied for two years by the Germans, from their western border with Europe up to the Ural Mountains. They were not about to make the same mistake again; their goal was to establish a "buffer" of docile if not friendly peoples, between them and the rest of Europe.

### A Confluence of Conflicts on Korean Ground

In 1947 Korea was divided at the 38th parallel and under the military rule of Russia and the United States. One of the reasons the United States wanted a base in Korea was to help its ally, the Chinese nationalist government. Chiang Kai-shek (or Jiang Jĕi, 1887–1975), a general and long-time leader of China, was fighting his political enemy, communist leader and military general Mao Zedong (1893–1976), for control of China.

# KIM IL SUNG

*1912–1994* Kim Il Sung was born Kim Sung Ju just two years after Korea had been annexed by Japan. Kim's family left Korea for Manchuria, China, in 1925, to escape from the oppressive Japanese colonial rule. Kim attended school in Manchuria and began participating in radical, communist youth organizations in his teens. He was arrested at the age of 17 for his subversive political activities. After getting out of prison, he joined with guerrilla fighters in their attacks on the Japanese at the border between China and Korea. At that time he changed his name to Kim Il Sung, after a legendary anti-Japanese fighter. He fought the Japanese in Manchuria in the 1930s and around 1941 was forced to flee to the Soviet Union. There he received military and political training.

When the Soviets arrived in the northern part of Korea after World War II to accept the Japanese surrender, Kim returned home with them, dressed in the uniform of the Soviet army. In 1948 the North held elections and, with substantial help from the Soviet commanders, Kim was made premier of the new communist Democratic People's Republic of Korea (DPRK) as well as head of the Korean Workers' Party. His compelling wish was to invade South Korea and reunify the country under his rule. The invasion took place in June 1950. The United States and United Nations unexpectedly came to the defense of South Korea, and Kim turned for help to the chairman of the new People's Republic of China, Mao Zedong. In October the Chinese entered the war. The war lasted until the summer of 1953, with millions of lives lost and both Korean states decimated, but little had changed. The dividing line between North and South Korea remained nearly the same, and the war ended in a stalemate.

After the war Kim established a rigid, militarized communist government, ruling under the name "Great Leader." He admired Soviet Premier Joseph Stalin (1879–1953) and developed his own status as an absolute ruler. He allowed no opposition in his country and was known to deal very harshly with any dissent. He developed a doctrine of nationalist self-sufficiency, known as "juche." From the 1950s to the 1970s Kim emphasized heavy industry and collective farming, and the economy of North Korea thrived. By the 1970s, however, the great costs of Kim's military and public works spending overran any progress in other areas, and North Korea's economy began to sag. It continued to fall during the 1980s. In 1991 the Soviet Union—North Korea's main sponsor and trading partner, and Kim Il Sung's mentor and model—dissolved. Kim, with his cult of personality leadership and his rigid Stalinist model of communism, came to seem to the rest of the world a dangerous remnant of a bygone era.

Because of its history of terrorism and Cold War hostility, many Western countries were nervous about North Korea's nuclear capabilities. In 1993 Kim announced that North Korea would withdraw from the longstanding international Nuclear Nonproliferation Treaty. After some major international tension, former U.S. president Jimmy Carter negotiated with him, and new talks between North Korea and the United States began. Kim died in 1994 after being the absolute leader of the country for 46 years.

---

Chiang and Mao, political enemies long before the Japanese invasion of Manchuria and China, had joined forces to beat back the Japanese as the world war broke out, and were succeeding up until the time of the Japanese surrender. After the war they returned to their political struggle, turning China into a battle zone once again. This internal war continued until December 1949, almost a year and a half after the two Koreas were created.

One other piece of the puzzle must be put into place. By 1947 it had become clear to U.S. politicians and military leaders that the Soviet Union was going to pose a threat to peace in Europe, a threat to which the United States could not respond effectively given its disarmament, without a long delay that could prove catastrophic to Europe and, in time, to the United States. Thus that year saw the passage of the National Security Act. Never before had the United States had a large, permanent intelligence agency and what amounted to a war council.

The National Security Act created the Central Intelligence Agency (CIA), the Department of Defense (the Pentagon) and Joint Chiefs of

NORTH KOREANS WORK IN FLOOD-DAMAGED RICE PADDIES AS PART OF THE UNITED NATIONS "FOOD FOR WORK" PROGRAM. NORTH KOREA, DEVASTATED AT TURNS BY BOTH FLOOD AND DROUGHT, HAS FACED THE PERIODIC THREAT OF STARVATION, EXACERBATED BY ITS ISOLATION. *(A/P Wide World. Reproduced by permission.)*

Staff, the National Security Council, and launched the Truman Doctrine, which basically announced that wherever communism threatened a government, the United States would offer that government its assistance. Thus, only three years after World War II, the United States was fully into a new war. This was a new kind of war, a war not in face-to-face confrontation or with the loss of American life, but a war nonetheless, involving a billion people in dozens of countries, costing hundreds of billions of dollars in the end, and which would eventually result in the death of millions—the "Cold War."

### North Korea as a New Nation

After the creation of the two Koreas in 1948, with Soviet help, North Korea immediately began to build up its military and establish an economic infrastructure that was suited to capitalizing on its natural resources—the mining of coal, metals, and other minerals, and refinement using coal and hydroelectric power, which were plentiful due to its mountainous terrain. This period saw huge advances in literacy and industrialization of the north; even today, with all its difficulties, North Korea is 99 percent literate and has life expectancies of 68 for men and 74 for women.

The new communist North Korean regime capitalized on a half-century of fear and hatred that had resulted from the brutal Japanese occupation, using the people's strong feelings to bolster its nearly limitless power. For many Koreans the new government did not represent a radical departure from their traditional Confucian values, but instead represented those values in a hierarchical system modeled on the centralized Japanese bureaucratic, authoritarian system. Even communism was not a new ideology to Korea, which had one of the oldest communist parties in Asia. The North Korean people were told that South Korea had been taken over by a puppet government for a new colonial power—that the Americans were simply replacing the Japanese. Many North Koreans were encouraged that their country was receiving the support of Russia, an ally that had assisted Korea in defeating the Japanese. With the people strongly behind the government North Korea was actually established on a strong foundation.

### The Korean War

The Korean War must go down in history as a deadly error on all sides. Kim Il Sung, backed, if not prodded, by Joseph Stalin (1879–1953), attacked South Korea just two years after the

North was created and just six months after Mao forced Chiang, the U.S. ally, to flee to Taiwan with a million of his followers. The United States still had hopes of Chiang's return to China, and General Douglas MacArthur (1880–1964), then governor of Japan and commander of the Far East forces, was sure of victory in Korea. Ultimately, MacArthur's poor judgment brought the seasoned Chinese Red Army into the war, which resulted in almost one million Koreans losing their lives, roughly 1.5–2 million Chinese deaths, and the conflict ending in a stalemate. Worse, the war strengthened an alliance of convenience between China and Russia that lasted more than a decade and reduced Chiang's already slim chances of a return to mainland China to zero.

After the Korean War ended in stalemate in 1953 the Cold War continued to deepen worldwide. The North Korean government, with a very strong propaganda program, continued to instill hatred among its people for the South Korean government, the United States, and Europeans in general. Although the Soviets had withdrawn their troops from North Korea at the end of 1948 and had never actively joined in the Korean War, the Soviet Union maintained a strong relationship with North Korea after the war.

## Covert Operations in North Korea

The Soviets saw in the North an opportunity to extend the Cold War into subversive, covert operations by helping the North become a source of terrorism. Playing into North Korea's willingness to involve itself in terrorism was its past experiences and its relationship with the West. The West had given every indication that it was bent on destroying the North: Koreans had already witnessed the European dominance over China, the U.S. "invasion" of South Korea, and the West's apparent effort to dominate the Arab world through the creation of Israel. Grateful to Soviet and Chinese supporters who they perceived to have saved North Korea from annihilation at the hands of the United States and its "puppet" government in the South, and lacking the ability to wage conventional war, the DPRK turned to the tools of the weak, fostering guerrilla movements and terrorist attacks, services for which it paid well.

Thus, in the 1950s North Korea honed its intelligence gathering, placing infiltrators in South Korea. During the 1960s these efforts combined with hundreds of commando raids and some assassination attempts; by 1968 a direct assault was attempted on the "Blue House," the South Korean equivalent of the White House. Terrorism towards the South continued into the 1980s and peaked in 1983 with the killing of 18 South Korean officials in Rangoon, Burma, narrowly missing then President Chun Doo Hwan (1980–88). On November 28, 1987, a Korean airliner on its way from Baghdad to Bangkok exploded in mid-air, killing 115 people on board. A woman arrested for planting the bomb was a North Korean agent who claimed to have received instructions to bomb the plane from Kim Jong Il, Kim Il Sung's son and successor.

## The Rise to Military Power

According to the Library of Congress, the rise of North Korea as an exporter of terrorist and guerrilla training and support by 1990 was extensive: "By 1990 North Korea had provided military training to groups in sixty-two countries—twenty-five in Africa, nineteen in Central and South America, nine in Asia, seven in the Middle East, and two in Europe." The report went on to note that more than 5,000 foreign personnel received training by North Korea, and thousands of North Korean military advisers, mostly from the Reconnaissance Bureau, were dispatched to about 47 countries. "North Korea is a convenient alternative to the superpowers for military assistance."

North Korea was active in the Middle East and North Africa during the 1970s and 1980s. North Koreans aided Egypt and Syria in their 1973 war against Israel (the Yom Kippur War) by piloting Egyptian aircraft, and they aided Libya in its border conflict with Egypt in 1977. During the 1970s North Korea began to focus on a massive arms trade. For the decade ending in 1987, again quoting from the Library of Congress study (citing the US Arms Control and Disarmament Agency as its source), the DPRK earned about US$3.9 billion from arms transfers to over 30 countries. It also spent billions importing arms from China and the Soviet Union. "Arms sales during the peak year 1982 represented 38 percent of North Korea's total exports," the Library of Congress reports. "Arms exports between 1981 and 1987 averaged around 27 percent of exports annually, with a 1981 high of 40 percent and a 1986 low of 14 percent."

By 2000 North Korea's military forces ranked fifth in size of all military forces in the world, with about 1.1 million men under arms (comparable to India with 1.1 million, Russia with 1.2 million, and the United States with 1.4 million; see the North Korea Advisory Group's 1999 Report to the Speaker, U.S. House of Representatives).

# KIM JONG IL

*1941–* Kim Il Sung fled to Siberia in the Soviet Union in 1941, and the next year his son Kim Jong Il was born there. The official line of the North Korean government, however, is that Kim Jong Il was born in North Korea, in a cabin on Mount Paektu. "At the time of his birth there were flashes of lightning and thunder, the iceberg in the pond on Mount Paektu emitted a mysterious sound as it broke, and bright double rainbows rose up," is the official biographical information. Either way, the family returned to North Korea after the Japanese surrendered, and soon Kim's father was absolute leader of the country. Kim's mother died when he was seven and a younger brother died as well. Kim was sent to Manchuria during the Korean War, but returned when it was over. He graduated from Kim Il Sung University in 1964.

His father decided to make him his successor in 1980, giving him several high posts in the government—he was a member of the politburo from the mid-1970s. In 1991 he took over as commander-in-chief of North Korea's military forces. In 1994 Kim Il Sung died. Although Kim Jong Il stepped in as leader in fact, if not in title (calling himself "Dear Leader" as

opposed to his father, the "Great Leader"), it was three years before he took over as head of the Korean Worker's Party, and there were rumors of a political struggle. It was the first communist hereditary succession in history.

Kim Jong Il had been associated with terrorist attacks before his father's death. South Korea in particular and the West in general, knowing little about him, painted him as a spoiled and vain playboy, given to drunken rampages and ruthless womanizing. But when Kim Jong Il visited South Korea in 2000, it was apparent to the world that he was an intelligent and discerning leader, regardless of his views.

Kim Jong Il has maintained power in the worst of economic and political circumstances, whether through ruthless tyranny or skillful leadership or both. He has kept the secretive nature of the North Korean world intact, and for all the intelligence and speculation of South Korea and the United States, we know very little about the man or his government. Assessments of the dangers that North Korea poses to South Korea, Japan, or the United States necessarily hinge on an understanding of Kim Jong Il.

## North Korea's Weapons of Mass Destruction

Starting in the 1980s North Korea turned its attention to increasingly sophisticated weapons systems, including nuclear, biological, and chemical (NBC) weapons of mass destruction (WMD). In the early 1980s the DPRK acquired a 300-kilometer range Soviet Scud missile. Using it as a model North Korea began to produce Scuds domestically. One of its biggest customers for these missiles was Iran, which used them in its war with Iraq. By the early 1990s the DPRK had developed the Nodong, a missile believed to have a range of 1,000 to 1,300 kilometers with a large enough diameter in the missile body to accommodate an early generation nuclear warhead. In 1998 the DPRK successfully launched one Taepodong 1 missile (a multi-stage missile that uses the Nodong as its first stage and modified Scud as the second stage, and a third stage that evidently failed) directly over Japan. With greater distance capabilities, but generally poor accuracy, this weapon showed that North Korea had enough

expertise to attack not only Japan but also the United States with NBC weapons, creating the possibility of at least isolated terrorist attacks. Japan and the United States reacted with concern and anger at this missile test, and North Korea has not launched any missiles since 1998.

Since the early 1980s North Korea was believed to have operated a large nuclear complex, Yongbyon, with the purpose of producing weapons-grade plutonium. A small reactor was put into operation there in 1985, and two more were believed to be in the works. By the 1990s U.S. intelligence indicated that the DPRK nuclear program had generated enough plutonium for one or two nuclear weapons and was capable of much more.

According to the Federation of American Scientists (FAS) North Korea began developing biological and chemical weapons in the 1960s and this work was ongoing through the present. Although the FAS concluded that the use of bio-

THEN-U.S. SECRETARY OF STATE MADELINE ALBRIGHT AND NORTH KOREAN LEADER KIM JONG IL MET IN PYONGYANG IN OCTOBER 2000 AS PART OF A U.S. DIPLOMATIC EFFORT TO ENCOURAGE GREATER OPENNESS IN NORTH KOREA AND CALM TENSIONS IN THE AREA. *(© AFP/Corbis. Reproduced by permission.)*

logical weapons was improbable and impractical for North Korea, it was believed that "if North Korea did choose to employ biological weapons, it probably could use agents like anthrax, plague, or yellow fever..." On the other hand North Korea's chemical weapons development, which started in the 1950s with the help of the Soviet Union, is believed to be ready for full use. North Korea has the capacity to produce bulk quantities of nerve, blister, choking, and blood chemical agents.

## The Agreed Framework of 1994

Fear of North Korea's potential to cause massive destruction had come to a head well before the 1998 launching of the Taepodong 1. In 1994 talks began in earnest that resulted in the 1994 so-called "Agreed Framework," which effectively halted North Korean production of weapons-grade fuel (principally plutonium), and committed both the United States and North Korea to working towards normalizing relations, making the Korean peninsula free from nuclear weapons, and strengthening the international non-proliferation regime. Further, to replace the loss of potential power from the nuclear power plant development that was halted, a Korean Peninsula Energy Development Organization (KEDO) was created

with the intent of building a light-water reactor. This has yet to begin.

## Intelligence Assessments on the DPRK's Weapons Systems

Despite North Korea's well-known concern for secrecy, much can be said about both the DPRK's weapons systems development and the motivations underlying the North Korean's actions. There exists direct testimony of high-ranking defectors, careful intelligence assessments assembled by such independent and respected organizations as the Federation of American Scientists, and many publicly available materials generated by the U.S. government.

Colonel Ju-hwal Choi is one example. Choi defected from the People's Army in North Korea in 1995. In his testimony before the U.S. Congress in 1997, he stated the following regarding his government's weapons of mass destruction. Note the motivations underlying its development of these weapons. He stated, "It is widely known in North Korea that North Korea produces, deploys, and stockpiles two or three nuclear warheads and toxic material such as over 5,000 tons of toxic gas.... North Korea acquires powerful and destructive weaponry with political and military purposes in mind. By having the weapons, the North is able to prevent itself from being slighted by ... major powers ... and also to gain the upper hand in political negotiations and talks with them."

From the viewpoint of traditional "power politics," (*realpolitik* or "realistic politics"), this is a very sensible statement. The use of military power for political coercion is a normal, traditional activity in international relations, as any world history or world civilization class will attest.

### Collapse of the Economy

Unlike other communist countries, North Korea maintained its rigid, state-controlled form of communism into the twenty-first century. Although the economic strategy was successful into the 1970s, by the 1980s North Korea was defaulting on its loans and its domestic production was decreasing. The great cost of its military overpowered the nation's economy. In 1989 the Soviet Union disintegrated, leaving North Korea without its accustomed sponsor and its major trading partner. Then agricultural disaster struck with the worst drought in the recorded history of Korea. On top of the natural disaster, the agricultural system had been poorly managed. A deadly famine struck the country in 1996 and had not yet been corrected five years later. North Korea is secretive about its internal affairs, but humanitarian organizations estimate that millions have died from lack of food and sanitation.

Regarding NBC weapons, North Korea has already indicated its willingness to sacrifice some measure of secrecy to assure greater U.S. compliance in lifting economic sanctions that have been ongoing since the Korean War. The concern with sanctions is due to the convergence of three developments: (1) the decline and finally end of significant Russian and Chinese economic aid; (2) the obsolescence of North Korean industrial structure and agricultural disasters; and (3) the policy of normalization (1998 "sunshine policy") advocated by South Korean President Kim Dae Jung, which has brought about the beginnings of a new trade regime and investment opportunities between the two Koreas. Further, both Japan and the United States (through the United Nations) have shown their willingness to aid the North with food and medical assistance averting the worst effects of their agricultural crisis.

Regarding Sino-Russian aid, relations between the DPRK and its two former allies and supporters have become increasingly difficult. The focus has shifted from cold war politics and Korean peninsula brinkmanship to managing economic globalization processes through various financial crises and adapting to a freer trade and capital flow regimen. North Korea, whether it admits it or not, is being left behind by the major powers, with its only legacy its ability to intimidate through promoting terrorism.

## RECENT HISTORY AND THE FUTURE

### Reassessment in 2000

In the United States for many years it was customary to characterize Kim Jong Il (currently North Korea's "Dear Leader" as general secretary of the Korean Workers Party, chairman of the National Defense Commission of the DPRK, and supreme commander of the Korean People's Army), his father Kim Il Sung (the "Great Leader," who ruled North Korea from 1948 until his death in 1994), and their government, as somehow aberrant, even insane. North Korea remained isolated and for the most part the people of the West, and particularly Americans, did not know anything about what was going on there.

By isolating North Korea from international relations—if not the human race—the U.S. government has done a disservice to the American people and their public assessment of U.S. foreign policy by keeping them uninformed. That the American people were uninformed about North Korea became obvious in the first visit of Kim Jong Il to Seoul in 2000. What a shock to see an educated, good-humored fellow treating the media, the president of South Korea, Kim Dae Jung, and all others he met, with respect and intelligent dialogue. The myth of his insanity, paranoia, megalomania, and so on, just evaporated.

A year after the Taepodong-1 missile was fired, the United States underwent a thorough reassessment of it relations with North Korea. In November 1998 President Bill Clinton (1993–2001) appointed a committee, headed by Dr. William J. Perry, to review the United States' policy toward the DPRK. The Perry Report, issued eight months later, found that any nuclear program in North Korea was destructive to world peace and must be stopped, but rather than using sanctions and isolation to achieve this end, it suggested diplomacy and engagement, with a goal of integrating North Korea into international relations. "By negotiating the complete cessation of the DPRK's destabilizing nuclear weapons and long-range missile programs, this path would lead to a stable security situation on the Korean Peninsula.... On this path the United States and its allies would ... move to reduce pressures on the DPRK that it perceives as threatening. The reduction of perceived threat would in turn give the DPRK regime the confidence that it could coexist peacefully...."

By 2000 the DPRK had taken the first steps needed to establish relations with the U.K. and the European Community (through its friends in Sweden). Then, for the first time, an envoy of North Korean leaders visited the United States. From this meeting, a joint communiqué was issued by the United States and the DPRK stating that they no longer had hostile intentions and would work to develop a new relationship free from the past.

With the meeting of South Korean President Kim Dae Jung and North Korean General Secretary Kim Jong Il, held June 13–15, 2000, in Pyongyang, more than one myth was dispelled. First, the two leaders agreed to work, both independently and together, for reunification, to settle humanitarian issues such as reuniting families, to promote balanced economic growth for Korea as a whole and across all areas (economic, social, and cultural), and to reciprocate Kim Dae Jung's visit to Pyongyang with a visit by Kim Jong Il to Seoul "at an appropriate time."

Shortly after the summit between the two Korean leaders, on June 19, 2000, the United States eased its economic sanctions against North Korea, allowing trade, personal and commercial transactions, and investments between the United States and North Korea. The U.S. counterterrorism or nonproliferation controls on North Korea, which prohibit exports of restricted military supplies and weapons, remained in place. North Korea also remained on the United States' list of seven countries that sponsor terrorism.

On June 30, 2000, delegates from the United States, Japan, and the Republic of Korea (ROK or South Korea) met in Hawaii for the Trilateral Coordination and Oversight Group meeting to assess relations with the DPRK. In a statement regarding the outcome of this meeting, the positive tone is reflected: "The delegations expressed their support for increased DPRK engagement with other countries as the DPRK addresses the concerns of the international community...."

Laxmi Nakarmi captured the feelings of many onlookers in a September 15, 2000, article on

THE MEETING OF NORTH KOREAN LEADER KIM JONG IL AND SOUTH KOREAN PRESIDENT KIM DAE JUNG, WHO MET FOR THE FIRST TIME ON JUNE 13, 2000, IN PYONGYANG TO DISCUSS RELATIONS BETWEEN THEIR TWO COUNTRIES, MADE INTERNATIONAL HEADLINES. *(© Reuters NewMedia Inc./Corbis. Reproduced by permission.)*

Asiaweek.com: "That North Korea is opening up there can be no doubt. The big question is whether the regime is changing for real—or simply trying to milk maximum concessions from the international community before reverting to its unpredictably dangerous self."

## Problems with the United States

President George W. Bush's administration (2001–) immediately took a harder line toward

North Korea than the Clinton administration had taken before it. Early in his administration Bush announced to South Korean President Kim Dae Jung that he would not resume talks with the North Koreans that had been started by his predecessor. He explained that he feared that North Korea was not keeping up its part in its agreements with the United States. His national security advisor, Condoleezza Rice, also took a harsh tone on the subject, and had been known at one time to call North Korea "the road kill of history."

When Bush did resume talks with North Korea it was to demand not only that the country stop exporting missiles and manufacturing nuclear weapons, but also that it pull its troops back from the border with South Korea. North Korea bristled under this demand, calling the United States "hostile." Since the September 11, 2001, terrorist attacks on the United States, the DPRK has supported some of the anti-terrorist agenda spelled out by the Bush administration, but failed to endorse the United States in its war in Afghanistan. North Korea has consistently asked to be taken off of the U.S. list of countries that sponsor terrorism and refuses to permit an inspection of its nuclear program.

It is apparent that North Korea's emergence from the cold war is a vital step toward containing, if not eliminating, global terrorism. North Korea has been the, one might say, "traditional" training ground for terrorists, and it has used terrorism itself in its efforts against South Korea. North Korea also has nuclear capabilities that are of concern to many nations.

In the aftermath of the terrorists attacks on the World Trade Center and the Pentagon, it is clear that economic globalization as a process cannot go forward, or even stay intact, in the presence of a significant terrorist threat. Given this, what problems are likely to emerge in North Korean relations with the United States, the European Community, and the rest of the world?

First, North Korea is likely to be under even more intense, effective, and sustained pressure to give up exporting terrorism or conducting terrorist acts itself. But will the United States be willing to pay the price to achieve this objective? One possibility for normalizing North Korea's international relations may be not a merger of the two Koreas, but rather a neutralization of both, making it a kind of "Switzerland of the Pacific." This could mean a withdrawal of U.S. forces from the region, one of China's long-cherished objectives.

It could also mean an economic development program designed to create an economic infrastructure on the Korean peninsula that will challenge Japan and significantly strengthen China's industrial north. Already South Korea is speaking of a railroad connecting Seoul and Pyongyang to Moscow. Such developments are a long way off, but as the pace of current events tells us, that doesn't mean that such developments are either unlikely or undesirable.

## BIBLIOGRAPHY

"Adversary Foreign Intelligence Operations," Section 3, *Operations Security Threat Handbook*, May 1996. Available online at http://www.fas.org/irp/nsa/ioss/threat96/part03.htm (cited December 21, 2001).

"Background Notes: North Korea," U.S. Department of State, October 2000. Available online at http://www.state.gov/www/background_notes/n-korea_0010_bgn.html (cited December 20, 2001).

Chadwick, Richard W. "Notes on the Cold War Structure in Korea: Can It Be Dissolved?" Available online at http://www2.hawaii.edu/chadwick/KINUessay.rtf (cited January 29, 2002).

The Cold War Museum: Links to the 1950s. Available online at http://www.coldwar.org/articles/50s/links.php3 (cited January 21, 2002).

"Inside the Secret State," BBC News Online. Available online at http://news.bbc.co.uk/hi/english/special_report/1998/09/98/korea_at_50/newsid_166000/166338.stm (cited December 4, 2001).

"Kim Jong Il: Playing a Poor Hand Skillfully," CNN.com/World, June 14, 2001. Available online at http://asia.cnn.com/2001/WORLD/asiapcf/east/06/13/bio.kim.jongil/ (cited December 18, 2001).

North Korea Advisory Group, Report to the Speaker, U.S. House of Representatives, November 1999. Federation of American Scientists. Available online at http://www.fas.org/nuke/guide/dprk/nkag-report.htm (cited December 21, 2001).

"North Korea: A Country Study," Library of Congress. Available online at http://lcweb2.loc.gov/frd/cs/kptoc.html (cited December 21, 2001).

"North Korea Special Weapons Guide," Federation of American Scientists. Available online at http://www.fas.org/nuke/guide/dprk/index.html (cited December 21, 2001).

"North Korean Mass Destruction Weapons, Prepared Statement of Ju-hwal Choi," 1997 Congressional Hearings, Special Weapons: Nuclear, Chemical, Biological and Missile. Available online at http://www.fas.org/spp/starwars/congress/1997_h/s971021choi.htm (cited January 22, 2002).

"Review of United States Policy Toward North Korea: Findings and Recommendations," Unclassified Report by Dr. William J. Perry, U.S. North Korea Policy Coordinator and Special Advisor to the President and the Secretary of State, Washington, DC, October 12, 1999. U.S. Department of State. Available on the World Wide Web at http://www.state.gov/www/regions/eap/991012_northkorea_rpt.html (cited December 21, 2001).

Wright, David C. "The North Korean Missile Program," Union of Concerned Scientists, November 2000. Available online at http://www.ucsusa.org/security/nk-miss-prog-dw.html (cited December 4, 2001).

*Richard W. Chadwick*

# THE MISSING GIRLS: SON PREFERENCE RESHAPES THE POPULATION IN INDIA AND CHINA

## THE CONFLICT

In the two most populous countries of the world, India and China, attention has lately been drawn to a disturbing trend in which some couples try to ensure male children by means of sex-selective abortion and infanticide. Because of these practices a significant imbalance has been noted in China and India, as well as Korea, Bangladesh, and some other countries. The imbalance will almost certainly mean that millions of young men will never marry, throwing the social structures out of line. Son preference not only disturbs the natural balance, but also reflects and perpetuates the inequality of women.

### *Political*

- In China the government's "one child" policy, aimed to curb the population explosion, probably caused a significant number of couples to abort female fetuses or kill female infants in order to try for a son, since they were only allowed one child.

- The governments' policies for population control in both India and China have indirectly added to the gender imbalance in the population.

### *Economic*

- In both China and India economic reasons for preferring sons are compelling. While daughters join their husbands' families, sons can supply a couple with an additional hand on farms or another income in the home, and can support them when they are too old to work.

- With the dowry system in place in India in modern times, multiple girl children have become an overwhelming expense when it comes to paying large dowries to their prospective husbands' families. Many poor people simply cannot afford to have them.

### *Religious*

- The ancient traditions of India and China still have a profound impact on the cultures in modern times.

A few years ago Malli, a young woman in India, delivered a baby girl. Instead of being greeted with joyful comfort and congratulations, she heard her mother-in-law speak in angry voice: "Again a girl! Are you not ashamed of yourself? The third time and still a girl." Both mother-in-law and husband had already threatened to send Malli to her parental home if she delivered a baby girl again. The fate awaiting the unwanted new baby girl and her helpless young mother was uncertain and not promising. This true story, reported by Shobha Warrier in *Rediff on the Net* (March 1999), is one among many. Stories of aborting and killing unwanted baby girls are generally untold and under-reported, but these practices are widespread in India and China and other nations, particularly in Asia. Population statistics provide evidence of a very large missing segment of the female populations of those countries.

There are several factors behind the imbalance in population ratios in terms of sex balance in India and China, the two most populous countries in the world. Scholars point out that the age-old tradition of son preference has combined with new technology and the introduction of government-sponsored family planning programs designed to control the rapid population growth in both countries. Fertility rates are dropping, while at the same time governments have increased control over population growth by making it difficult for couples to have large families. Wishing to ensure that they have boys (often a cultural preference)—and not having the assurance of being able to keep trying—couples are likely to perform pre-natal gender testing, now widely available through ultrasound. When the tests indicate a female fetus, many couples are taking the option of abortion. Along with this selective abortion and some cases

# CHRONOLOGY

*1961* India outlaws the dowry system, in which exorbitant sums of money are demanded from a bride's parents by the husband's family. The law is never enforced, and the practice continues.

*1979* China imposes the "one child" policy, in which the government limits couples to having only one child.

*1979* Ultrasound and other sex-determining technologies are introduced in China and India.

*1981–1991* There are 35 million girls less than would be expected in India's population.

*1992* China holds the International Seminar on China's 1990 Population Census, at which scholars present papers on the "missing girl" problem that surfaced in China's 1990 census.

*1994* The Indian government reports 5,199 cases of dowry death for the year, but some non-governmental organizations put the death toll as high as 25,000 each year.

*October 1994* The Chinese government prohibits the use of ultrasound for the purpose of sex-selective abortion in the Maternal and Child Health Law, which prescribes penalties for medical practitioners who violate this provision.

*November 1994* The United Nations Population Fund (UNFPA) and the government of the Republic of Korea sponsor the International Symposium on Sex Preference for Children in the Rapidly Changing Demographic Dynamics in Asia. Participants discuss indicators of son preference, the incidence of sex-selective abortion, and policy responses in Asian countries.

*January 1, 1996* The government of India bans prenatal sex determination, making it illegal for doctors to perform such tests, for women to undergo testing, or for relatives to encourage women to abort female fetuses. Still, the practice continues underground and the laws go un-enforced.

*September 1997* The World Health Organization reports that more than 50 million women are "missing" from the population in China due to sex-selective abortion, infanticide, or neglect.

*2000* A report by the UN Population Fund on World Population Day criticizes India for not doing enough to stop female infanticide and sex-selective abortion, stating that India has one of the worst sex ratios in the world. At the same time the UN praises India for making progress in slowing down population growth.

of killing female infants, the female mortality rate tends to be higher for girls than boys in many places, due to the poorer nutritional and medical care that is given to young girls. Consequently, there are significantly less females than males in the population.

The imbalance in the male to female ratio may result in some serious long-term social and economic consequences. Some population scientists maintain that if the current trend goes unchecked, women will eventually become an "endangered" sex in China and India, and in other countries engaging in selective abortion and infanticide. Due to this so-called "gender-cleansing," men will eventually face a "bride famine" for lack of females to mate. Beyond this, the practices have harsh social consequences for women, who are devalued by the very concept.

# HISTORICAL BACKGROUND

Son preference can be found in the history of any country and dates back to ancient times. In modern India and China the culture of son preference has been reinforced by economic needs as well as some unique belief systems. Most people in India and China today engage in agricultural production, using traditional methods. Since this kind of farm work is highly labor intensive, they need more laborers, and thus, sons come in very handy. Most farmers are quite poor—they need sons to generate family income. A daughter may be a helping hand to her parents before her marriage, but once she is married, she will live with her husband's family. If a couple has no son, their future may well be one of hardship and toil. In both countries there are only very limited public social security systems for the elderly, especially for the

A YOUNG GIRL HUGS A DOLL WHILE HER MOTHER SPEAKS WITH A FAMILY PLANNING WORKER IN CHINA. CHINA TRIES TO REIGN IN ITS FAST GROWING POPULATION BY PROMOTING FAMILY PLANNING AND CONTRACEPTION. *(A/P Wide World. Reproduced by permission.)*

rural population. Parents still rely heavily on their children—especially their sons—to provide for them when they get old.

Apart from purely practical matters, belief systems perpetuate son preference in both China and India. The particular beliefs are different in the two countries.

## China

Confucianism dominated China for more than two thousand years. One of the Confucian virtues is filial piety. There are three grave unfilial acts, and the failure to have a son is at the top of the three. The importance of having a son is obvious in a patrilineal society: only sons can carry on the family name. Without a male heir, the family chain is stopped. In the old days the failure to produce a son could be an excuse for a man to divorce his wife or to marry a number of concubines in order to guarantee a male heir. The Chinese have always valued boys more than girls. When a son is born, it is considered to be a "big happiness," while when a daughter is born, it is considered to be a "small happiness."

Historians have noted that female infanticide (the killing of newborn baby girls) was widespread in China in the nineteenth century and probably

for many centuries before. The practice decreased significantly after the Chinese Revolution in 1949. In the 1980s, however, the ratio of women to men once again began to drop. Many believe it was an indirect result of the People's Republic of China's imposition of the "one-child policy" of 1979. In trying to control population growth, the Chinese government limited couples to having only one child, and for some time the government strictly enforced this rule. Between 1982 and 1983 women who had already had a child were compelled by the government to use birth control; women who had unauthorized pregnancies were compelled to have an abortion. When a couple had two or more children, some were forced to undergo sterilization, while others were subjected to severe administrative punishment, such as heavy fines, or the loss of benefits, promotions, and even their jobs. It is likely that during those times a some parents chose to secretly abort, abandon, or even kill their female infants in the hopes of trying again for a boy, especially in the rural areas.

By the late 1980s China had eased up a bit on its population policies, but the trend of gender preference in individual family planning decisions seems to have taken hold. In September 1997 the World Health Organization reported that more

# IMPACTS OF CHINA'S ONE-CHILD POLICY

In January 1979 China's leaders announced a strict policy to control the nation's population growth. For the most populous nation in the world, limiting population growth is a primary concern. When the one-child policy was originally conceived, China was a developing nation with high population growth. It had to extend more of its resources towards its ever-increasing population rather than on modernizing its industry and technology to be more competitive with industrialized nations. Limiting population growth was seen as essential in helping China achieve modernization and increase the country's standard of living. The issue was considered so important that the *Beijing Review* warned in 1995 that if the population could not be controlled, it would "eventually bring this nation down."

China's efforts at population control have met with some success. Without the one-child policy, official estimates forecasted a population of 1.2 billion by 1986 and 1.5 billion by 1994. Jian Ding, writing in the *Beijing Review* ("Notes from the Editors: China's Population Hits 1.2 Billion," March 6–12, 1995), commented that "birth control has reduced China's population growth by 300 million over the past 20 years." As a measure of the policy's success, a July 2001 estimate had China's population at 1.27 billion, still far below the unrestricted estimate for 1994.

While China's population control measures have limited population growth, they have also changed Chinese society. Traditionally in China, sons are valued more than daughters. It is the son who is responsible for caring for his elderly parents. It is the son who continues the family line and who stays with the family after his marriage. In contrast, a daughter contributes little to the family's economy. She will grow up, marry, and leave home, ending her ties with the family that raised her. With these traditional beliefs still a part of Chinese society today, the demand for sons is unabated.

This demand has created a problem in that the one-child policy restricts a couple's odds of having a son. Many determined parents either disobey the one-child policy by continuing to have additional children until the desired son appears (subjecting themselves to fines and a loss of benefits granted to one-child families) or by taking other measures to assure that their first child is a boy.

These measures have a negative impact on girls. Through ultrasounds, parents can learn the sex of their child. If the child is a girl, parents may opt for a legal abortion and try again for a son. If an unwanted daughter is born, she may be abandoned, given away for adoption, or killed. Actions like these have greatly affected the birth ratio of children born after 1979.

Generally, the ratio of boys to girls in a society is roughly equal. In 1994 in China, however, the national birthrate was 117 boys to every 100 girls. According to "Major Figures of the 2000 Population Census (No. 1)," China's current national birth ratio is 107 boys to 100 girls (China Population Information and Research Center). The result of this imbalance, according to Luise Cardarelli in "The Lost Girls" (*Utne Reader*, May-June 1996), is that "there are now [at least] 36 million more males than females in China."

The imbalance in birthrates has significantly altered the face of Chinese society. When boys are ready to marry, many will not be able to do so, and this will directly impact traditional family roles, particularly that of the son's family caring for his elderly parents. Additionally, women, in such demand due to the "shortage," could become commodities to be bought and sold on a market that values their worth as human beings little in comparison to their worth as childbearers and family caretakers. This, in fact, is already taking place. A reported 8,000 women are kidnapped and forced into marriage in China each year, according to J. Manthorpe of the *Vancouver Sun* (1999).

The driving desire behind the one-child policy was to give China the chance to modernize, thus giving its people the chance for a better life. The highly uneven male/female birthrate, the uncertain and changing roles of women in society, the missing girls, and the millions of men without a mate are only some of the unpredicted effects—and hidden costs—of the population control effort. For the millions of missing girls in China, it is indeed a high price to pay.

than 50 million women were "missing" from the population in China due to infanticide or neglect—that is, the rate of women to men was very low and could not have occurred naturally.

The result has been a pronounced imbalance between males and females, with young men in China facing a future in which they are unable to find wives.

CHINA PROMOTES ITS "ONE CHILD FAMILY" POLICY WITH POSTERS, FAMILY PLANNING, AND OTHER MEASURES TO ENCOURAGE SMALL FAMILIES. (© Owen Franken/Corbis. Reproduced by permission.)

## India

In India people traditionally believed that daughters were liabilities and sons were assets. Boys were to be better treated and better educated than girls. Only sons were allowed to perform important religious rituals. For instance, according to the Hindu tradition, sons were needed to kindle the funeral pyre of their deceased parents and to help in the salvation of their souls. These cultural values remain very strong today.

In India, when a son gets married and brings a daughter-in-law into his family, he is providing for additional help around the house as well as a large dowry payment to the parents. The dowry system in India, a source of income for the groom's family, has become a terrible burden for many brides' families. A bride's parents may have to put their life savings into a dowry payment to give to their daughter's new family. If they have several daughters, their financial situation becomes almost unbearable.

India's dowry system has led to practices known as "dowry death" or "bride burning," in which husbands and in-laws have killed women (often by burning them to death and claiming it to be a kitchen accident) because they were unhappy with the amount of the dowry. In the old days

dowry was only meant to be a small gift a bride's parents gave to their daughter at marriage. The purpose of such gifts was to provide some financial security for her in case of her husband's death or any other calamity—the gift was considered the wife's property. In modern days the dowry has become a way for the groom's family to accumulate wealth. Dowry has been changed from a pure gift to required conditions. Quite often, the groom's family will demand a specific amount that the bride's parents are reluctant or unable to pay.

If problems arise in the payment of the dowry the consequences can be extreme for the wife. Bride-burning is widespread in India. The Indian government reported 5,199 cases of dowry death in 1994, but some non-governmental organizations put the death toll as high as 25,000 each year. Although the Indian government outlawed the dowry system in 1961, the practice continues. Alice W. Clark wrote in an article published by *Economic and Political Weekly* that the dowry system has contributed directly to the high female mortality rate in India: "In a patrilineal kinship system where marriages are arranged on principles of dowry ... and where women are objects of exchange along with other forms of wealth, excess female mortality is argued to be an inevitable outcome." Clearly, for a poor family, paying for dowries for several daughters is a frightening burden and would naturally lead to some attempt to limit the birth of daughters. Young women who have been subjected to great cruelty by husbands and in-laws may also think twice about bringing another female into the world only to suffer in the inhumane system.

## Modern Technology in the Aid of Patriarchal Values

Although the child mortality rate has come down in both China and India, the sex ratio of child mortality has continued to be skewed against female children. Modern technologies of pre-natal testing, particularly ultrasound (a diagnostic technique that provides two-dimensional images of organs and structures within the body) have helped those parents who insist upon having baby boys.

In China it is estimated that there are at least one million female fetuses aborted each year (and some figures are many times higher), much higher than the number of aborted male fetuses. Technologies to determine the sex of unborn fetuses were introduced in China during the 1980s. Among the different techniques, ultrasound is the most widely used, although it cannot accurately

ABORTION IS A GROWING RECOURSE TO INDIAN WOMEN EXPERIENCING UNWANTED PREGNANCIES. IT IS ALSO PREVALENT IN CHINA, WHERE POPULATION CONTROL EFFORTS GO AGAINST TRADITIONAL FAMILY PRACTICES AND RELIANCE ON BOYS. (*© Janet Wishnetsky/Corbis. Reproduced by permission.*)

determine the sex of the fetus until the second trimester of pregnancy. This results in late abortions, which are more controversial and can be harmful to the mother's health. Beginning in 1979 China has manufactured thousands of its own ultrasound machines and also imports machines to supply its heavy demand. The availability of ultrasound machines in China may contribute to the higher abortion rate for female fetuses.

The Chinese government prohibited the use of ultrasound for the purpose of sex-selective abortion by the Maternal and Child Health Law passed in October 1994, which prescribes penalties for medical practitioners who violate this provision.

India, too, began using prenatal techniques for sex determination in the late 1970s. When ultrasound appeared, it was used regularly to determine sex and then to abort female fetuses. In a January 6, 1994, episode of *ABC News PrimeTime Live,* it was estimated that more than three thousand female fetuses were aborted every day in India, at a rate of one million per year. A clinic in Bombay reported in the same year that, of 8,000 abortions performed after amniocentesis (a prenatal test) to determine sex, 7,999 of the fetuses were female. On January 1, 1996, the government of India banned prenatal sex determination, making it illegal for doctors to perform such tests, for women to undergo testing,

or for relatives to encourage women to abort female fetuses. The law stipulates fines and jail terms for people who engage in prenatal sex determination, but it has never been enforced and did not significantly change the number of selective abortions in India. The law banning selective abortions did, however, cause the prospering business to go underground, thereby raising the prices of testing and abortions considerably.

### The Population Ratio

Researchers find that there are some noticeable relationships between the size of a family and the chance of conceiving a boy in India and China. As the number of children increases in families, the likelihood of having boys also increases. As this phenomenon cannot be explained entirely by human biology, it is almost certainly human interference—the practice of selective abortion—that causes this result. Population scientists suspect that when the first baby is a girl the family will use whatever methods are available to them to carry only male pregnancies to term in the future.

Even without resorting to aborting female fetuses, couples may be controlling the gender makeup of their families. A 1993 study in China's Anhui province confirmed this hypothesis. Since

## STATUS OF WOMEN IN INDIA

There would not be a missing female population in India if women received equal treatment to men. Dowry deaths, bride burning, and female infanticide reflect deep and disturbing gender discrimination. It is important to remember that these particular practices are extreme cases and not the norm. India is in many ways a very modern country with active discussion of women's rights; it also has some very poor statistics regarding women. Some facts regarding the status of women in India follow:

- Women gained suffrage in India in 1950. But while the modern constitution provides for equal protection under the law for women, it also, for the most part, assumes a woman's position is as wife and mother. Husbands are regarded legally as "guardians" of their wives. Property rights and family law generally empower men. Rape is considered a crime against the husband of the victim.

- The government of India proclaimed 2001 Women's Empowerment Year, but the government has not accomplished most of its promised goals for women's empowerment. Notably, the Women's Reservation Bill, which would reserve 33 percent of the seats in India's Parliament for women, was deferred again, having been continually stalled since it was introduced in 1996.

- The Indian government has proclaimed its intent to educate its entire population. However, India has one of the lowest female literacy rates, at 37.7 percent, in Asia.

- The life expectancy of an Indian woman has risen from 32 years to 63 years in modern times. Malnutrition, AIDS, and other diseases, however, hit women in India at a much higher rate than men. Diet and health care are far inferior for lower income women and girls in India than for men. In India 460 out of every 100,000 women and 72 out of every 1,000 infants die during childbirth.

- Significant numbers of women in India are doctors, professors, lawyers, and other professionals. There are many women in the work force and women's jobs entitle them to health care and other benefits. However, many women in India work long hours in agriculture or domestic work or other jobs that do not earn them monetary wages. A study carried out in 1998 found that women are at work—either earning wages or in the home, or both—for significantly longer hours each day than men and that they sleep far less.

- Despite protective legislation, sexual assault and other types of violence against women often go unpunished in India. In particular, upper-caste men have a history of physically and sexually abusing Dalit, or "untouchable," women. India's criminal justice system has proven to be unsympathetic to women in most sexual assault cases, but especially when Dalit women are involved.

- There are laws in India to protect women from dowry killings or abuse, sex discrimination, child marriages, and numerous other gender-based abuses. But these laws have been largely unenforced.

---

1980, couples in Anhui with only a girl child have been slightly more likely than those with only a boy to have a second child; those with two girls have been 5 to 6 times as likely as those with two boys to have a third child. The interval between pregnancies was shorter when the previous child was a girl than when the previous child was a boy. It is apparent that these couples were attempting to control not only the size, but also the gender composition of their families.

The direct consequence of selective abortion or infanticide is the decline of the numbers of women in India and China's population. The measure of the balance of males to females in a given time period is called Sex Ratio at Birth (SRB). Under normal circumstances the population rarely has an absolute balance in the number of male and female babies born each year. The difference between the two sexes, however, should not exceed six percent. Because boys in general tend to have a higher mortality rate than girls, the gender imbalance will eventually even out. However, if the male/female ratio is greater than 1.06, then a real imbalance will occur.

In China and India, census data reveals that SRB has been increasingly skewed against females.

In China, for every 100 male babies born, there are only 82 female babies registered. By a conservative calculation there are 30 million females missing in China, and some estimates go as high as 50 million or more. The study in China's Anhui province confirmed that the overall sex ratio in that province was 1.18 male births per female birth, significantly higher than the expected ratio of 1.06. The sex ratio was low in 1980–86, when the national one-child policy was strictly enforced, and the ratio was significantly elevated before 1980 (1.18) and in 1987–93 (1.22). Last-born children, regardless of family size, had the highest sex ratio in favor of boys.

In India the 2001 census reveals that there are 1,000 boys for every 929 girls. (In the 1991 census the ratio was 1,000/945). This means that the male/female SRB ratio is 1.08: for every 1 girl that is born, 1.08 boys are born. In the states of Punjab and Uttar Pradesh, the SRB is 1.12. Between 1981 and 1991 there were 35 million girls less than the projected numbers. According to a study by Rami Chhabra, there was a total of about 11 million abortions in India in 1991, out of which 6.7 million were forced abortions undertaken mostly for female feticide.

DUE TO ATTEMPTS TO LIMIT POPULATION GROWTH AND A CULTURAL PREFERENCE FOR MALES, BOTH INDIA AND CHINA ARE EXPERIENCING AN UNNATURAL IMBALANCE OF BOYS TO GIRLS. (© *Sheldan Collins/Corbis. Reproduced by permission.*)

## RECENT HISTORY AND THE FUTURE

So what are the consequences of this strange war against baby girls? The first thing one can imagine is that millions of male bachelors will have to search to find a wife. Many of them will end up living alone all their life. Prostitution and violence against women may result. Studies of China's SRB show that the marriage market ratios are already starting to go out of balance and will become drastic if the imbalance of females to males continues.

The shortage of women has already resulted in kidnapping and in trading young girls to be brides by rural farmers. A group of scientists warned in an article published in *Science* (1995, 267/5199) that "on the longer term, masculinization of births will result in large cohorts of young unmarried males, posing social and cultural challenges in countries that are already undergoing rapid economic and political change," and, more importantly, that these trends are likely to "complicate efforts to increase the social and economic status of women and their control over reproductive decisions." In Guangdong province, the China news agency Xinhua reported, 500,000 bachelors are approaching middle age without hopes of marrying, because they outnumber women ages 30 to 45 by more than 10 to 1.

Scientists are not sure if this imbalance will be permanent. Ratios are low in the least developed rural provinces, high in more developed provinces, and low in the relatively modern cities of Shanghai and Beijing. Son preference as a rule is waning for couples in urban China. Many are quite happy when their only child is a girl. In the rural areas the government policy allows a couple to have a second child if the first child is a girl. This policy, while it may slightly decrease the number of selective abortions, could potentially encourage sex-selective procedures being used in order to make sure the second child will be a boy, and certainly seems to condone son preference.

The most important consequence of the practices of sex-selective abortion, infanticide, and son preference is social discrimination against women. Because women are not valued as much as men, parents are reluctant to invest in their daughters' nutritional, medical, and educational needs. Researchers in China's Anhui province found that baby girls are breastfed less than baby boys and have higher school dropout rates. This kind of neglect inevitably hurts the self-esteem of girls, lowers their motivation to learn, and makes them feel inferior to their male counterparts.

### Population Control

As mentioned earlier, India and China's governmental policies of population and family planning have contributed to the sex discrimination against female babies to a certain degree. Population control pressures are not likely to go away, since both China and India are still facing rapid growth in their population. At the turn of the twentieth century China's population was 400 million, and India's was 238 million. As the twenty-first century began India's population had increased four times, crossing the one billion mark; China's population had reached 1.26 billion. When you put the two countries' population figures together, it becomes an astonishing 2.3 billion, which makes up more than one-third of the world's total population. The land area of the two countries makes up less than 8 percent of the world surface areas.

To support 37 percent of the world population in that small a space is simply an impossible task. Food security is a general concern for both countries. In the early 1960s China had a major famine, which killed more than 20 million people. Half of India's population—525 million—still lives in absolute poverty, living on less than one U.S. dollar per day. There is no sign the population growth has been stabilized in the two countries. In fact, an additional 700 million will most likely be added to the combined population figures by the middle of twenty-first century. "Population explosion" is no longer a prediction, but a reality. It is the consequences of such an uncontrolled population growth the two countries have to find ways to deal with.

The urgent question is not about whether there will be population control, but instead, it is about how to do it. The changing balance of male/female population may be an unintended consequence of population control. People who, in better circumstances, would love and value their newborn daughters just like parents do elsewhere, are trying in their own ways to control their lives in an overpopulated, under-resourced world. Some of their female infants are "born to die" because, in a world with too many people, the value of human life is not always celebrated as it should be. Add to this factor the ancient value of son preference, and female infants will almost certainly have a lower chance of survival than male infants.

In fact, China has acknowledged that its one-child policy led to female infanticide and selective abortion. Although it has changed its strategy—providing incentives for couples to have only one child—the Chinese government believes that a one-child rule is necessary and that it has prevented more than three hundred million births since 1980. Lower population helps everyone's quality of life.

The United Nations Population Fund (UNPF) on World Population Day 2000 criticized India for failing to take action on its low ratio of women to men, one of the worst sex ratios in the world. At the same time the United Nations praised India for making progress in slowing down its population growth.

Some of India's state governments have established programs aimed at stopping female infanticide and sex-selective abortion while promoting population control. In 1992 the chief minister of Tamil Nadu enacted a program in which poor families that had one or two girls and no sons could receive monetary awards if one parent agreed to be sterilized. The same official established the "Cradle Babies" concept. In this concept, empty cradles were placed in government centers where families who so desired could abandon their unwanted female infants, rather than kill them. These programs were not particularly effective. Some non-governmental organizations have also been combating son preference practices. The Indian Council for Child Welfare has provided training programs on self-esteem, hygiene, and health for adolescent girls. As part of the training, the girls take an oath promising never to take part in female infanticide. Other programs emphasizing education and social strategies to raise women's status have been effective.

The governments of India and China must educate their people to overcome the traditional value of son preference. Special steps must be taken to protect females from becoming an "endangered" sex. The use of technologies must be regulated to prevent human engineering in the gender selection process, and to prevent the disturbance of the natural balance in the human species.

## BIBLIOGRAPHY

Aravamudan, Gita, "Born To Die," Rediff on the Net, October 24, 2001. Available online at http://www.rediff.com/news/2001/oct/24spec.htm (cited December 4, 2001).

Bannister, Judith, "Son Preference in Asia: Report of a Symposium," U.S. Census Bureau. Available online at http://www.census.gov/ipc/www/ebspr96a.html (cited December 3, 2001).

Chhabra, Rami. "Women's Status and Reproductive Health in the Context of Indian Family Planning Programme: A Review and Recommendations for the Future," in *Population Policy and Reproductive Health*, ed. by K. Srinivasan, New Delhi, Hindustan Publishing, 1996, pp. 267–75.

Clark, Alice W., "Social Demography of Excess Female Mortality in India: New Directions," *Economic and Political Weekly*, 1997, vol. 22, no. 17.

Ehrlich, Paul R. *The Population Bomb*. New York: Sierra Club/Ballantine, 1968.

"Evidence Mounts for Sex-Selective Abortion in Asia," *Asia-Pacific Population & Policy*, June–July 1995, Number 34.

Graham, Maureen J., Ulla Larsen, and Xiping Xu, "Son Preference in Anhui Province, China," *International Family Planning Perspectives*, Volume 24, No. 2, June 1998. Available online at http://www.agi-usa.org/pubs/journals/2407298.html (cited December 4, 2001).

Harriss-White, Barbara, "Gender-Cleansing: The Paradox of Development and Deteriorating Female Life Chances in Tamil Nadu," in *Gender and Modernity in Post-Independence India*, R. Sundar Rajan and U. Butalia, eds. New Delhi: Kali for Women, 1998.

Heyer, J., "The Role of Dowries and Daughters' Marriages in the Accumulation and Distribution of Capital in a South Indian Community," *Journal of International Development*. 1992, vol. 4, no. 4, pp. 419–36.

Hull, Terence H., "Recent Trends in Sex Ratios at Birth in China," *Population and Development Review*, 1990, vol. 6, pp. 63–83.

Jian Ding. "Notes from the Editors: China's Population Hits 1.2 Billion." *Beijing Review*, vol. 38, no. 10 (March 6–12, 1995), p. 4.

Kishor, Sunita, "May God Give Sons to All: Gender and Child Mortality in India," *American Sociological Review*, 1993, vol. 58, pp. 247–65.

Kumar, Dharma, "Male Utopia or Nightmares?" *Economic and Political Weekly*, January 15, 1983, pp. 61–4.

Lee, James Z., Wang Feng. *One Quarter of Humanity: Malthusian Mythology and Chinese Realities, 1700–2000*, Cambridge, MA: Harvard University Press, 1999.

"Major Figures of the 2000 Population Census (No. 1)." China Population Information and Research Center.

Available online at http://www.cpirc.org.cn/eindex.html [cited February 11, 2002].

Manthorpe, J. "China Battles Slave Trading in Women: Female Infanticide Fuels a Brisk Trade in Wives." *Vancouver Sun*, January 11, 1999.

Marquand, Robert. "In India, Moms Are Equal to Dad—Almost." *Christian Science Monitor*, March 4, 1999.

Miller, Barbara. *The Endangered Sex: Neglect of Female Children in Rural North India*. Ithaca, NY: Cornell University Press, 1981.

Mutharayappa, Rangamuthia, Minja Kim Choe, Fred Arnold, et al.: "Son Preference and Its Effect on Fertility in India," *National Family Health Survey*, March 1997, no.3.

Rajan, V.G. Julie, "Will India's Ban on Pre-Natal Sex Determination Slow Abortion of Girls?" Hindu Women. Available online at http://www.hinduwomen.org/issues/infanticide.htm (cited December 3, 2001).

Sakuntala Narasimhan. "Women's Empowerment Year: Beginning With a Bang, Ending With a Whimper." India Together, January 2002. Available online at http://www.indiatogether.org/women/opinions/year2001.htm. [cited 2-09-02].

Sen, Marla. *Death by Fire: Sati, Dowry Death and Female Infanticide in Modern India*. London: Weidenfeld & Nicolson, 2001.

"Sex Ratio at Birth and Son Preferences," *International Family Planning Perspectives*, 1998, vol. 24, no. 2, pp. 72–77.

Singh, Jyotsna, "India's Unwanted Girls," BBC News Online, July 11, 2000. Available online at http://news.bbc.co.uk/hi/english/world/south_asia/newsid_828000/828856.stm (cited December 10, 2001).

"Six Billion and Beyond," PBS Newsroom. Available online at http://www.pbs.org/sixbillion/india/in-status.html. [cited 2-10-02].

Tuljapurkar, Shripad, Li Nan, and Marcus W. Feldman, "High Sex Ratios at Birth in China's Future," *Science*, 1995, vol. 267, no. 5199, pp. 874–6.

Warrier, Shobha, "Again a Girl! Are You Not Ashamed of Yourself?" Rediff on the Net, March 1999. Available online at http://www.rediff.com/news/1999/mar/08woman.htm (cited December 3, 2001).

*Baogang Guo*

# RUSSIA AGREES TO TAKE THE WORLD'S NUCLEAR WASTE: BUT WHERE TO PUT IT?

## THE CONFLICT

With already serious nuclear waste problems and a very poor track record in nuclear safety, Russia has approved plans to import more spent nuclear waste from elsewhere in the world for reprocessing. Russia claims that it will use the profits to clean up its considerable nuclear waste problem, but there is worldwide skepticism about its ability to do so and fear of the consequences for the planet if its efforts are unsuccessful.

### Political

- The passage of the nuclear waste law contravened both the section of the Russian constitution covering popular opposition expressed through petitions and referenda, and in the process of legislative enactment itself, with all debate in Russia's upper legislative house being bypassed.

### Economic

- Every geographic and political entity that formed a part of the Soviet Union continues to be profoundly affected by the Soviet nuclear legacy, but none is capable of solving the environmental, social, political, or health effects through an application of its own resources.

- Economic sectors in other countries, such as England and Norway, are already being adversely affected by radioactive waste from Russia and the former Soviet republics.

- The full cost of cleaning up the Soviet-era nuclear mess will certainly run into the hundreds of billions of dollars. Serious aid to Russia and the former Soviet republics from other nations is necessary to cope with the tremendous nuclear waste legacy of the Soviet era.

On July 11, 2001, Russian president Vladimir Putin approved a law that clears the way for Russia to import approximately 22,000 tons of nuclear waste over a ten-year period. The storage, processing, and eventual disposal of that waste could, according to the plan's supporters, generate as much as US$20–21 billion for the Russian government, money that may be used to help clean up Russia's domestic nuclear waste problems. Despite serious opposition amongst the Russian public and the international community, and from environmental groups such as Greenpeace, the Russian government has indicated that it will move swiftly to implement the plan's broad outlines.

The passage of the law calls into question the health of Russia's democratic institutions. In September and October 2000 Russian environmental groups collected signatures petitioning that the government hold a referendum on the plan as it was then proposed. According to the Russian constitution, if a group or groups collect two million signatures, the president must call a national and legally binding referendum on the issue in question. Greenpeace Russia, which headed the collection process, claims that 2.49 million signatures were registered on the petition. After a brief period of consideration by the Russian Electoral Commission, however, over 600,000 of the signatures were arbitrarily rejected, leaving only 1,873,216 as "acceptable"—more than 100,000 too few to force President Putin to call a referendum.

No persuasive reason for the commission's rejection of approximately one-quarter of the petition's signatories has been forthcoming, and appeals against the ruling were rejected in Russian courts. Ironically the sponsors of the petition decided to aim for 2.5 million signatures rather

# CHRONOLOGY

*1942–43* The Soviet Union begins work on an atomic bomb project.

*July 1945* United States tests atomic device at Alamogordo, New Mexico.

*August 1945* Hiroshima and Nagasaki, Japan, are destroyed by atomic weapons.

*August 1949* The Soviet Union tests its first atomic device.

*November 1952* The United States tests a thermonuclear device.

*August 1953* The Soviet Union tests its first thermonuclear device.

*1954* The Soviet Union's first "commercial reactor" begins producing energy at Obninsk.

*August 1957* The first Soviet nuclear-powered submarine, the *Leninskii Komsomol,* is launched.

*September 1957* An accident at Mayak storage site releases large amounts of radioactivity.

*1971–72* The first commercial VVER-440 reactors go on-line at Novovoronezh.

*1973* The first commercial RBMK reactor goes on-line at Sosnovy Bor, near Leningrad (St. Petersburg).

*March 1985* Mikhail S. Gorbachev becomes the General Secretary of the Communist Party of the Soviet Union.

*April 1986* An accident in Reactor No. 4 of the Chernobyl Nuclear Power Station contaminates large areas of the western Soviet Union and eastern and western Europe. Nuclear power plant construction is halted while the accident is investigated.

*August 1991* A failed coup against Mikhail Gorbachev's leadership destroys the central communist authority in the Soviet Union. Belarus and Ukraine declare their independence.

*December 1991* Gorbachev resigns as general secretary, recognizes the end of the Soviet Union.

*1991–92* The Nunn-Lugar aid program to the Soviet Union and its successor states is established.

*1993* The Cooperative Threat Reduction nonproliferation assistance program is developed by the United States. More than $3 billion in assistance is transferred to the successor states of the Soviet Union in the 1990s.

*January 1995* A Norwegian scientific rocket places Russia on its highest level of nuclear alert.

*July 2001* President Vladimir Putin of Russia approves a law allowing for the importation of approximately 20,000 tons of foreign nuclear waste for cash.

than the required two million because they assumed that a 20 percent margin would be too great for the commission to reject on "technical grounds." Furthermore, the law did not proceed through the normal Russian legislative channels: approved by the lower parliament in December 2000, the bill should have been considered by the Federation Council, Russia's upper house, on June 29, 2001. Instead, the chairman of the council signed the bill without tabling it for debate, sending it straight to President Putin's desk for his signature, at which point it became Russian law.

Throughout the two-year process that led to the enactment of the nuclear waste law, observers constantly pointed out the disturbingly obvious point that Russia was in no condition to deal with its *own* nuclear waste, let alone to accept anyone else's. The country, and the other successor states of the Soviet Union, have been confronted by nuclear security and nuclear waste issues that would tax the resources of an economically powerful state—in the 1990s and beyond, the successors of the Soviet Union were anything but economically powerful.

Commenting on the plan in the July 3, 2001, issue of the *Christian Science Monitor,* the head of the Norwegian environmental group Bellona (which monitors nuclear waste problems in Russia's far north) Thomas Nilsen said, "I don't think you'll find any place else in the world where spent nuclear fuel is stored in such bad conditions. The first priority should be to secure spent nuclear fuel

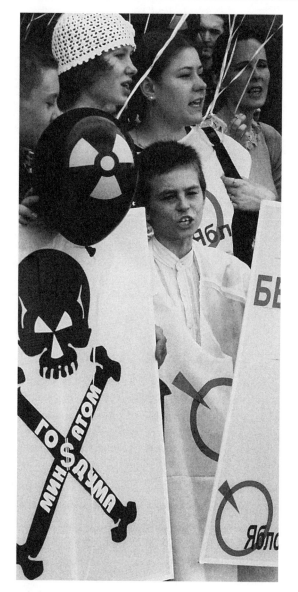

DEMONSTRATORS HOLD SIGNS THAT READ "DUMA EQUALS RADIATION." THEY ARE PROTESTING A PROPOSAL THAT WOULD BRING OTHER COUNTRIES' NUCLEAR WASTE INTO RUSSIA FOR REPROCESSING, WHICH WOULD BRING NEEDED REVENUE BUT UNWANTED NUCLEAR WASTE INTO RUSSIA. *(A/P Wide World. Reproduced by permission.)*

and radioactive waste already existing in Russia. You don't do that by importing more." There is, besides, a fear among opponents that any income generated by the processing, storage, and disposal of international nuclear waste will not be applied in cleanup efforts. Instead, it is feared that profits will finance the construction of nuclear power plants to expand Russia's energy supply.

In order to appreciate the strenuous objections to the new law, it is necessary to examine the

present situation regarding nuclear materials, both civilian and military, in the states of the former Soviet Union since the latter's collapse in 1991, and also to sketch the history of Soviet nuclear development during the Cold War. The history of the civilian and military nuclear programs are presented here separately and then examined together in the post-Soviet period. The reader is reminded, however, that the two programs were indeed intertwined throughout their histories and that one affected the other on a constant basis.

## HISTORICAL BACKGROUND

### Building the Bomb "On a Russian Scale"

Joseph Stalin, the leader of the Soviet Union during World War II (in Soviet history properly called the Great Patriotic War, from 1941–45), was well aware that the United States was considering the construction of a new kind of weapon—the atomic bomb—even before the initiation of the Manhattan Project in the United States in late 1942. Information had been supplied to the Soviet Union by a German-born but British-naturalized scientist, Klaus Fuchs. Fuchs had been reporting on Britain's experiments in the field in 1941 and 1942. When he joined the Manhattan Project in November 1943 he continued to pass information of high quality to his Soviet contacts. Initially, however, Stalin did not appreciate the significance of the atomic bomb, and he directed that only a small research endeavor should be undertaken.

At most two dozen Soviet scientists, led by physicist Igor Kurchatov (1903–60), worked on the project prior to 1944, and they focused their efforts primarily on the theoretical challenges of nuclear fission. In any case, in 1942 and 1943 the Soviet Union was still hard-pressed in its war with Nazi Germany, and more immediate production priorities, such as tanks and aircraft, occupied center stage. The equipment required by an atomic research program was simply unavailable to Kurchatov and his team.

The reports supplied by Fuchs after his move to Los Alamos, New Mexico (the headquarters of the Manhattan Project), along with the Trinity atomic test at Alamogordo, New Mexico, in July 1945, and the destruction of Hiroshima and Nagasaki, Japan, by atomic bombs the following month, all convinced Stalin that the Soviet Union could not afford to fall too far behind the American effort. The Soviet atomic bomb program was therefore reorganized, accelerated and, most of all, dramatically expanded in late 1945.

In January 1946 at a meeting with Kurchatov, Stalin is reported (in notes found in the Archive of the Kurchatov Institute in Moscow) to have said it was "not worth spending time and effort on small-scale work." Instead the Soviet scientific and engineering establishment would have to "conduct the work broadly, on a Russian scale, and that in this regard the broadest, utmost assistance" would be provided, especially an "investment of a decisive quantity of resources." It was a statement that signaled a shift of political emphasis: beginning in 1946 the construction of an atomic bomb would be the highest priority of the Soviet Union's political leadership, higher even than reconstruction of the damage inflicted by four years of terrible war with Germany.

Stalin got his bomb, and he got it quickly. In August 1949, only four years after the Manhattan Project had borne fruit in the deserts of New Mexico, the Soviet Union detonated its first atomic device. Characteristically, the news was kept a secret. It was high-altitude sampling by American aircraft over the Pacific Ocean that detected the unambiguous radioactive evidence of a Soviet nuclear test. The U.S. political and military establishment was shocked; all but the most hawkish of projections had bluntly stated that the Soviet Union would take until the mid-1950s to construct nuclear weapons. The Soviets had beaten those projections by more than five years.

The cost of that rapid development to the Soviet people and the Soviet environment, however, was enormous. It is significant that the man in charge of directing the overall atomic program was Stalin's secret police chief, Lavrentii Beria. Beria's other responsibilities included running the notorious Soviet concentration camp system, or *gulag*, where political prisoners and other "enemies of the state" were sentenced to long terms of hard labor in unspeakable conditions. Tasked with producing uranium for the atomic bomb program, Beria simply used concentration camp labor to mine and process the radioactive material.

No safety precautions, such as dust masks or protective clothing, were undertaken to shield the prisoners against the dangers of radioactivity. This use of slave labor was extraordinarily profligate in terms of human losses. The scientist Mikhail Klochko suggested that as many as 50,000 to 100,000 lives were lost in the process in the first decade alone, and other authorities concur that casualties were probably in the tens of thousands.

In addition to the mining and semi-processing effort, a series of processing and manufactur-

## ANDREI SAKHAROV

*1921–1989* The man most responsible for the development of Soviet thermonuclear weaponry was the gifted Russian physicist Andrei Sakharov. Born in 1921, he was brought into the atomic weapons program in 1948 by Igor Kurchatov. Sakharov derived many innovative solutions to problems encountered on the road to developing the so-called "superbomb." By his own admission, he worried little about the moral or philosophical implications of his early work. As time passed, however, Sakharov became more uncomfortable with his role as developer of "better" nuclear weapons for the defense of the nation. He became increasingly aware of the human costs of building and testing the weapons. He eventually openly criticized the Soviet policy of atmospheric nuclear testing in the aftermath of a truly gargantuan 50-megaton-plus test on the Arctic island of Novaya Zemlya in October 1961.

After criticizing this test and others, Sakharov was barred from direct involvement with the Soviet weapons program. In 1968 he published an essay entitled "Reflections on Progress, Peaceful Coexistence, and Intellectual Freedom," which called for the elimination of nuclear weapons and the establishment of political pluralism in the Soviet Union. After the essay appeared internationally, he lost all of the privileges accorded a member of the scientific elite, and became an "enemy of the Soviet state." As a dissident Sakharov continually spoke out against human rights abuses in the Soviet Union. Consequently when he won the Nobel Peace Prize of 1975, Sakharov was prevented from traveling to receive the award. His wife Elena Bonner accepted the prize on his behalf.

In 1980 Sakharov criticized the Soviet invasion of Afghanistan, for which he was exiled to the city of Gorki and prevented from contacting the outside world. In 1986 he was recalled to Moscow by Mikhail Gorbachev, where he became a tireless supporter of democratic change in the Soviet system. When he died in December 1989 while working as a member of a committee tasked with drafting a new, democratic constitution for the USSR, the nation lost perhaps its most powerful moral statesmen.

ing complexes were constructed, almost all of them in the interior of Russia east of the Ural Mountains. These centers, known only by postal code numbers and a name associated with nearby settlements, quickly grew into small cities closed to the outside world. In the late 1940s and 1950s

MAP OF SOVIET-DESIGNED NUCLEAR POWER PLANTS IN RUSSIA, THE COMMONWEALTH STATES, AND FORMER EASTERN BLOC NATIONS. *(The Gale Group.)*

at places like Chelyabinsk-65, Krasnoyarsk-26, and Tomsk-7, a massive research and productive effort grew up involving tens of thousands of engineers, scientists, and common workers.

Unlike the slave labor suffering in the mines, the scientists and engineers lived a cosseted existence by Soviet standards, supplied with the best consumer goods available, provided with lavish housing allowances (again, by Soviet standards), and given generous holiday benefits. Common workers at these sites, however, suffered a far more difficult existence, exposed on a regular basis to radioactive hazards that in many cases proved fatal.

Thus, very early in the program are seen two of the fundamental characteristics of the Soviet atomic effort: its secretiveness, remarkable even in comparison to the top-secret nuclear programs of the United States and, later, those of the United Kingdom and France; and its willingness to pursue whatever means were necessary to produce the required arsenal. Both of these characteristics would profoundly affect the Soviet experience with nuclear weapons, nuclear power, and the waste produced by both programs.

## The Expansion and Problems of the Nuclear Weapons Program

When Stalin died in March 1953 the Soviet atomic weapons effort was well advanced. The knowledge and technical expertise derived from the test of August 1949 and its aftermath allowed the burgeoning weapons infrastructure to develop techniques of repetitive and later mass production of weapons-grade plutonium and uranium. In 1953 the Red Army received its first shipment of deployable atomic weapons, and in August of that year the Soviet Union surprised the world once again, this time with its test of a thermonuclear (or "hydrogen") bomb, a weapon hundreds or thousands of times more powerful than those dropped on Hiroshima and Nagasaki. In doing so it demonstrated that the gap with the United States had closed dramatically—the latter had tested its first thermonuclear device not years but only months earlier, in November 1952.

The expanding nuclear weapons infrastructure that supported these remarkable advances was by no means trouble-free, however. Indeed, since the collapse of the Soviet Union in 1991 the true scale of the nuclear accidents, environmental contamination, and public health impact of the nuclear weapons program has become clear. At Chelyabinsk-65 (now called the Mayak Production Association) alone there were dozens, perhaps hundreds, of accidents in the 1940s and 1950s that claimed the lives of many plant workers.

Many of these accidents were caused by the feverish pitch of the work, which emphasized speed over safety and productivity over prudence. For example, if a reactor engaged in the production of plutonium for nuclear weapons became damaged, requiring repairs that would, if handled safely, keep it off-line for a year or more, then workers were sent in to repair it by hand, and to do so unprotected. Such an event occurred in June 1948, according to a September 1999 article in *The Bulletin of the Atomic Scientists*, and it involved the replacement of the entire reactor core—by hand—a process that led to "huge doses of radiation" to the personnel involved. But the repairs were completed within two months.

Chelyabinsk-65 was also the site of the largest accident in nuclear history prior to the 1986 accident at Chernobyl. In September 1957 a steel tank holding liquid nuclear waste exploded, spreading radiation over an area of 23,000 square kilometers, or approximately 9,000 square miles, and affecting approximately a quarter of a million people, ten thousand of who had to be permanently evacuated from their homes. As was the case at many other links in the nuclear weapons infrastructural chain, the plutonium and uranium processing at Chelyabinsk-65 was undertaken with little regard for the safe storage of waste. Indeed, for much of the complex's early life, waste generated was simply dumped into nearby rivers and lakes.

The River Techa was the destination for much of this waste, and radiation from Chelyabinsk-65 has been found in waters as far away as the Arctic Ocean, a thousand miles to the north. Closer to home the Techa represented the drinking water supply for approximately 125,000 people: when it became public knowledge that the water was highly radioactive the Soviet government resettled some 7,000 of them. Greenpeace estimates, however, that perhaps 8,000 residents who drew their water from the Techa have died of radiation-induced illnesses.

Similarly, another repository for Chelyabinsk-65's waste has the dubious distinction today of being the most radioactively polluted spot on the planet. For decades liquid and solid waste containing extremely high levels of radioactivity were dumped into Lake Karachay, close to Chelyabinsk-65. In 1967 the lake dried up and winds spread highly radioactive dust across a wide area, affecting tens of thousands of people both directly, as the dust was inhaled or ingested, and indirectly, as it contaminated their livestock and crops. The solution to the problem was typically Soviet: the entire lake-bed was sealed with concrete, a process not completed until the late 1990s.

The situation at Chelyabinsk-65 was not unique. Mismanagement of waste and disregard for safety were common characteristics at most of the nuclear production centers in the Soviet Union. Of course, the glaring question stands out: why was there such recklessness in the nuclear weapons program? The answer to that question is complex and consists of several aspects. First and foremost is the national security issue: the creation and maintenance of a nuclear arsenal comparable to that of the United States was seen by the Soviet leadership as the central guarantee of security during the Cold War. In essence, environmental or health problems were accepted as trade-offs in the creation, expansion, and maintenance of that nuclear arsenal. Second, in Soviet society information was an extraordinarily controlled commodity.

Events such as the accidents at Chelyabinsk that undermined the superiority of communism, or the infallibility of the Communist Party of the Soviet Union, were suppressed as a matter of course. Indeed, the initial response of the Soviet leadership to the Chernobyl disaster of April 1986 was to "hush it up," to deny that anything serious had happened. It was only when radioactivity was detected in large quantities in northern and western Europe and European experts confronted the Soviet Union with this incontrovertible proof that the true story became known.

Third, a balanced nuclear infrastructure, whether military or civilian, requires the creation of a so-called "complete cycle," involving the production, the processing, *and* the storage and disposal of by-products and waste. The storage and disposal of nuclear waste is, unfortunately, expensive; it is also crucial for environmental and human health. The Soviet economy could not encompass all three parts of the cycle, and concentrated primarily on weapons production. Whatever funds were left over were applied to the third leg of the cycle. They were not sufficient to do the job. As will be seen, the nuclear problem piled up as the Cold War matured and ended, to the extent that the states that succeeded the Soviet Union simply cannot deal with the problem without external aid in massive amounts.

## The Civilian Application of Nuclear Energy in the Soviet Union

The Soviet Union laid claim to the first civilian nuclear power station, which became operational at Obninsk, a small city in western Russia, in 1954. This was, however, a reactor primarily involved in the production of nuclear fuel for atomic weaponry, and it was not until the late 1960s that civilian applications of nuclear power began to expand in the Soviet Union. The country was extraordinarily gifted in terms of its fossil fuel resources, and so the rapid expansion of the nuclear power infrastructure after 1970 is somewhat difficult to explain in purely economic terms. There is no doubt, however, that the cutting-edge technology represented by nuclear power was attractive to the Soviet leadership.

During the Cold War, technological prowess was an important indicator of the strength of the communist system, and the broad application of nuclear power could, in the estimation of the Soviet leadership under Leonid Brezhnev (1906–82) and his immediate successors, demonstrate the superiority of the USSR in the world arena. Nuclear energy could also solve a problem confronting the Soviet economy in the 1970s. Although fossil fuel reserves remained vast, the extraction of coal, oil, and natural gas became increasingly concentrated in Siberia—a harsh, difficult, and therefore expensive environment in which to operate. The net costs of energy in the USSR began to rise in the late 1960s and 1970s and the establishment of a nuclear power grid promised to offset these rising costs to some extent.

Soviet nuclear power reactors were developed along two main lines. The first of these, a direct outgrowth of the reactors used by the military for the production of weapons-grade uranium and plutonium, was a simple type in which the nuclear reaction is "moderated" or controlled by graphite (the same material found in so-called "lead" pencils). The graphite, formed into rods that can be inserted into or withdrawn from the reactor's core, absorbs neutrons produced during the nuclear reaction. The amount of neutrons available governs the rate of the reaction and therefore the amount of power generated: as the rods are inserted, the reaction slows and generates less power, as they are withdrawn the reaction increases and generates more power.

Following experiments conducted at Obninsk in the 1950s and at the Beloyarsk station at Shevchenko (now Aqtau, a town in southwestern Kazakhstan) in the 1960s with graphite-moderated reactors, known by their Russian acronym RBMK, scaled-up commercial RBMK-based power stations were constructed at several sites around the western USSR in the 1970s. Another, larger RBMK plant became operational at Ignalina in Lithuania in 1983, and others were on the drawing board or under construction in the early 1980s.

Despite the fact that the RBMK formed the basis of this rapid expansion in the 1970s and early 1980s, it was nevertheless a profoundly flawed design. It became unstable when generating low levels of power, being prone to sudden "spikes" of energy that could raise the temperature within the reactor and, if unchecked, lead to a meltdown of the core—the so-called "China Syndrome" of popular imagination. Documents released since the collapse of the Soviet Union make it clear that the RBMK's design flaws were well known to both

MEMBERS OF THE INTERNATIONAL MOBILE RADIOLOGICAL LABORATORIES TEST THE SOIL SURROUNDING CHERNOBYL FOR RADIOACTIVITY LEVELS IN AN EFFORT TO LEARN MORE ABOUT THE EFFECTS OF NUCLEAR ACCIDENTS AND THEIR PREVENTION. (© *Reuters NewMedia Inc./Corbis. Reproduced by permission.*)

engineers and planners, yet RBMKs were not fitted with a secondary, reinforced concrete containment structure common in Western designs. That such domes were not constructed is again a consequence of economics: the main goal was the construction and operation of the reactor *itself*; "expensive" safety features were considered secondary in the design.

The other major Soviet reactor type was based on a pressurized-water design that employed water rather than graphite as the reaction moderator. Known as the VVER, this type was widely produced in the 1970s and 1980s, with reactors being constructed in Ukraine, Armenia, Russia, and in satellite states in Eastern Europe. In all, more than fifty VVERs were constructed during the Soviet period.

Though inherently safer than the RBMK design, VVERs nevertheless fall far short of western safety standards. Most lack secondary containment structures and they have poor emergency shutdown facilities. A measure of their unacceptability may be seen in the fact that, upon German unification in 1990, West German nuclear specialists inspected and then hurriedly shut down all five Soviet-designed VVERs that had been operating on East

German soil. Other Eastern European countries that still operate VVERs have come under heavy pressure from the western community since 1989 to shut down their reactors for the same reason.

Despite safety questions the VVER design was nevertheless seen as the centerpiece of Soviet nuclear power in the foreseeable future. Indeed, in the 1980s the future looked bright for the Soviet nuclear industry. New plants, based on VVER reactors, were being commissioned throughout the Soviet bloc, and dozens more were under construction or on the drawing board. Rosy projections foresaw nuclear power accounting for almost one-third of the Soviet Union's electrical generating capacity by the year 2000, and over half of the capacity for East European satellite states such as Hungary, Bulgaria, and Czechoslovakia. These projections and indeed the entire Soviet nuclear industry were thrown into chaos by the catastrophic accident at the No. 4 reactor of the Chernobyl nuclear power plant on 26 April 1986 (see sidebar). Many reactors under construction were suspended indefinitely whilst those on the drawing board were cancelled outright. Other plants underwent extensive modifications that improved their safety to a certain degree but not to western standards.

# CHERNOBYL

The accident that occurred at the Chernobyl nuclear power plant, 90 miles north of the Ukrainian capital, Kiev, at 1:23 AM on April 26, 1986, was the worst nuclear accident in history. An ill-conceived test of Reactor No. 4's safety equipment produced a power surge (to which the RBMK design was particularly vulnerable) that resulted in a steam explosion in the reactor's core. The lid of the reactor and the roof of the reactor building were blown off by the explosion, and graphite from the reactor's core sparked fires in and around the building. Immediate casualties—plant workers and fire-fighters—totaled 31, a casualty figure for the accident that is still used in certain circles today.

For days the exposed reactor burned, spewing unprecedented amounts of radioactivity into the atmosphere. Although it was detectable around the northern hemisphere, most of the radioactivity was concentrated in Belarus and Ukraine. Of particular concern were the radionuclides Iodine-131, which causes cancer of the thyroid, especially in children, and Strontium-90 and Cesium-137, both of which are concentrated in the food chain and cause a variety of cancers in humans, most notably leukemia. The zone immediately around the Chernobyl plant itself in north-ern Ukraine and the southern part of Belarus was worst affected: according to official statistics, and despite widespread evacuations totaling hundreds of thousands of people, approximately two million Ukrainians and two million Belarusians still live in areas suffering from contamination.

Direct casualties of the accident are much higher than the 31 reported at the time. According to David Marples, an expert on the accident and its aftermath, between 5,000 and 15,000 of the young men conscripted to clean up the region around the Chernobyl plant have died of a variety of causes, such as heart attacks, that should not affect people in their twenties and thirties. Total numbers of these so-called "liquidators" are exceedingly hard to determine, but there were somewhere between 200,000 and 800,000 involved in the operation. About 50 percent of the cleanup workers living in Ukraine are subject to various illnesses, including skin diseases and digestive and pulmonary problems. In addition, thyroid cancer rates have sharply increased in Ukraine and Belarus among those who were young children and teenagers at the time of the accident. The long-term health effects of the accident remain unknown, but many projections are grave.

---

The Chernobyl accident had a profound impact on Soviet society. Many commentators agree that the magnitude of the event undermined the authority of the Communist Party (under whose leadership such calamities were not supposed to happen). It unleashed long-simmering bitterness among the constituent republics of the Soviet Union—especially in Ukraine, on whose soil the accident occurred—against Moscow. It awakened an environmental consciousness among Soviet citizens, and it highlighted general economic and social ills in the Soviet Union. There is no doubt that Chernobyl forced a dramatic shift in Mikhail Gorbachev's policies of glasnost and perestroika, pushing them much further, and much faster, than Gorbachev and his reformist allies had intended. It is perhaps too much to claim, as some commentators have done, that Chernobyl "caused" the collapse of the Soviet Union. Still, it is important not to underestimate its impact either.

Chernobyl gave the Soviet people a basis upon which they could criticize other broad failures of the communist system. It was *that* attack upon its legitimacy that the Communist Party of the Soviet Union was unable to weather. Indeed, a last desperate attempt by communist hard-liners to "turn the clock back" on reform by ousting Gorbachev in August 1991 collapsed into farce as the army, the secret police, and the common citizenry simply refused to acquiesce in the face of this tawdry bid for power. Once the party itself was stripped of authority in real terms, the dissolution of the Soviet Union itself—which had been held together in large part by the threat of force or its application—was inevitable.

### The Nuclear Hangover: Post-Soviet Nuclear Power Issues in the 1990s

Ironically, the period immediately after the collapse of the Soviet Union was, relatively speaking, quite kind to the nuclear industry there. The 1990s were marked by sharp declines in the output of fossil fuels (crude oil production fell by almost half between 1988 and 1995, for example), as the energy sector struggled in times of economic chaos and deep cash shortages. Massive debts accrued to the energy sector as a whole, as consumers—from individual households to large industrial complexes—simply stopped paying their power bills. To a certain extent the nuclear industry was insulated from the most serious economic hardships by foreign aid, especially from the United States and, though shrunken from its high point in the mid-1980s, it still produced over 11 percent of Russia's electrical power in 1995 and output actually increased, albeit slowly, as the 1990s progressed.

Not surprisingly this performance led to the nuclear industry being hailed domestically as the answer to Russia's energy problems. In 1992 the Russian nuclear power industry (Rosenergoatom) announced that reactors whose construction had been suspended in the aftermath of Chernobyl would be completed and new reactors brought on line as well. However, the upbeat projections failed to take account of economic reality: Russia simply did not have the economic wherewithal to pay for such an expansion, and in the end only one of the long list of reactors was completed, at the Balakovo power station.

In other successor states of the Soviet Union the nuclear energy situation was, and remains, more complex. Ukraine, under heavy pressure to close the remaining three reactors at the Chernobyl plant, engaged in a long, difficult series of negotiations with the international community for aid to do so, and to construct coal-fired plants to replace Chernobyl's generating capacity. It took almost a decade and a $3.2 billion international pledge, but the last reactor at Chernobyl was finally shut down in December 2000. The problem facing Ukraine, Lithuania, and Armenia—states that had inherited nuclear power plants from the Soviet period—is that, relatively speaking, those plants generate much more of the state's electrical power than is the case in Russia.

Ukraine relies on its 13 remaining nuclear power stations for about one-third of the country's electricity; Lithuania's old and unsafe Ignalina plant accounts for about three-quarters of that state's electrical capacity; and the Metsamor plant in Armenia meets approximately 40 percent of the country's electricity requirements. Thus, shutting down the reactors is not a straightforward proposition: doing so will lead to a serious reduction in energy output, with the likelihood of economic

AN AERIAL VIEW OF REACTOR FOUR AT THE CHERNOBYL NUCLEAR PLANT SHOWS THE DAMAGE CAUSED BY AN EXPLOSION ON APRIL 26, 1986. DESPITE THE SEVERITY OF THE ACCIDENT, THE PLANT CONTINUES TO OPERATE DUE TO AN ENERGY SHORTAGE IN UKRAINE. *(A/P Wide World. Reproduced by permission.)*

instability to follow. Bilateral negotiations have therefore focused on replacing that energy shortfall, either through the building of fossil-fuel plants or through energy imports financed by Western credits.

Further compounding the nuclear power problem in these successor states is that none of them possess significant fuel reprocessing or waste storage facilities on their territory. During the Soviet period, as we have seen, those complexes were located on Russian soil; after the collapse of the Soviet Union other successor states had to conclude not always equitable agreements for their use. In any case, the reprocessing and storage facilities inherited by Russia were in an appalling state in their own right.

### Nuclear Weapons, Waste Problems, and the Western Response

The August coup of 1991 that led to the dissolution of the Soviet Union had an extraordinarily important side effect, the significance of which was not apparent at the time. In short, deeply disturbed by the implications of the coup, American legislators moved to establish a series of bilateral agreements between the United States and Soviet successor states covering nuclear weapons security, nuclear proliferation, and nuclear waste control. This range of agreements is the outstanding example of cooperation between the United States and the successor states of the Soviet Union.

The coup convinced U.S. politicians that it was in the best security interests of the United States to aid the Soviet Union in controlling its nuclear arsenal and supporting infrastructure. Upon the collapse of the USSR a few months later those plans were targeted towards the Soviet successor states. In its original form the assistance package, called the Nunn-Lugar program after its sponsors, senators Sam Nunn and Richard Lugar, called for Department of Defense funding of up to $400 million per year to assist the Soviet Union with the dismantling of a significant portion of its nuclear weapons arsenal as dictated by the Strategic Arms Reduction Treaty of July 1991. A highly popular bipartisan initiative, the Nunn-Lugar proposal passed the Senate by a vote of 86 to 8 and passed by acclamation in Congress.

Under the administration of President Bill Clinton (1993–2001) the Nunn-Lugar program was dramatically expanded and converted into a broad range of initiatives designed to aid the Soviet successor states not simply with dismantling nuclear weapons but with problems arising in the nuclear energy sector, with waste and reprocessing facilities, and with a potential "brain drain" of nuclear weapons specialists to emerging nuclear states such as Iraq or Iran. The umbrella covering these initiatives is known as the Cooperative Threat Reduction (CTR) regime, and between 1992 and 2001 more than $3 billion was transferred to the former Soviet Union under its auspices. It is by far the largest bilateral assistance program undertaken by the United States towards its former Cold War adversary.

Without that assistance, it is difficult to imagine just how serious the nuclear situation in the former Soviet Union might have become. It is impossible briefly to provide a comprehensive description of the state of the ex-Soviet nuclear infrastructure in the 1990s; however, a few examples may serve to illustrate the breadth, complexity, and gravity of the situation facing the Soviet successor states after 1991.

**Kazakhstan: The Reluctant Nuclear Power.**
Upon the collapse of the Soviet Union, the central Asian republic of Kazakhstan suddenly found itself to be the world's third-largest nuclear weapons power. Most of the USSR's powerful SS-18 intercontinental ballistic missile force was located on Kazakh soil, a force that comprised some 1,400 nuclear warheads—at least twice as many as the arsenals of the United Kingdom, France, and China combined. United States CTR programs and funding totaling $98.3 million facilitated the transfer of all warheads and missiles to Russia by 1995. In an operation entitled "Project Sapphire" and worthy of a spy novel, Department of Defense and Department of Energy personnel cooperated with the Kazakh government to spirit approximately 1,300 pounds of poorly secured, highly enriched uranium (enough for some 30 to 40 nuclear weapons) out of Kazakhstan in conditions of high security and absolute secrecy in the fall of 1994. The Kazakh government cooperated fully with the operation, partly because it did not want the material on its soil, and partly because the United States government reputedly paid approximately $100 million in cash and aid programs for the material. Department of Energy personnel involved in the transfer reported that almost all of the uranium could have been used almost "as-is" in a nuclear weapon.

**Norway Nearly Causes World War III.**
Unbeknownst to most people, the highest level of nuclear crisis alert since the Cuban Missile Crisis occurred in the early morning hours of January 25, 1995, when Russia believed it was possibly the victim of a sneak nuclear attack. A missile track suddenly appeared on Russian radar; emanating from an unknown location in the Arctic Ocean, the radar signature was similar to one that would be produced by a ballistic missile launched by a submarine lurking off Russia's northern coast. Such a missile attack, from "close by," gives minimal warning time and was therefore the standard strategy (well known to both superpowers) for opening a surprise nuclear attack during the Cold War. Russia's President Boris Yeltsin was awakened and alerted. For the first time in history Russia's nuclear "briefcase," through which civil authorities can communicate with their nuclear command-and-control infrastructure and order a nuclear weapons launch, was activated. Apparently, heated conversations between the president and his military staff ensued over the next ten minutes, as Yeltsin decided how to respond to this nuclear attack.

Only it was not a nuclear attack. The "missile" was in fact a rocket launched from Andoya in northern Norway carrying instruments to study the northern lights, part of an ongoing (and public) U.S.-Norwegian scientific program. Following standard procedure, both the United States and Norway had notified Russia of the rocket's launch time and trajectory profile several weeks earlier, but the message had somehow been lost after delivery and had never reached the proper authorities in Russia. Fortunately Yeltsin chose caution over launching Russian nuclear missiles against the United States.

After eight minutes of tracking, at which point only seconds remained before a Russian strike would have to be launched in response to the "attack," radar operators saw the "missile" reach its highest altitude, then fall back to earth far from Russian territory. Crisis was averted, but many commentators have argued that this event was an extraordinarily close-run thing; perhaps the closest the world had come to nuclear war. While it is true that Russian nuclear command-and-control functioned as it should have in the crisis—after all, no Russian missiles were launched—it must also be acknowledged that the crisis arose as a consequence of problems in that very system, as information vital to Russian national security was simply lost in the bureaucratic labyrinth.

### The Arctic Ocean's "Slow Chernobyl."

Scattered along the Arctic coastline of northwestern Russia are a series of decrepit naval bases, once home to the vaunted Soviet Red Banner Northern Fleet. When the Soviet Union collapsed in 1991, Russia inherited those bases and the naval vessels that comprised the fleet. Many of the vessels were nuclear powered, and throughout the 1990s Russia strove to find a way to deal with naval nuclear reactors and nuclear waste produced by decades of military mismanagement.

Roughly 300 nuclear reactors (some 20 percent of the world's total) are located in the region, along with tens of thousands of poorly maintained spent fuel elements, and a very large quantity of other assorted nuclear waste. When the Soviet Union collapsed, Russia found itself facing a decommissioning crisis. As late as 1998 almost two hundred nuclear-powered vessels awaited disposal, including approximately one hundred inactive nuclear submarines that lay tied up at dock or beached at shallow, isolated moorings, still requiring the removal of their nuclear fuel.

The condition of the submarines in particular deteriorated sharply in the 1990s. In some cases they have to be pumped with compressed air on a regular basis in order to remain afloat. Others simply sank at anchor; the condition of their reactors is unknown. While it would probably take decades

POWER PLANT EMPLOYEES PREPARE A NEW REACTOR FOR OPERATION IN ROSTOV, RUSSIA. *(A/P Wide World. Reproduced by permission.)*

for radioactivity to leak into the surrounding environment, the deteriorating condition of the vessels is cause for serious concern, as dilapidation sharply increases the problems (and costs) of decommissioning in the future.

This situation arose quite simply because Russia does not possess the decommissioning facilities nor the reprocessing capacity to handle the dozens of reactors and fuel that will be produced by the decommissioning process. In the early 1990s Minatom, the Russian Ministry for Atomic Energy, banned the use of the sealed casks that had been employed to transport naval nuclear waste to reprocessing sites at Chelyabinsk and elsewhere.

Unable to transport fuel elements that had been removed from submarines, the navy simply stored them in sites ranging in sophistication from semi-specialized facilities to shallow trenches dug in isolated areas on bases along the coast. According to the British Foreign Office, it will take decades to dispose of the nuclear material scattered along Russia's northwestern coastline, and it will be extremely expensive—perhaps $4 million to decommission each submarine, and tens or hundreds of millions more to move the nuclear material stored on land or on barges and deal with the current radioactive contamination.

These examples are provided to illustrate the two main problems that face Russia and the other successor states of the USSR. First, the Soviet-era nuclear infrastructure was unable to cope with the reprocessing and decommissioning requirements generated by nuclear power, nuclear weapons, and military nuclear reactors. The second problem was created by the economic crises faced by Soviet successor states in the 1990s: confronted by the more pressing problems of transition to a capitalist economy and dealing with the systemic economic and social dilapidation inherited from the Soviet period, nuclear issues were frequently marginalized or ignored altogether.

### Fixing the Problem at the Turn of the Century

The CTR program analysts quickly identified the depth of the problems and recognized that the fundamental first step in solving the nuclear crisis on a long-term basis was to upgrade Russia's reprocessing facilities; they were clearly the bottleneck that was choking even a partial solution to nuclear waste problems. Accordingly in 1992 the Mayak Fissile-Material Storage Facility (FMSF) initiative was added as part of the CTR program. This helped Russia build a large-scale facility at Mayak (the former Chelyabinsk-65) for the storage of plutonium and uranium from dismantled nuclear weapons. In all, approximately $450 million was allocated from U.S. sources for the construction of the site, with an opening date of 2002.

The FMSF was key to helping Russia meet its strategic arms reduction obligations which, according to the START I treaty signed by President George Bush (1989–1992) and President Mikhail Gorbachev, limited both the US and USSR to 6,000 strategic nuclear warheads. The establishment of a facility specializing in the storage of weapons-grade nuclear material would also lighten the burden on the rest of Russia's reprocessing infrastructure, allowing it to handle more material from the Ukrainian and Eastern European nuclear power programs, the Northern Fleet, and elsewhere. Thus, the FMSF and other facilities like it were seen as the keystone in any Russian plan to solve its nuclear waste and nuclear disarmament difficulties.

The FMSF program, however, has not been trouble-free. The facility as constructed possesses a much smaller capacity than originally intended, and the Russian government has insisted on converting the material to be stored there into a form that makes it almost impossible to identify it as originating in nuclear weapons. It has claimed that this is to prevent International Atomic Energy Agency (IAEA) officials, who would inspect the FMSF, from learning "state secrets" about Russia's nuclear weapons (the IAEA is a civilian organization).

This conversion to "generic" material means that it would be theoretically possible for the Russian government, if it so chose, to store material processed from commercial reactors or other non-weapons sources at the FMSF, in contravention of agreements concluded with the United States. It is even possible that material brought into the country under the new policy on importing nuclear waste could be semi-processed and stored at the FMSF, a policy that would violate both the letter and the spirit of the 1992 CTR initiative, jeopardizing both future FMSF funds and, probably, other CTR program funding as well.

The FMSF is in any case a storage facility, not a disposal site. In order to meet the disposal requirements of as much as 22,000 tons of waste over ten years, as outlined in the July 2001 law, a final location for the nuclear waste needs to be identified. At present the Russian government is considering an underground disposal strategy at one of four potential sites on Russian territory. These sites were being evaluated for their suitability, but prior to the passage of the nuclear waste acceptance law no final decision had been made as to which site was likely to be selected. Furthermore, the construction of such burial facilities will be expensive and the CTR program may not fund them if problems with the FMSF continue.

## RECENT HISTORY AND THE FUTURE

### Facing Realities

Whether the 2001 law on importing and processing nuclear waste translates into policy or not, it is clear that there are other, more fundamental issues facing Russia and the other successor states of the Soviet Union in the twenty-first century. Almost every part of the former Soviet Union is profoundly affected by the appalling Soviet nuclear legacy. None of the Soviet successor states is capable of solving the environmental, social, political, or health effects of that legacy through an application of its own resources. Nor will those effects disappear in the near term; radioactivity is a deeply pernicious and persistent phenomenon with an impact that lasts for generations, centuries, and, if unchecked, potentially for thousands of years. In short, it is not a phenomenon that can be ignored or simply wished away.

The government of Belarus is trying to do just that—returning formerly closed land to the plow in the south of the country, land heavily contaminated with cesium and strontium from the Chernobyl disaster. The decision is prompted by unavoidable economics: in 1995 the government spent approximately 20 percent of its entire national budget on combating the effects of Chernobyl. By 2000, although the health and environmental situation in the republic had not markedly improved, that figure had been slashed to 10 percent. The government simply could not maintain the necessary funding levels and so pretended that the problem was evaporating. A similar situation occurred in Ukraine, in which spending on Chernobyl's aftermath fell from 13 percent of budget in 1994 to only 4 percent by 2000.

In the chaos of the 1990s the nuclear waste issue was usually under-represented in political and economic calculations, as it had been during the Soviet period. Yet there was, and there remains, one vital difference between the 1950s and the 1990s: in the 1950s Western aid to the Soviet Union, the intractable enemy, would have been unthinkable. In the 1990s and beyond the Soviet Union has been replaced by a collection of states attempting, in a very real sense, to put the past behind them. As we have seen, the Cooperative Threat Reduction program initiated by the United States in the early 1990s and which continues today is without doubt the outstanding example of cooperation between the former Cold War enemy superpowers.

Despite problems that have cropped up with the Mayak Fissile-Material Storage Facility, on the whole Russia and other recipient states have adhered scrupulously to spending conditions and oversight mechanisms established by the United States. This behavior has been mirrored in almost all of the bilateral and multilateral agreements concluded between other Western states and Japan on the one hand and Soviet successor states on the other. The aid regime is therefore one of goodwill and trust but it is, unfortunately, still too narrow to tackle the full magnitude of the problem. The full cost of cleaning up the Soviet-era nuclear mess will certainly run into the hundreds of billions of dollars. That money will have to derive from further external aid: there is no realistic internal economic revival that can create wealth on such a scale.

A final characteristic of radioactivity is worth mentioning: as the world saw in 1986, radioactivity does not respect national borders. The farming industry in northern England is still affected by Chernobyl radioactivity, as are traditional reindeer-herding peoples in Scandinavia. Norway is deeply concerned that its fishing industry could be badly contaminated by nuclear waste leaking from submarines on the Kola peninsula. If the Soviet nuclear legacy is not solved, sooner or later it will affect peoples around the northern hemisphere.

Responding to the passage of the Russian nuclear waste law, John Reppert, head of the Belfer Center for Science and International Affairs at Harvard's Kennedy School of Government, noted in an interview with the *Christian Science Monitor* on July 3, 2001, that if Russia is "going to create the world's largest and least-safe nuclear-waste dump, then it will be a long-term consequence for the rest of the world." Russia is doing so precisely because it has identified a financial incentive of roughly $20 billion, income that is desperately needed; rather than condemn Russia, a far more prudent international response would be to advance that money in the form of aid in return for a guarantee that no importation of nuclear waste would occur. Such an international policy would be sensible not only in the short term but in the long term as well. As Carl Sagan stated in the early 1980s (in the context of reducing the numbers of the nuclear weapons whose manufacture produced the waste with which Russia and its neighbors now struggle), such a policy would not merely be wise, it would be "an expression of elementary planetary hygiene."

# BIBLIOGRAPHY

Dawson, Jane I. *Eco-Nationalism: Anti-Nuclear Activism and National Identity in Russia, Lithuania, and Ukraine.* Durham, NC: Duke University Press, 1996.

Holloway, David. *Stalin and the Bomb: The Soviet Union and Atomic Energy, 1939–1956.* New Haven, CT: Yale University Press, 1994.

Josephson, Paul. *Red Atom: Russia's Nuclear Power Program from Stalin to Today.* New York: W. H. Freeman and Co., 1999.

Marples, David R. *Chernobyl and Nuclear Power in the USSR.* London: Macmillan, 1986.

———. *The Social Impact of the Chernobyl Disaster.* London: Macmillan, 1988.

Marples, David R., and Marilyn J. Young, eds. *Nuclear Energy and Security in the Former Soviet Union.* Boulder, CO: Westview Press, 1997.

Nilsen, Thomas, Igor Kudrik, and Aleksandr Nikitin. *The Russian Northern Fleet: Sources of Radioactive Contamination.* Bellona Report No. 2, August 28, 1996. Available online at http://www.bellona.no.

Peterson, D. J. *Troubled Lands: The Legacy of Soviet Environmental Destruction.* Boulder, CO: Westview Press, 1993.

Tikhonov, Valentin. *Russia's Nuclear and Missile Complex: The Human Factor in Proliferation.* Washington, DC: Carnegie Endowment for International Peace, 2001. Available online at http://www.ceip.org/npp.

Wolfsthal, Jon Brook, Cristina-Astrid Chuen, and Emily Ewell Daughtry, eds. *Nuclear Status Report: Nuclear Weapons, Fissile Material, and Export Controls in the Former Soviet Union.* Washington, DC: Monterey Institute of International Studies and Carnegie Endowment for International Peace, 2001. Available online at http://www.ceip.org/npp and http://miis.edu.

*David F. Duke*

# SIERRA LEONE: LASTING PEACE OR A CRUEL MIRAGE?

In January 2002 the government and rebel leaders of Sierra Leone declared the end of the 10-year-old civil war in that country. An estimated 47,000 combatants had turned in their weapons, some of which were burned in a ceremonial bonfire outside the capital city of Freetown. At the ceremony the president of Sierra Leone, Ahmad Tejan Kabbah, pronounced: "Today we are happy that those flames of war are being extinguished. I declare the war is over and the curfew lifted." He added, "Go and enjoy yourselves."

Although apparently close at hand at the beginning of 2002, peace is like a mirage for the people of Sierra Leone. With warriors disarming, child soldiers being returned to their homes, and rebel leaders agreeing to stop fighting and join in the democratic process, everyone is hoping for an end to the war that has laid ruin to the land and traumatized its people. But after the horrors that have consumed the country since 1991 and the failure of several peace accords, it is difficult for many observers to get past doubt that the violence will end.

Civil war broke out in an already unstable Sierra Leone in 1991 when a group of rebels called the Revolutionary United Front (RUF), led by Foday Sankoh, rose up against the government. It is believed that the group was supported by Liberian rebel (later president) Charles Taylor. Although the RUF claimed to be fighting against a corrupt administration, any original ideology quickly dissipated when the rebels realized that Sierra Leone's greatest natural resource, its diamond mines, could bring them wealth and power beyond their wildest dreams. By 1994 the RUF occupied significant parts of Sierra Leone and had control of the diamond mines.

## THE CONFLICT

In January 2002 after a decade of civil war, peace was proclaimed in Sierra Leone and tens of thousands of soldiers disarmed as the country awaited democratic elections in May. Grave concerns remain, however, about the endurance of the fragile peace. At Sierra Leone's borders with Liberia and Guinea, continued fighting threatens the weak new government in Freetown.

### Political

- The rebel group that initiated the civil war, the RUF, was formed as a result of its leader Foday Sankoh's training in revolutionary camps sponsored by Libyan leader Muammar Qadhafi. The arrest of Sankoh and disarmament of RUF forces within Sierra Leone may not eliminate the rebellion if it is springing from regional sources.

- The war in Sierra Leone involves many other countries; peace negotiations that apply only within the country may not hold.

- The rebel RUF, under the peace accord, is transforming into a political party. Since many of Sierra Leone's citizens have been terrorized by this group, there is resentment that its leaders may be coming into power.

- The UN and the government of Sierra Leone have agreed to set up a small-scale international war crimes tribunal to try those most responsible for atrocities in the civil war. Some of the people responsible for war crimes, however, are in positions of power within Sierra Leone, and placing them on trial may stir unrest.

### Economic

- Sierra Leone's economy collapsed during years of war and the nation was rated as having the worst economic conditions in the world in 2001.

- Sierra Leone's diamond mines have provided funds to a wide variety of organized criminals, rogue governments, revolutionaries, guerrillas, terrorist organizations, and illicit businessmen throughout the world. It is not in their interest for peace to reign in Sierra Leone.

# CHRONOLOGY

*1991* The Revolutionary United Front (RUF) invades Sierra Leone, causing more than one million people to flee from their homes.

*1992* In a military coup, 27-year-old Captain Valentine Strasser overthrows President Joseph Momoh.

*1996* Sierra Leone has its first multiparty elections since 1967. Ahmed Tejan Kabbah is elected.

*March 29, 1996* Kabbah takes office as president of Sierra Leone.

*November 1996* The Abidjan Accord is signed by the Sierra Leone government and the RUF. It provides for demobilization and for the transformation of the RUF into a political party. Within a couple of months, however, fighting resumes.

*May 25, 1997* Johnny Paul Koroma and his Armed Forces Revolutionary Council (AFRC) overthrow President Kabbah in a military coup. The AFRC then allies with the RUF.

*July 19, 1997* Charles Taylor wins the presidential elections in Liberia.

*March 1998* ECOMOG, a West African Intervention Force led by Nigerian troops, storms Freetown; President Kabbah is restored to power.

*January 6, 1999* The RUF stage an attack on Freetown known as "Operation No Living Thing," killing more than 6,000 people and committing unspeakable atrocities on the residents of the city.

*March 1999* ECOMOG regains control of Freetown.

*May 1999* Kabbah and the RUF sign a cease-fire agreement.

*July 7, 1999* The Lome Peace Accord is signed. The accord awards blanket amnesty for rebels, allowing the RUF to transform into a legitimate political party within the Sierra Leone government.

*December 1999* The deadline for disarmament under the Lome Accord comes and goes and only a small percentage of fighters disarm. Violence continues as UN peacekeepers (UNAMSIL) begin to arrive to help with disarmament.

*May 3, 2000* The RUF captures 500 UNAMSIL peacekeepers.

*May 28, 2000* The RUF releases the last of the UN peacekeepers in Liberia, after the British marines arrive.

*May 7, 2001* The UN imposes sanctions on Liberia—a ban on diamond sales and travel by senior officials.

*May 15, 2001* A new peace accord is signed by Revolutionary United Front (RUF) rebels, the civil defense forces, and the Sierra Leone government.

*May 25, 2001* Hundreds of child soldiers are released in the town of Makeni, Sierra Leone, by the RUF as disarmament begins.

*January 18, 2002* The government and rebel leaders of Sierra Leone declare the end of the 10-year-old civil war in that country as disarmament is complete. Weapons are burned at a ceremonial bonfire outside Freetown.

The war that ensued was bloody and atrocious, notorious for its widespread and gruesome use of children in the military service on both sides. Child soldiers serving the RUF have been trained to attack and mutilate civilians, simply as a message to the population that their government cannot protect them. Not only the civilian population suffered from these atrocities; the children who were trained to kill were often subjected to terrible physical, psychological, and sexual abuse, and were forced into drug and alcohol abuse. Many have grown to adulthood in this environment and have never experienced peace.

Several peace accords have been negotiated in Sierra Leone since 1991, only to fall through.

Many former enemies now live together in "peace villages." Yet displays of common purpose during past peace negotiations have at times served to disguise efforts to rearm and regroup for the next battle. It is rumored that many rebels have turned in their guns during disarmament proceedings, only to use the US$300 they were given for obsolete weapons to buy newer and deadlier weapons for the next round of fighting.

This kind of ambivalence has been ever apparent. In June 2001, for example, during an intense firefight in the RUF stronghold of Kailahun, an on-the-spot cease-fire was negotiated between combatants on the front lines. They simply stopped fighting, claiming they were war weary

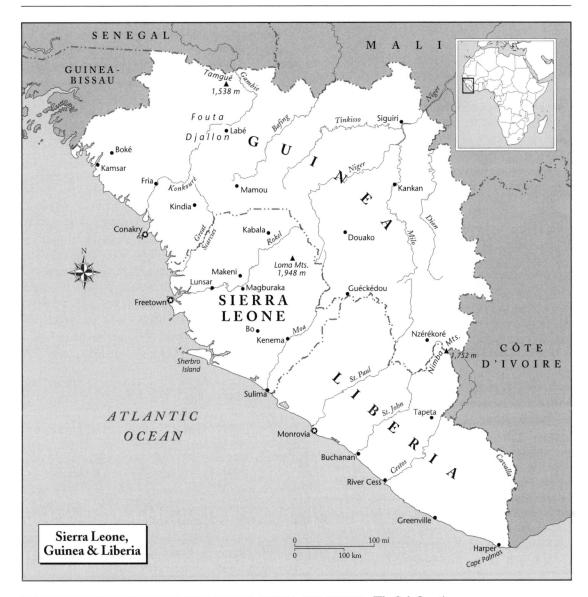

MAP OF THE REGION INCLUDING SIERRA LEONE, GUINEA, AND LIBERIA. *(The Gale Group)*

after years of killing each other with no obvious result for either side. On the other hand, when temporary peace has been achieved in the past, it has not always been appreciated. Ex-combatants in the peace villages complained about living in mud huts with thatched roofs, eating poor food, not having money, and not having status. A teenager who was, until recently, a general or colonel with his weapon at hand was "somebody," but today he is just another "nobody" in a run-down camp. Unless the ex-rebels and ex-government forces are given good educations and jobs, it is difficult to imagine this shaky peace lasting.

Although there is new hope in 2002 as the RUF disarms for peace, there is concern that the war in Sierra Leone has become a regional war; the country's precious diamond mines have attracted many other countries and revolutionary groups into the conflict. To establish lasting peace not only local players from Sierra Leone, but regional players from countries like Liberia, Côte d'Ivoire, Guinea, Burkina Faso, and Libya must be involved in negotiations or at least discouraged from buying conflict diamonds and supplying arms in exchange. The same is true of international players from a variety of nations such as Israel, South Africa, Russia, and Lebanon, and of terrorist groups like al-Qaeda, which has apparently been financing terrorist operations through profits made by trading the diamonds mined by the RUF in Sierra Leone.

# TROUBLE IN LIBERIA, 1980–2000

In 1980, during widespread food price riots in Liberia, a group of military officers led by Master Sergeant Samuel K. Doe carried out a coup d'etat in Liberia, killing its president, William R. Tolbert, and publicly executing 13 leading officials of his government. Doe, elected president in 1985, ran a corrupt and violent regime, and Liberia grew increasingly unstable. One of Doe's advisors was Charles Ghankay Taylor, who returned to his native Liberia from the United States to work in Doe's regime. But within three years, Taylor was accused of embezzling $900,000 from the government and fled to Boston to escape prison. The United States tried to extradite him, but he again escaped, making his way to Côte d'Ivoire.

Back in Africa, Taylor began to organize an insurrection, becoming the leader of the National Patriotic Liberation Front (NPLF). In December 1989 he led a military offensive against Doe's government in the mineral-rich area at the border of Liberia, Guinea, Sierra Leone, and Côte d'Ivoire. The war was vicious, and many local people fled across the border into Guinea, starting a refugee crisis there that remains today.

By 1990 there was a split in the NPLF. A rival group formed under the leadership of Prince Yormie Johnson. Johnson and his troops captured Doe and gruesomely tortured and mutilated him to death on videotape. Although both Johnson and Taylor proclaimed themselves president of Liberia upon Doe's death, a transitional government was formed with Amos Sawyer, a moderate academic, at its head.

Liberia was to be in a state of war for the next seven years. More than 250,000 people died in this war; at least half a million became refugees. Taylor repeatedly agreed to peace accords and then violated the terms. Taylor's NPLF fought ECOMOG troops, the Armed Forces of Liberia, and the United Liberation Movement of Liberia for Democracy (ULIMO). The country began to collapse under the economic and social toll of the violent war. Guinea, one of the founding members of ECOWAS, permitted ULIMO and the growing opposition to Charles Taylor to organize within its borders.

Gradually Taylor and the NPLF gained control of the country's infrastructure—transportation, banks, businesses. By 1995 he was Liberia's *de facto* leader. Taylor was feared as a brutal warlord, but in 1997 he won the presidential elections, promising to provide a strong and modern government and get the economy back on track. But five years after his election, the population of Liberia was still living in harsh conditions. The economy has not been revived, and many of the nation's institutions remain in shambles. Taylor's government has been accused of serious human rights abuses. Government security forces have beaten, tortured, and murdered insurgents and political enemies, and they have looted and raped civilians. Taylor has been accused of fueling the war in Sierra Leone and of possible involvement with terrorist groups. His government has been accused of discriminating against certain ethnic groups, of allowing child labor, and much more. The UN placed sanctions on Taylor and his government in 2001

In Liberia in 2002 there was great unrest. Guinea has continued to support ULIMO and another group of insurgents called Liberians United for Reconciliation and Democracy, who oppose Taylor's government. Taylor has sent military units to the border in response. Liberia, in turn, has sheltered Guinean insurgents. RUF commander Sam Bockarie crossed over into Guinea with a large RUF force to help reinforce Taylor's fighters there. There are many other rebel and militia groups at the borders of Liberia, Sierra Leone, and Guinea, and when battles erupt it is not always certain who is fighting whom or why. The hundreds of thousands of refugees in camps at the borders have been hit the hardest, and rescue efforts have been in place in 2001 and 2002 to remove them from the border area, where not only rebels and soldiers, but also the neighboring civilians have been known to attack them.

Tensions between Taylor and Guinean President Lansana Conte have been so bitter that even Taylor agreed to put West African monitoring forces at the borders. According to BBC African analyst Elizabeth Blunt, international alarm about the conflict has led some to theorize that Charles Taylor, with the backing of Burkina Faso, Côte d'Ivoire, Libya, and perhaps even France, is attempting to reorder West Africa, wresting power from the English-speaking countries and reducing American influence. Whether there is merit to the theory, Sierra Leone, with its weak new government, is in grave jeopardy of a coup or a new outbreak of war because of the ongoing conflicts between Liberia and Guinea at its borders.

The United Nations has its largest peacekeeping force—more than 13,000 people—in Sierra Leone. UN Secretary-General Kofi Annan and the Sierra Leone government announced in January 2002 that they would establish a war crimes tribunal to try those most responsible for atrocities. The tribunal will have a difficult and controversial task, since many of those who should stand trial are still in positions of political power and some are well-liked by the population. Indeed, during peace negotiations, the government has promised to create a multiparty system in which the RUF can participate as a political party rather than as a guerrilla group. Providing amnesty for the rebels is bound to stir up animosity from some of the victims of RUF abuse; prosecuting rebels, though, will also undoubtedly ignite protest among the factions.

### The Devastation

Sierra Leone has become a nightmarish landscape over the past ten years. "No hiding place from terror, no safe haven, no place to turn—that is how I would describe my country today—Sierra Leone," said historian and professor Dr. Sylvia Ojukutu-Macauley in an interview with the author. Sierra Leone has a population of 5,233,000 people. Despite being diamond rich and possessing other valuable commodities, Sierra Leone has the lowest per capita income in Africa. In fact, the United Nations Human Development Index rated Sierra Leone dead last in per capita income, health care, life expectancy, and educational levels in its July 2001 ratings of 162 countries of the world. The average person there earns less than $0.20 per day. The infant mortality rate is an appalling 148.6 per thousand. Well over half the population is under 14 years of age. Life expectancy is a mere 34.7 years. There is one doctor for every 11,000 people and most doctors live in the capital, Freetown. They seldom venture into the bush or forests, where most youth live, fight, and die. National health services have collapsed except in Freetown.

The educational system in Sierra Leone has virtually collapsed and the literacy rate has fallen to an all-time low of 31.4 percent. It is little wonder that war is seen as a principal trade for a young person. The only type of education readily available to children is training in the use of guns, bombs, rape, maiming, and murder. In the absence of alternatives, youth accept this nightmarish education and a way of life in which power and social recognition come from the barrel of a gun.

Between 50,000 and 75,000 people have died in Sierra Leone's civil war, largely in fights over the control of diamond fields. More than 20,000 others have been mutilated in RUF attacks that have left victims without hands, arms, feet, legs, ears, or lips. Two million people were living as refugees in neighboring countries in the year 2000. Even with the war officially at an end, hundreds of thousands of Sierra Leonean refugees are afraid to go home.

## HISTORICAL BACKGROUND

The Temne lived on the coast of Sierra Leone when the Portuguese arrived in the 1400s, the first Europeans to contact Sierra Leone. During the sixteenth century, Europeans frequently traded in Sierra Leone, bringing in cloth and metal goods and taking in exchange ivory, timber, and sometimes slaves. At about the same time Mende-speaking people from what is now Liberia migrated into Sierra Leone. They set up Sierra Leone's Mende states and soon were equal in number to the Temne. At the end of the seventeenth century, a British philanthropic company purchased land from some chiefs, including what is now the capital city of Freetown. There they established settlements for freed slaves. The first group arrived there in 1789. Almost all members of this group perished from disease or were killed by the Temne and the Mende. More freed slaves came from Nova Scotia and then from Jamaica by 1800. The purchased land became a British colony in 1808.

After abolishing the slave trade in 1807 the British began to patrol Africa's west coast, intercepting slave ships and forcing them into Freetown. An estimated 50,000 freed slaves were brought to Freetown in this manner and, although they came from all over Africa, many remained in Sierra Leone, where they became known as Creoles or "Krios." Most were Christian. They developed their own culture in Sierra Leone and prospered through agriculture and trade, forming an elite class that met with resentment from the indigenous groups.

For many years Europeans considered Sierra Leone the educational center of West Africa. Protestant missionaries established Fourah Bay College, a European-style university, there in 1827. Freetown became the headquarters of the British governor who also ruled the Gold Coast (Ghana) and the Gambia colonies. The entire country became a British protectorate in 1896, and English was the official national language. Several times during Sierra Leone's history as a British colony, the indigenous people rebelled against the

British and against the Krios, who dominated in economics and politics, but the British were too powerful for them.

## Transition to Independence

By the 1950s Britain introduced changes into the Sierra Leone government, allowing the people there more political responsibility. Sierra Leone achieved independence from Britain without violence in 1961. The country chose a parliamentary system, and Sir Milton Margai, leader of the Sierra Leone Peoples Party (SLPP), was elected prime minister. He died in 1964 and his brother Albert Margai succeeded him. Albert initially attempted to set up a one-party system, but was so violently opposed by the All Peoples Congress Party (APC) led by Siaka Stevens, he was forced to give up on the idea. In 1967 the APC apparently won a contested election. After this, Sierra Leone was cast into a series of coups d'etat. Stevens took office, but within minutes he was overthrown. Just a few days later, there was another coup, and the National Reform Council (NRC) took over. Several years later, another coup returned Sierra Leone to its parliamentary government under the rule of Siaka Stevens.

In April 1971 Sierra Leone became a republic; Stevens became its president. When general elections were held under the new constitution in 1973 there was so much violence that the opposition withdrew. In 1978 Sierra Leone became a one-party state. Stevens managed to survive two attempted coups and kept an iron grip on his power, forging and breaking alliances as needed, and relying on the military to quell the many rebellions. When Stevens stepped down in 1985, his choice for a successor was Major General Joseph Saidu Momoh, who was then chosen as president under the one-party system by the APC.

Unfortunately, Momoh was an inept politician. Under his seven-year-rule, Sierra Leone's economy collapsed. Corruption and mismanagement bankrupted the government. Unpaid civil servants were reduced to stealing office furniture, typewriters, and light fixtures and selling them to get money for food. In Freetown gas, electricity, and currency were scarce. Schoolteachers were not paid and the education system collapsed. Teachers demanded fees from parents to prepare students for examinations. Only professional families could afford to pay schoolteachers, so many children were on the streets without education, jobs, or hope. Many went to work in the diamond fields, but most of them got cheated out of the fruits their labor.

For years Siaka Stevens and then Joseph Momoh had smuggled diamonds out of Sierra Leone, along with hardwood and fish. According to William Reno in *Corruption and State Politics in Sierra Leone,* Stevens and Momoh used money from smuggled diamonds to buy rice from abroad. This rice was shipped to political bosses who distributed it to rural communities and urban constituencies in return for votes and political loyalty. At this time many Krios and others from Sierra Leone's professional classes used their political connections and influence to migrate to Europe and America.

Without this critical brainpower Sierra Leone slid from its place as a nation ahead of Malaysia and Singapore to a nation that ranked lower than Somalia and Rwanda in per capita income. Despite its gold, diamonds, bauxite, rutile, iron ore, fish, coffee, and cocoa, Sierra Leone became desperately poor. The population grew increasingly disgusted with their government as poverty gripped them. In the early 1990s prodded by the increasing protest demonstrations, Momoh was establishing a new constitution that would provide for a multiparty democracy in Sierra Leone. He was a little too late.

## The Revolutionary United Front (RUF)

In the spring of 1991 a tiny group called the Revolutionary United Front (RUF) invaded eastern Sierra Leone, announcing that it was going to launch an armed campaign to eliminate the corrupt politics and elitism of Momoh's government. The leader of this group, Foday Sankoh, was a charismatic man with a background of radicalism. As a student dissident in the 1970s, Sankoh had joined forces with others in Sierra Leone who wished to overthrow the corrupt government. He had been involved in a failed coup against former president Siaka Stevens in 1971, which earned him some time in prison. Upon release he was given a dishonorable discharge from the army. He was later fired from his job as a TV cameraman and he became very bitter.

In 1987 Sankoh went to Libya to join the military training programs sponsored by Libya's leader, Muammar Qadhafi, who hoped to initiate revolutionary movements throughout West Africa. While in Libya, Sankoh became friendly with some of the leaders of Liberia's rebel movement, the National Patriotic Front (NPFL). In 1990 Sankoh went to Liberia to fight in the NPFL's brutal campaign against the government, and while there he got to know the NPFL leader, Charles Taylor, who would become Liberia's pres-

# THE DIAMONDS AND INTERNATIONAL INVOLVEMENT

Diamond mines were discovered in Sierra Leone in 1930, and the country's diamonds quickly became known for their high quality as well as their abundance. In 1935 the huge international diamond trading company, De Beers, received exclusive mining and prospecting rights over the entire country for 99 years, but it was clear a decade later that they could not enforce these rights. In the early 1950s a diamond rush hit Sierra Leone; many countries became involved in smuggling, using Liberia as a diamond route. Diamond traders from all over the world opened offices in Monrovia. Even De Beers, foreseeing the inevitable, set up an office there not long before the colonial government took away its exclusive rights to the diamond mines. Israeli, Lebanese, Russian, and Italian organized crime got into the action.

Liberia had been heavily involved in Sierra Leone's diamonds since the beginning, but once the RUF started its rebellion in 1991, Liberia's forces had an official connection. Ian Smillie, Lansana Gberie, Ralph Hazleton, in their Partnership Africa Canada (PAC) report, conclude:

> By the end of the 1990s Liberia had become a major center for massive diamond-related criminal activity, with connections to guns, drugs and money laundering throughout Africa and considerably further afield. In return for weapons it provided the RUF with an outlet for diamonds, and has done the same for other diamond producing countries, fueling war and providing a safe haven for organized crime of all sorts.

The multibillion-dollar business of smuggling and trading "conflict diamonds" or "dirty diamonds" in exchange for small arms is vastly complex and involves people and institutions worldwide. One example of a diamonds-for-guns trader was a Ukrainian businessman named Leonid Minin, arrested by the Italian police on June 21, 2001, for supplying arms to the RUF through front businesses in Côte d'Ivoire, Burkina Faso, and Liberia. Italian court records show that Minin supplied the RUF with huge supplies of AK-47's, rocket launchers, self-propelled grenades, and anti-aircraft guns.

Minin and a Spanish associate operated companies registered in Milan, Italy, with headquarters in Monrovia, which shipped weapons to Liberia and from there to the RUF in eastern Sierra Leone.

During the Cold War the former Soviet Union flooded Africa with weapons. Consequently many African warlords possess Soviet-made weapons and prefer to buy ammunition and additional weapons that are compatible with current arsenals. The Moscow-based company Avia Trend supplies BAC-111s to fly weapons from Bulgaria via Ibiza, Spain, to Ouagadougou, Burkina Faso. Leonid Minin paid for these shipments through Swiss and Cypriot banks, according to records found by Italian police when they raided his Milan apartment. Diamonds worth hundreds of millions of dollars were found in Minin's apartment in Milan. It is clear from the records recovered from his apartment that his principal business partners included Charles Taylor, president of Liberia and Blaise Compaore, president of Burkina Faso.

Other well-known arms merchants have also been found to supply the RUF, and are paid in conflict diamonds. These dealers routinely break UN sanctions against supplying the rebels with weapons. Exotic, high-cost hardwoods are also used in payment for illegally supplied weapons to the RUF.

In 2001 international sanctions made it harder to sell conflict diamonds. Travel restrictions on Taylor and his cabinet made it hard for them to travel to Europe or elsewhere to put together arms for diamonds deals, which once enriched Taylor and the RUF. Sanctions were effective in smothering the arms trade and forcing combatants to make peace, like it or not. Thus, to the extent that the Taylor regime can no longer support RUF rebels with weapons, prospects for peace look bright. But, realizing how dependent they are on Taylor's success, some RUF commanders have crossed over into Liberia, where they are fighting anti-Taylor groups. They fear that if Taylor loses power an anti-RUF president will forever cut off their weapons supply.

ident in 1998. With Taylor's backing, Sankoh, by then in his fifties, returned to Sierra Leone and recruited young people there to join his Revolutionary United Front.

While in Libya Sankoh had been trained, along with other Liberian, Sierra Leonean, and Guinean exiles, in Muammar Qadhafi's insurgency techniques. Qadhafi introduced both Charles Taylor and Foday Sankoh to his revolutionary theory, teaching them, among other things, that politics and the control of a country should be in the hands of youth. In recruiting soldiers, Sankoh used some of Qadhafi's theory to

PEOPLE FLEE FROM SIERRA LEONE, WHICH HAS BEEN
DEVASTATED BY FIGHTING BETWEEN THE GOVERN-
MENT AND REBELS OF THE REVOLUTIONARY UNITED
FRONT, WHO TERRORIZED THE POPULATION. (©
AFP/Corbis. Reproduced by permission.)

proclaim against the current Sierra Leonean government's patron-client relationships, which used
diamond riches to reward only those in the president's small network and neglected the bulk of the
nation. Unemployed Sierra Leonean youth with
no prospect of gaining an education under the
official system rallied to this RUF message of
anger, and to promises of shared wealth in the
future.

As the RUF entered Sierra Leone, the public
was unaware of the group's existence and unpre-
pared for what was to happen next. Rather than
waging war against the army or the Sierra Leone

government, the band of young soldiers that comprised the RUF attacked defenseless rural civilians—elderly men, women, and young children. In
order to prove that the government was powerless
to help these rural civilians, the RUF butchered
them, murdering and raping and frequently using
their trademark atrocity of amputating limbs, particularly of children. Whatever ideals the group
may have started out with seem to have been
quickly lost. The two Libyan-trained dissidents
who had accompanied Sankoh as he began his
insurrection became disturbed by the atrocities
and tried to intervene. He had them executed.

When Sankoh and his soldiers entered a rural
region, he ordered the killing of traditional elders
and authority figures in areas that fell under RUF
control. All government officials were to be killed,
leaving no legitimate leaders to oppose the RUF
and, in effect, leaving villagers no alternative to
RUF control.

### Sankoh's Child Soldiers

Sankoh's success in taking over territory was
attributable in large part to his management of his
youthful troops, many of whom were young children. His initial mission, to recruit an army from
among Sierra Leone's poor and alienated rural
youth to overthrow the corrupt, wealthy, and powerful elite in Freetown, had strong appeal to many.
Beyond that, though, Sankoh made powerful use
of traditional culture, incorporating it into his initiation ceremonies for new recruits. Most of his
recruits were from the Mende tribe. Sankoh used
the Mende initiation ceremonies associated with
the "Poro" society for boys.

During a traditional initiation into the Poro
society, a boy meets the "bush devil" that seizes
him and abducts him from his mother. According
to Paul Richards, in *Fighting for the Rainforest:
War, Youth and Resources in Sierra Leone*, the RUF
convinced youth that since state schools had collapsed, it was the role of the RUF to step into the
breach, forcibly abducting boys from their mothers
and teaching them how to become men. Villagers
could in some way justify child abduction by the
RUF by likening it to the Poro initiation. In fact,
what the rebels did was introduce the children to
what is now known as "kalashnikov culture,"
teaching them to use modern weapons, training
them to become looters, military strategists, and
violent, ruthless killers.

The captives were vulnerable to their abductors. Poverty and lack of available educational
facilities meant that they had little to hope for in
their futures. And after capture, many suffered

from the "Stockholm Syndrome," a condition in which initially terrified captives subsequently identify with their captors. The RUF captors knew what they were doing. They would first treat the children with violent disrespect and force them to commit unspeakable atrocities. Then the captors would surprise their captives by being suddenly kind, respectful, and gentle with them. The result was predictable. Sierra Leone's abducted children became loyal to the very people who, in many instances, had forced them to kill their parents or brothers and sisters. The RUF commanders became more or less parental figures for these lost youth. Plied with drugs and alcohol, the child soldiers were stuck inside a culture of violence.

It was not just the RUF that used child soldiers, though. The Sierra Leone Army also used forced recruitment of children. For example, a child soldier named Ismael Baeh, who was forcibly recruited into Sierra Leone's army at age 14 described his recruitment like this (as quoted in the *Child Soldier Newsletter* in 2001): "I either had to join the Sierra Leone Army or to be killed—it was the only way to survive and to be alive. First of all they gave me a brief training in how to use a weapon…. the rebels were attacking where we were in the bush. I did not shoot my gun at first—but when you looked around and saw your schoolmates younger than you, crying while they were dying, their blood spilling all over you, there was no option but to start pulling the trigger."

## A Civil War

The Sierra Leonean Army under Momoh's regime was incompetent and could not clear the RUF from the diamond fields. In 1992, not long after the RUF first attacked, Sierra Leone Army officers overthrew Momoh. Frustrated by unreliable pay, poor equipment, lack of adequate training, and bad transportation, a group of young soldiers installed 27-year-old Captain Valentine Strasser as head of state. Composed of army officers, Strasser's National Provisional Ruling Council (NPRC) took over Sierra Leone. They promised to end corruption, improve living standards, and support the International Monetary Fund (IMF) and World Bank monetary reforms. The RUF was not appeased, however, and continued to fight the new government. For a time, Strasser's army kept the RUF in retreat in Liberia. Charles Taylor and his rebel troops in Liberia, however, came to the support of the RUF, perpetuating the war.

The familiar cycle of corruption, mismanagement, and misappropriation of government funds

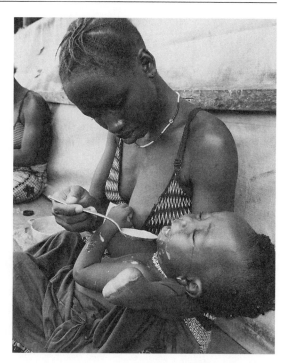

A WOMAN WHOSE HAND WAS CUT OFF BY REBEL FIGHTERS IN SIERRA LEONE FEEDS HER CHILD. REVOLUTIONARY UNITED FRONT REBELS HAVE MADE A PRACTICE OF VICIOUS ATTACKS ON CIVILIANS. *(© AFP/Corbis. Reproduced by permission.)*

repeated itself under Strasser. Optimism gave way to disappointment in Sierra Leone, and the fighting continued. Some soldiers became so corrupt that they were known as *sobels* or soldiers by day and rebels by night. Each unit claimed a part of the diamond fields and protected its turf against everyone, including the government that they were sworn to protect and defend. Meantime, the rebels were making headway throughout the country and rapidly approaching Freetown.

As the rebels advanced and the Sierra Leone Army was proving ineffective, Strasser began to rely heavily on Nigerian troops that came to his aid. He also privatized national security by hiring a South African firm known as Executive Outcomes to protect government-controlled diamond fields. Executive Outcomes worked with a rural militia made up of Mendes called the *Kamajors*. This militia, led by Hinga Norman, was one of several that had formed to protect the people in the countryside, since their government army was unable to help them—these came to be known as the Civil Defense Forces (CDF). The Kamajors went on to become a powerful fighting and political force. They were successful in hunting down and destroying RUF units. In addition, Strasser tried

SIERRA LEONE'S PRESIDENT AHMED TEJAN KABBAH AND REVOLUTIONARY UNITED FRONT LEADER FODAY SANKOH TALK DURING A DINNER AT PEACE TALKS IN LOMÉ, TOGO. THE TWO SIDES SIGNED A TREATY IN JUNE 1998 IN AN EFFORT TO BRING PEACE TO THE COUNTRY. *(A/P Wide World. Reproduced by permission.)*

to fortify the army with unemployed youth who were rapidly recruited to swell the regular army's ranks, but being poorly trained they were ineffective. The mercenary soldiers that were called in performed well and drove back the RUF, but they demanded such exorbitant payment that a scandal surfaced that brought down Strasser.

### *A Coup, an Election, and Another Coup*

In the mid-1990s civil society leaders demanded that Strasser organize elections and step down immediately. Strasser initiated the elections, but declared himself a presidential candidate. At 30 years old he was ten years too young to run as a presidential candidate under the Sierra Leone Constitution. His defense minister, Brigadier General Julius Maada Bio, overthrew him, and Strasser fled to Guinea. Bio then negotiated a settlement with the RUF and proceeded with national elections. Chairman of the National Advisory Council Ahmed Tejah Kabbah, a Mende representing the Sierra Leone Peoples Party, was elected in a highly tainted contest plagued by many irregularities, not the least of which was intimidation by the rebel troops. Since the RUF did not want the elections to go through, they used their most vicious tactics—notably cutting off people's hands—to deter them from voting. Kabbah won

and was sworn in anyway, and on March 29, 1996, Maada Bio handed power to him.

In November of that year the RUF and Kabbah's government signed a peace agreement called the Abidjan Accord. The agreement provided for demobilization and for the transformation of the RUF into a political party. Within a couple of months Sankoh was arrested in Nigeria. The RUF struggled over choosing a new leader, and the peace accord collapsed when fierce fighting once again erupted.

Kabbah lasted in office only fourteen months. On May 25, 1997, a soldier named Johnny Paul Koroma, heading the Armed Forces Revolutionary Council (AFRC), overthrew the president. Koroma was just out of jail for his part in a 1996 coup attempt, and he quickly formed a military junta to rule Sierra Leone along with his RUF allies. President Kabbah was evacuated to Guinea, along with 200,000 Sierra Leoneans.

### *Violent Years under AFRC/RUF Rule*

Under Koroma, Sierra Leone ousted Israeli and South African private security firms that had been central in the government's defense. The AFRC then suspended Sierra Leone's constitution and formed an alliance with the RUF, bringing chaos to the country. The RUF and the AFRC ravaged Freetown. At that point, Nigeria's dictator, Soni Abacha, with support from the United States and Britain, sent Nigerian troops into Sierra Leone, forming the backbone of the Economic Community of West African States Monitoring Group (ECOMOG) force.

The RUF demanded recognition as a legitimate government with the right to rule Sierra Leone and to control its resources. No government on earth recognized the RUF/AFRC government. It was a rogue state, a pariah. President Kabbah's government in exile held the distinction of being legitimate to most of the world. Britain, the United States, and the international community pressed for Kabbah's restoration to power. Nigeria, Ghana, and the Economic Community of West African States (ECOWAS) agreed and kept a regional peacekeeping force in the area to remove Foday Sankoh and the army junta and restore power to President Kabbah. In Sierra Leone new movements arose in opposition to the brutal junta, notably the Movement for the Restoration of Democracy. More civil defense forces emerged as the violent junta became increasingly unpopular.

### Battles in Freetown

In February 1998 the ECOMOG forces under Nigerian command stormed Freetown in an offensive against the RUF/AFRC forces, trying to get the junta out of the capital. In the terrible fighting that ensued, the RUF/AFRC soldiers carried out many atrocities, increasing their practice of cutting off the limbs of civilians, and burning and looting the city as they retreated. ECOMOG, with the help of the civilian militia groups, was finally able to force the RUF/AFRC troops out of Freetown, and in March President Kabbah was brought back into the capital. His rule, though, did not cover much beyond Freetown. In the ensuing fights around the country the rebels terrorized wherever they fought, destroying towns and villages in their path. Thousands of Sierra Leone's civilians fled to neighboring countries. The RUF secured solid bases in Koindu, Kailahun, and the Kono District's diamond mines by the end of that year. ECOMOG could not keep up with the rebels, and accused neighboring countries, particularly Liberia, of sending in troops to reinforce them.

By December 1998 the RUF had captured several key towns and villages within miles of Freetown. With Sankoh under arrest, RUF commander Sam "Maskita" Bockarie (often called "Mosquito") was taking the lead. He demanded that the government negotiate with him or he would attack Freetown. On the morning of January 6, 1999, the RUF entered the city to carry out "Operation No Living Thing." For several weeks, the hundreds of thousands of city residents were caught in a nightmare in which rebel soldiers raped, murdered, and mutilated residents, and burned down whole neighborhoods.

The city was for the most part without food, water, telephones, or electricity. When the rebels fought with ECOMOG soldiers, they often forced residents to serve as human shields. According to Ron Mitchell in *Sojourners* more than 5,000 people were killed in this attack alone [other estimates run as high as 7,000], 150,000 became homeless, 2,000 children were abducted by the rebels, and a significant number of aid workers, journalists, and businesspeople were abducted and later murdered. The majority of eastern Freetown's buildings were in ruins after the attack, some of them burned with people locked inside.

The children who, for the most part, carried out this operation had been fed a steady diet of cocaine, marijuana, free sex, and violence. They were on an insane rampage in Freetown. War correspondent Sebastian Junger in *Fire* described the battle for Freetown as follows: "It does not get any worse than January 6, 1999. Teenage soldiers out of their minds on drugs, rounded up entire neighborhoods and machine-gunned them or burned them alive in their homes.... They killed people who refused to give them money, or people who didn't give them enough money, or people who looked at them wrong.... They.... had been fighting since they were eight or nine, some of them, and sported names such as Colonel Bloodshed, Commander Cut Hands, Superman, Mr. Die, and Captain Backblast."

### The Lome Accord of 1999

By March Freetown was back in the hands of ECOMOG, and President Kabbah was convinced that he needed to negotiate peace, because military solutions could not hold back the RUF. In May 1999 U.S. Special Envoy Jesse Jackson, who had already formed a relationship with Liberian President Charles Taylor, put together a cease-fire, urging the Sierra Leone government to come to terms with the rebels. Kabbah signed the cease-fire agreement with the RUF in May. On July 7, 1999, the Lome Peace Accord was signed. The accord awarded a blanket amnesty for rebels, allowing the RUF to transform from a lawless guerrilla group to a legitimate political party within the Sierra Leone government.

In October Foday Sankoh and Johnny Koroma were brought back to Freetown. Under the accord, Kabbah was to preside over a transitional government in which the rebels would hold key posts until elections could be organized in 2001. Foday Sankoh was given the position of vice president in charge of the national minerals resources commission. Four other cabinet positions were given to RUF leaders. The blanket amnesty of the Lome Accord was controversial. Sankoh, responsible for countless deaths and atrocities, was awarded not only amnesty, but also a high government office without standing for election. To most people, giving him the post of overseeing diamond production was equivalent to letting a wolf guard the chickens.

The Lome Accord set a December 1999 deadline for disarmament. The deadline came and went and only a small percentage of combatants had turned in their weapons. Well into the year 2000, the peace in Sierra Leone was tense, with outbreaks of new violence and atrocities erupting regularly.

### The Abduction of the UN Peacekeepers

The United Nations Observer Mission to Sierra Leone (UNAMSIL) began arriving in the country at the end of 1999 to help with the disarmament. The peacekeeping troops in Sierra Leone would soon number around 11,000, but there were major delays in getting there. Great portions of the country remained under rebel control and neither the UN peacekeepers nor the ECOMOG troops were under a mandate to stop the violence. No matter what Sankoh had agreed to, there were now thousands of RUF youths in control of the eastern diamond-mining zone. They had no interest in disarming. Everyone feared sparking another battle and the civilian population was waiting out the upcoming elections in hopes that they would resolve lingering tensions. But on May 3, 2000, those hopes were shattered when RUF soldiers took 500 UNAMSIL peacekeepers hostage.

Britain sent in its marines to save the UN peacekeepers. Although all hostages were released by the rebels within three weeks, the abduction of the peacekeepers was the end of conciliation. Angry citizens mobbed Sankoh's home in Freetown, dragging him out and parading him around the city bloody and naked, until the authorities brought him into custody. UNAMSIL sent in more troops, more than 13,000, the largest peace-keeping mission in the world. Britain left its forces in Sierra Leone after its rescue mission and since then has taken a leading role in league with UNAMSIL to create an effective Sierra Leone army and a democratic government.

### The Liberian Connection: Charles Taylor

After the arrest of Sankoh, the RUF, led by General Issa Sesay, held on to the diamond mines and with them maintained significant control. Despite international efforts, a tremendous diamond mining and smuggling business under the RUF continued to exist well into 2001. Many of the children the rebels abducted as soldiers were put to work as miners. It is believed that the RUF sold the diamonds to smugglers at a discount, bringing in millions of dollars and supplying the rebels with arms.

It became apparent in a UN investigation that Charles Taylor, by then the established president of Liberia, and President Campaore of Burkina Faso, were supporting and supplying the RUF and were involved in the illicit diamond trade. A UN panel reported: "unequivocal and overwhelming evidence that Liberia has been actively supporting the [RUF] at all levels, in providing training, weapons and related materiel, logistical support, a staging ground for attacks and a safe haven for retreat and recuperation, and for public relations activities." The panel recommended an embargo on all diamonds and timber coming out of Liberia, as well as an air and travel ban for Taylor and his regime. The UN imposed some of these sanctions—a ban on diamond sales and travel by senior officials—on Liberia on May 7, 2001. There are many observers of the war who believe that Charles Taylor is, and has always been, the real leader of the insurrection in Sierra Leone.

On May 15, 2001, the Sierra Leone government and the rebels once again agreed to stop fighting and began to disarm. On May 25, 2001, 424 child soldiers were released in the town of Makeni, Sierra Leone, raising the number the RUF had released to more than 1,000. Many of the children were destined for camps and humanitarian programs sponsored by organizations such as UNICEF and Save the Children, where it is hoped they will get help in the long and difficult process of rehabilitation. British troops were at work training the government army troops. By the beginning of 2002, disarmament was complete. This time there was no blanket amnesty.

The UN and the government of Sierra Leone agreed to a military war crimes tribunal to try

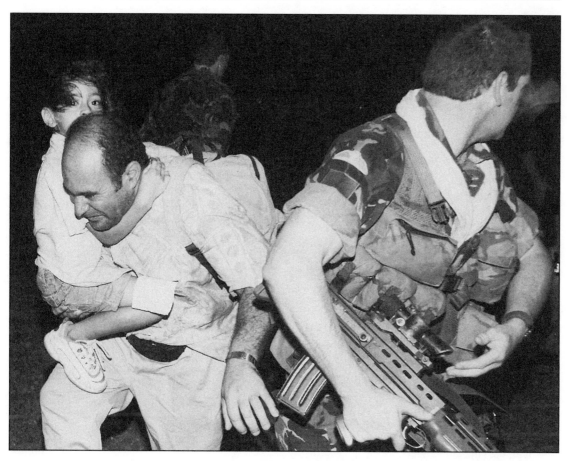

UN EMPLOYEES AND BRITISH CITIZENS ARE EVACUATED FROM FREETOWN, SIERRA LEONE. REBEL FORCES OVER-TOOK THE CITY AND TOOK 500 UN TROOPS HOSTAGE IN MAY 2000. *(© AFP/Corbis. Reproduced by permission.)*

those "most responsible" for the atrocities of the war since November 30, 1996, the date of the failed Abidjan peace agreement between the RUF and the government. Foday Sankoh will almost surely be tried for his part in war crimes. Nevertheless, the RUF still exists and is once again preparing to change from a military organization to a political party. Many of its members still call for the release of Foday Sankoh from prison.

## RECENT HISTORY AND THE FUTURE

Free, multiparty elections are to be held in Sierra Leone in May 2002 and UNAMSIL has received a mandate to help organize and monitor them. During 2001 the RUF changed to the RUFP (Revolutionary United Front Party). Although during peace negotiations the RUF urged a power-sharing interim government, it was not granted. They are not popular among the many people they have terrorized. Election results

may not be pleasing to them, and they have undoubtedly stored up arms in preparation for this.

With the huge UN peacekeeping force in place in Sierra Leone and billions of dollars coming in from all over the world, the prospects for peace are better than they have been in years. But many fear that the expenses of keeping peace in Sierra Leone have prompted too much international optimism. If the money and peacekeepers are withdrawn, trouble could quickly resume.

The year the rebellion began in Sierra Leone also marked the end of the cold war. When the cold war ended so did most foreign aid. Without aid, many of the state's institutions have collapsed, leaving an open door for opportunists who don't hesitate to use violence to take power. Thus, for the past ten years Sierra Leone has drifted from battle to battle. Peace for both the government and opposition groups has been regarded as an opportunity to recruit fresh forces, to rearm, and to reposition. Violence has been seen as a necessity for control of business and resources.

To many theorists, war as it has been undertaken in Sierra Leone is an extension of business. For the past decade in Sierra Leone war has been the nation's dominant activity, around which have grown many thriving businesses—most illegal and many profiting other nations, while Sierra Leoneans are impoverished. Paul Richards, in his book *Fighting for the Rainforest: War, Youth and Resources in Sierra Leone*, believes that this new Sierra Leonean model of war and peace, which he calls the "New Barbarism," is cultural. Those who have been left behind as the country collapses reorganize themselves into warlord groups in order to gain power, social recognition, and access to and control over resources. The two biggest issues facing the young population of Sierra Leone are education and jobs. With legitimate employment unavailable to them, many turned to warlords and violence to insure their survival and their livelihood.

In the last decade the World Bank and the International Monetary Fund have imposed "structural adjustment programs." These forced Sierra Leone to reduce the cost of government, leading to dramatic cutbacks in education and social service programs. Forced austerity measures also caused the government to reduce its armed forces, another source of employment for young people. The World Bank may have unwittingly become the RUF's ally in this way.

Cultures of violence evolve to fill power vacuums. Cultural clashes, environmental breakdown, overpopulation, and resource competition can provoke uncontrollable armed conflicts. Many of these conflicts are anarchic disputes that resemble banditry and criminal behavior more than they resemble political competition. Since terrorists attacked U.S. targets on September 11, 2001, many Americans are responding more attentively to the deep-rooted problems around the world. The United States's post-cold war foreign policy often sought insulation from foreign ethnic conflicts and weak governments threatened by collapse. But we now must wonder if these could be the forces that create and nurture future terrorists. It has become apparent that unless weak states receive help, they will provide fertile ground for the violent new cultures of the future.

# BIBLIOGRAPHY

Adedeji, Adebayo, ed. *Comprehending and Mastering African Conflicts: The Search for Sustainable Peace and Good Governance.* London: Zed Books, 1999.

Ayissi, Anatole, ed. *Bound to Cooperate: Conflict, Peace, and People in Sierra Leone.* New York: United Nations Institute for Disarmament Research, 2000.

Bangura, Yusuf. "Strategic Policy Failure and Governance in Sierra Leone," *Journal of Modern African Studies.* Volume 38, Number 4, 2000, pp. 551–57.

Bayart, J. K. *The State in Africa: The Politics of the Belly.* London: Longman, 1993.

Bender, David. *Urban Terrorism.* San Diego, CA: Greenhaven Press, 1996.

Blunt, Elizabeth. "The Guinea Conflict Explained." BBC News. February 13, 2001. Available online at http://news.bbc.co.uk/hi/english/world/africa/newsid_1167000/1167811.stm (cited January 22, 2002).

Bolton, John. "United States Policy on United Nations Peacekeeping: Case Studies in the Congo, Sierra Leone, Ethiopia, Eritrea, Kosovo, and East Timor," *World Affairs.* Volume 163, Number 3: winter, 2001, pp. 129–147.

Campbell, Greg. "Peace at Last in Sierra Leone?" *Christian Science Monitor.* Volume 93, Issue 160, July 13, 2001, p. 6.

Chabal, Patrick, and Jean-Pascal Daloz. *Africa Works: Disorder as Political Instrument.* Bloomington: Indiana University Press, 1999.

Chiahemen, John. "Sierra Leone Rebel Leaders Return Home," Time.com, October 4, 1999. Available online at http://www.time.com/time/daily/latest/RB/1999Oct04/83.html(cited January 21, 2002).

*Child Soldiers Newsletter.* The Coalition to Stop the Use of Child Soldiers, September 2001. Available online at http://www.child-soldiers.org/ (cited January 25, 2002).

Clarke, Michael. "Trouble Shooting for Peace," *World Today.* Volume 56, Number 6, June 2000, pp. 4–6.

Clausewitz, C. von. *On War.* Translated by J. J. Graham. Harmondsworth, UK: Penguin Books, 1968.

"Crisis in Sierra Leone" BBC News. January 16, 2002. Available online at http://news.bbc.co.uk/hi/english/in_depth/africa/2000/sierra_leone/default.stm.

Davidson, Basil. *The Black Man's Burden: Africa and the Curse of the Nation State.* London: James Currey, 1992.

Douglas, Mary, and A. Wildavsky. *Risk and Culture.* Berkeley, CA: University of California Press, 1982.

Doyle, Mark. "Refugees Flee Liberia Shooting." BBC News. January 27, 2002. [Cited 1-22-02]. Available online at http://news.bbc.co.uk/hi/english/world/africa/newsid_1785000/1785876.stm (cited January 22, 2002).

Fanthrope, Richard. "Neither Citizen nor Subject? 'Lumpen' Agency and the Legacy of Native Administration in Sierra Leone." *African Affairs.* Volume 100, Number 400, July 2001, pp. 363–86.

Farah, Douglas. "An 'Axis' Connected to Gaddafi: Leaders Trained in Libya Have Used War to Safeguard Wealth." *Washington Post.* November 2, 2001, p. A-22.

Francis, David. "Mercenary Intervention in Sierra Leone: Providing National Security of International Exploitation?" *Third World Quarterly.* Volume 20, Number 2, April 1999, pp. 319–338.

Furley, O. "Child Soldiers in Africa." In O. Furley, ed. *Conflict in Africa*. London: Tauris, 1995.

Goodwin-Gill, G., and I. Cohn. *Child Soldiers: The Role of Children in Armed Conflicts*. Oxford: Claredon Press, 1994.

Hirsch, John. *Sierra Leone: Diamonds and the Struggle for Democracy*. London: Lynne Rienner, 2000.

Huntington, Samuel P. *The Clash of Civilizations: The Remaking of World Order*. New York: Simon and Schuster, 1996.

Sierra Leone. Available online at http://free.freespeech.org/isierra-leone/civilwar/main.htm (cited January 22, 2002).

Junger, Sebastian. *Fire*. New York: W.W. Norton, 2001.

Kaplan, Robert. *Balkan Ghosts: A Journey Through History*. London: Macmillan, 1993.

Kaplan, Robert. "The Coming Anarchy: How Scarcity, Crime Overpopulation, and Disease Are Rapidly Destroying the Social Fabric of Our Planet." *Atlantic Monthly*. February, 1994, pp. 44–76.

Kpundeh, S. J. *Politics and Corruption in Africa: A Case Study of Sierra Leone*. Lanham: University Press of America, 1995.

Machel, Graça. *Impact of Armed Conflict on Children*. New York: United Nations, 1996. Available online at http://www.unicef.org/graca/ (cited January 22, 2002).

Mitchell, Ron. "Why Kosovo and Not Sierra Leone?" *Sojourners*, SojoNet. Available online at http://www.sojo.net/magazine/index.cfm/action/sojourners/issue/soj9907/article/990741c.html (cited January 2002).

Onishi, Norimitsu. "In Sierra Leone, War's Iron Grip Slowly Loosens," *New York Times*, May 26, 2001, pp. A-1, A-3.

Personal interview with Dr. Sylvia Ojukutu-Macauley, conducted by Dallas L. Browne, September 2001 at the University of Missouri, St. Louis Alumni House.

Ramsey, F. Jeffress, ed. *Global Studies Africa* ninth ed. Guilford, CT: McGraw-Hill/Dushkin, 2001.

Reno, William. *Corruption and State Politics in Sierra Leone*. Cambridge: Cambridge University Press, 1995.

———*Warlord Politics and African States*. London: Lynne Rienner, 1998.

———"The Failure of Peacekeeping in Sierra Leone," *Current History*. Volume 100, Number 646, May 2001, pp. 219–225.

Richards, Paul. *Fighting for the Rainforest: War, Youth and Resources in Sierra Leone*. Portsmouth: Heinemann, 1996.

Rutsch, Horst. "Peacewatch: Sierra Leone." *United Nations Chronicle*. Volume 38, Number 2, June-August, 2001, pp. 74–75.

"Sierra Leone and Liberia," Global Policy Forum, UN Security Council. Available online at http://www.globalpolicy.org/security/issues/slindex.htm (cited January 22, 2002).

Smillie, Ian, Lansana Gberie, and Ralph Hazleton. "The Heart of the Matter: Sierra Leone, Diamonds and Human Security," Partnership Africa Canada. Available online at http://www.sierra-leone.org/heartmatter.html (cited January 20, 2002).

United States Congress, House Committee on International Relations, Subcommittee on Africa. *Sierra Leone, Prospects for Peace and Stability: Hearing before the Subcommittee on Africa*. Washington, DC: United States Government Printing Office. Serial Number 106-26. March 23, 1999.

Wyse, Akintola. *Search Light on the Krio of Sierra Leone*. Freetown: Institute of African Studies, 1980.

———*Krio of Sierra Leone: An Interpretive History*. Washington, DC: Howard University Press, 1991.

Zack-Williams, Alfred. "Sierra Leone: The Political Economy of Civil War, 1991–98." *Third World Quarterly*. Volume 20, Number 1, February 1999, pp. 143–62.

*Dallas L. Browne*

# THE WORLD HEALTH ORGANIZATION TAKES ON THE TOBACCO INDUSTRY

## THE CONFLICT

Beginning in 1999 the World Health Organization undertook a series of meetings designed to create a Framework Convention on Tobacco Control (FCTC). Envisioned as a comprehensive, international, multilateral effort to reduce smoking rates, abate smoking-related illnesses, and regulate the trade, sale, and marketing of tobacco products, the FCTC marked the first truly global public health effort against tobacco consumption.

### Economic

- Tobacco companies have long argued that undue restrictions on the sale and trade of tobacco interfere with their ability to sell and market their product to consumers, an economic loss that is borne by their shareholders. The effort to reduce smoking also limits the revenue that national governments collect as taxes on tobacco products. In countries where the tobacco sector is state-owned, as in China, the potential economic loss from reduced tobacco consumption is considerable.

### Social

- Anti-tobacco efforts in more affluent, industrialized nations have been in place for a generation, and smoking rates have declined accordingly. Smoking rates in many less-developed nations, however, are just beginning to take off as consumers have more to spend on tobacco products. Because of these trends, the WHO predicts that smoking-related illnesses, finally declining in Western countries, will be a major source of mortality in coming decades unless aggressive anti-smoking efforts are put into place on an international basis.

### Political

- Although the WHO has issued numerous anti-smoking public health resolutions in past decades, the lack of any comprehensive strategy to help countries coordinate their efforts have rendered such initiatives largely ineffective.

At a Geneva meeting on May 24, 1999, the World Health Assembly's 191 members unanimously endorsed efforts to create a Framework Convention on Tobacco Control (FCTC). Although the assembly had passed 16 resolutions to govern the sale and trade of tobacco during the previous quarter century, the FCTC marked an important new step in coordinating public health efforts against tobacco-related diseases and regulating the production, distribution, and marketing of cigarettes throughout the world. As such, the FCTC was hailed by anti-smoking advocates as the first truly comprehensive program in the area of tobacco regulation and a first step in decreasing the number of smoking-related deaths and illnesses. Because its proposed mandate was so broad, however, the world's major tobacco companies immediately raised objections that the FCTC would impose unfair restrictions on the sale and use of their primary product, cigarettes, and infringe upon the civil liberties of smokers worldwide.

In taking on the global tobacco industry the World Health Assembly's administrative body, the World Health Organization (WHO) hoped to inject a sense of urgency in an increasingly crucial public health matter. With an estimated four million people dying each year from smoking-related illnesses—a figure that threatened to reach over ten million annually by 2030—the WHO viewed tobacco consumption as one of the greatest threats to public health in the twenty-first century. Indeed, with smoking rates soaring in developing countries, the WHO predicted that "the silent epidemic" would have an inordinate impact on countries least able to afford its long-term costs. In light of the immensity of the problem, the WHO set a target date of 2003 for the final resolution of the FCTC.

# CHRONOLOGY

**1946** The creation of a World Health Organization (WHO) is endorsed by 48 inaugural members at the International Health Conference in New York City.

**June 1948** The first meeting of the World Health Assembly, the governing body of the WHO, is held in Geneva.

**1964** The U.S. Surgeon General issues a report warning of the dangers of smoking.

**1966** Cigarette packages in United States begin to carry warning about the health risks of smoking.

**1971** Cigarette advertising is banned on United States television.

**September 1978** The WHO declares health as a fundamental human right at International Conference on Primary Health Care in Alma-Ata, Soviet Union.

**1989** The European Commission bans television advertising for cigarettes in member nations.

**May 1999** The WHO approves the beginning of multilateral negotiations on tobacco control under the Framework Convention on Tobacco Control (FCTC).

**October 1999** The first FCTC negotiations in Geneva result in twenty-five nations supporting a ban on cigarette advertising.

**November 1999** The WHO sponsors the "Women and Tobacco" conference in Kobe, Japan.

**2000** Estimates of global smoking rates indicate that 48 percent of men and 12 percent of women are regular smokers.

**May 2001** A second round of FCTC negotiations is held in Geneva.

**May 31, 2001** The first "World No Smoking Day" is held.

**Summer 2001** International controversy arises over a Philip Morris-sponsored report that concludes that the Czech government saved US$46 million from premature deaths of citizens due to smoking.

**Summer 2001** An internal report from three major tobacco companies outlines a plan to support self-imposed limits to cigarette advertising.

**November 2001** A third round of FCTC negotiations is scheduled.

**2003** A proposed completion date is set for FCTC implementation.

**2020** The WHO offers conservative estimate of number of smokers globally at 1.25 billion people.

**2030** The World Health Organization estimates ten million deaths annually from smoking.

In contrast, the international tobacco industry—dominated by Philip Morris (PM), British American Tobacco (BAT), and Japan Tobacco (JT), companies that held more than 42 percent of the global cigarette market—were wary of efforts that might impede their ready access to growing markets. As they had long argued, the decision to smoke was a matter of individual choice, one that should not be subjected to undue interference by public authorities. The tobacco lobby also feared that the costs of implementing the FCTC would be passed along to consumers in the form of higher taxes on tobacco products. Aside from these differences, however, there was some common ground between the outlined FCTC and the desire for limited regulatory measures on the part of tobacco companies. If increased vigilance over counterfeiting and smuggling cigarettes were implemented,

for instance, it would help protect the valuable brand names that were so immensely profitable to the major tobacco corporations.

Complicating matters was the difficulty in bringing so many nations together in support of one set of tobacco guidelines. Some countries, such as the United States and Japan, had powerful tobacco lobbies that greatly inhibited their national governments' willingness to endorse a strong set of FCTC measures. Other countries, most notably the People's Republic of China, were themselves in the business of trading and selling tobacco and derived a significant portion of their revenue from state-owned tobacco monopolies. Still other countries were not yet convinced of the need to press forward with the FCTC, especially with other, more immediate public health crises raging across the globe.

## HISTORICAL BACKGROUND

In the half century since its founding in 1948 the World Health Organization could point to a number of dramatic public health improvements that it had coordinated. In conjunction with numerous local non-governmental organizations (NGOs) the WHO contributed greatly to reducing the incidence of malaria, tuberculosis, venereal disease, poliomyelitis, and other viral diseases around the world. It also spearheaded a number of maternal health programs, helped to formulate nutrition and sanitation guidelines, and worked to ensure appropriate mental health treatments in its member states. In 1997 the tiny European nation of Andorra joined as the WHO's one hundred ninety-first member state; the following year, the organization celebrated its fiftieth anniversary as the world's most influential health agency.

Increasingly, however, the WHO raised controversy for its stance on public health issues. At its 1978 International Conference on Primary Health Care in Almaty, Kazakhstan (then called Alma-Ata as part of the Soviet Union), WHO delegates declared basic health care to be a universal right. Although the Declaration of Alma-Ata endorsed local control of health care policies by respective member states, it also expressed the belief in Section II that "the existing gross inequality in the health status of the people particularly between developed and developing countries as well as within countries is politically, socially, and economically unacceptable and is, therefore, of common concern to all countries."

Given the backdrop of both Cold War and North-South tensions, some observers took the Declaration as a not-so-veiled criticism of wealthier Western countries and their perceived lack of concern for conditions in less developed nations. In drawing a causal effect between reduced expenditures on public health and increased funding for military operations, the Declaration also took direct aim at the world's superpowers, then reaching the height of their struggle for Cold War dominance. Approved by the World Health Assembly and the United Nations General Assembly in 1979, the Declaration of Alma-Ata firmly linked public health issues with international political and economic concerns.

### Tobacco and Public Health Trends

The WHO's decision to prioritize tobacco consumption as a public health issue reflected both its willingness to influence long-term demographic trends as well as its desire to address the economics of the tobacco trade. Foremost among its concerns was the predicted growth in global mortality rates due to smoking. From a rate of four million deaths per year at the millennium, the WHO estimated that upwards of ten million people would die annually from smoking-related illnesses by 2030. By that date, about 70 percent of smoking deaths would take place in developing countries.

In addition to the obvious demographic trends, there were other reasons for the WHO's focus on anti-tobacco measures to assist developing nations. First, most Western governments—often urged along by non-governmental public health advocates—had already instituted an array of measures to lower tobacco consumption in their countries. Beginning in the 1960s official reports of the dangers of smoking became widely publicized in North America and Europe, leading to a gradual reduction in the incidence of smoking in industrialized nations.

In addition to the health scares Western governments implemented various public health measures to counter tobacco consumption. In the United States the famous "Surgeon General's Warning" of the dangers of smoking began to appear on cigarette packages in 1966; five years later, cigarette advertising was banned from television. Beginning with the state of Arizona in 1973, individual states also began to restrict smoking in public areas. Because of these public health campaigns, smoking rates for American men dropped from 44 percent in 1970 to 28 percent in 2000. Other countries were even more direct in taking anti-smoking messages directly to consumers; a series of large-print health warnings—accompanied by photos of smoking-induced maladies such as mouth cancer and brain cancer—helped Canadian smoking rates to plummet two percent annually from 1980 to 2000. Overall, after peaking in the mid-1970s, cigarette consumption in industrialized nations fell continuously over the next 25 years.

While the decline in cigarette consumption in Western nations was welcome news, the WHO predicted that developing nations were just beginning to see smoking rates rise. Outlining a four-stage process that linked tobacco consumption with economic development, the WHO explained tobacco consumption as a trend that increased along with disposable incomes in developing societies before leveling off and eventually declining decades later. In this model the least developed countries—including most of Africa, plus Afghanistan, Bangladesh, Nepal, and Haiti—had the lowest rates of cigarette consumption, mostly due to the extremely scarce amount of disposable income among the populace. In developing nations such as India, along with the newly industrialized Asian nations such as China, Hong Kong, and South Korea, smoking rates surged as consumers had more money to spend on brand-name cigarettes. For men in these countries, smoking rates approached 60 percent; for women, the rates were somewhat lower. For the third group of countries—including Japan and the eastern European countries of the former Soviet Bloc—higher mortality rates from smoking-related cancers caused a drop-off in the number of smokers as the dangers of smoking became more obvious. In the fourth group of countries—including the nations of North America and western Europe—smoking rates were in steady decline as older smokers died and public health warnings prevented more people from taking up the habit.

In essence, the WHO hoped that a set of FCTC guidelines would prevent people in the least developed nations from ever taking up the habit of smoking in the first place. Yet the challenge in accomplishing the task was far more difficult than simply modifying the four-stage model that it had developed. Indeed, in attempting to change the demographic trends of smoking, the WHO also confronted the economic realities of the global tobacco trade.

## WHO Charges of "Tobacco Neo-Colonialism"

Although the economics of tobacco consumption and its affect on developing economies was a less obvious part of FCTC discussions, it presented the most contentious part of the WHO's direction. Because a large share of the international tobacco trade was controlled by a handful of multinational corporations, these companies, called transnational tobacco companies or TTCs, were the targets of criticism from the start. The organization did not shy away from outright condemnation of the tobacco companies; in one paper commissioned by the WHO, Dr. Hatai Chitanondh, president of the Thailand Health Promotion Institute, labeled the marketing and promotion of cigarette smoking in developing nations as "tobacco neo-colonialism." He wrote in "Ownership of Tobacco Companies and Implications on Health," "The transnationals have been threatened by stronger laws and regulations in their countries and they must expand overseas. They try to shield an increasing proportion of their assets from lawsuits in developed countries. The TTCs would reap huge benefits from locating cigarette-manufacturing factories closer to tobacco growing areas. They also enjoy cheaper

A CARDBOARD COWBOY, REPRESENTATIVE OF CIGARETTE ADVERTISING, IS BURNED IN EFFIGY AT AN ANTI-SMOKING DEMONSTRATION. (© *AFP/Corbis. Reproduced by permission.*)

labor and transport costs." Chitanondh also accused the tobacco companies of using free-trade agreements to make inroads in developing nations; engaging in bribery, direct political lobbying, and superficial philanthropic efforts to gain access to markets; and introducing deceptively labeled "light" cigarettes—in fact, no safer than other cigarettes—to gain new consumers.

In a special conference held in Kobe, Japan, in November 1999, "Women and the Tobacco Epidemic: Challenges for the Twenty-first Century," the WHO also paid attention to the impact of tobacco marketing on women in developing nations. Although the estimated global rate of

## CIGARETTE CONSUMPTION IN ASIA CIGARETTES SMOKES PER PERSON AGE 15 OR OLDER

| Country | 1970–72 Cigarettes per year | 1980–82 Cigarettes per year | 1990–92 Cigarettes per year |
|---|---|---|---|
| Bangladesh | 510 | 680 | 990 |
| China | 730 | 1,290 | 1,900 |
| India | 1,010 | 1,310 | 1,370 |
| Indonesia | 500 | 950 | 1,180 |
| Japan | 2,950 | 3,430 | 3,240 |
| Malaysia | 1,400 | 2,050 | 1,630 |
| Philippines | 2,010 | 2,190 | 1,760 |
| Singapore | 2,510 | 2,550 | 1,610 |
| South Korea | 2,370 | 2,750 | 3,010 |
| Thailand | 810 | 1,080 | 1,050 |

CIGARETTE CONSUMPTION HAS INCREASED DRASTICALLY IN MANY ASIAN NATIONS. *(The Gale Group.)*

smoking among females was only about one-fourth that of males—at 12 percent versus 48 percent—the WHO feared that the number of women smokers was bound to increase as less developed nations experienced economic growth. Even if female rates of smoking stayed the same, however, the WHO was still concerned about their health. Because an estimated 60 percent of men in Asian countries were smokers, for example, the dangers of secondhand smoke for women and children were especially worrisome throughout the region.

In light of the aggressive marketing tactics to court female smokers the WHO held little doubt but that their ranks would increase. Again, the WHO singled out the development of "light" cigarettes as one deliberate attempt to get more women to smoke in the belief that the product was somehow safer than other cigarettes. The WHO also attacked tobacco company sponsorships of events and contests that targeted women, along with their philanthropic donations to women's organizations. Further, the WHO criticized efforts by tobacco companies to market cigarette smoking to women in developing nations as a symbol of progress and modernity. By emphasizing themes of independence, equality, and sexual attractiveness in their advertisements, tobacco companies had co-opted themes of women's equality to increase their sales.

### The International Tobacco Trade

Indeed, developments over the past two decades in the international tobacco trade seemed to bear witness to many of the WHO's charges. The most obvious trend in the tobacco industry was the tendency toward oligopoly, or control of the market by a few producers. In this case, just three publicly traded tobacco companies—Philip Morris, British American Tobacco, and Japan Tobacco—controlled about 42 percent of the global cigarette market. Philip Morris (PM) was the largest of the three major producers; with US$47 billion in tobacco sales in 1999, PM held about 17 percent of the world's cigarette sales. Led by its Marlboro brands—the best-selling line of cigarettes in the world, with 9.4 percent of the world market—PM derived about 54 percent of its revenue from tobacco sales.

Making a move to diversify its holdings and strengthen its bottom line in the face of enormous liability lawsuits in the United States, however, PM had long since ceased to be just a tobacco company. It acquired the Kraft brand name of familiar foodstuffs along with the Miller Brewing Company. Still, cigarette sales remained crucial to PM's long-term strategy. In 1999 the company paid $300 million to obtain certain brand names from competitor Ligget Group, Incorporated. The brands, which included Lark, L&M, and Chesterfield, were strong sellers in Europe and Asia, and PM spent part of its annual $813 million worldwide marketing budget to increase brand recognition even further. To its critics, PM's move to acquire the brands indicated its aggressive stance in going after markets in developing nations.

British American Tobacco (BAT), the second largest publicly held cigarette producer, also made headlines with its acquisitions in the 1990s. In 1994 BAT bought out the American Tobacco Company for $1 billion, gaining control of brand names such as Pall Mall, Lucky Strike, and Tareyton and about 17 percent of the U.S. market. In 1999 BAT paid about $7.5 billion for Rothman's International of Switzerland, then the world's fourth-largest cigarette maker. Through the deal, BAT added the Rothman's and Dunhill brands to its lineup. Unlike PM, however, BAT concentrated solely on its cigarette business. Although it had previously diversified into financial, insurance, and banking services, BAT split off into a separate company specializing in tobacco products in 1998. In 1999 BAT had tobacco sales of $30.4 billion.

The third-largest tobacco company, Japan Tobacco (JT), had perhaps the most interesting history of all the biggest players. Once a state-held tobacco monopoly, JT was privatized in 1994. The government retained a significant investment in the corporation, however, leading to inevitable charges of conflicts-of-interest by public health advocates. Indeed, smoking restrictions in Japan were some of the least obtrusive in the world, and health warnings included on cigarette packaging omitted any graphic statements about the product's health impact. With one of the highest rates of smoking in the world—at 133.5 packs per person each year—JT's 82 percent hold on its domestic market made the company a profitable one after it went public. In a bid to strengthen its market position outside of Japan, however, JT made the bold move to acquire R. J. Reynolds Tobacco Company's international tobacco operations for somewhat less than $8 billion in 1999. Through the sale JT acquired the rights to market the popular Winston, Salem, and Camel brands outside of the United States. In 1999 JT had tobacco sales of just under $30 billion.

In addition to the three major commercial producers, the state-owned monopoly China National Tobacco Company (CNTC) controlled a major portion of the global tobacco market. Although it was confined just to the People's Republic of China, the domestic market alone gave CNTC a hold on one-third of the world's smokers. Although CNTC kept cigarette prices low for Chinese smokers, the government nevertheless benefited considerably from the estimated ten billion dollars in tobacco taxes that it collected each year. The largest single source of tax revenue from the manufacturing sector, cigarettes contributed 12 percent of China's annual revenue.

Of all the major tobacco companies, PM was the most assertive in its public statements upholding its right to appropriately market and promote its tobacco products. Unfortunately, its tactics sometimes backfired, as in the case of a report commissioned by its subsidiary in the Czech Republic. The report, issued in July 2001, purported to show that the country had in fact saved 46 million dollars annually because of premature deaths from smoking-related illnesses. In arriving at the figure, the report noted the savings to the government from not having to pay out pensions, provide housing, or supply health care to elderly and ailing smokers. Adding tax revenues to the final tally, the report concluded that the Czech Republic had gained about $223 million in 1999 from the tobacco industry and consumption of tobacco products. Once the report was made public, the WHO and other public health agencies led an international outcry. For its part, PM quickly disavowed the study; in its apology, it admitted that the

## IMPORTED CIGARETTES MARKET SHARE BY PERCENTAGE

| Market Share in | 1985 | 1995 |
|---|---|---|
| Japan | 2% | 21% |
| South Korea | 2 | 6 |
| Taiwan | 0 | 22 |
| Thailand | 1 | 3 |

IMPORTED CIGARETTES HAVE GARNERED A GREATER SHARE OF THE MARKET IN MANY NATIONS WHERE THE PRACTICE OF SMOKING HAS INCREASED. *(The Gale Group.)*

report demonstrated "terrible judgment as well as a complete and unacceptable disregard of basic human values." With controversy raging over the Czech study, the WHO redoubled its efforts to get FCTC implementation underway.

### Towards a Framework Convention on Tobacco Control

After the World Health Assembly approved a FCTC drive in May 1999, it moved quickly through the WHO to schedule a series of meetings on the agreement. The first set of talks took place in October 1999 in Geneva with 150 WHO member nations attending. Although the first session did not formulate specific FCTC rules, it did end with 25 nations endorsing an outright ban on cigarette advertising. The Geneva meeting also resulted in a set of policy guidelines to serve as a blueprint for further discussions.

Foremost among the FCTC guidelines was a call for comprehensive restrictions on cigarette advertising and promotion in order to combat the incidence of smoking among young people and to prevent cigarette ads from crossing international borders. As visualized by the WHO, the restrictions would not just ban ads for cigarettes themselves, but would apply to any items carrying their brand names as well, such as sunglasses, backpacks, or other promotional items (a practice known as "brand stretching"). The WHO also hoped that a comprehensive ban on advertising would help to protect countries with advertising bans already in place such as Thailand, Norway, and Singapore. In Malaysia, for example, tobacco company-sponsored game shows reached across its borders to be seen by viewers in neighboring Thailand and Singapore, circumventing their complete bans on tobacco advertising and sponsorship.

A MAN SMOKING A CIGARETTE PEDALS HIS BICYCLE PAST A BUILDING PAINTED WITH "JOE CAMEL." CARTOON CHARACTERS SUCH AS "JOE CAMEL" ARE NOW FORBIDDEN IN CIGARETTE ADVERTISING BECAUSE OF CLAIMS THAT THEIR USE AIMS TO ENTICE CHILDREN TO START SMOKING. (*A/P Wide World. Reproduced by permission.*)

FCTC proposals also took direct aim at the political lobbying efforts by tobacco companies to influence legislation in individual nations. Noting that Philip Morris spent $60 million on 300 lobbyists in the United States alone, the WHO was deeply critical of the deep pockets that large tobacco companies could bring to bear on elected officials around the world. The WHO also bore down on non-tobacco subsidiaries of the major tobacco corporations, such as PM's Kraft Foods division, that participated in political lobbying. Going a step further, some FCTC supporters urged the WHO to take on an investigative role to monitor NGOs that were funded by tobacco companies.

In addition to demanding a more transparent political process through the FCTC, the WHO advocated greater disclosure of tobacco company information. In opening up internal health studies of cigarette carcinogens and publicizing the infor-

mation, the WHO believed that consumers would be better informed about the potential risks of using the product. The publicity would also help to counter tobacco company marketing efforts to portray "light" cigarette brands as somewhat safer to smoke than regular cigarettes. In conjunction with the full disclosure of the dangers of cigarette smoking, the WHO also supported international legal liability among the tobacco companies for damages caused by tobacco consumption.

In addition to these proactive measures, the WHO hoped that the FCTC guidelines would roll back free trade provisions that helped tobacco companies market and promote their products transnationally. With international free trade agreements reducing import and export restrictions, tobacco companies could claim that individual nations had no right to impose large excise taxes or product restrictions on cigarette imports. In putting tobacco products outside the realm of free trade agreements, the WHO thus hoped to empower individual countries to set their own standards on the importation and sale of cigarettes.

Finally, the WHO envisioned an FCTC that would set the groundwork for a sustainable, internationally oriented advocacy and watchdog group. The FCTC was proposed not just as a set of model practices, but rather as a group of policy initiatives that would be ratified by each member nation. In conjunction with the WHO, the FCTC provisions would then be enforced—through punitive actions such as sanctions and financial penalities—as a body of international laws. Although individual nations would come up with their own set of policies regarding tobacco control—in line with the Alma-Ata Declaration's statement in support of self-governance—corporations would be subject to the regulations of each individual nation.

### The Multinationals Respond

The international tobacco industry watched the WHO discussions closely and responded to WHO proposals at each step of the negotiations. For those who expected tobacco companies to revert to the adversarial stance that they had long held in respect to anti-tobacco initiatives, however, there was a surprising amount of support for the FCTC. The greatest area of common ground covered anti-smoking efforts geared toward children. Although tobacco companies had long been accused of targeting young smokers with ad campaigns such as R. J. Reynolds's "Joe Camel" character or PM's "Marlboro Man," the criticism over such practices—enhanced by severe advertising restrictions in many countries—had led to a disavowal of such marketing efforts on the part of the big tobacco companies.

One sign of the about-face occurred when the outcry over the use of Joe Camel—a cartoon image that critics charged was designed to appeal to children—led to a U.S. Federal Trade Commission complaint against R. J. Reynolds; in 1997 the company stopped using the character, even though it had been a major factor in increasing Camel's share of the eighteen-to-twenty-four-year old market from 4.4 percent to 7.9 percent. In addition to retrenching their advertising efforts, the major tobacco companies also endorsed educational programs to teach children about the dangers of smoking. Further, the tobacco industry supported policies to enforce national minimum-age requirements for the purchase of cigarettes.

Cigarette manufacturers also supported FCTC efforts to publicize health information to adult smokers, although they disagreed with the WHO about the extent of such warnings. While the tobacco companies agreed that such information should be widely available in order for adults to make a fully informed decision about whether or not to smoke, it insisted that graphic warnings on cigarette packages served no purpose other than to shock consumers. Photos of body parts riddled with cancer—such as the pictures of diseased brains and gums that appeared on Canadian cigarette packages—were simply too much for the cigarette lobby to endorse.

Addressing the economic dimension of the FCTC, commercial cigarette manufacturers also viewed the WHO's potential regulatory powers as an essential tool against international cigarette smuggling and counterfeiting. The problem was a severe one, with about one-third of all cigarettes around the world being purchased from unlicensed vendors. Some critics viewed the endorsement as a cynical attempt to protect valuable brand names from being associated with an inferior product; indeed, cigarette companies had an important financial incentive in keeping their products off the black market. As the major companies had long known, their success at marketing and promoting their products depended on controlling as many segments of the retail trade as possible. Without the ability to dictate product placement, quality assurance, and the retail price of their product, cigarette companies rightly feared the potential long-term consequences of black-market consumption.

In contrast to their support of vigilant anti-smuggling and anti-counterfeiting measures, however, the tobacco lobby was wary of endorsing increases in cigarette taxes. Claiming that exorbitant excise taxes would make cigarettes prohibitively expensive, the tobacco companies emphasized the right of individuals to choose to smoke. Once again, however, critics assailed their position as another attempt to preserve the tobacco lobby's own control of the cigarette market. Noting that consumers might "trade down" from brand-name substitutes in favor of rolling their own cigarettes—or simply give up smoking altogether—public health advocates pointed to the success of governments in lowering smoking rates by raising cigarette taxes. Some critics even charged that individual tobacco companies had often colluded with smugglers to avoid high excise taxes in the past, rendering their current stance on taxation and smuggling less than sincere.

Despite some of the fundamental disagreements over the FCTC, however, the world's largest commercial producer of cigarettes openly supported its development. In a speech before shareholders in April 2001, PM chairman Geoffrey C. Bible insisted that the only way to design an enforceable and fair FCTC was with the active participation of the tobacco industry. Bible also noted that the efforts of cigarette manufacturers to produce reduced-risk cigarettes with lower levels of carcinogens could only take place if international regulations assured manufacturers of specific production, marketing, and liability measures. Despite Bible's endorsement of the FCTC at the meeting, however, PM shareholders nonetheless rejected similar proposals to publicize the risks of smoking and secondhand smoke, end the use of animals in smoking studies, and supervise PM ads to make sure they did not appeal to children. Even as PM came out in support of the FCTC, then, its own policies continued to generate criticism from the public health sector.

## RECENT HISTORY AND THE FUTURE

While the momentum generated by the first round of FCTC talks made it seem that the WHO's targeted completion date of 2003 might be feasible after all, the second round of talks in May 2001 proved more contentious. NGOs such as the American Lung Association (ALA) and the Campaign for Tobacco-Free Kids (CTFK) were especially critical of the United States' participation in the talks. Although the Clinton administration had taken a hard line with tobacco companies by supporting a series of law suits against

A COUNTER DEPICTS THE NUMBER OF TOBACCO DEATHS BETWEEN OCTOBER 25, 1999 AND APRIL 30, 2001. THE COUNTER WAS INSTALLED AT INTERNATIONAL TOBACCO-CONTROL TREATY NEGOTIATIONS IN GENEVA, SWITZERLAND. *(A/P Wide World. Reproduced by permission.)*

cigarette manufacturers, the incoming George W. Bush administration (2001–) was far less adversarial with the tobacco industry.

The ALA and CTFK were especially concerned that U.S. delegates to the FCTC talks were rolling back key provisions that had already received general support in past negotiations. The Bush administration withdrew an endorsement to ban the use of terms such as "light" and "mild" in cigarette marketing, and fought against efforts to increase taxes on tobacco products to reduce their sales. The United States also declared its opposition to licensing tobacco retail outlets, even though such a system was generally viewed as one of the best ways to reduce smoking among children. In line with tobacco industry guidelines the United States also urged a new round of discussions on banning smoking in public buildings and other work places. Finally, the U.S. delegation worked to weaken the obligatory measures to be included in the FCTC in order to give individual states more freedom to implement or ignore the final agreement.

The United States was not alone in coming under attack by public health advocates after the second round of FCTC negotiations. Critics also accused Japanese delegates of trying to weaken the FCTC and renewed allegations that the Japanese government—with a profitable stake in JT—was trapped in a conflict of interest that rendered its participation in the talks counterproductive. Some observers even expressed the hope that the United States and other obstructionist nations would stay out of the third round of FCTC talks, scheduled for November 2001. As Clive Barnes of the British anti-tobacco group Action on Smoking and Health (ASH UK) told *Multinational Monitor*, "The U.S. contribution has been entirely negative: weakening, delaying, and deleting anything that might have substance. . . . It would be best if the United States goes home from Geneva, adopts its increasingly familiar ostrich, and stays out altogether."

In the end, the cigarette companies' own efforts to regulate the tobacco industry may prove far more influential in the short term than any official efforts. In August 2001 the advertising industry publication *Ad Age Global* reported that a study commissioned by PM, BAT, and JT had come up with a revised set of standards for limiting advertising and promotional efforts by the three largest commercial cigarette producers. Although industry commentators were tightlipped about the report, "International Tobacco Products Marketing Standards," they insisted that the joint effort demonstrated a definitive commitment to curb youth smoking around the world. Indeed, many of the proposed standards—such as banning any models who appeared to be under the age of twenty-five in cigarette advertisements—did show an effort to stay away from the youth market. Other measures went even further to preclude young people from being targeted by cigarette ads, such as a media ban at sites located close to schools or youth centers and a prohibition on cigarette product placement in television shows, concerts, and in night clubs.

In response to the report, public health advocates once again accused the cigarette industry of attempting to corrupt FCTC negotiations for its own benefit. In proposing their own voluntary restrictions, critics argued, tobacco companies hoped to forestall any meaningful and compulsory reforms coming out of the WHO. Further, the attempt to put forth guidelines authored by the tobacco industry was another way of fighting WHO's proposals for an outright ban on cigarette advertising, which 25 countries had endorsed at the very first FCTC session in October 1999. As well, the report convinced those skeptical of the good faith efforts of the tobacco lobby that the industry was continuing to act as an oligopoly, fighting any effort to decrease its control over the international tobacco trade.

# BIBLIOGRAPHY

Brown, Eryn, "The World Health Organization Takes on Big Tobacco (but Don't Hold Your Breath)," *Fortune*, September 17, 2001, 117.

"Bush Administration Faces First Test on Tobacco; Lung Association Urges White House to Back Tough Global Treaty." U.S. Newswire, April 26, 2001.

Chitanondh, Hatai. "Ownership of Tobacco Companies and Implications on Health." World Health Organization Web Site, Available online at http://tobacco .who.int/en/fctc/delhi/HATAI2000X.html (cited October 4, 2001).

"Countries Urged to Prevent Smoking Epidemic Among Women." *Women's Health Weekly*, August 5, 2001, 15.

"Critics Appalled by Report Highlighting Financial Benefits of Smokers' Deaths." *Canadian Press*, July 17, 2001.

"Declaration of Alma-Ata." World Health Organization-Denmark Web Site, Available online at http://www .who.dk/policy/AlmaAta.htm (cited October 4, 2001).

Eaton, Lynn. "Tobacco Companies Exploit Women, Says WHO." *British Medical Journal*, June 9, 2001, 1984.

"FCTC Primer." World Health Organization Web Site, Available online at http://tobacco.who.int/en/fctc/ primer.html (cited September 27, 2001).

Garrett, Laurie. *Betrayal of Trust: The Collapse of Global Public Health*. New York: Hyperion, 2000.

Kessler, David.*A Question of Intent: A Great American Battle with a Deadly Industry*. New York: PublicAffairs, 2001.

Kluger, Richard.*Ashes to Ashes: America's Hundred-Year Cigarette War, the Public Health, and the Unabashed Triumph of Philip Morris*. New York: Alfred A. Knopf, 1996.

Madden, Normandy, Margaret McKegney, and Anne-Marie Crawford. "Secret Report Reveals Big Tobacco's Retreat." *Ad Age Global*, August 2001.

Nullis, Clare. *Health Campaigners Fear Tobacco Treaty Will Be Too Weak*. AP Worldstream, April 29, 2001.

O'Dell, Larry. "Philip Morris Backs Tobacco Rules." Associated Press Online, April 26, 2001.

Parker-Pope, Tara.*Cigarettes: Anatomy of an Industry from Seed to Smoke*. New York: The New Press, 2001.

"Philip Morris Companies Inc. Comments Regarding Czech Study." Philip Morris Companies, Inc. Web Site. Available online at http://www.philipmorris .com/pressroom/press_releases/czech.asp (cited October 8, 2001).

"Philip Morris International and Philip Morris USA Discuss WHO's Proposed Framework Convention." Philip Morris International Web Site. Available online at http://www.pmfctc.com/content/fctc/ fctc_toc.htm (cited September 27, 2001).

Rubin, Daniel. "Europe Remains a Smoker's Haven." Knight-Ridder Washington Bureau, May 31, 2001.

Satcher, David. "Why We Need an International Agreement on Tobacco Control." *American Journal of Public Health*, February 2001, 191.

Weissman, Robert. "The Taste of the U.S.A." *Multinational Monitor*, June 2001, 6.

World Health Organization. *The World Health Report 1998: Life in the 21st Century—A Vision for All*. Geneva: World Health Organization, 1998.

Zegart, Dan. *Civil Warriors: The Legal Siege on the Tobacco Industry*. New York: Delacorte Press, 2000.

*Timothy G. Borden*

# WORLD TRADE CONFLICT: HAS THE THIRD WORLD BEEN CHEATED?

## THE CONFLICT

Third world countries, having entered into free trade agreements with Western nations in the expectation of securing greater opportunities for their exporters, complain that these agreements are being ignored or circumvented in the West. Trade barriers, although reduced on paper, continue to protect important products such as textiles and agricultural products in the Western markets. The figures on developing nations' exports are not encouraging.

### Political

- In the United States politicians hoping to keep the votes of American workers and farmers have turned against some of the WTO rules and oppose implementing some NAFTA agreements.

### Economic

- Many Western countries claim that the problem is not market access but the productive capacity of the third world. In many cases developing countries export far less than they could because they do not have the supplies—not because of trade barriers.

- In the early 1980s a deep economic depression hit many developing countries, rendering them unable to pay their international debts. Western banks, under the coordination of the International Monetary Fund, began to carry out rescheduling of selected countries' debts, but in return developing countries were expected to abandon their radical posture on trade issues.

"There is going to be blood on the highway!" "NAFTA is a trade pact, it is not a suicide pact!" So said Representatives Peter DeFazio (D-Oregon) and David Obey (D-Wisconsin) respectively in response to proposals by President George W. Bush (2001–) to implement the rest of the 1994 North American Free Trade Agreement (NAFTA) by permitting Mexican long-haul trucks into the entire lower-48 United States in stages. The fact that in signing NAFTA the United States had already promised to do this seven years ago made little difference to American politicians as they took steps in August 2001 to prevent the Department of Transportation from approving Mexican trucking company requests for greater access.

The politicians' opposition to granting the United States access to Mexican trucks is supported by James P. Hoffa, president of the American Teamsters, who represents tens of thousands of U.S. truckers. American truckers fear losing their jobs to low-cost Mexican trucking companies and have urged their union leaders to make their case. Hoffa plays on American fears of poorly maintained Mexican trucks plying the U.S. interstates. Relying on Transportation Department statistics that show that 36 percent of Mexican trucks inspected as they crossed into the United States in 1999 required repairs before being considered roadworthy, Hoffa warns that if tens of thousands of these trucks enter the United States, it will be a "recipe for disaster."

The Bush administration has sided with Mexican President Vicente Fox in arguing that these statistics are misleading. Currently, in spite of the NAFTA agreement, Mexican trucks are only allowed to travel 20 miles, or 32 kilometers,

## CHRONOLOGY

*1947* General Agreement on Tariffs and Trade (GATT) comes into effect.

*1949* The United States initiates the first foreign aid program.

*1964* The first United Nations Conference on Trade and Development (UNCTAD) convenes.

*1968* The Generalized System of Preferences (GSP) is established under GATT.

*1973* The OPEC Oil crisis begins.

*1974* Developing countries at the UN issue a Declaration and Action Program on the Establishment of a New International Economic Order.

*1974* The Multi-Fiber Agreement (MFA) is signed.

*1979* The GSP is expanded.

*1982* Third world debt crisis begins.

*1989* The Berlin Wall is taken down, symbolizing the end of the Cold War.

*1989* South Korea and Taiwan "graduate" from the U.S. GSP list.

*1994* The North American Free Trade Agreement (NAFTA) is signed by Mexico, Canada, and the United States.

*1995* The Uruguay Round of the GATT is completed, and the World Trade Organization is created.

*1997* The Asian financial crisis begins.

*1999* The Seattle ministerial meetings of the WTO occur amid protest.

*2000* The Bangkok meeting of UNCTAD takes place.

*2001* The Doha ministerial meeting of the WTO is planned.

into the United States before unloading all their goods onto U.S. long-haul trucks—a very inefficient practice to be sure. Because the trucks from Mexico only travel short distances, trucking companies dispatch older vehicles that are bound to have more problems. In fact such short-haul trucks owned by American firms in Kansas City have a 45 percent failure rate—much worse than for Mexican trucks, according to the *New York Times.* It is argued that if Mexican firms could enter U.S. long-distance service, they would use newer and safer vehicles, as they do at home. At any rate the question is largely moot since only two firms in the country are prepared to take full advantage of an open market.

Such is the dilemma of many third world countries: they willingly enter into free trade agreements with Western nations in the expectation of securing greater opportunities for their exporters, only to find agreements are ignored or circumvented in the interest of protecting particular groups of voters and supporters.

### The Problem from the Third World's Point of View

Before going farther, let us look carefully at the list of complaints being put forward by governments in the third world, also called the devel-

oping world. The crux of the matter lies in the failure of the West to meet expectations. For 60 years governments have agreed to alter policies that artificially raise the prices of imports so that locally manufactured goods are more competitive. Even though these trade barriers, such as tariffs (taxes on imports) and quotas (ceilings on the amount of a product that will be imported), are falling, there is no sign that third world exports to the West are rising as they should. Expectations were especially high coming off the most recent "round" of trade negotiations which ended in 1994, in which Western nations promised huge reductions in barriers to imports from third world countries. But the payoff has not materialized. The argument is ironically reminiscent of a longstanding complaint by the United States against Japan: the bottom line of all trade liberalization should be higher levels of trade.

What is happening, the third world countries say, is a subtle refinement of trade barriers, not their elimination. Certain products are being excluded with surgical precision. Although the overall tariff on all imports is only around five percent in developed countries, it is much higher for these products. Agricultural goods, for example, sometimes encounter tariffs in the hundreds of percent in the European Union and Japan, meaning that the price on the shelf of the imported good may be as much as four or five times what it is worth when it comes off the boat. Similar stories are heard with regard to third world exports of clothing, textiles, shoes, steel, and raw minerals. The Organization for Economic Cooperation and Development (OECD; sometimes known as the "rich countries' club") recently released a study showing that protection against agricultural imports was actually higher in eight out of ten wealthy countries in 1996 than it was in 1993, before those countries promised to lower barriers in the Uruguay Round of trade negotiations. This increase was due in part to the withdrawal of special allowances that permitted the poorest countries to sell their wares duty-free in the West. These so-called "preferences" were one of the things the third world bargained away in the hope of increasing overall access to foreign markets.

The net result is that the third world has found it harder, not easier, to sell its products to the West. Global agricultural exports by developing countries were only 30.7 percent of the total in 1996–97, a figure below its share of 31.7 percent in 1970–72, according to the World Trade Organization. In textiles there was an agreement to dismantle the 1974 Multi-Fiber Agreement (MFA), a treaty that had protected developed country markets from developing country textile exports, but this protection continues, particularly for finished goods (as opposed to raw materials—a phenomenon known as "tariff escalation"). The problem is particularly acute for the poorest of the poor countries, the so-called "Least Developed Countries." According to a joint study by the United Nations Conference on Trade and Development (UNCTAD) and the British Commonwealth, least developed countries' exports account for only one-half of one percent of the world's total in 1999—less than in 1990.

## HISTORICAL BACKGROUND

### How Did We Get Here?

The frustration over continued lack of access to Western markets is somewhat surprising, unless considered in context. After all, third world goods have been blocked for centuries—in fact, much of the point of colonialism was to find outlets for over-produced Western exports, not the other way around, according to Russian Communist leader Vladimir Lenin and other radical critics of imperialism. Even the notion of foreign aid was alien to governments until after World War II (1939–45). When the World Bank, now thought of as the primary multilateral development agency, was

founded, its principal focus was on rebuilding war-ravaged Europe. U.S. President Harry S. Truman (1945–53) inaugurated Western foreign aid in 1949 by urging increased private investment and lending to developing countries to help them increase production at home and purchases of Western exports.

Free trade, however, was always a matter primarily between Western countries and did not include third world products. When the United States and Great Britain spearheaded negotiations to begin removing trade barriers during the 1940s, although an invitation was issued to developing nations from Latin America to attend, it was just an afterthought; they played no significant role for many years. Naturally, most countries in Africa and Asia were still colonies and did not exist as politically independent entities and therefore played no part at all in the General Agreement on Tariffs and Trade (GATT; first signed in 1947, a forum to promote free trade between member states by regulating tariffs and providing means to resolve trade disputes) and other trade negotiating bodies. Tariffs were reduced for products rich nations sold to each other, such as refrigerators, automobiles, and ships. Agricultural and other primary products, as well as low-tech manufactured goods like clothing, were exempt from free trade deals. The United States took its agricultural price supports off the table in the mid-1950s, as did Europe a few years later. Unfortunately this meant that the types of goods developing countries were most likely to sell fell outside the expanding sphere of unregulated trade.

It was not until the 1960s that the ever-increasing number of newly independent developing countries began to take a stand on trade. Under the intellectual leadership of Raul Prebisch, a Brazilian economist, they demanded a one-sided bargain from the West. It involved granting developing countries free access to Western markets while at the same time erecting or preserving trade barriers against Western exports, particularly in the area of commodities, or primary products. The developing countries moved to create a new United Nations agency—the UN Conference on Trade and Development, where they would have the majority and therefore set the agenda and the rules.

UNCTAD represented a challenge to the GATT and Western domination of trade law. In an effort to co-opt third world countries, Western nations decided to concede many of their demands, on condition that the developing nations join the GATT, where Western nations

# KEY TERMS

**Agreement on Agriculture:** a treaty to lower barriers to agricultural trade negotiated under the auspices of the GATT.

**Agreement on Textiles and Clothing:** a treaty to lower barriers to textile trade negotiated under the auspices of the GATT.

**General Agreement on Tariffs and Trade; GATT:** an international organization that establishes rules in international trade.

**Globalization:** a term that describes the increasing interdependence of nations and societies in the context of global trade and travel.

**Generalized System of Preferences; GSP:** an arrangement that allows developed countries to import goods from developing countries with lower trade barriers than those offered by developing countries to developed country exports.

**Tariff:** a tax on imports.

**Tariff escalation:** the tendency for tariffs on raw materials to be lower than those on finished goods made from these raw materials.

**Market access:** the ability of foreign countries to sell their products to another country.

**Multi-Fiber Agreement; MFA:** a treaty that protects developed country markets from developing country textile exports.

**Non-tariff barriers:** policies, such as quotas or labor standards, that limit the number of imported goods.

**Quota:** numerical limit on an imported good.

**Subsidy:** payment by governments to producers to allow them to sell goods at low prices and still make a profit.

**United Nations Conference on Trade and Development; UNCTAD:** an international organization that promotes third world development through trade and aid.

**World Trade Organization; WTO:** successor to the GATT.

held much more influence. In the hope of eventually being fully integrated into the global marketplace, poor countries agreed and the notion of non-reciprocal trade was born. Essentially, the West agreed to give "something for nothing" in the short term, offering relatively free access to their markets to third world exports.

The arrangement was dubbed the Generalized System of Preferences (GSP) in 1968. Each Western country was free put the principles in place on a case-by-case basis, however. The result was a patchwork of complex rules that, in the end, mostly helped countries in the third world that needed it least. South Korea, Taiwan, Argentina, and Brazil, for example, had the industrial capacity to produce a large number of products for sale to the West and were successful in securing a presence in American and European markets. Countries like Bangladesh, Malawi, and Guyana, on the other hand, found it extremely difficult to produce enough goods for export, according to *OECD 1997*. When they did, these were more often than not agricultural products that were still covered by

high tariffs and low quotas. The same was true for textiles, which fell under the 1974 Multi-Fiber Agreement.

## Debts in Developing Nations

Even the surge of influence the third world experienced following the Arab oil embargo in 1973–74 and the resulting leap in petroleum prices proved short-lived. Developing countries were unable to secure Western support for such initiatives as price supports for commodities, cartels (producer-controlled mechanisms for limiting production) for such commodities as bauxite and coffee, or increases in foreign aid and technical assistance. This stemmed in large part from the Western decision to eschew the UN and retreat to more hospitable international institutions such as the International Monetary Fund (IMF) and the GATT.

The situation changed dramatically in the early 1980s when, following years of growth fueled in part by foreign borrowing and temporarily high commodity prices, a deep economic

## TARIFF ESCALATION INCREASE BY PERCENTAGE

| Tariffs Applied by | Manioc, roots, and tubers | | |
| | Fresh, dried | Flour, meal | Starches |
| --- | --- | --- | --- |
| European Union | 56.20% | 12.70% | 64.30% |
| Japan | 1.40 | 18.60 | 500.60 |

| Tariffs Applied by | Hides and skins | | |
| | Raw material | Leather | Articles* |
| --- | --- | --- | --- |
| European Union | 0.00% | 3.40% | 4.20% |
| Japan | 0.00 | 4.10 | 9.60 |

\* Excluding shoes

TARIFFS APPLIED BY THE EUROPEAN UNION AND JAPAN HAVE INCREASED MARKEDLY FOR MANY PRODUCTS. *(The Gale Group.)*

depression swept through the third world. Oil prices dropped from over $35 per barrel of crude to less than $10, while interest rates for short-term private borrowing increased to nearly 20 percent. Mexico, Brazil, and Venezuela—all oil exporters—found themselves unable to repay the quarterly interest payments and essentially defaulted on their foreign loans. Gradually, and for a variety of reasons, the economic troubles spread until almost every developing country was deep in arrears in loan repayments.

Since the debts were generally dollar-denominated and owed to Western banks, the developing countries could not simply print more local currency to get themselves out of trouble, as so many Western nations had done before them. Rather, they had to either sell more goods to earn the funds, attract more foreign investment capital, or ask for more loans to repay the old ones (this is called "rescheduling"). At any rate, nothing could be done without Western cooperation, and so the bargaining strategies changed almost overnight. Although there were attempts at organizing a coalition of debtors, these were quickly squelched as Western banks, under the coordination of the International Monetary Fund, began to carry out rescheduling of selected countries' debts. These deals came with significant strings, however: developing countries were expected to abandon their radical posture on trade and other economic issues. They were required to lower trade barriers to Western goods, make foreign investment safer

and more convenient, reduce subsidies to local producers, and eliminate price supports for basic goods, among other things. At the global level, any semblance of third world solidarity evaporated.

In time the third world liberalized, although not without considerable protest, given the horrendous toll on ordinary citizens these policies imposed. The West softened the blow slightly by creating a few preferential trade agreements (the Caribbean Basin Initiative, a series of acts starting in 1983 to promote economic development in Central America and the Caribbean islands through special treatment in the American market is perhaps the best known in the United States). But by the end of the 1980s, much of the Generalized System of Preferences was gone, either through concessions by developing countries or by the "graduation" of the more successful ones. South Korea and Taiwan were no longer eligible for special treatment in 1989. Third world countries were left to compete in the global marketplace as best they could in the face of ever-intensifying "globalization."

### The Uruguay Round of the Gatt

The proposal to draft a new set of trade rules under the rubric of the Uruguay Round of the GATT seemed to offer some promise to developing countries. They eagerly maneuvered to put their issues on the table. Thus negotiations began in the mid-1980s on trade in tropical goods, agriculture, textiles, and so forth. Added to the agenda was a proposal to strengthen and make the system fairer for settling disagreements among trading partners. Developing countries hoped that this addition would allow them to successfully charge Western powers with violating GATT's rules when the need arose in the future.

On paper the Uruguay Round was quite successful, from a developing country's point of view. The MFA was slated for elimination in an eight-year period beginning in 1995 when the Agreement on Textiles and Clothing went into effect. Tariffs against agricultural goods were to be reduced and quotas to be converted into more visible tariffs, to be reduced over time as well. Agricultural price supports in the West were to be reduced over time. In the end the developing countries succeeded in obtaining almost all of their negotiating objectives.

The devil, however, has been in the details of implementation. Because the language is vague and contains some loopholes, many Western countries are moving very slowly to put in place the agreement, while at the same time they are arguing that no violation has occurred. On the

A SIGN IN COLOMBO, SRI LANKA, DIRECTS TRAVELERS TO A FREE TRADE ZONE IN KATUNAYAKA. (© *Howard Davies/Corbis. Reproduced by permission.*)

other hand some countries are simply flouting the treaty and ignoring its provisions, much to the consternation of the developing world. In his summary of the most recent UNCTAD meeting in Bangkok, Thailand, in February 2000, Secretary-General Rubens Ricupero said, "What are [the diplomats] asking for?... They want the massive barriers to be dismantled in relation to trade in agriculture, textiles, and clothing and in the areas where tariff peaks and escalation still prevail, even after the implementation of the Uruguay Round Agreements."

An official summary of the meeting declared that many speakers from developing nations had opened their markets and strengthened their organizations and economies to better compete with industrialized countries, though without the benefit of equal liberalization. The summary also pointed out that implementation of agreements made during the Uruguay Round were uneven, and policy makers from developed countries were perceived to be bending under pressure for domestic protectionism.

Still others feel the inequity of the system is not inadvertent, but rather the result of a deliberate strategy on the part of the West to economically weaken the third world and bring about its virtual "recolonization."

### The Problem from the West's Point of View

In general most developed countries believe that their trade barriers are very low, both in comparison to years past and in comparison to developing countries' barriers. They are quick to point out, for example, that in general tariffs are extremely low—below five percent on average—and coming down.

The Uruguay Round, in particular, was a victory for developing countries, according to the developed nations. In the Agreement on Agriculture that came from the talks, most developed countries dropped tariffs by a significant margin. The European Union, for example, completely eliminated tariffs on coffee beans, cocoa beans, jute yarn, and paper. Canada eliminated tariffs on tea, fresh dried manioc, and paper products. Tariffs on other agricultural goods were cut by sizable amounts. Likewise, the commitment to phase out the Multi-Fiber Agreement will eventually result in much easier market access for developing countries.

The results of the Uruguay Round have been dramatic for some countries. Burkina Faso, for example, exports all of its goods duty-free worldwide, along with the Sudan, Djibouti, Lesotho, Guinea-Bissau, and several other of the poorest countries. Whereas almost half of Bangladesh's

MEXICAN TRUCKERS, WHOSE ROUTES TAKE THEM DAILY ACROSS THE U.S./MEXICO BORDER, WORRY THAT STRICTER REGULATIONS COULD PREVENT THEM FROM CROSSING ENTIRELY IN THE FUTURE. *(A/P Wide World. Reproduced by permission.)*

exports faced tariffs, now 98.62 percent of its exports are duty-free.

Developed countries have also maintained several preferential schemes whereby selected developing countries can export their goods duty-free. For example, nearly all imports from LDCs in Australia are duty-free, covered by the GSP. Likewise in Austria and Canada. This is true in spite of the fact that many developing countries have instituted new trade barriers of their own. For example, Argentina and several of the wealthier countries have aggressively pursued anti-dumping actions to block products they say are being sold below cost. Dumping violates World Trade Organization, or WTO, rules but is very tempting since it can dramatically increase a product's market share, even though it hurts profits in the short-term. The irony of this concern is that anti-dumping litigation is a tried-and-true practice in the West.

For most Western countries, the bottom line is that the problem is not market access, by and large, but the productive capacity of the third world. In many cases developing countries export far less than they could. Even before the Uruguay Round, for example, less than half the GSP quotas were filled, meaning that twice as many

exports could have been imported duty-free, except that there was no more supply from the developing world.

The problem, then, stems primarily from the poverty of third world economies and their inability to mass-produce goods for the overseas market. As we will see, this calls for a very different set of remedies than the developing countries have suggested.

This said, there are dissenting voices among the rich countries of the world. The Europeans have been more sensitive to the concerns raised by the developing world and have acknowledged that some third world exports still face high trade barriers. According to a recent European study, "more than 50 percent of [LDC] exports face a tariff barrier in the United States, Japan and Canada"—much worse than the 5 percent level in Europe. "If Canada, Japan and the United States follow the lead of the European Union, LDC exports will increase by approximately three percent." Europeans have been particularly sympathetic to the plight of the poorest nations and have even offered to eliminate all trade barriers on their exports, except where weapons and arms are concerned.

## LDC ACCESS TO DC MARKETS

| Nations Applying Tariffs | Portion of LDC Exports Facing Tariffs | Portion of LDC Exports Facing Tariffs over 5% |
| --- | --- | --- |
| Canada | 54.60% | 54.40% |
| European Union | 3.10 | 3.10 |
| Japan | 51.10 | 22.20 |
| United States | 48.70 | 47.00 |

LESS DEVELOPED COUNTRIES FACE STIFF TARIFFS IF THEIR GOODS ARE EXPORTED TO MANY MORE DEVELOPED NATIONS, INCLUDING CANADA, THE EUROPEAN UNION, JAPAN, AND THE UNITED STATES. *(The Gale Group.)*

## Opposition to the WTO

The focus of this debate ultimately centers on whether the WTO rules should be better designed and better enforced. This is not as esoteric as it may seem. Since late 1999, whenever the WTO has held large-scale meetings or, for that matter, whenever the powerful countries have gathered to discuss economic policy, they have been greeted by crowds of demonstrators. These protesters oppose the effects of "globalization" on all the weak and vulnerable. They charge the WTO and other economic organizations with numerous crimes and misdemeanors. For example, among its "Top 10 Reasons to Oppose the World Trade Organization," the Global Exchange network Web site includes that the WTO: "only serves the interests of multinational corporations"; "tramples over labor and human rights"; "is destroying the environment"; "is killing people"; "undermines local development and penalizes poor countries"; "is increasing inequality"; and "undermines national sovereignty."

At meetings in Seattle, Quebec City, Washington, DC, Rome, and elsewhere, tens of thousands of demonstrators have demanded access to the microphone in order to persuade diplomats to dramatically alter trading rules to allow governments to promote progressive policies through trade law. They argue, for example, that the policies that isolated the South African regime economically in the 1980s and led to the end of apartheid would be more difficult to put in place today since they would be viewed as WTO-illegal.

A common demand of demonstrators is for better protection of workers in what they call "sweatshops" in the developing world. In a famous story retold in *Life* magazine, Sidney Schanberg related an experience he had when he encountered children making soccer balls in Pakistan: "As I traveled, I witnessed conditions more appalling than [the last]—as children as young as six bought from their parents for as little as $15, sold and resold like furniture, branded, beaten, blinded as punishment for wanting to go home, rendered speechless by the trauma of their enslavement."

Demonstrators blamed the WTO's rules that liberate the forces of the market without providing any protections against its excesses, as in the case of the soccer ball makers in Pakistan. Interestingly enough, however, demonstrators soon discovered they were among the only voices defending the rights of workers in poor nations. As it turns out, third world governments are just as often sympathetic to the concerns of Western businesses that seek maximum latitude to set low wages. Thus, most developing countries have sought to prevent the imposition of new labor standards for fear of chasing away foreign investors. After all, part of the reason companies like Nike and Mattel set up facilities or subcontract to companies in the developing world is precisely because there is less government "interference" in the way the workplace is managed.

Indonesia has suppressed unions for years, for example, in order to prevent wages from rising as a result of strikes and union protests. It has also received a vast proportion of contracts from Western corporations until the late 1990s when its currency—and eventually its whole economy—collapsed. In other words depriving workers of Western-style rights is part of what gives developing countries a competitive edge. Mexico considers using local labor standards as a litmus test for blocking imports a barrier to free trade.

The same is true of environmental standards, which developing countries usually believe are another form of trade barrier. When the United

## WTO PROTESTS: EXCERPTS FROM "GLOBALIZE THIS!" BY THE GLOBAL EXCHANGE

November 30, 1999, marked a turning point in history. Tens of thousands of ordinary citizens took to the streets of Seattle to stop the World Trade Organization (WTO) from conducting "business as usual" (i.e., making rules for the entire planet that mainly serve the interests of large corporations)... When the meeting ended in failure on Friday the elitists had lost and the debate had changed forever... Seattle marked the greatest failure of elite trade diplomacy since the end of World War II... The Clinton team, led by U.S. Trade Representative Charlene Barshefsky, handled the controversy in Seattle so ineptly that the talks ended in total collapse... Most importantly, Seattle was the coming out party for a new global movement for citizen power that will certainly go on to bigger and better things.

Larger excerpt Available online at http://www.globalexchange.org/wto/GlobalizeThisIntro.html (cited February 6, 2002).

States imposed restrictions on imports of tuna in order to protect dolphins, Mexico and several other Latin American countries took it to court. The United States was found to have violated the free-trade rules of the WTO and was forced to work out another rule that would be mutually advantageous. On the other hand, U.S. rules to protect sea-turtles, although found to have violated WTO rules by one tribunal, were later approved, much to the dismay of developing countries.

Demonstrators and developing country governments, however, agree that Western governments are unfair in the application of their free trade rules and both groups argue for better market access and preferential treatment. They also agree that the free trade rules of the WTO tend to diminish the autonomy and sovereignty of developing countries.

### Efforts at Taking a New Approach

Western governments argue that the problem is not so much with market access questions. Rather they argue in favor of opening further all types of markets—to tear down the last remaining barriers to trade. This includes not only the types of barriers discussed earlier, but also the new barriers developing countries have erected. In order to accomplish all this, a new round of trade negotiations is needed.

In a recent joint statement by the key trade officials for the European Union and the United States quoted by Pascal Lamy and Robert Zoellick in the *Washington Post*, we find the following argument: A key goal of the cooperation between the United States and the European Union is to launch a new series of trade negotiations and overcome any lingering "stain" from the Seattle talks. "Why? Because we have a shared responsibility for the international economic system. Developing countries cannot expect to fare as well as the United States and the EU in a system of unbridled bilateralism. They would do much better under a multilateral trade round. Indeed, a new round is perhaps one of the most useful contributions we could make to the alleviation of global poverty, providing it is really a round for both growth and development."

The wording of the comment is rather unnerving, since it seems to imply a threat: the alternative to participating in a new multilateral round may be the collapse of the system and a reversion to country-by-country deals. Interestingly enough this threat may not be so idle. The United States has made clear that it intends to pursue not only a new multilateral negotiating round, but will also engage in bilateral talks with Laos, Jordan, and the Balkan states with strategic purposes in mind. Japan and Europe are also engaged in numerous bilateral deals, separate and apart from the WTO. The strategy has the effect of dividing the third world as some countries seek preferential deals at the expense of collective bargaining. The threat is also significant—it is certainly true that most developing countries could not hope to increase global market access through the means of bilateral deals alone.

Perhaps the most encouraging proposal, particularly for the poorest states, is the "Everything But Arms" initiative by the EU for LDCs. The idea is simple: all products exported to Europe from the LDCs would enter duty-free, unless they are weapons. This would mean the removal of escalating tariffs on products like chocolate and starch. Unfortunately, since its original promulgation in 2000, many governments in Europe have begun adding caveats and exceptions to the list, particularly in steel, textiles, and agriculture—the very areas that are most critical to the third world.

### Recent History and the Future

Once or twice each year, trade ministers from across the world gather for WTO policy meetings. The central question for the next few meetings will be whether to begin a new negotiating round. The United States and the European Union are

PRIOR TO THE UNITED NATIONS CONFERENCE ON TRADE AND DEVELOPMENT IN BANGKOK, THAI STUDENTS PROTESTED GLOBAL AUTHORITIES SUCH AS THE WORLD TRADE ORGANIZATION AND THE INTERNATIONAL MONETARY FUND BY BURNING PLACARDS BEARING THE ORGANIZATIONS' NAMES. (*© Reuters NewMedia Inc./Corbis. Reproduced by permission.*)s

determined to proceed, while the least developed countries have gone on record in opposition. In July 2001 trade ministers from these poorest countries declared that any new round would "have to take into account the inability of LDCs to participate effectively in negotiations on a broad agenda and implement new obligations due to the well-known limited capacity of the LDCs" (as quoted in the Marrakesh Declaration 2001) and that at any rate it was too soon to address such questions as rules on investment, environment, competition policy, and so forth.

But even before a new round can begin, U.S. negotiators will have to receive authority from Congress to sign any package deals—so-called "fast track" authority. At this point it is an open question whether Congress will be forthcoming. The Mexican truck situation has left a bad taste in the mouths of many legislators. Even Republicans, who would normally be expected to support President Bush, are advancing a farm bill that its supporters acknowledge provides new subsidies to farmers that are likely higher than permitted in WTO rules.

Many conflicting pressures will be brought to bear on the negotiators at the November 2001 meetings in Doha, Qatar. Western diplomats must weigh the need to protect essential industries and constituencies against foreign goods, while at the same time offering attractive enough inducements to secure developing country acceptance of a new round. The West may be in conflict with itself, however, as the Europeans brace for the introduction of the new currency—the euro—and the inevitable disruption this will cause. Likewise, the developing world is likely to lack the unity required to resist Western initiatives, as has been the case in the past. A likely scenario is that a new round may go ahead, but with a narrow agenda. It will bear watching, since the economic survival of billions hangs in the balance.

# BIBLIOGRAPHY

Das, Bhagirath Lal, "Strengthening Developing Countries in the WTO," Third World Network. Available online at http://www.twn.com (cited October 25, 2001).

Feinberg, Richard, and Valeriana Kallab, eds., *Adjustment Crisis in the Third World*. New Brunswick: Transaction Press, 1984.

"Farm Subsidy Foes Point to WTO Curbs," *Chicago Tribune,* August 31, 2001, p. A18.

"Globalize This!" Global Exchange, September 1, 2001. Available online at http://www.globalexchange.org/wto/GlobalizeThisIntro.html (cited October 25, 2001).

Khor, Martin, "LDC Ministers Not Prepared to Negotiate on New Issues" Geneva, 28 July 2001. Available online at http://www.twn.com (cited October 25, 2001).

Krasner, Stephen. *Structural Conflict: The Third World Against Global Liberalism*. Berkeley: University of California Press, 1985.

Lamy, Pascal, and Robert Zoellick, "In the Next Round" *Washington Post,* July 17, 2001, p. A17.

"In Rebuttal, Mexicans Dispute Claim Their Trucks Are Unsafe," *New York Times,* August 2, 2001.

Marrakesh Declaration of the Least Developed Countries, July 2001.

OECD, "Market Access for the Least Developed Countries: Where Are the Obstacles?" Paris: OECD, 1997.

Oxfam. *Rigged Trade and Not Much Aid: How Rich Countries Help to Keep the Least Developed Countries Poor*. London: Oxfam, 2001.

Raghavan, Chakravarthi, *Recolonization: GATT, the Uruguay Round and the Third World*. Singapore: Third World Network, 1990.

Raghavan, Chakravarthi, "Solidarity or Divide and Rule?" Third World Network, March 7, 2000. Available online at http://www.twn.com (cited October 25, 2001).

Ricupero, Rubens, "From the Washington Consensus to the Spirit of Bangkok: Is There a Bangkok Consensus or a Bangkok Convergence?" New York: UNCTAD, 2000.

Rothstein, Robert. *Global Bargaining: UNCTAD and the Quest for a New International Economic Order*. Princeton: Princeton University Press, 1979.

Schanberg, Sidney, and Marie Dorigny, "Six Cents an Hour," *Life,* June, vol. 19, no. 7, 1996, pp. 38–47.

Spero, Joan, and Jeffrey Hart. *The Politics of International Economic Relations*. 5th ed. New York: St. Martin's, 1997.

Stiles, Kendall, "The Ambivalent Hegemon: Explaining the `Lost Decade' in Multilateral Trade Talks: 1948–58," *Review of International Political Economy* vol. 2 #1 (Winter 1995), pp. 1–26.

———. *Negotiating Debt: The IMF Lending Process*. Boulder, CO: Westview Press, 1991.

"Top Ten Reasons to Oppose the World Trade Organization" Global Exchange, September 1, 2001. Available online at http://www.globalexchange.org/economy/rulemakers/ topTenReasons.html (cited October 25, 2001).

UNCTAD/Commonwealth. *Duty and Quota Free Market Access for LDCs: An Analysis of Quad Initiatives*. New York: United Nations, 2001.

UNCTAD, "General Debate 12–15 February 2000." New York: UNCTAD 2000.

United States Trade Representative, "US Wins WTO Case on Sea Turtle Conservation," June 15, 2001 (press release).

White House, "The President's 2001 International Trade Legislative Agenda," Washington: GPO, 2001.

"The WTO Erodes Human Rights Protections," Global Exchange, September 1, 2001. Available online at http://www.globalexchange.org/wto/CaseStudies .html (cited October 25, 2001).

WTO, Committee on Agriculture, Special Session, Submission by Cuba, Dominican Republic, El Salvador, Honduras, Kenya, India, Nigeria, Pakistan, Sri Lanka, Uganda, Zimbabwe, 28 Sept. 2000.

WTO, Annual Report 2000. Geneva: WTO, 2001.

*Kendall W. Stiles*

# United States Loses Seat on United Nations Human Rights Panel

On May 3, 2001, the United States failed to be reelected to its seat on the United Nations Human Rights Commission. This was the first time since 1947 that the United States had not been a member of this particular body within the United Nations (UN). The United States government expressed dismay and outrage over its expulsion from this commission.

What is so surprising about this turn of events is that it was America's friends and allies, not her adversaries, that led to her demise on the Human Rights Commission. Ironically, the Human Rights Commission currently has such new members as Sudan, Uganda, Sierra Leone, and Togo joining Syria, Algeria, Libya, Saudi Arabia, and Vietnam as already existing members. As President George W. Bush's administration noted, these countries have been continually under criticism for violations of human rights within their borders. In contrast, the United States has never been the subject of scrutiny of the UN Human Rights Commission, except on the issue of the death penalty, which the UN opposes and which still exists in the United States.

Reaction from the U.S. Congress was swift and predictable. Bipartisan condemnations came from both the House and the Senate. Senators Jesse Helms (R-NC) and Joseph Biden (D-DE) and representatives Tom Lantos (D-CA) and Henry Hyde (R-IL) all made threats to withhold American dues to the United Nations unless the situation was rectified. And, in some far corners of American society there emanated a renewed cry for the United States to end its membership within the United Nations permanently.

How did this seemingly strange set of circumstances arise? The United States has been one of

## The Conflict

The United States, long an outspoken advocate of human rights in other countries, lost its seat on the United Nations Human Rights Commission, signaling tense relations between the United States and other UN member nations.

### Political

- In the past decade, the United States has increasingly chosen to act unilaterally on matters of international concern.

- After the fall of the Soviet Union, the United States has emerged as the only superpower, throwing off the balances of power that existed during the Cold War and causing concern among many member nations.

- Within the United States, although polls show that a majority of the population supports the UN, there is a faction with strong representation in the U.S. Congress that distrusts the organization and seeks to lessen U.S. cooperation with member nations in international matters.

### Economic

- Back dues owed by the United States to the United Nations have at times during the past decade exceeded $1 billion, creating hostility among other member nations.

# CHRONOLOGY

*1921* The League of Nations is formed.

*1939* World War II begins.

*1944* At the Dumbarton Oaks Conference, China, the Soviet Union, the United Kingdom, and the United States work out proposals that will form the basis of the United Nations.

*1945* The United Nations is founded when representatives of 50 countries meet in San Francisco at the United Nations Conference on International Organization.

*1948* The Universal Declaration of Human Rights is put forth by the General Assembly, setting out basic rights and freedoms to which all women and men are entitled, including: the right to life, liberty, and nationality, to freedom of thought, conscience, and religion, to work, to be educated, and to take part in government.

*1950–53* In the Korean War, the United Nations calls for member intervention to halt North Korean aggression against South Korea and passes a resolution authorizing the use of force against the North Korean regime.

*1962* The UN helps to negotiate an end to the Cuban Missile Crisis.

*1968* The United States provides support and leadership in the UN efforts to develop arms control agreements, culminating in the Nuclear Non-Proliferation Treaty.

*1971* Communist China is admitted to the United Nations.

*1990–1991* The United Nations helps negotiate the Gulf War.

*1995* UN peacekeeping forces are sent to Bosnia-Herzegovina.

*1996–1999* The United States withholds UN dues, accumulating over a billion dollars in debt.

*1996* The United States promises to veto the reelection of Boutros Boutros-Ghali as Secretary General, forcing him to step down.

*1996* Kofi Annan becomes Secretary General of the United Nations.

*May 3, 2001* The United States is removed from the UN Human Rights Commission.

---

the staunchest proponents of human rights in the post-World War II era. How did it come to be replaced by states that have abysmal records in promoting human rights? The answer lies in the evolution of American involvement in the United Nations since its inception in 1945. The United States, while being a founding member of the United Nations and a permanent member of the Security Council, has never had a rosy relationship with the UN leadership.

As the 1990s progressed, support within the United States for participation in the United Nations decreased. Many politicians, with the ultra-conservative Senator Jesse Helms at the forefront, had become gravely concerned that the United Nations was becoming a quasi-sovereign entity rather than an organization comprised of sovereign states. Fears of UN control of American laws, particularly in the area of civil-military relations, and the use of American troops under UN command, became commonly expressed concerns. Many argued that the United Nations had over-

stepped its boundaries in its promotion of birth control policies, environmental standards, and the use of military forces abroad to enforce peacekeeping.

This distrust of the UN by certain groups in American society was not a new phenomenon. Throughout the Cold War many groups within the United States had viewed the UN as a liberal organization with socialist tendencies, bent upon global domination. During the Democratic administration of President Bill Clinton, fringe groups reacted strongly to incidents in which the government seemed to interfere in individual freedoms. Two key events in the early 1990s—the Ruby Ridge incident in northern Idaho in 1992, a week-long standoff between white supremacist Randy Weaver and Federal Bureau of Investigation (FBI) agents that ended when an FBI sniper shot and killed Weaver's wife, and the tragedy at Waco, Texas, in 1993, in which a 51-day standoff between the FBI and a group known as the Branch Davidians ended in a fire that killed 85

U.S. SENATOR JESSE HELMS, SECOND RIGHT, IS A VOCAL OPPONENT TO U.S. PARTICIPATION IN THE UNITED NATIONS. HERE HE ATTENDS A SENATE FOREIGN RELATIONS COMMITTEE MEETING WITH THE UN SECRETARY GENERAL AT THE UNITED NATIONS. *(AP/Wide World Photos. Reproduced by permission.)*

men, women, and children—triggered anti-government, anti-tax, and particularly anti-United Nations sentiments throughout U.S. fringe groups. The advent of the Internet made it easier for such groups to spread their beliefs.

In the late 1990s and continuing into the beginning of the twenty-first century, conflict grew between the United States and the UN over the failure of the United States to pay its dues to the UN. The unwillingness of the United States to shoulder its financial burden within the United Nations was just one problem. The United States' increased willingness to act unilaterally angered many of America's friends and allies. Hence, they retaliated in the only manner they could, and that was to vote the United States off of a key commission within the United Nations.

## HISTORICAL BACKGROUND

If we are to understand the current state of relations between the United States and the United Nations, we need to understand the role the United States has played in helping establish international cooperative ventures since the end of the World War I (1914–18). The devastation of both world wars caused world leaders to search for means to avoid further destruction and horror.

### *The League of Nations*

The roots of the modern-day United Nations can be found in the short-lived League of Nations that came into existence after the Treaty of Versailles ended World War I. The League of Nations was formed in 1920, with its first meeting taking place in November in Geneva, Switzerland. The League was founded with the goal of preventing another global conflict like World War I, which had just ravaged the globe. The League of Nations was to a great extent the brainchild of President Woodrow Wilson (1856–1924) of the United States. The core principles of the League were to promote peaceful cooperation amongst its members and to guarantee collective security for the countries that belonged to the League. Collective security in this regard refers to a system in which member countries would agree to defend any member nation that is threatened by foreign aggression.

Given the significant American involvement in designing the League's charter, it is surprising to note that the United States never joined the League of Nations. President Wilson had neglected to examine the domestic political environment in the United States at the time. The Senate was unhappy with Article X of the League's Covenant, which promoted the idea of collective security.

## SENATOR JESSE HELMS DELIVERS A SPEECH
## TO THE UNITED NATIONS SECURITY COUNCIL,
## JANUARY 20, 2000: AN EXCERPT

[Senator Helms has stated that the United States will pay its membership dues to the United Nations only if the UN agrees to reforms agreed upon by the Congress.]

In any event, Congress has written a check to the United Nations for $926 million, payable upon the implementation of previously agreed-upon common-sense reforms. Now the choice is up to the U.N. I suggest that if the U.N. were to reject this compromise, it would mark the beginning of the end of U.S. support for the United Nations.

I don't want that to happen. I want the American people to value a United Nations that recognizes and respects their interests, and for the United Nations to value the significant contributions of the American people. Let's be crystal clear and totally honest with each other: all of us want a more effective United Nations. But if the United Nations is to be "effective" it must be an institution that is needed by the great democratic powers of the world.

Most Americans do not regard the United Nations as an end in and of itself—they see it as just one part of America's diplomatic arsenal. To the extent that the U.N. is effective, the American people will support it. To the extent that it becomes ineffective—or worse, a burden—the American people will cast it aside.

The American people want the U.N. to serve the purpose for which it was designed: they want it to help sovereign states coordinate collective action by "coalitions of the willing," (where the political will for such action exists); they want it to provide a forum where diplomats can meet and keep open channels of communications in times of crisis; they want it to provide to the peoples of the world important services, such as peacekeeping, weapons inspections and humanitarian relief.

This is important work. It is the core of what the U.N. can offer to the United States and the world. If, in the coming century, the U.N. focuses on doing these core tasks well, it can thrive and will earn and deserve the support of the American people. But if the U.N. seeks to move beyond these core tasks, if it seeks to impose the U.N.'s power and authority over nation-states, I guarantee that the United Nations will meet stiff resistance from the American people.

As matters now stand, many Americans sense that the U.N. has greater ambitions than simply being an efficient deliverer of humanitarian aid, a more effective peacekeeper, a better weapons inspector, and a more effective tool of great power diplomacy. They see the U.N. aspiring to establish itself as the central authority of a new international order of global laws and global governance. This is an international order the American people will not countenance, I guarantee you.

The U.N. must respect national sovereignty. The U.N. serves nations-states, not the other way around. This principle is central to the legitimacy and ultimate survival of the United Nations, and it is a principle that must be protected.

"*Address by Senator Jesse Helms, Chairman, U.S. Senate Committee on Foreign Relations, before the United Nations Security Council, January 20, 2000,*" *Sovereignty International. Available online at http://www .sovereignty.net/center/helms.htm (cited September 5, 2001).*

Hence the United States never became a member of the League of Nations, although its diplomats often participated in League meetings in an unofficial capacity. Lack of American involvement was viewed by many during the interwar period as one of the main reasons why the League was so ineffective in promoting world peace and cooperation.

Despite the absence of the United States as a member, the League did have some limited successes during its existence. It was instrumental in curbing international drug trafficking, and it was moderately successful in assisting former colonies' transitions into statehood, particularly those that had been dominated by Turkey prior to World War I. Even in the area of peacekeeping, the League witnessed some moderate success, but for the most part the great powers attended to their own affairs without League involvement.

Due to its lack of internal cohesion and its inability to prevent German aggression after the rise to power of Adolf Hitler (1889–1945), the League of Nations became quite ineffective during the latter part of the 1930s. In 1946 it had dropped from a one-time high as a league of 63 member nations to become a mere shell. It voted itself out of existence in 1946 and much of its property and assets were transferred to the newly formed United Nations.

### The Formation of the United Nations

As World War II (1939–45) was winding to a close, representatives of 50 countries met in San Francisco at the United Nations Conference on International Organization. This meeting, which lasted from April 25 to June 26, 1945, established the United Nations. The delegates deliberated on the basis of proposals worked out by representatives of China, the Soviet Union, the United Kingdom, and the United States at the Dumbarton Oaks conference in Washington DC in August–October 1944. At this previous meeting it was generally acknowledged that the war would soon be over, with Germany and Japan defeated. There was a strong belief among the states that a new order needed to be devised to prevent a third major conflict on the scale of both world wars. It was also acknowledged that the United States was the only major state that could help lead the world, both economically and in terms of security, in the coming years. The Dumbarton Oaks conference called for a new security organization that built upon the collective security components of the League of Nations, but with more involvement by the great powers, especially the United States.

The representatives of the 50 countries signed the United Nations Charter on June 26, 1945. Poland, which was not represented at the conference, signed it later and became one of the original 51 member states. The United Nations officially came into existence on October 24, 1945, when the charter was ratified by China, France, the Soviet Union, the United Kingdom, and the United States, and by a majority of other signatories.

## Goals of the United Nations

The United Nations maintained the focus and emphasis that the earlier, ill-fated League of Nations had placed on collective security, and required that when states became members of the United Nations, they agreed to accept the obligations of the UN charter, a treaty that sets out basic principles of international relations. According to this document, the UN has several purposes. It strives to maintain international peace and security; it seeks to develop friendly relations among nations, particularly with regard to promoting international cooperation and respect for human rights; it serves as a forum where states can come together to air their grievances and attempt to solve their differences without resorting to violence. It should be noted that members of the United Nations are sovereign states. The United Nations is not a world government and it does not make laws. It does, however, provide the means to help resolve international conflict and formulate policies on matters affecting all of us.

Of the goals noted above, two are of special importance to the United Nations, and have benefited largely from American leadership in the post-1945 era. The central purpose of the United Nations is the preservation of world peace. Under the UN charter, member states agree to settle disputes by peaceful means and refrain from threatening or using force against other states. Over the years, the UN has played a major role in helping defuse international crises and in resolving a variety of international conflicts. It has undertaken many operations involving peacemaking, peacekeeping, and humanitarian assistance. It has worked to prevent conflicts from breaking out. And in post-conflict situations, it has increasingly undertaken coordinated action to address the root causes of war and to lay the foundation for a durable peace.

UN efforts have been quite effective in international crisis situations. Most people are familiar with UN involvement in the Korean War in 1950, when the Security Council called for member intervention to halt North Korean aggression against South Korea and passed a resolution authorizing the use of force against the North Korean regime. However, many are unaware that the UN was quite helpful in negotiating an end to the Cuban Missile Crisis in 1962. Throughout the post-World War II era, the UN has been involved in the Middle East peace process and was deeply involved in the 1973 Yom Kippur War, assisting in ending that conflict before it became more widespread. In 1988, a UN-sponsored peace settlement ended the Iran-Iraq war, and in the following year UN-sponsored negotiations led to the withdrawal of Soviet troops from Afghanistan. In the 1990s the UN was instrumental in liberating Kuwait through the Gulf War, and it played a major role in ending civil wars in Cambodia, El Salvador, Guatemala, and Mozambique, restoring the democratically elected government in Haiti, and resolving or containing conflict in various other countries. In the Gulf War of 1991 the UN acted as it had 40 years previously in Korea, by calling for troops and passing resolutions condemning Iraqi aggression against the Kuwaiti people. In the other conflicts, the UN worked as a mediator, providing assistance in ending the civil conflicts in ravaged states.

When it comes to peacekeeping and international security, the UN Security Council sets up the operations and defines their scope and mandate. Most operations involve military duties, such as observing a ceasefire or establishing a buffer zone while negotiators seek a long-term solution. Others may require civilian police or incorporate civilian personnel who help organize elections or monitor human rights. Some operations, like the one in Macedonia, were initially deployed as a means to help prevent the outbreak of hostilities. Operations have also been set up to monitor peace agreements in cooperation with the peacekeeping forces of regional organizations.

Since the UN deployed its first peacekeepers in 1948, some 118 countries have voluntarily provided more than 750,000 military and civilian police personnel. They have served, along with thousands of civilians, in 54 peacekeeping operations. In 2001, some 35,400 military and civilian police personnel were deployed in 15 UN sponsored operations.

## Human Rights at the United Nations

The other major concern that the United Nations pursues is the promotion of human rights around the world. The Universal Declaration of Human Rights was put forth by the UN General Assembly in 1948. What the Declaration does is set out basic rights and freedoms to which all women and men are entitled. These rights include the right to life, liberty, and nationality, to freedom of thought, conscience, and religion, to work, to education, and to participation in government. These rights are legally binding by virtue of two international covenants, and most member states of the United Nations are parties to these two documents. One covenant deals with economic, social, and cultural rights and the other with civil and political rights. Together with the declaration, they constitute the International Bill of Human Rights.

The Universal Declaration of Human Rights has established the foundation for more than 80 conventions and declarations on human rights, including conventions to eliminate racial discrimination and discrimination against women; support the rights of the child; examine the status of refugees; and prevent genocide. Its declarations have included concerns such as self-determination, enforced disappearances, and the right to development. With the standards-setting work nearly complete, the UN is shifting the emphasis of its human rights work to the implementation of human rights laws.

The High Commissioner for Human Rights coordinates all UN human rights activities, works with governments to improve their observance of human rights, seeks to prevent violations, and investigates abuses. The UN Commission on Human Rights, an intergovernmental body, holds public meetings to review the human rights performance of states. It also appoints independent experts—"special rapporteurs"—to report on specific human rights abuses or to examine human rights in specific countries.

UN human rights bodies are involved in early warning and conflict prevention as well as in efforts to address root causes of conflict. A number of UN peacekeeping operations have a human rights component. In all, UN human rights field activities are currently being carried out in 27 countries or territories. Promoting respect for human rights has become increasingly important to UN programs that promote development around the globe. In particular, the right to development is seen as part of a dynamic process that integrates all civil, cultural, economic, political, and social rights, by which the well-being of all individuals in a society is improved.

## Organization of the United Nations

In order to function and obtain its goals of international peace and cooperation, the United Nations has six main organs to manage and shape its activities. Five of them, the General Assembly, the Security Council, the Economic and Social Council, the Trusteeship Council, and the Secretariat, are based at UN Headquarters in New York. The sixth body, the International Court of Justice, is located at The Hague, the Netherlands.

Of particular interest for the human rights issue and for everyday management of the United Nations are the General Assembly and the Security Council. All UN member states are represented in the General Assembly, as a kind of parliament of nations that meets to consider the world's most pressing problems. Each member state has one vote in the General Assembly. Decisions on matters such as international peace and security, admitting new members, the UN budget, and the budget for peacekeeping, are decided by a two-thirds majority. Other, more routine matters are decided by simple majority. In recent years, especially after the end of the Cold War, great effort has been taken to reach decisions through consensus and compromise, rather than by holding formal votes.

As examples of what the General Assembly deals with on a regular basis, examine its 2000–2001 session. During this time the General Assembly dealt with more than 170 different topics, including globalization, nuclear disarmament, development, protection of the environment, and consolidation of new democracies. It should be noted that while the General Assembly represents world opinion and indicates current trends, it cannot force any member state to take action against its will.

When it comes to important decisions, much of the decision-making process reverts to the smaller body of the Security Council. For example, the Security Council makes recommendations to the General Assembly on the appointment of a new Secretary-General (the person who heads the United Nations as a whole) and on the admission of new members to the UN.

While the General Assembly has jurisdiction over routine matters facing the UN, the UN charter gives the Security Council primary responsibility for maintaining international peace and security. The Council may convene at any time, day or night, whenever peace is threatened. Under the charter, all member states are obligated to carry out the Security Council's decisions. Of course, it should be noted that there exists no mechanism to force member states to accede to Security Council Resolutions.

There are 15 members on the Security Council, with China, France, the Russian Federation, the United Kingdom, and the United States being permanent members. The other 10 are elected by the General Assembly for two-year terms. Decisions made by the Security Council require nine affirmative votes. Except in votes on procedural questions, a decision cannot be taken if there is a "no" vote, or veto, by any permanent member. Hence, through much of the Cold War the Security Council was often ineffective due to superpower vetoes. The one major exception, as discussed below, is the UN resolution to aid South Korea in the Korean War, during which the Soviet Union was boycotting the Security Council due to issues over the status of divided Berlin and the exclusion of Communist China from UN membership.

When the Security Council encounters a threat to international peace, it initially examines means by which the dispute can be settled peacefully. It may suggest principles for a settlement or undertake mediation. In the event of fighting, the Security Council will attempt to arrange a ceasefire. It may send a peacekeeping mission to help the parties maintain a truce and to keep opposing forces apart. It should be noted, however, that any peacekeeping mission must be requested by the warring factions. The UN has no power to send troops abroad without consent of its members, and it cannot send peacekeeping forces without explicit permission from the combatants.

The Security Council can take measures to enforce its decisions. It can impose economic sanctions or order an arms embargo. On rare occasions, the Security Council has authorized member states to use "all necessary means," including collective military action, to see that its decisions

A MICHIGAN MILITIA SUPPORTER, WAVING THE U.S. FLAG, DEFIANTLY STANDS ON THE FLAG OF THE UNITED NATIONS DURING A PROTEST OF UNITED NATIONS DAY. *(A/P Wide World. Reproduced by permission.)*

are carried out. (It again should be noted that the final decision made by the Security Council is not binding on the remaining members of the United Nations. States cannot be forced to commit troops to UN missions abroad.) The final decision on whether force should be used or not is voted upon in the General Assembly, and final commitments are at the discretion of the member states.

### United States Relations within the United Nations

As a founder of the United Nations and a permanent member of the Security Council, the United States has played a major role in the United Nations and its activities since 1945. The United States has been a prime mover in UN actions, from the interventions in Korea and Kuwait, to the promotion of human rights and international peacekeeping around the globe, to encouraging economic assistance to struggling countries. However, American relations with the UN have not always been entirely friendly. As the years have passed, many American political leaders have become disgruntled with the UN, viewing it as encroaching on American sovereignty. In the

UNITED NATIONS HIGH COMMISSIONER ON HUMAN RIGHTS MARY ROBINSON SPEAKS AT A PRESS CONFERENCE ON THE 50TH ANNIVERSARY OF THE UNITED NATIONS UNIVERSAL DECLARATION OF HUMAN RIGHTS. *(A/P Wide World. Reproduced by permission.)*

logical differences spilled over into the UN as well. East versus West scenarios became familiar voting patterns within the UN General Assembly, as states tended to vote with their superpower patrons and allies rather than acting out of their own volition.

The first major military action of the post-World War II era occurred when North Korea launched an invasion of South Korea in June 1950, and South Korea quickly appealed to the UN for help. The Security Council voted to send troops from member states to assist the South Koreans, and under American leadership the United Nations embarked upon its first military intervention. The conflict ended in 1953 with an armistice that holds to this day.

In 1956 a crisis developed in the Middle East between Israel and its Arab adversaries, and both superpowers, the Soviets and the Americans, became involved as they helped the UN moderate the Suez Crisis. Again the UN prevailed in restoring peace to the region.

In the 1950s the popularity of the UN was quite high in the United States. Most citizens supported UN ideals of peacekeeping and its attempt to solve conflicts by nonviolent means. With such a short time between the end of World War II and the start of the Korean War, much of the world's population was highly motivated to see the international peacekeeping ideal become a reality. It seemed only natural that the United States, which came out of World War II still-powerful, would assume a major share of the responsibility for getting the UN started and functioning. And, with the exception of the Soviet Union, most members of the UN were willing to allow the United States to play a leading role in UN actions.

### The 1960s

The decade of the 1960s witnessed decolonization on a major scale around the world, and the first use of UN peacekeeping forces in Cyprus, where conflict between Greek and Turkish Cypriots raged. The UN during this time period was largely concerned with issues of human rights and assisting former colonies in their transitions to independence. With its concern for promoting peace in the international arena, the United Nations provided a forum for discussions and debates on various issues relating to weapons and armaments and their spread in the international system. The United States provided support and assistance in all of this, as well as being a critical actor in developing various arms

remainder of this section, American relations with the rest of the United Nations are examined as they progressed decade by decade, with an emphasis on the emerging tensions that culminated in the May 3, 2001, decision to exclude the United States from the human rights panel.

### The 1950s

In the 1950s, as through much of the Cold War, relations within the United Nations were dominated by the superpower rivalry. With the United States and the Soviet Union both permanent members of the Security Council, their ideo-

control agreements, culminating in the Nuclear Non-Proliferation Treaty of 1968.

However, cracks were beginning to appear in global support of the United States as a dominant power. Many countries, particularly in the Third World, were becoming increasingly wary of American involvement in Vietnam and its support of non-democratic regimes.

### The 1970s and 1980s

The next twenty years saw a remarkable change in the attitudes of other countries toward the United States, and these attitude changes were reflected at the United Nations. American involvement in Vietnam had never found much approval worldwide, and its lack of commitment to the promotion of human rights in many of the countries it supported against communism angered many other members.

As an example, the United States was quite supportive of dictatorships within Latin America, notably in Chile and Argentina, where human rights abuses were rampant. But since these countries were opposed to communism, the United States turned a blind eye to the violations that took place within them. Many UN members took the United States to task on this, stating that it was hypocritical to preach human rights and link them to issues such as trade, while still interacting with abusive dictatorships.

During the Ronald Reagan and first George Bush administrations, American foreign policy focused almost exclusively on combating Soviet influence around the world. Jeanne Kirkpatrick, the U.S. ambassador to the UN, made it abundantly clear during her tenure under the Reagan administration that the United States would not conform to anyone else's standards. Kirkpatrick routinely maintained that the United States was not bound by any UN resolution that it did not favor. It was under her tenure that the United States began to go into arrears with its debt to the UN.

### The 1990s

Times changed dramatically in the early 1990s. The collapse of the Soviet empire in Eastern Europe in 1989 led to a major change in how the superpowers dealt with one another. This was coupled with the Iraqi invasion of Kuwait in August 1990 and the Gulf War in 1991. The UN Security Council authorized the removal of Iraqi troops from Kuwait, and the United States built a military coalition to drive Saddam Hussein from Kuwaiti territory. This American leadership led many states to believe that the United States was ready for a new role in the international arena. President George Bush proclaimed a "New World Order," and many states felt that a kinder, friendlier relationship between the UN and the United States was in order.

In spite of American success in the Gulf War, many states around the world were becoming increasingly agitated with American behavior. There was widespread condemnation of American actions on human rights, for example. The United States continually traded with China, which had a horrible human rights record, but consistently scolded other states for not behaving in more proper fashion.

## RECENT HISTORY AND THE FUTURE

If we examine the last five years of the 1990s and the beginning of the twenty-first century, we see the culmination of years of frustration and disagreement between the United States and the United Nations come to a head. In 1996 the UN Secretary-General Boutros Boutros-Ghali was forced out of office. During Boutros-Ghali's tenure at the head of the UN, the number of UN peacekeeping missions greatly increased, with missions in Cambodia, Somalia, Rwanda, and Bosnia. The missions were complicated and controversial, with varied results. Boutros-Ghali was particularly criticized for the lack of force used by the UN in Bosnia. Beyond this, American politicians charged the UN with corruption. In fact, in the 1996 presidential campaign, Republican Robert Dole ran on a platform of opposition to allowing U.S. soldiers fight under Boutros-Ghali and the UN. Finally, when Boutros-Ghali sought a second term, the Clinton administration said it would veto his nomination in the Security Council.

The Secretary-General quipped after leaving his post that he would now have more time for flying black helicopters, imposing global taxes, and writing laws for the entire world. He was satirizing the image held by a segment of the American population who viewed the United Nations as a global government bent on eradicating national sovereignty worldwide. These beliefs, while quite far-fetched, resonated among numerous politicians in Washington DC.

When the 1994 midterm elections were held, the Republican Party emerged in control of the

A CHILD HOLDS A SIGN URGING PEOPLE TO "GIVE PEACE A CHANCE" ON INTERNATIONAL HUMAN RIGHTS DAY. THE UNITED STATES WAS REMOVED FROM THE UNITED NATIONS' HUMAN RIGHTS COMMISSION. *(A/P Wide World. Reproduced by permission.)*

ducted by Zogby in April 1999 found that 70 percent of Americans surveyed had a favorable opinion of the United Nations, and 61 percent believed that the United States should pay its back dues to the UN.

In light of all this public support for the United Nations among the American public, why is there so much friction between the United States and the UN? The answer lies in the changing political landscape of international politics as we enter the twenty-first century. The United States is currently the sole superpower, and has begun to experiment with a lessening of its international commitments. In 1999, for example, the United States refused to (re)ratify the Comprehensive Test Ban Treaty on nuclear weapons, and has begun to pursue the development of a national missile defense system. The desire of the United States to act unilaterally in regard to security issues has been building over the past decade. This specter of American isolationism has many American allies worried. When this is coupled with American refusal to support international environmental treaties like the Kyoto Protocol, the worldwide effort to curb climate-changing emissions, there is bound to be some backlash.

The United States learned on May 3, 2001, that it had alienated many of its friends and allies. Much of this can be attributed to the United States's desire in the past decade to act in a more unilateral fashion on a variety of international issues. Its removal from the Commission on Human Rights was the only means by which many members of the United Nations were able to successfully express their displeasure over recent American actions on the global stage.

The world has changed in the last decade, with the collapse of the Soviet empire and the rise of nationalism around the globe, once firmly kept in check by the superpower rivalry. Voting blocs within the UN General Assembly are no longer centered around superpower influence, but around the interests of rich nations and poor nations.

UN Secretary-General Kofi Annan has expressed an interest in the United States returning soon to the Human Rights Commission and hopes that the United States will stay actively engaged in UN activities. As long as the United States continues to search for unilateral solutions to global problems, it will be faced with criticism from friends and enemies alike. But if it returns to more cooperative behavior that marked its early years in the UN, then it will most likely see its stature rise again on the UN stage.

U.S. House and Senate for the first time in over 20 years. Many members of the Republican Party, especially Senator Jesse Helms of North Carolina, were quite critical of President Clinton's policy of aggressive multilaterilism in regard to the United Nations. These politicians were very suspicious of UN activities, particularly when it came to having American soldiers serve under UN auspices on peacekeeping missions.

Starting in 1996, and continuing until 1999, the U.S. Senate refused to pay the membership dues that the United States owed to the United Nations. By the time Boutros-Ghali left office, the United States owed $1 billion. But a faction in Congress was against paying it. There was fear that the "New World Order" as espoused by President George Bush five years earlier was granting too much power to the United Nations. Senator Helms was increasingly vocal about reforming the UN to conform to American interests and status. If the UN would not conform, Helms advocated a U.S. withdrawal from the United Nations.

After being threatened with the loss of its vote in the General Assembly, the United States began to pay its back dues in 1999. And, despite the rhetoric of many of the political leaders in the United States, there was a fair amount of public support for the UN and its policies. A poll con-

## BIBLIOGRAPHY

Diehl, Paul. *International Peacekeeping.* Baltimore: Johns Hopkins University Press, 1994.

Diehl, Paul, ed. *The Politics of Global Governance: International Organizations in an Interdependent World.* Boulder, CO: Lynne Rienner Publishers, 2001.

Hook, Steven W., and John Spanier. *American Foreign Policy Since World War II.* 15th ed. Washington, DC: CQ Press, 2000.

Ostrower, Gary. *The United Nations and the United States.* New York: Twayne Publishers, 1998.

Ruggie, John Gerad. "The United States and the United Nations: Toward a New Realism." *International Organization* 39, 2, 1985.

Russett, Bruce, ed. *The Once and Future Security Council.* New York: St. Martins Press, 1997.

United Nations Web Site. Available online at www.un.org (cited September 12, 2001).

*Christopher Sprecher*

# CONTRIBUTORS

**Gina Amatangelo** is a Washington Office on Latin America (WOLA) Fellow, specializing in U.S. drug control policy toward the Andes region. Prior to joining the WOLA staff, Amatangelo worked from 1998 to 2000 as campaign associate for Amnesty International USA, where she coordinated the organization's corporate accountability project and developed strategies for grassroots country campaigns. As a 1997 recipient of the Amnesty International USA Patrick Stewart Human Rights scholarship, she worked with the Andean Information Network in Cochabamba, Bolivia, to document human rights violations that occurred in the course of U.S.-funded anti-narcotics operations.

ENTRIES: The Expanded U.S. Drug War in Latin America: A Downed Missionary Plane Places the Spotlight on the Andean Initiative

**Baogang Guo** is an assistant professor of political science at Dalton State College. He received his B.A. and M.A. from Zhengzhou University in China, and his Ph.D. from Brandeis University.

ENTRIES: The Missing Girls: Son Preference Reshapes the Population in India and China

**Sonia G. Benson** is the editor of volume 4 of *History Behind the Headlines*. She received her M.A. from the University of Michigan and has worked as an editor and writer in reference publishing for 12 years. She is the author of a two-volume reference book on the Korean War.

ENTRIES: The Afghan Taliban Strikes Out; Hard to Say Sorry: Indigenous Australia's Reconciliation Movement

**Jessica Blitt** received an M.A. in International Affairs from the Norman Paterson School of International Affairs in Ottawa, Ontario, and a B.A. in Peace and Conflict Studies from the University of Toronto. From November 2000 to May 2001, she worked in Bosnia and Herzegovina for the Democratization Department of the Organization for Security and Cooperation in Europe (OSCE). She has also researched and worked in Sri Lanka and the Philippines. Her publications include, *Ecoviolence: Links among Environ-*ment, Scarcity and Violence, which she co-edited with Dr. Thomas Homer-Dixon.

ENTRIES: The Lockerbie Trial on Trial: Was Justice Served?

**Michael P. Bobic** earned his B.A. in political science from Berea College (1985) in Kentucky. He earned his M.A. in 1992 and Ph.D. in 1996 in political science from the University of Tennessee, specializing in national institutions and research methods. Dr. Bobic is currently employed at Emmanuel College in Franklin Springs, Georgia, as an assistant professor of political science and as the director of institutional research. He and his wife live in upstate South Carolina.

ENTRIES: Quitting the Kyoto Protocol: The United States Strikes Out Alone

**Timothy G. Borden** completed his doctorate in history at Indiana University and holds degrees in economics and international relations from Brown University, and in labor history from the University of Toledo. He has worked as a consultant in the areas of international relations and public policy in addition to teaching at Indiana University and the University of Toledo. Dr. Borden's work has appeared in *Labor History, Michigan Historical Review, Polish American Studies, Northwest Ohio Quarterly,* and the *Organization of American Historians Magazine of History.*

ENTRIES: The World Health Organization Takes On the Tobacco Industry

**Dallas L. Browne** is chairman of the Department of Anthropology at Southern Illinois University-Edwardsville. He is also president of the St. Louis Council on Foreign Relations and chairman of the CFR Board of Directors. He is under consideration to become Honorary Counsel for the Republic of Tanzania. He is completing a book-length biography of Allison Davis, the first African American ever awarded tenure on any faculty in the United States..

ENTRIES: Libya, Qadhafi, and the African Union; Sierra Leone: Lasting Peace or a Cruel Mirage?

**Sapna Butany-Goyal** is currently a student in her final year of a combined Bachelor of Law/Master of Arts at the

University of Ottawa and the Norman Paterson School of International Affairs in Ottawa, Canada. She is also currently serving a term as editor-in-chief of the Ottawa Law Review, a legal journal. Sapna's research interest involves the United Nations International Human Rights Regime, as well as various aspects of international law. She will spend her articling year as a clerk at the Federal Court in Ottawa.

ENTRIES: International Military Tribunals: Bringing the World's Worst to Justice

**Richard W. Chadwick** earned his Ph.D. at Northwestern University in 1966, specializing in the modeling of foreign policy decision-making. He has since held positions at Yale, Harvard, System Development Corporation, CALSPAN, Inc., and has had research positions in Mannheim, Zurich, Canberra, Australia, and elsewhere. He has lectured throughout China on management theory for economic development. As a tenured professor at the University of Hawaii, he has taught international relations for over 20 years, specializing in Asia and the Pacific. Among his most recent works are essays for the Korean Institute for National Unification, the journal *Simulation & Gaming,* and a USCINCPAC presentation on the uses of global modeling for decision-making.

ENTRIES: North Korea: The Hermit Kingdom in the Global Era

**Peter Cole** is professor of journalism and head of the Department of Journalism Studies at the University of Sheffield in the United Kingdom. He entered university education after a long career in national newspaper journalism. He reported politics for the *Guardian,* before becoming news editor and then deputy editor of that paper. He was founder editor of the *Sunday Correspondent.* He was News Review (opinion) editor of the *Sunday Times.* Earlier in his career he was New York correspondent for the *London Evening News.* Cole writes and broadcasts widely on media matters, and for six months in 2000–2001 wrote a weekly column for the *Guardian* on press coverage of the euro debate. He speaks frequently at conferences. He is a board member of the Society of (UK) Editors, and a board member of the National Council for the Training of Journalists. He is an economics graduate of Cambridge University.

ENTRIES: The Euro Versus the Pound: Britain and the European Single Currency

**David F. Duke** is an assistant professor of history at Acadia University, Nova Scotia, Canada. He received his Ph.D. from the University of Alberta in 1999 on the subject of the environmental history of the USSR. His current projects include a comparative study of the environmental policies of the United States and Soviet Union during the Cold War. He is editor of the forthcoming *Russia and Eurasia Documents Annual: 2000,* published by Acadamic International Press.

ENTRIES: Russia Agrees to Take the World's Nuclear Waste: But Where to Put It?

**Richard Louis Edmonds** is editor of the *China Quarterly* until the summer of 2002 and senior lecturer in Geography at King's College in the University of London. Dr. Edmonds has written extensively on inland

China, Japan, Taiwan, Macau, and Hong Kong. He is the author of *Macau* (Oxford: Clio Press, 1989), and *Patterns of China's Lost Harmony: A Survey of the Country's Environmental Degradation and Protection* (London: Routledge, June 1994). Currently he is working on environmental problems in China and transition issues in Macau.

ENTRIES: The Sanxia (Three Gorges) Project in China: A Crisis in the Making?

**Erica L. Fraser** is a graduate student at the University of Illinois at Urbana-Champaign, currently working on her Ph.D. in history. She completed her Bachelor of Arts (Honours) degree at the University of Calgary in 1998 and her Master of Arts degree at the University of British Columbia in 2000 before moving to Russia for a year to teach English and continue to study the Russian language. Her major field of interest is the history of the Soviet Union, particularly during World War II and the early Cold War period. Her doctoral dissertation will examine how the Cold War was experienced in Russian culture.

ENTRIES: Post-Cold War Espionage Between the United States and Russia: How Has the Mission Changed?

**James Frusetta** is a doctoral candidate in modern European history at the University of Maryland College Park, focusing on Southeastern Europe in the early twentieth century. He was an NSEP Graduate Fellow in both Macedonia and in Bulgaria and is currently a Fulbright fellow in Bulgaria, working on the dissertation "Bulgaria in Macedonia: Intersections between Bulgarian and Macedonian National Identity."

ENTRIES: Macedonia Faces Division and Violence

**Douglas M. Gibler** received his Ph.D. from Vanderbilt University in 1997. He served as assistant professor at Vanderbilt and as lecturer in International Policy Studies at Stanford University before arriving at the University of Kentucky. Doug has taught classes on the causes of war, American foreign policy, international organizations, international law, international relations, and American government. His research interests focus on the prevention of mass military conflict broadly, and specifically, on the role that interstate alliances play in the onset of conflict and the preservation of peace. His research has been published in such journals as *International Studies Quarterly, Security Studies, International Interactions, Journal of Peace Research,* and *Conflict Management and Peace Science,* and as chapters in several edited volumes. Gibler is currently working on a book-length assessment of military alliances since 1648.

ENTRIES:Defending Against the Indefensible: Creating a National Missile Defense in the United States

**Thomas Haymes** is an analyst and consultant on a variety of topics in international relations and group dynamics. He has an M.A. in International Relations and an M.A. in German and European Studies, both from Georgetown University. He was formerly Africa analyst for Stratfor, Inc., an Austin, Texas-based intelligence firm and is author of analyses and publications on nationalism, ethnonationalism, and international politics. He is currently working on a book on decision-making and is a founding partner of Global Synergies, an international consulting and software services company based in Austin, Texas.

ENTRIES: Côte d'Ivoire: A Cosmopolitan Society Descends into Political Chaos and Violence

**Colleen Hoey** has a Masters in international affairs with a specialization in conflict analysis. She has worked for international organizations at the UN, government, and NGO levels. Currently she is attending McGill Law School in Montreal, Canada.

ENTRIES: Africa's Ivory Trade: Fighting for the Bearers of "White Gold"

**Alynna Lyon** is an assistant professor of political science at Southeast Missouri State University. She received a Ph.D. in political science from the University of South Carolina (1999) and her research focuses on the relationship between ethnic conflict and international politics. Her recent publications include "Separatism in Chechnya: The Role of the Jihad," in Rolin G. Mainuddin's (ed.), *Religion and Politics: An Examination of the Explosive Interactions*. In 1999 she was the winner of the Ethnicity, Nationalism, and Migration Section of the International Studies Association Graduate Student Paper Competition for her work entitled: "Rethinking Intervention in Ethnic Conflict: Blueprint for Assistance or Aggravation?" Dr. Lyon's other teaching and research interests include the United Nations, conflict resolution, third world politics, and human rights.

ENTRIES: Reading, Writing, and Warfare: Children in Armed Conflict

**Vinayak Narain Srivastava** completed his higher education and research from University of Agra, Agra, Jawahar Lal Nehru University, New Delhi, and University of Cambridge, U.K. He has worked at Centre for Policy Research and Institute of Social Sciences, New Delhi, and is presently working as a Fellow, Centre for Contemporary Studies, Nehru Memorial, Museum & Library, Teen Murti House, New Delhi. His primary field of study and research is political economy. Areas of research interests include politics, economy, and society of India, the former USSR, and Russia and Central Asia; local governance in India and the issue of political identity formation contingent on sociocultural and civilisational attributes. He has written a book entitled *The Separation of the Party and the State: Political Leadership in Soviet and Post-Soviet Phases* published by Ashgate, U.K., in 1999. He has also contributed to newspapers and is nearing completion on a monograph on local governance in India. Srivastava is a member of the editorial board of the forthcoming Journal *Contemporary India* to be brought out by the Centre for Contemporary Studies, Nehru Memorial, Museum & Library, Teen Murti, New Delhi.

ENTRIES: India's Caste System under Attack: The Dalit Movement

**Thomas D. Reins** received his Ph.D. in 1981 from Claremont Graduate School and currently teaches at California State University, Fullerton. Previously, he has taught at the University of California, Riverside, California State University, Los Angeles, and Chapman University. His research interests include the global drug trade and drug trafficking in Asia, especially China. He has published reviews, articles, and chapters in the *Journal of Asian Studies, Journal of Third World Studies, Modern Asian Studies, China Review International, Magill's Guide to Military History*, and other publications.

ENTRIES: The Spy Plane Incident: China-U.S. Relations

**Christopher Sprecher** received his Ph.D. from Michigan State University, in 1999 in the field of international relations. He is visiting assistant professor with the Department of Political Science at Texas A&M University. Sprecher is coauthor of an article in the *Journal of Peace Research*. His current research is on: alliance behavior; deterrence theory; crisis escalation in enduring rivalries; and empirical testing of formal models.

ENTRIES: United States Loses Seat on United Nations Human Rights Panel

**Kendall W. Stiles** is an associate professor of political science at Loyola University, Chicago, where he teaches international law and organizations. He has written several books and articles on a variety of international institutions and problems, including the IMF, the WTO, human rights law, and the UN. His most recent work is *Donors, NGOs and the Intermestic Policy Circle in Bangladesh*, to be published by Praeger Press in 2002. The second edition of his text, *Case Histories in International Politics*, was published by Longman Press in 2001.

ENTRIES: World Trade Conflict: Has the Third World Been Cheated?

**Allen Wittenborn** spent two years in Turkey with the U.S. Air Force. He has an A.B. in Chinese-Japanese literature, an M.A. in international relations, and a Ph.D. in Chinese-Japanese intellectual history. Wittenborn published *Further Reflections on Things at Hand*, a study of twelfth-century Chinese thinkers, as well as several articles on current affairs in China, Indonesia, and Burma. He is also certified as "expert witness" in political asylum cases concerning Asian refugees. Wittenborn has worked, lived, and/or traveled in every country in Asia except North Korea, Brunei, and the Philippines. He is currently professor of Asian Studies and history at San Diego State University. He has a special interest in the modern history and society of China, Indonesia, Malaysia, and Burma and is currently researching the Chinese Nationalist troops in Burma after WWII.

ENTRIES: Japanese Voters Seek Change as Their Economy Deteriorates: New Prime Minister Vows to Break Political Logjam

# General Bibliography

*This bibliography contains a list of sources, primarily books and articles, that will assist the reader in pursuing additional information on the topics contained in this volume.*

## A

Alexander, Yonah. "Commentary: Terrorism in the Twenty-first Century: Threats and Responses," *The World and I,* June 1999.

Amirahmadi, Hooshang, ed. *The Caspian Region at a Crossroad: Challenges of a New Frontier of Energy and Development.* New York: St. Martin's Press, 1999.

Amstutz, Mark R. *International Conflict and Cooperation: An Introduction to World Politics.* New York: McGraw-Hill Companies, 1998.

Arendt, Hannah. *The Origins of Totalitarianism.* reprint, New York: Harcourt Brace Jovanovich, 1973.

Arrighi, Giovanni. *The Long Twentieth Century.* New York and London: Verso, 1994.

Avruch, Kevin. *Culture and Conflict Resolution.* Washington, DC: U.S. Institute of Peace Press, 1998.

## B

Bairoch, Paul. *The Economic Development of the Third World since 1900.* Berkeley, CA: University of California Press, 1975.

Barkan, Steven E., and Lynne L. Snowden. *Collective Violence.* Boston, MA: Allyn and Bacon, 2001.

Bartlett, C. J. *The Global Conflict: The International Rivalry of the Great Powers, 1880–1990.* New York: Addison-Wesley Longman, 1994.

Bercovitch, Jacob and Richard Jackson. *International Conflict: A Chronological Encyclopedia of Conflict Management, 1945–1995.* Washington DC: Congressional Quarterly, 1997.

Blaker, James R. *United States Overseas Basing: An Anatomy of the Dilemma.* New York: Praeger, 1990.

Bradbury, Jonathan and John Mawson. *British Regionalism and Devolution: The Challenges of State Reform and European Integration.* Regional Policy and Development Series 16, London: Jessica Kingsley Publishers, 1997.

Brown, Michael E.. *The International Dimensions of Internal Conflict.* Cambridge, MA: MIT Press, 1997.

## C

Collins, Joseph J. and Gabrielle D. Bowdoin. *Beyond Unilateral Economic Sanctions.* Washington, DC: Center for Strategic and International Studies, March 1999.

## D

Deudney, Daniel H. and Richard A. Matthew, eds. *Contested Grounds: Security and Conflict in the New Environmental Politics.* Albany, NY: State University of New York Press, 1999.

Diehl, Paul and Nils Gleditsch, eds. *Environmental Conflict.* Boulder, CO: Westview Press, 2000.

Dieter, Fleck, Michael Bothe, and Horst Fischer. *The Handbook of Humanitarian Law in Armed Conflict.* New York and London: Oxford University Press, 2000.

Drezner, Daniel W. *The Sanctions Paradox: Economic Statecraft and International Relations.* Cambridge, MA: Cambridge University Press, 1999.

## E

Ebel, Robert and Rajan Menon, eds. *Energy and Conflict in Central Asia and the Caucasus.* Lanham, MD: Rowman & Littlefield Publishers, 2000.

*Encyclopedia of World History.* New York and London: Oxford University Press, 1999.

## F

Fukuyama, Francis. "Rest Easy. It's Not 1914 Anymore," *New York Times,* 9 February 1992.

# G

Gall, Susan B., ed. *Worldmark Chronology of the Nations.* Farmington Hills, MI: Gale Group, 2000.

Gall, Timothy L., ed. *Worldmark Encyclopedia of Cultures and Daily Life.* Farmington Hills, MI: Gale Group, 1997.

Ganguly, Rajat and Raymond C. Taras. *Understanding Ethnic Conflict: The International Dimension.* New York: Addison-Wesley Longman, 1998.

Gilpin, Robert and Jean M. Gilpin. *Global Political Economy: Understanding the International Economic Order.* Princeton, NJ: Princeton University Press, 2001.

Goldstone, Jack A., Ted Robert Gurr and Farrakh Mashiri. *Revolutions of the Late Twentieth Century.* Boulder, CO: Westview Press, 1991.

Gottlieb, Gidon. *Nation Against State: A New Approach to Ethnic Conflicts and Sovereignty.* Washington, DC: Council on Foreign Relations Press, 1993.

# H

Haass, Richard N. *Conflicts Unending: The United States and Regional Disputes.* New Haven, CT: Yale University Press, 1990.

Haass, Richard N., and Meghan L. O'Sullivan, eds. *Honey and Vinegar: Incentives, Sanctions, and Foreign Policy.* Washington, DC: Brookings Institution, 2000.

Hahnel, Robert. *Panic Rules!: Everything You Need to Know about the Global Political Economy.* Cambridge, MA: South End Press, 1999.

Hodgson, Marshall G. S. "World History and a World Outlook." In *Rethinking World History: Essays on Europe, Islam and World History.* New York: Cambridge University Press, 1993.

Hoffman, Stanley. *World Disorders: Troubled Peace in the Post Cold War Era.* Lanham, MD: Rowman & Littlefield, Publishers, 2000.

Homer-Dixon, Thomas F. *Environment, Scarcity, and Violence.* Princeton, NJ: Princeton University Press, 1999.

Hudson, Christopher, ed. *The China Handbook: Prospects Onto the Twenty-first Century.* Chicago, IL: Glenlake Publishing Company, 2000.

Hunter, Shireen T. *Turkey at the Crossroads: Islamic Past or European Future?* Brussels, Belgium: Centre for European Policy Studies, 1995.

# K

Kakar, Sudhir. *The Colors of Violence: Cultural Identities, Religion, and Conflict.* Chicago, IL: University of Chicago Press, 1996.

Kaplan, Robert D. *The Ends of the Earth: From Togo to Turkmenistan, from Iran to Cambodia—A Journey to the Frontiers of Anarchy.* New York: Vintage Books, 1996.

Kanet, Roger E. *Resolving Regional Conflicts.* Urbana, IL: University of Illinois Press, 1998.

Katz, Richard S. *Democracy and Elections.* New York and London: Oxford University Press, 1998.

Keegan, John. *A History of Warfare.* New York: Vintage Books, 1994.

King, Anthony D., ed. *Culture, Globalization and the World-System: Contemporary Conditions for the Representation of Identity.* Minneapolis, MN: University of Minnesota Press, 1997.

Kohn, Hans. "Nationalism," *International Encyclopedia of the Social Sciences,* 11: 63–39.

# L

Lal, Brij V., and Kate Fortune, eds. *The Pacific Islands: An Encyclopedia.* Honolulu, Hawai'i: University of Hawai'i Press, 2000.

Lambert, Richard D., Alan W. Heston, and William Zartman. *Resolving Regional Conflicts: International Perspectives.* London: Sage Publications, 1991.

Lawson, Stephanie. *Tradition Versus Democracy in the South Pacific: Fiji, Tonga and Western Samoa* (Cambridge Asia-Pacific Studies). London: Cambridge University Press, April 1996.

# M

Mayall, James, ed. *The New Interventionism, 1991–1994: United Nations Experience in Cambodia, Former Yugoslavia, and Somalia.* Cambridge, MA: Cambridge University Press, 1996.

———. *World Politics: Progress and Its Limits (Themes for the 21st Century).* Cambridge, MA: Polity Press, 2001.

McNeill, William H. *Plagues and Peoples.* New York: Anchor Books/Doubleday & Co., Inc., 1998.

McRae, Rob and Don Hubert, eds. *Human Security and the New Diplomacy: Protecting People, Promoting Peace.* Montreal, Canada: McGill-Queen's University Press, 2001.

Miall, Hugh and Tom Woodhouse, et al. *Contemporary Conflict Resolution: The Prevention, Management and Transformations of Deadly Conflict.* Cambridge, MA: Polity Press, 1999.

Mitchell, C. R. *The Structure of International Conflict.* New York: St. Martin's Press, 1990.

# N

Nash, Gary B., Charlotte Crabtree, and Ross E. Dunn. "In the Matter of History." In *History on Trial: Culture Wars and the Teaching of the Past.* New York: Alfred A. Knopf, 1998.

National Commission on Terrorism. *Countering the Changing Threat of International Terrorism.* Washington, DC: U.S. Congress, 2000.

Nye, Joseph S. *Understanding International Conflict: An Introduction to Theory and History.* New York: Addison-Welsey Longman, 1999.

# O

O'Brien, Patrick K. *Atlas of World History.* New York and London: Oxford University Press, 1999.

Osborne, Milton. *The Mekong: Turbulent Past, Uncertain Future.* New York: Atlantic Monthly Press, 2000.

# P

Paris, Erna. *Long Shadows: Truth, Lies, and History.* Bloomsburg, 2001.

Prendergast, John. *Frontline Diplomacy: Humanitarian Aid and Conflict in Africa.* Boulder, CO: Lynne Rienner Publishers, 1996.

# R

Ramsbotham, Oliver, Clive Ramsbotham, and Tom Woodhouse. *Humanitarian Intervention in Contemporary Conflict: A Reconceptualization.* Oxford, England: Blackwell Publishers, 1996.

Ramsbotham, Oliver and Tom Woodhouse. *Encyclopedia of International Peacekeeping Operations.* ABC-CLIO, 1999.

Ratcliffe, Peter. *Race, Ethnicity, and Nation: International Perspectives on Social Conflict.* London: UCL Press, 1994.

Rayner, Caroline, ed. *Encyclopedic World Atlas: A-Z Country-by-Country Coverage.* New York and London: Oxford University Press, 1994.

Reich, Walter, ed. *Origins of Terrorism: Psychologies, Ideologies, Theologies, States of Mind.* Washington, DC: Woodrow Wilson Center Press, 1998.

Rochards, Andrew. "Meaning of 'Genocide'," *Times Literary Supplement,* 15 May 1998.

Rothchild, Donald and David A. Lake, eds. *The International Spread of Ethnic Conflict: Fear, Diffusion, and Escalation.* Princeton, NJ: Princeton University Press, 1998.

# S

Sachs, Wolfgang. *Global Ecology: A New Arena of Political Conflict.* London: St. Martin's Press, 1993.

Schlesinger, Arthur Meier. *The Disuniting of America: Reflections on a Multicultural Society.* New York: W.W. Norton, 1998.

Schnaiberg, Allan and Kenneth Alan Gould. *Environment and Society: The Enduring Conflict.* New York: St. Martin's Press, 2000.

Shawcross, William. *Deliver Us from Evil: Peacekeepers, Warlords and a World of Endless Conflict.* New York: Simon and Schuster, 2000.

Simmons, Aan G., and Ian G. Simmons. *Changing the Face of the Earth: Culture, Environment, History.* 2d ed. New York and London: Oxford University Press, 1993.

Smith, David A., Dorothy A. Solinger, and Steven Topik, eds. *States and Sovereignty in the Global Economy.* New York: Routledge, 1999.

Snooks, Graeme Donald. *The Dynamic Society: Exploring the Sources of Global Change.* New York: Routledge, 1996.

Spencer, Metta, ed. *Separatism: Democracy and Disintegration.* Lanham, MD: Rowman & Littlefield Publishers, 1998.

Staub, Ervin. *The Roots of Evil: The Origins of Genocide and Other Group Violence.* Cambridge, MA: Cambridge University Press, 1992.

Stearns, Peter N. "Nationalisms: An Invitation to Contemporary Analysis," *Journal of World History* (Spring 1997): 57–74.

Sulimann, Mohamed. *Ecology, Politics and Violent Conflict.* New York: St. Martin's Press, 1998.

# V

Von Hippel, Karin. *Democracy by Force: U.S. Military Intervention in the Post-Cold War World.* Cambridge, MA: Cambridge University Press, 2000.

# W

Walter, Barbara F. *Civil Wars, Insecurity, and Intervention.* New York: Columbia University Press, 1999.

Weart, Spencer R. *Never at War: Why Democracies Will Not Fight One Another.* New Haven, CT: Yale University Press, 2000.

Weaver, Frederick Stirton, and Ron Chilcote. *Latin America in the World Economy: Mercantile Colonialism to Global Capitalism.* Boulder, CO: Westview Press, 2000.

Wippman, David, ed. *International Law and Ethnic Conflict.* Ithaca, NY: Cornell University Press, 1998.

*Worldmark Encyclopedia of Nations.* Farmington Hills, MI: Gale Group, 1998.

Wolfe, Patrick. "Imperialism and History: A Century from Marx to Postcolonialism," *The American Historical Review* 102 (April 1997): 388–420.

Worsley, Peter. *The Three Worlds: Culture and World Development.* Chicago, IL: University of Chicago Press, 1989.

# Z

Zhang, Wei-Wei. *Transforming China: Economic Reform and its Political Implications.* New York: St. Martin's Press, 2000.

# INDEX

*Page numbers in boldface refer to a topic upon which an essay is based. Page numbers in italics refer to illustrations, figures, and tables. A number followed by a colon refers to the volume in which you will find the given page reference(s).*

*Index*

# C

Canton system, China, 4:79
Carajas Iron Ore Project (1982), 1:15
CARAT Act (1999, U.S.), 3:68–69
Carbon dioxide
    emissions credits, buying and selling, 4:166–167
    Kyoto Protocol's focus on, 4:169–170
    rainforest destruction and, 1:18
Cárdenas, Lázaro, 1:62, 3:181–182, 185
Cardoso, Fernando, 1:14
Caribbean Basin Initiative, 4:292
Carnation Revolution (1974-1975), 2:183
Cartels
    Colombian drugs, 1:*72*, 75, 2:174, 4:18
    diamond industry, **3:61–72**
    Mexican drugs, 2:174–177
    movement into Ecuador, 3:97
    OPEC, 1:196, 200
    *zaibatsu*, Japan, 4:149, 150, 151
Carter, Jimmy, 2:137
de las Casas, Bartolomé, 2:73
Casement, Roger, 3:202
Cash crops. *See* Agriculture; *specific crops*
Caspian Sea drilling rights, **3:26–36**
Caspian Sea region, 3:*28*
Castaño, Carlos, 4:19
Caste system, India. *See* Dalit Movement
Castilla, Ramón, 3:210
Castillo, Rene, 2:*173*
Castillo Armas, Carlos, 2:127
Castro, Fidel, 1:94–101, *95*, 3:*85*
Catechists and Mexican reform, 1:63–64
Catholic Church
    Chiapas, 1:59–60, 63–64
    China, 2:45
    East Timor, 2:92–93
    Ecuador, 2:100, 103
    Northern Ireland, 2:223–225
    Peru, 2:237
    Uganda, 3:308–310
Catoca Diamond Mine, 3:*70*
Cattle industry
    Brazilian rainforest and, 1:16
    mad cow disease, United Kingdom, 2:112, *118*
Caucasian mummies in China, 3:46
Caucasus. *See* Armenia; Azerbaijan; Nagorno-Karabakh
*Caudillos*, Venezuela, 1:304
CCP (Chinese Communist Party), 1:286, 2:44–45, 3:38, 44–48
Ceausescu, Nicolae, 3:103
Census undercounting, Albanians, 4:207
Central Intelligence Agency. *See* United States Central Intelligence Agency
Central Selling Organization (CSO) (diamonds), 3:65–66
Central Tibetan Administration (CTA), 2:278–279
Ceylon. *See* Sri Lanka
CFU (Commercial Farmer's Union) (Zimbabwe), 2:311
Champagne Diamonds, 3:67
Chan, Anson, 3:153, 154–155
Charlottetown Accord (1992, Canada), 3:23
Chaudhry, Mahendra, 3:129, 133
Chávez Frías, Hugo, 1:303–304, *305*, 307–309, *309*
Chechen-Ingush Republic. *See* Chechnya
Chechens, deportation by Soviet Union, 1:51–52
Chechnya
    chronology, 1:47

demography, 1:48–50
elections, 1:53, 54
ethnic groups, 1:48–49
human rights violations, 1:47–48, 56–57
independence from Russia, **1:46–57**, 1:*55, 259*, 263–264, 4:107
map, 1:*48*
mass media, 1:52
oil industry, 1:49–50, 54, 56
Russian reporting on, 3:233–236
Chelyabinsk-65 nuclear accident (1957, Soviet Union), 4:253
Chemical warfare training, United States Army, 3:*286*
Chemical weapons and bioterrorism, current threats, 3:288–290
Chen Shui-bian, 1:284, 292
Cheney, Dick, 4:*170*
Chernobyl nuclear accident (1986, Soviet Union), 2:251, 4:256, *257*
Chernobyl soil testing, 4:*255*
*Cherokee Nation v. Georgia* (1831), 2:201
Chiang Ching-kuo, 1:291
Chiang Kai-shek, 1:286–287, *287*
Chiapas (Mexico). *See* Mexico
Child protection agencies, 4:60
Child soldiers, **4:49–61**, 4:*51, 52, 57*
    Sierra Leone, 4:264, 270–271, 273
Childhood, debate on definition, 4:53–55
*Children: The Invisible Soldiers* (Brett, McCallin), 4:53
Chile
    chronology, 1:205
    drug trade, 1:75
    economy, 1:204–208
    elections, 1:206, 208
    human rights violations, 1:208–209
    map, 1:*212*
    nationalist politics, 1:206–207
    relations with United States, 1:206–207
China
    ballistic missiles, 4:223
    Chinese emigration to United States, 2:295
    chronologies, 1:285, 2:43, 52, 3:41, 4:63, 77
    civil war, 2:278
    communes, failure of, 3:45–46
    cultural influence on Korea, 4:227
    Cultural Revolution (1966-1976), 2:45, 280, 3:47–48
    economy, 2:54–62, 3:149–150
    Falun Gong, **2:42–50**
    family planning policy, 3:49–50
    Hong Kong, **3:146–156**
    international relations, history of, 4:78–80
    invasions and defeats, nineteenth century, 4:79–80
    involvement in Angola, 2:16, 19
    involvement in Korea, 2:152
    Islam in Xinjiang Province, **3:37–52**
    maps, 1:*288*, 2:*44*, 3:*39*, 4:*64*
    nationalities of Xinjiang-Uighur region, 3:47
    "one nation, two systems," 1:290, 292, 3:151
    population control policy, **4:238–247**
    reform era, 3:48–50
    relations with former Soviet republics, 3:38–39
    relations with Taiwan, **1:284–294**, 1:*290, 293*, 2:281, 3:150, 4:77–78
    relations with Thailand, 3:8
    relations with Tibet, 2:45, 276–281

Index

# D

# E

*Index*

# H

*Index*

# I

## J



## K

Index

# M

## N



*Index*

# O



*Index*

# P

# Q

# R

# S

*Index*

# U



*Index*

Index

# V

# W

# X



# Y



# Z



Index